Digital Marketing Analytics:
Making Sense of Consumer Data in a Digital World

CHUCK HEMANN
KEN BURBARY

Digital Marketing Analytics

ISBN-13: 978-0-7897-5030-3
ISBN-10: 0-7897-5030-9

Library of Congress Cataloging-in-Publication Data is on file.

Printed in the United States of America

Fourth Printing: April 2014

Trademarks

Warning and Disclaimer

Bulk Sales

Que Publishing offers excellent discounts on this book when ordered in quantity for bulk purchases or special sales. For more information, please contact

U.S. Corporate and Government Sales
1-800-382-3419
corpsales@pearsontechgroup.com

For sales outside of the U.S., please contact

International Sales
international@pearson.com

CONTENTS AT A GLANCE

TABLE OF CONTENTS

6   Tools: Audience Analysis   85

7   Tools: Content Analysis   97

8   Tools: Engagement Analysis   113

Foreword

"We have two ears and one mouth so that we can listen twice as much as we speak."
—Epictetus

"Data! data! data!" he cried impatiently. "I cannot make bricks without clay."
—Sir Arthur Conan Doyle

"The geeks shall inherit the earth."
—Scott Monty

When I decided to become a classics major in my undergraduate university, I didn't really have an expectation as to how the lessons in ancient history, drama, architecture, politics, and culture would remain with me in throughout my professional career. At the time, my sole desire was to expand my academic horizons beyond the heavy science commitment that a pre-med/biology concentration would otherwise allow. While I posited that the use of Greek and Latin roots in medical terminology would be helpful, I was also keen to broaden my knowledge base beyond my narrow focus on the life sciences.

While I eventually moved to the business side of healthcare (and later biotech, pharmaceutical, and high-tech—the last of which fueled my interest in social media), I found that it was the humanities rather than the sciences that continued to forge a lasting impression in how I perceived and thought about the world around me, particularly with respect to consumer behavior. No other quote has quite stayed with me like this one from the Roman orator and politician Cicero:

"If you wish to persuade me, you must think my thoughts, feel my feelings, and peak my words."

For in observing human behavior over the course of history, it became fairly obvious that we haven't changed much in the 2,000 years that separate us from Cicero. Certainly, the industrialization and technological advance of our physical world has moved us far beyond anything the ancient astronomers could have imagined, but fundamentally, we still want the same things that we've always wanted: what's best for ourselves and those we care about, the need to be heard, and the desire to be part of something bigger than ourselves so that we can make a lasting impact on the world. If we as marketers and communicators can grasp that reality and ensure that we're thinking about the needs of consumers in this digital age, we'll find that awareness will be repaid by more attention, trust, and loyalty.

If we revisit that Epictetus quote—a saying that nearly every reader may recognize as emanating from their grandmother—we can immediately understand its great wisdom: listening trumps talking. And perhaps we can even, with a certain degree of emotional intelligence, understand our great failure in this post-mass marketing digital age, as we've rushed to find even more people, likes, followers, and audiences who'll be the recipients of our "messages."

Ever the master logician and thinker, Sherlock Holmes opined for more data before he could apply his reasoning. For years, marketers have been data-driven in their product research, consumer assessment, and audience segmentation exercises to help bring a product to market. And we stand on a threshold of Big Insights (derived from the ubiquitous "Big Data") that should allow us the unprecedented ability to predict needs and products.

Marketing Science has been the stronghold of most of data-driven portions of marketing to date. However, the rise of social media has granted us access to unfiltered consumer data in real-time, or near real-time, that can influence the direction and even the creative elements of campaigns. In the 2012 presidential election, we saw how the information crunchers and back-room data geeks managed to steer the already nimble Obama-Biden campaign machine to a decisive victory based largely on studying the numbers and helping the front line apply its efforts to the right markets and the right people at the right time.

Rest assured that this is the very type of marketing expertise that will be highly valued in the future. The geeks shall truly inherit the (marketing) earth.

What Chuck and Ken have developed is a definitive handbook to help you navigate the important analytical and technical aspects of modern marketing. From listening to planning, search to response, launching products to supporting customers, and more, digital and social media play a central role in your ability to successfully integrate with the world around you. Read, study, and enjoy this book.

And always listen to your grandmother.

—Scott Monty
Global Head of Social Media
Ford Motor Company

About the Authors

Chuck Hemann, Director of Analytics for WCG, has spent the last eight years providing strategic counsel on digital analytics, measurement, online reputation, and social media. He was previously VP of Digital Analytics for Edelman Digital and VP of Digital Strategy and Analytics for Ogilvy Public Relations. He has worked with global brands from Intel to General Mills to Pfizer.

Ken Burbary, Chief Digital Officer at Interpublic's Campbell Ewald, has 16 years of online marketing and advertising experience, including a deep background in digital and social media. He served as VP–Group Director, Strategy and Analysis at Digitas, working with global brands from American Express and Bank of America to P&G and GM.

Dedication

This book is dedicated to my mom, grandmother, and grandfather. Without their consistent encouragement and guidance, I would not be where I am today. There is not a day when I am not thankful for everything you have done for me.
—Chuck

This book is dedicated to my family. They gave me the inspiration to embark on this journey and provided much support, encouragement, and understanding throughout the process. I would not have been able to do this without their love.
—Ken

Acknowledgments

From Chuck

Raise your hand if you have ever thought about writing a book. The number of you now raising your hands is probably pretty small. It is not that you don't have a lot of experience; rather, it is that you have to make sure all that experience lands on the page for the reader. Up until last year, I would have put myself squarely into the camp that said they would never write a book. However, after going through the process of writing this book, I can say that it is the most professionally gratifying experience I have had to date.

A book like this does not happen without a lot of support. First and foremost, I would like to thank my mom and sister Marie for being amazing cheerleaders. They were always there, checking on progress and offering encouragement throughout the process. There are many who suggested we write this book, but the loudest voice was Stephanie Wonderlin. I can't thank you enough, Stephanie, for suggesting that I go down this road.

Thank you to Jim Weiss and Bob Pearson at W2O Group for not only supporting me in this endeavor but also bringing me to such an amazing firm. I have learned a lot while working for you and appreciate everything you have done for me. Also, a huge thank you to my team at WCG (current and former)—Brandon Watts, Meredith Owen, Emma O'Brien, Natalie DeNike, James Wade, Justine Braun, Shruti Saran, Allison Barnes, Jackie Birnbaum, and Jessica Pina—who have supported me throughout this project.

I would also like to thank Scott Chaikin, Chas Withers, Keith Mabee, and Rob Berick for giving me my first agency job at Dix & Eaton. If you had not taken a chance on me back then, I would not be where I am today.

Thank you to Aaron Strout and Spike Jones for your friendship and also your guidance while we were writing this book. Your perspective as authors was invaluable to us throughout the process.

I also want to thank several friends and mentors who provided support for me as we were writing the book. Thank you to Tom Webster, Tamsen Snyder Webster, Justin Levy, Michael Brito, Kyle Flaherty, Greg Matthews, Colin Foster, Andrew Nystrom, Summer Boone, Jason Falls, Lauren Warthan, Heather Whaling, Amanda Kleinhenz, Samia Joseph, and Lisa Grimm. I very much appreciate all you have done to support me.

Thank you to Katherine Bull, our acquisitions editor, who has patiently worked with us every step of the way. This book would not have happened without the faith you have put in us. I cannot thank you enough. Thank you also to Charlotte Kughen, our development editor, and Don Martelli, our technical editor, for their tireless work in making sure this book sings for the reader.

Thank you also to Ken Burbary, my co-author, for agreeing to embark on this journey with me. It could not have been completed without your expertise and knowledge.

Finally, I would like to say thank you to all the clients I have worked with over the years. All of you have taught me a lot about business and marketing, and I hope I have added value to your business during our relationship.

From Ken

Before setting out on this adventure, I never imagined what an amazing and terrifying process writing a book could be. I survived, but only thanks to the love, help, and support of so many wonderful people in my life. I would like to thank my family for being so supportive, understanding the sacrifice that this "second job" required. The encouragement, support, and at times tough love you gave me were incredible, and I wouldn't have succeeded without you.

I'd like to thank many other people, from friends to professional mentors and peers, but there simply isn't enough room to mention them all. A special thank you to the following people, whose advice, opinions, or expertise helped me throughout the writing of this book. Thank you Tom Webster, Aaron Strout, James Sanders, Adam Cohen, Lucy-Shon, Bill Silarski, and Noah Mallin.

Finally, I would like to thank two people without whom this book wouldn't have been possible. Katherine Bull, our acquisitions editor at Pearson, exercised herculean patience when dealing with this first-time author throughout the process. Your understanding, coaching, and flexibility are appreciated very much. Thank you also to Charlotte Kughen, our development editor, and Don Martelli, our technical editor, for their great work on this book. Thank you to my co-author and friend Chuck Hemann. I am grateful for having the opportunity to work with you on this project together and can't thank you enough for the help and understanding you've shown along the way. It's been a wild ride; this book wouldn't have happened without you.

We Want to Hear from You!

As the reader of this book, *you* are our most important critic and commentator. We value your opinion and want to know what we're doing right, what we could do better, what areas you'd like to see us publish in, and any other words of wisdom you're willing to pass our way.

As an associate publisher for Que Publishing, I welcome your comments. You can email or write me directly to let me know what you did or didn't like about this book—as well as what we can do to make our books better.

Please note that I cannot help you with technical problems related to the topic of this book. We do have a User Services group, however, where I will forward specific technical questions related to the book.

When you write, please be sure to include this book's title and author as well as your name, email address, and phone number. I will carefully review your comments and share them with the author and editors who worked on the book.

Email: feedback@quepublishing.com
Mail: Greg Wiegand
           Editor-in-Chief
           Que Publishing
           800 East 96th Street
           Indianapolis, IN 46240 USA

Reader Services

Visit our website and register this book at quepublishing.com/register for convenient access to any updates, downloads, or errata that might be available for this book.

Understanding the Digital Media Landscape

When digital marketing and advertising began in the 1990s, the promise of digital channels was to deliver the right message to the right audience at the right time—a game-changing upgrade over traditional media channels. Digital media has been sold as a nirvana of data collection, analysis, and measurement that would yield the most efficient, optimized programs one could hope for. Fast-forward 15 years, and we've learned that achieving that reality isn't impossible but can be far more difficult than it seems at first glance.

Today's digital media landscape is more complex than ever before. The continuous and rapid introduction of new platforms, tools, data sources, and media consumption devices (such as mobile devices and tablets) have created an environment that can make any marketer's head spin. The challenge now lies in identifying which unique composition of all those choices is required to produce the outcomes needed to achieve your digital goals and objectives.

Digital media is great at creating data about who you are, what you like and dislike, and where you've been online. This book helps you work smarter by providing you with the approach and information you need to understand and utilize the data that exists across the entire digital landscape. Hopefully the original digital promise that got everyone so excited in the first place will become a reality for you, and you'll have a better understanding of why digital channels continue to draw more investment in time and money away from traditional media channels.

Digital Media Types

From the mid-'90s until the present day, the digital media landscape has undergone tremendous change. For a good 10 years there were two dominant media types, although we've relabeled them through the years. The first is *paid media*, either in the form of paid search (think Google AdWords) or display advertising (think DoubleClick banner ads). Paid media is literally just that—digital media channels that a brand pays to utilize.

The second is *owned media*. This is a generic term for any media asset or platform that a company owns, controls, and utilizes to reach a prospective audience. Some of the most common forms of owned media are dot-com brand websites, email marketing to subscribers, and company blogs. For both paid and owned media, clicks still rule as the dominant data to collect and analyze. However, tracking what happens after a user clicks on a link can be useful, but it can't answer all the questions.

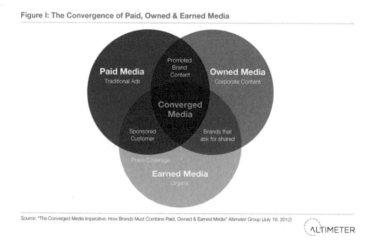

Figure I: The Convergence of Paid, Owned & Earned Media

Source: "The Converged Media Imperative: How Brands Must Combine Paid, Owned & Earned Media" Altimeter Group (July 19, 2012)

ALTIMETER

Figure 1.1   *Paid, earned, and owned media are converging to the point where one type of media has a direct impact on the other.*

Source: *"The Converged Media Imperative: How Brands Must Combine Paid, Owned & Earned Media," Altimeter Group (July 19, 2012)*

In the past several years, there has been the emergence of a third media type, called *earned media* (see Figure 1.1). Some say it's new; others think it's simply a new label for what public relations professionals have historically called *free media*, something generated by word of mouth, buzz, or a communication "going viral."

With Facebook eclipsing 900 million users and Twitter closing in on 150 million, owned and earned media are now richer sources of data that include new data types that weren't available to marketers in the past—specifically those types that involve user behaviors, intentions, and affinities. The new era of engagement has resulted in a data explosion that takes us beyond analyzing clicks, counting advertising impressions, and adding up website page views.

The data and tools available today can give you the insight you need to improve marketing and advertising performance. You can now better understand both the qualitative and quantitative dimensions of a prospective audience. You can use this knowledge to personalize user experiences and facilitate a real value exchange that meets users' needs and expectations. Simply put, you've never been in a better position to generate the desired outcomes and predict future behavior thanks to the robust ecosystem of data and analytics tools. Over the course of the next several chapters we will dive into these tools, which include search analytics, social media monitoring, and social media engagement.

Each media type contains several channels that serve a purpose and play a role in your marketing mix. The data and analytics associated with each helps you determine how much or how little of a role each should play. No digital strategy can succeed based on only one media type.

Paid Media

Paid media is a more mature media type than some of the other digital media types. It has well-established methods of targeting, audience segmentation, and measurement. Additionally, paid media programs contain real-time measurement capabilities, which allow companies the opportunity to assess and change course if necessary. However, because the way paid media programs are executed is well-established, the models have not evolved to meet the impact of owned media channels (such as Facebook, Twitter, YouTube, and so on).

Paid search is still one of the best places to get insights and understanding about an audience. Several search engine and third-party analytics tools work with search data to identify user, behavioral, and intention insights. Read Chapter 5, "Tools: Search Analytics," for more information on paid search data and analytics.

Paid display, otherwise known as banner advertising, is suffering these days due to "banner blindness." Banner blindness happens for one very clear reason: utter saturation of the digital landscape with all types of banner advertising units, including standard ads, rich media ads, interactive game ads, and social ads. Consumers have become so attuned to seeing display ad units on web pages that they block them out. Banners are essentially background noise most of the time. The net effect is declining views and click-through rates (CTRs).

Performance of banner ads varies due to many factors as well as the banner type. The average CTR for a standard banner ad unit is estimated to be around 0.1% or 0.2%, depending on banner type. This means that if 1,000 people see a banner, only 1 or 2 people click it. This is subpar performance by any standard, and it compares unfavorably to seemingly less attractive digital options, such as email (or even traditional marketing options such as direct mail).

The upside of the paid display market is its well-established methods for targeting and measurement. Publishers and ad-serving platforms have become quite advanced in their usage of cookies for collecting data and tracking an audience. In fact, it's big business. According to a 2012 cross-industry study by Krux, data collection and audience profiling grew 400% over the prior year. This means, for example, that the average number of data-collection events associated with a single web page visit increased from 10 to 50.

Targeting is done through a combination of both first- and third-party data. What does this mean? It means the company (first party) that owns the website you land on is directly capturing data about you and your visit. Third-party collection is responsible for the lion's share of data collection growth. In fact, the number of data collection companies has doubled, with more than 300 companies observed in the 2012 Krux study, compared to 167 the previous year. Targeting is done through a variety of creative cookie wrangling and has been aided by the integration of social technologies into owned media assets.

An example of targeting that is quite common, and yet not well known, is popular social sharing widgets such as ShareThis. It's a simple proposition for website owners: A company can easily install a preconfigured social sharing widget to allow sharing of their brand content across major social networking platforms and/or email. ShareThis is free, and it takes little time to get it installed and running. The catch, though, is data leakage. The sharing widgets are voluntarily leaking data about users to third parties.

In exchange for freely distributing a sharing widget, companies like ShareThis target users by tracking users' sharing activity through the network of websites that have the widget installed. They collect data about what users like, read, share, save, and more. This data is then augmented with additional targeting data and sold at a premium.

To truly understand the magnitude of data generation and collection that occurs, you can do a fun exercise using a browser plug-in. The developer disconnect.me has created a plug-in for the Google Chrome browser called Collusion that graphs in real time all the data collection that occurs during your web browsing. Figure 1.2 maps the web of data collectors associated with just 15 minutes of a web surfing session. Collusion provides an effective way to see a visual representation of data leakage.

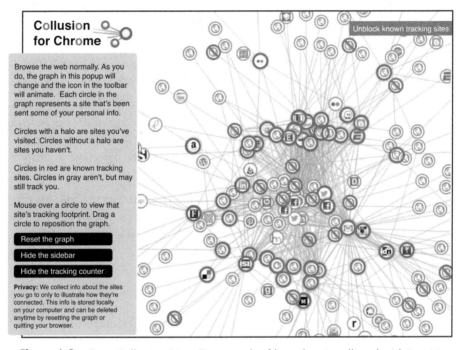

Figure 1.2   *Data Collection Map: An example of how data is collected with just 15 minutes of a web surfing session.*

Source: Google

The end result is a robust data set that can be sliced and diced using data management platforms (DMPs) such as Demdex or BlueKai. DMPs are cookie data warehouses married to analytics engines that have massive horsepower. They are designed to clean, manage, and integrate data with all different types of first-party and third-party data that a company might have or purchase.

DMPs offer advanced capabilities to find trends and to understand and segment audiences based on user attributes, media consumption habits, and more. Many large corporations with complex segmentation needs, such as those within the Fortune 100, have migrated to utilizing DMPs to increase performance and improve efficiency through optimization and targeting.

We identify some paid media data sources that you can use to gain deeper audience insights and understanding in this chapter.

Owned Media

It's not just the emergence of earned media that is new to the digital data and analytics landscape. Owned media assets offer more options than ever to gather competitive intelligence, user experience feedback, real-time site analytics, and testing for site optimization in addition to richer-than-ever-before clickstream activity analysis.

Your goal should be to tie the insights and data from each media channel to one another to tell a deeper story. These are not redundant analytics options, meant to be an either/or decision. Remember, they complement one another.

Trying to decide which of the data and analytics options to implement can be overwhelming. Your choice depends on your defined goals and learning agenda. You can read more about the details of defining clear and specific objectives in Chapter 2, "Understanding Digital Analytics Concepts."

Developing a learning agenda is a useful technique in defining the boundaries of where to focus your analytics efforts. Such an agenda essentially defines the specific questions you are trying to answer about your audience and acts as a guide for your analysis during a project to keep you focused.

 Note

It's now the big data era. Massive amounts of data and processing are available, but you don't need all of it. Many companies are struggling with digital analytics because they are trying to collect everything. Resist the urge to collect and analyze all the data these platforms make available. Remember that although they're interesting, many digital data sources are diagnostic measures at best, and some lack the ability to take action. Applying the "So what?" test is a simple and helpful way to avoid chasing shiny objects that have no real business value. Ask yourself, "So what? What action can I take based on this data?" If the answer isn't clear, you're probably just playing with a tool that spews data rather than valuable insights.

In the following few sections, we dive into each of the considerations for analytics on your owned media properties.

Competitive Intelligence

Keeping an eye on competitors is nothing new. There is quite a bit to pay attention to these days, and there are many tools aimed at helping you understand what your competitors are doing on both their owned media assets and social media platforms. You should use a combination of free and paid tools to access the data you need for competitive intelligence.

> ✉ *Note*
>
> You'll see that using a combination of free and paid tools to perform adequate analyses is a theme of this book.

Free tools from Google, Alexa, and Compete can provide competitor website and audience profile data. Paid versions of these tools offer more robust data on consumer behavior data that you can use to answer specific questions such as these:

- Which audience segments are competitors reaching that you are not?
- What keywords are successful for your competitors?
- What sources are driving traffic to your competitors' websites?

It's not difficult to gather competitive intelligence data when it comes to social media. Most of this data is freely available to anyone who is interested in it. Quick-and-dirty approaches using free versions of tools such as SimplyMeasured can provide a wide range of competitive intelligence across several social platforms, including the following:

- Facebook competitive analysis
- Facebook content analysis
- YouTube competitive analysis
- YouTube channel analysis
- Twitter profile analysis

These higher-level reports do not always provide the depth you need. To get more information, you can use specialty tools that focus on particular social platforms and can provide more detailed data and metrics. For example, EdgeRank Checker focuses exclusively on Facebook analytics for a specific industry and compares them to your brand page. Reports like the ones you get from EdgeRank Checker provide analysis and insight into post-grading, page recommendations, trending of post performance over time, and keyword engagement analysis.

Clickstream (Web Analytics)

Counting onsite activity using web analytics is the oldest form of digital analytics. (Remember log file analysis of website hits?) Thankfully, web analytics tools have come a long way since those days and now offer a full suite of advanced measurement and analytics features, including the following, among many others:

- **Custom dashboards**—Leading platforms offer the ability to create custom dashboards, personalized to your site and conversion events, including threshold notifications for key events and custom key performance indicators (KPIs)/goal definition.

- **Content analytics**—Content is king. Identifying best- and worst-performing content is invaluable. You cannot optimize what you don't measure, and content analytics gives you a window into what content users are consuming and interacting with most (and least). Internal page analytics and local site search reporting also provides useful insights into what users are looking for.

  In addition to content analytics, several leading web analytics platforms, such as Adobe Omniture and Google Analytics, also allow for content experimentation. This feature gives you the ability to test variations of content and user experience on your website pages in order to determine which specific permutations yield the most conversions and highest user satisfaction.

- **Mobile analytics**—The mobile web is in the midst of an explosion, and it hasn't yet reached critical mass. Mobile analytics is no longer only a nice-to-have feature; it's a core requirement to provide an effective mobile experience, whether through a mobile-optimized site or mobile application. Web analytics tools have incorporated mobile support, and they offer a robust set of features to measure any mobile content across any mobile device. Mobile analytics provides answers to common questions such as these:

  - Where is my mobile traffic coming from?

  - What content are mobile users most interested in?

  - How is my mobile app being used? What's working? What isn't?

  - Which mobile platforms (and versions) work best with my site?

  - How does mobile users' engagement with my site compare to traditional web users' engagement?

Conversion Analytics

Your website exists for a reason. More specifically, it exists for a set of specific conversion events. Leading web analytics platforms provide insights regarding this key area and answer questions about how onsite user behaviors lead to conversions (regardless of what those may be—sales, registrations, leads, and so on).

One of the most advanced capabilities offered in the area of conversion analytics has to do with multichannel funnel attribution. You're no longer limited by the "last click" attribution problem. You can now gain insight into how much each digital marketing or advertising channels are contributing to specific conversion goals, including paid search, paid display, social marketing, email marketing, and more.

Another useful feature is user experience path visualization, which enables you to determine the highest-performing visitor conversion paths. What are the most common and highest-performing entry points onsite? Where are users getting stuck along the path? What step in the user experience journey causes the most abandonment? These are all key questions involved in optimizing the user experience.

Finally, some leading platforms, such as Blue Fountain Media, offer attribution modeling. Want to build predictive models to attribute conversions to specific channels to better gauge your channel mix and investment? Now you can.

Custom Segmentation

Custom segmentation enables you to personalize your web analytics in the way that's most relevant to your business. It allows you to define custom variables and classify individual user segments or groups.

Analyzing your traffic in aggregate might be interesting, but it isn't advised. As Avinash Kaushik—one of the foremost experts on all things web analytics—has repeated over the years, data in the aggregate is useless. You must segment or die. This has never been more true than it is today. It's one of the biggest issues we currently face with social platforms and the data they generate. Most social platforms provide vast amounts of data, but in the aggregate, which is not terribly useful. Facebook, for example, provides basic segmentation by certain demographics, such as age, gender, location, and a few others, but as of this writing, it doesn't allow page administrators to segment their audiences in a meaningful way.

With custom segmentation, you can divide your audience into segments that mirror your customers and prospects, and this enables you to optimize and personalize the user experience for each. Custom segmentation also enables you to drill down into specific subsections of a site, such as visitors that converted or paid user behavior versus organic user behavior.

Visual Overlays

Visual overlays are a nice-to-have but useful method for viewing web analytics data in a visual format. This typically includes overlays in the form of heatmaps, clickmaps, and geomaps that show physical locations of website users.

API Integration

We live in a world of application programming interface (API) integration. Mashing up one data type with another can reveal new and incredible opportunities. Thankfully, leading web analytics tools provide APIs for precisely this purpose. The ability to connect website user data with other types of data is a reality. Chapter 23, "The Future of Digital Data: Business Intelligence," touches on this topic.

Social Media Reporting

Some people like to categorize any social profile in the earned category, but we disagree. There is a difference between real "earned media" through word of mouth, buzz, and so on and direct investment in maintaining a brand presence on a social platform. Maintaining a brand presence requires investing time and money on behalf of a brand, which is why we have included social reporting in the owned media category.

Many web analytics tools now provide varying degrees of social analytics reports. These channels do not exist in silos but must work together. Converged media is the future. In an effort to measure the specific effect that social activities have on the metrics and goals that matter, we see these tools in the early stages of social attribution. There are indeed limitations now, but they offer the ability to

- Identify which social referral sources send the most engaged visitors to your site.
- Learn which brand content social visitors engaged with most and what visitors are sharing most.
- Learn how users engage with your brand content offsite, on websites that are not your own.
- Segment and measure the performance of individual social media campaigns.
- Create custom segments for users on individual social networks, such as Facebook and Twitter. This is a useful feature because segmentation enables you to truly understand the differences between your user groups and provides you with insight to optimize and personalize the user experience.
- Identify which user-generated content is responsible for amplifying brand content; this contributes to true "earned media."

These social report integrations for web analytics tools do have some shortcomings. Data quality concerns, reporting inconsistencies, and overall data coverage are issues. For example, Google Analytics currently supports some major social platforms in its tracking, but it excludes others. This creates blind spots and can lead to questionable analyses and decision making, based on a false view of user behavior and the digital landscape.

Although an integrated solution containing both web analytics and social analytics is ideal, at this point you are better served by using best-of-breed tools for each. The social analytics landscape is immature, fragmented, and, frankly, a mess. There is too much choice, there are too many redundant tools with little to no differentiation that have created an incredibly frustrating and difficult experience for buyers. The future holds more mergers and acquisitions to reduce these problems, much as it did in the early days of digital with the early web analytics vendors.

User Experience Feedback

There are tools that enable you to gather very specific qualitative user feedback through onsite surveys. Some call this "voice of the customer," and others call it "visitor feedback." All these tools share a common functionality, which is a continuous and consistent measurement of the user's website experience.

Clickstream analysis can provide insight into the volume of activity by page and conversions. It's a starting point, but it provides an incomplete picture of overall site activity, and it's why companies try to collect specific feedback. User experience feedback can be crucial for answering the following questions and determining how users feel about the overall website experience:

- How would you rate your overall website experience?
- What was the primary purpose of your visit?
- Were you able to complete your primary task?
- Could anything about your website experience be improved?

Site-survey solutions, such as those from iPerceptions and ForeSee Results, provide additional benefits, such as web analytics integration, threshold-based alerts to notify you about significant changes, and benchmarks of vertical industries for comparisons.

The combination of quantitative clickstream analysis to determine what is happening onsite and qualitative user experience feedback can answer many questions about what is working with an owned media asset and what needs improvement.

Real-Time Site Analytics

The newest kid on this block, real-time analytics, overlaps with traditional web analytics in terms of technical capabilities, but real-time analytics runs at hyperspeed. Real-time analytics is all about what's happening on your website *right now*.

Real-time solutions from companies such as Chartbeat and Woopra were created to solve problems for those on the frontlines who are responsible for managing publishing and media sites, but they're useful for just about any company. The assumption is that the end users are in sales, marketing, or content roles and aren't looking to immerse themselves in data and reports. They're focused on optimizing the user experience for each audience segment in real-time.

Real-time analytics tools provide analysis and reporting of what users on your site are doing on a second-by-second basis. You can use these tools to determine how active your users are on a page, what page interactions they are most engaged in, and what content topics and types are most consumed, shared, and ignored. Whereas web analytics focuses on clickstream analysis, real-time site analytics focuses on everything else that happens between clicks.

2

Understanding Digital Analytics Concepts

Communicators have had a love/hate relationship with numbers for as long as there has been a communications profession. Writing; interacting with clients, colleagues, and reporters; and doing high-level research are all things that are more comfortable to communicators than numbers. Unfortunately for those numbers-averse professionals, the explosion of digital media has also led to the explosion of available data with which to analyze program and campaign performance.

One of the most common reasons for aversion to numbers is a lack of familiarity with key terminology. There is a lack of clarity around what each of the metrics means, which metrics are most important, how each of the metrics is collected, how to develop goals, and which metrics fit those goals. This chapter helps you understand how to set proper goals and objectives, what the key metrics are for digital analytics, and how these metrics can be aligned with traditional tactics.

Starting at the Top

Before you dig into specific metrics, it is important that you understand how to determine the right metrics for your campaign. Public relations textbooks have been teaching students for years how to set measurable goals and objectives, but the communications landscape is changing. Public relations professionals have new channels and new available tactics for reaching customers that might not be covered in a textbook.

However, just because the channels are new does not mean the way we arrive at metrics should change. What are the components of a measurable goal? There are three things that every practitioner—digital or otherwise—should know:

- **Behavior**—This is the most critical component of goal setting. Are you trying to increase awareness with your target audience, or are you trying to get your target audience to take some sort of action? Take a moment to sit down and write out what your desired behaviors are from the program.

- **Amount of change**—It is important to identify how much you want the behavior to change. It can be expressed as a raw number (for example, the number of new people entering a store is expected to go up by 5,000 customers) or as a percentage (for example, the number of new people entering a store is expected to increase by 10%).

- **Time**—Every goal should have a time element. Whether it is a year, a month, or a week, professionals should be looking to identify how long the program or campaign will last.

There are a lot of metrics available to you, but the metrics that you actually use to gauge the success of a program should flow from the behavior you are trying to affect. For example, if you are trying to raise awareness, an appropriate metric might be impressions, page views, or reach. Similarly, if you are trying to drive consumers to a website, then tracking the number of clicks and visits would be most appropriate.

Spending the time to outline the behaviors you are looking to change, how much you want to change them, and how long it will take you to potentially change them is critical. Without that grounding, there is a very good chance you will be analyzing too many data points, analyzing the wrong data points, and, most importantly, not truly understanding how your program is performing.

Determining Your Owned and Earned Social Metrics

Social metrics are likely to be the most familiar metrics to communicators because these days very few programs are executed without a social component. An abundance of metrics are available to professionals, which makes landing on the "right" metrics all the more challenging. To add a layer of complexity, social metrics can be broken down into two different groups:

- **Owned social metrics**—These are metrics related to the social channels (Facebook page, Twitter account, YouTube channel, and so on) that you are currently maintaining.

- **Earned social metrics**—When communications programs are developed, professionals design them in the hope that conversation will take place outside owned social channels. Every conversation about the program or the brand that you did not directly "pitch" would be considered earned.

The following sections dive into the specific metrics for the owned and earned categories. Keep in the back of your mind that the metrics described here are the most common metrics. The metrics that you pick for your program must align with the behaviors you are trying to change. Examining other metrics can be interesting, but may be a waste of effort.

Owned Social Metrics

If you are a communicator who is currently developing a program for your company or client and are not including a social media component, you are most likely in the minority. That is not to say that social media belongs in every program, just that in the majority of cases, some sort of social activation makes sense.

There are a number of ways to approach this topic, but we thought it would be most helpful to break down the top metrics by social media platform that communications professionals are using today. Please note that these are the metrics for the top social media platforms. There are a number of fringe social media channels that we do not explore here.

 Note

The following sections describe the key owned social media metrics across the bigger social media networks. There are obviously others available to you, and you should always be looking to tie your metrics choices to the behaviors you are trying to change, but these are a good place to start.

Facebook

Facebook is the most popular social network and boasts more than 900 million users. There is a pretty good chance that if you are reading this book, you maintain a page for a brand or client, and you have a personal page that you use to share photos, favorite articles, and news about yourself. If you are managing a Facebook fan page, you have access to Facebook Insights. Facebook Insights is Facebook's free analytics platform that enables page owners to see metrics on how their pages are performing.

If you have logged into Facebook Insights recently, you know how daunting it can be. There are a lot of possible metrics, and it is not completely clear how you decide which ones you should be using. The answer to which metrics you should pay attention to depends on the behavior you are trying to change. However, there are popular metrics that almost every communications professional looks at when evaluating the page's performance. Here are the most popular:

- **Total likes**—Probably the most common and easiest to understand, total likes is the number of people who have "liked" your page.
- **Reach**—Facebook breaks down reach into organic, paid, and viral. *Organic reach* is the number of people who have seen a post in the news feed, in the ticker, or on the page itself. *Paid reach* is the number of unique people who have seen an advertisement or a sponsored story. *Viral reach* is the number of unique people who have seen a story about a page published by a friend.
- **Engaged users**—This is the number of people who have clicked on one of your posts during a given time. It provides a good benchmark for how many people are actually reading your Facebook page's content.
- **People talking about this (PTAT)**—PTAT is a combination metric that includes the number of likes, comments, shares, and total stories created over a 7-, 14-, or 28-day period.
- **Likes, comments, and shares by post**—The preceding metrics in this list are page-level metrics, but there are some post-level metrics you should also watch. *Likes* refers to the number of people who have clicked the Like button on a post, and *comments* refers to those who have contributed some opinion on a post. *Shares* refers to the number of people who have posted your content on their page.

Twitter

Unlike Facebook, which provides users with an extensive analytics platform, Twitter is largely bereft of data. If you are managing a Twitter account for a brand, there is very little data available to you outside number of followers and lists. In later chapters we will go into greater detail about social media management system (SMMS) that can be helpful in collecting more data. For now, here are some common metrics you can examine for Twitter:

- **Followers**—Similar to likes on Facebook, this is the number of people who have decided to track your brand's account.

- **Retweets**—This is the number of people who have shared your content with their followers.

- **Replies**—Replies refers to how often someone has mentioned your brand directly on Twitter.

- **Clicks and click-through rate (CTR)**—Clicks refers to the number of times people have clicked a link that you shared, and the CTR is the number of clicks divided by the number of people who had an opportunity to click, typically expressed as a percentage. It is important to note that without the use of a link-shortening service, such as bitly, tracking clicks is not possible. Posting directly to Twitter or Facebook does not allow you to track the number of clicks on a post.

Note

Link shortening services take an extremely long web address and shorten it to fit within the context of a character limited tweet or Facebook post.

- **Impressions**—Impressions refers to the number of times someone viewed or had the opportunity to view your content. Impressions on Twitter is somewhat controversial as some analytics tools calculate impressions by including replies. If you reply to someone on Twitter, the only people who see it are you, the recipient, and the followers who overlap. If you are using a social media management tool, you should ask to see how it is calculating impressions. If you are calculating impressions manually, you should exclude replies from your analysis to get the most accurate count.

YouTube

Like Facebook, YouTube offers channel owners a robust analytics platform for tracking performance. There are metrics related to how the channel itself is performing, as well as how specific videos are resonating with your target audience. There is a lot of data available to channel owners, and these are the most popular metrics:

- **Views**—Views on YouTube can be broken down into how many times someone saw a video or the YouTube channel itself.
- **Subscribers**—This is the number of people who have signed up to receive your content since you posted it.
- **Likes/dislikes**—This is the number of times a viewer had selected whether they like or dislike a video. This is typically expressed as a raw number, but it can be aggregated to show a ratio of likes to dislikes over the span of several videos.
- **Comments**—This is the number of times someone has offered an opinion on a video or your channel.
- **Favorites**—This is the number of times viewers have clicked on the Favorite link to show how much they like a particular video.
- **Sharing**—This is the number of times your video has been posted on another social network. YouTube aggregates sharing into a single metric.

One important note about YouTube is that in many instances, the engagement numbers can be combined into one number. So, for example, if you are the channel owner, you can combine likes, comments, and favorites into one number that shows engagement overall. Or, similarly, you can combine the numbers and divide by the total number of videos to achieve an engagement rate.

SlideShare

One doesn't normally think of SlideShare as a popular social network, but, according to Quantcast, the site receives almost 33 million visitors globally each month. It is a valuable place to provide thought leadership and, if you are managing the communications for a public company, it's a place to share earnings announcements, investor presentations, and other documents of interest to key stakeholders. There is not a lot of data available, but channel owners can find some metrics:

- **Followers**—This is the equivalent of a like on Facebook or an account follower on Twitter. When you decide to follow someone or a brand on SlideShare, you receive notifications when new content has been posted.
- **Views**—This is the number of times someone has seen something you have uploaded to your channel (documents and presentations).
- **Comments**—Viewers of your content have the opportunity to add to the discussion by contributing their point of view. This metric measures the number of such comments.

- **Shares**—Every piece of content that you upload can be shared to multiple social channels. It is important to track how often your content is "picked up" and "placed" elsewhere, as it provides a strong barometer for how well it is resonating.

Pinterest

One of the fastest-growing social networks, with approximately 12 million users, Pinterest offers users space to create virtual pinboards for images of interest across the Internet. Companies are just now starting to create branded channels on Pinterest, and data on just how well those channels are performing is fairly limited. Pinterest has yet to build out an analytics platform for its users. However, there is some data you can capture manually:

- **Followers**—As with the other social networks listed earlier, followers on Pinterest is the number of people who have elected to view your content.
- **Number of boards**—This is the number of separate pinboards you have created for your account. Companies that are currently using Pinterest typically create pinboards based on product categories.
- **Number of pins**—This is simply the number of images or videos that have been "pinned" to a board you own.
- **Likes**—As is the case with the other channels, users can click the Like button for individual pieces of content. This metric counts those clicks.
- **Repins**—If you like something that another user has pinned, you can click the Repin button to share it with your Pinterest followers. This metric counts the number of repins.
- **Comments**—As with the other channels, users have a chance to offer their own perspective on a piece of content. This metric counts those comments.

In a recent announcement, Pinterest disclosed that it received $100 million in funding, including money from a Japanese-based ecommerce company called Rakuten. As Pinterest explores more ecommerce opportunities, it is likely that its analytics offerings will improve.

Google+

As with Pinterest, brands are just now truly exploring the possibility of creating a Google+ presence. And like Pinterest, Google+ does not offer its users very much data on how the channel is performing. There are some metrics users can look at, but collection at this point is manual:

- **Number of people who have an account circled**—This is the Google+ equivalent of likes, followers, or fans. It is the number of people who have put you in a circle in order to track your content.

- **+1s**—Clicking the +1 button on Google+ is the equivalent of a like on Facebook, SlideShare, or YouTube. This metric counts the number of such clicks.

- **Comments**—Like every other channel, users can offer their unique perspective on a piece of content you have posted. This metric counts the number of such comments.

 Note

There has been widespread speculation about the integration of Google Analytics (discussed in later chapters) into Google+. But that hasn't yet happened.

Flickr

Flickr, the largest photo-sharing site, does not offer its users very much in the way of metrics. It is very top level and doesn't dig into how a photo might be resonating with your target audience. That being said, the area of visual analytics is exploding as visual channels (such as YouTube, Flickr, and Pinterest) achieve higher levels of adoption. If you are posting photos to Flickr as part of your program, what can you track? Here are the possibilities:

- **Views**—This is the number of people who have seen a photo that you have uploaded. Views can also be the total number of times people have viewed your sets of photos.

- **Favorites**—As is the case with YouTube, users can click the Favorite link to show appreciation for a piece of content. This metric counts the number of such clicks.

- **Comments**—As on the other social media networks, Flickr users can offer their perspectives on a piece of content in the form of a comment. This metric counts those comments.

⚲ *Tip*

Although most of these metrics are for networks themselves (for example, likes on a Facebook page), you can also gather post-by-post data, if necessary.

Earned Social Media Metrics

The best communications programs have tactics that resonate with the target audience using the appropriate channels, but the explosion of social media has created a second layer of performance that requires examination. This additional layer is earned coverage, or, in the case of social media, earned conversations. When communications professionals create content to post on owned social media networks, they hope the content will spread. This dissemination could come in the form of sharing, which we covered earlier in this chapter, or it could come in the form of organic chatter in the broader community.

There are two different kinds of earned social media metrics that communicators can track:

- **Earned conversations**—These are social media conversations that are taking place outside the owned social media properties

- **In-network conversations**—Communicators should be looking to foster a sense of contribution in the online community. Tracking this kind of content separately is valuable in determining how well it does in driving action, typically additional engagement.

Much of this data is captured using social media monitoring software, which is covered in the next two chapters, but these are the primary data points most communicators gather when evaluating earned conversations:

- **Share of voice**—Most communicators are familiar with the concept of market share, and this is fairly similar. Share of voice tracks, typically in percentage form, how much conversation is happening about one brand versus another.

- **Share of conversation**—Share of conversation is often overlooked and, in our view, is a more accurate gauge of how aware people are of a product or campaign within a broader industry than share of voice. This metric tracks, typically in percentage form, how much conversation is happening versus the broader industry.

- **Sentiment**—The topic of sentiment is highly controversial. Simply put, it is the amount of positive, negative, or neutral (with gradations in between) conversation that is happening about a brand or product.

- **Message resonance**—Chances are good that your company, and in turn your communications program, is trying to advance some message or messages. Knowing how well (or not) a message is being received by the community is vital. Again, you'll learn more on tracking things like message resonance with social media monitoring software later on in Chapter 3, "Picking the Tools of the Trade," and Chapter 4, "Tools: Social Listening."

- **Overall conversation volume**—Tracking the volume of conversation over time is critical in understanding how well a message has been received. Similarly, it is important in understanding how visible a brand is to the community. If your conversation volume trend line looks like a rollercoaster, then it is likely time to start revisiting your social media strategy.

The other element of earned social media metrics is in-network conversations. These are conversations, or content, that the community generates on its own and posts to owned properties. These are easier metrics to understand and gather because they are almost identical to the metrics outlined earlier in the section for specific social media channels. The only difference is that instead of looking at higher-level page performance (likes, followers, subscribers, and so on) communicators should be looking at post-level data (comments, likes per post, shares per post, and so on).

Social media data is abundant, and as it becomes more mainstream, more data will become available. Because of that abundance, it is easy to become distracted by all the potential data points. If you focus on the metrics we have listed and how they apply to your goals, you will not go wrong. That being said, social media data is only one piece of the puzzle. There are other digital components communicators need to gather, as described in the remainder of this chapter.

Demystifying Web Data

Most communicators have had at least some exposure to web analytics tools, such as Google Analytics, Webtrends, and Omniture. However, web data tends to be the most confusing of all digital data sources.

The good news for communicators is that almost regardless of which tool you decide to use to gather web data, the outputs look very similar. The bad news is that, as with social media, there is a lot of web data available.

Where should communicators begin? Whatever tool you select, the vendor will likely offer a training program, but regardless, the web metrics you decide to measure should line up with the behaviors you are trying to change. If you keep your eye on measurable goals, picking the right metrics in a sea of data will not be a challenge. So, what are some metrics that communicators typically use? There are a number of things you can do to track the effectiveness of a website and how it interrelates with other channels. Suffice it to say, though, that the following metrics are the most popular metrics communicators are using today:

- **Visits**—Depending on the platform in question, visits is the number of times people have been on your site. Visits are considered to be unique in that if I come to your page, click a few links, and then leave, that is one visit. If I return to your site quickly, that is considered part of the same session.

- **Unique page views**—This is the number of visits during which a specified page(s) was viewed once.

- **Bounce rate**—Bounce rate is expressed as a percentage and is the number of visits in which a person left a site from the initial entry page.

- **Pages per visit**—This is probably the easiest metric to understand. It is simply the number of pages a person viewed during a single session. It is important to understand how many pages and which pages a person visited during a session to see which content resonated.

- **Traffic sources**—This is not one metric, per se, but knowing the traffic sources is helpful in matching up content from social channels to website presence.

- **Conversion**—Conversion is probably the most controversial metric because it is one that does not apply to all situations. In some cases, companies are using digital media channels to build awareness. In those instances, conversions do not apply. If you are tracking conversion, it is the number of times someone has taken an action on your page—or a dollar figure expressing the amount spent on the page. If a visitor downloads a white paper, buys something from your site, or even signs up for coupons via email, the action is counted as a conversion. Whatever it is, conversion is an important metric for communicators to track. It is a clear way to demonstrate the value of a program.

Searching for the Right Metrics

Search analytics suffers a similar fate to web analytics, in that there is a lot of confusion around what to measure and how to measure it. Some of that is due to the mysticism behind Google's ranking algorithm, but the majority of it is due to search analytics being a relatively new field for many communicators.

For years, search analytics has been an area where specialists have come in and offered counsel to companies. Recently, a link has been created between social media and search analytics that makes it imperative for communicators of all disciplines to have at least a basic understanding of search data. The data collection and metrics themselves are not so mysterious if you know how to break them down into manageable chunks. Search analytics is typically broken up into two categories.

- **Paid searches**—A paid search is any form of online advertising that ties an ad to a specific keyword-based search request.

- **Organic searches**—Organic search results are listings on search engine result pages that appear because of specific relevance to search terms.

Both types of search analytics have metrics tied to them. The following sections deal with each one individually.

Paid Searches

As described earlier, a paid search is any form of advertising that ties an ad (creative and text) to specific keywords in order to appear more prominently in search results. It has often been the purview of search engine optimization (SEO) and search engine marketing (SEM) professionals. But now that the communications disciplines (such as public relations, marketing, digital media, social media) have come together, it is important for all communications professionals to understand the various metrics that can be tracked when executing a paid search.

We are going to sound like a broken record throughout this book, but the paid search metrics (assuming that there is a paid search component to a program) should align with the behaviors you are trying to change. Here are some of the most popular paid search metrics:

- **Impressions**—An impression happens when a paid search ad appears on the search engine results page. This metric counts the number of such impressions.
- **Clicks**—This is probably the easiest metric to understand. It counts the number of times a user clicks on an ad and visits the predetermined landing page.
- **CTR**—The CTR is often expressed as a ratio, and it is the number of clicks an ad gets versus the number of impressions received.
- **Cost per click (CPC)**—CPC is the average amount an advertiser would pay for a click.
- **Impression share**—This is the ratio of the impressions your ad received to the possible impressions it could have received. This is similar to the share of conversation in social media analytics.
- **Sales or revenue per click**—Quite simply, this is the amount of money generated per click received on an ad.
- **Average position**—This metric measures where your advertisement appeared on the search engine results page.

There are 10 or 20 additional metrics that could use with paid searches, depending on your goals. However, the metrics listed here are the most popularly used and referenced. If your program has a paid search element, and you are not using one or more of those metrics, you should probably rethink your measurement plan of attack.

Organic Searches

Organic search results are listings on search engine pages that are tied to a specific keyword and are not being driven by an advertisement. The good part about organic search metrics is that even though users are not necessarily taking an action, through the use of tools (see Chapter 5, "Tools: Search Analytics," for more details), we can generally know what people are looking for.

It sounds a little creepy, but if you visit a search engine and enter a word or phrase, there is likely someone on the other end analyzing that behavior. Understanding organic search behaviors is critical because there are some industries that see very little volume of conversation online. Or, in a traditional sense, they see very little mainstream press attention. The online community might not be participating, but they are most assuredly trying to learn something about the subject. That is where search analytics comes in.

Whether or not you have a paid search component to your program, you should be trying to understand the organic search landscape. What are the metrics that communicators can use? The following are a handful of the ones that are commonly used:

- **Known and unknown keywords**—How many keywords do you know that are driving people to your website? How many do you not know? Is there an opportunity to optimize your content based on those unknown keywords? It is very possible that your unknown keywords are also unknown to your competitors.
- **Known and unknown branded keywords**—Similar to the known and unknown keywords, communicators need to understand which words about their brand are being used most often.
- **Total visits**—Ideally, you are tracking total visits to your website in your web analytics platform, but this metric could also fall under the organic search bucket as well.
- **Total conversions from known keywords**—If you are properly optimizing your content based on known keywords people are using, then you should see an uptick in conversion. Again, in this case, conversions could be a dollar figure, downloads, signing up for a newsletter, and so on.

- **Average search position**—Yes, this metric overlaps with paid searches, but it is important to know where you rank in search engine results pages, based on your top known and unknown and branded or unbranded keywords.

The search analytics tools might be complicated, but the individual metrics are not. Social, web, and search metrics are the three primary buckets that communicators need to be familiar with. We have identified the most popular in each of those categories, but you should not feel constrained to these lists. If there are two or three in each category that make sense for your program, use them.

 Tip

Do not get stuck in the trap of trying to measure everything just because the data is available.

Once you have picked your social, web, and search metrics, where do you go from here? If you have been paying attention throughout this chapter, you will probably realize that we have left out one very important piece of the puzzle: traditional analytics. The next sections tackle this subject.

Aligning Digital and Traditional Analytics

Just because digital media has exploded and subsequently created an abundance of data does not mean that traditional media and analytics is dead. In fact, when used together, digital data can strengthen traditional data and vice versa.

The best measurement approaches examine traditional media trends alongside digital media trends. Communicators everywhere are attempting to come up with integrated programs and should therefore be developing integrated measurement programs to more accurately gauge effectiveness.

At this point, communicators may be more familiar with traditional metrics than with digital metrics, so we have outlined what traditional research tactics you should continue to engage in even if you are gathering mountains of digital data.

Primary Research

The mainstream and digital trade press have published a number of articles arguing that surveys and other forms of primary research are dead. In fact, with rare exception, primary research is still a very important input for companies of all sizes.

> ✉ *Note*
>
> When we say *primary research*, we primarily mean surveys and focus groups.

As abundant as digital data is, there are certain things that it cannot entirely answer for communicators. Some of those measures include the following:

- **Brand reputation**—We have seen a number of studies attempting to tie social presence to overall brand reputation, and, at least at this point, those studies are incomplete. Unless communicators ask very specific questions of the target audience, it would be very difficult to use online sentiment and volume to ascertain how a brand is currently perceived. Some decent assumptions can be made, but the story is incomplete.

- **Message resonance**—Message resonance is a metric included in the social analytics section, but it is still something that requires offline testing. Just because an online audience is picking up a key message does not mean it is because of the company's program. Plus, hard as it is to believe, there are some targets that are still much more likely to engage offline than online.

- **Executive reputation**—Despite the growth in the number of brands engaging in social media activities, the corporate executives at those brands have not adopted social media at the same rate of speed. Those executives that do are genuinely embraced by the online community following the brand if they communicate authentically. When the communication is authentic, the brand does see a benefit. How much benefit? It is hard to tell without asking the online community following your brand, "Why?"

- **Advertising performance**—To date there has been very little experimentation in the testing of ads online. Typically the ads are produced, run on traditional channels, and then posted to social networks. Not only is posting advertising verbatim to social networks not interesting, there is also a small chance it will resonate if it contains no comedic value. Testing advertising in small, highly targeted focus groups is still the most effective method.

Traditional Media Monitoring

Social media monitoring software has made most of the traditional media monitoring platforms obsolete. However, there are still plenty of publications that the traditional platforms pick up that social ones do not. If you were to ask about building a list of reporters for a traditional media outreach, the first place to turn would not be a social monitoring platform.

We are not advocating that communicators should go out and spend big money on traditional media monitoring platforms. What we are advocating is that if you need to find recent articles in the mainstream press, you should pick the right tool for the job. In almost every case, the right tool for the job is a traditional monitoring platform.

Traditional CRM Data

The field of social customer resource management (CRM) is growing, but it is still limited to a specific channel. There is still valuable intelligence on our customers that we need to be leveraging from traditional CRM databases. Now, the goal here isn't to abuse the wealth of data digital media creates on our customers by just dropping it into a database and forgetting about it. Rather, the goal is to look for trends we can identify from our traditional databases, look for the similarities and differences in online behavior, and try to understand how that can be used to the company's advantage.

Toward the end of the book (see Chapter 22, "Social CRM"), we talk at greater length about social CRM and how it is changing the field of analytics. For now, it is just important to know that the traditional CRM database still has value in understanding consumer behavior.

Bringing It All Together

At this point, you should be more familiar with setting proper goals, potential digital metrics and what they mean, and how you can continue leveraging traditional activities to help better inform digital ones. Assume for a moment that you have built your program, have begun executing your program, know which metrics you are going to use, and have begun collecting data. Now what should you do? That is the million-dollar question, right? How often should you report? What should the reporting template look like? What should you report to your boss versus to other internal stakeholders? The answer to all of those questions is, of course, "It depends on the company." However, there are some generally accepted practices that communicators can follow. Read on.

The Reporting Time Line

How often you report depends a lot on your boss and how thirsty for data you are. The best measurement programs utilize a combination of approaches. Those programs produce a monthly snapshot with a high-level synopsis of how core metrics are tracking. Then every quarter, those same companies produce a deeper dive that shows how the targeted behavior has changed.

 Tip

> Arm yourself with data. The more data you have, the better you can under-
> stand how behaviors have changed. Data eliminates anomalies and allows
> your communications to truly take hold with the target audience.

The Reporting Template

There are a number of templates available to communicators, and oftentimes a simple email or Word document with key metrics tracked over time and an executive summary would suffice. However, most of the best-practice measurement programs create scorecards and build presentations based on those scorecards. The scorecards are typically integrated (traditional and digital together) and provide a snapshot and deep-dive into how the program performed.

 Tip

> Consider creating a simple matrix that shows the desired behavioral
> changes across the top and the channels used to affect those behaviors
> along the left-hand side.

Different Strokes for Different Folks

Not everyone within an organization needs to see a deep-dive report. Your boss probably wants to see it, but your boss's boss probably wants something more condensed. That can be as simple as a bulleted email with key highlights or as complicated as a truncated scorecard matrix. Figure out what your bosses would like to see and how often they would like to see it.

You now have a solid foundation for setting measurable goals, understanding what metrics matter and what the individual metrics mean, and knowing how the metrics can be utilized with traditional research techniques and how you bring it all together for either a monthly or quarterly (or both) report. Now, we will dive into each of these areas more deeply!

3

Picking the Tools of the Trade

The practice of digital analytics involves both tools and the human analysts who use them. Tools make the data collection process easier and give an analyst a jumpstart on providing actionable insights. They also provide a way to scale data collection and insights across a large company.

The tools are critical, but so is the analyst. The analyst provides valuable context on the business, the goals of the data collection and research, the ability to cross-reference multiple data sets toward the solution of a business problem, and, most importantly, the selection of the tools themselves. There is a world of data available to communicators and analysts alike, and there are many tools available to collect that data.

In previous chapters, we talked about how the amount of data has exploded as social media networks have exploded. There are hundreds, or maybe even thousands, of tools that help companies collect data across a wide variety of subjects. Over the course of the next few chapters, we dive into the tools for social media listening, search analytics, audience analysis, content analysis, engagement analysis, and influence analysis. In this chapter, we discuss how you go about picking a social media listening and engagement tool.

Identifying a Social Media Listening Tool

Since 2007, the social media listening market has undergone a dramatic transformation. As social media has grown, more established traditional media monitoring companies such as Cision, Factiva, and PR Newswire have developed solutions for clients to track social media conversations. At the same time, a number of startups have been founded to track social media conversations. Startups like Radian6, Techrigy's SM2 platform, Crimson Hexagon, Visible Technologies, and Sysomos were formed in order to take advantage of this newly growing industry. As a result of the growth of this market, it has become very difficult to select a tool.

It has become difficult to do the proper due diligence because it isn't always clear which tools should be evaluated. In addition, a number of tools that have been developed are better for midsized businesses than for enterprise customers. Unfortunately, unless communicators spend a considerable amount of time using the tools themselves, they may not necessarily be able to make that distinction.

If you are currently evaluating social media listening tools or considering a change in tools, what should you be looking for in a solution? There are a number of features that you should be mindful of when making your decision:

- **Data capture**—Before going any further, let us dispense with the notion that there is a tool that offers 100% data capture. There is not one, and even if there were, you would not want it. A tool capturing 100% of the content would gather a lot of online spam, which would make the process of developing insights more difficult.

- **Spam prevention**—This goes hand-in-hand with data capture, but how good is the tool in reducing spam?

- **Integration with other data sources**—Social media listening tools have begun to integrate other digital data sources. Can your tool do this?

- **Cost**—This is an obvious one, but it should not be the only consideration.

- **Mobile capability**—Social media listening tools have begun to develop mobile applications so that communicators can track conversations while on the go.

- **Application programming interface (API) access**—Most tools offer users the ability to collect data and then repurpose it.

- **Consistent user interface**—If the user interface is difficult to use, it is time to look at another solution. For example, some of the tools available on the market utilize flash technology, which can make it unstable.

- **Workflow functionality**—With your social media listening tool, can you easily route mentions to other members of your team?

- **Historical data**—It is important to have as much data as possible in order to identify trends.

Let's dig into each of these items in more detail.

Data Capture

As mentioned earlier, there is no tool on the market right now that captures every possible mention or site. The reality is that if there were a tool that captured everything, users would be so inundated with spam that it would be difficult to decipher anything meaningful from the data. However, there are some things you should look for about the way a tool captures critical data:

- **Channel capture**—Some tools are better at capturing blogs than forums. Others do not capture very much visual content even though manual searches reveal content being posted on those channels. Ask the tool salesperson questions about how data across Twitter, blogs, forums, and other social media networks is gathered.

- **Twitter access**—There are tools that gather only a random sample of tweets, and others that have access to all. Ask how much Twitter data is gathered in the platform.

- **Full-text versus content snippets**—Not every tool offers you the ability to see the full text of the post within the platform. Some offer only content snippets. If having access to full text is important to you, ask the salesperson about this.

- **Categorization of mentions**—This is probably the most critical component of data capture, and the one that is the most difficult to solve. The conundrum is that it is very difficult to determine what is a blog and what is a mainstream news outlet these days. However, before you make a decision on a social media listening tool, you should go through the blog and news mentions to make sure you are comfortable with how they are being categorized.

In Chapter 4, "Tools: Social Listening," we dive into even more specifics about social media listening tools. Who are the key players on the market today? What are the pros and cons of using one of those tools? For now, the features listed in the following subsections should provide you with an understanding of the core functionality to be aware of when making a buying decision.

Spam Prevention

Spam prevention goes hand-in-hand with data capture. As mentioned earlier, 100% data capture truly is not possible. Even if it were, users would be spending half of their day sifting through a large amount of spam. Some tools are better than others at eliminating spam, but it is definitely something users should be asking about during the process of buying a spam filter. Does the spam filter learn as you mark items as spam? How rigorous is the spam filter "out of the box"? These are the two primary questions you should be asking your salesperson.

Integration with Other Data Sources

Social media listening tools have evolved considerably over the past five years, and one of the areas where that evolution has been most noticeable is in the integration of other digital data sources. Social media listening requires integration of disparate data sets.

 Note

Throughout the book, we preach integration of disparate data sets.

There are two primary data sources that social media listening tools are currently integrating that you should inquire about when making a decision:

- **CRM**—Can existing customer resource management (CRM) data be easily imported into your listening tool? Or can you export data from your listening tool into your existing CRM database? Either way, be sure to ask whether it is possible.

- **Web metrics**—A few of the available tools on the market provide access to web data. If you can get web data, use it. It can be valuable in determining how your consumer goes from talking about your brand to visiting your homepage.

Cost

We mentioned earlier that cost should not be the only consideration when you select a tool, and we stand by that recommendation. An inexpensive tool might be priced right, but it might not be the best tool for the job. One of the questions communicators often ask us is, "Can social media monitoring be pieced together with free tools?" Many small- to medium-sized businesses cannot afford enterprise-sized listening tools.

It is true that some of these tools can be expensive if you are monitoring a large volume of conversation. However, there are a couple cost considerations involved in picking a tool:

- **Free tools may actually be rather expensive from a time and actual dollar perspective**—Just because it is free does not mean a tool is the most comprehensive or affordable. If a tool is free, it is likely only capturing a small segment of the conversation. To get an accurate read, users might be forced to use multiple free tools and piece together the information.

- **Solutions for smaller businesses**—There are solutions available for small- to medium-sized businesses, and some of the tools that might be considered enterprise tools do have pricing available for smaller organizations. Do your homework to see what paid options are available before trying the free tool route.

Mobile Capability

Some of the social media listening providers, such as Radian6, have developed mobile applications that give users the ability to monitor conversations on the go. Most of these applications offer a high-level look at how conversations are trending, whereas the more advanced applications have workflow functionality and the ability to monitor social channels within one interface.

If your current solution does not offer mobile capability, ask when it might be coming. Managing conversations when you are not in front of your computer is critical in this 24 hours/7 days a week/365 days a year response culture that has been partially created by the explosion of social media.

API Access

API access is one of those items that is critical only for the heaviest of social media listening users, but it is critical as communicators look to combine conversation data with other digital data sources. When picking a tool, consider bringing in information technology (IT) professionals (or market research, if appropriate) to ask questions about the tool's API capabilities. Most of the tools currently available on the market do have this capability; it is just a matter of how reliable it is.

Consistent User Interface

This might seem like a really obvious item, but unless you spend a considerable amount of time using one of these tools, you do not realize how unreliable they can be. These tools are technology, so there is a good chance there will be glitches at some point in time. However, consistent issues such as data changing or modules not loading means it is time to start considering other solutions.

A component of a consistent user interface is a robust customer support team. It should be easy for users to reach customer support either through the telephone, email, or social outreach. We think that if you are not contacted with a potential solution within an hour, that is poor customer support. Why an hour? Quite simply, a crisis in social media can explode in a short period of time. If a user is in the middle of a crisis and cannot access the tool the way he or she needs to, that is a serious issue. Most providers have strong customer support, but feel that out as you are making your decision, either through questions of the salesperson or asking close peers.

Workflow Functionality

The ability to monitor conversations in real-time and then route them within the organization for potential response is critical. Users should have the ability to easily send conversations about topics of note to other users within the organization.

How does having the workflow functionality benefit you? Quite simply, it makes monitoring multiple topics easier. If you are in charge of monitoring conversations for multiple brands or topics, there are likely to be others within the organization who have more knowledge if a response is required. Having the ability to send a conversation in real-time to someone else often can lead to a speedier, more accurate response.

Historical Data

Some tools come equipped with historical data going back approximately two years. Others, however, provide only 30 days of data when you first start using them. Even if historical data isn't offered out of the box, the chances are good that you will be able to access it for an additional fee. Check with your provider to ensure that you have access to the extra data. It is critical in understanding the long-term conversation trends.

Tip

Picking a social media tool is not easy. Using the items listed here to create a matrix of functionality for yourself can help you evaluate tools. A
simple Microsoft Excel grid with the social media listening tools on the left,
and the variables we have listed above would suffice.

Understanding Social Media Engagement Software

Social media engagement software has exploded over the past two years, as large
companies have looked for ways to make social media activities easier to scale. It is
not always practical to sit by your computer to post something to an owned social
media channel, it's not always easy to triage mentions or conversations to more
appropriate people within the organization, and it's not always easy to ascertain
how successful social media activities have been. Engagement software can help in
all these areas.

There are a number of ways that you can use social media engagement software
to help manage a brand's presence. However, as with social media listening tools,
there are a number of available options for communicators to pick from. The
numerous choices and the relative newness of the industry have made the buying
process a little muddy. In addition, two recent acquisitions have made the buying process rather uncertain. First, business hardware and systems manufacturer
Oracle purchased Vitrue. Shortly thereafter, Salesforce.com purchased Buddy
Media. Vitrue and Buddy Media were two of the largest providers in the social
media engagement software space. (Read more in Chapter 8, "Tools: Engagement
Analysis," about how these tools have evolved and where they will go from here.)
Here are some things you should consider when making a purchase:

- **Easy-to-navigate user interface**—As with social media listening tools,
  you want the interface to be easy to use without being overly flashy.

- **Reliability**—In addition to being an easy–to-navigate user interface, a
  tool must be reliable.

- **Robust analytics dashboards**—This is an analytics book, right? Users
  should be able to extract data about how their posts are performing.

- **Beware of the black box algorithm**—Some tools offer users a black
  box calculation in order to demonstrate the value of a single post. Be
  wary of such calculations if they cannot be explained easily.

- **Mobility**—As with social media listening tools, you aren't near your computer 24 hours a day, 7 days a week, and 365 days a year. The ability to manage social media channels on the go is essential.

- **CRM "hooks"**—Can you take the interactions you are currently having through social media engagement software and plug them into your CRM database? Or can you take the data you currently have in your CRM database and plug it into your social media engagement software?

- **Social governance**—It is critical to have one central junction to manage access, permissions, and approvals.

- **Monitoring platform integration**—Some tools on the market have partnered with listening providers, but this is still something that is relatively new.

As we did for social media monitoring tools, let's dig into each of these considerations in more detail.

Easy-to-Navigate User Interface

Before going any further, please note that *easy to navigate* does not mean the same thing as *fancy* or *sexy* or *sleek*. Some of the available tools have very slick interfaces, which might mask deficiencies in other areas. Certainly, it would be great if a tool looked great, but when evaluating tools, you should consider function over form. A "pretty" user interface will not help if you are in the middle of a crisis and need to post content.

When evaluating a user interface, there are five things to keep in mind:

- **Ability to schedule content**—Scheduling content keeps someone from having to be at the computer 24/7/365. Most of the tools currently on the market have this functionality, but check before buying.

- **Ability to post to all major social channels**—Again, this is a core functionality of most tools, but ensure that users can post to Facebook, Twitter, and YouTube without difficulty.

- **Uploading multimedia content**—Is it easy to attach photos and/or videos when uploading a post? Visual content is becoming increasingly important for brands, so if you cannot upload multimedia content with a post, it might be time to look elsewhere.

- **Geo-targeting**—This is a feature of some tools, but not all. When posting information about an event in Chicago, for example, chances are good that your fans in Dallas do not care. The more relevant the content is to a particular audience, the more engagement it is likely to receive. Check to see if the tool currently in place allows for this kind of targeting.

- **Post tagging**—Post tagging is a critical component for reporting down the line, and it is an often-overlooked feature. Properly tagging posts will save the user from having to go through every single post at the end of the month to determine how certain post topics performed.

Reliability

It seems that reliability would be another obvious point, but it is often surprising how unstable these platforms can be. There are often issues with double posting, inability to upload multimedia at random times, broken links, and out-of-date data. An occasional outage is certainly understandable, but constant technological challenges means it is time to look elsewhere. Your community expects flawless execution when you contribute content, so ensuring that the technology helps deliver that is critical. Insist on a test period before signing an agreement to check for any of these glitches.

Robust Analytics Dashboards

This is an analytics book, and you might have wondered about the purpose of this section if we had not covered analytics. The analytics platforms of social media engagement tools are a big source of frustration because some of the tools that are thought to be best in class have some of the least valuable analytics platforms. Just because it is not an analyst who typically interfaces with one of these tools does not mean the analytics dashboard should be dumbed down. What should an analytics dashboard contain? The following are a few possibilities:

- **Everything available through Facebook or YouTube Insights**—It should be very easy for a social media management system provider to gain access to the Insights data via the API and include it in your dashboard. But just because it is available does not mean it is being pulled in. If there are things that you would like to see in your analytics package that are not currently there, you should ask immediately.

- **Twitter data**—Gathering data on Twitter is a little more complex than gathering it on Facebook and YouTube as there is not currently an analytics platform, but at the very least, the engagement software tool should give you access to impressions, clicks, retweets, and replies.

- **Competitive data**—There are tools currently on the market that offer Facebook data on competitors within the publishing platform. Such competitive intelligence is invaluable as you evaluate your own page's performance.

- **Link-shortening integration**—Whether it is bitly or another customized link-shortening service, users should be able to use their tool of choice. bitly and others like it gather data on clicks, which is valuable information to obtain.

Beware of the Black Box Algorithm

In Chapter 9, "Tools: Influence Analysis," when we dig into influence analyses, we talk at greater length about black box algorithms, but social media management tools have begun incorporating their own algorithms to gauge the performance of individual posts. In most instances, the formula is meant to place a dollar value on a specific post or set of posts. Although the idea is interesting and worth consideration, the fact that the algorithm is not often published makes it very difficult to defend. If you do not feel comfortable standing in front of the chief marketing officer and defending a calculation, do not use it.

Mobility

Does the platform you are currently using offer you the ability to now or in the future access the publishing engine or data via a mobile device? Again, you probably do not want to be tethered to your computer 24/7/365. Not every application currently has a mobile application, but asking if one is in the works is critical.

CRM Hooks

Valuable data is gathered through social media engagement software. Data is available about how people talk about a brand, how they engage with the brand, how the brand has responded to customers, how long it has taken the brand to respond to customers, and what the resolution was to the customer's problem. The good part for the brand is that this type of data has been captured in traditional CRM databases for years. Now it is time to look for ways to incorporate that data with social media engagement data. Some tools have those hooks today, but check to see when you're going through the purchase process.

Social Governance

Social governance is critical. You need to ensure that as social media spreads throughout an enterprise, there is one location through which to manage access, permissions, and approvals so the appropriate people engage at the appropriate time. Included in governance is digital asset management so the brand "voice" is maintained at every touchpoint. Setting up social governance procedures ensures that a global strategy can be executed while maintaining local market flexibility.

Monitoring Platform Integration

Monitoring platform integration has the most promise and value for communicators. Some tools, like Spredfast, currently have partnerships established with social media listening tools. However, the marketplace has yet to see a truly integrated engagement and listening platform tool. The winning platform will be the one that contains full-scale listening capabilities with the ability to engage in real-time plus gather data on that engagement. There have been rumors about such integrations occurring, but it has not come to fruition yet.

Purchasing Social Media Engagement Tools

Now that we have given you an outline of what you should consider when purchasing social media listening and social media engagement tools, it makes sense for us to provide some guidance on how you should make the decision. Just as there is a lot of confusion about what features to look for, there is uncertainty about how the decision to buy is made.

Of course, there is an element of cost to be considered, but that is not what we mean here. In most cases, there will be multiple people from multiple departments using these tools. There are hundreds of available tools to potentially buy. How do you decide which tools to evaluate? Additionally, ensuring that growth occurs at a manageable pace is critical. Finally, it is important that the buying decision be made with a long-term partnership vision and not the idea of a company/vendor relationship.

Who Decides Which Tool to Buy?

Everybody wants to be the person who makes the final decision. In large companies where there are multiple decision makers, finding one single person to make the call is likely going to be a challenge. However, the decision to buy a listening tool or engagement software is probably being led by someone in communications—either public relations or marketing. That person, whoever he or she is, should be the final decision maker after consulting with a cross-functional team. The cross-functional team should include representatives from the following departments:

- **PR or marketing**—As mentioned earlier, one of these departments is likely driving the ship toward an eventual purchase. Someone from the other department should be on this team, as well.

- **Legal**—Someone needs to be there to negotiate the final contract terms.

- **Procurement**—Someone also needs to be there to write the check, of course.

- **Customer support**—Many social media programs now have a dedicated customer support function. It is important that they be consulted on any specific needs related to both a listening tool and engagement software.

- **IT**—IT professionals have largely received a bad rap in social media circles, but in this case, they serve a vital purpose. There is often a random technology issue that keeps listening and engagement tools from working properly inside companies. Having IT in the room early might mitigate some of those challenges.

Which Tools Should You Evaluate?

During the past four or five years, there have been a number of horror stories about companies evaluating hundreds of different tools before making a final decision. Not only is that a colossal waste of time, but there is a very good chance that you would not have noticed much difference between the tools after the fourth or fifth one.

How should your company decide which tools to evaluate? Well, a good initial criterion would be what we have listed in this chapter. However, there are other things you can do to narrow the list:

- **Do some initial research**—If you were to do an Internet search on "social media listening," you would find a bevy of recent blog posts to read. A lot of research has been done on the tools already, and you should take advantage of that.

- **Ask your peers at other companies**—Whether it is over Twitter, Facebook, Google+, or any other social channel, there is a good chance some of your peers have faced a similar decision. Ask them which tools they looked at before making a decision.

- **Pick one or two tools from the enterprise and midsized class**—A number of tools fit into both of these categories, but it doesn't make sense to look at all enterprise tools or all midsized tools. There are a couple reasons for this. The first is that you will likely not see much variation in the two sets. The second is that in some cases, the midsized tool is looking to step up in weight class and might offer you better pricing or more opportunities to grow together.

How many tools should you evaluate before making a decision? No more than five. Trust us. You will not see much variation after the fifth tool.

How Do You Manage Growth?

There are countless examples that we could point to of companies purchasing either a listening tool or an engagement solution and immediately deriving value from using them. That is the good news. The bad news is that good news does not stay contained for very long, regardless of the company size. So, instead of having a small, contained team that can manage the relationship and the tool, growth goes out of control.

Of course, the goal is for as many of the right people as possible to be engaged with the tool, but the expansion has to be gradual and manageable. Before a new part of the organization can take part, there has to be a sound business problem it is trying to solve. Also—and this is not a miniscule concern—someone within the organization is paying for the tool. If another part of the organization wants to take part, it might make sense for that group to pony up some cash to pay for it.

How do you Establish a Long-Term Partnership with Your Listening Provider?

If you have been active in social media for any length of time and have seen the evolution of social media listening tools and engagement software, you know that the innovation contained therein has been a result of client demand. When signing a contract, explore the possibility of working out a relationship with the product development team. If the development team shows interest in building a relationship, chances are good that the tool will grant that access. It should be more about building a long-term relationship and not a company/vendor relationship. If you focus on the former, the tools will grow with you.

Conclusion

In this chapter, we outlined the considerations for purchasing a social media engagement and social media listening tool. Also, we outlined the ways in which the ultimate decision should be made. Over the course of the next few chapters, we outline a similar process for other digital analytics tools, as well as go into more detail about social media listening tools.

4

Tools:
Social Media Listening

In Chapter 3, "Picking the Social Tools of the Trade," we talk at length about how to go about picking a social media listening provider. It is not an easy decision and should involve multiple internal stakeholders. Remember, if you are maximizing social media listening's value to the organization, you are thinking about applications that extend beyond public relations and marketing. Listening has value to human resources, product planning, corporate strategy, and investor relations, just to name a few.

In Chapter 3 we also briefly mention that the social media listening space has undergone a considerable transformation over the past six years or so. Not only have the tool features become more robust, but also the sheer number of them available to brands has become almost unmanageable. There has been some consolidation in the social media listening space, and that trend will continue for the foreseeable future. But that consolidation does not make the buying decision very easy right now.

Chapter 3 outlines several things to look for when evaluating a social media listening tool (depth of data capture, cost, ability to track multiple channels, and so on), so we do not repeat that here. Instead, this chapter dives deeper into the tools themselves, with a focus on the following three areas:

- **Where the tools have come from**—It is important to understand how the tools have evolved from their origins—not just how they have evolved since social media listening came into vogue about five years ago.
- **Where the tools are currently**—We dig into the crowded space of social media listening tools, with a particular focus on an analysis of the top listening tools available on the market today.
- **Where the tools go from here**—How will social media listening continue to evolve? The evolution could include everything from expanding the scope beyond public relations and marketing to developing a social intelligence supply chain to developing a social media command center.

It is very likely that the next five years of social media listening will evolve at the same rate as the previous five years. The tools themselves are not cheap, and when you combine the tool cost with the human resources required to use the tools, you have a considerable budget outlay that requires justification. Our intention is to arm you with enough knowledge to maximize your investment in a listening tool.

Social Media Listening Evolution

If you are involved in public relations and marketing activities—whether as a student or as a corporate or agency professional—you have had some exposure to traditional media monitoring tools. You have probably heard of tools such as Factiva, Cision, and BurrellesLuce. These three tools are some of the best tools available for monitoring traditional media. They capture a large chunk of the printed publications around the globe, and public relations professionals have been using them for years.

In most cases, internal communications teams have used these tools reactively. Public relations professionals pitch a story and then use a traditional media monitoring tool in order to track when it is published. But using media monitoring tools in that way is a terrible use of resources because you could complete the task with free tools (for example, Google Alerts). Here are some other ways you utilize traditional media monitoring:

- **Pitch ideas**—When you are curious about whether someone has written about your topic before, media monitoring tools can be an excellent source for information. By entering specific keywords, you can identify articles from pretty much any publication that fits your topic area.

- **Measurement/reporting**—Media monitoring tools can help if you are trying to gauge the number of mentions your brand has had in a month, quarter, or year. They also provide a central repository where you can read articles and assess whether a key message has penetrated the market.

- **Understanding media tendencies**—By spending a little time developing a strong keyword set and honing your target pitch market, you can easily understand what reporters and bloggers have been writing about during a predetermined period. That is valuable intelligence when you are developing a pitch.

You might be saying to yourself, "Well, no duh, of course these tools can be used for more proactive research efforts." If you are indeed saying this, consider yourself advanced. The reality is that most communications departments have not used these tools proactively for years. Companies have not treated these tools as valuable media research vehicles but rather as a commodity that they have always had access to.

When social media listening tools hit the market, they faced their own battles. Communicators everywhere heard the term *monitoring* and had flashbacks to the nightmare of their first attempts using Factiva or Cision. To be fair, social media was still in its infancy at that stage, so very few people were clear about why they should be paying attention to online mentions. It was clear that a culture shift needed to take place for social media monitoring to really take hold.

The companies that had tools available on the market in those early days had a daunting task. Not only were they launching very new software to most communicators, they also had to overcome the negative stigma of monitoring being a commodity-based business. Even the word *monitoring* needed to be thrown out. Think about that term for a second. What image does it conjure in your head? To us, monitoring sounds like a passive activity. We take some action, and then we monitor to see if it is effective. There is nothing inherently wrong with that, but it isn't something that warrants significant investment.

So what did the social media monitoring tools do? There are four things they did to overcome the stereotypes inherited from the traditional media-monitoring world:

- **Rebranded itself as listening**—Think about the term *listening* for a second. What image does it conjure in your head? For us, it sounds very proactive. We listen and then we take an action shortly thereafter, if not simultaneously.

- **Actively evangelized and provided thought leadership**—Two of the early pioneers in the social media listening business, Marcel LeBrun and David Alston, and the other founders of Radian6, were actively attending conferences, offered thought leadership in terms of blog posts and whitepapers, and spoke at multiple high-profile events to spread the word about the values of listening. (Read more about Radian6 later in the chapter.) They did not just put up a booth and hope people would show. Instead, they offered a unique perspective that the market had not heard before.

- **Created "pretty" and usable dashboards**—Up until the point where social media listening tools hit the market, media monitoring tools were very difficult to use and were not offering the most visually appealing outputs, which might have been offputting to users. That changed as Radian6 and others came onto the market.

- **Aggregated data**—Aggregation of data sounds like a simple thing, and something that traditional media monitoring had already mastered, but it was a milestone when social media listening tools started to offer social media mentions in one location. Before that, communicators had to piece together the data from multiple sources, without ever knowing whether they had all the bases covered.

When companies started purchasing social media listening tools, they primarily used the tools for reputation management. Companies were just starting to dabble in social media and had seen instances where reputations were damaged by using social media technologies incorrectly or where social media learned of issues companies had in providing great service to its customers.

From there, companies started using listening to inform communications planning—primarily online communications. Communicators and researchers alike had an opportunity to learn several things about their brand that they previously were not able to access, including the following:

- **Location of conversations**—In the age of traditional media monitoring, communicators had some knowledge of where, geographically speaking, mentions of the brand were happening. With social media listening tools, the information was even more specific because communicators could see geography and channel (blog, forum, news, Twitter, and so on).

- **Sentiment**—Before online listening became popular, one of the only inputs communicators had to gauge brand perception was offline surveys. Now, there was a second input to gauge the brand's value to multiple stakeholders.

- **Key message penetration**—Because social media listening was near real-time, communicators could more immediately understand how messages were resonating with key stakeholders.

- **Key influencers**—Communicators have also known, or thought they have known, who is driving brand perceptions. Unfortunately (or fortunately, as the case may be), listening to social conversations has turned that notion on its head. Social media listening tools have given communicators greater clarity about who, specifically, drives perception.

As mentioned in Chapter 3, most companies that conduct any sort of online listening today study these areas. That chapter also talks about using listening data for proactive content development, which is not being implemented as often as it should be. Whether social media conversation data was being used for reputation management or proactive planning, it became clear that marketers were sitting on a pile of data that could be extremely valuable to the organization.

Back in 2009, we introduced the concept of the *social analytics lifecycle* (see Figure 4.1). Our vision was that several parts of an organization could use social media listening data. Inherent in our model is the belief that marketers can drive business intelligence—not just intelligence for communications planning.

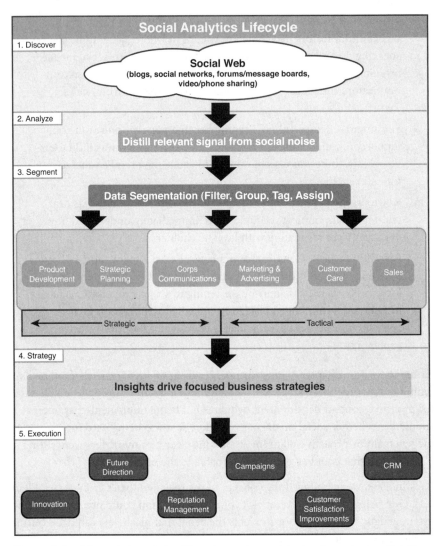

Figure 4.1 *The social analytics lifecycle can be used to develop a body of intelligence from social conversations that covers an entire organization.*

The social analytics lifecycle concept has five distinct stages:

- **Discover**—During the discovery stage, the organization gathers all data relevant to the brand from social channels. This could be mentions of competitors or the industry. Ideally, it is a combination of mentions of the brand, competitors, and the industry.

- **Analyze**—In the analysis phase, a human interacts with the data to determine what is signal and what is noise. What are the pieces of data that the organization could take action on?

- **Segment**—After the data is parsed for how actionable it could be, it is shared with all parts of the organization. When we developed this model, we envisioned applications for product development, strategic planning, corporate communications, marketing, customer care, and sales. (We will dig into these specific use cases in coming chapters.)
- **Strategize**—The insights the organization has come up with after reading the data—regardless of segment—need to be formed into a strategy.
- **Execute**—Whether it is marketing, public relations, or customer-care activities, an organization needs to develop tactics in order to execute on the insights developed in the strategy phase.

After developing this model, we realized that it was a bit of future state. Most companies were still using listening data for strict reputation management, and the companies considered to be the most "advanced" were using it for proactive planning. That being said, some companies adopted a similar model in order to develop a social media listening command center. Later in this chapter we discuss the concept of the command center in more depth.

It was not an overnight transition, but the invention of social media listening tools forever changed how companies monitored media. The term *monitoring* is still being used, but only as a fundamental way to understand what social media listening tools can do. Not only has social media obliterated the mindset that monitoring is a commodity, but it has also armed communications with even more organizational firepower.

This brings us to 2010–2011, when social media listening became more accepted and necessary. There were a number of solutions available on the market by that time, and companies were really starting to wrap their collective heads around the value of this new data source. The present-day listening market, though, is beset with a new set of challenges and tools.

Social Media Listening in the Present Day

As more companies started looking to social media listening data as valuable intelligence on their customers, the number of available tools on the market exploded. News wire services such as BusinessWire and PR Newswire, which are companies that previously had a traditional media-monitoring footprint, began to develop their own solutions. In addition, previously unknown providers developed a number of new technologies that offered organizations a way to monitor social media conversations.

In late 2010/early 2011, the social media listening landscape could be summed up in one word: confusing. There were literally hundreds of tools available at varying price points, all offering "special" variations on the data. Co-author Ken Burbary created a wiki to capture all the available tools on the market. The tool is still maintained today and has almost 230 different solutions included. Whereas we live and breathe social media analytics, the average consumer of these tools does not. Doing the kind of due diligence outlined in Chapter 3 is not possible when there are hundreds of available tools.

Although the market was relatively juvenile, it was clear that consolidation needed to take place if for no other reason than it would make the purchasing decision easier for large companies. The first domino fell in June 2010, when Marketwire acquired Sysomos. While PR Newswire and BusinessWire were attempting to build their own listening footprints, Marketwire decided to go the acquisition route. At the time, it seemed like a strange acquisition because Sysomos was viewed largely as a middle-of-the-road player. It had a small gap in its forum (or group) capture, and it was capturing only a sample of Twitter mentions. The influx of cash coming from Marketwire helped Sysomos close the gaps in data capture and continue building out its offering.

Since 2007, Sysomos has gone from being just another social media listening tool to one of the top two or three tools that companies look at when making a buying decision. What does Sysomos look like today?

Understanding Sysomos

Sysomos's platform has undergone significant upgrades since 2007. It has seen so many upgrades that it is now considered to be one of the top listening tools available. Sysomos now captures all available data from Twitter, and also captures the majority of mentions coming from blogs, forums, news channels, and other social channels. It captures only a percentage of publicly available Facebook content, which is a quality it has in common with many other social media listening tools. To capture any more than what is publicly available would violate Facebook's terms of service and the privacy of its users.

The platform itself is broken into two different pieces: MAP and Heartbeat. Users of Sysomos can take advantage of one or both platforms with a single seat license. The MAP platform is seen as an ad hoc research tool, whereas Heartbeat is used for ongoing tracking. The following sections dig into each of these options individually.

Sysomos MAP

MAP offers a simple Boolean query constructor where users can input a series of keywords in order to track mentions of an event, a brand, competitors, or the industry (see Figure 4.2). It gathers the same data as Heartbeat—from news, blogs, forums, Twitter, YouTube, Facebook, and other social networks.

WHAT IS A BOOLEAN QUERY?

Boolean searches enable you to combine words and phrases using the words AND, OR, NOT, and NEAR (otherwise known as Boolean operators) to limit, widen, or define your search.

Historical data, automated sentiment, geography, gender, top keywords (displayed as a word cloud), the ability to save search queries, and nodal relationships between words are displayed in the MAP dashboard. Users can prepopulate a list of the sources they would like to be included in the output. What is most important, though, is that users can export almost everything they see from MAP. This matters most for heavy users who want to manipulate the data in different ways. Users can export the data in its entirety or as a sample set of the overall mentions.

It is worth noting that historical Twitter data is not available in Sysomos MAP. Until recently, Sysomos offered users only a sample of the available tweets. Now the platform is pulling in all available mentions, so to avoid data inconsistencies, we recommend that you pull a sample when you export mentions.

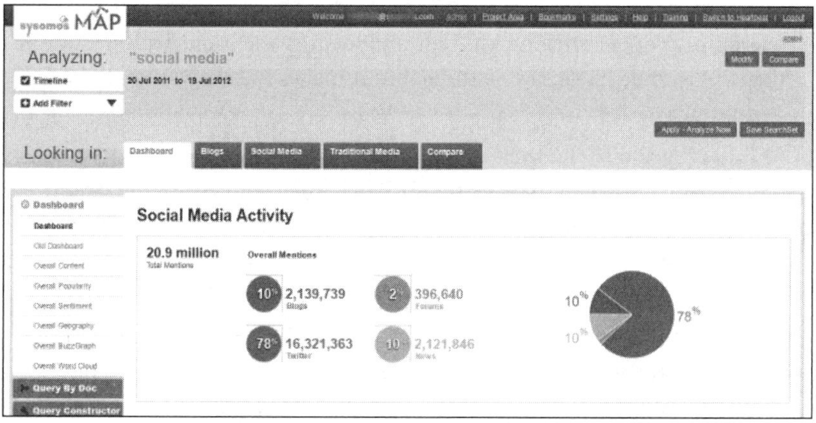

Figure 4.2 *Sample Sysomos MAP output for the keywords* social media.

One thing that Sysomos does well is filter out a lot of spam. It is not perfect by any means, but Sysomos filters out a lot of the noisy blog and Twitter spam that other tools pick up. In a few recent comparisons, Sysomos offered about 5% to 7% less spam than its nearest competitors. Although that might not seem like a large difference, if your brand experiences 10,000 social media mentions or more a day, this could shave off a significant amount of analysis time.

In addition, Sysomos offers a robust online and offline training program for users. If we have not made it clear yet through our discussions in Chapter 3 and here, these tools are not necessarily the most intuitive for people who do not use them frequently. Training programs are critical to achieving widespread enterprise adoption.

If you are going to be conducting a lot of ad hoc social media conversation research, Sysomos MAP is a great tool for the job.

Sysomos Heartbeat

The Heartbeat platform (see Figure 4.3) is Sysomos's version of an advanced social media analysis tool. It offers a lot of the same things that MAP offers, including historical data, capture of almost every media channel, complex Boolean queries, top keywords, nodal relationships between words, geography, and demographics. Heartbeat's query constructor is set up in a similar fashion to the MAP query constructor, but Heartbeat's version offers you the ability to add more terms to the words you would like to track.

Where does Heartbeat differ from MAP? It offers users four distinct things that MAP does not:

- **Topic tags**—Users of the Heartbeat platform can apply tags to mentions for easy categorization later. For example, you could include a series of product attributes as tags and identify mentions with those tags. It sounds like a simple thing, but it makes the analysis on the back end much easier.

- **Managing social channels**—With this relatively new addition to Heartbeat, users can manage the social channels of their brand or client from one interface. This single interface is huge in the development of more fluid content, as discussed in Chapter 3. Users can see mentions come in real time, develop content for response in real time, and then post the content without ever leaving the platform.

- **Trend analysis**—Users can see how the volume of conversation has trended over time for their company versus key competitors.

- **Share of voice**—On the right side of the Heartbeat interface, users can see how mentions of their brand stack up versus competitors.

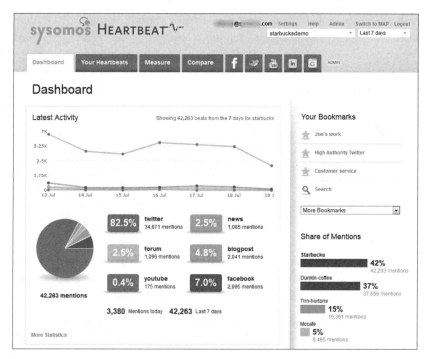

Figure 4.3   *Sample Sysomos Heartbeat for Starbucks over a period of seven days.*

Sysomos's platform is strong, and it's suitable for customers of all sizes. Although it might look like it plays to an enterprise-only audience, it has value to many small- and medium-size businesses as, at a minimum, a way to aggregate mentions of the brand in one platform.

Over the past several years, Sysomos's main competitor has been Radian6, the company that changed the listening landscape and marketing forever. We take a look at them next.

Radian6's Effect on the Marketing Community

In 2007, Radian6 was a young, upstart company that claimed to be able to monitor social media conversations. During those early days, there were online conversations taking place about brands, but not nearly at the level that is seen today. Twitter and Facebook were a fraction of their current sizes. Blogs were prevalent, but they had not been adopted by the mainstream press to the extent that they are today. People were talking to each other in forums, but forums had not become the information treasure trove they are today. Tracking news mentions was still the most popular form of monitoring.

The Radian6 crew—led by the talented quartet of Marcel LeBrun, Chris Ramsey, Chris Newton, and David Alston—set out to change how companies were monitoring mentions of their brands. Radian6 was one of the original companies to talk about monitoring as *listening*. LeBrun et al. positioned the Radian6 platform as a tool for proactively gaining insight into what customers want from the brand on an hourly or, at worst, daily basis. Radian6 was present at every conference and on every online channel where someone had a question about social media listening.

In essence, Radian6 was a major driving force in the advent of another customer intelligence input, which has fundamentally changed marketing forever. It put real-time data about customers into the hands of marketers, who have in turn used that data to build successful programs, develop new forms of content, and solve customer care issues; this data has therefore become an even more valued component of the enterprise.

Sure, there were other tools available on the market at that time, but Radian6 was the most successful in achieving mindshare with key decision makers in those early days. What else did the company do to bring listening to life?

- **Community management**—We cannot emphasize enough how different Radian6's tools were from what most in the media research and marketing worlds were used to dealing with before 2007. When most had issues, they turned to Twitter, forums, and blogs to ask questions. When they did, Radian6 was right there to respond.

- **Thought leadership**—As mentioned earlier in this chapter, social media listening tools have done a tremendous job of building thought leadership in the space. That thought leadership has led to greater mindshare among potential customers. Radian6 was the clear leader in developing thought leadership during those early days.

- **Customer-first mentality**—Anyone who has been with Radian6 since the beginning knows that the past couple years have been trying from a customer service perspective, but in those early days, Radian6 was very available for customers. What do we mean by "trying"? Radian6's customer base grew at a rate that was unsustainable for its customer service personnel. When the rate of change equalized, customer service greatly improved.

- **Better dashboard**—As social media grew, some of the world's largest brands were faced with having to digest tens of thousands of mentions each day. That was not something many organizations were prepared to handle, but Radian6's dashboard was so well put together that it made digesting information much easier. Part and parcel with making listening approachable, Radian6 developed a dashboard that provides ample detail, but is simple in design. (See Figure 4.4.)That is not an easy thing to accomplish.

Figure 4.4 shows an example of a Radian6 dashboard. It is worth noting that although Radian6 has changed the dashboard visually and added new features, what it captures has stayed largely the same.

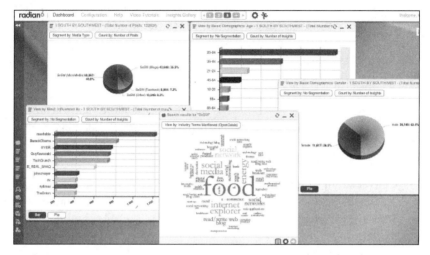

Figure 4.4 *Radian6's dashboard, showing conversations about the South by Southwest Interactive Festival.*

The main dashboard screen is useful, but the configuration screen is where the data capturing process begins. To begin capturing data, you need to enter the following elements:

- **Visibility**—You can make profiles visible to all users within your environment, or you can restrict access to people who are working on a particular project.

- **Languages**—The default setting captures all languages that Radian6 currently tracks.

- **Media types**—You can specify which type of media you'd like to track. For example, if you would like to track only news, this feature enables you to do that. As with languages, the default is to track all media types.

- **Regions**—You can specify geographic regions that you'd like to track. For example, if you are interested in capturing only mentions in the United States, you can set up your profile that way.

- **Source filters**—As with Sysomos, you can create a list of sources from which you want to pull mentions.

- **Keywords**—The keywords section is broken down into simple and advanced. Simple keywords are just free-form words like *social media*. The advanced query constructor enables you to set up keyword groups, do proximity searching, and exclude words from the profile capture.

Radian6 has worked hard to make the process of creating a profile easier, and we think it has been mostly successful. The keyword constructor takes some getting used to if you are not familiar with Boolean query construction, but Radian6 offers training to new users. If you are not familiar with constructing the queries, you can contact Radian6's customer support center, which will work with you to develop the right keyword set. That back-end work ensures that the dashboard output is useful, regardless of the use case.

These are the primary elements of the Radian6 dashboard:

- **River of News**—The River of News displays all mentions that you are trying to capture. The display defaults to chronological order, but you can segment based on a number of other metrics, including Twitter followers, inbound links, Twitter following, and so on.

- **Conversation Cloud**—This displays the top keywords used in conversations that include the words you have entered in the configuration screen. It is a pretty standard word cloud that is available in most platforms.

- **Topic Trends**—The Topic Trends widget shows volume of conversation over time for the keywords you have entered. The default view is pure volume, but you can also segment it by things such as media type.

- **Topic Analysis**—The Topic Analysis widget is most commonly used to display share of voice, or the percentage of conversation happening about your brand versus competitor brands. It is displayed as a pie chart, and you can also segment it multiple ways.

In addition to the initial dashboard, Radian6 provides several related products to assist users with engagement, data flow management, and insights development.

- **Radian6 Insights**—Via plug-ins to the social media dashboard, Radian6 offers users more data through third-party platforms. For example, you can now purchase access to OpenAmplify and OpenCalais, which are both natural language processing engines that help improve text analysis and sentiment scoring within the dashboard. In addition, you can purchase a Klout plug-in that you can use to ascertain the scores of Twitter users talking about your brand. These plug-ins are relatively inexpensive and offer stronger text analysis than the traditional Radian6 dashboard.

- **Engagement Console**—This product is meant to bridge the gap between social media listening and engagement. It enables you to read and post from one platform. It has much of the functionality of the standard dashboard, as well as workflow capabilities to assign responding responsibilities to people within the company. This product has been slow to get off the ground, mostly because companies are utilizing separate social media engagement solutions.

- **Summary Dashboard**—If you are looking for a solution to provide to executives, this is probably your best bet. It provides data such as a top-level look at share of conversation, breakdowns by media type and volume, and a word cloud to identify top words people are using.

- **Mobile**—This application for the iPhone shows a top-level look at conversations in your topic profile. It is unclear whether the application will be released for the Android or tablet.

Radian6 is not without issues. The platform typically has slightly more spam than Sysomos, for example, and is not preloaded with historical data. You can add historical data, but it comes at an additional cost, based on the amount of data you want. Also, because the platform is based in Flash, there can be issues with data reliability. It is often the case that if you create a widget, log out, and then log back in, the numbers in the widget change significantly. If you are using Radian6, we recommend that you frequently export mentions or widgets in order to preserve the data you have previously gathered.

Radian6 was involved in the second falling domino in the social media listening consolidation game. In March 2011, Salesforce.com acquired Radian6 for $326 million. The full effect of that acquisition has yet to be realized, but it is likely that in the near future, there will be tighter integration with Salesforce.com's CRM products.

Radian6 and Sysomos are not the only two listening platforms available on the market. There are others that have gained some market share in recent years.

The Best of the Rest

There are almost 230 platforms that organizations can utilize for social media listening. Not only does that make for difficult buying decisions, but it makes the process of doing due diligence on the tools nearly impossible. In addition, reviewing all 230 tools for you in this book would be completely impractical and—dare we say?—boring.

Sysomos and Radian6 are two of the most popular tools, and they are in almost every consideration set when companies are evaluating listening tools. In our experience, there are two others that appear almost as frequently: Visible Technologies and Crimson Hexagon.

Visible Technologies

Visible Technologies has been around as long as Radian6, and it offers a very similar service. It is tailored to enterprise-size clients, so its price tag is rather high. Visible Technologies collects data from Twitter, blogs, LinkedIn, YouTube, Facebook (publicly available content only), news, forums, and so on, just like Sysomos and Radian6 do. Users can create unlimited search strings, which is a valuable option for organizations that are actively testing conversation levels around key product attributes. The data is also available in multiple languages, which is helpful for companies whose base of operation is overseas. See Figure 4.5 for an example of the Visible Technologies standard dashboard.

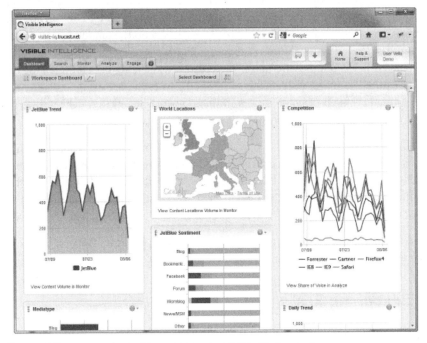

Figure 4.5   *A sample dashboard view for Visible Technologies.*

These are the key analytics components of the Visible Technologies dashboard:

- **Trend analysis**—Much like Sysomos's Heartbeat and Radian6's Topic Trends, Visible Technologies allows you to see how volume has fluctuated over time.

- **World locations**—Visible Technologies provides a heat map so that you can see what countries are driving mentions about a brand.

- **Competition trend line**—A line graph shows how volume of conversation is trending for a brand and its key competitors.

- **Sentiment**—Using automated sentiment scoring, which is only somewhat reliable, you can see how many positive, negative, or neutral mentions have been made about a brand.

- **Topic discovery**—This helps a user discover unique topics that are being discussed about a brand that you might not be currently aware of or tracking.

- **Prominent terms list**—This list provides a rundown of the words most commonly used in conversation.

- **Site-level demographic and psychographic analysis**—Based on self-reported data, Visible Technologies offers you some high-level information about who is talking about you.

Like Sysomos's Heartbeat, Visible Technologies also offers you the ability to engage in conversations directly from the platform (see Figure 4.6). This includes mentions on Twitter and Facebook, which is an invaluable resource if you are looking to develop content on-the-fly, based on listening findings.

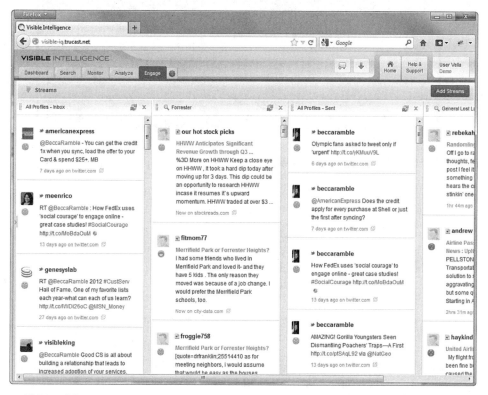

Figure 4.6 *The Visible Technologies sample engagement dashboard view.*

The engagement platform also has workflow functionality so that a user, or set of users, can assign tasks to other members on the team. This is a critical feature, as most companies have multiple people reading and responding as the organization becomes more socially mature.

It is unclear where Visible Technologies will go from here. Our assumption is that they will remain private for the foreseeable future, especially after receiving a large amount of venture capital funding shortly after the Radian6 acquisition was announced.

Crimson Hexagon

The other platform that we consistently encounter is Crimson Hexagon (see Figure 4.7). Crimson Hexagon is not purely a social media listening tool, though it offers users that functionality. Its main differentiator is its opinion analysis engine, which aims to go a level deeper than the text analysis that other providers offer.

Figure 4.7   *Sample Crimson Hexagon summary output.*

Using a sophisticated natural language processing engine, Crimson Hexagon offers deeper dives into online perceptions than the other tools listed here. Its greatest value is in opinion analysis, so if you are planning to use Crimson Hexagon, do not view it as you view Radian6, Sysomos, or Visible Technologies. Rather, view it as a potential add-on to your other listening efforts.

International Listening: The New Frontier

One type of listening that we have not talked about so far is international. Many brands are starting to ramp up social media capabilities overseas, and it is only a matter of time until there is a need for robust global listening tools. There are several reasons global listening has not taken off so far:

- **Cost**—Not only does it cost money to recruit, train, and retain talented analytics professionals in these markets, but also the tools themselves can be expensive, based on the markets you analyze.

- **Existing tools are below average**—Many brands are utilizing the tools already listed. Unfortunately, the global capabilities in these tools, particularly in terms of sites captured, are lacking.

- **Foreign languages**—Part and parcel with our second point, the tools covered earlier are not satisfactory for listening to mentions in foreign languages, unless you build the profile in that language.

If you hope to expand your listening efforts internationally, we recommend looking closely at Brandwatch and Brandtology. Both offer similar outputs to Sysomos, Visible Technologies, and Radian6, but both have greater "chops" in Western Europe and in Asia. Most importantly, they offer clients the data and the analyst to either translate or interpret. If your organization is struggling to identify internal resources for this effort, either Brandtology or Brandwatch could be your resource for global listening.

What's Next for Social Media Listening?

Predicting what's next in a market that is as volatile as social media listening is like playing the lottery, but it is important to keep pushing the envelope forward so that the tools stay useful and we deliver the best possible insights. What we know definitively, however, is that the tools will change in some way to meet evolving client demand. Also, companies will find new ways to use listening data.

We expect social media listening to change in six ways:

- **Consolidation**—Radian6 and Sysomos have already been acquired by much larger entities. It would not be surprising to see Visible Technologies and Crimson Hexagon get acquired in the not-so-distant future. There are still too many tools on the market to pick from, and there is not much differentiation between them at this point.

- **Tighter CRM integration**—Taking raw, unstructured social media conversations and cross-referencing against a CRM database lets you get even greater insight into how your customers behave. Pay attention to how Radian6 integrates the existing Salesforce.com products into its dashboard for keys to how this will evolve.

- **Command center development**—Made popular by Gatorade and Dell, many companies are establishing a listening command center internally to track mentions. A command center is staffed nearly 24 hours a day, 365 days a year as an early warning system. These command centers are also being used to proactively track mentions for communications planning. Our hunch is that command centers will keep proliferating because they offer an internal rallying point for social media activities.

- **Engagement software integration**—Chapter 8, "Tools: Engagement Analysis," talks about engagement analysis tools, but note that listening providers are already starting to develop this capability internally. Visible Technologies and Sysomos already offer it as part of the package, and Salesforce.com plans to merge Radian6 with its recent acquisition, Buddy Media. This is an important trend to watch, especially as listening tools look to expand outside the analytics community and into the community manager crowd.

- **Influencer Analysis**—This industry is just too big for the listening tools to not offer a more robust solution. Radian6 is already partnering with Klout, but it would not surprise us to see one of the solutions develop a proprietary algorithm to include within its base dashboard offering.

- **Making the lifecycle real**—Earlier we talked about using listening data outside public relations and marketing. We will talk about some of those use cases in later chapters, but as more case studies come to life, more organizations will begin using listening to supplement research being done in other areas of the organization.

What shape social media listening tools take in the 12 months or more from now is yet to be determined. We can assure you that as social media conversation data becomes more pervasive within companies, so too will new enhancements to the tools in order to meet those needs. It has been an amazing transformation over the past five years. The next five years is shaping up to be just as interesting.

5

Tools:
Search Analytics

Social listening can be incredibly useful in mining social data for opportunities, but the volume of data and potential opportunity pales in comparison to ones that lie in search. More specifically, search analytics can aid you in understanding how to best be discovered, both naturally through organic search, but also through paid search (advertising) opportunities. Discovery has never been more important than it is today. As discussed in Chapter 1, "Understanding the Digital Media Landscape," there has been an explosion of content and data, and there's a lot of activity as consumers interact with the content. In addition, historically well-defined boundaries between search, advertising, and branding have blurred. There are no more silos; all the channels must support one another. What you do with your outbound marketing efforts now has a direct effect on your ability to get discovered. This is due to changes in how the major search engines (Google, Yahoo!, and Bing) have evolved their algorithms in the past several years to incorporate new inputs, such as social and location data.

All this translates to a significant amount of digital "noise." Cutting through the clutter and positioning your brand, your digital outposts, and your brand content in the best possible way to be discovered is more critical today than ever before. In order to successfully do that, brands need to first understand how they are currently positioned, how consumers are currently behaving in terms of searching for relevant content and experiences, and what competitors are actively doing to capture consumer attention first. This chapter describes the opportunities available to marketers to do all these things by demonstrating how to deploy search analytics. It also describes the diverse ecosystem of tools available to perform search analysis techniques and activities.

Understanding the Basics of Search

It is important that you understand the size and scale of the search opportunity. According to the 2011 to 2016 Digital Marketing Forecast Report by Forrester Research, in 2012, companies spent a combined $41 billion on digital marketing across all channels (see Figure 5.1). Search marketing accounted for more than $21 billion of that (roughly 52%), more than all other channels combined (social media, email marketing, mobile marketing, and display marketing). Why was so much money, time, and attention focused on search? Because it's the first place consumers go, and it's also the activity they spend the most time on.

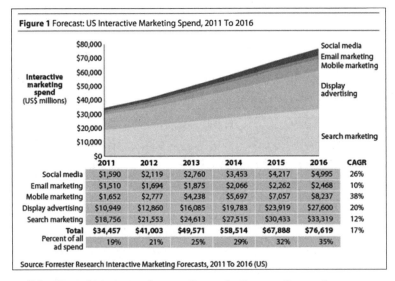

Figure 1 Forecast: US Interactive Marketing Spend, 2011 To 2016

	2011	2012	2013	2014	2015	2016	CAGR
Social media	$1,590	$2,119	$2,760	$3,453	$4,217	$4,995	26%
Email marketing	$1,510	$1,694	$1,875	$2,066	$2,262	$2,468	10%
Mobile marketing	$1,652	$2,777	$4,238	$5,697	$7,057	$8,237	38%
Display advertising	$10,949	$12,860	$16,085	$19,783	$23,919	$27,600	20%
Search marketing	$18,756	$21,553	$24,613	$27,515	$30,433	$33,319	12%
Total	$34,457	$41,003	$49,571	$58,514	$67,888	$76,619	17%
Percent of all ad spend	19%	21%	25%	29%	32%	35%	

Source: Forrester Research Interactive Marketing Forecasts, 2011 To 2016 (US)

Figure 5.1 *Digital Marketing Forecast Report by Forrester Research.*

According to Google's Zeitgeist (http://www.google.com/zeitgeist/2012/#the-world), there were more than 1.2 trillion searches on Google during 2012. Search dominates because there simply isn't any other channel that offers brands access to such a large, relevant audience. Despite the emergence of other channels, such as social media or mobile channels (and they are stealing percentage share from search), people still rely on search more than anything else.

Aside from the large quantity of information on search that's available to analyze, there's an upside in the fact that the information is freely available (for the most part). There are limitations, but the major engines, such as Google, provide a wealth of tools that help you assess and analyze consumer behavior through the lens of what the consumers search for. That said, it's important to draw some boundaries around the specific use cases for search analytics. Search analytics can help you with quite a bit, but like every other tool and technique discussed in this book, it works best when you're aiming at solving specific problems. You need to choose the proper tool for the job.

Search Analytics Use Cases

One of the most prevalent themes in this book is content creation, targeting, and optimization. There are many analytics approaches and tools aimed at this topic, from understanding audience content consumption so that you can create an initial content strategy to optimizing specific content and messaging in the wild. Because Chapter 17, "Search Analysis," is dedicated to detailing the specific use cases for search analysis, we'll keep it brief here and simply identify the specific ways in which search analytics can support content development for any digital marketing initiative:

- **Choosing paid advertising messaging (search engine marketing)—** Paid search campaigns are simply advertising links to brand content, based on relevant searches. There are many tools available to uncover the most popular searches and thus the critical search terms associated with them, which yield more consumer searches converting into visits to your site or consuming your content.

- **Choosing natural search messaging (search engine optimization)—** Natural, or organic, search is still a continuous effort for which every marketer needs to plan. Being found naturally, without assistance from paid advertising, is one of the most difficult problems for marketers to stay on top of. Doing so is part art, part science. It's not just about having the most relevant keywords woven throughout your brand content. You also have to include key variables that search engine algorithms consider, such as link building, and consider local search optimization. Fortunately, there are many tools to help with this, both free and paid. You'll read more about those tools later in the chapter.

- **Identifying and choosing brand associations**—Branding used to be unrelated to discovery. Specifically, optimizing for discovery and external brand communications weren't integrated such that both contributed to a common goal and/or objective. In many instances, they actually work against each other. Consider that the content (for example, keywords, tagging, and links) a brand publishes has a *direct* effect on the likelihood that it will be discovered. Failure to connect these two initiatives results in a gigantic missed opportunity.

  Most brands still treat branding as being unrelated to discovery. However, that's changed, and it won't ever be the same again. In an effort to add more relevance and cater to brands, Google started emphasizing the importance of branding in its search results in 2011. Similarly to how the Brand Tags (http://www.brandtags.com) project creates associations between consumer sentiment about the brands they do business with, there are search tools that allow marketers to understand how they should position their product(s) or service(s) against competitors, based on how consumers view them and search for them.

- **Identifying trends and seasonal changes**—Consumer behavior—specifically how people search and what they search for—isn't consistent year round; it changes over time. Interest in specific topics or categories picks up and peaks at different times throughout the year. Understanding these trends and, more specifically, what they look like in your industry or for your product category, can be gleaned by using search tools. And you don't have to limit your investigation to your company or product. Because search data is freely available, you can learn about your competitors as well, and you can use the knowledge you gain to make more informed decisions about appropriate allocation of resources, whether that's paid advertising dollars or internal resources associated with content development, social media support, or publishing efforts.

- **Supporting new product/market launches**—Whether you're launching a new product in an unknown category or expanding an existing product into a new market, search analysis can provide insights that lead to an understanding of nuances. For example, a new market might place greater emphasis on a specific product attribute that hasn't played a big role in its traditional market. How consumers in different markets search can reveal key differences in product or category attributes across various geographies and can help marketers gain a sense of where interest is greatest for individual product attributes.

This enables you to tailor market-level messaging for paid advertising, brand content, and social media publishing to the nuances and needs of each market.

- **Brand audits**—Audits provide helpful summaries of how consumers currently think, feel, share, and act toward a brand in digital channels. Agencies frequently conduct brand audits to inform advertising campaigns, product launches, and development of digital strategies. How consumers search about a brand and what keywords they associate with a brand is important when planning any of the aforementioned initiatives. The tools described later in this chapter provide marketers the ability to perform these audits.

Free Tools for Collecting Insights Through Search Data

At their core, most of the search tools we cover in this chapter excel at one very specific thing: quantifying search volume (queries) for specific keywords and providing related keyword associations for additional context. In addition, there may be other features, such as the ability to segment and target by geography or time period.

Google Trends

For several years, the most popular tool for analyzing search data has been Google Trends (formerly called Google Insights for Search). This tool provides the ability to easily identify the most popular search trends along with the ability to quickly and easily search and explore what consumers are interested in based on Google search queries. You can find Google Trends at www.google.com/trends.

In the example shown in Figure 5.2, we've used two terms: *digital analytics* and *social analytics*. Notice that the initial view provides search volume trending beginning from 2007. This is based on an index, rather than total number of searches, with 100 on the index representing the peak search volume for the provided terms. You can easily modify the date range to suit your needs, going as far back as 2004. However, there may not be search data available for certain terms that weren't popular until after that date. As you can see in Figure 5.2, social analytics interest skyrocketed during 2007 and significantly outpaces digital analytics in overall search queries. Further segmenting this volume, though, can reveal additional details that might be useful to you.

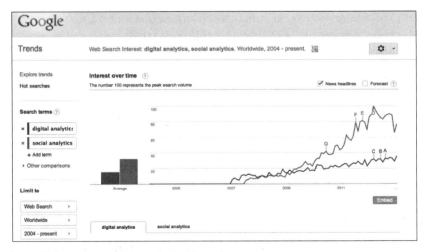

Figure 5.2   *The Google Trends dashboard.*

Google Trends is fairly flexible, enabling you to include search operators to refine your queries to match exact phrases with quotes, to combine terms using the + operator, and to exclude undesirable terms by using the – operator. Figure 5.3 shows an example that uses related terms.

Related terms	Top	Rising
digital marketing analytics	100	
marketing analytics	95	
digital media analytics	50	
digital analytics association	20	
video analytics	15	
digital analytics jobs	15	
strategy analytics	15	
social media analytics	15	

Figure 5.3   *Google Trends analysis of related terms.*

Figure 5.3 shows the most popular searches that match the terms provided, along with the corresponding index number to give you a sense of how popular that related term is, based on overall search volume. Basically, these terms represent the ones that are most interesting to consumers. It's important to note that Google Trends automatically categorizes the top searches and assigns each to a specific industry or topic, so there might be some classification errors in certain instances. However, for the most part, the data is accurate across billions of searches.

By default, Google Trends provides a list of the top 10 terms, but you might want to explore more. You can easily view additional terms by downloading the data locally. You can easily export the data for additional analysis. Thanks to the automated classification, the filter feature enables you to view search volume and associated keywords by specific category. In the example in Figure 5.4, we've filtered the two searches by industry and show only the search volume and keywords associated with advertising and marketing.

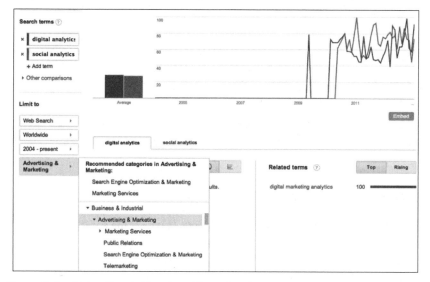

Figure 5.4 *Using Google Trends to filter related terms.*

As discussed in previous chapters, segmentation is essential. As we've just shown, Google Trends provides the ability to easily segment by time (date range), industry or topic, and also location. Location helps narrow the scope of interest across the keywords you're interested in and can help you decide not only which geographic regions to focus on but even which cities have the most interest, based on relevant search volume. In some cases, location data is available even at the metro level. Google Trends defines metros as geographic areas within major metropolitan areas of the United States, as defined by Arbitron, Inc., a major media and marketing research firm.

Google Trends breaks out the location view into two separate views, as shown in Figure 5.5. The example in the figure uses an interactive heat map to show each country and its index number. The right-hand view shows region by default but can be toggled to show the same data by city, in list view. You might be surprised in this particular case to see that when it comes to social analytics, India, not the United States, is the clear winner in terms of interest in this topic (and it's not even close)!

There is one final location feature worth noting. Google Trends enables you to play back the search interest to see how popularity of the specific terms has changed over time and across regions. Clicking the Play button animates the heat map to visually represent changes over time. The darker the shade of color for each region, the more popular that search term is for that region.

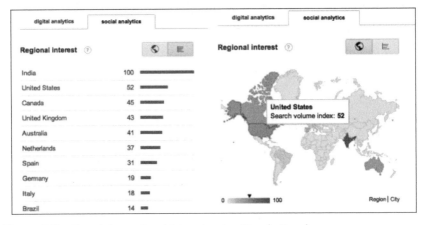

Figure 5.5   *Examining regional interest, using Google Trends.*

One of the most convenient features of Google Trends is the ability to easily embed any of the charts into a separate web page or document (for example, a slide presentation). Google Trends provides native embed functionality directly in the tool, and using it takes only a few clicks. Google continues to add features and functionality to Google Trends to both segment the data in the most relevant way possible and analyze and present the data in easily digestible ways. This is a huge opportunity for brands or marketers, and one they must capitalize on, as it provides a direct window into what consumers are interested in, including the date and location of that interest. You can use this information to focus on developing content to target popular topics among the desired audience, using keywords you can have confidence in. You can use this tool to learn how to speak the language of your audience.

YouTube Trends

YouTube is not only the most popular video destination hub on the Web, but it's also the second-largest search engine. As of this writing, approximately 72 hours of video are uploaded to YouTube each minute. More than 4 billion hours of video are consumed each month on YouTube. All this content and consumption generate significant amounts of digital data for analysis. As Google has done for traditional searching, YouTube has developed its own trends tool for video. YouTube Trends (http://youtube-trends.blogspot.com) describes itself as "a new destination for the latest trending videos and video trends on YouTube and a resource for daily insight into what's happening with web video."

Based on viewership data, as well as YouTube search data, YouTube Trends takes the pulse of what's happening on YouTube at any given moment and helps identify emerging trends that might reflect broader, cultural trends. It can be useful to both media and brand-focused marketers. YouTube algorithmically generates topics for classification based on the metadata assigned to individual videos. Metadata includes keywords contained in the video title or description, as well as any keyword tags the user applies to classify the video when he uploads it.

Let's take a look at the specific features and functionality of YouTube Trends, which include the following:

- **Identify Trending topics**—This feature looks at topics in which a set of videos are currently rising in popularity. This can be useful for identifying popular topics that might be relevant for brand content publishing on YouTube or even paid advertising messaging on YouTube (TrueView in-stream campaigns).

- **Identify Trending Videos**—This feature looks at individual videos that are popular due to offsite activity. These videos are receiving significant views and consumption because they were embedded in popular third-party websites, not on YouTube.

- **Popular This Month**—This feature shows a collection of the most popular videos being viewed and shared during the past month.

In addition to the snapshot-type data about what's trending, an interactive dashboard provides more granular information. The YouTube Trends dashboard provides some of the same segmentation capabilities as the Google Trends tool, such as the following:

- **Location Filtering**—YouTube Trends automatically detects a user's country-specific content preferences and then uses this as the default choice in the dashboard. However, you can override the default and select another country. Not all countries are available. The tool currently supports the top 50 countries, based on viewership data and usage. From there, you can drill down the location filter to the state or city level, based on available data, as shown in Figure 5.6.

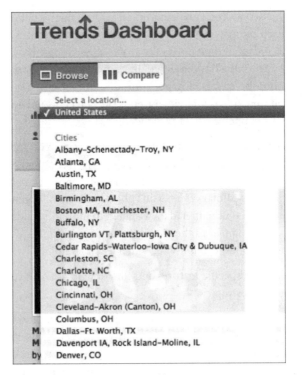

Figure 5.6   *The YouTube Trends location filter.*

- **Demographic Filtering**—The tool enables you to view trending video information, based on age group segmentation (see Figure 5.7). There are seven unique age groups, from 13–17 years old up to 65+ years and everything in between. Although we certainly prefer to gather much more data about a target audience, this traditional demographic information can be useful for understanding video content nuances among difference audience segments. A caveat worth noting is that YouTube collects age and gender demographics from logged-in users via their YouTube account profiles. So, in essence, this is self-reported data, and it exists for only a subset of the entire user population.

Trends Dashboard

☐ Browse   ▌▌▌ Compare

🔽 United States

👤 25-34 years old

All   Male   Female

Figure 5.7 *The YouTube Trends demographic filter.*

- **Comparison**—This is perhaps the most interesting and useful feature that the YouTube Trends tool has to offer. It enables you to make up to three comparisons across different audience segments and provides the trending videos for each group selected. For example, in Figure 5.8, we're trying to identify differences in video consumption among women between the ages of 35 and 44 in three unique geographies: Austin, Detroit, and Boston. The tool allows you to easily customize each group.

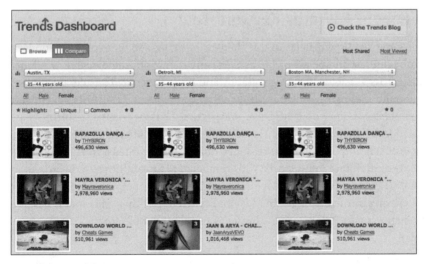

Figure 5.8 *The YouTube Trends comparison tool.*

One of the points we really drive home in this book is that digital analytics provides many opportunities. Arguably the most important opportunity is understanding the target audience and its needs, preferences, and behaviors. The YouTube Trends tool offers keen insight into how specific audience segments are consuming video content. You can use what you learn with it as input for a variety of content strategy, content development, or advertising messaging initiatives.

- **Most Shared**—This feature lists the most shared videos on Facebook and Twitter during the past 24 hours. This is useful for understanding and tracking content distribution across social platforms. You can combine this information with data from Facebook Insights to understand the virality of a new brand video and to determine the propensity consumers currently have for sharing it.

- **Most Viewed**—This feature shows a collection of the most viewed videos during the past 24 hours that were uploaded within the past month. The YouTube Trends tool is helpful, but it lacks some of the features you see in other tools covered in this chapter and others throughout the book. Namely, it doesn't include the ability to export, manipulate, and work with the data with your own hands. For now, it's basically a reporting tool. However, there is still value in using YouTube Trends, and if you're considering reaching an audience through video content, then you should have this dashboard in your toolkit.

The Google AdWords Keyword Tool

The tools mentioned so far in this chapter do a good job of helping you understand search interest and behavior in aggregate and then, with some degree of segmentation across variables such as geography and time, they may reveal opportunities for outbound messaging, whether through branded content or advertising. However, what the tools don't do is help you understand the larger digital footprint of associated terms that a brand has. Consumers make associations between brands and their digital outposts. For this reason, Google has integrated a freely available keyword research tool into its AdWords campaign platform (https://adwords.google. com/o/KeywordTool). The Keyword Tool is useful for helping inform and refine advertising through Google, but it's not limited to just that. This tool is designed to enable anyone to explore the brand associations people are making in greater detail.

The Keyword Tool is designed for anyone who is planning on using Google AdWords. But of course, if brands are targeting their paid search advertising based on popular keyword searches in Google, then it makes sense for you to be doing the same for discovery purposes regarding the keywords on your website and social media outposts because the AdWords Keyword Tool results are the keyword searches of real people using Google. Figure 5.9 shows the Google AdWords Keyword Tool dashboard.

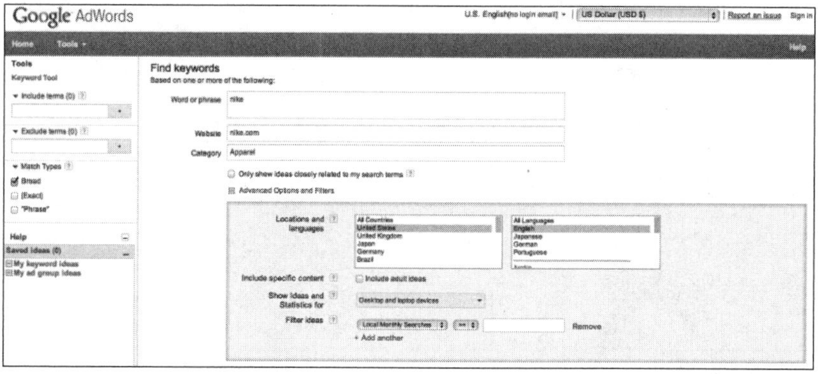

Figure 5.9   *The Google AdWords keyword tool.*

Unsurprisingly, Google offers a robust set of targeting options within the Keyword Tool (see Figure 5.9 and 5.10). The brand associations are derived from actual search queries and their effectiveness at increasing targeted website traffic. To start understanding what keywords and topic associations are most relevant, simply enter the desired keywords or phrases, along with your website URL and the category (industry) that is most appropriate. The example shown in Figure 5.8 uses Nike and Nike.com.

The Keyword Tool has some advanced targeting options and filters that are worth highlighting:

- **Location**—This option filters search results by geography, down to the country level.
- **Language**—This option filters results by language. It currently supports 42 unique languages globally.
- **Device Type(s)**—This is one of the most interesting and useful options, particularly given the explosion of mobile devices. From a search perspective, mobile behavior can be quite different from computer behavior. Google provides several filtering options, by device type, including the following:
  - Desktop and laptop searches
  - All mobile device searches
  - Mobile WAP device searches
  - Mobile devices with full Internet browser searches

- **Ideas (Data Sources)**—This feature enables you to filter your ideas by different statistics and view the results across different dimensions. For example, you can filter by competition (low, medium, high) for a particular keyword or by global monthly search volume.

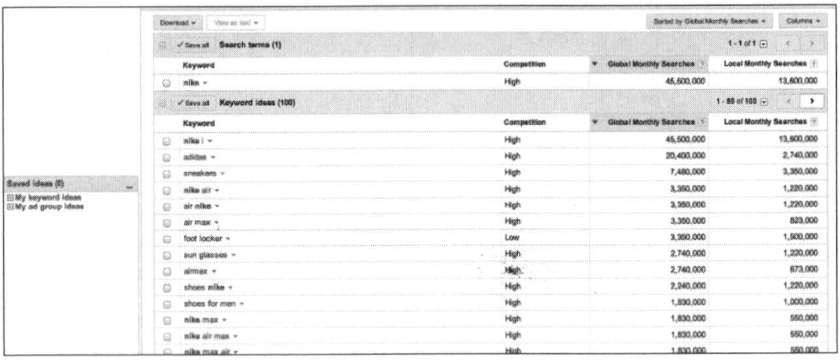

Figure 5.10   *The Google AdWords Keyword Tool – Standard View.*

By using the Keyword Tool, you can get a clear understanding of what keywords and topics consumers most associate with your brand, based on the terms provided, that yield the most traffic. Focusing on these keywords in your messaging, site content, link building, and external content development for publishing will give you the greatest chance of maximizing your potential traffic, conversions, and audience engagement.

Yahoo! Clues

Yahoo! Clues (http://clues.yahoo.com) is a freely available trends reporting tool that operates by categorizing and classifying daily search volumes on Yahoo.com. This product competes with Google Trends, but it offers some things that Google Trends doesn't. It also displays the data in a more visual and friendly manner than Google Trends.

One of the most noticeable differences between Yahoo! Clues and Google Trends is the inclusion of demographic data on the searchers. Yahoo! Clues automatically includes age groups and gender integrated into search volume reporting, which makes for a single unified view. In this instance, this tool is easier to use than some of the other tools if you're interested in a quick snapshot of which age groups and/ or gender might be most interested in your brand or your terms.

For example, say you're looking at search volume for the Nike Fuel Band, a wearable, health-focused electronic device that tracks your personal activity and movement. Figure 5.11 shows the Fuel Band searches over time and the age groups that are responsible for the share of search volume. In this case, men aged 25 to 34 are responsible for 21% of all Fuel Band searches.

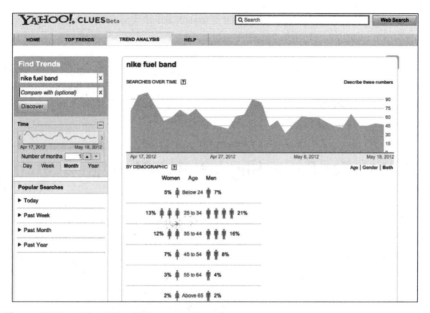

Figure 5.11   *The Yahoo! Clues trends tool.*

Like the other tools, Yahoo! Clues also shows results by geography, in an interactive map that you can drill into for additional detail. The example in Figure 5.12 shows trend data at the city level for Fuel Band searches.

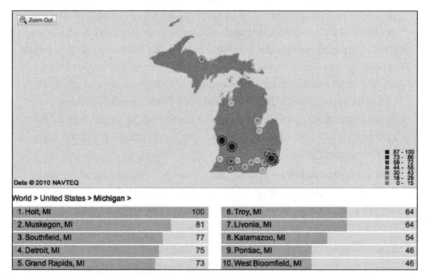

Figure 5.12   *Geographic filtering in Yahoo! Clues.*

Yahoo! Clues provides the ability to customize the date range, compare with additional terms or topics (although the comparison feature is not quite as robust as the YouTube Trends comparison tool), and include related terms and keywords that are relevant to the provided terms. The uses for this tool are similar to the uses of the other search trend analysis tools, but Yahoo! Clues is based on a different set of data. Although Google still commands approximately 67% market share of search, according to December 2012 comScore research, Bing and Yahoo! are noteworthy, at 16% and 15%, respectively, and you should consider them in your research and analysis, particularly if you know your audience indexes heavily on the use of those engines.

Paid Tools for Collecting Insights Through Search Data

The free tools we've covered can be incredibly helpful, and in many cases they will be sufficient for your needs. However, certain use cases require that you upgrade from free to paid tools that provide a robust feature set and are designed to handle all the nitty-gritty details necessary to research, analyze, and optimize discovery, particularly for search engine optimization (SEO). The tool providers sell to both brands and agencies, and the tools are used to measure and manage search-related marketing activities, including but not limited to the following:

- **Keyword research**—The paid tools can be used for deep keyword research analysis in the same manner as the free tools.

- **Competitive analysis**—Competitive analysis is typically focused on share of voice, also referred to as share of search. This feature enables you to specify competitive brands and/or URLs for analysis, which are then compared against the category, as well as your brand, and provide reporting on market share based on specific terms. This type of analysis can be incredibly useful when you're just beginning your effort to optimize your brand's discovery potential. It also gives you the ability to peek into your competitors' keyword and page optimization strategies so that you can identify and uncover your highest-potential competitive opportunities.

- **Social media analysis**—You can integrate and analyze social media data to reveal the areas that will boost SEO performance. You can identify what specific keywords and pages should be targeted with social media management—for example, tweets, posts, likes, and shares.

- **Search opportunity modeling/forecasting**—Some tools provide automated analysis based on your inputs. This analysis can help you model specific scenarios, predict the value of the SEO you're considering, and ultimately the impact it will have on your business performance.

- **Qualitative and quantitative analytics**—Many tools offer integration with voice of customer survey providers and leading web analytics platforms, such as Adobe Omniture SiteCatalyst, Google Analytics, Webtrends, and Unica.

- **Local search**—Search is increasingly more local. Consumers seek local results in their search queries, and engines have responded by including more local results integrated within search engine results pages (SERPs) to increase relevancy and user satisfaction. Marketers and brands are feeling the impact of this change, and it's a painful one. Local search puts greater emphasis on the ability to optimize local search and vary optimization efforts for discovery by location. You can imagine how this can quickly get unmanageable for brands that have a significant need for local search or a number of retail locations in different geographic locations. How can you efficiently manage local search at scale? Some tools that are now emerging have the capability to address this particular pain point.

Although this list is robust, it's far from covering the entire spectrum that professional paid search and SEO platforms cover. The landscape is littered with both full-service search analysis tools and specialty tools that focus on a particular niche aspect of search analysis. There are hundreds of tools. We've created several good lists that you're encouraged to explore:

- **KissMetrics Indispendisble SEO Tools**—http://blog.kissmetrics. com/6-indispensable-seo-tools/
- **SearchEngineWatch 43 Paid Search Tools**—http://searchenginewatch. com/article/2066594/43-Paid-Search-Marketing-Tools-And-When-To-Use-Them
- **140 SEO Tools**—http://www.seocompany.ca/tool/seo-tools.html

Given the diversity, depth, and complexity of the tool space, the following section focuses on a single enterprise SEO platform to finish the chapter.

The BrightEdge SEO Platform

Chapter 8, "Tools: Engagement Analysis," focuses on several of the well-known social media management system vendors, such as Buddy Media, Vitrue, and Sprinklr. What makes those vendors so attractive is that they have developed one-stop tools for all things engagement management across major social media platforms. BrightEdge (http://www.brightedge.com) is the equivalent for SEO. It's designed to put all your search analysis and reporting in a single, integrated dashboard. Rather than using 10 different search analysis tools, you simply log in to one. There are advantages to this approach—such as convenience and simplicity—but you give up some of the specialty features and functionality that more diverse toolboxes can deliver. Figure 5.13 shows the BrightEdge dashboard.

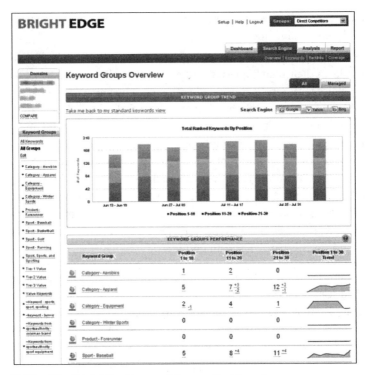

Figure 5.13   *The BrightEdge Keyword Groups dashboard.*

After logging in, you immediately see your brand keyword groups overview, how your terms are currently ranking in SERPS by positions 1–10, 11–20, and 21–30 for each major search engine. This is a very helpful visual snapshot of current performance. Also included is the trending of each specific page on your site over time against the various SERPs positions 1–30. At a glance, you can see how performance has changed over time, and you can evaluate which optimization efforts have been successful.

Another view of the platform is the previously mentioned competitive analysis that BrightEdge calls Share of Voice (SOV). SOV factors the rank position of your specified keywords and number of keywords ranked against your competitive set of brands/companies. Figure 5.14 shows an example of the output of SOV analysis.

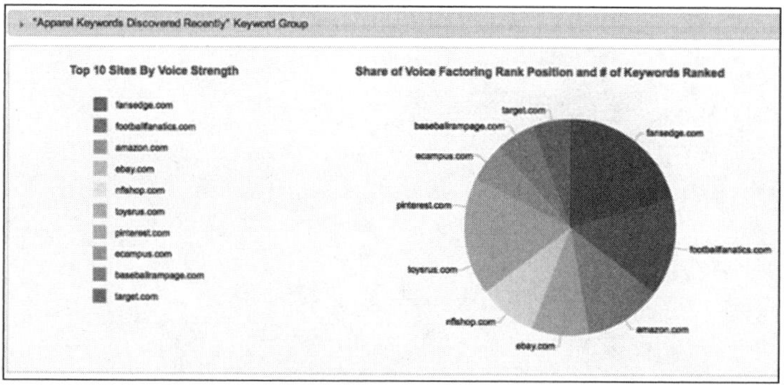

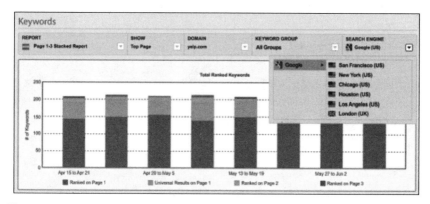

Figure 5.14   *The BrightEdge Share of Voice report.*

Given what a challenge local SEO can be and how few tools provide capabilities in this area, we want to share how BrightEdge approaches this problem. Figure 5.15 is a snapshot of a local SEO report, pulled from BrightEdge. You see the familiar keyword group report, by rank and position, but you can toggle through various local markets. This enables easier reporting and management of local market optimization activities.

Figure 5.15   *BrightEdge local SEO.*

Wrapping up Search Analytics

This chapter provides an overview of various search analytics tools. These tools enable marketers to understand terms, topics, and associations that are linked to desired business outcomes. In the right hands, these tools have powerful capabilities. A well-defined plan, accurate keywords, and a skillful analyst can often find insight gold, given the time to do so. Try incorporating some of these tools into your next research plan and infuse the findings into your strategic planning.

6

Tools:
Audience Analysis

Digital marketing and advertising do not operate like broadcast mass media (or at least they shouldn't). Instead of the same standardized message being served to a mass audience, every single visitor to an online property experiences some degree of personalization. Whether it's through opt-in subscriptions, saved user account preferences, or cookie-based targeting, your web experience isn't the same as mine, quite often even if we're on the same site.

The best way to demonstrate this at work is through a seemingly simple Google search. Google goes to great lengths to understand its users—and to understand them better than you might realize. It stockpiles all types of data about you and your preferences to deliver personalized search results. Chances are that your search results are never going to be the same as mine. This is due to a variety of factors. Several things can potentially affect the outcome of a Google search. Consider the following examples:

- **Location-based results**—Google auto-detects your location, using either your IP address or the My Location feature in the Google toolbar (if you have it installed).

- **Personal history**—If you have not disabled it, Google remembers your past search history, constantly assesses that against future searches, and then serves up a new result set.

- **Browser type**—Depending on the browser type, Google can access prior browsing history and use that history as an input for determining which result set to provide. Previously visited sites affect search results.

- **Device type**—Google has been auto-detecting the type of device you're using and serving up different results based on the device for some time. For example, mobile search queries receive different results than desktop or laptop queries, even for the same term(s).

These are four of the most common factors, but they're not the only ones. The point here is that Google exerts a significant amount of effort to learn enough about users to deliver a deceptively simple yet incredibly effective user experience.

It's not obvious on the surface, but creating successful, personalized user experiences can happen only with a keen understanding of the audience and their needs, expectations, and behaviors. This requires pulling in digital data from a variety of sources and performing rock-solid analyses. The end result is a clear picture about what makes an audience tick, and it is something that you can begin to align against as you develop your marketing and advertising plans. We call this process *audience analysis*.

What Is Audience Analysis?

Audience analysis isn't new, although most people other than professional writers probably aren't familiar with it. Traditionally, audience analysis is the process by which technical writers determine the most important characteristics of their audience in order to choose the best style, format, and information when preparing a document or speaking. Basically, it's an approach to user research which ensures that you are delivering value to the target audience.

Audience analysis involves several research activities that reveal key information about what matters most to the audience you're trying to reach, just like Google does. We've adopted this traditional concept and made some adaptations to reflect the specific needs of profiling a digital audience.

The term *audience* itself can be used as an acronym for remembering this technique:

Analysis—Who is the audience?

Understanding—What is the audience's knowledge and attitude toward the brand?

Demographics—What is the audience's age, gender, education, location, and so on?

Interest—Why is the audience reading, sharing, and interacting with your brand content?

Environment—Where does the audience spend time online?

Needs—What are the audience needs associated with your brand, product, or service?

Customization—What specific needs and/or interests should the brand address in order to add value for the audience?

Clearly, some of these activities aren't new to digital media; we've been capturing these types of data and using them to target users for years in online marketing and advertising programs. What's new, and different, is the ability to go beyond basic demographic data and augment that layer with additional sources, such as psychographic, behavioral, and even user-interaction data based on social network activities.

Social networks are a rich source of these data types. Facebook's meteoric rise can largely be credited to the mountains of self-reported personal data its 900+ million users have provided to the company. Facebook might very well be the largest source in the world of consumer activity, interest, opinion, attitude, and values data.

Audience analysis brings together several of the different tool types we've covered in previous chapters and combines their outputs to formulate a holistic view of a particular group of online users. There are techniques that you can apply to data garnered from existing tools and combine with supplemental metadata to enhance your knowledge and understanding of the audience.

Audience Analysis Use Cases

The audience analysis approach is comprehensive, and if followed in its entirety, it can require a significant amount of effort. Thankfully, it doesn't mean you have to do everything, every time. Like most of the topics we talk about in other chapters, everything begins with goals and objectives. In this instance, it depends on the use case. Audience analysis can be quick and dirty or more rigorous and formal, depending on the use case.

The following are some common use cases for audience analysis:

- Digital strategy
- Content strategy
- Engagement strategy
- Search engine optimization
- Content optimization
- User experience design
- Audience segmentation

The following sections examine these use cases in more detail.

Digital Strategy

In addition to having clearly defined business objectives, developing a robust digital strategy requires having a clear understanding of the market, your competitors, and your audience. You'll be trying to find customers but first need to have identified their needs, wants, and expectations. If you identify those, you'll be successful. If you ignore them, your digital strategy will rest on delivering content and experiences that offer little to no value. Getting clarity through audience analysis is key to ensuring that you'll succeed.

An audience analysis supporting a digital strategy initiative tends to be more comprehensive and lengthier than other strategies. This is due to the complexity of the digital landscape. We no longer live in a "if you build it, they will come" digital era. Social technologies and mobile devices have accelerated the fragmentation of the Internet. Your audience is scattered like bits and pieces across a vast network of sites and platforms. This means you have to source data from more platforms of several different types.

Content Strategy

Optimized content allows digital interactions to reach their greatest potential. Content strategists view content, regardless of type (text, images, audio, video, and so on) as products. They therefore plan, design, research, and test content, just as you would a product, to ensure that content has value to the recipient. In order for content strategists to be effective, they require as much input about the audience as possible.

Content strategists work with many inputs to understand their users prior to moving forward. User research includes demographic, behavioral, and psychographic information, personas, and user experience flows, to name a few. Digital analytics provides this data.

Engagement Strategy

After your company has made a decision to utilize a social platform and create a brand presence, engagement activity isn't far behind. Brands develop engagement strategies to maximize the number of desired outcomes produced on social platforms. However, even the best-laid plans can go awry and require course correction. Engagement analytics to the rescue!

Analyzing engagement activity reveals insights about what your audience likes, thinks, and needs. Almost every major social platform has a native engagement analytics tool. A diverse third-party engagement analytics ecosystem also exists. The problem is not lacking analytics tools to measure and optimize your engagement, but having too much tool choice.

Search Engine Optimization

Search engine optimization (SEO) is not new to digital marketers. It's never been easier to get your content published and distributed, but unfortunately that means it's also never been more difficult to be discovered through organic searches. A growing trend also affecting SEO is the inclusion of social data signals into search engine algorithms.

Content Optimization

It's not enough to optimize your website content to maximize discovery; you must also infuse the content distributed in your social status updates, tweets, blog posts, comments, and so on. This means the output of the SEO analysis has multiple uses.

User Experience Design

The online landscape is chock full of complex systems. User experience design is important for simplifying things enough so that users can complete desired tasks and leave a digital experience satisfied. Digital analytics plays a big role in informing user experience designers about what steps along a consumer journey are providing what users need and which steps are broken, causing dissatisfaction and abandonment. Web analytics, site surveys, and social analytics can reveal a combination of what people are doing and saying about their experience. Designers can incorporate these feedback mechanisms as input and optimize user flows accordingly.

Audience Segmentation

As described in Chapter 1, "Understanding the Digital Media Landscape," segmentation is critical. Your audience is made up of unique segments, each with a specific set of online behaviors. Using a number of third-party analytics tools, you can begin to build custom segments that reveal key behaviors and activities for you to align your marketing against. A good example of this is Forrester's Technographics, which handles segmentation and how consumers behave online.

Audience Analysis Tool Types

We have provided a high-level description of the uses for audience analysis. Now let's dig into the tools you can use to execute with. The tool landscape is saturated is many categories. Remember to follow the steps outlined in Chapter 3, "Picking the Tools of the Trade," to ensure that selecting a tool isn't a painful process and that you end up with a tool that meets your needs.

Inside a digital analyst's toolbox, you'll find the following types of tools:

- **Search insights**—Search insights tools are useful for mining search engine volume patterns across geography, industry categories, time, and properties to find actionable insights. Google Insights for Search is a useful free solution, and companies such as Hitwise and Compete offer their own premium paid versions.

- **SEO**—You can use SEO tools to monitor, track, and manage both your own and competitor keyword rankings. The landscape is saturated. Leading paid tool providers are SEOmoz and BrightEdge. Although these tools are impressive, there are many suitable free tools, such as Microsoft SEO Toolkit, Searchmetrics Essentials, Tynt, and Google AdWords. This list doesn't even come close to scratching the surface of the universe of SEO tools in the marketplace. Depending on your level of expertise and willingness to do the work, you can opt for completely outsourcing the work or doing it yourself. There is an SEO tool that will meet your needs.

- **User surveys**—Surveys capture answers to custom questions from website visitors. They offer advanced features such as skip logic, randomization, website integration, reporting, and analytics. Surveys are a valuable source of qualitative feedback that you can tie to web analytics data to connect what an audience says with what it actually does. Options such as SurveyMonkey, Polldaddy, and Zoomerang offer low cost, and premium solutions from companies such as QuestionPro offer custom variable capture, advanced segmentation, and filtering.

- **Website profiling**—Website profiling services do exactly what the name suggests: You can enter a website URL and get back a site profile that reveals site traffic statistics, search volume, demographic data on visitors, related sites, and more. Alexa, Google Ad Planner, and Compete all offer free tools that provide this functionality.

- **Web analytics**—Traditional web analytics tools collect and report on data to optimize website usage. These tools are primarily used to gauge overall traffic volumes, but they are also a rich source of behavioral data. Analyzing clicks can provide some value, but we live in an era that requires you to go well beyond counting clicks in the aggregate.

  Web analytics can reveal behavior patterns that tie back to several of the use cases referenced earlier, particularly user experience design. (Optimized user experience design = a happy audience!) Many web analytics tools allow for custom segmentation and multivariate testing. For example, these methods enable you to experiment with and understand which specific content types (text, image, video) an audience most desires by testing different variations. It takes time up front to define and plan what behavioral tests you want to execute, but tests can reveal specific insights that relate to audience intent, likes, and needs.

- **Social listening**—Hundreds of social listening tools exist in the marketplace. Their roles in supporting an audience analysis are to identify the sources (both media type and individual URL) of relevant social conversation about your brand or product/service and to provide some demographic and psychographic data. Refer to Chapter 4, "Tools: Social Listening," for details on how to select a listening tool and considerations for using social listening.

  One aspect of social listening that is unique to audience analysis and that we cover in this chapter is how to utilize custom tagging and classification to better understand your audience opinions, likes, and sentiment about specific brand, product, or services attributes.

- **Influence analysis**—It is important to identify individuals responsible for driving action among relevant members of your audience. This category is covered in greater detail in Chapter 9, "Tools: Influence Analysis."

- **Sharing analysis**—There are tools specifically dedicated to tracking share activity of content across digital platforms. These tools provide a window into the type of content that's most desirable and most interesting to your audience through URL-shortening services such as bitly and free sharing tools such as AddThis and ShareThis that provide reporting. For a more customized paid offering, you can try something such as Meteor Solutions platform.

- **Social profile and activity analysis**—Social profile and activity analysis is one of the features most commonly found in third-party social analytics tools currently on the market. Whether you're performing an analysis of your own brand or a competitor's social profile, these tools detail your engagement activity, friends/fans/followers, and published content to reveal insights and trends.

For example, SocialBro, a third-party tool designed to manage your Twitter community, provides the following type of analysis at the account level:

- Users by location

- Users by language

- Users by number of connections

- Users by posts per day

- Users by time zone

- Users by profile/bio data

This information is interesting but not all that useful, until you apply the newest feature—the ability to apply the same analysis at specific Twitter lists. Now we're taking steps in the right direction: segmentation! You can begin to customize engagement toward reaching a specific audience and their interests by applying social analytics tools like this but at a narrower band of your followers, not in aggregate.

As more social analytics tools provide segmentation capabilities, their usefulness will increase. This is the biggest advantage that web analytics, search analytics, and paid media analytics have over social analytics at this stage. The rapid rate of innovation and change among the tools in this category is producing some hits, but there are also some misses when it comes to functionality.

One final note about this category: As of this writing, the social analytics category is a wide spectrum of capability and specialization. On one of end of the spectrum exists specialized one-offs that focus narrowly on an individual social platform, such as SocialBro for Twitter or EdgeRank Checker for Facebook. At the other end of the spectrum live the social analytics dashboards. These solutions support and provide analytics for all major social networks.

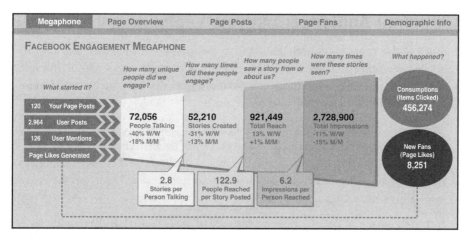

Figure 6.1 *Facebook Engagement Megaphone.*

Source: SimplyMeasured

SimplyMeasured is an example of a social analytics dashboard. It provides intuitive and visual dashboards that give detailed reporting on the following:

- YouTube channels
- YouTube competitive analysis
- Klout audience analysis
- Twitter follower analysis
- Facebook fan page analysis
- Facebook content analysis
- Facebook page insights
- Facebook competitive analysis
- Google+ page analysis

SimplyMeasured is far from being the only full-spectrum dashboard provider. Several of the social media management system (SMMS) tools described in Chapter 3 also provide analytics dashboards for the social networks they support. Market leaders such as Vitrue, Buddy Media, and HootSuite are good places to start if you have those needs. Jeremiah Owyang, an industry analyst at Altimeter Research Group, has compiled a comprehensive SMMS list, which you can find online at http://www.web-strategist.com/blog/2010/03/19/list-of-social-media-management-systems-smms/.

Additional Audience Analysis Techniques

Much of this chapter has been dedicated to the specifics of what audience analysis is, why you perform it, and the specific uses for audience analysis output. In this section, we get into the specifics for some techniques that you can use to get more out of these tools than is provided out of the box.

As stated in Chapter 3, the business of digital analytics isn't completely about tools, and, in our opinion, it never will be. The quality of an analysis is directly tied to the quality of the human analyst and the analysis techniques the analyst applies to various digital data types. Tools can make an analyst more efficient, but they won't magically provide the answer by themselves.

Rightfully so, social data analysis is a big area of focus these days. Brands are trying to get answers to audience questions such as these:

- What conversations are taking place about my brand?
- What topics and/or themes are most talked about?
- How does my audience feel about specific brand, product, or service attributes?

Social listening tools don't give you answers to these questions. Instead, they provide a starting point for them. Let's break down where the job of social listening tools ends and the analyst's job begins. Given the three questions we've offered, tools try to provide answers using word clouds, word frequency, or overall sentiment reporting. None of these adequately answers the questions if your goal is to take action and optimize content marketing or engagement efforts. This is where custom tagging can create supplemental metadata that enhances your analysis and delivers actionable insights instead of only interesting information. Social listening tools also offer insight into how your competitors are being talked about online.

Conversation Typing

In order to understand audience preferences and get answers, you need to apply custom tagging. Several of the leading listening platforms allow for this in their tools, but you need to plan for it up front in order to realize maximum value.

A common approach you can take that applies custom tagging is called *conversation typing*. At a high level, it is as simple as segmenting your conversations into the most common types. However, it's based on the specific conversation types that you care about and define up front.

As an example, owners of a larger brand might find thousands of relevant monthly conversations among their audience about one of their products or services. Those conversations share this common trait, but at the same time fall into very different groups, or types. Common conversation types such as complaints, compliments, or company announcements exist across all categories. There are also conversation types unique to a brand, product, or service. Adding these custom elements to your conversation analysis yields much greater understanding about what your audience is discussing and truly cares about.

For example, say that you're looking at a product review, or a conversation surrounding a specific event or conference. This type of custom tagging can be useful when applied at the next level down—product or service attributes. Instead of learning the number of conversations about a brand's latest new product—a new gaming console, for example—wouldn't it be even better to know specifically what percentage of your audience discussed product issues with accurate gameplay, skepticism about a particular product attribute, or commentary about the overall product experience? The overall list could look like this:

Standard/Custom Brand Response	Online Community Comment Type
Standard	Complaint
Standard	Compliment
Standard	Company Announcement
Custom	Product Attribute 1
Custom	Product Attribute 2
Custom	Product Experience Feedback

There is no limit to what you can create and apply, although the more granular you get, the more work you must do. The point here is that your analysis is now more relevant than ever before to your business. Instead of being brand relevant at a high level, the analysis now has laser-like precision to specific areas of your business. This is highly targeted social data analysis.

Classifying the standard data through human analysis and custom tagging turns interesting data into useful data. For example, a brand could use the insights it uncovers to update product development efforts and fix bugs, alter the product development roadmap to reflect feedback about the audience experience, or even inform outbound marketing and advertising efforts based on the feedback learned from examining conversations about specific product attributes.

Event Triggers

It's one thing to understand the breakout of different conversation types that are being had about you instead of a single, aggregate number of brand mentions. You can do more to understand what your audience is doing and what is driving those conversations so that you can optimize your media mix, content marketing, and engagement strategies based on a keen understanding of what events are triggering the conversation types that are most beneficial to you and your brand.

Event triggers analysis is something we first encountered while working on a large social listening program for a Fortune 50 brand. It was imperative for the company to understand the quantity and type of conversations about its product—and also what was causing the audience to have the conversations. So we developed a technique that we called *event triggers*.

The event triggers technique is essentially what the name implies, but you won't find it in any social listening tool as an out-of-the-box feature. This technique comes after the conversation typing method described earlier has been completed. Event triggers analysis is a natural extension of that analysis. Building on the example previously used, the process is to examine all conversations of a particular type and to identify the root-cause event that sparked it in the first place. Although there are limitations to the technique and using it is not always possible, in many cases it doesn't require much more effort to identify and link the conversation back to a specific event.

Using our gaming console example, there could be any number of unique events responsible for triggering relevant conversations. Following a similar methodology to conversation typing, you might expect to find gaming shows or conventions, industry product reviews, PR announcements, competitor announcements, or consumer-generated product reviews as the events triggering relevant conversations.

The value in this technique is that it enables you to reveal enhanced insights that improve product attributes, make your marketing and/or advertising initiative more effective through optimization efforts, and reveal new opportunities that weren't previously identified.

7

Tools: Content Analysis

"Content is king" has been a mantra to marketers since Bill Gates made it popular in his 1996 essay on the state of the Internet. It focused on what would be responsible for driving digital revenue and growth in the years to come. However, Mr. Gates wasn't the original creator of the idea. Media magnate Sumner Redstone first coined the phrase in the early '90s. Since then, we've seen an unprecedented explosion of data and content creation across traditional digital and emerging social and mobile platforms.

To put this trend into context, consider the following quote from IBM research on big data: "Every day, we create 2.5 quintillion bytes of data. So much that 90% of the data in the world today has been created in the last two years alone." A significant portion of this data is content—content in the form of digital pictures and videos; posts to social media sites; text/copy on websites, blogs, and forums; and many other forms.

For marketers, the good news is that it's never been easier to produce and distribute content to an audience. The bad news is that as a result, it has never been more difficult to get noticed. More competition puts a bigger emphasis on making sure you know that your content meets the needs and expectations of the target audience. Enter content analysis.

Content analysis isn't new. It was originally developed in the 1930s to identify key properties and patterns in large amounts of information, such as the most frequently used keywords or the most important structures of content communications. Several aspects of content analysis have been enhanced since then and applied to other disciplines, such as marketing.

Due to the growth of digital, social, and mobile usage, combined with the rapid rise in content creation, marketers have never been in more need of the benefits that content analysis can provide to support their content marketing and distribution efforts.

First, let's look at the emergent trend called *content marketing*, or as some industry leaders—such as Shiv Singh, Pepsico's global head of digital media—refer to it, a *brand-led original programming*.

Simply put, content marketing works. The more nuanced answer is that no single media type alone can meet the needs of both marketers and consumers. Recent research from the Altimeter Group has labeled the current future of marketing the "Converged Media Era." We couldn't have articulated it better and believe market forces and consumer trends have finally forced a much-needed convergence of traditionally separate media types, working together to satisfy the needs of the consumer and cultivate relationships between brands and consumers. What are the three types of media we are talking about?

- **Paid media**—Media that a brand purchases
- **Owned media**—Media that a brand owns or controls
- **Earned media**—Media created and/or shared by consumers

Each of these media types serves a specific purpose and has its own unique role in a marketing communications plan. Relying wholly on paid media isn't a viable strategy anymore. (Was it ever?) Relying wholly on earned media or user-generated content won't work, either. Brands have become publishers, and rightfully so. Who better to tell the brand story? No one else understands the customer's needs, wants, and preferences better, and no one else is in better a position to deliver value in the form of custom content to meet those needs.

Owned media is the brand's best opportunity to tell a story—what the brand stands for, how a product or service benefits the consumer, or simply why people they trust find a brand relevant and useful. Paid and earned media can play roles in generating reach and awareness, which amplifies content created by the brand. And when it comes to building relationships with customers, content marketing works. According to a 2012 study by the Custom Content Council (http://customcontentcouncil.com), 90% of consumers find custom content useful, and 78% believe brands that provide custom content are interested in building good relationships with them. Useful? Check. Trustworthy? Check.

This means that the way we create and manage digital content has never been as critical as it is now. Historically, this was limited to the content placed on the brand website, whether a corporate website, a microsite serving a specific initiative, or even direct marketing content via email. That's too narrow a view in 2013 and beyond. The scope of brand content now extends beyond the website. Digital content has no borders. Digital leakage is a fact of life. Your content will flow like water through the digital landscape, and it will be consumed, altered, and shared by consumers along the way.

The riddle that marketers need to solve involves understanding the content needs of the audience, how the audience consumes content, and how to deliver on that. In order to make sense of all this, there are many tools and techniques available to get to the heart of the matter, including answering key questions such as these:

- What content should we be creating?
- What content types will work best?
- What topics and content types should we avoid?

This chapter covers some of the tools available and provides specific details on analysis techniques that you can use to gain a robust understanding of an audience and what content types and messaging should be used to reach them.

Content Audits

Often, marketers believe they understand what consumers want to hear from them. Often, marketers are wrong. The brand might want to talk about its products, services, or latest deals or promotions. Consumers don't necessarily have an aversion to that content, but they are looking for a shared value exchange—something in it for them. They are voting either for or against a brand with their time and attention, and consumers give either a direct or implied endorsement in the form of likes, shares, retweets, favorites, ratings, and reviews.

There is no universal definition of *content audit*. It can mean different things to different people, but at the core, content audits involve inventory and subsequent analysis of *all* content about a brand, product, or service (not just website content). The objective is to first learn what content exists and then identify patterns in content types and apply business-specific metadata to reveal consumption habits and trends. This can and should include social media content (conversation analysis) as well as both brand-published content and content from earned media conversations. Content audits are a combination of manual tasks and automated tools that can be executed in an informal or formal manner. This chapter explores the range of analysis that you can perform, and the next section begins by highlighting the main things to look for when performing an audit on any content source. The first step is developing your content audit checklist.

Content Audit Checklist

- **Content type**—What type of content is it? Text copy, audio, video, imagery, document? A website alone most likely has many different content types. It's important to understand all of the various ways in which you can tell your story as a brand.

- **Ownership**—Who created the content? Who maintains it? This might be an easy question to answer for smaller brand websites or microsites. However, most large corporations rely on content from various groups within the organization. It's important to understand who owns what and who is responsible for each piece of content on the site.

- **Topics**—What is the content about? This can be as simple as assigning a piece of content to a simple category, such as product. Or you can take it several levels of classification deeper, assigning specific product attributes. We revisit this technique later in the chapter.

- **Keywords**—What keywords are associated with this content? Has it been tagged properly? Does it contain any metadata with descriptive keywords in it? Are consumers using certain terms in conjunction with that content? Understanding "related keywords" is especially helpful at optimizing your content for discoverability. You need to consider search engine optimization (SEO) when developing a content strategy. Every occurrence of a brand publishing content, whether on a website or through social media platforms, is an opportunity to increase the likelihood of being discovered through search.

Now that we have shown you what should be audited, it is important to understand how to audit it.

Content auditing for smaller sights or brands can be done manually, using a tool as simple as a spreadsheet (see Figure 7.1).

	A	B	C	D	E
1	Name	Content Type	Ownership	Topic	Keywords
2	car safety info	image	marketing	product features	car, safety, features, consumer
3	car interior	image	advertising	product features	car, interior, features
4	car handling	video	marketing	product features	car, performance, handling, horsepower, mph
5	press release	text copy	public relations	product launch	car, product, press release, new, launch
6	faq	text copy	customer service	product support	faq, customer service, troubleshooting, help
7	consumer survey	web survey	customer intelligence	customer research	survey, customer needs, preferences, opinion

Figure 7.1 *Content audit spreadsheet.*

For brands with a larger digital footprint or with many websites, this approach wouldn't suffice. There needs to be some automation of the content collection that can then be augmented with custom metadata for later analysis. Some effective tools on the market can be used to accomplish this. PageTrawler, currently a free service, is such a tool.

As described on its website, PageTrawler is a simple content-auditing and site-mapping tool designed for people who make websites, including user experience designers, content strategists, marketers, information architects, and more (see Figure 7.2). PageTrawler essentially takes a single input, a URL, and then crawls that site to identify each page and collect additional information about it. PageTrawler then combines all this data into a CSV file that can be downloaded and further edited. PageTrawler provides the following data for each unique URL:

- **Page title**—The unique page title of each URL crawled
- **Page header 1**—Classification of the topic or main theme of content within the page
- **Page header 2**—Additional classification of subtopics within the page
- **Page depth**—The number of links from the main or index page of the site
- **Page owner**—If available
- **Page goal**—If available
- **Date crawled**—The timestamp from when the data was collected
- **Metadata keywords**—Additional keywords used to describe the content on the specific URL

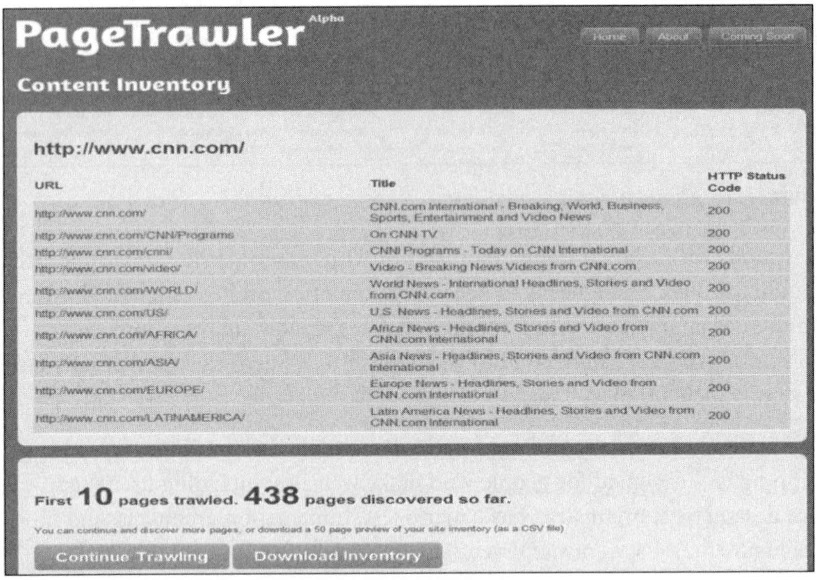

Figure 7.2   *The PageTrawler interface.*

PageTrawler is currently in an early alpha phase, but it is a useful tool that can save a lot of time and energy when you're beginning to take an inventory of your content, especially when it's spread across multiple sources on the Web. The integration of web analytics data with the data PageTrawler collects provides a richer perspective on web content. Not only can you quickly inventory what content exists, but you can also get context on how valuable it is to consumers who visit those pages. This is exactly what PageTrawler is working on integrating into the product in future phases. Later releases of the tool will include the following web analytics data:

- **Broken links**—Problems with content links
- **Page visits**—The number of visits to the specific URL
- **Time on page**—The time spent on the specific URL
- **Page exit rate**—The percentage of visitors who saw a page, which was the final page viewed in the visit
- **Page bounce rate**—The percentage of visits that are single-page visits

Real-Time Analytics

There is another method and category of tools to aide in a content analysis that has emerged during the past 18 months, particularly in the media and publishing industries. Companies such as *The New York Times*, Time Inc., and Mashable are all using real-time analytics tools. The companies' use of real-time analytics tools signals a shift to reliance on real-time analytics to understand content consumption activities among website visitors as well as other aspects of the user experience on any given URL that has been tagged with a real-time analytics tool. Before we dive into how this works, we offer a brief explanation of what real-time analytics tools are and how they differ from traditional web analytics platforms such as Google Analytics, Omniture SiteCatalyst, and WebTrends.

Real-time analytics, sometimes called real-time web analytics, give you the ability to do just what their name implies: watch what users are doing on your website live, literally as it happens. It's tremendous eye candy, and the dashboard is constantly in motion, providing you with the ability to see individual visitors to a specific URL—even a specific content area within a page—and watch what happens. Are users responding favorably to the latest product post? Are they seeing the promotional content that was brought up to a more prominent area of the page in the latest redesign? Real-time analytics tools can help you quickly observe, analyze, and optimize by answering questions like these quickly rather than waiting through the delay that comes with traditional web analytics reporting.

You might be wondering how the tools work. Think of them as essentially hyperactive web analytics tools, capturing data much more frequently than a traditional tool would. Real-time analytics tools are pinging a tagged web page and loading user interaction data into a dashboard every 10 or 15 seconds. Combine that with some creative cookie data wrangling, and you have a real-time pipeline of data from each individual who visits the website, delivered to a constantly updated dashboard. The top tier of tools in this space come from companies such as Chartbeat, Woopra, Clicky, and even Google Analytics, which has added a real-time view within its standard dashboard. Let's take a look at a couple of them in greater detail.

Chartbeat

Chartbeat (see Figure 7.3) is one of the better-known tools in the real-time analytics category, although it is not necessarily the most feature-laden tool of the bunch. What it offers is a fantastically designed dashboard that makes it easy to visually follow what is happening with users engaged on the site at any given moment. Chartbeat positions itself as a tool for the "frontline doers"—day-to-day marketers in the trenches rather than the back-office analysts who work with data all day. With Chartbeat's dashboard, you're only a click or two away from knowing the following:

- How long has a given user been actively engaged on a single page? It's time to reconsider the popular time-on-site metric. Finding out how many peoples are actively engaged can be a good measure of truly successful user experience.

- Is a user reading, writing, responding on a page, or idle? This is important because traditional web analytics rely on the page view metric. The page view alone cannot tell you what someone is doing; it only tells you if the page was loaded.

- How many pixels on a page has the user scrolled? This information is most useful for understanding consumption levels of content not contained in the initial visible area of a page.

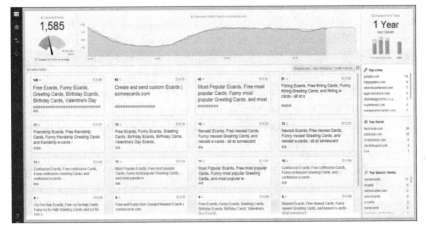

Figure 7.3 *A sample Chartbeat dashboard.*

Some Chartbeat customers, such as Business Insider, have gone one step further and now share their real-time statistics in the form of an Engage-O-Meter (http:// www.businessinsider.com/business-insider-reader-meter-chartbeat-2011-8), a widget on the website that shows the number of currently engaged users. Chartbeat is not free, but it's very reasonably priced. The pricing is tiered based on site traffic, but you can get started for $10 per month for a site with up to 1,000 concurrent users. Chartbeat is a low level of investment for potentially highly valuable consumer feedback that you can use to optimize content types, positioning on a page, and other aspects of the user experience.

Woopra

If there is a pioneer of real-time analytics, then Woopra is it. Founded in 2008, before real-time analytics were even discussed in marketing, Woopra is arguably the most sophisticated of real-time analytics tools on the market today in terms of breadth of features and capabilities. Like Chartbeat, Woopra enables you to monitor your content and site in real time, but it takes things even further, enabling you to isolate and segment key categories of your website visitors. This sort of segmentation enables you to understand what content works with what specific audience.

In addition, Woopra provides the ability to do real-time monitoring of what's happening with your key success events and conversion goals.

Consider the example in Figure 7.4, which shows various success events on a brand website and the distribution of current users across them. Woopra lets you closely monitor specific aspects of the user experience within a page and content consumption rather than only aggregate page-level activity.

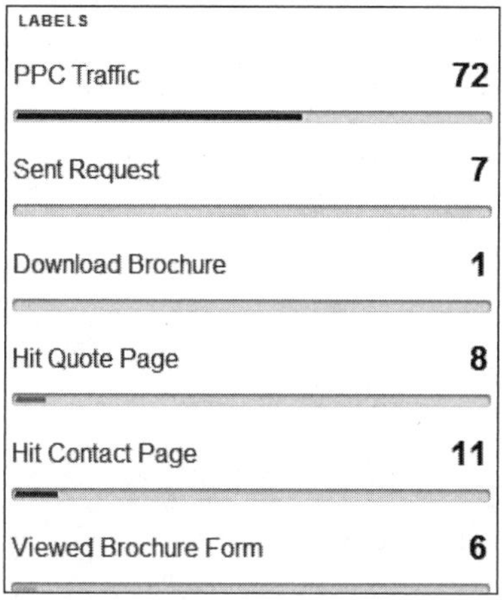

```
LABELS

PPC Traffic                    72
━━━━━━━━━━━━━━━━━━━━━━━━━━━━━

Sent Request                    7
───────────────────────────

Download Brochure               1
───────────────────────────

Hit Quote Page                  8
▬──────────────────────────

Hit Contact Page               11
▬▬─────────────────────────

Viewed Brochure Form            6
───────────────────────────
```

Figure 7.4 *Woopra segmentation.*

In addition to these core features, Woopra also provides the following capabilities:

- Detailed information about every individual that visits your website and the content each one consumes
- Live views of what activities are happening within every page on your website
- Customizable tracking of success events and conversion goals
- Ability to track custom JavaScript and Flash events
- Unique campaign tracking
- Clickstream path analysis
- Download monitoring and tracking
- Outbound link monitoring and tracking
- User retention analytics

Woopra (see Figure 7.5) follows a volume-based pricing structure, but it's based on the total number of actions per month. In the real-time analytics world, the page view is not a reliable indicator of user engagement; thus Woopra defines an action as any page view, download, outgoing link clicked, or any other custom event set up in the system. The basic commercial plan can be purchased for as little as

$11.95 per month for up to 200,000 actions per month. It's a cost-effective method for getting instantaneous feedback on what your audience members are engaging with, what content they are responding to, and what content is being left to wither and remain little used.

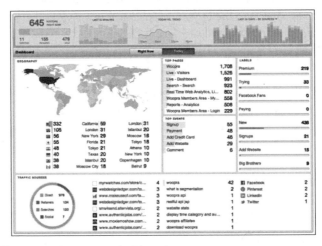

Figure 7.5   *A sample Woopra dashboard.*

Whether you're cataloging your content using the approach described earlier or keeping a finger on the pulse of what content is most desirable using real-time analytics, these activities are merely the first step in navigating the maze of content choices facing brands today. These activities can help tell you what content you have, but this is just the beginning. Next, we walk through some techniques and tools for analyzing content consumption data to understand whether what you have is what consumers want and in the format they prefer.

Optimizing Content Distribution

Now that you understand what types of content are available to you and how to optimize and segment it based on a particular audience type, it is time to start thinking about how the content is delivered. Optimizing content creation and distribution just begins when you click the publish button.

Depending on the target audience, the willingness to share and use content can vary dramatically, especially when it comes to social media platforms. Having scale in social media platforms—that is, a large numbers of followers—does not guarantee large numbers of corresponding calls to action.

There is increasing value in understanding the "flow" and engagement of well-constructed content that will enable you to make course corrections in order to maximize the engagement potential of a single piece of content and win consumer attention. Tools in this niche space are aimed specifically at measuring the effectiveness of content, at a specific time, to a specific audience, and quantifying the attention it earns. There are a lot of tools available on the market to distribute content, but the best in our view is SocialFlow.

SocialFlow (see Figure 7.6) is a unique technology and analytics platform that enables marketers to see real-time conversation activity based on content consumption and interaction across social platforms such as Facebook and Twitter. The platform applies proprietary data collection and analysis to identify the content that is garnering the most attention. It's an elegant technology solution that embraces the philosophy put forward by Thomas Davenport in his bestselling book from a decade ago, *The Attention Economy: Understanding the New Currency of Business*. The main premise of the book is that consumer attention is the scarcest of online commodities. Brands are in an increasingly difficult position of having to cut through a sea of noise and win consumer attention. Therefore, companies that learn how to effectively capture and keep consumer attention will beat the competition.

Two critical factors determine the effectiveness of your content in winning consumer attention:

- **Timing**—Timing is everything. SocialFlow knows this and tracks, monitors, and predicts audience availability and content interest to identify the optimal time to reach an audience. Basically, it's a tool that identifies what Google calls the Zero Moment of Truth (ZMOT). How an individual decides what to buy, what action to take, and so on while online boils down to pivotal ZMOTs. SocialFlow seeks to tip the odds in your favor by getting your content to the right audience during the ZMOT. It does this by looking at how much of an active audience is available at any given moment that will be receptive to a particular tweet or Facebook post.

- **Relevance**—Relevance is a match between the content being shared and how language (topics and/or keywords) has historically performed with the audience you're trying to reach. There is more to SocialFlow's secret sauce, but this essentially is what makes up the proprietary content scoring algorithm called AttentionScore.

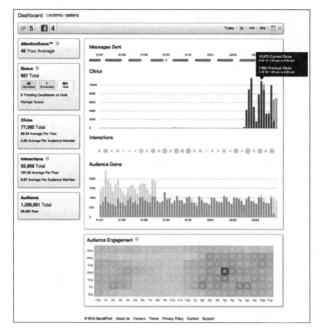

Figure 7.6   *A sample SocialFlow dashboard.*

SocialFlow helps you ensure that your content is published within the window of opportunity that has the maximum potential for engagement and influencing behavior. AttentionScore is a real-time content score for every piece of content published and tracked by SocialFlow. It provides a single number that demonstrates the effectiveness of your content's ability to capture audience attention. It helps you understand what content topics and types are resonating the most and at what times.

Analyzing Content Consumption

So far, we've focused on content audits and analysis of what is mostly brand content contained on corporate websites or campaign microsites. That represents only one side of the content-analysis coin. The other is analysis of relevant consumer conversations and content they are sharing to determine the most prominent topics and keywords of interest to your target audience. This starts to blend with some of the techniques and tools we cover in other chapters devoted to social listening. That's because social listening tools are like digital Swiss army knives, capable of solving many different problems, depending on the questions being asked and the problem you're trying to solve.

In the case of content analysis of social conversations about a brand, product, or service, the key is to go beyond counting raw mentions and augment the automated analysis that comes from a social listening tool such as Radian6, Brandwatch, or Visible Technologies with your own custom classification of conversations, based on specific topics and/or content types.

Let's forgo the specific details of a social listening tool and dive into the technique of analyzing and classifying social listening data to understand content types and needs. In this example, which is based on a real project from a former client that is confidential, let's assume that a social listening tool has been used to create queries to gather social conversation data around a new product launch, specifically a new video game console and associated game titles that will release with it. The key to extracting very specific, actionable insights that can inform content strategy and optimization to meet audience needs is to ask very specific questions. The way to ensure that this happens is to create a learning agenda.

Learning Agendas

Creating a learning agenda is a fantastic technique that we developed in the early days of social listening (otherwise known as social media monitoring) to get additional value out of the exercise. A learning agenda allows you to go beyond counting mere brand mentions and total volume of mentions by media type or identifying influencers based on how noisy they are in social media. A learning agenda enables you to focus your analysis on specific brand or on product or service attributes and to filter out the false-positive mentions that social listening tools capture; therefore, you can keep and analyze only the conversations that matter.

In the years we've been developing social listening programs for clients, including many Fortune 100 brands, one of the things we've most consistently seen is a lack of a learning agenda. Lacking a clear and understandable set of guidelines to guide your research and analysis often results in disappointment with the final results, or it yields results that demonstrate that lots of consumer activity is occurring on social platforms, but it fails to identify actionable next steps.

A learning agenda acts as a lens to filter all the social data you collect in order to determine whether it's relevant and should be kept for analysis or discarded and ignored. Let's get to brass tacks and develop a sample learning agenda, building on a new product launch of game titles for a new console.

Let's get some of the most obvious questions out of the way first. What is a learning agenda? It can be a Word document or PowerPoint slide that captures the specific questions you want to answer. A learning agenda doesn't have to be complicated. In our example, let's say that the following questions are important to the product manager and serve as a learning agenda:

- How are consumers reacting to the game's price?
- Do consumers feel that the game is relevant to them? Are they expressing interest, excitement, or intent to purchase?
- What are the barriers to consumer purchase?
- What are consumers' expectations for performance?
- Do consumers think the game will deliver on its promise?
- How are serious gamers reacting to the game? How are casual gamers reacting? Are they acting as brand advocates and amplifying key features of the game to their friends?

Now, on the surface, none of these questions seem to be directly about content, but the answers to them will have a direct effect on the content and messaging that the brand should use to market and promote the new game title. Let's walk through how to tease out these answers.

We need to transform each of the questions defined in the learning agenda into a set of search queries to be used as inputs with a social listening tool. It's important to note that this is an iterative process. Constructing the right set of queries that finds *only* social conversations related to these types of questions is more advanced than brand-level social listening. You might need to refine keywords through a few iterations and also utilize exclusions to filter out unwanted results. Don't become discouraged if this takes some time. The results in the end will be well worth the effort you put into query tuning. Assuming that you have well-constructed queries and are receiving relevant social conversation data, next comes the most important step in this process: applying custom metadata through a classification process.

Classifying Results for Content Analysis

Classifying results for content analysis is critical for unlocking the value and insights from your social data. Without this technique, you're just collecting a set of conversations that share one common attribute: a set of keywords. However, not all those conversations are about the same topic. In fact, those conversations most likely contain a wide range of topics that are relevant to you as a marketer. The key to determining how much or little value they contain is to segment the conversations into more specific and discrete topics and attributes.

Before we dive into examples, it's important to make clear that this is a process—and it is a manual, human one at that. There is not currently any pieces of marketing analytics software that can do as good a job as a human at interpreting the data, making judgment calls, and classifying the social data collected into meaningful information in the context of your particular brand, product, or service. This is true because every company is different. Every industry is different. Each has its own vocabulary, jargon, and nuances. Simply stated, there is no standard across all industries. So the magic happens through a combination of tools and human analysis, as it always has. There is no silver-bullet solution available.

Let's look at some examples. First we'll dig deeper into the following item from our learning agenda: "What are the barriers to consumer purchase?"

Before we begin analysis of any data returned from social listening queries related to this question, we define the criteria we'll use to evaluate each piece of social data—in this case, a conversation—against. For barriers a consumer may potentially perceive when considering a new game console and new game title, we start with the following:

- **Performance**—Are there any issues that degrade the user experience?
- **Competition**—Are the new console and title differentiated from competitive offerings on the market?
- **Price**—Are consumers citing any issues with the initial price points?
- **Miscellaneous/other**—There are always some conversations that don't fit nicely into any of the other categories. This is the catchall category for those conversations.

After you've defined the initial criteria, it's time to get to work sorting and classifying your data according to the list. Now remember, this is only an initial list; it's not comprehensive. You are likely to discover new categories throughout the analysis that you need to add to the list. Let's face it; brands and marketers work diligently to understand their target audiences. Research, testing, and surveys help, but there are still blind spots. There are things consumers see differently or feel about a product that we, as marketers, just didn't anticipate. So it shouldn't be surprising that throughout our classification process in this example, we identified additional barriers consumers cited in social conversations that we hadn't initially thought of. It's time to revise the list with the following:

- **Relevance**—Does the new product resonate with consumer preference? Is it relevant to them?
- **Space**—Consumers are confused about the physical space requirements to play with the hands-free console. How much space is required?
- **Peer perception/looks**—Will I look silly playing hands free, without a standard controller? Is it awkward? What will my friends think?

We've completed the first step of the classification process: We've collected data for the third question in our learning agenda and segmented that into seven subtopics that are consumer barriers to considering this new product. But we're not done yet.

The next thing to do is to quantify the distribution of the data across the seven categories, and then prioritize consumer needs and issues. This will ultimately answer the original content questions and reveal the key points that need to be integrated into a content strategy.

For the sake of brevity, we won't go through all the details associated with quantifying the results. It's actually fairly straightforward: Complete the classification and tally the results. The final results of this example are shown in Figure 7.7.

Barriers	% Share of Voice
Performance	24
Competition	15
Price	14
Relevance	27
Space	7
Peer Perception	8
Other	5

Figure 7.7 *Social data classification results.*

This approach yields specific, relevant, and, most importantly, actionable insights to the business. It takes raw, unfiltered consumer feedback and uses the insights to transform or optimize the brand content that is distributed across paid and owned media channels, by the brand, to consumers, essentially maximizing the potential resonance of the message. That's the upside, the true value of this approach. The downside is that it takes effort, planning, and time. You must balance when and where it makes sense to deploy this technique rather than use a down-and-dirty, more automated approach using higher-level classification and/or text analysis in the form of word clouds, for instance.

There are times when it is sufficient to use tactics such as word clouds, counting raw mentions, and so on to be directionally correct, but when it comes to making strategic decisions about an audience, strategizing about content, and meeting consumer expectations, the tools and approaches described in this chapter yield the most rewards and actionable insights. Use your judgment and apply these tools and techniques where appropriate.

8

Tools:
Engagement Analysis

At this point in the book, you have no doubt determined that there is an abundance of data available through digital and social media, that there are a number of tools available on the market, and that analytics is the lifeblood of any digital marketing program.

One of the primary ways people use digital data, or insights from that digital data, is to develop content. That content could be for your website, Facebook page, Twitter account, LinkedIn presence, or YouTube channel. Your brand's content is the fuel for your digital marketing program. Without content that truly resonates with your target audience, the chances of your program succeeding are quite small. Your content can be written words or visual material, depending on the message you are trying to convey.

In Chapter 11, "How to Use Listening to Inform Marketing Programs," we talk specifically about how you can use social listening data to shape marketing programs. For now you just need to know that you should be using the information you gather online about your customers to inform your content development. You should be using the words your community is using and developing content for the networks that your community participates on the most.

Content development can take place at the beginning of a digital marketing program, in the middle, or even at the end. After you complete a conversation audit (as described in Chapter 11), one of the next steps is to take an inventory of existing content in order to assess its appropriateness, given the conversation audit findings. The next step is to create new content, depending on how much content currently exists. The next step, and a step that never truly ends, is to tweak your listening program based on the conversation audit to consistently feed insights to your content development team for the purpose of developing new content that resonates with your community.

That is where engagement analysis comes into play and, more specifically, social media engagement software (SMES). SMES is sometimes called social *content* management software, or social CMS. Whatever words you use to describe the tools, SMES offers brands and the agencies that represent them a way to more effectively create, post, and analyze content. In just minutes you can take one piece of content and upload it to one of these software solutions and distribute it across multiple social channels.

The bad news for those attempting to select an SMES solution is that—as with the listening tools—there are many tools on the market today. The number of currently available tools makes selecting an SMES solution very difficult. Refer to Chapter 3, "Picking the Tools of the Trade," to find out how to select a tool.

This chapter focuses on the following four topics:

- **Introduction to SMES**—You might be asking why you would utilize SMES when you could post directly to any of the social channels. Read more about the reasons you might want to use SMES in the section, "Introducing SMES."

- **Availability of tools for small to medium-size businesses**—A number of tools are available for small and medium-size businesses, but two of them stick out above the rest: Argyle Social and HootSuite. We dive into what makes these tools excellent later in this chapter.

- **Availability of tools for enterprise customers**—A number of quality tools are available for enterprise customers. This chapter covers Spredfast, Wildfire, Sprinklr, Awareness, Inc., Vitrue, and Buddy Media (now part of Salesforce.com). All of them have their own individual nuances, and all are highly recommended.

- **The future of SMES**—In some ways, the future of SMES has already begun to unfold, with large CRM players such as Salesforce.com and Oracle acquiring Buddy Media and Vitrue, respectively. We expect this merging of tools to continue over the coming months and years. Later in this chapter, we examine what such mergers mean for the industry.

Introducing SMES

There is a very real possibility that you have been posting natively to social channels. By *posting natively* we mean posting a piece of content that you have created directly to Facebook, Twitter, YouTube, or any of the other popular social media networks. Posting in this manner is easy, and it does not require investment in a tool or in education for using new software. However, if you are posting natively and represent a company with more than 1,000 employees, you are in the minority.

In January 2012, the Altimeter Group released a report titled "A Strategy for Social Media Proliferation." In the report, Jeremiah Owyang, Partner at Altimeter Group, released some excellent data about SMES adoption, as well as some helpful tips for organizations looking to utilize this software more effectively. One noteworthy finding is the more widespread adoption of SMES tools in 2011 than in 2010. The report indicates that in 2012, 64% of companies with more than 1,000 employees were using SMES solutions.

Interest from venture capital firms in acquiring an equity stake in the engagement tools and a clear lack of ability for these tools to differentiate themselves has resulted in an explosion of available tools. The Altimeter Group report mentions at least 35 different tools, which makes this a very crowded field of tools to pick from. The report identifies another issue: The available tools have a difficult time satisfying enterprise customers. That lack of satisfaction is a result of three factors:

- **SMES tools lack monitoring integration**—Some of the tools covered in this chapter—such as Spredfast—have light capabilities when it comes to monitoring social media conversations. This "complaint" is one of the reasons the Salesforce.com acquisition of Radian6 and Buddy Media makes a lot of sense. We expect to see more of this type of feature integration in the coming months and years. We will talk about both of these points later in this chapter.

- **The tools rely on an API**—SMES tools rely on the application programming interfaces (APIs) of the social media networks in order to survive. Fundamentally, the end user creates a piece of content and uploads it to the SMES tool, and then the content is posted to a social network via an API. If you have ever worked with the API of one of these tools, you know that APIs can be unreliable. This unreliability does not work for brands that require flawless execution in terms of posting content to social media networks.

- **Technology is not helping organizations scale**—One of the benefits of SMES tools is the ability to help organizations scale social media efforts, while bringing much of the capability in house. Unfortunately, that is not happening often enough with the existing technologies. On the flipside, organizations are not using the tools to their maximum benefit.

The SMES space does not have only negative qualities. Benefits of purchasing an SMES solution include the following:

- **Using robust analytics dashboards**—Most of the available solutions utilize a social network's API to pull in available data from that site, but the best ones include other metrics (for example, competitor data) in one easy-to-read dashboard. These dashboards are generally collaborative in nature and help with brand/agency coordination.

- **Scheduling content**—SMES solutions keep us from being tied to our computers at all times. Having the ability to schedule content and have it be reliably posted is a huge advantage. Read the section, "Scheduling Content," later in the chapter for more about this.

- **Posting to all major social channels**—Most of the tools covered in this chapter have the ability to post to Facebook, Twitter, LinkedIn, Google+ and YouTube.

- **Uploading multimedia content**—Brands sometimes post more than written content to social media networks. Oftentimes they include pictures or videos with written posts. Most of the available tools offer the capability to include visual content with posts. If the tool you are currently using does not, it is time to switch. Visual content is important because not every one of your stakeholders learns via text. A balance of text and visual content is essential.

- **Geo-targeting**—Geo-targeting enables you to "send" content to an audience that lives in a particular geographic area. This is a feature of most tools that are currently available.

- **Post tagging**—Analytics dashboards and post tagging are intertwined. All platforms give users the ability to label posts for future reporting.

Remember that Chapter 3 discusses some of these benefits at a very high level. In the coming sections, we will dig into each of them in more depth.

Using Robust Analytics Dashboards

One of the best parts about these tools is that they offer strong analytics dashboards to users. You might be thinking that the platforms themselves offer strong analytics, so why would dashboards be beneficial? Anyone who has used Facebook Insights knows how unreliable it is and how incorrect the data it yields can be. Although the Facebook Insights data issues might carry through to an SMES tool, at least with a dashboard, the data will be more neatly organized and more easily exportable for further analysis.

The same thing is true for Twitter. If you manage a Twitter presence, you know how difficult it is to get quality data about how a post performed. The best you can often do is know how many people are following the handle, how many people have listed it, and how many it currently follows. This is useful information, but only in a very limited way. By integrating with link-shortening services (or using their own link-shortening services), SMES tools offer all those metrics plus replies, retweets, total clicks, click-through rate, and often even the average number of engaged followers. One could make the argument that the purchase of an SMES tool to manage nothing but Twitter would be a worthwhile investment.

The tools discussed in this chapter have strong analytics offerings. They all present data in slightly different ways, but for the most part, they display the same types of things. The analytics offerings from these tools typically take the form of per-post and overall channel performance. Figure 8.1 shows an example of a per-post analytics dashboard from Spredfast.

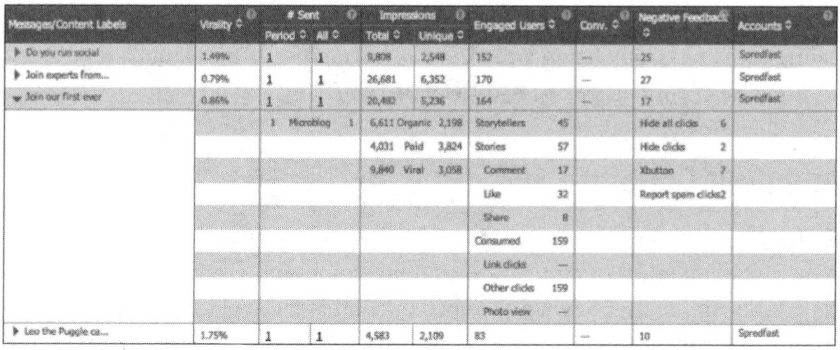

Figure 8.1   *The Spredfast message dashboard.*

Figure 8.1 shows a series of Facebook posts within the Spredfast platform. This per-post analytics dashboard shows virality, which is the number of people who have created a story from a post, as a percentage of the number of people who have seen it; total impressions (broken down by organic, paid, and viral); unique impressions; engaged users; and any negative feedback. Most importantly, it shows the message and content labels for the most popular content, which makes it easy to identify positive and negative trends in the content.

Another approach is to offer a high-level analytics view to users. Such an overview will likely show the size of your network and any engagements that might have happened with your content. Figure 8.2 shows a sample of what a high-level analytics dashboard might look like. This is the first thing users see when they visit the Measure tab in Argyle Social.

Figure 8.2   *The Argyle Social dashboard overview.*

Each of the tools covered in this chapter has strong analytics capabilities, and new features are constantly being added. It is a huge plus for these tools to be able to tell users what content performed the best.

Scheduling Content

Managing social media networks is a very difficult job. Community managers have to develop content, post content, respond to comments (when necessary), and triage attacks on the brand when they occur. All this takes place in a rapid cycle that is unlike anything most marketers have had to deal with in their careers. A community manager for a large brand needs to be a very strong writer, communicator, and strategist.

That role of community manager also requires almost 24-hours-a-day, 7-days-a-week attention. However, asking that person to post natively to one of the social networks on that sort of schedule is unrealistic. Community managers must be able to schedule content in the future and have it be posted as planned, without hiccup. The scheduling functionality of these tools looks similar to the normal content uploading view. The only difference is that instead of scheduling immediately, users can select a future date and time for a post. Figure 8.3 shows Sprinklr's primary content management view, in which users can select whether the post will go live immediately, will go live in the future, or will be repeated at different times.

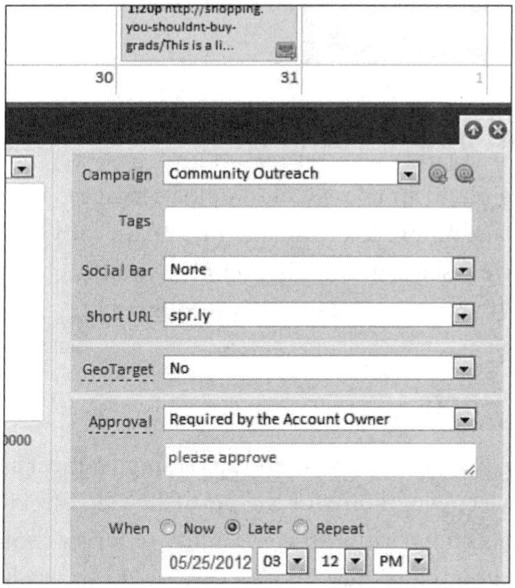

Figure 8.3   *Scheduling content in Sprinklr.*

The ability to schedule content is a pretty straightforward feature, and your SMES tool should have it. If it doesn't, start looking for a different tool.

▶ *Caution*

Although it's helpful to schedule posts in the future, there are some risks to doing so. For example, on the day of the Newtown, Connecticut, school shootings in 2012, several brands continued posting content that was very marketing oriented. Some people perceived this as insensitive, and there was a serious backlash on a social media network. Always be mindful of what content is being scheduled as well as world events. You can always remove or change the schedule for a piece of content.

Posting to All Major Social Media Networks

Most, if not all, of the SMES tools post to Twitter, Facebook, LinkedIn, and YouTube by now. Some are adding channels such as Pinterest and Instagram. Your SMES tool should give you the ability to post to the big three social networks at a bare minimum.

In addition, the fact that some functionality does not currently exist doesn't mean it is not available. Some solutions allow you to innovate. If you are a good customer of a vendor, it may be helpful to you in return. For example, you could be included in a beta launch of new social media networks being included in the platform.

Uploading Multimedia Content

Does your existing platform allow you to upload images? What about videos? Can you include an image or a video with a text post? As with scheduling functionality, most of the tools we discuss in this chapter give you the ability to include multimedia in your posts. If your tool does not, start looking for a new solution.

Geo-Targeting Posts

Refer to Figure 8.3 (the Sprinklr content uploading feature) and notice that one of the options is to select geography for the post (the GeoTarget option). Most of the tools covered in this chapter offer the capability to target content to a specific geographic area, based on major metropolitan areas. For example, if you were holding an event in Chicago and wanted to create content for only that market, you could do that by selecting Chicago for geo-targeting. Then, only people who have indicated that they live in Chicago will see that post. In theory, if you have a lot of fans within that particular geographic area, you should receive higher levels of engagement because the post is more targeted.

▶ *Caution*

Geo-targeting functionality exists only with Facebook posting. Users cannot geo-tag posts for Twitter, for example, through any of the SMES tools. It's important to be aware of this as you create content for your various channels, especially if you often cross-post the same content on Facebook and Twitter.

Post Tagging

Tagging posts isn't difficult, but it's often done in a sloppy fashion, if it's done at all. The idea of post tagging is that the user of an SMES tool would upload the verbatim text of a post and apply a word, or even a phrase, to the post. What does this do? It enables users to more accurately measure how posts have performed at the end of a program or cycle. Instead of combing through all the verbatim text for every post you have ever done, you can simply export all your posts (with data included) and sort by a specific tag. If you are at all familiar with Microsoft Excel, the rest should be pretty self-explanatory.

Let's look at some examples of tags you could potentially use. Let's say you are managing the corporate social presence for General Electric. Your boss comes to you and says that he would like to highlight technology innovation, leadership, profitable products, financial performance, and corporate citizenship. All these terms could and should be your post tags when you are uploading content using an SMES. You could create some variations on these tags as well. For example, you could label products by specific business unit to create a subtopic for profitable products. This would give you the ability to slice the data in such a way that you could report to your boss about which business units had the highest-performing content.

Using an SMES Tool for a Small to Medium-Size Business

One of the questions we are often asked is what is the best tool for the small to medium-size business? Most of the social media management tools that are widely known fall into the enterprise customer category. However, there are almost as many tools for small or medium-size businesses as there are for enterprise customers.

If you are currently working for a small business—either inside or outside the company—there are tools available for you to effectively manage a social media presence. One thing to note, though, is that some of the tools for this category of companies do not fit all the criteria listed earlier. They might give you a great interface you can use to post content but be lacking in analytics capabilities. Similarly, you might be limited in the social networks to which you can post from one of these platforms.

There are a number of tools available for small businesses, and our favorites are HootSuite and Argyle Social. Both have strong publishing interfaces and pretty good analytics capabilities. Are those analytics capabilities as good as some of the enterprise solutions discussed later in the chapter? No, but they do provide strong direction on what content is performing the best. Let's examine each of these tools individually.

HootSuite

For a small fee of $9.99 per month, you can access an unlimited number of social profiles, schedule messages, receive one analytics report, designate one additional user, see Google Analytics integration, use Facebook Insights integration, and develop unlimited Facebook applications. However, HootSuite does not allow you to geo-target or do enhanced analytics. In addition, a HootSuite Pro account allows for a limited number of users. If you have more than two people who will be accessing these tools, it might be wise to search for a different solution.

HootSuite enables you to manage the entirety of your social footprint. You can manage your Facebook, Twitter, LinkedIn, Google+, Foursquare, Myspace, WordPress, and Mixi pages from the main HootSuite interface. The integration of Facebook Insights, Google Analytics, and click data through Ow.ly, a link-shortening service offered through HootSuite, is a powerful combination for tracking leads generated and conversions from social media activities. Furthermore, there are a variety of custom reports you can build for an additional fee.

One of the best features of HootSuite is the ability to collaborate internally before responding to a social media post externally. Using a tool called HootSuite Conversations, users of the platform can ask questions of an internal team, read the responses, and then post appropriately, based on the group's decision. To have everything within one platform is invaluable and saves you from having to follow chains of emails from various people within your company.

Finally, HootSuite allows you to manage its dashboard through a mobile application. With an iPhone, Android device, BlackBerry device, or iPad, the dashboard will be fully functional on your device. This is an excellent feature that prevents practitioners from having to sit in front of their computers 24/7/365.

Argyle Social

Argyle Social has many of the same features as HootSuite, but it's packaged differently. One area where HootSuite and Argyle Social differ is in the ability to post to many different social networks. Unfortunately, Argyle Social allows its users to post only to Facebook, Twitter, LinkedIn, and a blog. These may be the primary social channels that brands are using today, but this is a gap you might want to keep in mind.

The nice thing about Argyle Social is that you can post photos, schedule posts for the future, include trackable links in status updates, and set up publishing content workflows. With publishing content workflows, someone in your organization can create content, and then someone else can approve it before it goes live. In addition, if you decide to create content to be posted at a later time, all your content can be viewed in Argyle's content calendar view. Figure 8.4 shows an example of how this looks.

Figure 8.4 *The Argyle Social content calendar.*

The differentiator between Argyle Social and HootSuite is the Argyle Social's robust analytics offering. Users of Argyle Social can integrate Google Analytics and a number of Facebook and Twitter metrics, as well as actively track goals. Most importantly, though, is Argyle Social's ability to track social return on investment (ROI). Users can track ecommerce transactions as well as micro-conversions (for example, paper downloads, signups, demo video views) in the same analytics suite as the other metrics. This ability to track top-of-the-funnel activity with bottom-of-the-funnel activity is incredibly powerful. The best part is that the technology to track this sort of conversion is very simple to use if you simply involve your IT or web analytics team.

Understanding the Enterprise SMES Landscape

There are many SMES tools for enterprise customers. We could cover a dozen or two different tools here, but that wouldn't be productive. We have done a lot of work to vet these tools for our clients and have narrowed the list considerably. The five tools that we feel you should consider researching to examine how they would fit your organization are Spredfast, Wildfire (now part of Google), Sprinklr, Vitrue (now part of Oracle), and Buddy Media (now part of Salesforce.com).

Spredfast

Spredfast introduced its social media management system (SMMS)—a social CRM—in 2010. Designed primarily for enterprise companies, Spredfast relies on its comprehensive social CRM dashboard. Although Spredfast has not been around as long as some of its top competitors in the social CRM space, it is regarded as one of the first to aggregate social media engagement and campaign management across major social media channels and leading blog platforms. In addition to social media channel and campaign management, Spredfast integrates a robust social data analytics suite, as well as several solutions for social media project/team management.

There are several benefits to utilizing the Spredfast platform:

- **Flexibility and collaborative nature of social media campaign management**—Spredfast is an intuitive multiuser platform. It allows many social marketers to participate in campaigns across the enterprise. Project leaders are able to assign tasks, create posts, and establish access and permissions for each team member to ensure that only approved content is published.

- **Social platform integration**—Spredfast displays social media content from any linked social media platform, enabling marketers to quickly create content and respond to social conversations in real time. Figure 8.5 shows Spredfast's Social Inbox, which brings together brand social presences and provides light monitoring capability.

- **Robust analytics and reporting**—Spredfast integrates with analytics platforms from all social media channels. In addition, Spredfast integrates with Google Analytics and Adobe's Omniture product. Finally, Spredfast offers additional tools for processing social data across campaigns, regions, and more—allowing you to track performance and ROI for each piece of content distributed.

- **Macros for custom automation**—Users responsible for responding to, curating, and assigning social engagement tasks have the ability to bundle repetitive actions into a single step.

Figure 8.5   *The Spredfast Social Inbox.*

We have only two criticisms of Spredfast:

- **Relative newness to the market**—More and more companies release products for SMES every day. In this increasingly saturated field of competitors—many that have specialized in CRM and collaborative tools outside social media for years (such as Salesforce.com and Oracle)—Spredfast has been challenged to scale on pace with the industry. Although its analytics dashboard is the best in the industry, in our view, the content management portion of the platform has not been clearly differentiated.

- **Dashboard complexity**—From a user interface perspective, Spredfast is intuitive for most communicators who have experience using these types of tools. If you have not had experience with these tools, setting it up can be daunting.

Spredfast is an excellent tool that continues to evolve rapidly. We would not be surprised to see it become one of the top three SMES tools for enterprise customers.

Wildfire

Wildfire, a division of Google, provides SMES software solutions to more than 20,000 customers globally. Wildfire serves 30 of the 50 most valuable brands in the world. Widely known for its Facebook brand page management applications and its social content development templates, Wildfire also provides enterprise solutions for social CRM via several additional products and services. Wildfire users can manage internal project and campaign teams, create workflow automation, and customize permissions and access for individual team members. Rounding out its services are real-time social engagement, social media ad management, and a social listening and data and analytics suite. Users of Wildfire receive four primary benefits:

- **Promotion Builder**—This is Wildfire's leading product, a platform from which users are able to develop engaging and interactive promotional campaigns to be distributed via social media. Promotion Builder facilitates in-depth demographic and psychographic targeting, aimed at driving accelerated channel growth and fan/follower acquisition.

- **Page Manager**—This product is a custom toolkit for marketers to rebrand their Facebook presences. This feature also incorporates design templates and tools for further customization of Facebook pages over what Facebook itself makes possible. Through Page Manager, content distribution can be scheduled and targeted to more effectively drive engagement.

- **Messenger**—For brands not in search of a major social CRM overhaul or behemoth enterprise solution, Wildfire's Messenger is a low-intensity option that gives users the capability to manage workflow, real-time engagement, and community-building functions. This is useful for marketers who more focused on developing content, promotions, and campaigns but who have a high volume of brand-related communications to address in real time as well.

- **UI/UX**—Wildfire's interfaces, dashboards, and configurations are simple, intuitive, and easy to use. With fewer bells and whistles than some of its main competitors, Wildfire lowers the threshold for proficiency, allowing a greater number of team members to use the tool more effectively and quickly.

Unfortunately, because Wildfire is focused mostly on the application development side of the SMES ledger, it fails enterprise customers in several ways:

- **Analytics and monitoring**—Because Wildfire is focused on content and engagement, it has slightly less capability in social media monitoring and analytics than its competitors. However, the analytics suite does integrate with outside data sources and has customizable features for in-depth analyses and ROI tracking.

- **Facebook focused**—Wildfire has devoted a large percentage of its efforts to Facebook page management and design templates specifically for Facebook content development. Although this is an important feature, marketers increasingly are approaching social media in search of balanced and fully integrated models for distributing content across social platforms. Aside from its Messenger feature, Wildfire offers very little in the way of creating social content across multiple platforms in the way that it does for Facebook.

- **Lack of historical data archive**—Wildfire is not capable of archiving historical data. The analytics available are based solely on data generated from the outset of a brand's relationship with Wildfire. This can pose a problem when trying to compare social media data from campaigns that predate a brand's partnership with Wildfire to campaigns launched from Wildfire's platform.

Wildfire is a great tool if you are focused almost exclusively on Facebook and the production of high-quality Facebook applications. However, if you need more robust Twitter management, for example, you might want to look at some of the other tools.

Sprinklr

In 2009, Sprinklr was launched in order to help enterprises successfully adapt to the realities of a world dominated by online media. It was founded on the belief that the way people communicate with each other around the world is changing. We communicate with each other via Facebook posts, blog posts, tweets, texts, Instagram photos, and pins on Pinterest. This foundation assumes that enterprises form different relationships with customers than they used to. These relationships are more interactive and not push-messaging oriented. Of course, Sprinklr is 100% right with its approach.

Sprinklr is competing with Spredfast right now for the position of top independent SMES tool. Like Spredfast, the Sprinklr tool has a lot of excellent features. Here are its main strengths:

- **Creating rules to automatically tag or highlight audience members**—Users can create profile tags based on specific industry verticals and passion toward the brand (see Figure 8.6). If you are integrating your social interactions with your existing CRM database (read more in Chapter 21, "Social CRM"), this is an invaluable feature.

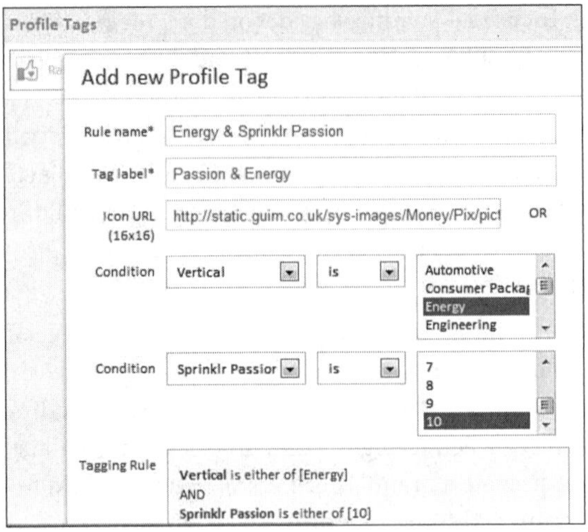

Figure 8.6   *A Sprinklr profile tag.*

- **Optimizing messages based on past performance**—As with the Spredfast dashboard, Sprinklr users can see how individual posts have performed. Users can see tags, reach, number of clicks, retweets, and replies. High-level data is useful, but per-post data is invaluable for current and future content development. See Figure 8.7 for an example of the message optimization view.

	Message	Type	Tags	Reach	Clicks	Filtered Clicks	Retweets	Replies
	The 1 Good Reason Daily is out! http://t.co/tgnmkINt ▸ Top stories today via @tomharrigan @robbin_g	Mention		6847	551	0	0	0
	The 1 Good Reason Daily is out! http://t.co/tgnmkINt ▸ Top stories today via @hunchfree @bigryanpark @nielsenwire @scanlife	Mention		6854	551	0	0	0
	The 1 Good Reason Daily is out! http://t.co/tgnmkINt ▸ Top stories today via @startabuzz @tparish	Mention		6844	550	0	0	0
	The 1 Good Reason Daily is out! http://t.co/tgnmkINt ▸ Top stories today via @steviedove	Mention		6861	535	0	0	0
	Social Media Analytics book signing @the Hospital Club - Lo - My book signing @ the Hospital Club - http://www.youtube.com/watch?v=TnV3gFO_mvM	Mention	Singapore, Logan, Virgin Atlantic, Heathrow	8010	394	135	0	0
	http://somema.org testing web analytic	Update		4590	18	12	0	0
	this is a test message http://cnn.com	Update		16	7	4	0	0

Figure 8.7   *Sprinklr message optimization.*

- **Searching, filtering, and analyzing audience members**—Much like the first benefit of being able to tag or highlight audience members, the Sprinklr dashboard offers detailed profiles on any audience members that you select. Figure 8.8 shows the audience member view.

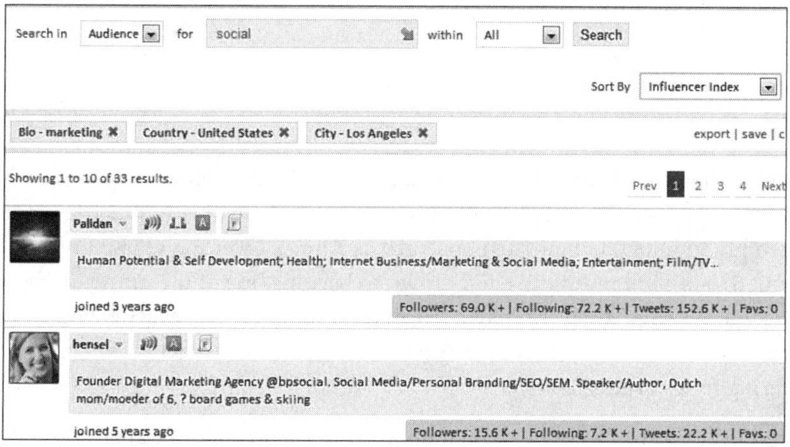

Figure 8.8 *The Sprinklr audience member view.*

- **Avoiding spammers**—One of the problems brands face is spammers coming in and mentioning the brand or its products in an effort to hijack the conversation. The Sprinklr dashboard provides a spam index from A to F (A being not a spammer and F being a spammer). Users can assign people mentioning the brand one of these grades. Figure 8.9 shows the spam index view.

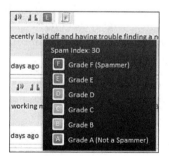

Figure 8.9 *The Sprinklr spam index.*

Sprinklr's content management platform and analytics dashboards are among the best in the industry. In fact, many customers who were long-time Buddy Media and Vitrue customers migrated to Sprinklr when those two organizations were acquired. As mentioned earlier, Sprinklr and Spredfast are in a race to see which one becomes the frontrunner in SMES technology for enterprise customers. Before they can do that, however, they need to make their user dashboards easier to utilize. As with Spredfast, if a user is not familiar with these technologies, using Sprinklr "out of the box" can be challenging. Sprinklr does offer training, but marketers have busy schedules and often want solutions that are plug and play. Whichever company solves the training problem first and adds integration to media monitoring platforms (read more about that in a moment) will be the winner.

Vitrue

Vitrue's goal is to help marketers manage their presence on Facebook, YouTube, Pinterest, Instagram, and other platforms. One of its strongest qualities has been its ability to integrate new partners (such as Klout). Over the years, it has received about $30 million in funding and grown to become one of the most popular solutions for big companies. In May 2012, enterprise software company Oracle purchased Vitrue for $300 million in order to provide a social networking platform offering to its larger clients.

The Vitrue platform can be broken up into the following three areas:

- **Publishing**—Users can post content to Twitter, Facebook, Google+, and other platforms through Vitrue. Content can be scheduled in advance, it can be geo-targeted, and it can include multimedia elements. Like users of Argyle Social and the other SMES tools we have investigated here, Vitrue users can view future content in a calendar format.

- **Tabs**—Vitrue tabs provide custom Facebook modules to create content, as well as deploy and track content. These tabs can be targeted to regions, cities, zip codes, languages, brands, and products. The tabs can be customized for mobile use and, most importantly, they can incorporate other social channels as necessary.

- **Analytics**—Vitrue provides information on everything from top engaged users, to post engagement rates, to complete platform metrics, to the ability to track Facebook fan growth.

It is too soon to pronounce a final verdict on Vitrue as an SMES platform. How it integrates into Oracle's other services is still somewhat of a mystery at this writing. Vitrue, in our view, also has a much weaker analytics offering than Sprinklr and Spredfast. Brands are becoming increasingly reliant on the data that social and digital tools provide. If an analytics dashboard is incomplete, many brands will look elsewhere. Again, how Oracle helps improve this for Vitrue is yet to be determined. However, Vitrue has the potential to be a very powerful tool for enterprise customers with Oracle backing it.

Buddy Media

Buddy Media was recently acquired by Salesforce.com and reintroduced as part of its fully integrated and comprehensive Social Marketing Cloud. Buddy Media's offerings have been enhanced by the support of Salesforce.com's infrastructure and the partnership created when Salesforce.com also acquired industry leading social media conversation site Radian6. Previously, Buddy Media was known for its capabilities in supporting brands' launching, maintaining, and managing their Facebook presences across multiple countries and languages. Salesforce.com highly touts the integration of Buddy Media and Radian6 into its Social Marketing Cloud, saying that it can now provide a comprehensive social CRM platform. From our perspective, there are five primary benefits to utilizing Buddy Media:

- **Social content creation/social integration**—The Social Marketing Cloud enables customers to integrate any of its 50 social applications and leverage content-generation templates for contests, video sharing, photo galleries, and more. Whether or not a social channel is the desired medium of distribution, the Social Marketing Cloud supplies marketers with tools to add socially engaging elements to content meant for any digital medium.

- **Engagement and workflow automation**—Responding to customer queries and managing the influx of general social communications about brands are focal points for the Social Marketing Cloud. Through its dashboard, marketing and communications leaders can easily route communications and assign tasks. The Social Marketing Cloud also incorporates an if-then feature that enables users to create rules to automate a series of responses based on the keywords in any given communication about or directed to a brand's social presence.

- **Segmentation and targeting**—Buddy Media has added to the Social Marketing Cloud technology that allows customers to target social media users by sentiment, age, location, emotion, and intention. In addition, Buddy Media has made available more than 1,700 third-party social enterprise apps on AppExchange.

- **Real-time listening capabilities**—Customers are able to leverage the Social Marketing Cloud to incorporate social listening data from more than 400 million sources across the Web and social media platforms. Conversations happening on sites such as Facebook, Twitter, YouTube, and LinkedIn—as well as blog content—are captured and can be aggregated across keywords, sites, languages, location, and more. A new app for iOS even allows listening via mobile devices.

- **Social ads**—The Social Marketing Cloud provides a platform within its dashboard for launching, managing, and even automating data-driven changes to social ad campaigns.

Salesforce.com's acquisition of Buddy Media and its relaunch of the Social Marketing Cloud incorporating Buddy, Radian6, and its existing CRM capabilities have created an incredibly powerful combination. However, there are some negative features of this offering:

- **Cost**—Starting at $5,000 per month, the Social Marketing Cloud could potentially be cost prohibitive for small to midsize brands or for large companies looking to augment an already established protocol for social engagement, analytics, and CRM.
- **Flexibility/Scalability**—Although packed with advanced features, the Social Marketing Cloud is an end-to-end solution. Aside from its listening and analytics capabilities powered by Radian6, it appears to be difficult to incorporate the Social Marketing Cloud's social engagement and CRM features without total buy-in. This might be the right solution for an enterprise looking to establish a social CRM or make a wholesale move of its social CRM to the cloud, but for a company in search of specific solutions for social content development and engagement, the Social Marketing Cloud is likely to be far too broad in scope.
- **Support**—Although Buddy Media University has been integrated with the Social Marketing Cloud's support/training service, the fact that Salesforce.com has more than 100,000 clients globally increases the probability that flexible and real-time support from inside the Social Marketing Cloud will be hard to deliver.

The Social Marketing Cloud represents the future of SMES tools. How well Salesforce.com incorporates these three tools is yet to be determined, but it could be a game changer for enterprise customers.

The Future of SMES Tools

What the future holds for SMES tools is up in the air, but we think that the last six months of 2012 foretell what might lie ahead. The acquisitions of Buddy Media and Vitrue by Salesforce.com and Oracle, respectively, seem to indicate that a period of consolidation is likely ahead. Social media listening tools have undergone a similar period of acquisition to the point where there are between three and five tools considered in any purchase decision-making process. Sprinklr and Spredfast could be targets of consolidation, depending on the size they achieve, but any commentary on an acquisition would be purely speculative at this point.

Communicators should also be on the lookout for two other trends in regard to SMES tools. The first trend is building a more robust social media monitoring capability. The Altimeter Group report, "A Strategy for Social Media Proliferation," notes that enterprise customers are looking for the ability to create content and monitor social media conversations in a more robust fashion. Some platforms have gone the acquisition route, whereas others, such as Spredfast, have partnered with companies like Crimson Hexagon. Either way, these SMES platforms need to develop stronger monitoring capabilities. The second trend is integration with CRM platforms. We discuss the concept of social CRM in Chapter 21, but for now suffice it to say that brands of all sizes are clamoring for the ability to engage in social media and then cross-reference with data from a company's CRM database. It should not be too hard to integrate the SMES and social CRM platforms, but it is right now.

Based on these two trends, we think the Social Marketing Cloud holds tremendous potential. Over the coming weeks and months, we will be watching as the Social Marketing Cloud offering takes shape. If done right, it could become like the ThomsonReuters offering to the investor relations (IR) constituency today. In that model, ThomsonReuters holds a very large market share because it is essentially a one-stop shop for everything an IR professional might need. Until the Social Marketing Cloud offering is more clearly defined, we recommend looking at all of the tools we have outlined here. It would be a good starting point for creating, measuring, and analyzing your performance on social media networks.

9

Understanding Digital Influence

In August 2010, Jay Baer, chief executive officer of Convince & Convert and a well-known blogger, wrote that influence mining would become the next gold-rush topic. More than two years later, we can definitively say that he was right. Not only has it become a gold-rush topic, but online influence is one of those topics that sparks considerable debate in digital marketing circles. Before we go any further, it is worth a mention that digital influence is really the replication of what consumers would do with friends and family offline. It's just that the interactions now happen much more frequently and in a different forum.

We have talked at length through the first eight chapters about the abundance of customer data available to marketers. That data can be used for making decisions, or it can be used to develop lists of people who might be influential in shaping a brand's online identity. Note that we were very careful to qualify online identity versus offline identity. We elaborate on that idea when we discuss some of the failings of online influence analysis later in this chapter.

Not only is influence mining a gold-rush topic that could have multiple data inputs, but it is also a topic that can be sliced and diced into many different pieces. For the purposes of this book, we look at five core elements of digital influence:

- **The reality of digital influence**—Some argue that digital influence, or the presence of influencers, is misguided. The argument is that what really takes place is that large groups move topics forward.

- **Modern-day media lists**—For many in public relations fields, working from a predetermined list of targeted media is commonplace. That kind of thinking is not only antiquated but also patently false.

- **Tools of the trade**—As is the case with social listening and search, a number of tools are available to marketers to measure influence. Those tools have pros and cons, both of which are discussed in this chapter.

- **Online versus offline influence**—There is a distinct difference between someone who moves conversation online and someone who causes behavior change offline. There is a link between the two, but right now tools are not tapping offline influence. Particularly, online influence tools do not tap into word-of-mouth suggestions between friends and family. We investigate this phenomenon further in this chapter.

- **Using the influencer list**—It is not enough to just create a list of influencers. You have to create strategies to use the list.

Fundamentally, the influence question is one of measuring and analyzing human behavior. Why does someone decide to create an abundance of content about a particular topic? Why does someone gather content from a particular source? Why does an influencer's content "move" more than someone else's? These are all questions we ask when trying to determine someone's influence on a particular topic or idea. Will we ever land on a common point of view regarding online influence? Before answering this question, let us discuss the five elements of digital influence.

Understanding the Reality of Digital Influence

Think about how you make decisions in your everyday life. Where do you turn for information? Who do you ask for advice? What sources do you trust to give you accurate information? Is this group of people and sources a large crowd or a very small one? If it is the former, how large is that group? If it is the latter, is it the same four or five people every time?

These are questions consumers of goods and services (and information) do not even think about. If you need to buy a new television, for example, you instinctively know how you have done that in the past and then take action. If your source has been Amazon.com, you sit down at the computer or pull out your smartphone and start looking at the options. You do not necessarily think about what sources you turned to previously, or even who you may have asked. You know you need to take some sort of action.

Part of what makes the topic of digital influence so challenging is that there is not a "why" button associated with any of the influence tools discussed in this chapter. Or, in the case of analyzing social conversations, not every consumer explains why he took the action that he took. Similarly, when you analyze the traffic patterns of a website, there is not an explanation provided for why someone clicked on a particular link. You can speculate based on informed opinion, but that is all you can do.

The good news is that there is informed, academic debate on both sides of the digital influence question. There are basically two camps on the digital influence question: those who say that a small group of people can move a topic, and those who say that a larger community drives a topic forward. Both sides have really strong points of view that require some further examination.

The "Tipping Point" Phenomenon

Let's bring the conversation back into the communications realm and a little out of the social science discussion. How often have you watched a news cycle for your company or client following an announcement? Have you ever paid attention to how much volume of conversation there is or how long it lasts? Have you looked at who was driving that particular news cycle? In our experience, the answer to the latter question is often a limited number of people. Whether it is one person or five is irrelevant. There is usually a single source that picks up the story first, followed by a wave of "copycats" who follow or syndicate the news.

How does a news cycle begin or spread? Obviously, it is started by an idea or, in the case of communications, a piece of content. That piece of content could be in the form of a press release, an interview, or even a statement posted on a website. Whatever form it takes, someone will find it and write about it. How much attention it gets overall is a function of a lot of things—and beyond the scope of this discussion. What's important to know, though, is that there is a single person who finds it and spreads the idea. This is an example, albeit rudimentary, of the idea Malcolm Gladwell wrote about in his book *The Tipping Point*.

In the book, Gladwell argues that ideas and behaviors often spread like infectious diseases. He says that these ideas and behaviors often start with one "carrier" and then make their way into the entire ecosystem. Although Gladwell was not talking about digital influence, per se, you can see how his ideas could be applied to this area. An idea or a statement, in the case of a brand, is created and posted online. That is followed by an enterprising blogger or mainstream news source picking up the idea and writing about it. After the blogger or mainstream news source picks it up, other bloggers, news sources, and interested parties begin to syndicate the idea. Eventually, you reach a place where a lot of people are talking about the idea (with the volume depending on how interesting the idea is), which was started with a small group of interested individuals.

We are aware that we just took a pretty complicated psychological concept and broke it down into a handful of small tidbits, but that's the idea, in principle. In the case of communications, a small group of individuals create the news. As Gladwell would say, these individuals create the "tipping point" whereby the rest of the community pays attention.

One of the criticisms of this approach is that a brand does not have, in most cases, a single consumer, and by identifying individuals, you ignore the rest of the people who buy your product. We dive into this in more detail later in this chapter, when we talk about using an influencer list, but the truth of the matter is that not every consumer is a content creator. If we are talking about furthering a message online, we certainly care most about the content creators. In the case of the online world, the number of content creators is actually a very small group.

What are the other criticisms of the influencers model? Who is arguing the other side of this debate?

The Community Rules Phenomenon

On the other side of the digital influence debate are those who believe that the community, or a larger group of individuals, drives a topic or an idea forward. This group does not believe that one influencer, or a small set of influencers, drives an idea forward. It believes in the power of the community at large to drive an idea forward.

This theory gained traction thanks to Duncan Watts, then a researcher at Yahoo! and now the principal researcher at Microsoft. In a paper titled "Influentials, Networks, and Public Opinion Formation," Watts argued that ideas are driven by a critical mass of easily influenced individuals. He also argued that highly influential people do not drive large-scale changes in public opinion; instead, large-scale change is driven by easily influenced people who influence other easily influenced people. Essentially, Watts argues that it is better to reach a large group of people than a smaller group of people. By reaching a larger audience, he says, a brand (or person) can change public opinion more quickly.

Generally speaking, this model fits the mindset of the communicator who is looking to maximize reach as well as impact. We have all heard of a communicator who is trying to achieve as many impressions as possible, right? This approach has been around for many years, and there really is not anything wrong with it. It is the way most communicators have been measured and are continually measured. It isn't necessarily a good barometer to measure overall impact, but it is one measure in a set of many other metrics.

The bigger issue with this approach, especially in the context of social media, is that trying to reach an entire community is very difficult—and very expensive. Most brands do not have enough staff members who can actively influence a large community. It is why many have taken to identifying influencers to help spread a particular message.

Whether you agree with the influencer model or the community model, the common thread is reaching a core group of people to spread an idea. That, at its heart, is influence. The only difference is the number of people you are trying to reach and how you are trying to reach them.

Developing a Modern-Day Media List

Those who have grown up in traditional public relations firms are no doubt intimately familiar with the media list concept. In case you do not come from that world, we take a moment to explain how these lists come together:

1. **Identify the pitch idea**—The first step is identifying what the pitch is going to be about. Essentially, you determine what message, or news event, you are trying to convey to the author.

2. **Determine the media type**—If you lump mainstream news and bloggers together when you are only trying to reach bloggers, you might confuse people who are trying to take action on it. Therefore, you need to determine the media type.

3. **Identify the "beat"**—Most likely there is a target beat that you will be looking for at the different media outlets.

4. **Select a tool**—Most corporations and agencies have access to media list generators, such as Cision, for downloading a list of media. When you have a tool, you can download your media list.

5. **Lightly scrub the list**—You need to identify the people you have a relationship with already and check to see if any of those reporters have moved on.

6. **Begin pitching**—After you scrub the list, you can start pitching the reporters on your news idea.

Public relations professionals everywhere have replicated this approach for decades. The lists are constantly recycled, with notes being added periodically as people change beats or leave an outlet. It is not a bad concept, but it really is only a starting point. The problem with this approach is that the lists are static, and if you are at all familiar with the online world, you know that it moves very quickly. It is not enough to download a list and use it for months on end anymore. The other reality is that just because a list of reporters has been downloaded from a tool doesn't mean the people are influential. Additionally, the news landscape is constantly evolving (reporters leaving publications, going to new publications, retiring, and so on) so that lists are very hard to keep fresh.

Paul Dyer, head of the engagement practice for WCG, wrote a couple years ago that if your agency hands you a pitch list sorted by circulation, you should fire that agency. He is right, of course. Communicators can become significantly more sophisticated in how they develop a media list.

So, how can you tweak this old-school media list approach to fit today's modern world? How do you create a list of influencers and not just a list of media everyone will know? Following these seven suggestions will help you create a more effective media list:

- **Use Google and blogrolls**—You do not need to come up with sophisticated Boolean queries. All you need to do is know how to properly format keyword strings based on your topics. After you have identified sources, check the sites they are linking to and reading. They are most likely good sources for content.

- **Think relevance first**—It isn't enough to just identify someone's beat. If you are targeting health care reporters, for example, you need to realize that there are a number of different subcategories within health care. Your job is to find the people who are the most relevant to the story you are trying to tell.

- **Think syndication second**—Because this is a chapter on influence, it is important to bring up syndication. You do not want to target only people who write a lot. You want people who write a lot and have their writing shared by others in large numbers.

- **Think post volume third**—If you have identified relevant people, chances are good that those people are also frequent writers on your subject. When people care deeply enough about a topic to write about it, quite often they also post frequently.

- **Think reach fourth**—There is a reason we have identified reach fourth. If you are identifying people who write a lot, are relevant, and receive widespread syndication, reach will take care of itself.

- **Tools still matter**—As much as it might have seemed like we were being negative about tools like Cision, they still do have their place as a starting point for research.

- **Refresh frequently**—Do not refresh your list only once per year, especially if you are in a tumultuous industry category. Communicators should refresh their influencer lists every quarter.

 Tip

Do not fall into the same trap communicators have fallen into for years. Take the time to build a list that is relevant and full of people who are widely syndicated and reach a lot of people. If you do, your messages will resonate better.

Using the Tools of the Trade

If you are at all familiar with the concept of digital influence, you are probably wondering how we have gone this far without talking about tools. A number of tools are available on the market today, mostly web-based tools that offer users the ability to identify and rank influencers. Fundamentally, these tools enable social scoring. Marketers can use these tools to rank one person against another. The efficacy of this approach is the subject of discussion in a moment, but for now, let us dig into each of the tools, starting with the most controversial: Klout.

Klout

Klout defines itself as a tool that analyzes data across multiple social media channels in order to determine a person's influence. Ever since it broke onto the scene a few years ago, it has been the subject of much consternation, as individuals have struggled to understand how the scores are determined. Initially, Klout was measuring online influence using data captured from only a handful of networks. However, over the past few years, it has expanded to include metrics from Instagram, Foursquare, YouTube, LinkedIn, Google+, and so on. With the addition of new networks has come the addition of new metrics so that now the algorithm includes 400 metrics.

Entire books have been written about Klout. In February 2012, Mark Schaeffer released a book titled, *Return On Influence: The Revolutionary Power of Klout,*

Social Scoring, and Influence Marketing, in which he details Klout's evolution, how brands are using it, and its effect on marketing as a whole. We are not going to get into that much detail here, but we do dissect a few elements of Klout's platform:

- **Scores**—The Klout scores are easily the most polarizing aspect of the platform. They're calculated in a way that is largely unclear to the marketing world.

- **Topics**—Klout has recently added topics, which could be an interesting way to identify potential influencers.

- **Klout perks**—Over the past few years, Klout has been working with brands to take advantage of its platform with special perks programs. These perks programs are where Klout adds the most value to brands.

- **Klout's future**—The Klout platform and algorithm are constantly changing. Later in this section, we predict what we expect Klout to unveil next.

Let us dig into the scores first, since they are probably what most marketers know about Klout.

Klout Scores

The way Klout comes up with an individual's score is unclear at this moment. We know that it is based on an indexed and weighted scale from 0 to 100. We also know, based on what has been published on Klout's website, that it includes up to 400 metrics in the final calculation. The good news is that we know users have the ability to include multiple channels in their score. Users can include Facebook, Twitter, YouTube, LinkedIn, Flickr, Google+, Instagram, and Foursquare in their scores. At a minimum, the score has the ability to represent the entirety of someone's online presence.

Unfortunately, the positives do not outweigh the uncertain aspects of the scoring mechanism:

- **Algorithm ambiguity**—As noted earlier, about 400 metrics go into calculating the score. What those metrics are is a complete mystery. We can speculate based on channels analyzed (for example, number of followers on Twitter), but it would only be speculation.

- **Weighting uncertainty**—We know that Klout measures multiple channels, but which channels receive the most weight—Twitter, Facebook, other channels? How are the channels factored into the final analysis?

- **Score comparisons**—One of the favorite pastimes of marketers, done in a joking way or not, is to compare scores. However, it is not clear how Klout indexes people against each other. Is it based on work in similar industries? Is it based on the number of channels being analyzed? These are big questions if we are to take the scoring seriously.

- **Fluctuations in scores**—We respect Klout's desire to tweak the algorithm in order to make the scores as real as possible, but monthly, even daily, fluctuations are not realistic. A person's influence should not move two points or more in a given week.

- **Post volume**—It has always been assumed that frequency of posts is a component of the score, but what is the ideal amount to be posting to boost your score?

Klout could silence many of its critics by posting some components of its algorithm. In an ideal world, it would post the algorithm in its entirety for people to study, but we need to be realistic. The algorithm is part of Klout's intellectual property, and we respect the desire to protect it. However, a simple posting of metrics or a quick explanation on weighting could go a long way.

Klout Topics

Klout has rolled out special pages in order to identify a list of people who could be influential on topics of interest. These pages are very much in the early stages, as many topics have not been populated, but eventually these pages could serve as a starting point to identify influencers.

How does it work? Users of Klout can give other users +Ks, which basically serves as an endorsement of a user's work on a particular topic. The more +Ks a user receives, the more influential he or she becomes about a particular topic. Figure 9.1 shows a sample topics page.

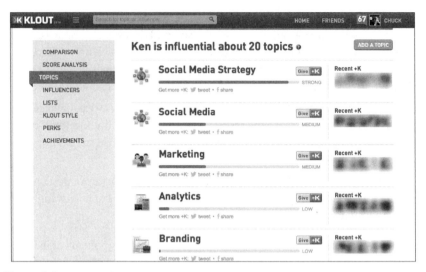

Figure 9.1   *Ken Burbary's active topics on Klout.*

Figure 9.1 shows topics Ken generally talks about online. That's the good news about Klout topics. The bad news is that it is very easy to game. Because there are no controls on who can give a +K and on what topics, the giving of +Ks might not actually represent what a person is talking about online. In addition, the practice of "Klout bombing" has developed, as a humorous way to poke fun at Klout and people online by giving them +Ks in completely afield topics. Topic pages would offer a good starting point to identify influencers if Klout developed an easy mechanism whereby users could delete topics or prevented users from gaming the system.

Klout Perks

Klout perks are exclusive products or experiences that you earn based on your influence score on the platform. Perks are delivered to users via email and so essentially function as email marketing. Users can be targeted based on score, demographics, locations, channels, or topics. When a brand engages Klout to run a perks program, it is given access to an interface to target Klout users it is looking to reach based on those criteria. It's an easy way to filter out the inaccurate aspects of Klout upfront, and it's a way to access some compelling data after your Perks program has expired. Not many brands have taken advantage of the program because of Klout's negative stigma, but more brands should be considering it as a potential way to activate a set of influencers.

Klout's Future

There are a number of things that Klout can do to improve its image, most of which we discuss in the preceding sections. More clarity around the score and a tighter leash on the topics would be great places to start. Klout has been making several changes to its platform of late, which does make it more visually appealing (see Figure 9.2). The changes also offer a unique perspective for how individual posts are performing over time.

Figure 9.2   *A sample profile page from Klout.*

Klout has also made changes to its overall dashboard page (see Figure 9.3), which provides a breakdown, by channel, of how the score was calculated. What goes into the channel scores is still a mystery, but this is a step in the right direction.

Figure 9.3   *A sample dashboard page from Klout.*

At a high level, a brand marketer would know how a person stacked up on a certain channel without ever having to engage with Klout in a perks program. That's helpful. However, Klout still has a long way to go before serious marketers embrace it as the true standard on influence. If Klout released the algorithm, that would be a positive step toward greater acceptance.

PeerIndex

PeerIndex is the largest of Klout's web-based application competitors, and it positions itself in a very similar way to Klout. It gives users an index score between 0 and 100, shows who they influence, shows who influences them, and shows what topics they are talking about most. Unlike Klout, however, PeerIndex measures only your Facebook and Twitter presence, which severely limits its ability to truly gauge online influence. However, it does offer more visibility into its scoring mechanism, which offers a leg up on Klout. There are three elements to the PeerIndex score:

- **Authority**—This is how much other users in your ecosystem trust you or rely on your recommendations. It is calculated based on the topics you are most actively talking about online.

- **Activity**—Essentially, your activity score is calculated by examining how much relevant content you are creating compared to others in the ecosystem.

- **Audience**—This is PeerIndex's proxy for reach; it is calculated by looking at the number of people who took action on a post. In our view, this is a more accurate measure than just looking at raw number of followers or fans or subscribers.

PeerIndex also offers brands the opportunity to partner with them to deliver perks to customers. It functions much in the same way as Klout's program does, by allowing brands to target based on geography, score, demographics, and so on. Also like Klout, PeerIndex is making significant changes to its dashboard view (see Figure 9.4). Over the past few months, it has rolled out a new platform that offers a cleaner look. All your scores, who you influence, who is influencing you, and your topic breakdown are on one screen.

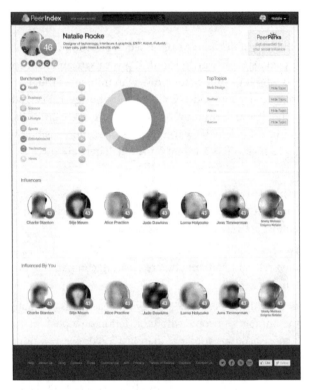

Figure 9.4 *A sample PeerIndex user dashboard.*

Where PeerIndex will go to compete with Klout is an unknown at this point. Klout's mindshare advantage makes it very difficult for other tools to compete. PeerIndex offers more transparency on its scoring, which should help somewhat. Adding in a relevancy factor, or even offering brands the ability to interact more frequently with someone on the PeerIndex team to develop insights from the score, could be beneficial.

Kred

Kred functions in a very different way than Klout or PeerIndex. It isn't set up in the typical dashboard view, like those other two platforms. Instead, Kred is broken up into six disparate elements that all have interesting utility:

- **People**—Users can view other users' social graphs, as well as their most influential content over the course of the past three to four years.
- **Events**—Users can enter any active hashtag in order to see who is moving conversation about a particular topic.

- **Communities**—Users can see how people are connected by topics and affinities, as well as what they are talking about, in real time.

- **Books**—Users can check out what people are reading and discover the most popular words they are using to describe those items online.

- **TV shows**—Users can see a real-time overview of what people are thinking and linking to from their favorite shows.

- **Movies**—Are you curious about whether a movie is worth seeing? The movies feature shows users a gallery of tweets, pictures, and hashtags about the latest releases.

Because Kred is so topics focused, it could be the most useful tool for brands to identify people who are talking online about issues they care about. The platform is still in its infancy, and time will tell whether Kred evolves to look more like Klout or PeerIndex.

TweetLevel and BlogLevel

TweetLevel and BlogLevel are two different tools created by Jonny Bentwood, head of analyst relations and strategy for Edelman Public Relations. Unlike Klout, these tools do not try to measure influence across every social channel. Rather, TweetLevel focuses on measuring a user's Twitter influence, and BlogLevel measures blog influence. This makes them fairly limited in terms of gauging someone's ability to move content across multiple channels, but it does not mean these tools lack value.

Unlike Klout and PeerIndex, TweetLevel and BlogLevel are upfront about their algorithms and what goes into their scores. For TweetLevel, there are about 14 metrics, whereas BlogLevel uses about 8 metrics. Each algorithm uses a weighted approach that takes into account four different factors:

- **Influence**—Things such as inbound links, Google PageRank, and Twitter inbound links are weighted in this bucket for BlogLevel. For TweetLevel, the frequency with which someone's Twitter handle is mentioned is weighted most highly.

- **Popularity**—BlogLevel and TweetLevel both approach popularity using reach-related metrics such as page views and Twitter followers.

- **Engagement**—Engagement metrics can include things like comments, retweets, and overall syndication of content.

- **Trust**—Although Edelman admits that measuring trust through an automated tool is challenging, BlogLevel and TweetLevel analyze proxy measures such as inbound links and percentage of retweets versus overall tweets.

Users can look at how an individual performs in aggregate or at one of these weighted categories separately. The other valuable component of both BlogLevel and TweetLevel is topic pages. If you are curious about how a hashtag has performed and who has used it, TweetLevel is a good starting point. If you are curious about which blogs are writing about a topic of interest, check out BlogLevel. Again, it is worth noting that because these are single-channel tools, they should not be used to demonstrate how influential someone is online.

Developing Your Own Influence Tool

Although Klout, PeerIndex, Kred, TweetLevel, and BlogLevel all do an excellent job at aggregating a large amount of data, they are still black boxes in many regards. If you do not feel comfortable defending the list that you have assembled and run through one of these tools, you should not use them. You can create your own approach just by taking a little bit of time to collect information. If you choose to develop your own approach, here are some things you should think about:

- **Platforms for analysis**—If you were developing a Twitter influencer approach, it probably wouldn't make sense to look at blogs. But, if you were trying to develop an online influence approach, you would probably want to look across multiple platforms.

- **Date range**—Our preference is always for a longer data capture period—preferably 12 months—but that kind of effort can be labor intensive. Narrowing the range to 6 months should eliminate any random anomalies that might skew data.

- **Metrics for analysis**—As we have outlined in previous chapters, an abundance of metrics are available for use. You do not need to use them all, but you should be sure that you are representing reach and engagement metrics at least equally.

- **Weighting**—Think about what you are trying to achieve with your program. If it is maximum engagement, then you probably want to weight engagement metrics more highly. If it is reaching the most people, then you probably want to weight the reach metrics more highly.

You can do all this work in Excel if you have someone on the team who possesses a good understanding of Excel formulas. It might take a little more work than running a Google search and dropping names into Klout or a similar tool, but the results will be more reliable.

Online Versus Offline Influence

One of the places where tools like Klout do not excel is measuring the effect of offline word-of-mouth influence. If you were to recommend a particular brand of television, for example, to a friend over dinner, the online influence tools would have no mechanism to capture that recommendation unless you voluntarily offered it up while making an online purchase. We have not yet encountered a tool that would serve as a good proximity for offline influence, but we should assume that it is coming.

On the surface, an influencer list is excellent for identifying who will drive reach and engagement simultaneously. It is less clear how it will cause offline behaviors to change unless we utilize primary research to test and ask the critical question "Why?" A sensible approach to bridging the online and offline research gap would be asking simple questions in market research testing about how a certain purchase decision was made. For example, it would be wise to always ask how a person found out about a particular product or service. If it were online, then it would be worth asking an additional question of where, specifically, the person learned about it.

The good news is that the topic of online influence is relatively new, as is the topic of offline influence. We are likely to see a tool developed by someone soon that tries to bridge the gap. In the meantime, though, the two analyses are mutually exclusive. You still need to do offline behavior testing and mirror that with activities you are seeing online.

Using the Influencer List

Although this book and chapter focus mostly on the analytics behind influencer analysis, we would be remiss if we didn't spend some time talking about how brands can utilize influencer lists. What good is an influencer list that you have spent a considerable amount of time creating if you don't use it? If you don't develop an activation plan, the list becomes merely a fancy dust collector.

It isn't enough anymore to think about using the development time needed to build a list as a pitch-only investment. The reality is that a list has applications that stretch well beyond earned media. The list has paid, earned, and shared media applications as well. See Figure 9.5 for a detailed outline of this model.

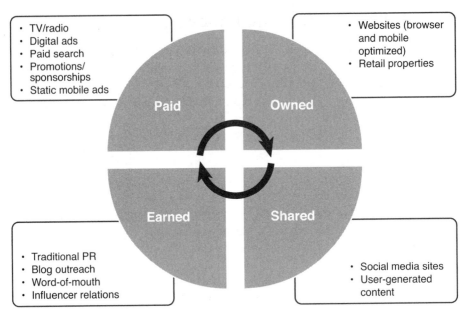

Figure 9.5 *An integrated media mix for influencer lists.*

Let us take a moment to dive into each of these elements:

- **Paid media**—Because we have taken the time to identify people and outlets that are offering the most relevant content, it can be assumed that these sites might also be quality locations for banner advertising. Similarly, these influencers can be excellent test subjects for television and radio advertising.

- **Owned media**—Aggregating influencer content on your owned properties can be a valuable approach. Instead of consumers being inundated with your static marketing copy, bringing in relevant influencer content (assuming that it is not bashing the brand) can offer website visitors valuable information.

- **Shared media**—As with owned media, sharing influencer content on shared media properties (for example, your Facebook brand page) can be a useful way to supplement content development and generation, and it also offers people a unique voice.

- **Earned media**—This is the most obvious application for influencer lists, and it mirrors very well traditional public relations activities. Fundamentally, it involves using the influencer list in the manner described earlier in this chapter, in the section "Developing a Modern-Day Media List." You have, in theory, developed a fluid media list that is highly relevant to your topic, and it should be a constant source for pitching ideas.

There are additional ways to segment the earned media targets from your influencer analysis. If you have done your homework, you will have identified people who are clearly influential but not the best outreach (earned media) targets. Specifically, there are four ways to break down the earned media targets (see Figure 9.6):

- **VIPs**—These are the people you would bring to corporate headquarters or to whom you would give special access to company personnel and products, when available.

- **Exclusive access**—You want to build a good relationship with these people because they generate a lot of conversation. They should also be receiving special content and first looks on new products.

- **Pitch list**—If you are announcing a piece of news, these are the people to whom you would send the press release. They drive conversation, but they aren't necessarily your most vocal brand advocates. This group is much less likely to write about you than the VIPs or exclusive access crowd.

- **Listening only**—This is where most of the negative influencers reside. They drive conversation, but they would never be invited to headquarters or given access to company executives. It is important to keep tabs on them because they might be the likely source of an online crisis.

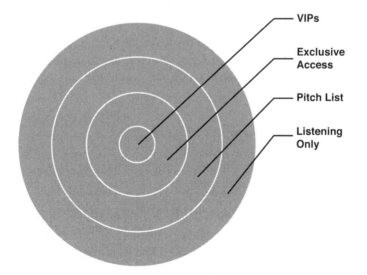

Figure 9.6 *VIPs, exclusive access, pitch list, and listening-only earned media targets.*

The development and use of influencer lists is a growing field. Public relations professionals have been reaching out to influencers for years. Now you have access to more data you can use to determine whether, for example, a mainstream news reporter is *actually* an influencer. What data you collect to ascertain influence is also evolving, as is how you crunch it. As Jay Baer has said, this is a gold-rush topic that has a lot of people trying to solve the issues identified here. Who knows? Perhaps two years from now, all these issues will have been solved, and communicators will have a concrete approach. Until then, consider the advice we have given you throughout this chapter. It will help make your influencer analyses more accurate and effective.

10

Developing Your Social Media Listening Program

Up to this point in the book, we have provided you with the basics of digital analytics, the available tools and how to pick them, and a high-level understanding of the current digital media landscape. The earlier chapters are meant to give you the proper foundation for the next step, which is putting those ideas and concepts into action.

Chapters 3, "Picking the Tools of the Trade," and 4, "Tools: Social Listening," specifically cover how to evaluate the listening tools and which tools are considered "best in class." Those chapters also provide an overview of the market and where it is headed. There is not a one-size-fits-all tool available today, which means you need to do due diligence before you make a purchase.

Inherent in the criteria we outlined in Chapter 3 is a basic understanding of what you are trying to achieve by listening to social media conversations. Without a clearly defined goal or goals, the rest of the research conducted before you make a purchase will be for naught. Knowing what you are trying to achieve is the foundation for evaluating the tool and for outlining your program after the tool is selected. Do not make the mistake of picking a tool before you have outlined a goal and an approach.

After you have picked the goals and tools, you still have to develop the program. What does the program development phase look like? It involves the following:

- **Listening trends across companies**—There are some things that you can learn by evaluating how most organizations conduct listening programs presently and how you can extend those programs.
- **Understanding what listening can do for the brand**—Listening data can extend well beyond the public relations and marketing functions.
- **Training, reporting, and scope**—After you select a tool, you still have to figure out how to train the people who will use it, how you will generate reports from it, and what the scope of your program will be.

In this chapter we dig into each of these elements to provide a roadmap for developing a social media listening program.

How Other Companies Are Listening Today

As the social media listening tools have evolved, so has the application of listening data by companies. In the early days of social media's evolution, companies were monitoring social conversations in order to protect their reputations. From there, the ways companies used listening data changed dramatically. Companies began to lightly monitor for mentions of their brands, competitors, and industries. After that process took hold, a few listening programs morphed into providing strategic recommendations for communications programs. Now some companies are using listening data across the entire enterprise.

Using Listening Data for Program Planning

Using listening data to protect a brand's reputation is still important, but now in almost every case, companies are using the information to inform strategic decisions. To be clear, listening data is not a replacement for other data sources. In fact, conversation data is made more valuable when it is paired with other marketing data inputs, such as surveys and focus groups.

The process of analyzing data for strategic decision making is very linear, meaning that brands gather data, use data, and then measure the effect of the program. The diagram in Figure 10.1 from David Armano, executive vice president, Global Innovation and Integration for Edelman Public Relations, explains using listening data for strategic planning perfectly.

Figure 10.1   *Listening data for program planning.*

Source: David Amano, Edelman, edelmandigital.com (2011)

To understand Figure 10.1, it is important to break down its component parts.

- **Data**—The data portion represents all the conversations gathered about the brand, competitors, and industry topics.

- **Analysis**—This is where the human analyst interfaces with the conversation data collected to start deciphering its potential meaning.

- **Insights**—The insights are the combination of the data, business knowledge, and the analysis coming from the analyst.

- **Planning and strategy**—In this phase, the analysts and the communications team meet to discuss how the data and insights collected can be used to inform a program for moving forward. It is critical that you take into consideration all elements of communications when you apply the data.

- **Program**—After the data has been collected, analyzed, and put into a plan, it is time to implement the idea.

- **Measurement**—Finally, after the program is implemented, you gather data to understand whether the program was successful.

The life cycle of this approach typically lasts several weeks to several months. Although you can collect data throughout the cycle, companies that adopt this approach often do not. The data is gathered at the end. This approach has both advantages and disadvantages. First, here are the advantages:

- **Easy implementation**—There is not much that deviates from a traditional communications planning process, which communicators are likely to be familiar with.

- **No additional resources**—Most companies already have internal resources in-house that can tackle each of these phases.

- **Allows for integrated communications**—The purpose of the planning and strategy phase is to develop a program that covers all kinds of media, not just digital media.

Now, here are some of the drawbacks of this approach:

- **Rigidity**—Communicators who are familiar with various types of social media implementations know that there is a very good chance something unexpected will occur. Because this process does not necessarily allow for data gathering and strategic alteration while a communications program is being executed, a turning of the conversation tides will most likely be missed.

- **Periodic measurement is missing**—Waiting months to gauge the effectiveness of a program simply is not practical in the real-time data world where communicators dwell.

- **Very public relations and marketing centric**—Understanding that the primary audience reading this book is composed of public relations and marketing professionals, the visual does not take into account applications outside these two functions.

Most companies are using this approach to dive into proactive listening. However, there is room to evolve beyond this very linear approach.

Utilizing Listening Data for Ongoing, Proactive Communications

When the true power of social media conversation data is really understood within a company, there is a greater desire to apply it to more than campaign planning or outside a public relations and marketing setting. More people within the organization want to be involved and glean their own insights for their own purposes.

Similarly, public relations and marketing pros have gathered conversation data and used it proactively to meet a particular objective. The natural inclination is to gather more data at varying stages of a program. Those professionals will also be looking to leverage that data with other parts of the organization, just as much as other parts of the organization will want to be involved. Remember that in the digital marketing world, as in so many other spaces, knowledge is power. If you are in a position to know more about your customer than the competition, you will win.

David Armano has developed a visual (shown in Figure 10.2) that helps explain how the same conversation data can be used for ongoing, proactive communications.

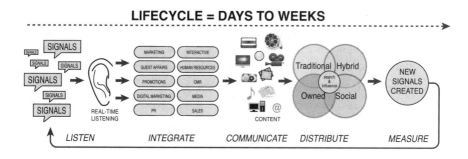

Figure 10.2   *Listening data for proactive planning.*

Source: David Amano, Edelman, edelmandigital.com (2011)

Let's dissect the various phases of this approach, as we did with Figure 10.1:

- **Signals/listen**—In this phase of the approach, you are listening for all mentions of the brand, its competitors, and industry topics. The key differentiator between this and the previous visual is that listening is happening in real time and not only at the beginning of the project.

- **Integrate**—Notice that several aspects of the organization are reflected here. The reason for that is that quite often there is conversation data you can gather that would be applicable to customer service, product development, or even human resources. It is important that as real-time listening is taking place, the data is funneled to the right places within the organization..

- **Communicate/distribute**—Because this process allows for gathering data in real-time, it also allows for much more fluid content development across several types of media channels.

- **Measure**—As this process unfolds, new signals or conversations are being created about the program or brand. This approach enables you to gather that feedback and measure in almost in real-time.

Just as is the case with the other listening model, there are positives and negatives to this approach. First, here are the positive aspects of adopting this approach:

- **Maximum flexibility**—Because data is being captured in real-time, content can also be developed in real-time to meet community demand.

- **Integrated approach**—This is where the two models overlap. Data is being captured for multiple organizational purposes, which means content can be developed to solve multiple business problems.

- **Real-time measurement**—Unlike the first model, this model allows for capturing data more regularly, which should lead to more frequent measurement. More frequent measurement leads to a better understanding of how content or a program itself is resonating.

- **Shorter life cycle**—The other model requires weeks, if not months, to work through. From start to finish, this model takes only a few days, or at most a few weeks. If you are under pressure to deliver something for your boss, a shorter time line is usually preferred.

The following are some of the potential drawbacks:

- **Internal resources**—This approach requires not only digital analytics expertise but also community managers who understand how to apply the data in real-time. There are not a lot of those kinds of professionals out there, so keep this in mind before adopting this approach.

- **Internal stakeholder buy-in**—The model does not work to its full potential unless stakeholders outside public relations and marketing are on board. Showing those stakeholders applicable social conversation data will likely bring them into the fold.

- **Lack of data**—There are some industries, such as some business-to-business companies, that see very little conversation volume. A lack of data means that it is more difficult to glean insights.

- **No rigidity allowed**—If it takes your legal department a week to approve content, this might not be the right approach for you. This approach requires speed and flexibility. A monthly content calendar and this kind of listening approach will not mix well. A lack of data often means that it is more difficult to glean long-term behavioral insights.

You might be wondering which approach is right for you. The answer is that it depends, and it's probably some combination of both. If you are doing marketing or public relations for a consumer brand that is developing lots of original content then the second approach makes more sense. If you are doing marketing or public relations for a B2B industrial manufacturing company, though, the first approach probably suits your needs. That said, as you become more sophisticated with digital media, you can evolve into the second model.

Understanding What Listening Can Do

Now that we have detailed the two primary approaches to listening, it is important to have some grounding in what listening can do. Social media conversation data is powerful and provides a window into consumer behavior in a way that marketers have never seen. It is also a real-time source of information that shows how a program is performing. Before moving any further, though, it is worth reiterating an idea we discussed in Chapter 2, "Understanding Digital Analytics Concepts": Social media conversation data is not a replacement for all other kinds of research. Market research is evolving to be sure, but the ultimate power of listening data is realized when it is brought together with other data sources.

Listening can do five things for your organization:

- **Real-time content development**—We discussed this briefly in earlier in the chapter: Gathering conversation data can only help improve the quality of content produced.
- **Better relationships with your customers**—When a brand responds to a tweet or a blog post, there is a very good chance that the customer will appreciate it. That appreciation is likely to translate into more positive posts about the brand.
- **Product knowledge**—Is the product performing in the manner in which it was intended? If not, your consumers will be talking about it online.
- **"Marketing through conversation"**—Jason Falls, CEO of Social Media Explorer, talks frequently about the concept of subtly marketing to consumers by listening to related conversations.
- **Business intelligence**—As a social media listening program evolves within an organization, there will be opportunities to use the data in more ways to gain competitive advantage.
- **Crisis Mitigation**—Paying attention to online conversations can also help to provide an early warning system in the event that a crisis unfolds online. There will be more on listening during a crisis in Chapter 12, "Using Listening Data to Anticipate a Crisis."

As usual, there is more to the story for each of these benefits. Read on.

Real-Time Content Development

When discussing the two primary listening models earlier in this chapter, we talked about how listening data can be used to tweak content in real-time. The speed at which social media moves requires brands to be more flexible than ever before. Populating a content calendar with a month's worth of content without understanding whether the community cares is likely a recipe for disaster.

Unfortunately, some brands are constricted by a legal department that does not quite understand social media. The reaction to a difficult legal review process is typically defeat, but all is not lost if the legal team is strict and requires a long lead time for approvals. There are things PR and marketing pros can do to leverage conversation data in real-time, thereby allowing for more real-time content development:

- **Align listening efforts to key message points**—Instead of listening to the broader conversation about your brand, try listening to only those conversations that match your key message points. In theory, they have already been approved by your legal department, which should make content development easier.

- **Involve legal early and often**—This is a broad social media maxim, and it is especially true in the content development game. The earlier your legal team understands what you are trying to do and that it isn't a threat, the more flexibility you will have to develop new content.

- **Find the value sweet spot**—If you are listening to online conversations and developing content to match, there is likely a point where you are achieving maximum return for your organization. Do a little research to find that point and then exploit it to your advantage.

- **Set up a "hotline" for quicker approvals**—Whether it is the legal department or some other part of the organization, find a way to circumvent the traditional approval process by setting up a hotline. If there is an ally within your legal team that you can go to directly, do it. Even if there is not someone like that, if you plan early on in the process, you will likely be able to send content to someone in near real-time and achieve more rapid approval.

The reality is that real-time content development probably does not make sense for every brand. However, it is safe to say that using a canned content calendar that is completely locked is not an effective strategy either. If you can listen in real-time and develop content in real-time, that is great. If you have to use one of the approaches outlined in this section, do that. Whatever course of action you take, do not get locked into a content calendar that does not meet the needs of the community in question.

Developing Better Relationships with Customers

Have you ever had a company respond to something you have said online? How did that make you feel? It probably made you feel special, right? Is your company currently listening for those types of opportunities? There are people talking online about you or your competitors every day. It is true that some brands receive quite a few mentions on a daily basis, which does make it hard to read and respond. However, if the experience is positive, it does not take a very detailed response to make them happy. For example, if one of your customers tweets about having just purchased an item from a very helpful salesperson, a simple response like "Thank you very much for the kind words. We appreciate the feedback" can go a very long way. It is worth noting that having a cross-functional committee is imperative to be able to read and respond in real-time—especially during a crisis.

Receiving negative feedback from a customer is a little more challenging. Following these steps can help you handle this situation:

1. Acknowledge the feedback publicly and suggest that the conversation be taken offline.

2. Note to the angry customer that you care about the feedback and are constantly listening.

3. Ensure resolution (as best as possible) of the matter quickly and professionally. Customers are aggravated by unresolved issues, especially if a resolution was promised.

4. In whatever software solution your company is using, document all the elements of the situation. You never know when that issue may come up again.

Gaining Product Knowledge Through Listening

There is some overlap between listening to develop a better relationship with customers and listening for product knowledge. You can gain valuable intelligence about how a product is performing just by listening for mentions of it. Is the widget your company manufactures constantly overheating during use? Is that a known issue? If not and it has just been uncovered through listening, you might be able to prevent a more widespread crisis. If so, listening to those mentions might help you understand the full scope of the product issues.

This type of listening does not need to be for just crisis prevention or communications. It could also be to listen for new applications or releases. It is always surprising how a customer base can totally redefine your product's use case. If those same customers were redefining it in a useful, profitable way, it would probably be something the product development team would want to know about. Either way, involving the product team in the listening process can only help you. These are the people who build stuff that help to make your organization money. If you can make them smarter, you will be an internal champion.

Marketing Through Conversation

The flipside of listening to conversations in order to develop a better relationship with your customers is listening in an intrusive way. This is where the science of developing a keyword profile and entering it into a listening tool comes together with the art of a response. It does not always make sense to respond, and only a very in-tune community manager understands the right and wrong times to get involved. However, there are times when the community is talking to each other and you can subtly insert yourself into the equation. For example, if you are the community manager—a person or persons who is available to respond to an online group of individuals who are talking about a particular subject or brand—for a hotel chain and notice a person asking about hotels in San Francisco, there might be an opportunity to share your hotel's locations in San Francisco with that customer.

The trick, as with anything else online, is having a proven track record of adding value. If the online community knows you have added value to them, they are most likely going to be accepting of your marketing to them occasionally.

Listening to these kinds of conversation is a little trickier than listening to mentions of a brand, product, or competitor name, however. In this instance, it is listening to mentions of the industry. Depending on the industry in question, that might increase the volume of conversations to sift through.

 Tip

Before embarking down this path, you need to ensure that there are adequate resources to listen for these mentions.

Gathering Business Intelligence

It should be crystal-clear by now that we are firm believers in utilizing listening data for more than just public relations and marketing activities. It is true that those two departments have the greatest need for listening, but other parts of an organization can gain valuable intelligence by listening to online chatter. There are a few different types of business intelligence that you can gather:

- **Executive/corporate reputation**—If you are currently working with or for a public company, there is a very good chance you are doing some reputation testing. Analyzing online conversation can give you similar insight into how your customers and key stakeholders view executives and the company at large.

- **Human resources**—Listening for human resources issues goes hand-in-hand with corporate reputation, but if you are actively recruiting online, it is important to understand how current and prospective employees are talking about you. If you do not, and issues are identified with the hiring process, there is a very good chance that a prospective employee in the future will find that information.

- **Insight into the buying cycle**—By now, you are probably familiar with the traditional marketing funnel. Each of the stages of the funnel contains customers who are likely talking online. One way to digest a large number of conversations is to break up those conversations into their respective funnel pieces. That way, you can truly understand how your customer goes from product awareness to purchase. Who wouldn't want to know that?

- **Employee activity online**—Employees are a very important asset for a company, and knowing how those employees behave online is critical. We are not suggesting that you turn into Big Brother, but monitoring activities to see how they might be helping or hurting the brand is valuable intelligence.

Those are five primary ways in which companies can derive value from listening activities. Utilizing listening for program planning or new content might be all you need. That is totally fine if that is your use case for listening data. However, if that is all it is being used for, you are leaving a lot of value on the table. You should start small by utilizing listening for content development and slowly make your way into these other areas. Before you know it, you will be delivering more value than you've ever expected to your company.

Implementing Your Listening Program

Now that we have gone through the process of identifying the two primary models for listening and all the potential benefits of listening to an organization, it is time to start listening to conversations. At this point, you should have clear goals for your listening efforts and resources lined up to complete the work. This is the moment of truth, where you actually begin listening to online conversations and start to develop actionable insights from that listening.

This all sounds easy now that the ducks are in a row, but just because you have gotten this far does not mean everything falls into place. There are still a few elements that we need to discuss before you can kick your listening program into high gear. We discuss each of the following items in more detail in the sections that follow:

- **Tools**—In Chapters 3 and 4 we talk about how to go about choosing a tool and what tools are available on the market. After that process is complete, there are a few additional items that need to be checked off the list.

- **Training**—Now that you have a listening tool internally, how are people being trained on how to use it?

- **Reporting**—When discussing the different listening models, we briefly touched on how to funnel information throughout the organization. However, a more formal reporting mechanism should be developed before launching the program. In addition, there are some best practices that you can follow when developing the reports themselves.

- **Response protocol**—If there is a positive mention of your brand, do you understand who within the organization should respond? What if there is a negative mention?

Before any of these other things can take place, your listening tool needs to be set up with the proper keywords, among other things.

Sharpening Your Listening Weapon

Now that you are at the stage where you are starting your listening program, you need to consider the following things regarding your tool:

- **Your dashboards**—Most of the tools we outline in Chapters 3 and 4 offer users the ability to create custom dashboards. Depending on the type of your company, it might make sense to break up your dashboards into PR/marketing, product, reputation, human resources, and customer service categories. If you do this, everyone can stay focused on his or her part of the pie.

- **Number of users**—Will there be one person who owns the dashboards for your organization? It is best practice to have multiple people within the organization accessing the data, but you have to decide that on a case-by-case basis.

- **Tool integration**—Whatever your listening approach, are there other tools that might need to be incorporated, such as search tools, social media engagement software, or web analytics? Make sure those ducks are in a row before you begin listening.

When you've made all these decisions, you are ready to start listening. Well, almost ready to start listening. Have the appropriate people been trained?

Developing Your Training Program

Assuming that there will be multiple people within the organization utilizing your listening tool, you should develop a training protocol. Even if there aren't currently multiple people using the tool, there could be in the future, so determining a rollout plan is key. Regardless of the tool selected, the training program should be as hands on as possible. If you are currently using listening tools, you know that the only way to truly learn how to use them is to work with them directly.

There are a few things you need to know before you develop your training program:

- **Take advantage of vendor training**—Most of the tools we have talked about have comprehensive training programs or, at a minimum, dedicated support personnel to help users. You should use your vendor's training program as much as possible.

- **Start with a core team**—Regardless of how many users there are, the training should involve a core team of social media leaders within the company. Ideally, the core team would be someone from PR, digital marketing, legal, CRM, human resources, and consumer insights or market research. Those core team members can then turn around and train others on their respective teams.

- **Gradual expansion is best**—Do not make the mistake of trying to expand too quickly. Slowly work with the core team to expand to other parts of the organization. If expansion happens too quickly, there is extreme pressure on the core team managing the project to maintain standards that have been developed.

- **Create incentives for completing training**—We would like to think that people will be interested in participating in the training without any incentive, but we also are not naive. A possible incentive, or penalty, could be that if a person or persons does not complete the training program, he or she cannot do listening for your organization.

What should be included in the training program? It does not need to be anything complicated, but a few staples should be included:

- **Keyword building**—If you have a list of keywords you are using for other programs, that would be a great place to start. If not, try listing terms related to the industry and the brand. You could also do a few keyword searches using a search engine to see what words appear that you could add.

- **Metrics provided by the listening tool**—It does not need to be all inclusive, but a recap of the top-level metrics provided by your listening tool would be helpful.

- **General listening tool functionality**—Depending on the audience, the training should focus primarily on how the listening tool operates. Things such as how to enter keywords, how to extract data, and how to create modules or widgets are all good things to include in the training program.

- **Key contacts**—You can provide this information in a meeting or in some sort of document. Letting people know who the main points of contact are for the program and tool is important.

This is a training program in a nutshell. Before you officially launch your listening program, you need to make sure a training program is in place and has been conducted.

Setting Up a Reporting Template

After developing a training program, it is important to determine how reporting will be done. In addition to determining how it will be done, a decision needs to be made about how often a report will be completed and shared. As usual, it depends on the internal expectation and appetite for information. Regardless of the listening platform or whether data is being captured for only the brand name, there are some easy ways to set up your reports to fit any audience.

You should create your reports by applying the five Ws:

- **What**—What are people talking about when they reference the brand, competitors, or the industry?
- **Where**—Where are people talking about the brand? Are they talking about the brand on forums or blogs?
- **When**—When are people talking about the brand? Does it happen on the weekend? Does it happen on Monday or over the weekend?
- **Who**—Who is talking about the brand? Are they the core audience? Is it men and women? Is it only men who are talking?
- **Why**—Why are people saying the things they are saying? It can be difficult to identify consumer intent based on reading online conversations, but with a little digging, you may be able to do it.

When the report is properly framed using the five Ws, it will be easier to determine how often a report should be compiled. How often you assemble reports depends a lot on your organization's desire for information, but there are other factors as well:

- **Dynamic versus static content**—If the brand is embracing a model similar to the first listening model, it likely would not make sense to report more than once a quarter.
- **What does the boss want?**—If the boss were looking for regular information, it would make sense to develop a simple, one-page report for him or her every month that provides a recap of performance.
- **Internal versus external resources**—If the internal resources are available to handle regular reporting, use them. If you can utilize an agency to help put together reports every month, use it. If you have neither, then it makes sense to scale back the reporting requirements.

Reporting is where all the hard work to pick a tool, set up a tool, and train people on how to use a tool comes together. You should make sure the reports you develop are as actionable as possible, or the investment in listening will be questioned. This could change during a crisis, however. We will dig into more specifics of crisis monitoring in Chapter 12.

Responding to Online Conversations

If you're using the second listening model, responding to online conversations is an important component of your plan. However, it is not as easy as reading the comment and then responding, especially if the comment is negative. Also, if the comment falls outside the typical public relations or marketing function, it might be necessary to get support from within the organization. How does the response process work?

The simplest way is to develop a response flowchart. David Armano has created an excellent sample flowchart for brands to utilize (see Figure 10.3).

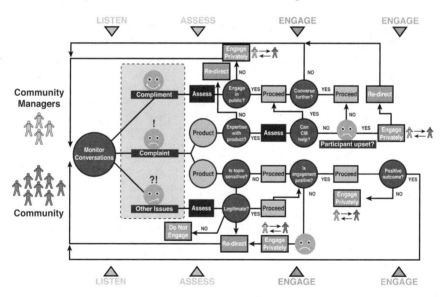

Figure 10.3   *Response Flowchart.*

Source: David Amano, Edelman, edelmandigital.com (2010)

This looks like a complicated visual, but when you see it broken down into its component steps, you see that it is not very difficult to build:

- **Resources**—It takes community managers and analysts working together to fulfill the listening portion of this flowchart. Have those people been identified internally?

- **Compliment/complaint/other issues**—Can you distinguish between what is a positive comment, what is a negative comment, and what are the other comments? Which bucket the conversation falls into might change the way it is routed within the organization.

- **Identify known issues**—This flowchart comes together when a list of known positive, negative, and other issues are identified. A component of identifying known issues is determining who within the organization should answer. For example, with a known product issue, it might make sense for someone in product marketing to respond.

- **Engage**—Not everything that gets mentioned online deserves a response. If it does, ensure that the proper response is crafted and approved ahead of time. If the conversation does not deserve a response, then collect the data for future use.

- **Assess the outcome**—Was the response to your comments positive? Did the customer feel like the issue was resolved? If so, consider the case closed. If not, start the process all over.

This chapter covers the most common models for listening, a breakdown of what listening can do for a brand, and how you can implement a listening program to achieve maximum value. From here, we dive into how to use listening for multiple parts of the organization.

11

How to Use Listening to Inform Marketing Programs

In this book, we have talked at length about basic digital analytics concepts, the tools of the digital analytics trade, and how to begin developing a social media listening program. After reading the first nine chapters, your brain was probably swimming with potential opportunities to use the data to inform your communications programs. It is why Chapter 10, "Developing Your Social Media Listening Program," offers some initial thoughts on how to develop a social listening program. It is also why the next several chapters (Chapters 11 through 14) dig into the various use cases for social and digital data. The possibilities for the data are endless, especially as the tools themselves evolve to meet customer needs. It is important to note that there could be other use cases in addition to the ones we present. What we offer are the use cases most commonly used by organizations of all sizes.

The most common use case for social and digital data is marketing. That is, you take the data points created by your customers' online activities, develop insights from them, and then use those insights to alter or create marketing strategies and tactics. Most companies began listening to social conversations about their brand either in response to a crisis or to prevent a crisis from occurring. That activity quickly transitions into using the data for marketing and public relations programs.

Where should you get started using listening for marketing programs? The first step is to refer to the two different listening models described in Chapter 10—using listening data for program planning and using listening data for ongoing, proactive communications. For the purposes of this chapter, we focus most on using listening data for program planning.

Recall from Chapter 10 that the programming planning model includes six core elements:

- **Data**—The first phase of the model is to gather the data you are interested in capturing. It could be all social media conversations, or it could be a combination of social media conversations and searches. Whatever the data is, it needs to be captured in a clean way before it can be analyzed.

- **Analysis**—In the analysis phase, a human goes through the data and cleans it in order to begin deciphering its potential meaning.

- **Insights**—The insights are the combination of the data, business knowledge, and the analysis coming from the analyst.

- **Planning and strategy**—This phase of the process takes the insights gathered from the research and begins to implement some sort of action plan.

- **Program**—We do not spend much time discussing the program in this chapter, but it is literally the actual implementation of the plan that is developed from your research.

- **Measurement**—After the program is implemented, you gather data to understand whether the program has been successful.

There are a number of different data points you could gather to help inform a marketing program. However, in this chapter we focus mostly on social media conversations. Other data points are also discussed, but a lot of the data that goes into the communication planning phase comes from social media conversations. All the available social media conversation data can be easily categorized into three different types of projects:

- **Conversation audit**—A conversation audit is the initial step into social media that many organizations take. This process involves digesting everything that can be found online about a brand, its competitors, and its industry in order to fully understand the current landscape.

- **Influencer analysis**—Understanding who drives the share of conversation (you'll read more on this in a moment) about your brand is critical. Chapter 9, "Tools: Influence Analysis," covers the tools and techniques of influence analysis at length; this chapter discusses how those analyses can be used to inform marketing programs more directly.

- **Social brand benchmarking**—Before you spend time building your digital footprint, you should have a clear understanding of what your competition is doing online—that is, understanding what the competition is doing across all online channels, not just Facebook.

The following sections talk about how each of these different analyses is conducted, what you should expect to get out of them, and where they fit in the planning continuum outlined earlier.

Understanding the Conversation Audit

At one time, social media was highly experimental. The early adopters at the enterprise level were working under the belief that launching a presence in social media would offer a closer connection to customers. Although that proved to be the case, some of those early brands were placing "bets" on channels that could have failed just as easily as they succeeded. We realize that pointing out social media success stories as possible failures probably is a little confusing, but hear us out.

If you are managing the digital marketing, traditional marketing, or public relations for your company, or if you are working for an agency, wouldn't you like to have access to data about how your customers (current or potential) are behaving online? Wouldn't you like to know the kinds of words they are using to converse? Wouldn't you like to know their preferred channel for conversing? These are just a handful of things you could learn from a conversation audit.

The conversation audit has become a critical input into the digital marketing planning process. It is not that the days of social media experimentation are over. Quite a bit of experimentation still takes place. However, the difference today versus five years ago is that experimentation is now done more thoughtfully and is only a small slice of a digital marketing budget. Today, communicators of all kinds are looking for data and justification for launching a particular online strategy or tactic.

Note

Although in most cases a conversation audit is done at the start of a program, it can often be done after social strategies and tactics have already been implemented. The audit can also follow any other preliminary listening efforts that might have taken place.

The following sections describe the steps needed to complete a conversation audit.

Scoping the Conversation Audit

The possibilities with a conversation audit are endless. If you are working for or representing a large brand (such as Disney, Dell, Pepsi, Coca-Cola, or Cisco) you are likely faced with a diverse business with multiple products or business units or both. Because of that diversity, a conversation audit could easily go from being a very good idea with strong insights to being a really bad idea with hundreds of slides of data telling no real story. How do you avoid the second scenario? As with any other project, developing the proper scope helps mitigate the possibility of receiving a data dump at the end of the project. There are six key steps involved in developing a proper scope:

- **Outlining the brand objectives**—Whatever the communications program, it is imperative that the business objectives be clearly defined. Without those brand or business objectives in mind, the insights delivered from the research are likely to be flawed.

- **Determining an area of focus**—A conversation audit is meant to be comprehensive. However, *comprehensive* can be a bad word when it leads to a mountain of data and very little insight. It's important to define what you are going to be searching for when conducting the analysis.

- **Developing a set of keywords**—After determining the scope, creating a set of keywords is essential. It cannot be a random set of media monitoring keywords that have been used forever, though you could make such a set as one input. There are often several different inputs to a set of keywords. We offer more detail on this in a moment.

- **Understanding data inputs**—While using the term *conversation audit* might signify only the use of a social media listening tool (see Chapters 3, "Picking the Tools of the Trade," and 4, "Tools: Social Listening"), in reality it could be much more comprehensive and include other data inputs.

- **Defining the research question(s)**—Outlining the question(s) you are trying to answer with your research is critical to an excellent end product. In Chapter 15, "Formulating Your Research Plan," we talk about developing your research plan and hypothesis.

- **Building a time line**—The research you are going to conduct cannot go on forever. When does the project begin and end? When are the interim check-ins for the project? How much data will you be collecting for the project? A typical conversation audit encompasses about 12 months worth of data. It is worth noting that not every social media listening solution comes with 12 months of data automatically. Oftentimes you need to request the additional data, and often you have to pay an additional charge.

If you walk through all the steps in this list, your conversation audit scope should be good, and your resulting research report will be very insightful. There still remains the problem of needing all the information in one place; this is critical because we are all busy and attend too many meetings. If a critical project partner misses a meeting about a conversation audit, that person needs to know where to find the documentation. The scoping document helps ensure that knowledge transfer is seamless. This document should be broken up into the following sections:

- **Details of the project**—This could be something as simple as the owner of the project within your organization, to the original requester, to the amount of budget being allocated for the project.

- **Project scope**—This part of the document will have the brands to be included in the analysis, the products, the regions, the languages, and the time frame for the analysis.

- **Situation overview**—This part of the document states why your organization is conducting this research. This is essentially the same as the brand objectives outline earlier in this chapter.

- **Research objectives**—Who is talking about the brand online? What are the key topics of conversation? Where do the majority of conversations take place? These are just a few of the sample research objectives or questions you could ask.

- **Existing data**—There may be data that the team needs to reference as part of the conversation audit. This data could include existing market research, search analyses, web traffic data, or any brand plans. This section of the document can include links to those documents or, at minimum, the key takeaways from each of those other pieces of research.

- **Type of deliverable**—In most instances, the type of deliverable will be outlined as a presentation with key insights. However, people in your organization might want multiple formats (for example, a Microsoft

Word document, PowerPoint presentation, or Keynote presentation) for delivering the data. Ensure that you know all the format types needed before getting to the end of your project.

- **Desired delivery date**—Again, these projects cannot go on forever, but they can be labor intensive. Give your team some time to produce the report but be clear in the scoping document what your expectations are for the date of delivery.

When your scoping document is created, you can actually begin the conversation audit. The next section outlines all the elements of a best-practice conversation audit.

Elements of a Conversation Audit

When your scoping document has been created, it is time to start conducting your research for the conversation audit. By this point, you should have decided on your social media listening tool and should have developed a set of research questions you want to answer with your research. You should also have a firm understanding of the topics you are researching, the brands you are including from an internal perspective, and the competitors (or peers) you are using for comparison.

Even when you have a well-crafted scoping document, there is still a very real possibility that you are infected with analysis paralysis, and you download hundreds of thousands (if not millions) of conversations, analyze them, and put them in a slide deck that completely lacks any insight to help the business. The reality of social media data is that it is plentiful, and analyzing it can often be daunting. A scoping document helps, but some guideposts about what should be in the report are even more helpful.

Our best suggestion is to ask around before trying to determine where those guideposts truly lie. Ask other divisions within your company if they have conducted this type of research. Ask your peers at other companies if they have done a conversation audit. Heck, ask an open-ended question about conversation audits on social media channels if you think you would get a good response.

You may be hoping that we'll provide you with those guideposts. We can give you some ideas, but keep in mind that they are general suggestions. What we suggest below is generic help that comes from our experience doing hundreds of such audits for brands of all sizes. The following list addresses several things you should be trying to answer with a conversation audit. What you pick from this list needs to be based on your brand's objectives and the research questions you are trying to answer:

- **Current share of voice**—Share of voice is the percentage of conversation happening about your brand versus about competitor brands. Those competitor brands should have been identified in your scoping document.

- **Current share of conversation**—Share of conversation is the percentage of conversation happening about your brand versus about the entire category. For example, if you are conducting a conversation audit for Dell, one of your measures could be looking at the volume of conversation about Dell versus about personal computers. The share of conversation would be calculated by dividing the volume of conversation about Dell by the volume of conversation happening about personal computing. In our experience, this number almost never exceeds 5%.

- **Location of conversations**—Your conversation audit should identify which channels contain the most conversation. That could be Twitter or news, as is typically the case if you are conducting a conversation audit at the corporate level. It could also be blogs and forums, as is often the case with brand-level analyses. Wherever those conversations take place, you need to know about them.

- **Key conversation themes**—A critical input to developing social media content is understanding what the online communities already talk about. This could be themes that mention your brand, only the competitors, or only the industry. A conversation audit should help you identify what people are passionate about when mentioning you and also where the opportunity lies when your competitors are mentioned.

- **Individuals or outlets driving conversation**—The conversation audit should begin to identify which people are mentioning the brand, competitors, or the industry most often. We talk more about influencer analyses later in the chapter.

- **Keywords people are using online**—Much like identifying the themes, the conversation audit is meant to identify what words people use when mentioning your brand, competitors, or the industry. The goal of identifying the keywords people are using is to ensure that your content also uses those words. This helps you speak the community's language, and it also helps with natural and paid searching. (Refer to Chapter 5, "Tools: Search Analytics," or see Chapter 17, "Search Analytics," for more information on search analytics.)

- **When conversations take place**—If you have conducted any conversation audits in the past, you have likely seen a volume line graph with spikes showing peaks in conversations. You should be looking for when people are doing the most talking about your brand or the industry in order to properly sync your content with that trend. This part of the analysis should also help you understand which conversation themes have really resonated.

- **Search keywords/volume**—Although this is meant to be a discussion of social media research, search activity does play a role. Identifying the top words people are using in searches and cross-referencing against the words people are using in online conversations can be powerful when it's time to develop your content.

These are the high-level elements of the conversation audit. Obviously, the amount of research you do against any one of these points can be quite extensive, based on the volume of activity and your overall goals for the project. However, every one of these elements should be included in your conversation audit at some level. If you do not include one of them, you will leave a gaping hole in the finished product that might result in missing a key insight that could help the business.

 Note

Much of this section on conversation audits references the use of social media listening tools. If you need a refresher on those tools as you read this section, please refer to Chapters 3, 4, and 10.

Fitting the Conversation Audit into the Program Planning Continuum

It should be relatively obvious that a conversation audit is most useful when it is completed before you create digital strategies or tactics. A conversation audit is a rich source of intelligence about your customers, the industry, and your competitors. It's so rich that coming up with a digital strategy, or even developing content without conducting the audit, would be terribly shortsighted. If you move ahead with the development of a strategy and tactics before conducting a conversation audit, you could enter the community talking about something completely different from what the community actually wants to hear. Trust us when we tell you that doing that is far worse than spending four to six weeks conducting a conversation audit and determining what people would like to hear.

All this being said, a conversation audit could be conducted at the end of a program in order to either change the course of or gauge the effectiveness of your program. Yes, it is a measurement tool as much as it is a planning tool. A company that conducts a conversation audit at the end of a program or while a program is currently under way typically does it to inform the future state. That is a perfectly acceptable use for an audit, but it's important to know that it might result in the revelation that your current program strategies and tactics are flawed based on the research.

▶ *Caution*

> Before moving on to talk about influencer analysis and its role in inform-ing marketing programs, we should note that the conversation audit is not a be-all, end-all solution. Sure, it has tremendous value and gives us great intelligence on our industry and customer. However, it should never be assumed that what is unearthed in the conversation audit is the entire story. Tom Webster, vice president of strategy and marketing for Edison Research—an organization that conducts market research and exit polling worldwide—is fond of saying that social media research (or, in particular, conversation audits) can allow us to ask better questions as marketers. We completely agree with this sentiment. A conversation audit is only one piece of the marketing planning process.

Identifying Online Influencers

In Chapter 9, "Tools: Influence Analysis," we talk about the various influencer analysis tools on the market. Klout, PeerIndex, Kred, and each of the other tools postulates that its particular technology can help brands of all sizes identify who is influential online. Each tool's free, web-based application assesses the impact of the written or digital word of people who are contributing content. At least that is what the tool vendors tell us they are doing when they are gauging someone's online influence.

We talk at length about the influence tools in Chapter 9, and here we want to just point out the influence tools fail in two significant ways:

- **Lack of clarity about metrics**—All the tools make claims about track-ing cross-channel influence, but if you enter someone's name into one of the tools and receive a score of 79, for example, nobody is quite sure how that score was derived.

- **Lack of any broad-scale relevance**—If you enter "Ken Burbary" or "Chuck Hemann" into Klout, for example, you are likely to notice that both of us have some influence on the topic of digital measurement or analytics. This makes sense. However, what if you enter our names into Klout, notice that we have high scores, and then include us in an online influencer list strictly because of that. You might laugh about this, but—trust us—it does occur. Just because a person has a high score according to one of those tools does not mean that person is influential.

We are not saying that the influence tools have zero value. Most of the topics they associate with people are real. We are saying, though, that the scores themselves are not helpful. What would be more helpful is conducting your own analysis of the online landscape in order to determine who is relevant and matters to your brand. Before you panic about conducting another research project, let us set your minds at ease:

- **Data is abundant**—If you learn nothing else from this book, we hope you take away that social and digital media is an abundant and rich data source about your customers.

- **Data is accessible**—Nothing about the data collection that we talk about in the rest of this section is difficult. If you know how to conduct Google searches and are familiar with intrasite searches for any web-site, then you will be able to get this data for yourself.

- **No advanced algorithm is needed**—It is possible to gauge online influence without using a complex algorithm. If you would like to build something like that, do not let us stand in your way. However, for the average marketer, a scaled-down approach is perfectly accessible.

- **Basic Excel skills are all that is required**—If you would like to use SPSS Statistics or some other advanced statistical modeling tool, feel free to do that, but you don't have to. If you have a strong understanding of Microsoft Excel, then you will do just fine with influencer analysis.

- **Thousands of names would be overkill**—Paul Dyer, head of Media and Engagement at WCG, talks about the identification and creation of influencer lists and the modern-day media list and says that having too many names is unnecessary. He is right, of course, and as is the case with a traditional media list, there will likely be a core set of individuals you know can be "money in the bank" for the brand. In addition, there is no need to identify thousands of names because the chances that you will perform outreach to all those names are slim to none. Find a core set of influencers—50 to 100 people overall—and reach out to them as appropriate.

Hopefully you are feeling that an influencer analysis is an approachable undertaking for your brand. These are some elements that belong in an influencer analysis:

- **Focus on relevance first**—The natural instinct is to search for publications that reach the most people. Although that might be a successful strategy in some instances, the largest publications write on a variety of topics. They might or might not be interested in your brand or your pitch idea. You want to identify those people who are writing a large percentage of their content over a given time period on the topics you care about. That should be your primary focus.

- **Focus on syndication second**—Some sample syndication metrics include how often a post or a piece of content is retweeted, how often it is shared on Facebook, and how often it is commented on during a given time period. Syndication metrics are a useful barometer for how likely a message is to spread when it is introduced to the marketplace.

- **Focus on reach third**—We are not crazy enough to think that reach has no part of an influencer analysis. However, we do feel strongly that it should not be the only thing used to measure influence. Unique monthly visitors, total page views, inbound links, Twitter followers, and blog subscribers are all examples of reach metrics.

- **Determine the time frame for your analysis**—We recommend using at least 12 months' worth of data to prevent certain events from skewing the data, but we understand that for bigger industry categories, this might not be possible. You should be aiming for at least 6 months' worth of data, however, when you conduct the analysis.

- **Think about the weight you would give to certain metrics**—We have not outlined a series of metrics here—just broad concepts—but you should think about whether you would weight retweets of on-topic content more highly than unique page views, for example. Not all metrics are created equal. Some will be more important to you than others. You should give those metrics more weight in your final analysis.

- **Weighting certain networks more highly than others**—Just as you would weight certain metrics differently, you should also give greater weight to some networks than others. If previous experience tells you that blogs are most important to your brand, give bloggers more weight in your final analysis. A simple way to think about this weighting concept is to determine what channel is driving the majority of the conversation. If it is blogs, news, forums, Twitter, or even video content?

- **Think about all potential online channels**—Coming up with a list of bloggers and media who are influential to your category is nice, but it's even better to develop a list of influencers across news, blogs, Twitter, video, forums, and so on. The Internet is much larger than any one channel, and calling a list of bloggers the people who matter most to the brand would be disingenuous. Your category is likely going to have people talking across a variety of networks. You should know who they are before you call your list "final."

At the end of your analysis, you should have a highly targeted list of people who are widely syndicated, widely read, and, most importantly, highly relevant. Because the data is so abundant and accessible, it would be foolish to fall into the trap of downloading a media list from a tool and using it verbatim. Take the time to conduct research using the components and ideas outlined here. We think you will find that you'll gain more traction and create additional stories that would have never been possible with a "canned" media list.

 Tip

Not everyone in your new influencer list is a potential outreach target. You will likely identify folks who have influence on the community but are overly negative toward the brand. You should include those people in your listening program as "people to watch."

Conducting Social Brand Benchmarking

After you have completed an influencer analysis, your next step should be to conduct social brand benchmarking. This might sound like something that would be covered along with the conversation audit, and it could be. However, our experience indicates that doing it as a separate analysis can be very valuable. Your conversation audit is already chock-full of intelligence about the key themes of conversation online. An influencer analysis shows you who is driving conversation online. What you do not have is a sense of how the competition is utilizing social media.

What does a social brand benchmark look like? A social brand benchmark has two primary elements:

- **Social channel presence**—At a high level, understanding where your competitors are currently engaging online is very helpful. When you are conducting this analysis, think of this portion of the project as understanding the size and scope of the presence.
- **Content analysis**—It is not enough to know whether one of your competitors has an online presence. You need to understand what kinds of content that competitor is posting and how successful it is in generating interest from the community.

Where do you begin to assess your competitors' online presence? Bob Pearson, president of W2O Group—a strategic communications consulting firm and parent company to Chuck Hemann's agency, WCG—frequently talks about the 10 channels of online influence. Table 11.1 outlines these channels of online influence and why they matter. It is important to know how your competitors stack up on all these channels. Do they have an active podcasting program? What does their video presence look like? Knowing where your competitors are currently "playing" is the first step in the process.

Table 11.1   The 10 Channels of Online Influence

Influence Areas	Trend	Relevance
Audio	Favorite of sales force customers on the go.	Podcasts of all types, plus audio tracks of video segments are an undefined area of online, yet have growing utility.
Blogs	More than 200MM; trend is to have multiple blogs, multiple languages.	You should know the top influencers by topic who drive relevant share of voice. The numbers of influencers are small; precision is key.
Data/Slides	60mm unique slides at SlideShare.	A great location to share all public presentations.
Forums	The engine of conversations online; often patient driven.	Knowing who is driving conversation in forums is key. You should treat high volume moderators with the same respect as you do journalists.
Images	Is all content tagged to effect natural search?	Companies often forget to tag all content in the 10 languages that reach 90% of the online population.
Micro Blogging	An effective way to alert influencers, help propel news cycles.	A great opportunity to build a network of influencers who want to share your news in real time. Twitter is a prime example.
Search	Yes, Google is #1, but YouTube is #2.	You need to know the influencers on the first screen for our brand and key topics. You also need to understand where people are taken when they search.
Social Networks	The communities that are often the "first place to go" online.	The day often starts and ends with Facebook, MySpace, or Orkut (or other) depending on where you live.
Video	Consumption habits are starting to favor video versus copy.	There are more than 50 video sites, which sometimes house ratings and reviews of your products, to analyze.

Influence Areas	Trend	Relevance
Wikis	Free online peer edited online encyclopedia.	Nearly every topic has a Wikipedia entry, which means it could be the first information a consumer finds about any topic he is seeking information about.

Source: Bob Pearson of W2O Group.

A simple way to approach the table shown in Table 11.1 is to count the number of podcasts, or videos, or Twitter followers, or images, or any other channel listed in Table 11.1 for your top competitors and industry. Although counting is not terribly insightful, it will give you some idea of what channels the competition thinks is important.

The next step is to understand what kinds of content your competition is producing on each of those channels. The following are some simple ways you can do this across a network:

- **Examine content engagement**—Whether it is Facebook, Twitter, or YouTube, an abundance of engagement data is available. An analysis could include an examination of posts on Facebook to determine how many likes, comments, and shares a competitor received, on average. What would be even more helpful is to categorize the posts by subject or type to truly understand what posts performed well.

- **Post frequency**—Are your competitors posting on Saturday? Do they post seven times per week? Just because they are posting on Saturday doesn't mean you should post on Saturday, but if those posts receive engagement, you should at least consider it.

- **Earned versus shared versus paid content**—The analysis does not need to be all about what the competitor brand is doing on shared channels, or even through earned media. You might discover that a competitor brand is advertising on a well-known industry forum. It might not be engaging, but clearly it found the network valuable enough to pay for advertising space. Does that mean you should be doing the same thing? No, but it could mean an open opportunity for you to engage with the community rather than buy its attention.

- **Presence of your target audience**—This might come out during your conversation audit, but as you are examining the competitor presences on the 10 channels of online influence, you should qualitatively assess whether you believe your target audience is participating. If it is not, it might be time to look elsewhere.

Conclusion

We have given you three different ways to use social listening data to improve marketing programs. Brought together, the conversation audit, influencer analysis, and social brand benchmarking are powerful sources of information about your customer. We highly recommend that you conduct one—if not all three—before launching your social or digital efforts. Not only will they be more focused and easier to manage, but also the return on those efforts will be higher.

Before we move on to the other use cases in the following chapters, we thought it would be helpful to share a perspective about the value of social data from one of the early adopters: Intel Corporation. Intel was one of the first brands to adopt and embrace the power of social media, and it has now begun leveraging the data available to improve programs across the enterprise. Ali Ardalan, media and analytics strategist for Intel, offered the following perspective on the value of social networks and social data:

> The concept of an "Open Brand" where customers and firms can communicate directly on a more frequent basis allows for new, more consistent global relationships. Intel has traditionally communicated through television, print, billboard, and radio advertising with customers. This is necessary for driving awareness & preference of branded Intel technologies "inside" of partner computing devices. Seeking to modernize, in 2005, we redeveloped our online presences, updated our branded logo, embraced SEM/SEO, deepened investment in banner & rich media advertising and in 2008/2009 launched Social Media as a center of excellence in our marketing strategy organization.
>
> With this evolution, digital data became essential in the way we conduct and tune our modern business. Digital data is essential for firms, who desire to look at an end-2-end picture of their business, and the meaningful transactions that they conduct with customers. Today's firm's must scorecard clearly defined conversion based metrics and yet also review on a regular basis softer, more directional business indicators many of which are digital.
>
> In our integrated media center of excellence (COE), we set annual strategies for our paid, owned and earned programs, analyzing progress by audience each quarter; metrics targets and guard rails, many of these digital, keep our business on track. We use historic digital data as an input into planning our annual modeling as we forecast investment scenarios. We evaluate and tune the effectiveness of our reach and the depth of our engagement in quarterly campaigns with digital data. Events, product launches, partner programs, promotions every aspect of our communication today has digital metrics associated with

it. We also benchmark our impact, share of voice and performance among external competitor, partners and brands whom we admire. Benchmarking data is oftentimes difficult to come across; digital metrics tend to be some of the more readily available figures, which we can use consistently over time.

As we look into the future, our industry will continue to evolve with various form factors of computing devices. New more open methods of communication building open the value seeded by social networks like Twitter & Instagram will emerge. The future for us is tied into the way we embrace appropriate messaging across these avenues, we segment our audiences and we seek to understand the new value creation steps in the journey with our brands. This journey is no longer linear for our customers; it varies by market, and does not always fit into a tradition sales funnel.

When we speak at conferences and meet our peers in different places, we see each company going through this evolution at a separate pace, and with varying degrees of openness. Some organizations embrace these new methods in silos, perhaps within one or two business units only—their task over the next 5-10 years is to pioneer, demonstrate the value of new methods and seek deeper integration and consistency in methods across their firm. In other industries the task will be to work more collectively with partners but to dig this down in granularity on a daily basis, or to help spur a similar evolution in their channel organizations and ecosystems. I think of the automotive, healthcare and manufacturing sectors where we have hundreds of thousands of dealers, doctors and resellers many of whom benefits of these modern methods have likely not yet been fully realized, due to the challenges of scale, resources and in some the need for sensitivity and privacy. We also now have new data that is being created at an extraordinary pace. Medium/Long strategies for effective management of big data, cloud computing solutions which scale more effectively, effective us of SaaS tools, side by side with enterprise data and the impact of "data scientists" working closely with each organization in a firm will become essential components for all brands seeking to continue leading their industries. The next decade is going to be extremely exciting for us numbers guys. ;o)

12

Using Online Data to Anticipate a Crisis

Almost every company faces a crisis situation at some point. Whether that crisis is a plant closing, large-scale layoffs, or executive management changes, a company's value is always under threat. Good communications departments have developed crisis plans that account for these types of issues, and they are constantly tweaking those plans to match how the business is moving. Not-so-good communications departments are caught blindsided by issues and are usually inundated with press attention.

Social media amplifies the flow and volume of news during a crisis. If the Wall Street Journal, New York Times, or Associated Press pick up a story about your brand, you are likely going to face hundreds of additional articles and thousands of tweets. In addition, bloggers who are not necessarily friendly to your brand will pick up the story and offer their own slant. Those bloggers might have limited reach, but it takes only one with a network the size of the Huffington Post to help make a small crisis into a big one.

Crisis does not just impact mainstream news, the blogosphere, or the Twittersphere; it can also affect searching. One of the stories we love to tell is that if you do a Google search for Exxon, you still see mentions in the first two results pages of the *Exxon Valdez* spill, which occurred more than two decades ago. Google indexes all the attention that Twitter, blogs, and news sources give to an event and makes it available for years after. Therefore, a crisis does not last a month or two anymore. It has the potential to live on for years after the fact because of search engines.

There is good news in of this for brands. Understanding that a crisis is always right around the corner is a good first step. In addition, taking the time to develop a crisis plan that includes social media is essential. One of the elements of crisis plan development is taking the time to document all potential issues. In our experience, brands are aware of at least 90% of issues that the company could face. These issues could come from operational challenges, customer service complaints, product disputes, and so on. Wherever the issues come from, the company has likely heard of them before. It is also our experience, however, that most brands do not document those issues correctly.

This chapter examines how brands can utilize listening data to anticipate a crisis and, if a crisis does arise, how to ensure that mechanisms are in place to gather conversation data and react to it.

Developing a Modern-Day Issues Management Plan

As mentioned earlier, a brand is aware of approximately 90% of issues that arise. Unfortunately, most of the time those issues are not well documented in a communications crisis plan. The obvious question is "Why not?" The reality is that all it would take is for the corporate communications team to sit down with business unit leaders for a day and whiteboard all the potential scenarios. Everyone is busy, but we're talking about protecting the brand's value. But we digress.

WCG, a full-service communications consultancy based in San Francisco, and the firm that employs one of the authors of this book (Chuck), has developed an excellent model—the modern-day issues management plan—to tackle these issues (see Figure 12.1).

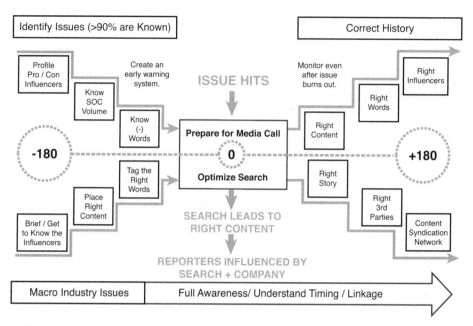

Figure 12.1   *WCG's approach to issues management.*

Although the model looks very complicated, it is in practice very simple. It relies on social media listening efforts to essentially create an early warning system for a crisis. It is based on the premise that a brand does not need to go on the defensive when a crisis strikes. In fact, it can go on the offensive to correct the record. There are three distinct phases to this approach:

- **Identify known issues**—This takes some diligence, but the known issues must be documented. Not only must the known issues be documented, but several other elements must be researched and outlined as well.

- **Face the crisis day**—If you currently work for a brand or an agency that represents a brand that has faced a crisis, you know what that day looks like. It's typically chaotic. However, if you have done the due diligence in the first phase, you may be able to reduce the crisis tidal wave.

- **Correct history**—After the issue hits, you can leverage the things you have learned in the first phase to help correct the record.

Let's dive into each of these issues in more detail.

Identifying Known Issues

Taking the time to identify known issues is a critical step in mitigating the damage that can be done in a crisis situation. Not only that, but this upfront work might also help prevent a crisis from ever seeing the light of day online. To identify the known issues and properly prepare for a crisis situation, you should do the following:

- **List the known issues**—You should identify a core team of individuals to list all the known issues the team members could face in their parts of the business.

- **Know the share of conversation volume**—How much conversation is taking place about your brand right now versus about the general industry? Do you know?

- **Profile pro and con influencers**—Knowing who drives conversation for the brand, both positively and negatively, is key.

- **Brief and get to know influencers**—The brand does not need to invite every one of the influencers to headquarters, especially if they are not friendly, but you should know everything you can about them ahead of time.

- **Place the right content**—Based on what you know influencers are writing about, and what issues could arise, are you posting the right kinds of content online?

- **Know the positive and negative words**—When people search for you, do you know what words they are using? Do you know if those words are positive or negative?

- **Tag the right words**—Are you using the words people are using in conversations and in searches to appropriately tag content on social and web properties?

The next several sections cover these elements in more detail.

Listing the Known Issues

We have said it several times throughout this chapter so far: Making the effort to list your known issues is essential. You do not need a huge team of people to create the list, but the list needs to be comprehensive enough so that you are not surprised when an issue arises.

Also, in case you are concerned about adding another thing to your already overflowing plate, the job of listing the issues is not the exclusive job of the corporate communications or marketing departments. If you reside in one of those groups, you will likely be asked to lead the charge, but you are going to need help. Where should that help come from?

- **Legal**—The legal department is most likely the best source of information on known issues facing the company. The legal team gets a bad reputation in some marketing circles, but it is their job to protect the company. As such, they are constantly researching and identifying issues that may affect the brand's value.

- **Human resources**—The HR team will be aware of any employee issue that might make its way online. Ask them to be involved in your crisis SWAT team, but if they won't, at least pick their brain for potential issues.

- **Customer service**—Customer service folks are often your first line of defense with customers. They are aware of issues your customers might be having with the product or service. There is a very good chance they will have a list of known customer issues that you can use to begin the online research process.

- **Business unit heads**—The men and women leading the individual business units are very close to the business. They will know issues with the product or service that you can build upon.

- **Senior executives**—The executive team might direct you right back to any one of the four different groups already mentioned, but conducting an interview with the CEO would not be out of the question. He or she will respect the fact that you are trying to protect the brand.

What do you do after you have talked with each of these constituent groups and listed issues you are already familiar with? You begin the research process, of course! The first step is knowing the issues. The second step is researching whether people are already talking about those issues online.

Knowing the Share of Conversation Online

After you have identified your issues, you can begin conducting research to see if people are talking about or searching for them. It is imperative that you know where you stack up in terms of share of conversation online. As a reminder, share of conversation is the amount of conversation taking place that mentions the brand versus the amount of conversation that is happening about the entire product category.

How do you know if people are talking about or searching for these issues? You can follow these four easy steps:

1. **Develop keyword strings**—Based on the issues, develop a list of keywords that match those issues. This will take a little bit of time to properly hone, but it is the most important step to gathering the most relevant content.

2. **Build a dashboard only for issues**—If you are monitoring for multiple things (customer service, marketing, public relations, and so on), be sure that one of your listening dashboards is dedicated to known issues.

3. **Check frequently**—Do not assume that building the dashboard is the last step. It is important to check frequently to see if anything pops up on the known issues. Also, do not assume that just because you only see one mention of the issue that a crisis is not under way. These are known issues for a reason, and any small post can turn into a big deal online.

4. **Formulate a response plan**—If one of these issues crops up online, do you have a plan to respond? If a response is warranted, who within the organization will deliver it? Who approves the messaging? David Armano of Edelman Digital has developed an excellent community management map that can also double as a response protocol (see Figure 12.2). It might look daunting, but the biggest step in developing this map is listing the known issues, which you should have done already.

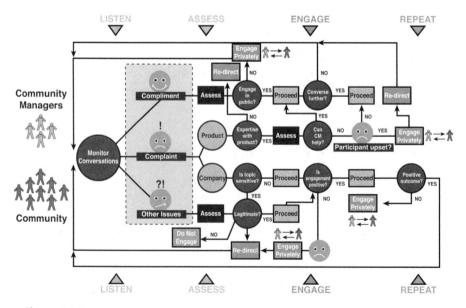

Figure 12.2 *Sample crisis response protocol.*

One of your other dashboards should be actively tracking overall brand mentions, and that is where you can ascertain the current share of the conversation. It is important to know it before a crisis so you can benchmark how big the crisis was when you assess your response after the crisis subsides.

Knowing Profile Pro and Con Influencers

A component of listening to the known issues and identifying any that are currently being talked about is nailing down the people who are driving the share of conversation online. These people could be talking about you or the issues positively or negatively. They could be talking in forums or on blogs or on Twitter. Regardless of who they are, where they are talking, and the sentiments they express about the issues you care about, you need to identify who those top people are. If you spend the time to identify who these people are, then when a crisis does hit, you know who to share content with in order to spread your message.

In Chapter 9, "Understanding Digital Influence," we talk at length about identifying influencers, the tools, and how you can conduct this analysis yourself. If you are not using one of the tools we talk about in that chapter, we encourage you to reference the section "Developing Your Own Influence Tool." It can help you nail down this phase of the online crisis management process.

Briefing and Getting to Know the Influencers

Before a crisis hits, take the time to really know who your influencers are and where they typically produce content. This is Essential Public Relations 101. Building a relationship and offering something of value to these people helps you if a crisis does hit. If you wait until a crisis hits and you have never talked to these people, they are not likely to help you. Take all the opportunities that are presented to you in peacetime to build those strong influencer relationships.

We cover how to get to know the influencers in Chapter 9, where we walk through the four different levels of outreach: VIP, exclusive access, pitch list, and listening only. The listening-only influencers are those who are difficult to "pitch" or might be more negative toward the brand.

Placing the Right Content

In Chapter 2, "Understanding Digital Analytics Concepts," and Chapter 3, "Picking the Tools of the Trade," we talk at length about using listening data to inform content development in real time. It is a similar idea here: After the known issues and influencers have been identified, you should be looking for any opportunity to share relevant content with the community. This content does not need to be 100% issues related, however. If it is, it obviously cannot be something that would tip the community off to a potential product or service issue.

A good example of placing the right content is related to the customer service angle mentioned earlier. If you have talked to your customer service team and realized that long hold times are an issue and then realized after analyzing social conversations that this is the subject of some discussion online, what should you do? Well, a practical approach is to interject pieces of content on shared channels (such as Facebook or Twitter) that talk about how you are addressing longer-than-normal hold times. Although it isn't a full-blown issue yet, it could be if it got into the hands of the right influencer. However, if you have taken the time to put out specific pieces of content about the issue, you can neutralize some of that impact.

Knowing the Positive and Negative Words

It isn't enough to just know the issues and the influencers. You need to be intimately familiar with the words people are using in conversation. Chances are good that there are anywhere between 10 and 15 "money words" that people use in connection with one of these issues. Do you know them? If not, spend time doing research, looking at social conversations and identifying those words.

How do you identify the money words? A number of tools are available, and at least these two simply must be in your arsenal:

- **Wordle**—If you have ever developed a word cloud showing the most popular terms, it was probably developed by Wordle. Wordle is a free web-based application that enables users to copy and paste a large number of words into the system to see which words are used most frequently. Figure 12.3 shows an example of a Wordle.

- **Textalyser**—Textalyser works in much the same way as Wordle, in that it requires users to copy and paste a large amount of text into the system. The difference is that instead of giving you visual output, Textalyser gives more quantitative output that shows the number of times a keyword or phrase was used.

Figure 12.3   *A sample word cloud identifying the top keywords/phrases.*

How do you use these tools? Wordle is better for presentation purposes, such as showing your boss or executive management the topics that are being used most. Textalyser is best used as a preliminary research tool and for identifying the words you should be including in your content.

Tagging the Right Words

After you have identified the keywords people are using online, it is important to cross-reference those words against the words you are using on all your properties. Do they match the words you are tagging on your website? If not, why? The goals should be to customize your content to what the community is looking for and also to make it as visible as possible.

Are these words the same words you are using in social media posts? If not, why? Again, you need to ensure that you are giving the right content and that it is very visible. What about on your blog? The same idea fits. Conduct an inventory of the words you are using in tags versus the words you have identified that match these issues.

If you go through these seven steps, you will have a firm grasp on the identity of known issues and will create a best-in-class crisis communications plan. Not only that, but these steps help make facing the day of a crisis a little easier. What happens when the crisis hits, though? How do ensure that you are taking the right steps from an analytics perspective? Read on.

Crisis Day Monitoring and Ongoing Reporting

So a crisis has hit, and you have done your upfront research. Obviously, on the day a crisis hits, everyone is frenzied. There is certainly no time to do any in-depth research, which is why the steps we outlined in the preceding section are so important. What are the next steps?

1. **Deal with the issue hitting**—For the sake of this discussion, we assume that you have done the upfront research. When the issue hits online, you should activate the crisis protocols you have put into place.

2. **Develop a content plan**—When you know who is calling and who is talking online, it is easier to know what types of content you should be posting. Again, if you have done the upfront research, this should not involve much heavy lifting. A component of the content plan is also determining how frequently you will be posting.

3. **Determine your reporting plan and cadence**—There are things you should be reporting on in real time, and there are others you should save for after the crisis.

Let's dig into each of these steps in a little more detail.

Dealing with the Issue Hitting

On the day an issue hits, you do not have time to identify influencers, determine the share of conversation, or figure out what words people are using in conjunction with this issue. If a known issue comes to light and you have done your research, all that should be required is to activate your crisis protocols. These are the specific protocols that should be in place:

- **Form a monitoring team**—If you are a marketer or corporate communicator, you will not have time to monitor online conversations on the day of the crisis. Before a crisis hits, you should identify who needs to be on the monitoring team. It could be more junior members of your team, but this is also an excellent place to utilize an outside partner. When an issue hits, this team will need to be activated to offer real-time support.

- **Activate the war room and crisis response team**—You should have a previously designated physical location where you and the crisis response team will gather. It should have phones and computer access, and it should be away from the rest of the team. You need to focus on what's happening with the crisis, and you can't risk any distraction.

The crisis team members vary from organization to organization, but most times this team involves marketing leaders, corporate communications, HR, legal, and senior executives.

- **Develop a schedule**—Depending on how big the crisis is, you will likely want to create a schedule that shows who is on duty and who is off duty. You should assume that everyone is on duty until some sort of formal schedule is created.

When the issue hits, you should be ready with all these things. Trust us: The online world will not wait for you to have all your ducks in a row.

Developing Your Content Plan

You know the issues people talk about online. You know the issues facing your business. You know the words people are using online. You know what people are searching for. Based on all this research, you should develop pieces of content that you can utilize if a crisis hits. It might be necessary to develop content on-the-fly, especially if an issue is unknown. However, developing that content is challenging.

Your posting cadence is also critical. It depends somewhat on the news flow, but as the crisis evolves, you should determine how often you should be posting online. It could be once, with a simple statement after the crisis breaks, or it could be frequently, as news develops. Either way, you should be prepared to post content within six hours of the crisis breaking.

As you develop your crisis content plan, you should also keep the following in mind:

- **Consider the social platform**—You can probably repurpose content on Twitter and Facebook, depending on what the crisis is about. However, it might make sense to develop something more unique for each channel, if the crisis warrants.

- **Ensure that the initial response is on the channel where the news broke**—If the news broke in an online mainstream news outlet, then that is where you should respond. (In the initial research, you will have identified influencers, including those from mainstream news, and your list should make the initial response easier.) If the crisis was spawned on Twitter, then you should develop a piece of content that fits the Twitter audience.

- **Keep the top keywords in mind**—You have already identified the top keywords in your research. The posts you develop, regardless of channel, should utilize those keywords.

- **Use senior executives**—This would be a good time to take advantage of your senior leaders who are already using social media. If they aren't using social media, use their voice in your posts. After the Domino's Pizza crisis in 2009, the company's CEO, Patrick Doyle, become the immediate face of the content they were posting. Positioning your senior leaders in this way gives your constituents confidence that you are taking the crisis seriously. This can also be an opportunity to convince your executives that they should be more active online.

- **Be flexible**—We said just a few paragraphs ago that developing some static content would be a good tactical move, and it is. But you should be flexible with your content, based on how the news cycle develops.

Developing Your Reporting Plan and Reporting Cadence

Depending on how big the crisis is, you might be inundated with thousands of posts over a very short period of time. Digesting and offering insights on that much data in a crisis situation is very challenging. If you have activated your monitoring team (internally or externally), you will also need to determine how frequently you are reporting, what you are reporting on, and what your postmortem reporting plan will be.

A component of the reporting plan is utilizing a tool that provides information in near real time. Check Chapters 3 and 4, "Tools: Social Media Listening," to find out more about tools that could fit the bill. If your business is in a category that is constantly under threat of crisis (for example, the airline industry), you should ensure that your monitoring tool can handle volume as it comes through in a timely fashion.

The following sections talk a little more about reporting frequency, contents, and how you should be reporting after a crisis ends.

Reporting Frequency and Contents During a Crisis

In the early days of a crisis, you should be planning on reporting fairly regularly. If the crisis is generating a lot of online attention, you might want to consider developing a report every hour. If the crisis is generating some attention but the news is not changing much, it might make sense to do a couple reports. What should be in your reports, and in what format should you present them?

- **Email**—If you are in the middle of a crisis, it will probably not be practical to create a fancy PowerPoint presentation. An email should be perfectly sufficient to deliver the news.

- **Executive summary**—Every report should contain a few sentences on what is happening online. Think about developing something that's very high level—even a bullet point format that sums up the period's activities.

- **Volume of conversation**—This is an obvious one, but it is helpful to see how much conversation is taking place online about the crisis.

- **Locations of conversations**—Do the conversations take place in blogs or forums? Most crisis situations see mentions coming from news and Twitter, but every situation is slightly different.

- **Sentiment**—Do not try to have someone on the team read the conversations and then assign a sentiment score to them, but it is helpful to offer a qualitative snapshot of the sentiment of online conversation.

- **Top sites**—Which sites are generating the most buzz? Buzz in this case is most often a proxy for the number of shares on Twitter and Facebook that an article is receiving.

Do not obsess about making the format beautiful. What you really want to convey is a pulse check on what's happening, and content flow can change based on what is happening in conversations at that moment.

Reporting Frequency and Contents After a Crisis

After a crisis is over, you should plan on doing a deeper dive into how the crisis unfolded online. This is your opportunity to highlight what happened, how it happened, and how you reacted to make sure further brand value was not lost as a result of the crisis. Your monitoring team should be involved in putting together this report, whether that is your agency or an internal team. The following should go into the post-crisis report:

- **Executive summary**—One slide that talks about what happened during the crisis is an imperative. This might be the only slide your executives read, so be sure it tells the story you want to tell about the crisis.

- **Volume of conversation**—Again, it is helpful to see how much conversation took place during the crisis.

- **Locations of conversations**—Identifying whether Twitter or blogs drove the crisis coverage will help provide a barometer for where you can expect crisis coverage to originate the next time.

- **News cycle analysis**—It is important to analyze how the news cycle unfolded. How many mentions did it take before the peak was reached? How long did the news cycle last? Who drove that initial spike? These are all things you should be trying to answer in the report.

- **Sentiment**—Depending on the crisis, it would be helpful to look at overall online sentiment during that period. You can then further break down sentiment by media type to see where the most positive, negative, and neutral conversations came from.

- **Influencer coverage**—If you have done your upfront analysis, you will know who typically drives share of conversation for the brand. Did they cover the crisis? If so, how did they cover it? This does not need to be a quantitative analysis. Rather, it is most important to show how the influencers covered it.

- **New influencers**—Are there people who generated a lot of news attention that could be considered influencers in the future? If so, consider adding them to the list of sites/sources you are actively monitoring.

- **Key subtopics**—If the crisis is long enough, there is a good chance that subtopics will develop. What are they, and should you add them to your known issues list in the future?

The post-crisis report should be viewed partially as reporting on what took place during the crisis, but also as an update to the benchmark research you conducted in the first phase of the crisis planning process. To ensure that you have gathered all the relevant data, you should wait at least a month after a crisis to conduct this report. You might be able to glean valuable intelligence as mentions continue trickling in after the heat of the crisis begins to subside.

Correcting the History After a Crisis Is Over

After a crisis is over, you have the opportunity to assess how the team performed. How effective was your team? How effective was your pre-crisis research in saving you valuable time during the crisis? How good was your reporting during and after the crisis? Are there things you wish you would have reported on either during or after the crisis? The good news is that none of these things are set in stone. In fact, the best crisis plans set up the company for success during the crisis but are fluid enough to change based on a specific crisis experience.

For measuring the impact of your initial crisis planning, after the crisis subsides is the best time to evaluate some of your original research. It is also helpful to identify important third parties who came to your aid and to tweak your content syndication plan.

Evaluating Your Preliminary Research

You shouldn't be surprised that we advocate ongoing measurement of your communications efforts—crisis situation or not. There is no better time to evaluate how effective your initial crisis planning research was than after a crisis is over. Here's what you should you be looking at when you evaluate your preliminary research:

- **The right influencers**—Did you reach out to the right people during the crisis to help spread your message? Were they effective in spreading that message beyond their initial post? Did any new people emerge as influential that you could use in a future crisis? These are some of the questions you should answer to ensure that you can continue pumping out content that helps you correct the perceptions people might have developed about your brand during the crisis.

- **The right words**—The keywords you identified by using Wordle or Textalyser should have been used in the posts you issued during the crisis. Were they used appropriately? After doing the post-crisis report and looking at the keywords people were using, do they still match up?

- **The right content**—Your preliminary research should have shown what types of content resonated most about a particular issue. Is that content still the same, or is there some nuance you can make to ensure that you keep reaching people with the right content?

- **The right story**—Does your message about a particular issue need to change in the wake of the crisis? Maybe you will never talk about that issue again unless another crisis develops, but analyzing whether the message is still resonating is critical.

Identifying Key Third Parties and a Content Syndication Plan

When a crisis situation ends, you have a great opportunity to see which third parties came to your aid. This is not necessarily individual bloggers, mainstream news reporters, or Twitter users. It may be that key third-party organizations utilized their own social properties in order to defend your point of view. If a crisis event crops up again, these groups will likely come to your aid again. It is important to identify any potential "friendlies" that could help you in a future negative situation.

Also, this is the time to test whether your content syndication plan was effective in spreading the message. The following are some key questions to ask yourselves about the content syndication plan:

- **Did the influencers move content?**—When you reached out with a specific message, did they accurately portray your point of view? If not, it might be best to think about another source as the "tipping point."

- **What channels drove the most syndication?**—We know that Twitter tends to be a strong driving force for additional mentions, but was it really during the crisis? Or was Twitter just a megaphone for other people's content?

- **Did you have the right blend of original and static content?**—We mentioned earlier that it would be helpful to have some canned content at the ready, but you also need to be flexible enough to develop content based on how the news cycle develops. Did your mixture of new and old content work for you?

- **Did you achieve the volume you expected?**—You benchmarked the volume of conversation before the crisis, so you can see how much volume—generated by both you and other parties—occurred during the crisis.

Crises can be painful. However, if you take our advice, your crisis situation will be a little less painful. We promise. Utilizing social data before, during, and after a crisis can be invaluable in finding the right content mix, finding the right issues, finding the right channels, and, most importantly, protecting your brand from future attacks. What are you waiting for? Start tapping into social data today to prevent or mitigate the effects of a crisis tomorrow!

13

Improving Customer Service

We are living in an exciting and transformative business environment. Innovations in technology, such as social networking and communications mobility, have changed (and continue to change) consumer behavior—permanently. Consumer expectations have changed, too. These are not trivial changes; the changes define expectations about how companies market and sell products and services and also how customers are serviced and valued by the companies they do business with. The Internet has accelerated these changes like no other development. Online-only businesses, such as Zappos, have completely changed the game and raised the bar for customer experience and customer support. These expectations are not limited to Zappos or the category it does business in but rather have leaked into all industries. Consumers now expect companies to meet their needs on the customer's terms, not the company's.

As a result, you have to provide customer service and support in places where it might not already exist, across social media platforms such as Twitter or Facebook, and across mobile or tablet devices. Gone are the days when a company thought it could simply build out a call center to handle customer service via a toll-free number and keep customers satisfied. We live in a multichannel customer service world, including assistance via live agents on a brand website, email, social media outposts, and smartphone apps.

Why does this matter? It matters for many reasons, but we'll look at just two of most important ones. First, customers who have good customer service experiences are likely to purchase again, according to a December 2012 study from eMarketer titled, "Best Practices for Building Loyalty in Customer Service Experiences (see Figure 13.1)." There is no rocket science here: If companies are able to meet customer expectations and provide satisfactory outcomes during customer service experiences, the customers remain loyal to the brand. However, it's much easier said than done today, given the options customers have to engage with brands.

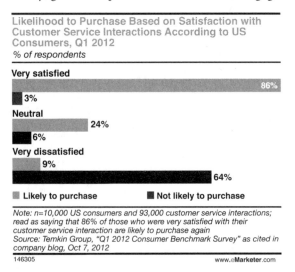

Figure 13.1   *eMarketer customer service survey from 2012.*

The second reason it's critical to deliver on customer expectations during a service experience is also nothing new: It's word of mouth. Both satisfied and unsatisfied customers tell other people about their experiences, positive and negative. Unsurprisingly, customers who have negative experiences tell *more* people. According to the 2012 Global Customer Service Barometer study conducted by American Express, customers who feel like they have a good customer service experience with a brand tell an average of 15 other people. On the other hand, customers who are disappointed with a customer service experience with a brand tell an average of 24 additional people. Combine those numbers with the fact that these consumers now live in a hyper-connected world, and it's easy to see how delivering exceptional customer service has never been more important to keeping current customers and acquiring new ones.

This is an easy sell to most companies, but successfully operationalizing it—and understanding where the opportunities are to gather insights that can improve customer service—can be complex. For starters, the fragmentation of media channels means customers have a plethora of choices in engaging with a company. The table in Figure 13.2 from the eMarketer study highlights the most common channels that customers use to obtain support.

Importance of Select Digital Channels Throughout Stages of the Purchase Process According to Online Shoppers Worldwide, April 2012
scale of 1-5*

	Awareness	Choice	Transaction	Delivery	After-sales care
Internet site	3.94	3.92	3.80	3.92	3.94
Email (such as newsletters, offers)	3.56	3.47	3.34	3.71	3.79
In-store technology (such as kiosks)	3.31	3.33	3.41	3.25	3.28
Social media	3.09	2.99	-	-	2.99
Smartphones (specific apps)	2.88	2.82	2.81	2.93	2.91
Phone (via call center)	2.67	2.63	2.70	2.87	3.08

Note: Australia, Brazil, Canada, China, Finland, France, Germany, India, Italy, Mexico, Russia, Spain, Sweden, Turkey, UK and US; *1="not at all important" and 5="extremely important"
Source: Capgemini, "Digital Shopper Relevancy: Profiting from Your Customers "Desired All-Channel Experience,"July 10, 2012

143535   www.e**Marketer**.com

Figure 13.2   *eMarketer customer service data on channel usage.*

What's most interesting in Figure 13.2 isn't the traditional leading channels but rather the trend that the data indicates: a shift away from established channels such as live agents, interactive voice recognition (IVR), and web self-service to emerging channels such as text/SMS messaging, social media, and mobile applications. What's the common denominator driving the shift? Immediacy. The ability for customers to "get my questions answered quickly" is the overwhelming reason (79%) for the shift from traditional customer service channels to emerging ones. Social networks and mobile media technologies have been so broadly adopted, across all major age groups, that it's altered customers' expectations for acceptable responses from the companies they do business with.

The second and third reasons customers prefer the group of emerging channels reveal key insights about the mindset of the modern-day consumer. Number two (51%) is "can multitask" and number three (46%) is "most efficient communication method." When you look at these data points holistically, you see that they reveal a trend for which you should develop a plan of action. Digital customers live in an always-on, instant-gratification world that provides practically unlimited choice. Catering to the customers' specific needs and channel preferences on how to best serve and support them is the only sustainable scenario. If companies don't remove barriers to efficient and effective customer service experiences, customers will abandon them for a competitor.

With some emerging channels, such as customer conversations and interactions on public social networks, data isn't locked in corporate databases behind a firewall but is freely available, both to a company and its competitors. Herein lies a unique opportunity to apply digital analytics to reveal hidden insights that you can use to improve customer service. Let's get into the details of what approaches are available to collect this information and look at some case studies of companies that have already extended their customer service initiatives into emerging media channels such as social networks.

The Social Customer Service Conflict

Despite the growing trend of consumers desiring customer service and issue resolution in new digital channels, most companies have been slow to embrace the opportunity and implement the necessary changes within their own organizations. Social media has changed everything when it comes to supporting customers. Customer service hours are different from standard corporate hours. When you add social media to that mix, it creates an environment where customers want and expect support when they need it. You can call it *ad hoc support* or *customer service on demand*. Whatever the name, the expectation is there, thanks to companies like Dell and Comcast, early pioneers in the area of experimenting with social media to help customers.

There is a conflict, and several obstacles must be overcome. Although an organization might aspire to provide social service to customers, some companies don't have the internal resources to support it. According to research on social media and customer service conducted by SAP and Social Media Today, more than 77% of companies currently invest less than $50,000 in social customer care. To put that number in context, consider that Fortune 100 companies spend hundreds of millions, even billions, on customer service and support programs. As of 2013, there is still a considerable lack of resources being allocated to social media with the purpose of formally providing customer service and issue resolution.

Another obstacle facing companies tackling social customer service is integration—or lack thereof. The proliferation of channels is exacerbating the silo problem that companies have. Customers don't want or need another digital silo. Companies bear the burden of integrating social service channels into traditional channels to ensure that customers are interacting with them using a single, continuous communications channel. For example, customers want to be able to start a conversation in one channel (such as Twitter) and have it seamlessly carry over to email or the brand website, without the need to start the conversation all over again. You've likely experienced this at one time or another, having been asked to provide your name, address, or account number redundantly after being transferred for the sixth time. This is a symptom of lack of integration. We revisit this topic in a case study later in the chapter.

Related to integration, the third obstacle is inefficiency. Most social service programs are still in their infancy and thus immature. They struggle with meeting customer expectations for response times, providing appropriate coverage (responding to all inquiries), and finding appropriate answers. Research from the Social Customer Engagement Index says that 66% of companies providing social service are responding within four hours or less to customer inquiries. The reasons for efficiency issues tell the real story, however. These are the top four reasons:

- Finding the answer (41%)
- Waiting for guidance on how to answer (34%)
- Finding the appropriate message to answer (27%)
- The current tool does not make it easy to respond (7%)

These issues indicate process, education, and training/policy issues within the company, not problems inherent in any social platform or technology. These specific issues have been addressed with traditional customer service channels such as call centers and live agents, and it's a matter of formally extending those more mature business processes into new channels and areas, such as social media and mobile technology. Later in the chapter, we look at how some companies are doing that, but first, let's dig beyond the obvious answer to why you should support customers in social channels. We look at the three main areas of opportunity to utilize digital analytics to improve customer service.

Beyond issue resolution, why should you support customers in digital and social channels? What's in it for the company, other than just a new expense? The answers are simple but present an incredibly powerful opportunity to learn and then optimize the customer experience to improve brand loyalty. The result is a longer-term relationship with the customer. The following sections describe three ways you can do this.

Understanding the Customer

Who is the customer? It's a simple question, but it's difficult to answer based on the data sources and research you use. Don't guess who the customer is; know! The tools covered in previous chapters enable you to use the appropriate digital service points to collect data about the individuals you're interacting with. Finding this information is critical because segmentation plays as important a role in customer service as it does in marketing and sales.

Recent data from OurSocialTimes.com (See Figure 13.3) demonstrates that demographics affect channel preferences for service and support. For example, younger age groups, filled with people who are digital natives, unsurprisingly skew higher toward using social media for customer service. In fact, 15% of consumers ages 16 to 24 prefer to interact with companies' customer service on social media over any other method. Three out of four people in this group indicate that the first thing they do when encountering a problem with a product is go online to find help. These percentages are lower for older age groups: 8% for people in the 25 to 34 age group and 5% for people between 35 and 44, but the numbers are growing overall. This trend isn't specific to the youngest group.

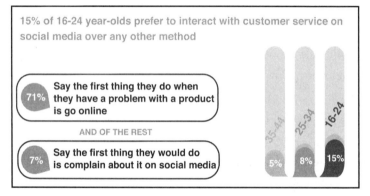

Figure 13.3   *Our Social Times customer service survey on demographic characteristics of social media users seeking customer support.*

Forrester's research on customer service interactions indicates that emerging channel usage has grown 18% for live chat, 20% for SMS, and 19% for Twitter. Applying digital analytics to precisely identify which channels your customers want to use is critical. You can't, and don't, need to provide service on all of the channels. Identify the ones that matter and then deploy them according to best practices for those channels.

Understanding Customer Intent

You don't need a sledgehammer to drive in a finishing nail. In customer service in digital channels, you need to use the right tool for the right job. You can use both social and web analytics to understand customer behavior on specific channels, and you can make changes to guide customers to the appropriate channels, depending on their issue. Twitter and Facebook might be great for time-sensitive, lower-complexity requests where email wouldn't be nearly as effective. Conversely, time-intensive or complex customer requests are better suited for live agents or web chat.

Performing an inventory on existing customer service requests and mapping out their complexity to channel likelihood for resolution can be a helpful exercise to prioritize decisions on what problems to solve and where. Maximize the value of the channel to deliver a satisfactory experience. Knowing what a customer came there for and wants to accomplish is key in doing so.

Personalizing the Customer Experience

Customers seek personalized service. It can be a point of differentiation in many categories. Knowing who the customer is and knowing her preferences (past purchase history, past service issues, communication needs) is easier if you're talking about a customer relationship management (CRM) database that supports a call center. What about personalization for a Twitter interaction? This requires a level of integration previously not asked of companies; it also requires connective tissue between customer databases, commerce platforms, product databases, recommendation engines, content management systems, and third-party social platforms. This is the emerging domain called *social CRM*, with players like Salesforce.com, Oracle, and Jive. We cover them in more detail in Chapter 21, "Social CRM."

Let's now begin to dig into the models or approaches companies have taken to provide social service and what aspects of those you may take for your own purposes to improve customer service for your organization.

Social Customer Service Models

It's appropriate here to introduce the idea of a maturity meter for customer service when describing the different approaches companies have taken to offer support in social media. A three-stage maturity model can be used to evaluate social service efforts. The three stages are ad hoc, limited, and enterprise. This section covers cases of different companies at each stage and describes the data and analytics available and how companies can utilize those to produce better customer service outcomes by understanding, more precisely, who their customers are and what they are trying to do.

The Ad Hoc Stage of Customer Service

Most companies take an ad hoc approach to social customer service at the onset. It often originates through the good intentions of a single individual within a company. In other cases, it starts for the opposite reason: The company is dragged into a social service interaction on Facebook by a vocal customer with immediate needs. The ad hoc stage is informal and inefficient in that it can't easily scale without major changes to address foundational gaps in the company. At this stage, companies do not have formal objectives, policies, and education internally. Data collection and analysis are minimal, if they exist at all. The priority is on handling frontline requests.

The Limited Stage of Customer Service

The limited stage of social customer service is more coordinated and organized than the ad hoc stage in that multiple individuals support the effort, and the company has a mechanism for more meaningful data collection and reporting. Some objectives have been set, and processes have been put in place, but this stage is still limited in that it lacks integration with the rest of the company, both culturally and systematically. The connective tissue described earlier, which is necessary to provide personalized customer service interactions between different data sources, is still missing at this stage. Data collection and analysis begin to emerge here, with an emphasis on counting activity—but that is not necessarily the most reliable indicator of customer satisfaction.

The Formal Stage of Customer Service

The formal stage of social customer service is full-scale support for all products and services across the company. It includes everything mentioned thus far, in addition to dedicated teams, governance, workflow, and crisis preparation. One of the most important distinctions between this and the other stages is the connection of different business units/groups within the company, which is an effort that directly increases coordination and efficiency and decreases duplication of efforts to resolve customer issues. This integration includes aggregation of data specific to customer satisfaction rather than social data and metrics associated with marketing or brand building.

The following section provides a specific example of a company that is serving and supporting customers in social environments.

Delta Air Lines

Airlines are easy targets for criticism about how they handle customer issues. However, Delta Air Lines deserves credit for embracing emerging trends and leveraging new communication channels (both social and mobile) to reduce customer issues and provide satisfactory responses more quickly and efficiently than it did in the past. Delta is a pioneer when it comes to social customer service. It was one of the first brands in the category to officially support customers on Twitter, and it was the first to implement a booking engine on Facebook as well. It has evolved its social customer service program over time as the company has learned what things work better than others. Like most other global brands, Delta is present on the social media outposts you'd expect: Facebook, Twitter, YouTube, a corporate blog, and more (see Figure 13.4).

Figure 13.4   *Delta's social media presence.*

Delta took a strategic approach when considering how to solve customer needs via social channels, and it decided to create something entirely new, dedicated to assisting customers via social media. In May 2010, @DeltaAssist was born. It looks different now than it did back in 2010, but the primary charge remains the same: "Serve as a way to interact and engage with customers in a meaningful way." @DeltaAssist was originally staffed with 4 customer service agents, officially providing answers Monday through Friday from 8:00 a.m. to 6:00 p.m. EST. That didn't last long, as customer issues don't punch a clock. The program has evolved and is now staffed by 15 agents who provide continuous coverage 24 hours a day, 7 days a week to resolve customer issues.

Any successful initiative begins with clearly defined objectives, and Delta is very specific about what assistance this social service program will and will not provide to customers. The following services are offered, and for each we show an example of a customer request and @DeltaAssist response:

- Answers to questions on policies and procedures (see Figure 13.5)

Claudia Valovic Owens

Why does Delta and other airlines advertize "compassion airfare" when in reality you don't make any concessions for people with a sick loved one? My mother is 92, sick and dying, and I am struggling to afford a flight from Boston to FT Lauderdale. You offered me $540 RT fare when I can get $318 on flight websites. I do not call that helping someone to fly to be with a sick relative.

Like · Comment · 14 hours ago

 Poley King The $540 is a discounted fully flexible ticket should needs ✕ change while you are in FL. The $318 fare is a restricted fare. if you know exactly what date you were coming back the standard fare is a better option. If your wrong about the return date the cheaper fare can cost alot more than the flexible ticket

4 hours ago · Like · 👍 2

Figure 13.5   *Delta policy for customer service online.*

- Travel help (for example, airport, online bookings, posttravel questions; see Figure 13.6)

 18 Frank Belford 13 @belfordfl   14 Dec

@DeltaAssist I was hoping you could help me change my seat on Dl811 tonight. Currently in 15e but I see 17F is open

Retweeted by Delta Assist

Expand

Figure 13.6   *Delta assistance customer service through social media.*

- Rebooking assistance, which is incredibly convenient and worth using if you fly Delta

- Complaint resolution (see Figure 13.7)

 65 Delta Assist 48 @DeltaAssist   27 Aug

@GALDYTROIN I understand your frustration & I'm sorry that this has happened. Was the gear damaged during baggage handling? ^TW

Expand

Figure 13.7   *Complaint resolution by Delta online.*

- Random/fun information and answers to questions (see Figure 13.8)

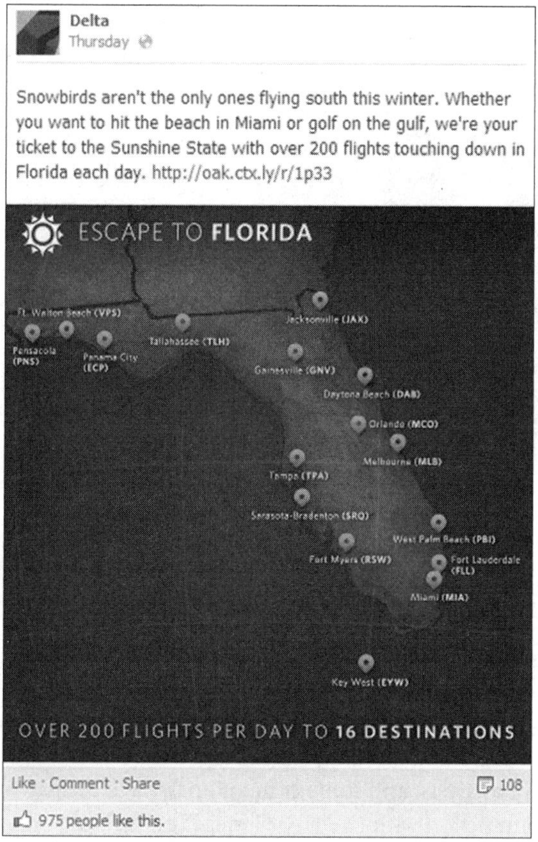

Figure 13.8 *Delta's use of social customer service includes fun information.*

One of the benefits of having a single dedicated account for serving customers is clarity and responsiveness. By funneling all customer service requests online to the @DeltaAssist handle, Delta has reduced response time considerably. A study done by WaveMetrix in September 2012 demonstrates just how much response time has been reduced. WaveMetrix compared Delta with four other airlines (see Figure 13.9) to determine which companies have the most timely responses to tweets. Delta easily won on responsiveness. There is an added benefit to having the separate handles: Because all customer issues are directed to @DeltaAssist, the main social profiles for the Delta brand are not littered with customer posts about complaints or problems. This all but ensures that Delta will have the lowest response time unless a competitor copies Delta's approach and validates Delta's operational structure for having a dedicated team of agents supporting social media.

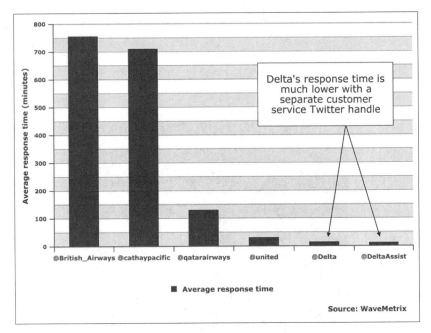

Figure 13.9 *WaveMetrix's comparison of airlines' tweet response times.*

Initially, the data and metrics that Delta collected were limited to counting activity. Metrics included such things as overall volume of mentions of Delta, automated sentiment analysis, and some content analysis to identify key topics being discussed in conjunction with Delta Air Lines. You can see some of this detail in Figure 13.10, which is output from the Visible Intelligence platform. For more information on Visible Intelligence and its features, please read Chapter 7, "Tools: Content Analysis."

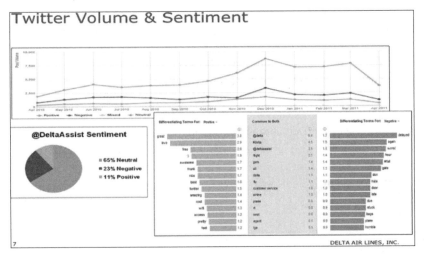

Figure 13.10 *Delta's metrics for social customer service.*

As we've discussed throughout the book, it's essential to align social goals to business goals in order to enable the development of a relevant measurement strategy. Over time, Delta has matured and evolved its own social customer service measurement approach to be consistent with how the company measures customer service effectiveness. Instead of relying only on total volume of mentions, tweets, and followers, the health of the @DeltaAssist initiative is viewed through the same lens as the traditional customer service channels in the company. Specific metrics such as resolution rate, response rate, and compliments are key performance indicators (KPIs) that are tracked each month. The volume of inbound requests is part of that, but it is not a true indicator of how @DeltaAssist contributes to keeping customers happy.

14

Launching a New Product

Launching a new product is not an easy task for any company, even for the big brands like P&G and Coca-Cola. In most cases, the market, regardless of category, is saturated, and consumers are creatures of habit. According to strategic brand positioning expert and consultant Jack Trout, consumers repeatedly buy the same 150 items, which constitute as much as 85% of their household needs. In addition, only 3% of new consumer packaged goods meet or exceed their first-year sales goals. Product launches fail for a variety of reasons, but a large percentage of them can be attributed to lack of preparation by the company.

Some of the reasons product launches fail are internal issues within a company, such as the inability to support fast growth after a product gains some traction in the market. Or a product might be truly original and revolutionary, but the company finds there isn't a market for it. (Segway personal transporters are a good example of this.) Most common is a scenario in which consumers feel that a product has failed to live up to its claims and/or benefits, and so the product receives harsh criticism and consumer bashing. Microsoft suffered through this in 2007, when it launched Windows Vista, with exceedingly high consumer expectations. Unfortunately for Microsoft, Vista was littered with so many compatibility and performance issues that even loyal Microsoft customers rejected it and viewed it as a massive failure. (This failure created the opportunity for Apple to run its "I'm a Mac" advertising campaign.)

Having a clear understanding of where new opportunity exists in a market depends on knowing consumer needs, wants, and preferences. This is absolutely crucial to new product success, and failure to do due diligence, where possible, to gather insights is akin to failing to prepare and increases the likelihood of mistakes and missing the mark during product launch.

Failing to conduct due diligence is not a one-time problem, either. Products that start out strong can quickly have trouble remaining successful during a growth phase. Before we talk about how to apply some of the digital analytics capabilities discussed earlier in the book, it's worth spending some time looking at the product lifecycle. Understanding the different phases of the product lifecycle and what you need to do in each one, from a marketing and/or advertising perspective, will provide a structured approach to guide your decision making on how and when to best apply digital analytics capabilities in the support of any product initiative. Let's take a look at the product lifecycle.

General Overview of the Product Lifecycle

The concept of a product lifecycle is essential to any professional in marketing, and it's taught as part of the curriculum in many degree programs. However, it needs to be augmented by appropriate digital analytics capabilities at specific phases to truly help you make informed marketing decisions. Essentially, any product goes through a lifecycle that has the phases shown in Figure 14.1. Within each of these phases, companies alter their marketing mix (product, pricing, distribution, and promotion) to account for the unique challenges faced within each phase:

- **Development**—Development is an internal phase that some omit completely when discussing this concept. During this phase, the product is being developed and made ready for release to consumers. At this point, the product is not in the market.

- **Introduction**—During this phase, the product is launched to the market, with the goals of generating awareness and achieving market penetration. Basically, the company is establishing a foothold for the product in the category.

- **Growth**—After the product has been accepted by the market, the company seeks to build brand favorability and increase market share.

- **Maturity**—At this stage, aggressive growth is no longer possible, as the category has matured and competitors offer similar products. The company seeks to defend its market share and maximize its profit margin.

- **Decline**—Inevitably, sales decline because a product is less desirable among consumers. The company must decide to either discontinue the product or relaunch it with new features and benefits.

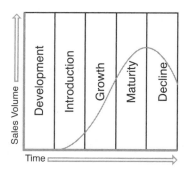

Figure 14.1 *The product lifecycle.*

The opportunities to reduce risk and refine product marketing initiatives are realized through preparation and continuous optimization. Fortunately, you now have the ability to accomplish these things because the consumers you're trying to reach are hyper-connected and have a propensity to share their product opinions and brand experiences across the digital landscape. By harnessing digital analytics capabilities, specifically social listening and search analysis, you can begin to improve your understanding of what the consumers you're trying to reach truly think, want, need, and expect from your brand and your competitors. (After all, open data cuts both ways.)

In this chapter, our approach has a goal of shifting (upward) product diffusion curves across the entire lifecycle by capturing deep consumer insights that enable you to make the necessary optimizations or course corrections. The diffusion curve is represented by the top line spanning all of the phases in Figure 14.2. Digital analytics can help you realize the goal of optimizing a new product launch by capturing consumer feedback and behavior and distilling it down into specific answers that ultimately tie back to product success or failure.

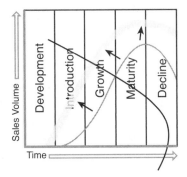

Figure 14.2 *New product launch—diffusion curve.*

The following sections outline each of the middle three product lifecycle phases. We provide unique considerations for each, along with the specific digital analytics you should consider as you answer specific questions associated with the goals and challenges for each phase.

The Product Lifecycle Introduction Phase

Recall that during the introduction phase, the product is introduced into the wild. (See Figure 14.3.) During development, assumptions have been made about the target audience, how the audience will perceive the new product, how the product is positioned to address specific end customers, and the value the product will provide to users. These assumptions will have been thoroughly examined, discussed, and vetted internally prior to launch. That said, they are simply hypotheses based on the best data available during the development phase.

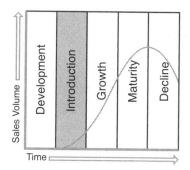

Figure 14.3   *The introduction phase of the product lifecycle.*

The rubber meets the road when a product is launched, so there likely isn't a more important time to be collecting and analyzing consumer data and feedback about the product, as well as the specific product attributes that you've positioned in your marketing mix and messaging. This analysis will enable you to identify bad assumptions and make adjustments as quickly as possible, as well as identify new opportunities that weren't discovered during the product development phase.

As mentioned in the preceding section, the introduction phase has fairly simple business objectives:

- Generate awareness.
- Establish a foothold in the market.

You need some initial considerations (the "what") as a starting point to guide the activities you'll perform (the "how") to generate the outcomes and benefits of this analysis (the "why"). The following are some examples of considerations in the introduction phase:

- What are the emerging trends in the category regarding new product usage and repurposing? What trends are developing?
- What factors of influence are fueling consumer advocacy for Product X's new usage?
- What are the consumer likes/dislikes about current promotions and offers? Which promotion/offer channels have the most impact on consumers?
- Where do consumers find the most utility for Product X?
- Which meal occasions are the most relevant for Product X? Why?

Figure 14.4 lists activities that revolve around collecting, tracking, and monitoring key performance indicators and consumer feedback throughout the introduction phase, by customer segment (if applicable).

Activities: (how)

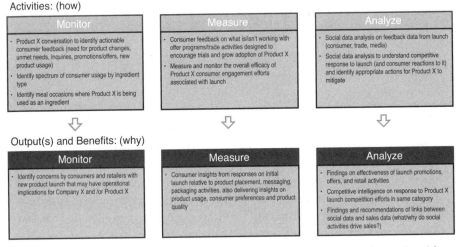

Output(s) and Benefits: (why)

Figure 14.4 *Examples of activities during the introduction phase of the product life-cycle.*

Let's apply social listening analysis to solve this problem and capture data that can help you understand if you're generating awareness and penetrating the market to effectively lead to sales. The first step is planning. Remember that you get out of social listening what you put into it. A concrete and specific plan will yield detailed insights that you can actually act on. Let's walk through a hypothetical scenario in which you will generate a learning agenda (covered in previous chapters) for a mainstream consumer household product you might buy from a company such as P&G, Kraft, or General Mills. The following sections examine some of the broad questions you might want to answer after a product launch.

What Is the Consumer Reaction to Product X?

Are consumers responding favorably to their initial exposure to the product? Are there specific product attributes they like/dislike? Are there specific product attributes they prefer over others or prefer against competitors? Specific queries can be created within your social listening tool to reveal consumer conversations that answer these questions. This specificity, when combined with sentiment analysis, can produce insightful findings.

It's not enough to count mentions of the new product, use automated sentiment analysis, spit out the answer, and call it a day. That might produce eye-candy charts, but it won't generate anything the business can use to validate that a new product launch is heading down the right path in terms of acceptance or to point out a fatal flaw. It's more effective, yet more time-consuming, to break down the "consumer reaction" according to the specific product attributes and any key messaging being used in the marketing and advertising of the product.

In this example, Product X—a cooking ingredient, let's say—has four specific key attributes. Consumers are reacting favorably to the first three (for example, taste, price/value, quality) but unfavorably to the fourth, a new use for the product (for example, as a cooking ingredient). The product's growth strategy might rely on positive consumer reaction to the new use. It's imperative to monitor this closely and not let the overall picture (three out of four positives) alter consumer perspective on that specific product attribute.

In summary, remember to think critically about both product performance and market acceptance as a whole but also about product attributes that are strategically important to both the short- and long-term business plans.

What Are the Consumer Concerns About Product X?

This is an important question to answer, but it is one that is difficult to predict ahead of time. What specifically should you be using to find and collect the relevant consumer conversations? Our experience has shown that it's an organic activity that is best done after you've already performed social listening and analysis about general consumer reaction (as described in the previous section). The reason for this is simple: You don't know what you don't know.

You can identify certain categories ahead of time, but there are always some categories (sometimes a few, sometimes many) that weren't on the radar earlier and need to be factored into your plans, based on how consumers are reacting. As described in Chapter 4, "Tools: Social Listening," about segmentation of social listening data is key. Your data for Product X can be first categorized into a bucket for "consumer concerns." Within that data set, you can further refine the data into subsets of concerns. For example, the concerns could be extensions of the four attributes we listed earlier. Detailed analysis of the fourth attribute (a new use as a cooking ingredient) could possibly reveal that awareness is high for the new use for the product, but the actual experience is poor. Consumers could be citing issues with inconvenient packaging or saying that the product itself isn't living up to the new use claims (as in the Microsoft Vista example). Perhaps Product X isn't moist enough and needs to be reformulated.

These are examples of the specific types of consumer feedback that can be gathered and applied to product attributes, in sufficient detail, to take action. You don't necessarily need to change the product. It could just as easily be that the target audience in this case needs education about the new product use and the content/messaging in the marketing and advertising needs to be adjusted to clarify and eliminate any confusion in the minds of the consumers.

What Are the Consumer's Unmet Needs?

Meeting consumer needs is obviously critical, but identifying those needs can be tricky. This is another activity best performed after your broader consumer reaction data collection has been done. Trying to predict unmet needs and search for consumer conversations via social listening tools is difficult because of the previously mentioned "don't know what you don't know" condition. The broad search will collect all types of reactions/conversations about the product. After the segmentation has been done, there will be a set of data that just doesn't fit into another category. Call it miscellaneous or other—the label doesn't matter. This is often one of the most revealing areas for identifying unmet needs. Consumers will provide opinions and ideas that don't fit neatly into another category. Taking the time to perform a qualitative analysis on this data set is worth doing and may very well uncover that elusive diamond in the rough.

The Product Lifecycle Growth Phase

In the growth phase of the product lifecycle (see Figure 14.5), the market has accepted the new product, and it's a race to grow and build market share. Here, the goal is not to generate awareness, because that has been done, but to differentiate the product in the category, building brand preference and capturing customers from competitors. This is more difficult, and the challenges associated with this phase are very different from those in the introduction phase.

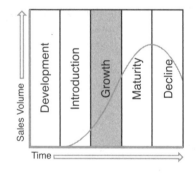

Figure 14.5   *The growth phase of the product lifecycle.*

This phase focuses on the triggers that are responsible for generating product advocacy, brand favorability, and adoption among the target audience. Knowing how and why these triggers occur can reveal how to fuel them through marketing and advertising efforts, which in turn drives growth. Robust analysis helps you clarify the appropriate marketing mix to deploy during the growth phase in order to achieve your growth objectives.

As in the introduction phase, you need some initial considerations (the "what") as a starting point to guide the activities you perform (the "how") to generate the outcomes and benefits of the analysis (the "why").

The following are some examples of considerations in the growth phase:

- What online communities and dynamics are shaping the conversation about Product X and driving incremental adoption of cooking by consumers with Product X?
- What efforts can be made to fuel/grow customer advocacy within these communities?
- Which events and/or triggers are responsible for generating spikes in conversation about Product X? What can the company do to increase the volume of these triggers?
- How do these spikes in conversation correlate to sales of Product X?
- What is the appropriate media mix to drive growth and adoption?

Figure 14.6 lists activities that revolve around monitoring and measuring both consumer and retailer promotional efficacies to identify optimal marketing and engagement levers across specific marketing channels. Applying social listening can help play a significant role in solving any issues while also enabling your organization to understand how to drive product promotions. Effectively following the trends in social conversations can enable you to introduce marketing strategies and tactics to drive spikes in advocacy that eventually could lead to further sales.

Activities: (how)

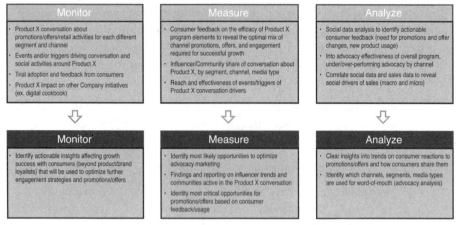

Figure 14.6   *Examples of activities during the growth phase of the product lifecycle.*

Again, the first step is planning. Let's continue with our example of Product X and generate a specific learning agenda that supports the growth phase. The following sections examine the broad questions you might want to answer in a growth scenario.

What Are the Communities, Sites, and Social Platforms in Which Product X Is Being Discussed, Shared, and Evaluated?

Engagement is one thing, and activity on any social platform is another. What's important to take away from both engagement and activity is understanding what advocacy looks like for your product/brand within that engagement and activity and to identify the strongest sources of that advocacy. It's important to remember the goal and to identify insights, trends, or patterns that can be fueled to emerge in other areas of the market. This will drive direct sales growth and also generate more advocacy, which in turn drives future growth.

When we use the term *advocacy*, we are using a particular definition. Many of the social listening and analytics tools covered in this book provide the ability to identify advocates or influencers using their own formulas/secret sauces. That's okay, as each one has pros. In this case, however, we're focused less on identifying a specific individual advocate and more about the source of that advocacy (what caused it) and where it occurred (the source).

For example, there are several potential sources of advocacy, such as ratings and reviews on Yelp and other similar sites, as well as sharing and endorsements of coupons and special offers across social platforms like Facebook, Twitter, or

Pinterest. Was it the positive review about the quality of Product X (a specific attribute, not the product as a whole) that drove new interest and consideration? Or was it the discounted offer for first-time buyers that was shared heavily on Facebook? Assessing qualitative feedback from consumers via social listening data and comparing it with quantitative data from social sharing of offers and coupons will help you find the answer.

These are a few of many potential sources that play an important role in the brand marketing mix when you're attempting to achieve growth through acquiring customers. You need to understand which sources to ignore and which ones to double down on, in terms of investment to fuel more growth. For that you need to create and develop specific channel tactics, but doing so will help you optimize the entire marketing mix, from a strategic perspective.

Who Are the Influencers in the Product X Conversation?

This question is related to the previous question, but it's unique. We don't cover this in great detail here; read Chapter 9, Tools: Influence Analysis," for more information. It's a point worth mentioning here, though, because an outreach program might be a component for driving growth, particularly in an established category. There may be a set of key influencers on topics relevant to your product who can play a role in driving growth through word of mouth to their followers, thus reaching friends of friends, who are consumers not currently exposed to your brand and/or product. For details on how to approach this, revisit Chapter 9.

What Is the Consumer Reaction to Retail/Promotions for Product X?

Brands discount heavily to lure new buyers in many categories, and this one is no different. However, each promotion is trying to resonate across a specific product attribute or set of product attributes to entice new customers. Is it all about the quality of the product, the best possible ingredients? Or is it a balance of price and value? The buyer wants to feel like the value and benefits are there for a reasonable price. Targeting promotions highlighting different product attributes across different segments of the target audience is a complex process.

It's not about the numbers or conversions associated with each promotion. Those are obviously key inputs for assessing marketing performance. However, the role of social listening in this phase, and the theme throughout this chapter, is to give brands a tool or mechanism to capture consumer opinions and attitudes about specific promotions in order to optimize their promotional marketing mix. That might mean changing where certain promotions are being executed or the specific language and pricing associated with a promotion.

In the example of Product X, the conversation associated with promotions cover many subtopics, but the common ones revolve around the following categories:

- **Product evaluation**—Consumers express intent or consideration for trial, to give the product a chance.

- **Sales**—Consumers share specific offers or coupons with their friends, along with their opinion of the value of an offer relative to the product.

- **Recipes**—Consumers share or describe their planned or favorite recipes for the product, along with the promotion.

- **Nutrition**—Consumers share nutritional information about the product, including their opinion on the health benefits of the product (or lack thereof).

- **Consumption**—Consumers share their favorite ways to consume/use the product (snack, in certain dishes, and so on).

- **Other/misc.**—Consumers share something related to the promotion that doesn't fall into the other five categories. As indicated earlier, this category can be a rich source of insights for unmet needs or unanticipated uses. Do not discard this data without analysis just because it looks minimally useful in an unattractive category. Dig in and explore.

The Product Lifecycle Maturity Phase

In the maturity phase of the product lifecycle (see Figure 14.7), the product strategy is simple: "Defend your turf." This means staving off threats from mature competitors that offer similar products and squeezing every cent out of each transaction to maximize profit margins. Competitors might introduce new features to differentiate their product from yours. Keeping an eye on consumer reactions to competitors and how they view differentiation is a high priority in this phase. Another important area of focus is understanding what changes have occurred since the product introduction and growth phases. It's important to understand what has changed from the baseline data and benchmarking regarding consumer awareness of the brand and product, consideration and intent to purchase the product, brand loyalty, and even sentiment of specific product attributes. Have those changed over time, and, in the maturity phase, are they declining? If so, why?

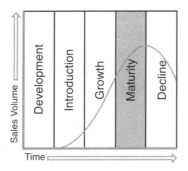

Figure 14.7 *The maturity phase of the product lifecycle.*

Another possible way to extend the maturity phase of a product for longer volume and sales is to utilize cross-selling opportunities with other products in the company's portfolio. What products could be packaged together for combination sales? How do consumers view the various packaging options, and are they helping extend the mature product's sales?

As with the other phases, we establish initial considerations (the "what") as a starting point to guide the activities you'll perform (the "how") to generate the outcomes and benefits of this analysis (the "why").

The following are some sample considerations in the maturity phase:

- What activities are most commonly performed and/or discussed among consumers that can be highlighted to extend the length of the maturity phase for Product X?
- What consumer trends and preferences have emerged for Product X? Of these, what has changed from the original data, baselines, and assumptions?
- What topics should the company monitor continuously throughout the maturity phase for Product X?
- What key brand advocates and influencers have emerged in the maturity phase, and how should they be engaged moving forward?
- What other related products do consumers show interest in that could be opportunities for combination meals and occasions (cross-selling)?
- What are consumers saying about direct competitors and their products? Are they citing any perceived differentiation or new features?

Figure 14.8 lists activities that revolve around identifying aspects of consumer attitudes that identify relationships between components of Product X program and business performance, with a focus on maximizing sales volume and closely monitoring competitors. Again, the first step is planning. Let's continue with our Product X example and generate a specific learning agenda that supports the maturity phase.

The following sections examine some of the broad consumer questions that were asked in the initial product introduction phase to understand changes in the market and consumer attitudes about the product.

Activities: (how)

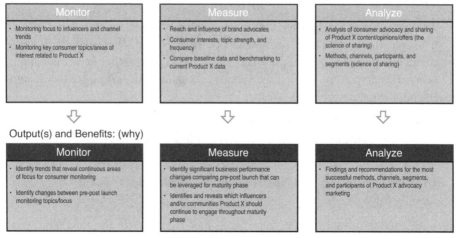

Figure 14.8 *Examples of activities during the maturity phase of the product lifecycle.*

What Consumer Trends and Preferences Have Emerged Around Product X Use?

When we walked through the introduction phase earlier in this chapter, we looked at important aspects of how consumers are reacting to the product and product attributes that we made a point to collect and analyze. You use this baseline information to build a marketing mix and a go-to-market strategy for the relevant channels. As mentioned previously, consumer attitudes, opinions, and behaviors change over time. The information distilled from the introduction phase has a shelf life. It expires, and you must gather and compare new information against the original to understand changes and trends that directly affect the length and duration of the Product X maturity phase.

This means dusting off those queries in your social listening tool and using them as a starting point for this phase. You might need to make tweaks and edits to refine the focus, but the exceptions will be minor.

What Related Products Do Consumers Show Interest In?

For a company with a diverse, yet related, product portfolio, determining what related products consumers are interested in can help extend the life of a mature product. The focus is on trying to collect data on any related uses and topics consumers associate with conversations about Product X and to identify any potential complementary products that can be combined into a more attractive package.

For example, Product X could be paired with other cooking ingredients to make a variety of recipes. Are consumers talking about specific recipes or ingredient pairings that coincide with any products in the current portfolio? Such conversations provide opportunities to examine in this phase. Any social listening tool will suffice, as the ability to capture relevant consumer conversations, and thus data, is dependent on the specificity and relevance of your search queries, not the technology or the tool.

Conclusion

This chapter has described an approach you can adopt to harvest relevant consumer feedback about your product, regardless of where it falls in the lifecycle. This information, while not the end-all, be-all, can have tremendous value. It can also be used to make near real-time optimizations to marketing and advertising campaigns or identify how competitive products are getting a leg up on you in the minds of consumers, based on differentiated positioning and relevance to consumer demands.

Will everything you find be valuable to your brand or product marketing? Absolutely not. We hope you understand that the approach described here is yet another key way to capture critically important consumer feedback about a product throughout the course of its lifecycle. You should not rely on it as the single source of truth but should combine it with other product feedback and consumer data to paint a comprehensive picture of product performance against consumer attitudes and needs. In the next chapter, you'll discover more about how to formulate your research plan.

15

Formulating Your Research Plan

Throughout this book, we have dissected all the various tools you can use to gather and analyze social, search, and engagement data. Chapters 4 through 9 deal with everything from picking a social listening provider to understanding the current digital influence toolset. Understanding the available tools, the pros and cons of each, how to pick them, and how to eventually use them is critical.

However, understanding the tool landscape is only one part of the puzzle. Companies of all sizes are also looking to use cases. If a company is to select a tool like Radian6, for example, how can it expect to use it? Similarly, how are other companies utilizing tools like Radian6? In Chapters 11 through 14 we have drilled into such use cases. Those use cases range from very basic—such as using data for marketing programs—all the way to more advanced—such as using listening to inform new product launches.

It is important to lay the foundational elements as explained in the first several chapters. Our experience shows that companies still are not clear on how to select tools, analyze data, and then apply it. They are weighed down by the amount of available data and the lack of internal headcount that is required to push a digital analytics agenda forward. The first few chapters of this book have shown you a clear roadmap for not only tool selection but how you can ultimately use the data you're collecting.

Those chapters are also the foundational elements for the next several chapters in the book. In the following sections, we dive deeper into developing reports for manageable consumption, building out a best-practice scorecard, and understanding how this all ladders up the holy grail of return on investment (ROI).

A critical part of any digital analysis is a research plan. You don't need to have a panic attack. This is not a return to your high school science class, but it is a critical step to informing your eventual reporting. In Chapters 4 and 10, we discussed social media listening and talked at length about properly scoping your program. This research plan is how you do just that. Without such a plan, your listening (or, really, any form of digital analysis) has the possibility of being unclear and unusable. Where do you begin? The research plan starts and ends with sources and methods.

Developing Your Source List

One of the reasons we have focused on several different kinds of digital analytics tools in this book is that we firmly believe in the interplay between the various channels. Developing a new piece of content for your website can affect search, social, and paid media programs. Similarly, social media activities can have a profound effect on search visibility and can provide valuable input to the development of paid media programs.

Think about it for a moment: If you do a Google search for your name, what typically appears? The social networks you are currently using, right? On occasion, you also see a particular piece of content near the top of the results. Social media affects searching and vice versa. In Chapters 6, 7, and 8 we talk at length about using tools to assess your audience, content, and engagement efforts. Using data from those tools in combination with social media listening data can be very powerful.

We don't want to belabor the point, but it is important to understand that we are talking about digital media for a reason. All the types of digital media, social media included, rely on each other to deliver maximum value for the brand. When you are developing your research plan, you should take into consideration all digital media.

The first step in developing the plan is to identify your sources. (Well, really, the first step is to identify your goals, but we assume that you've already done that.) As we've mentioned several times throughout the book, in addition to having a lot of data available to you, there are many tools you could potentially select for the job. We assume that if you have reached the point of developing a research plan, you have already selected your tools. If you haven't, though, go back and read Chapters 4 through 9 before finishing this chapter. Next, we dig into each of the pieces of the source list.

Identifying Data Sources

This is likely to be very obvious, but a critical part of a research plan is identifying your data sources. Again, the data can come from a number of digital analytics tools. We do not necessarily have a preference, as each tool has strengths and weaknesses, and all have different roles. In addition, you should take into account the goals of your program. For example, if it is a traditional public relations activity, some of these tools might not apply.

Although each tool has different strengths and weaknesses, there is a standard toolkit that you should assemble when building your research plan, including the following things:

- **Social media listening tools**—You expected this one, right? Social media listening is one of the hottest things in social media marketing today. It offers tremendous insight into how your customers behave online. Whether you are planning to use Sysomos or Radian6, your research plan should include gathering data from this source. If you need guidance on which tool to pick, go back to Chapter 4, "Tools: Social Listening," for a more detailed analysis.

- **Search tools**—In Chapter 5, "Tools: Search Analytics," we talk about search analytics tools, and in the lead-up to this section, we talk at length about the interplay of digital media. Search and social media are inextricably linked. One of the most popular search analytics tools is Google Insights, and it should be in your research plan toolbox. Google AdWords is another possibility, especially if you are trying to assess keyword possibilities and overall volume.

- **Social network insights**—Facebook Insights and YouTube Insights, for example, are great sources of data if you are conducting an analysis of social conversations and how each of those networks has performed for the brand. Typically, we have used the data provided by these insights platforms as a good compliment to data and insights derived from reading social conversations. This is particularly helpful if you are trying to understand whether top-performing content themes on

Facebook match top social media conversation themes on other platforms.

- **Traditional media monitoring tools**—Traditional media monitoring is not the focus of this book, obviously, as we are focusing on digital monitoring, but it can be an important tool in your toolset. Social media monitoring tools capture a significant number of online news sites, but tools such as Factiva and Cision have even greater news media capture capabilities.

- **Engagement tools**—Again, this applies only if you are using one of the tools identified in Chapter 8, "Tools: Engagement Analysis." As with social networking insights data, the data provided by engagement tools can provide a window into how content themes match up across channels.

These are not the only data sources, obviously, but they are the most popularly used sources. Remember that not every tool is required for every job. Think about the overall goal of the program and your research before narrowing down the tool selection.

Picking the Channels for Analysis

After you have selected your data sources, the second most important step is picking the channels you are going to analyze. Picking the channels is not as simple as saying you are going to track everything. If you glean nothing else from this book, we hope you take away that providing proper scope around what you are collecting leads to better insights.

What do we mean by picking the channels for analysis? When you are developing your research plan, we want you to figure out whether you are going to track only blogs, for example. If you are planning to use this data to inform a traditional public relations program, then maybe you only want to utilize news. Here are some channels that are typically analyzed when conducting this type of research:

- **News**—News outlets are the usual suspects that you should be familiar with by now. *The New York Times*, *Wall Street Journal*, and *USA Today* are examples.

- **Blogs**—It is becoming increasingly difficult to discern a blog from a news outlet these days, but blogs are the most common channel identified for developing research plans.

- **Comments**—Blog and news comments can also be a source of conversation data to analyze, as well as fodder for the research plan.

- **Groups or forums**—These are often closed networks of people who are talking about single, or related, subjects online. A good example of a group or forum is Babycenter.com, which is dedicated to all things "mom."

- **Twitter**—Twitter is one of the most common channels analyzed, as brands of all sizes attempt to determine how it can be best leveraged. It is also typically a large source of mentions for brands. One thing to note, though, is that not every tool pulls in the entirety of Twitter mentions. See Chapter 4 for a more detailed discussion.

- **Facebook**—In the same camp as Twitter, Facebook is one of the channels most commonly included in research plans. It's important to understand, however, that listening tools do not capture all available Facebook content. They only pull in what is publicly available. So, if you are including Facebook in your analysis, it is important to denote that Facebook volumes may be higher, but data is currently unavailable.

- **Video/images**—As the importance of visual content grows, so will the importance of tracking video and image sites such as YouTube and Flickr.

Depending on your business and research goals, these channels might vary. Do not feel obligated to track them all. Only track those that help you meet your goals.

Identifying Search and Source Languages

Identifying what search parameters and source languages you will use has as much variability in the research plan as any we have talked about so far. One of the reasons there is so much variability is that there is a lack of clarity around what tools to utilize in what markets. In Chapter 4, we talk a little bit about global listening tools—such as Brandwatch and Brandtology—but those tools are the new frontier of social media listening.

The other reason for the variability is available resources. *Resources* in this case can refer to money and human resources. There are not many people floating around who have experience conducting global listening, especially in the more remote parts of the world. Tools such as Brandwatch and Brandtology can be expensive, depending on the markets and languages you are planning to analyze.

Most tools, though, have relatively strong capabilities in markets outside of North America, if you are trying to gather English-only mentions. In almost every case, companies start with global English and expand from there. Organizations with heavy operations overseas need to think about global analytics. Where is a good place to start?

It probably does not make sense for your organization to listen to every language around the globe. Nor would it make sense for your organization to monitor every country's activity. The most sensible place to begin is by narrowing down to the markets in which you currently do business. From there, you can select the right tool(s) to gather that data. If that isn't an option, another possibility is to narrow down by a specific set of languages.

According to Common Sense Advisory, there are 12 languages that reach 80% of the world's online population. Chinese is the most prominent language, reaching almost 23% of the world's online population. English is second, with almost 22%. If you are looking to conduct global analytics, these are the other languages you should be capturing:

- Spanish
- Japanese
- Portuguese
- Arabic
- German
- Russian
- French
- Indonesian
- Korean
- Italian

It is not imperative for you to capture all these languages, certainly, but this list is a good starting place if you are launching a global analytics project. After you have identified the data sources, the languages for analysis, and the channels for analysis, you have completed about half of your research plan. The next step is to clearly define the methods for the analysis.

Nailing Down the Research Methods

A critical part of a research plan is the research methods you will utilize after the data has been identified and gathered. In the first part of this chapter, we talk about what the right data sources are and which languages and channels you should capture. That is only part of the equation. It is a critical part of the process, obviously, but without a consistent set of methods, the analysis or project can fall apart.

Several components are involved in finalizing your research methods:

- **Hypothesis**—Do not worry about whether your science teacher is looking over your shoulder and grading your hypothesis, but it is important to have some general statements about what you are expecting to see in the analysis.

- **Time frame for analysis**—It is not practical to gather all the available information on the Internet. Nor is it practical to gather information for all time. You need to select a specific time frame in order to properly scope your analysis.

- **Project team**—Not everyone in the organization is going to be involved with your research project, so it's important to clearly define roles.

- **Depth of analysis**—It might sound like we are beating a dead horse, but the amount of data available to you is incredible. Because of the volume of information, your analysis can be very granular. Before you start analyzing the data, determine how deep you want to go with the project.

- **Coding framework**—You should have a standard approach to coding mentions or pieces of data as you are conducting the analysis. By coding, we simply mean noting the topic mentioned in the post, the sentiment of the post, or the location of the post (blogs, Twitter, forums, and so on).

- **Sentiment approach**—How people are talking about your brand online (positive, negative, or neutral) is important. Is it the most important metric? No, it is not that important in every case. If you have a consumer brand, though, it might be very important to understand. As with the coding framework, you should have a standard approach to measuring sentiment; otherwise, the results could be inaccurate.

- **Spam/bot filtering**—Because of the way the tools we have talked about in previous chapters work (that is, using keywords to gather information on the Internet), you are likely to capture mentions that you do not care about or that are spam. Before conducting the analysis, your team should have a clear understanding of how to treat those mentions.

Over the course of the next several sections, we dive into each of these components in more detail.

Developing a Hypothesis

The hypothesis development process is the single best way to ensure that your research is focused. Without a clearly defined hypothesis, you could end up producing a research report that does not tell a clear story. It does not need to be a hypothesis in the way that you learned all throughout your high school and collegiate education, but it needs to be a statement you can use to guide the data collection and analysis processes.

Simply put, a hypothesis is a proposed explanation for some kind of phenomenon. There are several kinds of hypotheses, but the most common form is the scientific hypothesis. A scientific hypothesis can be tested using the scientific method.

This book does not include a discussion of the scientific method (consult your old textbooks if you would like to take that trip down memory lane), but it is important to note that the hypotheses that you develop for your digital analytics programs should be testable. That is, it should be a statement (or statements) that you can prove or disprove using data.

What is the most important element of a hypothesis? Simply put, unless you have outlined the behavior you are trying to analyze, your hypothesis is incomplete. The following are a few examples of hypotheses you might come up with:

- Conversations mentioning the brand are taking place in news and blogs, and they are not representative of our target audience.
- Corporate responsibility mentions will be the most referenced messaging pillar from the list of five core messages.
- Overall sentiment about the brand will be neutral to positive.
- People talking about our brand online will be offering new product ideas or requesting a heightened level of customer service.
- Industry conversation themes will be in alignment with the brand's messaging pillars.

✉ *Note*

These are just five examples of potential hypotheses. Note that these hypotheses do not apply to a specific brand, and you should consider your own situation before developing a hypothesis statement. Do not fall into the lazy marketer trap of copying and pasting what we have listed here.

Those statements seem straightforward, right? It should be relatively easy to develop hypotheses for your brand. However, if you are struggling to develop your own brand's hypotheses, what can you do? Try the following:

- **Preliminary research**—You probably have a set of media-monitoring terms laying around that you can pop into Google for some initial searching. By this time, you have also selected a social media listening tool. Input some of the social media monitoring words into that tool and see what you come up with after a cursory review. The key is that it does not need to be an exhaustive search.

- **Gathering existing market research**—See if you can obtain the volumes of offline testing your market research team has already done. It can be a valuable source for developing a hypothesis statement.

- **Interviewing communications colleagues**—Some of your compatriots in the communications or marketing functions might have some knowledge based on work they have already completed.

- **Asking your online community**—If this is a standalone research project or you're just attempting to verify some assumptions after you have launched an online presence, asking your community to provide input can be helpful. There is a very good chance that your community will offer up an opinion if asked and that can serve as a good behavior (or question) to test.

Creating a hypothesis is the most important step in developing the methods portion of your plan. Without it, all the work you have done to narrow and identify sources of data will be for naught. You will just end up testing everything, which will make your final report a lot less helpful for those who read it. Do not skip this step, even if it takes you an additional week to land on the right hypotheses after an internal review.

Time Frame for Analysis

It would be impossible for you to gather every single mention about a brand, its competitors, and the industry for the entire time the Web has existed. Not only would you be unable to digest that amount of information, but it would lead to a serious issue with spam collection. (We discuss the issues with spam later, in the section, "Spam/Bot Filtering.")

The other reason capturing all the available data is impractical is incomplete data. It is not discussed much within digital analytics, marketing, and public relations circles, but oftentimes a shortcoming of this kind of research can be incomplete information. By that we mean that a blogger might mention the brand in January but delete the post in March. When you conduct the analysis in April, you cannot capture that piece of content. Another example is an individual who is active on Twitter when he mentions your brand but then goes several months without activity and has his account suspended.

Aside from the issues related to data degradation and spam, another important reason to identify a time frame for the analysis is the length of time it takes to properly analyze behavioral trends. Looking at a short window might provide some interesting information, but it would be very difficult to establish any long-term trends in consumer behaviors.

On the flip side, it is possible to look at a time frame that is too long. For example, if you were to gather two years worth of conversation, a trend that you identify at the beginning of that cycle might no longer be a trend 20 months or so later. It could very well be a trend, but you would need to do additional testing with more recent data to verify that.

Where is the happy medium? Best practices suggest that data should be captured over a 12-month period. Utilizing a 12-month window lessens the possibility that holidays (if applicable), quarterly earnings events (if applicable), and crises (if applicable) will unnecessarily bias the data. It also enables you to accurately assess behavioral trends online. The 12-month time window also eliminates a lot of concern about data degradation. If collecting data for 12 months results in too much data to analyze, a compromise solution is to gather 6 months of data.

 Note

Although narrowing down the window might cut down on the amount of data to gather and analyze, it might also create a seasonality bias in the data. If your company has clearly defined "busy seasons," and your analysis does not include those times, you might get inaccurate results and develop poor insights.

Identifying the Project Team

The project team is one of the most crucial elements of the research plan. It is not enough to develop your hypotheses and identify the data sources. Without a team behind the project, there is a good chance the project will not be completed and the organization will not benefit from its insights. These are the most crucial roles to identify within the project team:

- **Project leader/champion**—This person does not necessarily need to be the one who does the work, but she needs to be the person who assembles the research plan. She also should be the one who helps to evangelize the need to complete the project and gather the insights.
- **Research leader**—The research leader could be the same person as the project leader, but oftentimes the roles are separated. The research leader is the one who ensures that the parameters identified in the research plan are followed.

- **Analyst**—In all likelihood, the analyst is the person who completes the research in conjunction with the research leader. He could come from any part of the organization, but the best analysts understand the tools and the business needs. They are the people who can properly blend those two elements into actionable insights for the business.

- **Research Quality Assurance (QA)**—Someone on the team should be designated to double-check the coding. This could be the analyst working on the project or the research leader. Read more about coding in the following sections of this chapter.

- **Content strategist/engagement leader**—This person works hand-in-hand with the analyst, research lead, and project lead to develop insights from the data. Without this person, all that is completed is the collection of a massive amount of data.

These people can come from any part of the organization. Ideally, you want to form a hybrid team between marketing and market research, but if the team members are coming from one area or the other, that is okay. As long as the people have knowledge of the tools and the business, the project will be successful.

Determining the Depth of Analysis

Depending on the volume of data in question, the time frame you are using, and whether you are expanding the scope behind your own brand (to competitors and the broader industry), it might not be possible to read and code every mention. We will talk more about the coding process in a moment, but the depth of your analysis is an important consideration. There are four different methods of analysis that you can pick from for your project:

- **Automated**—Many of the tools we have talked about in this book offer automated dashboards that count mentions across a variety of potential metrics. This is not a very desirable state, though, as the data has not been vetted for spam or checked for relevancy.

- **Manual**—Whether or not you decide to go with a manual process of reading and analyzing every post depends on the size of the project. If you decide to analyze only content that mentions your brand, and there are not many mentions, then doing the analysis manually can work. If yours is a company the size of Disney, however (which means you have tens of thousands of mentions per day), then a manual process won't work.

- **Hybrid**—Most companies take a hybrid approach, in which they rely on an automated dashboard and supplement it with manual analysis.

- **Random sampling**—This method utilizes all the data you can gather from the tool(s) you are using and then randomly samples a selection of those mentions. How large the sample is depends on the confidence interval you are comfortable using. The confidence interval indicates how reliable your data will be. If you are familiar with political polling, you have no doubt seen mention of plus or minus 5% next to the results. It is similar with digital data. After the random sample is pulled, a manual process ensues.

Which method you choose depends on your particular project, but we recommend that you use a random sampling method. Such a method boils down a large number of mentions into a manageable size and offers the best approach to manually reading posts and offering insights.

Building the Coding Framework

Before you freak out at the term *coding*, let us explain what we mean by it. Coding the random sample—assuming that you choose the random sample method—involves applying a qualitative label to a much larger post. For example, if a mention of a brand took place in *The New York Times*, then a possible code for that mention could be "news." It really is not more complicated than this. However, it is important that the team working on a project agrees on the set of variables that will be coded for at the start of the project. The following are some examples of codes you can use for your project:

- **Media type**—This basic tag assesses whether the mention came from a news, blog, forum, Twitter, comment, video, or image site.
- **Sentiment**—Sentiment coding is simply understanding whether a piece of content is positive, negative, or neutral. Read more about sentiment in the next section of this chapter.
- **Messaging pillar**—Most companies have a set of messages they are trying to convey to the marketplace. One of your tags should be which bucket that mention falls into.
- **Company spokesperson**—This is an obvious yes or no tag to include in the analysis.
- **Type of post**—Is the post a customer complaint, or is it a product mention? Could the mention be categorized as an HR issue? Capturing the type of post helps you segment and share the data with other parts of the organization, if appropriate.
- **Target journalist or media outlet**—Again, this is an obvious tag, but you should be able to sort based on the tag and see whether a majority of mentions came from target publications.

Depending on your particular project, there could be dozens of different codes you can use. The most critical thing is to establish them ahead of time.

Taking a Sentiment Approach

Online sentiment is probably the most controversial subject in the digital analytics community today. The debate is centered around two different core topics:

- **Automation versus manual**—The social media listening tools we have mentioned throughout the book all have an automated sentiment-scoring tool. Unfortunately, those automated sentiment-scoring tools are far from accurate—primarily because they have a hard time discerning sarcasm from authenticity. However, manual sentiment analysis introduces issues of human bias and scale that have yet to be overcome.

- **Value to the brand**—It is important to note that online sentiment is not necessarily a proxy for overall brand reputation. It is possible that during a period of crisis, the two could be related, but it is not always the case. Some brands place too much emphasis on online sentiment, whereas others do not look at it at all. The answer lies somewhere in the middle of those two extremes.

The most common scale for online sentiment analysis is positive, negative, and neutral. However, this scale does not allow for very much interpretation. In addition, not every post is overly negative or positive. In longer-format posts (such as blogs or news), there will likely be elements of positive, negative, and neutral mentions woven throughout. Our preference is to utilize a five-point scale for scoring sentiment:

- **Positive**—The positive posts will likely be the most obvious. They are the posts that advocate for the brand in some way or that compliment an action the brand has taken. These posts are also often endorsements of the brand to friends and family members.

- **Somewhat positive**—A step below the positive mentions, somewhat positive can be tempered endorsements of the brand. These mentions might mention the brand positively but may do so only briefly in the course of a post.

- **Neutral**—The neutral posts are probably the hardest to classify because it is often difficult to determine the intent from a casual read of the posts. Furthermore, some posts say positive and negative things in a period of a couple of paragraphs. Typically though, these posts don't advocate for the brand in anyway, and they likely just mention the brand's name.

- **Slightly negative**—These posts often use negative terms in association with the brand, but one of the key differentiators between slightly negative and negative is that slightly negative posts do not focus on your brand exclusively. The person might say that he or she "dislikes" the brand but in the context of a post that is totally irrelevant to you.
- **Negative**—Negative posts focus exclusively on the brand and are hypercritical of its actions, behaviors, or messaging.

There is no perfect solution to the sentiment question. There are tools currently on the market, such as Clarabridge, that are trying to lend more validity to automated sentiment scoring. Until that process becomes more accurate, brands need to rely on manual scoring by humans. As long as the scale and types of posts that fall into each part of the scale are decided upon ahead of time, it is still the best solution.

Filtering Spam and Bots

The final portion of your research plan should be an outline of how to deal with spam and bots. There is a tremendous amount of spam on the Internet, and it varies in volume, depending on the brand you are analyzing. In some instances, we have encountered a spam-to-real content ratio of 90%:10%. In niche markets, such as business-to-business technology, there is often less spam because there is not the ability to capture traffic from genuine sources.

Spam and bot filtering is only one part of the process. The other part is factoring in news or press release syndication. Some tools filter out press release syndication, but others capture it. Those instances are, technically speaking, a mention of the brand, but they are mostly noise. They do not necessarily contribute anything to brand reputation or value. Our recommendation is to exclude such instances from your analysis.

So there you have it. These are the elements of a research plan. The plan is a critical component to direct your research and ensure that actionable insights follow the analysis. These steps do not necessarily need to be done in sequential order, but it is important to map out the sources and methods completely.

16

Making Reports Easy to Understand and Communicate

In the last several chapters we have talked at length about the different use cases for social media listening data. You should now have a better understanding of how that data can be valuable for groups other than public relations and marketing. Remember the maxim that we have reiterated throughout this book: "Knowledge is power." If you are the person feeding information to product planning, strategic planning, or customer service, then you are at the seat of power within your organization.

Knowing the different applications of social media listening data is helpful, but unless you have a firm understanding of how to build a research plan (see Chapter 15, "Formulating Your Research Plan") and deliver insights, you will be sitting on a pile of data with little meaning. Insights are critical in fueling the communications strategies and tactics for your organization. A component of developing insights is knowing how to deliver a report.

It's important that you get reports right. Why? Because if you do not, all the research you have done on tools and all the time you have spent building your research plan will go to waste. This chapter provides an overview of what your reports should contain. We dig into the following specific topics:

- **Report construction**—If you have developed your research plan, building a report should be a piece of cake. We'll offer some tips and tricks on how to construct a report.

- **Report delivery**—If we do nothing else in this chapter, it is our hope that we arm you well enough that you do not fall victim to data dump syndrome. The reports themselves must present insights that inform strategies and tactics; they cannot be slide after slide of only data.

- **Report use cases**—Not everyone in your organization needs to see every piece of data that you have collected. For example, you will likely need to create a report for just your executive team. That report should include the key takeaways, a few of the most important data points, and a description of how the data is going to be used.

- **Central repository of information**—The reports that you construct will have limited long-term value unless you develop a program or repository for the insights that you have gleaned.

Reports are where the rubber meets the road. Taking the time to build an appropriate internal toolset will pay off for your organization. This is where understanding the social media listening applications will benefit you the most. This is also where building your research plan in advance will save you a tremendous amount of time. Without further delay, let's get into how to build reports.

 Note

In the coming sections we talk about how reports are constructed for public relations and marketing. However, the concepts are broad enough to be applicable to other parts of the organization, if such a use case exists for your company or client.

Constructing Reports

This chapter is about building better reports, and it makes sense to start with an explanation of how to construct reports. When you read this section of the chapter, it'll be obvious if you did not read Chapter 15. In Chapter 15, we talk at length about building a research plan. If you launched right into data collection and analysis, your report is likely going to fall victim to "data dump syndrome." What does that mean? It means putting together dozens of slides that do not tell the full story. It also means you have a whole lot of data and probably not a lot of insights.

How do you combat this problem? Much of the answer to this question lies in Chapter 15, but there are a few other things you can do to prevent being infected by this syndrome:

- **Build your reports from back to front**—This is not necessarily intuitive for most people; the next section includes more explanation of this concept. The idea is that you start at the back of your presentation and move forward.

- **Ensure that you have a reasonable hypothesis**—If you have a set of hypotheses, your presentation will be focused. If you cast the net wide, collect a lot of data, and then try to put all that data into a presentation, you will be swimming upstream.

- **Focus on the Five Ws**—It is easy to lose track of the story you are trying to tell as you are sifting through a mountain of data. Every slide or insight you deliver should be based on the five Ws (who, what, when, where, and why). You'll learn about this in the section, "Focusing on the Five Ws," later in this chapter.

- **Formatting reports**—Some of this will be covered in this chapter in the section, "Building a Report from Back to Front," but there are some tips and tricks in order to properly format your reports that we cover throughout the chapter.

- **Watching your report time frame**—In several chapters we have talked about ensuring that you have a large enough data set to properly identify trends and develop insights. The actual development of the report is no exception, but there are some subtle nuances.

In the next several pages, we dive into each of these topics individually.

Building a Report from Back to Front

Again, building a report from back to front isn't intuitive. You might be saying, "Are you telling us to start with the last slide first?" Yes, that is exactly what we are telling you to do. Why? Doing so can help you deliver cohesive, concise, and focused reports. This approach ensures that your report clearly conveys the most important takeaways. Otherwise, your takeaways may get buried.

How do you go about building your report in this way? There are four key steps to pulling it off successfully:

1. Conduct initial research—At this stage, there is no need to build a comprehensive social media listening profile, but it's great if you do have one. Whether you use a social media listening tool or Google Insights (see Chapters 5, "Tools: Search Analytics," and 6, "Tools: Audience Analysis," for more details) or just a regular Google search, you should do some initial searching in order to get a sense of the current online landscape. This research does not need to be comprehensive but is meant to be directional.

2. Develop your hypotheses—If your hypotheses lack focus, the report will too. What is an example of a hypothesis statement that can be used to properly build a report? An example might be "We expect to see the majority of conversations online mentioning a particular product." If, when conducting the research, you realize that the hypothesis statement is true, you can spend several slides digging into the details of that conversation. If it proves not to be true, you can spend several slides discussing what was being mentioned online. (Chapter 15 really digs into how to format a research hypothesis.)

ρ *Tip*

How many hypotheses should you have? There is no clear-cut answer to this question, unfortunately. However, three to five different hypothesis statements is typical. This number of hypotheses will give you a solid foundation of data and will result in a sufficiently concise report that people in your organization can digest it.

3. Build your strategic and tactical recommendations—You can refine these recommendations as you start to collect data to either prove or refine your hypothesis statements, but before you put the final report together, jot down a few things you might be able to do tactically as a result of developing the report.

4. Create the report outline—Ultimately, the outline of the report will be in the front of the presentation. After you do your initial research, write your hypothesis statements, and formulate initial strategic and tactical recommendations, it is time to start creating the outline. The outline will lead to a more concise and clear final report.

If you use the method of building reports from back to front, your final reports will be clearer and likely containing insights that you can take action on.

> ✉ *Note*
>
> We are aware that this approach might seem like a self-fulfilling prophecy. By developing hypotheses ahead of time, you could introduce bias into the data collection and analysis process, and you could possibly miss out on valuable intelligence. The hypothesis statements are meant to be a guide only. When you dig into the data, if you realize that there is some new groundbreaking insight that deserves to be reported on, you should report on it. Nothing is stopping you from expanding beyond your initial hypotheses.

Ensuring That You Have a Reasonable Hypothesis

As mentioned in Chapter 15 and the preceding section, you need to have a reasonable hypothesis before you can develop a concise and cohesive report. The hypothesis statement should be based on your initial research and knowledge of the business. Similarly, you should take into account what the goals of your communications program will be. The more input into the hypothesis that you can offer, the better the hypotheses and the report will be.

The following are some examples of hypothesis statements that you can use for the purposes of your report:

- "A majority of conversations taking place online reference customer service issues."
- "Conversations taking place on forums focus on three main product attributes."
- "Mentions of the CEO include discussion of overall leadership and take place in mainstream news outlets."
- "There are few or no blog conversations that mention the brand or competitor brands."
- "Women who are parents will be the primary audience talking online about the brand and competitors."

A hypothesis statement should represent some element of the Five Ws, which are covered in the next section. For the moment, though, it is important to note that you should not skip the hypothesis step. Doing so is a sure-fire way to develop "data dump syndrome."

Focusing on the Five *W*s

Aside from building your hypothesis statements and your initial recommendations, there is no more important component to a clearly laid out report than focusing on the five *W*s:

- **Who**—The "who" is the people who are talking about the brand, its competitors, or its industry online. The "who" could be the demographics of the people who are talking, whether they are influential or not, or even whether they are employees of the company.

- **What**—The "what" is the key topics people talk about online. It can be based on the hypothesis statements you have outlined in the previous step, or it could be based on your deep-dive research. This can also be used for creating both paid and earned content that affects search engine optimization (SEO).

- **Where**—The "where" is the location of conversations taking place online. You will most often see "where" defined as news, blogs, Twitter, Facebook, YouTube, forums, and other social networks.

- **When**—The "when" is the date/time element of your research. Are people talking on the weeknights, or are they talking on the weekends in the early morning? The good news is that most social media listening tools offer the capability to identify this data point. Identifying when people are talking can be helpful as you line up your content schedule.

- **Why**—The "why" involves understanding the rationale for the behavior of people mentioning the brand, competitors, or industry online. It can partly be answered through reading social media conversations but requires additional research inputs—namely surveys and focus groups. Social media listening data can serve as an input to those surveys and focus groups to try to answer that "why," however.

Every slide or bullet that you put together for your report should attempt to answer the five *W* questions. You won't be able to answer all five *W*s in every bullet or slide, but your goal should be a minimum of three. When the report or bullets do not include enough of those elements, you often are left with very ambiguous statements that are difficult to act on.

 Tip

An example of an ambiguous comment would be noting in the report that 40% of the conversations are taking place on Twitter. Although it's helpful to know where people are talking, this statistic leaves out who is doing the talking, when they are talking, and what topics they are talking about.

Formatting Reports

It is common for social media listening reports or even reports that are augmented with other digital data sources (for example, engagement or search data) to be presented in Microsoft PowerPoint or Keynote. In our view, creating such a presentation is the best way to compile the mountain of data you have collected and then convey a story to your key internal or external stakeholders.

The following elements should be in every one of your reports:

- **Project overview**—Every presentation you create should have one slide that outlines the goals of the project. Amazingly often, the goals are not clearly outlined. Without a project overview slide, the rest of the presentation will fall flat.

- **Hypotheses**—If you are testing hypotheses—and we sure hope you are!—they should appear on a separate slide. It is also worth noting on this slide whether the hypotheses were proven to be true or slightly off, just to provide context.

- **Methodology**—The methodology should include how much data you collected, where you collected it, who collected it, when it was collected, and what was collected.

- **Executive summary**—The executive summary should include the top three to five findings from the research. The key element here is that every bullet you put on the executive summary slide should be actionable. There should be some way for the organization to develop a communications strategy to combat or amplify what you have found.

- **Top-level data**—The handful of slides that follow the executive summary should focus on the most important data and analysis captured in your report. They should seamlessly flow from the executive summary and are likely to be based on your original hypotheses.

- **Top-level recommendations**—The recommendations should flow from the executive summary slide previously presented. They should appear on a series of slides—likely three to five tactics or ideas that can be executed. They can include social media tactics or any other communications medium, based on your findings.

- **Everything else**—We do not mean to minimize the amount of work you have done to put together the report, but the rest of the report is just backup. It shows that you have done the work required to develop the insights and recommendations but really is valuable only to the numbers junkies (we mean that in the nicest way possible) on your team.

How long should a report be? The answer, as you might suspect, is that it depends on the depth of the research and the number of questions you are exploring. A typical report following the format described in this section would be anywhere from 15 to 20 slides. You should reasonably assume that getting your audience to pay attention after about 20 or so slides will be challenging. Keep it brief and stay focused on the story you are trying to tell. Large amounts of data can often lead to large amounts of slides, which can often lead to presentations that are not digestible. Keep the presentation simple and germane to the story you are trying to convey.

Understanding Your Report Time Frame

How much data you collect and present is entirely based on the scope of the project. However, you should always err on the side of including more data in your upfront analysis. Why? There are two primary reasons:

- **More data eliminates anomalies**—Major news events tend to skew the data either positively or negatively. However, when you include an ample amount of data, those news events have less of an effect.

- **More data is a more accurate predictor of how behaviors have changed**—If you have been actively communicating with your community and want to see how the behavior has changed, the best course of action is to look at the 12 months leading up to the communications and then as much time after as possible. The behaviors you are trying to change and influence do not change overnight. Putting out an advertisement today does not mean people will be aware of your product tomorrow. Similarly, just because you begin posting a link to new content today does not mean people will engage with it over the long term.

Other data sources should follow a similar rule. If you collect 12 months worth of social media conversations, you should also collect 12 months worth of search data. Or, if your research project calls for website data, then you should collect 12 months worth of that as well. Consistency is key. It will be very easy to poke holes in the methodology if you do not follow the same script with all the data you are gathering.

Now that you know the key tips and tricks for developing a report, it is time get down to creating it. Then you can deliver it, as described in the next section.

Delivering a Report

You have done a lot of work on collecting a pretty large amount of data, ideally over the past 12 months. You have developed hypotheses. You have built slides that outline what the data is telling you. You have created some preliminary recommendations based on that data. The bottom line is that you have done a tremendous amount of work to get to this point. But you are not done yet. There still is the very important step of delivering your report.

One consideration is to whom you should deliver your report; we talk about that in the next section. Another important consideration is *how* to deliver the report. It is not enough to compile the report and send it out via email. You could do that, but you would be leaving the report open to wild interpretation that may not be helpful. You have likely spent hundreds of hours compiling the report, and you want it to be well received. Providing a voiceover with additional context can help.

If sending out the report via email, even with a voiceover, is not the right approach, how should you deliver it? The best approach is to deliver it in person. How should that meeting be structured? There are four steps to a successful review of a report:

1. **50% review**—Your report may be further along than 50%, but this is the opportunity for your stakeholder group to provide feedback on the report itself. It is also their opportunity to ask questions or make additional data requests, based on their specific needs. This review session will ultimately lead to a more focused report for all of your stakeholders.

2. **Final review**—After you have incorporated the input of your stakeholder group, you should set up a second meeting where you can go through the report in more detail. Ideally, you should set up a one- or two-hour meeting in which you go through the slides described earlier in this chapter. In this session, you can talk through the findings with your stakeholder group and begin discussing how to act on the recommendations.

3. **Strategy and tactical workshop**—Now that you have a mountain of data and some initial recommendations, it is time to put that information to good use. The group you invite to this workshop is likely smaller than the first two review session groups, including mostly the people who will be executing against the data and recommendations.

4. **Debriefing and next steps**—You need to debrief with the larger stakeholder team, discussing what worked and what didn't with the research project. This is also an opportunity to discuss what project the team will undertake next. Will the next project be a continuation of the research already done? Will it be an exploration of a theme or themes

you have identified in this report? Those are just a couple of the things that could be discussed in the debriefing meeting.

You must do a lot of work to put together a research report, and you don't want to miss out on the chance to deliver your findings in person. Presenting strong insights in person about your customers to senior executives will help them to remember you. In the executives' minds, you will forever be the person who understands the customer. Remember: Knowledge is power.

Understanding Report Use Cases

Until now, we have been speaking in generalities about what should go into a report. We have talked about ensuring that your slides include some reference to the five Ws (who, what, when, where, and why). We have talked about how to deliver a report. We have talked about how a report should be structured. We have talked about how much data should be included in a report. What we have not talked about yet, however, is to whom you should deliver the report.

If you sat down and listed all the people who would be consuming the report you are developing, you might find yourself with a list of about 10 use cases. I am sure you could guess without us telling you that developing 10 different versions of the same report is silly. If you tried to develop 10 different versions of the same report, you would be working on it for quite a long time. In most situations, there are just 3 primary use cases that you should always consider:

- **Executive**—The executive within your company is not going to read a 50-page research report. Yes, we are sure that there are exceptions who will read the whole thing, but the majority of people will not. They probably won't even read the 15 or 20 slides that we described earlier. You have to create a slimmed-down version for your executive team.

- **Management**—The management level includes the people who are likely to take action based on your data and findings—typically the public relations and marketing people within your company. They will be the ones expected to develop strategies and tactics based on your findings.

- **Analyst**—Analysts want data. They will find value in the recommendations, but these folks will be "geeking out" on all the additional data slides in the back of your presentation.

Let us dig into each of these use cases in a little more detail.

The Executive-Level Use Case

The executives within your company are busy. They deal with operational challenges, human resources problems, product issues, and many other things that come up during a normal workday. Most of them find value in new research, even if it is in a channel they do not fully understand. This is especially true if you offer significant consumer, product, or customer service insights. If your research and data focus on those three areas, you will likely get their attention.

However, you will not have their attention for a long period of time. You might have a grand total of 15 minutes with an executive to share your findings (if you are lucky). That does not give you much of an opportunity to go into great depth. You probably cannot even utilize the slide format outlined earlier for your report. Here's what you can share that will get the executives' attention:

- **Project scope**—It is important to keep this part brief because executives do not care about the intricacies of the tool or date range you selected. They also do not care about the total volume of data you collected. The project scope should be very high level on the project's goals and its approach. You should use no more than three or four bullets on this slide.

- **Key data points**—As with the project scope, the executives are not going to care about all the data you have. They will likely appreciate that you have gathered it, but they will not have time to get into it in great detail. You should give the executives two or three things that they should take away from the meeting.

- **Key recommendations**—We have presented these types of reports to a number of executives over the years, and the response is almost always the same: "This is great, but what are we going to do with it?" The recommendations do not need to be finalized, necessarily, but they should be ideas that could be executed based on the data. You will either get a "go" or a "no," and having preliminary ideas is a great way to get immediate sign-off on any sort of tactical implementation you have considered.

- **Next steps**—You don't need to say much about next steps, but it is important to give executives an understanding of what will happen when you all leave that room. It could be more research, or it could be more meetings to develop the tactics as a result of the research. Whatever it is, make sure the next steps are concretely outlined for your executives.

With executives, you might have an opportunity to present 4 or 5 of the 50 or more slides you've prepared. You might find this scary, or you might feel like your work is being minimized, but set those feelings aside. Presenting those 4 or 5 slides could give you greater visibility to the executive team. That is a pretty big deal at most companies. (And remember: Knowledge is power.)

The Management-Level Use Case

Those in the management level are the people who are going to be using the data most often within your organization. If your project has executive-level sponsorship, the management-level people will also be responsible for developing strategies and tactics as a result of the research. Most often, they are the marketing and public relations people within your organization.

Some people in the management level will want to see the entire report. We know plenty of people within the marketing and public relations professions who love to see numbers. Unfortunately, we know just as many who are so numbers averse that their peers who are effectively using data to hone strategies and tactics are lapping them. What does the management-level use case look like? It looks a lot like the executive-level use case, with a few notable additions:

- **Project scope**—Like the people at the executive level, those in the management layer care about how the project was completed. Unlike the executives, though, this audience is likely to care more about the tools, the date ranges, and the volume of data collected.

- **Key data points**—Again, like the executives, the managers want to know the key data points. During your 50% review, this team might identify those for you, but if not, err on the side of including too many. You can always cull the list down after the broader team has an opportunity to review it.

- **Additional "noteworthy" data**—There might be elements that you have excluded from the executive report because it would be too long. If so, this is the group to share that information with.

- **Recommendations**—Based on the data you have collected, the managers are going to want to know all the potential applications for it. This is where you can go above and beyond what you share with the executives and discuss more ideas. The managers are likely closer to their particular piece of the business on a day-to-day basis, and therefore they might be able to use the data to identify some recommendations that you would not. That is perfectly okay. In fact, we encourage it with the reports we prepare for companies.

- **Next steps**—The managers care about next steps, and the next steps can be the same as what you share with the people at the executive level.

The Analyst-Level Use Case

The analysts—the "data geeks" as we like to affectionately call them (and ourselves sometimes)—are the men and women who sift through mountains of data and deliver insights in order to make communications programs (and the business overall) more effective. They are your organization's eyes and ears—and oftentimes the brain. Without consumer insights people, many communications programs would miss the mark, leaving many people in the management level looking for new employment.

We are obviously biased as we ourselves come from the analyst-level world (at least we started there). We can't overstate the importance of the role analysts play in the digital analytics process. They are most often involved in selecting the tool, creating the project scope, writing hypotheses, crunching the data, developing the insights, and determining how best to mesh what they have found with existing research. These are significant tasks. And all the while they must measure the progress of existing communications programs.

What do the analyst level care about in this context? Well, there is a good chance that these folks put together the report. If they did not, however, they are sure to care about everything the managers care about, plus all the available raw data. That raw data might lead to additional research projects or the refinement of existing projects.

You have a lot of data, and you have reported on its various findings to the different internal stakeholders. It is time to move on to the next project. But before you move to the next project, there is still a critical question that needs to be answered: How is this information stored in order to ensure that you are constantly able to tap into it and learn about what your customers are saying? The last section of this chapter covers how to build a central repository of information.

Building a Central Repository of Information

The field of digital analytics has come a long way in the past five years. Significant innovations in the area of data capture and analysis have taken place as social media has exploded and presented much new information for public relations and marketing. There has even been progress with combining multiple data sources to offer the best insights. We know, it sounds silly, but until very recently, the people who held the search data were not always excited to compare notes with the person who held the social data.

What we as an industry have not gotten good at yet, however, is building a central repository for information. You see, in most cases, the reports are developed as we have outlined in this chapter, put into PowerPoint, shared, and then stored on a hard drive somewhere. That is useful only for the person who has the report on his or her desktop. Nobody else in the organization will see consistent, long-term value from it. This model also opens up the organization to knowledge-management issues if the person who owns the presentation leaves the company.

You can see the problem, can't you? Well, the good news is that there are a couple solutions available for building a central repository:

- **Command center**—No, we are not talking about the bridge of the *Starship Enterprise*. Many companies, including Dell, Gatorade, and Cisco, have created social media command centers to serve as central repositories of data collection and insight development.

- **Web-based application**—Several companies specialize in the development of dashboards that live remotely on individual desktops.

Command Centers

The command center concept became popular after Dell developed a physical location (see Figure 16.1) where people on Dell's Social Media and Community team (affectionately called SMaC) could monitor conversations around the globe. These command centers capture all kinds of data, much of it centering on the five *W*s concept covered earlier in the chapter.

A command center is usually a single location with multiple monitors and multiple individuals reading conversations on a nearly 24/7 basis. It can also be a source of information for public relations, marketing, customer service, social media, crisis managers, community management professionals, and consultants within the organization. The people who work in the command center utilize listening tools and categorization/routing techniques in order to put the data in the hands of the people who need it most.

The command center is the primary source of data, but it is not the only place for gathering information on key stakeholders online. The people who work in the command center could be market research professionals, but quite often they are a random collection of people from within the organization who have some social media responsibility.

Figure 16.1   *Dell's Social Media Command Center, located at the company headquarters in Round Rock, Texas, serves all of the company's global needs.*

A command center can provide an organizationwide rallying point for social media, but there are some drawbacks:

- **Physical and technological infrastructure costs**—The tools and the physical space needed to power a command center in this way are not cheap.

- **Scalability questions**—If all the data is being collected in the command center, how do people who are not near the room take advantage of it in real-time? They need someone who is actively monitoring within the command center space to send them the details. This is not an efficient use of anyone's time.

- **Available talent to work in the command center**—There is a dearth of available digital analytics talent, and command centers require strong communications and technical skills in order to operate effectively.

Command centers are very cool spaces, but they require a significant investment. Technology—in terms of data gathering and display, human talent, and physical location—costs need to be considered. However, using a command center is one effective way to centralize data gathering and insights development within your company.

Web-Based Applications

An alternative to creating a physical command center location is to build a web-based application that can live on multiple desktops within the organization. It provides data in real time across a number of different channels and networks, and it has the added benefit being a lot more cost effective than a command center.

During last year's Consumer Electronics Show (CES), Intel Corporation was featured in several industry trade magazines for its Social Cockpit (see Figure 16.2). The Social Cockpit is a web-based application that gathers data from multiple sources. Although not as flashy as a physical space, it is visually appealing enough to get people excited about the data.

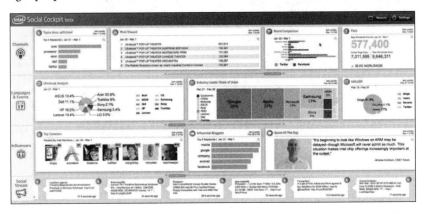

Figure 16.2 *The Social Cockpit captures data from across the web and serves it up in an easy-to-read application.*

A web-based application captures social media network data, conversation data, and anything else the team might need to do its jobs more effectively. The data presented can then be used to develop content, alter tactics, and even solve customer service issues, if necessary.

The most valuable part of this type of centralized data application is that it is completely customizable. If you want to see only social media conversations about your brand, you can do that. If you want to see only social network data, you can do that also. What is key is that you develop a set of goals, use cases, and requirements before building an application like this.

The market will continue to go down one of these two paths—command center or web-based application—as the centralization of data becomes more important. Not every company is there yet. Plenty will continue to execute reports as we outlined at the beginning of this chapter, and that is okay. However, as your organization becomes more familiar and more interested in this kind of data, the need to build a repository of information will grow. Do not wait to be asked. Get ahead of it and start thinking about how you can build either a command center or a web-based application in order to house the information.

17

Search Analysis

In Chapter 5, "Tools: Search Analysis," we describe some of the tools available to assist in gathering digital insights from search data, and we also highlight the most common uses for such analysis. In this chapter, we dig deeper into how to perform some of these activities and identify where they can be used to support digital strategy development, influence content strategy and planning, and inform advertising messaging and content.

Although analyst firms, agencies, and brands have developed a bevy of digital strategy frameworks, these frameworks all follow a common approach. Digital strategy is a broad term but essentially involves the research, planning, definition, and creation of a go-to-market plan for digital channels, with the end goal being a return on that investment—something affecting the bottom line in a reasonable period of time. Figure 17.1 shows an example of a digital framework we've followed with some clients that has served us well.

Digital-Marketing Strategy Framework

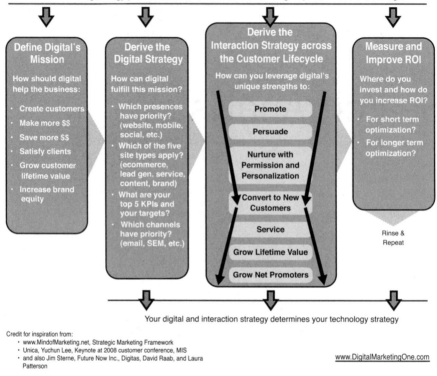

Figure 17.1 *A digital strategy framework.*

When you're developing a digital strategy, digital analytics serve as a rich input that helps you understand a target audience across many different dimensions. (See Chapter 6, "Tools: Audience Analysis," for a complete breakdown of the different methods for profiling an audience.) In this chapter, we dig into search data and link it to the audience analysis method, as well as describe how to create search term maps to visualize keyword and brand associations.

Search analysis is based on customers' actual search queries, so it includes relevant, timely, and specific information about what consumers are searching for. The search terms reveal the topics consumers are interested in, which you can then dissect to inform content strategy and planning. Throughout this book, we've hammered home the point that content is king. Content strategy is a process that breathes life into content marketing programs and branded content initiatives.

Content strategy deals with one of the biggest—yet not-so-obvious to many organizations—problems that marketers face today: organizing and planning content. In order to be relevant to your audience, you need to have remarkable content.

However, let's be clear: Your content needs to be remarkable to your audience, not every audience, which means relevancy is crucial. How can you ensure that your content is delivering on those key requirements? By understanding the topics the audience is interested in, based on mining data that reveals what customers search for.

Finally, paid advertising can benefit from search analysis, whether it be paid search (search engine marketing) or paid display (banners/online listing management (OLM)/rich media), in the same manner that content strategy can—through knowledge of keywords and topics relevant to consumers or of interest to consumers. By understanding audience intent and interests through search analysis, you can tailor the specific combination of keywords, topics, and phrases contained in advertising copy or even a landing page (the destination page a consumer visits after clicking a link within a paid advertising unit).

Let's begin by classifying the common search analysis use cases we identify in Chapter 5 and putting them into one of the three categories that they best align with. Remember that these are the use cases:

- Choosing paid advertising messaging
- Choosing natural search messaging
- Identifying and choosing brand associations
- Identifying trends and seasonal changes
- Supporting new product/market launches
- Conducting brand audits

Anyone interested in or responsible for developing a digital strategy will be most interested in the last four use cases. Someone focused on content strategy and planning will be more likely to focus on the first four use cases. Finally, for paid advertising, the first two use cases are most beneficial. Table 17.1 shows a summary of these use cases.

Table 17.1 Search Analysis Use Case Matrix

Use Case	Category 1	Category 2
Choosing paid advertising messaging	Paid advertising	Content strategy
Choosing natural search messaging	Content strategy	Paid advertising
Identifying and choosing brand associations	Digital strategy	Content strategy
Identifying trends and seasonal changes	Digital strategy	Content strategy
Supporting new product/market launches	Digital strategy	
Brand audits	Digital strategy	

Now that we've established the relationships and links between the search analysis activities and the specific business activities that digital marketers execute, let's dig into each area in greater detail.

Search Analytics for Digital Strategy

Identifying brand associations, tracking seasonal trends, and performing audits are common activities that you can do at any point for a brand. Supporting a new product launch is obviously more situational and might not be relevant to your needs all the time, so this section focuses on the audits and tracking seasonal trends.

We focus on brand associations because they provide clues about how consumers think, feel, and view your brand. They aren't reasons for consumers to buy into a brand or buy a brand's product(s). Instead, they provide a sense of acquaintance and differentiation that consumers feel about the brand—any feeling about a brand that is deeply embedded in the consumer's mind. These brand associations are unique to each brand and not replicable. Identifying these crucial associations is of great value to a brand, as it can serve as fuel that will power a successful digital marketing plan.

Brand associations are formed in a variety of ways, including but not limited to the following:

- Consumer contact with the brand or company employees
- Brand advertising
- The price point at which the brand product or service is sold
- Perceived product or service quality
- The category in which the brand has positioned itself
- In-store displays
- Word of mouth
- Opinions of friends, family members, or influencers
- Competitor messaging and/or brand advertising

Understanding these perceptions is simultaneously every marketer's aspiration and challenge. When you successfully identify and understand consumer brand associations, you can have confidence in your strategic planning, digital channel priorities, and content/messaging effectiveness. Digital analytics, holistically, can reduce that gap between the brand and the consumer by accurately identifying where the opportunities exist to shrink that gap.

A big part of developing a digital strategy is having very specific goals but also having a keen understanding of the target audience. That will be used to set digital channel allocations and priorities across the paid–owned–earned media spectrum. A classic mistake when developing a digital strategy is to try to be everywhere, across all channels. But the digital landscape is far too large, far too deep, and far too complex for *any* brand to successfully pull this off. It's also unnecessary, even for big brands with a wide customer base. Trying to be everything to everyone in digital media is a recipe for failure.

Let's look at BMW as an example and dive into more detail using the Google Trends tool described in Chapter 5. Figure 17.2 shows how you can use Google Trends to identify the brand associations consumers are currently making about BMW based on their search behaviors. You can look at different views of the data, starting with overall volume of searches using various phrases.

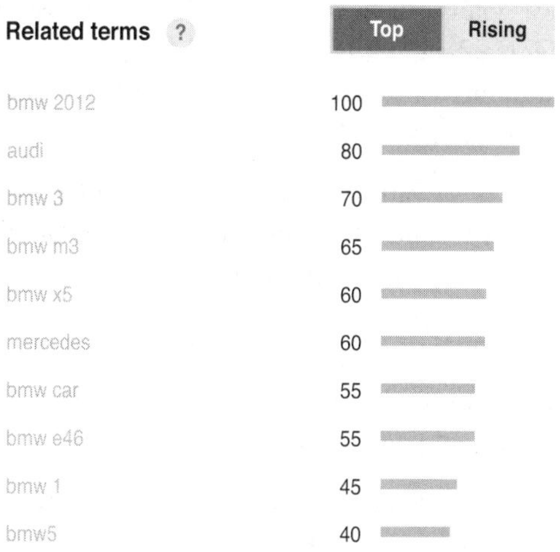

Related terms ?		Top	Rising
bmw 2012	100		
audi	80		
bmw 3	70		
bmw m3	65		
bmw x5	60		
mercedes	60		
bmw car	55		
bmw e46	55		
bmw 1	45		
bmw5	40		

Figure 17.2 *BMW search volume.*

At first glance, you can see that the search volume analysis reveals some interesting details, about the most popular BMW products (models) and also about which competitors are perceived to be closely related to the BMW brand. Regarding BMW products, you can extrapolate from this data that consumers are still interested in 2012 model year vehicle information, based on the terms yielding the most search volume (notice the index number of 100).

The second product-related observation reveals the BMW models that consumers are most interested in. In descending order, they are BMW 3, BMW M3, BMW X5, BMW car, BMW e46, BMW 1, and BMW 5. This information should be combined with other digital analytics data to verify consumer preference and priority. You should not give any single data source complete confidence and trust. You can combine product intent insights with web analytics and/or social analytics data to validate what you see (see Figure 17.3). If consumers visiting the BMW website also shows the popularity of these BMW products, based on visits, views, time spent on those product pages, you can assume that it is a more reliable and accurate indicator of consumer interest and intent.

Figure 17.3   *Brand association analytics trifecta.*

The same reliability is true of consumer preferences based on insights from social data. We can cross-reference the specific BMW product priorities from search analysis with the analysis of relevant mentions of the same BMW products from social listening data. Are consumers talking about these BMW products using the same priority and/or volume as they are searching for information about them? You can gather all three data inputs and align them side-by-side to identify important consistencies and inconsistencies that you need to explore further in order to land on a reasonable explanation.

The second important observation is related to competitive positioning. In this instance, you see that Audi and Mercedes are being searched for most often in association with the BMW products listed earlier. This means BMW should be focusing on what these competitive brands are doing to reach consumers, their brand campaigns, content, and messaging. You can see that consumers perceive Audi and Mercedes to be most closely associated to BMW, rather than, say, Lexus, Cadillac, or other perceived competitors.

The next tab, Rising Searches, provides a useful view for identifying emerging consumer interest and topics. Figure 17.4 provides a list of the topics and terms that are rising in popularity based on consumer search behavior.

In this view, you can identify the recent BMW products, campaigns, or initiatives that are resonating with consumers, capturing attention, and generating awareness and interest. It's a helpful way to gather performance feedback on what products are emerging interests on the minds of consumers and then prioritize initiatives accordingly. In this instance, the BMW HP4 (high-performance motorcycle) is breaking out relative to the others. Based on this knowledge, it would be prudent for a marketing manager to reexamine other digital media investments promoting the product, as there is clearly consumer interest. There might be additional opportunities to augment a current advertising campaign or share more relevant content about this product through social channels. Think real-time marketing. Paying careful attention to signals like this can increase your opportunities to deliver the right content to the right audience at the right time.

Related terms ?	Top	Rising
bmw hp4		Breakout
bmw championship 2012		+2,150%
bmw 2013		+750%
bmw 4 series		+250%
bmw m4		+170%
bmw f30		+140%
bmw 2012		+120%
bmw i8		+60%
bmw 328i		+50%
autoscout		+ 40%

Figure 17.4 *BMW rising terms.*

As we've described, search can be useful in identifying what topics or products consumers are interested in learning more about, but it doesn't necessarily give you all the qualitative feedback you'd like. In the BMW example, it would be ideal to learn more about some of the topics of interest that consumers are searching for. Sure, we've identified some products that are generating consumer interest, but what specific product attributes are consumers interested in? What product attributes are favorable and unfavorable? What products are generating consideration? In order to learn more, and hopefully answer these questions, you can take the outputs from search and use them as inputs in a social listening exercise that will dive deeper into the consumer conversation around those products. Then you apply text analytics to those conversations to ultimately reveal answers to your questions. Hopefully you see the pattern: Search analysis working together with social analysis or web analytics can be much more powerful than using only one tool on its own. Integration of digital analytics sources and data can help you begin to tell the entire story rather than just one or two chapters.

When formulating an approach to your digital initiatives, you need to have your finger on the pulse of consumer interest before you can begin to develop channel priorities, content plans, and advertising messaging. You should use the search analytics tools combined with the approaches described in this chapter to provide clarity before you move on to content strategy and planning.

Search Analytics for Content Strategy and Planning

Figure 17.5 is part of the content strategy process, as published by the Content Marketing Institute (http://contentmarketinginstitute.com/2011/04/5-things-about-content-strategy/). As you can see, one of the goals of any content strategy or content marketing initiative is to provide engaging, relevant content to a particular target audience. Content strategists will tell you that planning for content is the most significant part of the content strategy process, and you can't over-invest in this area. The more time you put into it up front, the better the benefits down the road, such as minimizing confusion, managing expectations, and providing a better understanding of user content needs across the organization. Also, content strategy helps you ensure that your plan understands the content needs of all stakeholders. For example, you can make sure community managers get the brand content they need to publish and distribute across social media platforms, not just content necessary for the brand website or paid media advertising units.

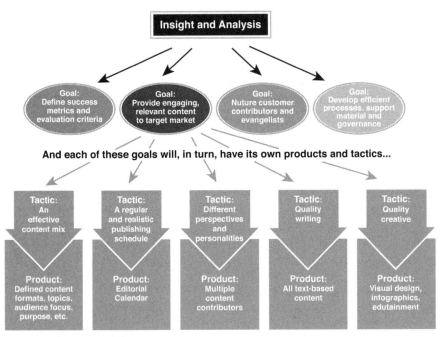

Figure 17.5   *Sample content strategy process.*

Content strategists use a variety of methods to discover the types of content an audience requires. Content strategy often involves information architecture activities such as content audits, mind-mapping, cart sorting, sketchboarding, user research groups, and focus groups. We suggest adding search analysis to that mix, as it can provide additional insights that reveal content topics that you should include when planning for content.

As discussed previously, search analysis excels at identifying specific keywords and topics that are already of interest to consumers because it's based on actual search queries, in the moment. This makes search analysis a perfect complement to the activities listed earlier that are currently used to identify user content needs. It won't answer questions like "What content formats or types should I be creating?" but it will address questions like "What topics and keywords should my content include?"

As in the previous example, using tools such as Google Trends, the Google AdWords Keyword Tool, Yahoo! Clues, or even the Bing Keyword Research Tool shines a light on the keywords and topics that might be necessary to include in your content planning. (We cover all these tools except the Bing Keyword Research Tool in Chapter 5.) Why? Quite simply, the more keywords and topics included in your content plans that are currently of interest to consumers, the more likely you'll be discovered. However, relevancy does expire, and because content marketing is an evergreen process (continuously executing and optimizing), search analysis should be performed regularly to ensure that your content publishing is aligned with consumer needs and current interests and intent. The frequency should be determined by how often you publish content. In a real-time marketing scenario, this could be a daily exercise, although that's likely overkill for most brands.

This approach is actually quite simple. It involves capturing keywords and topics from search analysis and comparing them against the content topics and keywords that arise from the other content-planning activities listed earlier. There will be overlap, and the keywords are the sweet spot in terms of targeting and should manifest as core components of your content planning—and ultimately within the content that is published across the brand's digital ecosystem, whether it be the brand website, microsites, landing pages, email marketing, social media content, or even YouTube channel content. Relevancy is the name of the game: Distribute relevant content to your audience, and they will reward you.

Search Analytics for Paid Advertising

Keyword research is the number-one activity you need to perform when it comes to paid advertising, particularly for paid search advertising. However, it applies to paid display advertising, too, although a lot less than to search advertising. As with the use cases that support content strategy and planning, search analysis can support your digital paid advertising efforts by acting as a compass, directing your keyword and topic decisions for advertising messaging. The more likely you are to utilize keywords that are representative of what consumers are seeking, in the moment, the more likely it is that you will be rewarded, regardless of whether it is through clicks on ad units or in terms of increased search engine rankings through improved organic page listings.

The process is actually identical to the one we just described for content strategy and planning: You capture consumer interest in the form of relevant keywords and topics through search analytics tools listed in Chapter 5 and compare those to the content and messaging you're using in your paid media advertising units.

Does your messaging include the most prominent and popular terms that consumers are currently searching for? If no, why not? If yes, are there opportunities to test variations of related keywords (see Google Trends related terms) to improve the performance of your current ads? You have myriad optimization opportunities for paid media copy and messaging; you can use search analysis to align your advertising copy with the terms that consumers are thinking about and using most often in their searches. These are the types of considerations marketers must make when thinking about paid media content or copy optimization. Many tools allow multivariate testing of various ad copy versions to identify the ones that yield the greatest performance. You have an opportunity to leverage search analysis to constantly gather the most relevant, timely keywords and topics that remain at the top consumers' minds and thus reveal consumer intent. Get searching and make keyword research a standard component of your strategic, content planning, and paid media processes.

18

ROI = Return on Investment

By this point in the book, you have probably guessed that we think digital media is important. We're not the only people who think so. According to a recent report from Econsultancy, 68% of companies report that they expect increases for their digital budgets over the next 12 months. Anecdotally, we have heard from several client-side marketing professionals that digital spending is going up, while television spending is decreasing.

This is not a trend that is likely to slow, especially as brands attempt to continue to capitalize on a new channel that allows them to more frequently communicate with key stakeholders and drive new business leads. What is also not going to change is the abundance of data available to communications professionals. In fact, the amount of data is likely to go up from here as social media becomes more mainstream.

The availability of data means communicators can no longer hide behind the lack of available numbers to prove whether a program was successful. It is all there; you just need to spend time creating your goals and setting up the mechanisms necessary to collect and analyze data. The problem is often determining what to track.

In Chapters 1, "Understanding the Digital Media Landscape," and 2, "Understanding Digital Analytics Concepts," we talk about some of the foundational elements of digital analytics, including setting measurable goals. Without those measurable goals, the rest of the measurement process falls apart. If you set proper goals, you should have an abundance of potential metrics to choose from. One of those metrics is return on investment, or ROI.

ROI and social media have a love/hate relationship. Companies are struggling to determine whether ROI should be captured and what actually goes into an ROI calculation.

ROI is the gain from any spending minus the cost of the investment divided by the cost. Dividing by the cost of the investment gives you a percentage gained or lost. It is really quite simple. Why then, according to a latest study from Awareness, Inc., do a majority (57%) of marketers still struggle with this concept?

The reasons are many, and we examine them throughout this chapter. We also dig into the other variations of ROI, which, for all intents and purposes, are not valid with senior executives. Finally, we talk about some of the considerations for actually calculating the ROI of your programs. Although we think ROI is important, it does not make sense to evaluate it in every instance.

Defining ROI

The concept of ROI is not a complicated one. To reiterate, ROI is the gain from any spending minus the cost of the investment divided by the cost. This calculation yields a percentage either gained or lost from your investment. This makes sense, right? Unfortunately, the advent of social media has made calculating ROI a little more complicated. Some people have attempted to circumvent the need to calculate the financial return from a social media program by creating different acronyms.

We do not mean to insinuate that the people who have come up with these acronyms have sinister intent. In fact, we think those who have created the acronyms are simply attempting to help those who struggle to capture social media's value to the organization. Unfortunately, senior executives are not likely to understand or even accept any variation on ROI. Your immediate boss might accept some alternatives, but in our experience, senior leaders recognize only ROI as financial return on investment.

In the coming pages, we outline all the different variations on ROI so that you can understand what each of them means and why they are problematic.

Return on Engagement (ROE)

One of the original variations on ROI is return on engagement (ROE), which measures the effect your organization's social media activities have on engagement rates. It assumes that engagement with content leads to greater awareness, which then leads to higher likelihood of consideration, which then leads to greater likelihood to buy.

The math behind ROE tends to vary, which is one of its primary issues, but it is calculated primarily by understanding the effect a community manager has on talking to someone after that person has mentioned the brand online. For example, if your company's community manager reaches out to someone who has made a complaint about the brand and is able to rectify that complaint, then a potential ROE calculation might be the time it took to make the contact and resolve the issue.

Another way ROE can be calculated is by looking at the percentage of engaged users within the community. This calculation varies by social media network. Here is how it is calculated for Facebook, Twitter, and YouTube:

- **Facebook**—The number of engaged users is calculated by adding the number of likes on a post, the number of comments on a post, and the number of shares on a post, and then dividing that sum by the number of fans (or likes).

- **Twitter**—The number of engaged Twitter users is calculated by adding the number of replies to the number of retweets and dividing it by the number of followers.

- **YouTube**—There are a couple ways to calculate engaged YouTube users. The first is to add the number of comments, the number of ratings, and the number of likes, and then divide that sum by the number of views of a particular video. Another variation is to add those same engagement metrics and divide the sum by the number of subscribers.

Knowing the number of engaged users and capturing the instances in which the community manager for your company improves or helps your customers are both valuable. However, it is very difficult to capture the financial effect, especially when looking at just the number of engaged users. The following are some of the other issues with ROE:

- **Fuzzy math**—We have highlighted a couple different ways ROE can be calculated in this chapter, and there are likely many others that we have not covered here. When you are reporting results to upper management, it is imperative that the math be clear and defendable. Although both of the methodologies we have outlined here are defendable, the effect on the organization is not clear.

- **Determining whether engaged users equal sales**—The fact that 25% of your fans on Facebook or followers on Twitter are engaged with your content does not necessarily translate into sales. To make that sort of correlation, you would need to do a lot of work on the back end to track your fans' or followers' activity. (We present more on this concept in the upcoming pages.)
- **Focusing on the wrong part of the funnel**—ROE is not a substitute for ROI because it isn't meant to capture sales. ROE is an appropriate calculation if you are focusing on creating brand awareness and being more actively considered before a buyer makes a purchase.

ROE is a fine metric if you are trying to understand how an audience reacts to your content online. It is not, however, a method to track the financial performance of your social or digital media campaigns.

Return on Influence

Likely the most popular variation on ROI is return on influence, which is an attempt to calculate how a particular activity in social media changes behavior. This variation on ROI is so popular that books have been written on the subject. In 2012, Mark Schaefer wrote *Return on Influence* (McGraw-Hill, ISBN: 978-0-07-179110-6), which talks about, among many other things, the importance of engaging influencers through social media marketing activities. This book provides a lot of detail about how to identify influencers, who is an influencer, and how to work with influencers. We cover these concepts in Chapter 9, "Tools: Influence Analysis."

The fundamental issue with the notion of return on influence is that it is not necessarily tied to a sales behavior. Sure, digital marketers could design a program in order to engage influencers to ultimately result in an increase in the number of purchases, but that is not often done. Most often digital marketers create influencer programs in order to grow volume of conversation and increase reach. A sale that results from that activity is great, but digital marketers often do not set up the mechanism to track that sort of behavior.

The other fundamental issue with return on influence is that those who espouse its value assert that each entry into a social conversation creates influence or a transaction. For example, in September 2011, Amy Jo Martin, CEO of Digital Royalty and Digital Royalty University, argued that every tweet, retweet, or engagement with content is a transaction. She also asserted that digital marketers can divide

the total revenue generated via social efforts by the number of social media fans/
followers to get a per fan/follower value. This, she argued, is how the return from
social media activities should be calculated. We have identified several issues with
this approach, including the following:

- **Tweets, retweets, comments, and likes are not transactions**—Think
  about your own activity online for just a moment. When you click
  the Like button or retweet someone, is your next action to go and buy
  something from that brand? In most cases, the answer to that question
  is "no." How often have you retweeted or liked something because a
  friend of yours works for the brand? These activities *might* lead to a
  transaction, but they are not direct transactions.

- **The fan/follower value calculation is flawed**—Looking at the dollar amount spent on social activities and dividing it by the number of
  fans or followers acquired is inherently flawed. The primary reason
  it is flawed is that it does not take into account the way in which fans
  are acquired. Some fans are acquired organically, and some fans are
  acquired through the utilization of paid media or advertising. Each of
  those activities has different levels of return, depending on the organization. It is a big leap—one we are not comfortable making—to assume
  that a like equals increased likelihood to buy.

- **Not all fans are created equal**—Just because I like, retweet, or even
  comment on a post does not make me more likely to buy. In fact, I
  could be the exact opposite of the brand's target audience. Therefore,
  if I retweet or share a piece of information, have I helped the brand?
  Perhaps I have in terms of raising visibility or growing reach, but there
  is a very good chance that my "share" will not reach anyone who is a
  likely buyer of the product. Is that valuable to you as the brand
  manager?

- **Changing behavior is important but not inherently financial**—We
  take a very literal approach to ROI. ROI is, without doubt, a financial
  metric. Return on influence and the previously discussed ROE are not
  necessarily financial results. They do enable you to track the effect
  you are having on certain behaviors, which is great. However, causing
  people to retweet, share, or even speak more positively about a brand is
  not the equivalent to a sale.

We are not trying to be overly negative toward anyone's work. We are only trying
to shine a light on the idea that return on influence is not a financial metric, which
is what your CEO or CMO will be expecting you to provide. As with calculating ROE, calculating return on influence can help you understand how you have
affected behaviors. It is not, however, helpful in determining how often your end
consumer will eventually ring the register.

Return on Experience

Perhaps the most radical variation of ROI is return on experience, which takes the notion of ROI and completely stands it on its head. The idea is for the brand to go above and beyond what the customer expects and earn outsized exposure by shocking the customer. Some believe that this type of shock to your customer will earn rapid word of mouth and will therefore reduce the cost per customer acquired.

Thankfully, this particular variation on ROI has not been widely applied. You can see some of the major flaws with this approach, right? The primary issue is that the brand has no way to scale this sort of measurement. "Shocking" individual customers, who then in turn create positive word of mouth, is great. However, for a company like Dell, which has several hundred customer interactions online per day, tracking this sort of activity simply is not feasible without an army of measurement professionals.

The other issue with this approach is that it is inherently not a financial metric. If your community manager creates an amazing experience for your customer, it might lead to an additional sale or sales from that person's peers, but how do you know? You would need to set up the mechanisms to track that person's activities, and if you did that, you would not be tracking return on experience. You would in fact be tracking return on investment.

Unfortunately, there are other variations to ROI that we are not dissecting here. We think you understand our point by now that ROI is a financial metric and that the variations we have outlined simply are not. Are they valuable to your brand? Potentially, but not as a way to track the direct effect your activities have had on the business. ROI in the truest sense of the word is an important metric for digital marketers to be tracking. Is it the end-all, be-all metric that some make it out to be? No, it is not the only metric you should be tracking. However, it is the metric your senior executives will care about the most. Because it matters to your senior executives, it should matter greatly to you. These are the people who control your career and your budget.

Properly Tracking ROI

Now that you know more about incorrect variations on ROI from social media activities, it is time to dig into how you can properly capture ROI. Before we get into the proper way to capture or calculate ROI, it is important to note that not every campaign requires calculating a financial impact. Recall the discussion in Chapter 2 about how important it is to set measurable goals. Sometimes increasing sales is the primary goal of a campaign, but not in every instance. Sometimes the goal of a campaign is to build awareness and brand affinity. Those two things might have some relationship to sales, but they aren't sales on their own.

The other thing worth mentioning before we get into properly tracking ROI is that tools are required in order to properly capture the financial return of your programs. We talked about many of those tools in Chapters 3 through 9; a proficiency in Microsoft Excel or other statistical modeling software (for example, SPSS) might be required. This might necessitate bringing in outside support. Keep in the back of your mind that capturing ROI requires tools that not everyone within your organization may know how to utilize.

So what are some of the ways you can capture the ROI from your social media programs? In July 2012, the Altimeter Group, an organization that provides research on a variety of communications topics, released a paper titled "The Social Media ROI Cookbook" (http://bit.ly/PEVy58). In this paper, Susan Etlinger and others outlined six excellent approaches for measuring the revenue effect of social media. Those six approaches can be broken down into two categories: top-down and bottom-up. We think this is a helpful framework for anyone trying to understand the financial impact of communications efforts.

Understanding the Top-Down Revenue Measurement Approaches

"The Social Media ROI Cookbook" outlines three different ways brands can measure the top-down revenue effect of social media activities. It is important to note that these three approaches are typically the most popular with brands. They are often the easiest to capture, and they require the fewest number of internal resources. Unfortunately, they are often high level and difficult to scale. These are the three types of top-down revenue measurement approaches:

- **Anecdote**—This is probably the most common of the three, and it involves a verbal "share" of a relationship between a social media activity and a sale.

- **Correlation**—A correlation analysis takes a certain type of social media behavior and tries to establish a relationship between it and some other activity.

- **A/B, multivariate testing**—In this type of analysis, a marketer attempts to understand the effectiveness of two versions of some type of content (for example, a web page, a marketing email, or a social media advertisement) in order to determine which has the best response rate. Multivariate testing can be thought of as many different A/B tests happening simultaneously.

The following sections describe each of these three methods in a little more detail.

Anecdote Analysis

This is likely to be the least concrete of the models we talk about here, but an anecdote is simply a verbally expressed relationship between social (or even digital) media and sales. Altimeter indicates that this is likely to be seen in large, often B2B, companies with high consideration and long sales cycles, but it would not be hard to visualize a consumer example of this type of activity.

An example of this sort of anecdotal relationship could be something like you tweeting that you're interested in buying a car. Let's say that Scott Monty, global social media lead for Ford, follows up on your comment with a reply directing you to the Ford.com website. You might then reply to Scott to indicate that you are now much more likely to buy a car, thanks to his outreach. Is it a direct sale? No. Did Scott just create an opportunity for a sale to take place? Absolutely. And that kind of activity needs to be tracked whenever possible by the measurement or market research team.

You can probably see some potential issues with this approach. Although it is valuable for Scott Monty and people like him to create these kinds of opportunities for the brand, it is not practical for him to reach out to everyone who talks about buying a car. Scott and individuals like him are not scalable. The other issue is that the process of finding these conversations can be automated, but the outreach is still very manual. Such a manual process creates strain on existing resources. However, in some smaller companies, this sort of anecdotal feedback can help achieve buy-in for additional social media activities. At a bare minimum, it demonstrates that your customers are online and looking for information.

Correlation Analysis

A correlation analysis is simply an attempt to establish a relationship between two different variables. This type of analysis is used to identify patterns in behavior. It could be anything: comparing likes on Facebook to sales, the relationship between engagement on Twitter and in-store traffic, or even more advanced models that look at economic indicators and marketing activities.

The best thing about this type of analysis is that it can establish a relationship between social strategies, tactics, and business outcomes. It's a well-established statistical approach so unlike return on engagement or return on influence you should not receive any pushback from internal stakeholders who are questioning the methodology.

However, the issue with this approach is that it is very manual. Each time you would like to understand the relationship between your social media activities and some other behavior, the analysis has to be re-created. A trained analyst (another issue with this approach, by the way) needs to capture the relevant data for the social activity and the other variable you are testing it against. Furthermore, the analyst needs to spend time outlining all the other variables (and their data sources) needed to properly conduct the analysis.

A number of tools make this process a little easier, but the primary tool of the trade is Microsoft Excel. The input might be a social media listening tool, or even an email service provider, but most of the work takes place in Microsoft Excel. There are other tools, like MarketShare, that help with even more advanced analysis. MarketShare can help you understand the consumer journey and what economic or environmental factors affect your marketing efforts.

A/B: Multivariate Testing Analysis

Multivariate testing is a method of testing a particular hypothesis using complex, multivariable systems. It is most commonly used to test market perceptions. Multivariate testing is a quickly growing area as it helps website owners ensure that they are getting the most from the visitors arriving at their site. Areas such as search engine optimization and pay-per-click advertising bring visitors to a site and have been extensively used by many organizations. Multivariate testing allows Internet marketers to ensure that visitors are being shown the right offers, content, and layout.

This type of analysis is probably most familiar to digital marketers who have been engaging in this type of work for years. Those of you who are familiar with this type of approach have probably utilized this methodology in order to understand how a particular advertisement—traditional display or social media advertising—is resonating with your core audience. It can also be used to compare different tactics across multiple populations.

Like correlation analysis, A/B testing provides strong insight into how social strategies and tactics affect business outcomes. It is also widely accepted as a practice of measurement by digital marketing professionals. However, it requires trained analysts who know how to define the variables needed for the test. It is also manual, which means that every time marketers want to understand the relationship between variables and their effect on the business, the analysis needs to be created from scratch.

Also, as with correlation analysis, this type of analysis is often done in Microsoft Excel, but it could include data inputs from social media monitoring software, web analytics tools, or even social media engagement software (such as Oracle or Buddy Media).

The three top-down revenue-tracking approaches discussed here offer marketers insight into how social media programs are performing. They are not, however, without issues. The primary issue is that these methods are not very scalable. They require the presence of human beings who have deep knowledge of tools and statistics. Even through the math behind these analyses is solid, there may still be an element of uncertainty about how a campaign performed. With correlation and multivariate analysis, there are several variables in between the social activities and the business outcomes that need to be tested in order to truly establish a relationship. The bottom-up approaches described in the next section provide more granularity.

Utilizing Bottom-Up Measurement Models

The bottom-up measurement models offer a bit more detail than the top-down approaches. This does not make them better than top-down approaches, as each organization needs to consider its goals before picking an approach. The reality is that both types of approaches need to be utilized in some form to tell a complete story.

"The Social Media ROI Cookbook" describes three primary methods of tracking revenue impact using bottom-up techniques:

- **Linking and tagging**—Probably the most familiar method for seasoned digital marketers, linking and tagging uses a series of codes in order to track how a person comes to purchase your product.
- **Integrated**—Just as the name implies, integrated measurement utilizes multiple techniques in order to gather information about how a particular person makes a purchase.
- **Direct commerce**—This is probably the first "no duh" approach that we have outlined, but the direct commerce route utilizes some sort of selling functionality within the social network your brand is utilizing.

Let us dig into each of these in more detail.

Linking and Tagging Approach

Simply put, the linking and tagging approach enables marketers to apply a short link, ROI tag, or cookie to a site in order to track the source of a conversion. A short link is simply a long URL that has been shortened using one of a number of link-shortening services (such as bitly or tinyurl). Marketers can use a shortened URL to easily track clicks to a web property or an ecommerce site where the end user may make a purchase.

A cookie is usually a small piece of data sent from a website and stored in a user's web browser while the user is browsing a website. When the user browses the same website in the future, the data stored in the cookie can be retrieved by the website to notify the website of the user's previous activity. This allows a marketer to follow a particular person's path to purchase as she lands on the page and eventually surfs around it before buying.

A linking and tagging approach is widely applicable to any setting where a good or service is being sold online. It can be applied to the actual consumption of content on a website (such as whitepaper downloads or application submissions) that the brand could consider to be conversions. The good news is that it is also the industry standard for conversion attribution and allows for deep understanding of consumer behaviors online.

The bad news with a linking and tagging approach is that it does not account for any macroeconomic trends. For example, if the economy is going through a recession, or even if more people have become predisposed to purchasing in brick-and-mortar stores, the linking and tagging approach will not suffice. The other concern is that links often break, which prevents tracking of the activities post-click.

What types of companies should be utilizing linking and tagging? The answer is probably every type, but these methods are primarily for brands that have an ecommerce presence, are selling a lower-consideration item (think cereal and pet food), or have a longer sales cycle. In some cases, you might want to think about conversion a little differently. You can set up a tagging structure that enables you to track things like white paper downloads as conversions or as leads generated. Those generated leads are just as valuable in the short term in industries that see longer sales cycles.

Integrated Approach

The integrated measurement approach utilizes an application, typically installed on a social property (most often Facebook) in order to track the user's activity. This application can be a way to serve up special content to users or direct them toward a place where they can either receive a coupon or make a purchase directly.

The best part about an integrated approach is that it tends to be very data rich. Here's what this means for communicators:

- **Understanding consumer behavior**—If you build an application that serves multiple types of content, these apps can help you understand what consumers want to see based on what they interact with the most.

- **Gathering consumer data**—Most of these applications "force" users to enter a name and an email address. The email address can be valuable when it is cross-referenced against an existing email database. However, the best applications gather that information as well as other demographic characteristics that can be very valuable for future testing.

- **Coupon redemptions**—For many B2C companies, these applications can offer the ability to serve up multiple types of coupons and track redemptions. While not a sale, per se, the download of a coupon is a pretty good indicator of a sale.

There are other types of integrated measurement approaches. The most popular, and the one that seems to be growing rapidly these days, is the utilization of digital focus groups. The concept is similar to the concept of a traditional focus group, in that a small group of people are brought together in order to learn something about how consumers are behaving.

Digital focus groups differ from traditional focus groups in that they are online (obviously) and often are served up questions at varying intervals. For example, say that you are the head of marketing for a major technology company that recently launched a new smartphone device. You have a group of influencers who drive awareness of the product, and you would like to ask them a few questions. As the marketer, you could invite them to the digital focus group and ask questions about upcoming content, new product features, existing product features, and the competition to better understand their behaviors. It does not need to be a group comprised only of influencers, obviously, but you can see how you can use this method to test the effectiveness of content and even see how certain features might be driving sales. When you know what those features are, you can create content around those ideas to drive additional purchases.

The primary challenge with this type of integrated measurement approach is that the metrics are very siloed. Building a Facebook application is great and can be a source of great information about your customers, but it is limited to only people who are existing fans. What about the effect paid media has on your fans? The data is available, but it's not conveniently presented side-by-side with other Facebook data very often. With silos can come confusion about what the data actually means.

Direct (Social) Commerce Approach

One of the easiest ways to know whether your social media activities have driven sales is to sell directly through a particular channel. The most common method of doing this today is by creating a storefront on a social platform, such as Facebook, and selling your products directly from there. Tools such as 8thBridge, Moontoast, and Spiceworks allow users to create this sort of environment.

The direct (social) commerce route is the newest and has the most potential for direct correlation to sales. It is not something that very many have undertaken so far, and it probably will evolve to something well beyond a Facebook storefront. Bob Pearson, President of W2O Group, an integrated communications agency based in San Francisco, talks about the birth of social commerce in seven different dimensions:

- **Multichannel marketing**—This represents the shift from two marketing channels to five pillars (.com, brick-and-mortar, partners, employees, and customers).

- **New media networks**—Individual communities are forming across a variety of social media channels.

- **Customers reached through search**—Many of your customers might turn to a search engine before they ever look to you for information.

- **A new content model**—This should go without saying, but customer-driven content drives the highest conversion.

- **A new approach for retail**—By understanding the effectiveness of each partner or OEM, you know how to build the right retail mix by brand, geography, and topic.

- **More effective media planning**—Using data, we can become even smarter about how we target different types of paid, owned, earned, or shared media activities.

- **New demand**—Creating new demand requires a focus on the broader community and not the influencers in order to drive sales.

Will this type of direct commerce become more popular over the years? It is hard to say. However, we have outlined several other ways you can track the ROI of your social media activities in the preceding sections. You do not need sales to occur directly on Facebook in order to show impact.

Before we close this chapter, we want to offer one relatively large statement: Engaging in social media activities is not entirely about the sale. Sure, in cases where we can track a direct business outcome, we should be doing it. However, social media can be about more than just the sale. There are other metrics you should consider when gauging the effectiveness of your social media program:

- **Share of Conversation**—This metric tracks the volume of conversation mentioning your brand against the volume of conversation happening for the entire industry. Note that share of conversation in many industries has been correlated to market share, which is a strong, more financially oriented metric.

- **Share of Voice**—This metric tracks the volume of conversation happening about your brand versus about competitor/peer brands.

- **Sentiment**—Sentiment is a widely contested subject, specifically in how it is calculated and whether it is valuable at all. However, we believe it is worth tracking in order to gauge overall brand perception.

Is it the end-all, be-all for brand perception? No. But tracking it is directionally appropriate.

- **Message Resonance**—There are invariably two or three key messages you are trying to get across to key stakeholders. Testing whether your community is talking about those messages is important.

- **Reach to Core Audience**—We realize that *core audience* is a broad term that has specific metrics assigned to it, based on the social media network in question, but we feel it is important to include here. Should it be used in isolation? No. Tracking reach alone can be misleading. However, tracking reach among your core audience can be useful in determining how often you are in the end consumers' consideration set.

There are other metrics, but these are five big ones you should be tracking in addition to financial performance. ROI is an interesting topic in the social media world, and we think it's one that needs to be solved sooner rather than later. CMOs are not tolerant of things like return on influence or return on engagement already, and time is wearing thin on their support for a measurement report that includes only soft metrics. Whether you are utilizing a top-down or bottom-up revenue tracking approach, the bottom line is that you need to be tracking ROI somehow. Do not be in the position of not tracking it when your CMO comes around to the importance of seeing the financial impact of these activities.

19

Creating the Best-Practice Measurement Scorecard

Understanding how your digital media program is performing has been an underpinning concept of the entire book. When we dissect how to build a social media listening program in Chapters 4, "Tools: Social Listening," and 10, "Developing Your Social Media Listening Program," we talk about how insights feed program planning and further listening. Chapters 5, "Tools: Search Analytics," 7, "Tools: Content Analysis," and 8, "Tools: Engagement Analysis," talk about how other digital media data—search, content, and engagement—can teach us how our campaigns are performing and how our stakeholders are reacting.

Chapters 1, "Understanding the Digital Media Landscape," and 2, "Understanding Digital Analytics Concepts," dissect the basics of digital media analytics. They discuss the various metrics you can utilize for your digital media program. They define various terms you have probably read online and throughout this book, and they talk about the importance of constantly gathering data to fuel content, program, and tactical development.

Everything in this book up until this point, while obviously focusing on other elements of digital analytics, has dealt with measurement in some way. What do we mean when we say *measurement*? Measurement in digital media terms is the quantitative and qualitative assessment of how a strategic or tactical element has performed. For example, if your brand is using a Facebook page to raise awareness, one of the ways you could quantitatively assess the impact of those efforts is by tracking impressions.

It seems pretty straightforward, right? Unfortunately, the topic of digital media measurement is one that has been challenging for many communications practitioners. To be frank, it is one that has challenged those same practitioners since before digital media became as large as it is today. The following are some of the challenges of digital media measurement:

- **Different channels**—For all intents and purposes, these channels are brand new to people. Because of that newness, there is a lack of clarity about how the channels fit into the overall marketing mix most effectively.

- **Different metrics**—With different channels come different metrics. Some, such as impressions, are familiar, but many are different from what you might have tracked in the past.

- **Volume of data**—Digital media creates a lot more data for marketers and communicators to sift through compared to other channels. The first 19 chapters of this book talk about how to properly scope your analytics efforts, but there is still a lot of data to go through.

- **Measurement frequency**—The volume of data creates uncertainty about how often data should be captured and analyzed.

- **Lacking measurement fundamentals**—Putting aside the digital media component for a second, the measurement fundamentals of many communications professionals are lacking. It is not something that's taught in school with any kind of rigor, and many professionals have an aversion to numbers. This is still prevalent today.

Over the course of this chapter, we dive into many of these elements to give you the building blocks to make your measurement efforts more successful. Measurement is not hard if you know how to do it properly.

Understanding Measurement Fundamentals

Measurement fundamentals are not being taught as often as they should be to young communications professionals as they enter the workforce. Measurement is sometimes a small part of a college course, and in some instances, internships offer the opportunity to learn some of the basics. Those basics, though, are not being uniformly taught. Because those basics are not being taught, the introduction of new channels leads to more confusion.

A greater emphasis was put on those fundamentals in 2007, when Katie Paine published, *Measuring Public Relationships: The Data-Driven Communicator's Guide to Success*. If you are a communications practitioner and you have not read this book, we highly recommend that you do. Katie goes to great lengths to detail all the basics of how to measure communications activities.

You might be thinking, "Yeah, but it was published in 2007. That was well before social media really exploded." The great thing about Katie's book, and all of her writings following the publication of the book, is that they stand the test of time. Whether we are discussing traditional public relations or online marketing, measurement is measurement. The process is still the same as it always was when outreach to the mainstream press and traditional marketing activities were all we could do.

Here's what the measurement process looks like in practice:

- **Benchmark research**—Many of the chapters leading up to this one talk about gathering data at the start of a program to inform planning. It is the first, and most-often skipped, step in the measurement continuum.

- **Strategy development**—Based on the benchmark research, communications strategies should be developed.

- **Tactical elements**—All the tactics you identify for your program should support the strategy and be strongly rooted in benchmark research.

- **Measurement practice**—This is the meat of the chapter, but how do you measure each of the tactical elements to prove how the overall strategy was successful?

Now let's dig into each of these practices individually.

Conducting Benchmark Research

Chapters 4 and 10 talk at length about using social media listening to inform program planning. Chapter 3, "Picking the Tools of the Trade," talks about using search analytics tools to understand how people experience your brand without necessarily talking about you. Those are both critical inputs to the benchmark research process, but they are not the only ones.

The benchmark research phase is meant to be inclusive of whatever information you can get your hands on. It should include existing market research on related subjects, and it should include search data, social media data (if applicable), and traditional media data (if applicable).

The following steps are required to conduct good benchmark research:

- **Setting a goal**—Ideally, this is done by a group of people involved with the program, but it should be very clear to all stakeholders. An example of this might be attempting to improve customer service through the use of Twitter. If that is your goal, you can then begin to research how other companies are using Twitter to achieve a similar goal. One very important part of the goal is ensuring that it is measurable. You can read more on measurable goals in the next section, "Strategy Development."

- **Picking the tools**—Depending on the goal of the program, the next step is to identify which tools you will use to collect and analyze data. If you are reading this chapter and still have not selected a tool, please refer to Chapters 4 through 9.

- **Conducting the research**—Assuming that you have developed a research plan (see Chapter 16, "Making Reports Easy to Understand and Communicate"), you are now ready to begin collecting and analyzing the data.

- **Developing your key findings**—If you have collected a mountain of data—and chances are you have—consult Chapter 16 on making your reports easier to understand. They should provide an actionable, go-forward insight to begin developing the strategies. You don't need to have volumes of pages or slides.

- **Additional research needs**—Based on the findings in your report, you should develop a set of additional questions or hypotheses that might require further testing. This additional testing can be done as the program gets under way, or even after. Whatever the appropriate cadence is for your brand, the research you do in this benchmark phase will likely uncover additional questions that you should address.

After your benchmark research is complete, you can begin the strategy development phase.

> 📩 *Note*
>
> Benchmark research is the primary input for communications strategies
> and tactics. If any one of the aforementioned steps is skipped or is not
> fully completed, there is a very good chance your strategies and tactics will
> be unsuccessful. Do not skip a step.

Strategy Development

After the benchmark research, which really provides the foundation for everything
else in this process, strategy development is the most critical. It is how the tactics
are developed. It is how the program itself is measured. It is what you are trying
to achieve by launching the program in the first place. You can see where we are
going with this. The strategy is not an insignificant step and should not be treated
as such.

These are some of the things you should keep in mind when you are developing
your strategy?

- **It should be measurable**—A strategy that is not measurable is a recipe
  for disaster. Why? Well, think about what might happen if you launch
  a program, and your boss asks you how you did. What would your
  answer be? If your strategy is measurable, you can quickly respond
  with an answer your boss will respect.

- **It should be based on the benchmark research**—Don't fall victim to
  "checking the box" syndrome. Don't conduct research and then set it
  aside because it flies in the face of the strategy you planned before the
  research was conducted. Use it. Base your strategies and tactics on it.
  That is what it is there to do for you.

- **It should be easy to map tactics against**—This speaks to the first point
  about it being measurable: The tactics you develop should easily flow
  from the strategy statement. The statement shouldn't be ambiguous
  nonsense that someone who wasn't involved in the process early on
  would have a hard time understanding.

- **It should allow for an integrated tactical approach**—This book does
  not delve deeply into communications tactics, but we make mention
  throughout about the importance of integration. Strategy development
  is no exception to this rule. Different communications tactics can
  feed off each other, which only improves overall results. Think about
  the strategy in terms of how well it brings in many communications
  disciplines.

- **It should be based on multiple input sessions**—If a program is meant to be integrated, then the input into the strategy should also be integrated. There should be a project owner to be sure, but multiple stakeholders should have input. This input early on will save you headaches down the line, when people question results or the approach.

If your strategy statement adheres to each of those elements, you will be off to the races and looking good to your boss. All this being said, strategy statements are still a challenge for many communicators, so we thought it might be helpful to offer up a few sample strategy statements for guidance:

- **Enable brand advocacy**—Provide information to enable members of the online community to be advocates for the brand.
- **Build product awareness**—Communicate with key stakeholders in an effort to raise awareness of the product.
- **Ensure message penetration**—Raising awareness for the company's efforts in the area of corporate social responsibility.
- **Drive purchase intent**—Creating a greater share of conversation to drive greater purchase consideration among key stakeholders.

▶ *Caution*

Don't fall into lazy marketer syndrome again and just copy and paste these strategy statements. Yours should be customized based on your benchmark research and all the considerations listed earlier.

Tactical Elements

The tactical elements chosen for your program should flow seamlessly from the benchmark research you have conducted and the strategy statement(s) you have developed. The tactics should be integrated, which means that the tactics you identify to achieve your goals should be ones that include traditional and digital elements.

These tactical components should also have data available for you to measure success. The chances that they will not in this day and age are small, but you should be sure that you can collect data on the progress of the campaign. Without that data, your hard work to get to this place will really be for naught.

This book deals with the analytics and measurement components of communications, so we aren't getting too much into the details of developing tactics. However, here is a list of potential tactics you could implement after conducting your bench-mark research and strategy development:

- Building a Facebook brand page
- Establishing a Twitter customer service account
- Launching a YouTube channel to share product videos
- Developing a new paid media program to support a product launch
- Outreaching to mainstream news outlets to further a particular message
- Activating bloggers to grow the share of conversation

Measurement Practices

After your program has been implemented, it is time to start measuring your prog-ress. By now, your strategy is clearly defined, you have done your initial research, your tactics have been developed, and you are already starting to affect behavior (hopefully). If you have done all the work leading up to this point, the measure-ment itself should be pretty easy. We aren't talking about advanced statistical measures in most cases. We're talking about tracking things in Microsoft Excel and transferring the information to a Microsoft PowerPoint presentation.

As you develop a measurement plan, there are several things you should consider:

- **Data collection procedures**—Depending on the tactics you have decided to implement, there should be clear expectations about how you are going to collect data. Our recommendation is that you collect it frequently to prevent any issues with missing data after the campaign is over. You can always collect it and sit on it until you are ready to measure.

- **Metrics to gauge success**—After your procedures are in place, you should consider which metrics you are going to track. You can't track everything, and the metrics you do track should support whether the overall strategy has been successful.

- **The measurement team**—The measurement team could be the same people who developed the program, and it could be your market research team. It could also be your agency, if applicable. Whoever it is, make sure the roles are identified before you start measuring.

- **Tools**—If you are launching a mostly social media–based program, then a lot of the data will come from platform-specific insights tools (for example, Facebook Insights, YouTube Insights). If your program includes multiple communications disciplines, and it probably should, then you need to identify what tools you will use to collect that data.

- **Reporting**—Before you share findings with internal stakeholders, you should consider how you would like to present the information. Different stakeholders should see different kinds of reports. See Chapter 16 for more detail on presenting your findings.

After reading this section, you might be wondering if we are going to touch on measurement frequency. The good news is that we are—but not until the next section. Before we do that, we think it's important to discuss one other core measurement tenet: the difference between outputs, outtakes, and outcomes. Even with the introduction of new digital media, the three O's still apply. What do we mean by outputs, outtakes, and outcomes?

- **Outputs**—This is the production of a physical product. For example, if one of the components of your tactical plan is to create a blog, then an output would be the number of posts you have written. These are important to capture, but outputs is the least valuable of the three O's.
- **Outtakes**—Outtakes are the things that your key stakeholders will glean or absorb from the program. For example, if you are trying to convey to the market that your company is active in corporate sustainability, an outtake would be how well that message resonates after the program has concluded.
- **Outcomes**—What are the quantifiable changes in behavior that you have impacted as a result of the campaign? Outcomes are the most valuable O, but they're also the most difficult to track. It requires robust benchmark research—which we hope you will complete after reading this book—and then rigorous post-campaign testing to ensure that the behavior has actually changed.

Your campaign's measurement program should have elements of all three O's in it, with as much focus on outcomes as makes sense. The outcomes are the metrics that will resonate most with your boss and continue to gain budget for you and your team. Tracking those metrics will also show your boss that you are serious about doing something other than racking up fans and followers.

Now, let's focus on how often you should be measuring and what each of your reports could look like.

Developing Your Measurement Reporting Cadence

You have an abundance of digital data available at your fingertips. If you include it with the abundance of offline data available, you are probably feeling a little overwhelmed right about now. In addition to the challenges presented by having to build a communications program (it is not easy, as any practitioner will tell you), you now have to collect a mountain of data and figure out what do with it.

So what *do* you do with it? What's an actionable insight? Where should you collect the data? The latter two questions are covered in the first nine chapters of the book; more germane to our conversation here is the question of how often you should be measuring. And what should be included in each of the reports? It's a complicated question, and it's one that both of us are famous for dodging when asked. Of course, we are not dodging it to be difficult, but the reality is that measurement frequency depends on a lot of different factors, including the following:

- **Content dynamics**—If you are developing relatively static content that will not be changing much over the course of the campaign, you can get away with a longer time between measurement reports. However, if you are going to need data to inform content in real time, you might need to alter your approach to more regular reporting.

- **The boss's expectations**—Some bosses like to see information frequently and others less frequently. Your boss's expectations can determine how often you are required to report. That being said, our recommendation is to set your boss's expectations early and tell him or her how often it makes sense, based on the program you've developed.

- **Internal resources**—Throughout this book, we talk about the internal resource burden of digital analytics. Measuring digital media programs is no exception. It takes people and money to gather and analyze data. If you do not have the internal resources or an agency to support you, then you might need to scale back reporting expectations.

- **Platforms in use for the campaign**—Twitter, for example, is a very fast-moving platform. So are Facebook and YouTube, to some degree. Traditional media, however, does not change as frequently. Think about the tactics you are implementing before you go down the road of constant reporting.

With all this in mind, what does the measurement cadence look like? We think it can be broken down into five intervals, as shown in Figure 19.1.

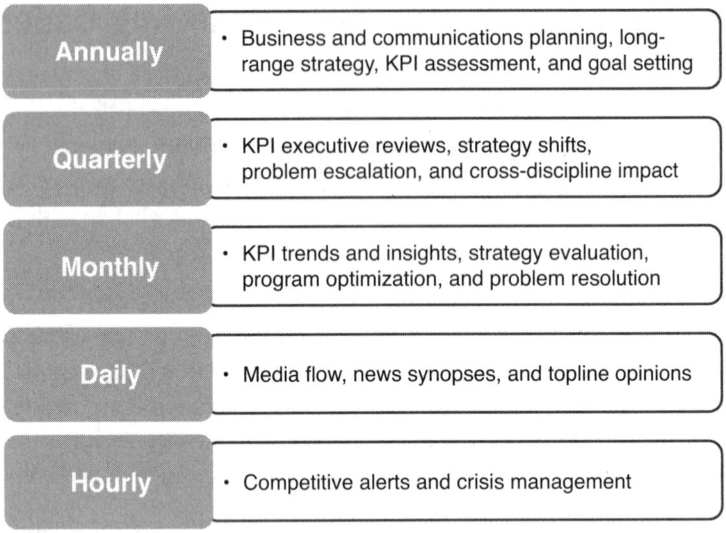

Figure 19.1 *The various potential measurement frequencies for digital analytics programs.*

Over the course of the next several sections, we dig more deeply into each of these frequencies. Chances are good that you will use bits and pieces of each, but it depends on many of the factors listed earlier in the section and your overall campaign.

Annual Reporting

Regardless of your campaign, almost every brand will undergo some form of annual reporting. It is an opportunity to assess the program you have launched, but also the program in conjunction with all the other communications activities undertaken by your organization. There are three primary benefits to completing an annual report of activities:

- **More accurate gauge of behavior change**—Over the course of a 12-month period, the people you are looking to influence will likely have been exposed to whatever message you are trying to convey to the market.

- **A large data set to analyze**—The more time that goes by, the more data you will have at your fingertips. The more data you have at your fingertips, the greater the likelihood that the trends you identify are real.

- **Greater ability to impact long-term strategy**—These annual reports are meant to feed into the following year's planning cycle. The first two points in this list speak to the reasons, but you should be using annual reports to feed strategy development.

Annual reports can be powerful. Because they take a long time and a lot of data to complete, unfortunately they are not very nimble. Yes, they do feed the following year's strategy, but anyone who has recently developed a social media program knows how quickly the social landscape evolves. New channels are developed. Existing channels are changed. This does not allow for much in the way of flexibility.

 Note

Annual reports always need to be supplemented by more frequent reports. However, just because you do more frequent reporting does not mean you can avoid a yearly rollup. It is a critical component of your measurement strategy.

Quarterly Reporting

Quarterly reporting is the most frequent type of measurement currently being completed by brands. It offers a robust data set to pick from and offers the flexibility to change tactics if something is not performing well over the course of a campaign. It also allows for the ease of completing two different kinds of reports:

- **Key Performance Indicator (KPI) executive review**—This is a top-level synopsis of findings for the c-suite (think Chief Executive Officer, Chief Marketing Officer, and Chief Financial Officer). Think of this as a scoreboard with qualitative assessment included. (See Figure 19.2.)

- **Marketing/communications management**—This is a more detailed dashboard that shows how each of the channels performed during the quarter (see Figure 19.3).

We are often asked for examples of these kinds of measurement reports, and so we provide them to you in Figures 19.2 and 19.3. Please note, however, that these examples do not contain any metrics. It is our firm belief that if you go through the processes we have outlined in this chapter, filling in these metrics should be easy. You should choose metrics that make sense for your campaign—not just ones we say are important.

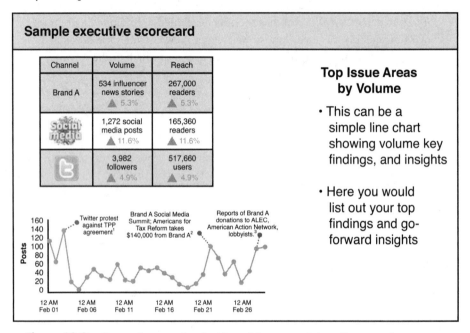

Figure 19.2 *A sample executive dashboard from a social media campaign.*

Notice that the executive dashboard is very basic. It has key findings, key metrics, volume of activity, and that is all. The details change based on what you know your executives care about, but this is a sample of what one could look like for a social media campaign.

The marketing and communications management dashboard looks very different, in that it includes a lot more detail on how the campaign has performed. It also tends to be cross-channel so that each of the teams contributing to the effort can understand how each channel has affected the other.

Sample full scorecard

Channel	Volume	Reach	Engagement	Themes	Key Findings by Channel
f	7 posts ▼ 36.4%	910 impressions ▼ 36.4%	65 likes, 14 comments, 6 shares ▲ 6.3%		
t	87 tweets ▼ 23.7%	11,310 impressions ▼ 23.7%	100 retweets ▼ 29.1%		
g	5,116 search phrases ▲ 6.0%	1,030,000 total searches ▲ 4.9%	19,065 search to site visits ▲ 5.7%		
Blog #1	694 page visitors ▼ 12.5%	694 page visitors ▼ 12.5%	167 Facebook likes, 28 Tweets 7+1s ▲ 55.4%		
Brand A website	241,670 global rank --N/A	96,071 page views ▲ 1.2%	2.75 pages/ visit ▼ 3.1%		
Brand B website	34,984 total visits ▲ 4.6%	24,830 unique visitors ▲ 8.2%	00:03:28 avg time on site ▼ 3.7%		

Figure 19.3   *A sample full scorecard showing cross-channel impact over the course of a quarter.*

The full scorecard shows volume of activity (outputs), reach and engagement (out-takes), top themes by channel, and the key findings highlighting behaviors we are seeing on each of the channels (outcomes). You can quickly see how this would be too much for an executive, but someone who is managing the program on a day-to-day basis would find this level of intelligence invaluable.

🔍 *Tip*

This type of scorecard can be adapted for a monthly view, but you need a lot of quantitative and qualitative work to pull that together. If you have a measurement team, this could be a good option to scale down into a monthly report.

These reports also allow for issue escalation, if necessary. Chapter 12, "Using Listening Data to Anticipate Crisis," discusses how you can use social media listening data to prevent or mitigate a crisis. A quarterly report is often instructive in identifying issues that might not have hit your radar yet. If new issues are uncovered by a quarterly report, you can insert those into the crisis analytics modeling detailed in Chapter 12.

Finally, quarterly reporting allows for the accurate assessment of cross-channel impact. We have talked at length about the effects that searches and social media have on one another; assembling multiple metrics across communications disciplines can help you assess that impact.

Monthly Reporting

A monthly report is essentially a "skinny" version of a quarterly report. It provides top-level insights on the overall objectives (goals) of the campaign. Everything included in a monthly report should support the overall goal/objective statement(s). This is a helpful, short-term view that shows how the overall approach is tracking. A monthly report is not meant to have the final say on how a campaign is performing, but it can be a helpful interim indicator.

A monthly report also enables you to optimize the program you are currently executing. For example, if your benchmark research indicates that your community on Facebook is very interested in recipes but your monthly report indicates that posts with videos of celebrities are performing best, perhaps next month you should consider tweaking your content. Similarly, if you are using Twitter to perform customer service and you note that a new issue is arising in conversations, it might be time to update your known FAQs document. Monthly reports are excellent at helping you change midstream, while keeping the strategic objectives intact.

Tip

It is important not to overreact to a monthly data point. As we have noted throughout this chapter, the behaviors we are trying to affect take a long time to change. Overreacting to an individual data point might cause a program course correction that is not needed.

Like a quarterly report, a monthly report can assist you in identifying new problems or issues. If there are new issues that arise as you are assembling the monthly report, refer to the crisis modeling described in Chapter 12.

Daily/Hourly Reporting

Daily and/or hourly reports should be the most infrequently used of the measurement models outlined here. Unfortunately, they tend to be the models used the most often. Why do we say they should be used infrequently? There are two reasons we do not recommend doing daily or hourly reporting:

- **Not an accurate barometer of long-term trends**—Just because a group of people are tweeting or posting about a topic today does not mean they will be talking about it tomorrow. They might still be talking about it, and you certainly should be keeping an eye out for those mentions, but you shouldn't overreact to one data point. If it becomes a trend over the course of 30 days, then it's worth including in your long-term reporting.

- **Drain on resources**—Assembling quarterly and monthly reports takes time, but daily reports are the ultimate drain on resources. One person has to take time out of his or her already busy schedule to collect the data ad hoc, analyze it, and assemble it into a report. This takes the person away from other projects, of potentially higher strategic value, that he or she might be working on.

If you are going to disregard our advice in this area, that is fine; you know your brand better than we do. However, all we ask of you is to keep your daily reports brief and low tech. A Word document or a simple email should suffice to deliver a daily report. And a daily report should include a couple graphs—most likely showing overall volume for the day—along with a couple bullet points assessing qualitatively how the day unfolded.

Many brands have gotten away from this daily reporting for the two reasons we list earlier. It is not practical to report on activities daily in most cases. There is not enough data to provide a meaningful analysis, and many of those emails and Microsoft Word documents go unread. Save yourself energy and time by abandoning daily reporting if you can.

Tip

The one exception to the daily reporting rule is in the event of a crisis or single-day event. If your brand is faced with a crisis, you need to do more active reporting to ensure that you stay on top of any trends or additional news events that arise.

This all seems so simple and formulaic, right? We have outlined all the steps required to develop a best-in-class measurement program. Even if you do not undertake any kind of heavy reporting, at least we have given you the keys to the car so that, if desired, you can ramp up your efforts in this area. If you follow the steps—from benchmark research to the measurement plan—and use the measurement frequencies and reporting styles we have outlined in the following list, you shouldn't go wrong.

We are leading up to something, as you can probably tell. However, there are several places where marketers and communicators can go off the rails:

- **Volume of data**—There is a lot of data available to gather and collect. It is not easy to collect all this information. However, if you follow our advice from Chapter 15 in which we discuss the requirements of a research plan, the volume of data should not be an obstacle for you.

- **Lack of clarity on metrics**—One of the hardest things to do in measurement is to identify metrics that accurately support the overall goals and objectives. There is not a manual for it. You tend to know it when you see it. Don't worry if the metrics don't perfectly align with the objective right away. If you are unclear, ask someone in your market research department. Or, if you are working with an agency, ask the agency's in-house measurement expert to provide some guidance. One way or another, you will get the answer you need.

- **Lack of clarity on measurement frequency**—Even though we just spent a section discussing this, there is likely still some confusion about how often brands should be measuring. The short version is that if you are planning, an annual report is best. If you are assessing campaign performance and making strategy changes, then a quarterly or monthly report is sufficient. You should use daily and hourly reports only in a crisis. You may do bits and pieces of each, but choose wisely based on your own internal resource requirements.

- **Lack of objective setting**—This is the biggest reason measurement programs at companies fail: They skip the benchmark research and instead guess what the objectives of the campaign should be. Please do not be the brand that contributes to the measurement chaos we have seen over the past decade or more. Follow the steps from benchmark research to measurement that we list in this chapter, and you will not go wrong. We promise you.

Measurement is a big issue for brands, as discussed in this chapter. In addition to our recommendation of Katie Paine's book, we highly recommend that you check out the website of the Institute for Public Relations (www.instituteforpr.org/research/commissions/measurement/) on measurement and evaluation. It provides a number of resources you can use in the event that you have questions.

20

Mobile Analytics: How Mobile Is Different than Other Digital Channels

This book has covered all manner of digital analytics— everything from studying the demographic characteristics of your audience to understanding how your core consumers search for information to analyzing how people are reacting to your content on your shared social channels. The common tie is that each of these elements is part of a broader digital marketing program. However, there is one other characteristic that adds some complexity to what we have talked about so far: how the individual behaves while he or she is not in front of a computer.

Consider for a moment how you consume information. How often are you in front of a computer? There is a good chance that between 8:00 a.m. and 5:00 p.m. you are in front of your computer nonstop, but that is only 9 hours of a 24-hour day. Chances are good that during some portion of the other 15 hours, you are on your phone, tablet, or some other mobile device. Whether you are checking out the latest app, reading a newspaper online, or playing a game with your family, you are probably accessing mobile devices more than you realize.

Because using mobile devices to consume information has become so common, more marketers are trying to understand how they can reach consumers on the go. Companies are developing apps and new websites in order to capture consumers wherever they live. Large B2C brands are tapping into apps like Shopkick and Apple's Passbook in order to deliver deals to customers.

One new technology is geo-fencing, which is a virtual perimeter for a real-world geographic area that enables companies to know exactly when potential customers are passing by a store or location. These geo-fences are dynamically generated—as in a radius around a store or point location. Alternatively, a geo-fence can be a pre-defined set of boundaries, such as school zones or neighborhood boundaries. This technology allows companies to deliver a piece of information, typically a coupon, only when consumers are in the area.

More and more companies are partnering with Foursquare and other location-based services to offer things like special perks for the mayor of a certain location, free or discounted merchandise, and tips for customers who are visiting a certain location. For example, American Express has partnered with Foursquare to enable its card members to sync their cards for the purposes of unlocking special deals. This is not the only partnership Foursquare currently has, but it is one of the biggest relationships in terms of company size. We expect more partnerships like this to develop as the location-based mobile market continues to evolve.

Even with its explosion, mobile marketing remains a relatively undiscovered and untapped method of communicating with customers for most companies. If your company has a mobile team, it is likely very small, and the activities that team is undertaking are probably limited to things like making sure the homepage is optimized for mobile devices. That is not an insignificant venture, mind you, but there are many other tactics that could be deployed. One of the reasons some mobile marketing tactics have not been deployed yet is a lack of an appropriate appreciation for how big this space has become.

This chapter discusses mobile marketing in the following ways:

- **Current trends in the market**—We outline the size and scope of the current mobile market.
- **Where mobile goes from here**—In 2012, the mobile market continued to grow and mature. In 2013 and beyond, we are likely to see similar growth in the market and adoption of mobile marketing by large companies. We identify and analyze some of the big trends that are likely to emerge.

- **What changes in the market mean for digital analytics**—This is a book about digital analytics, after all, and in the last section of this chapter, we examine the current state of mobile analytics and where we need to go from here.

Without further delay, let's look at the current mobile market dynamics.

Understanding the Current Mobile Market Landscape

Mary Meeker, partner at Kleiner, Perkins, Caufield & Byers (KPCB), is one of the foremost authorities on trends associated with the Internet. Meeker has a long history dating back to her days at Morgan Stanley, where she published seminal reports such as "The Internet Report," which contains vital information about how the Internet exploded during the dot-com boom of the mid- to late 1990s.

Meeker is one of the leading voices on trends related to mobile adoption around the world. Her Internet Trends report (http://www.slideshare.net/kleinerperkins/2012-kpcb-internet-trends-yearend-update) is one of the most widely consumed pieces of research on the subjects of Internet and mobile adoption. It is chock-full of information compiled from a series of credible sources and then published for KPCB clients and to a broader audience through SlideShare.

The report that Meeker publishes is more than 100 pages long, so we can't cover everything in it here. Over the coming sections, though, we discuss the topics that are most germane to our discussion of mobile marketing and analytics so that you can begin to wrap your head around the potential value that mobile marketing can bring to your business. We encourage you to download the report and consume it in its entirety.

Growth in Smartphone Adoption

One of the things that most of us who work in some sort of marketing-related profession take for granted is the use of a smartphone device. Many assume that all those who utilize mobile technology are doing so from a smartphone device. But that could not be further from the truth. There are still many people using older cellular technology, like flip phones. One of the most interesting trends in Meeker's report is the growth of smartphones, and how much penetration those devices have worldwide. Figure 20.1 shows Meeker's market-by-market breakdown of the number of smartphone subscribers as of the fourth quarter of 2012, what the adoption level was as a percentage of the overall subscribers, and the growth year-over-year.

1.1B Global Mobile 3G Subscribers, 37% Growth, Q4 – @ Only 18% of Mobile Subscribers

Rank	Country	CQ4:11 3G Subs (MM)	3G Penetr ation	3G Sub Y/Y Growth	Rank	Country	CQ4:11 3G Subs (MM)	3G Penetr ation	3G Sub Y/Y Growth
1	USA	208	64%	31%	16	Canada	16	62%	34%
2	Japan	122	95	9	17	Taiwan	14	48	17
3	China	57	6	115	18	South Africa	13	21	49
4	Korea	45	85	10	19	Turkey	13	20	62
5	Italy	44	51	25	20	Portugal	13	78	19
6	UK	42	53	25	21	Vietnam	12	11	358
7	Brazil	41	17	99	22	Mexico	11	11	55
8	India	39	4	841	23	Malaysia	10	27	7
9	Germany	38	36	23	24	Sweden	10	73	25
10	Spain	33	57	21	25	Philippines	10	11	45
11	France	30	45	35	26	Saudi Arabia	10	19	17
12	Indonesia	29	11	27	27	Netherlands	9	44	34
13	Poland	28	57	17	28	Egypt	8	10	60
14	Australia	22	76	21	29	Austria	7	58	24
15	Russia	17	8	45	30	Nigeria	6	6	51

Global 3G Stats: Subscribers = 1,098MM   Penetration = 18%   Growth = 37%

Note: "3G includes CDMA 1 x EV-DQ and Rev. A/B, WCDMA, HSPA: One user may have multiple mobile subscriptions and may be counted as multiple subscriber. Source: Informa WCIS+   7

Figure 20.1 *Smartphone adoption worldwide. (Source: Informa/Internet Trends by Mary Meeker, December 3, 2012.)*

There are three interesting things for marketers to consider when reviewing this smartphone adoption data:

- **The opportunity in China is huge**—Notice that China has the largest number of smartphone subscribers, at 270 million. However, this is a very small percentage of the overall number of mobile subscribers. China has become a very important market for many companies, and its adoption of mobile devices is likely to make it a more important market.

- **Smartphones are not ubiquitous**—As mentioned earlier, there is an assumption that every person utilizing a mobile device is doing so from a smartphone. Even in the United States, where we are constantly inundated with advertising for such devices, only 48% of the mobile subscribers are using smartphones. The market is going to get bigger from here as the devices get better and more cost-effective.

- **Growth overall is huge**—Marketers need to consider how their content is going to be viewed, consumed, and shared on a smartphone. Although some people are still utilizing older technologies, a smartphone growth rate of 42% needs to be taken seriously.

We expect smartphone adoption to continue growing at a rapid rate. Are we expecting it to grow at a 42%-per-year clip? No, but it will continue to grow. You need to consider how your content is being or will be viewed on these devices.

The Battle Between iOS and Android

There is a clear divide developing around the world between those who utilize iOS devices from Apple and those who use Android devices. It is widely assumed that Apple's iOS operating system used on the iPhone, iPad, and iPod mobile devices trounces its Android counterparts. Apple advertising constantly inundates us, and its fans are rabid. If you participate on Twitter or Facebook, there is a very good chance that you see someone posting about his or her Apple device at least once a day.

What is actually taking place, though, is that Android devices are growing at an even faster pace worldwide than iOS devices. Figure 20.2 shows the number of units shipped for iPad, iPhone, and iPod as of the third quarter of 2012. What's noteworthy is that iPad growth is three times larger than the growth of the other two devices.

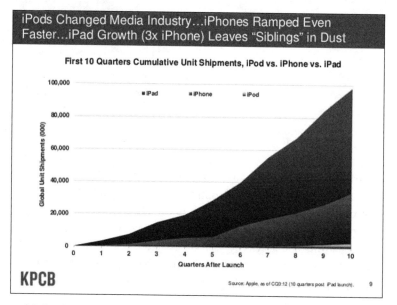

Figure 20.2   *Number of iPhone, iPod, and iPad units shipped worldwide as of third quarter 2012. (Source: Apple Inc./Internet Trends by Mary Meeker, December 3, 2012.)*

This is an impressive growth trajectory, given how long those devices have been available to the market at a cost-effective price point. However, Android devices are still growing more quickly than iOS devices worldwide. In fact, Android devices are growing six times faster than iOS devices. Android devices are taking more of the market because Android is a more open platform for developers, has greater device security, and has more widespread availability. Figure 20.3 shows the current growth trajectory for Android devices.

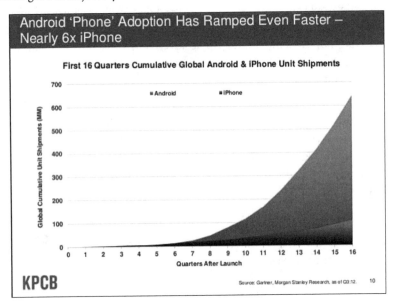

Figure 20.3   *Worldwide adoption of Android versus iPhone devices. (Source: Gartner, Morgan Stanley Research as of third quarter 2012/Internet Trends by Mary Meeker, December 3, 2012.)*

What does this trend mean for marketers? We could spend a lot of time talking about the intricacies of developing content and sites for both iOS and Android, but that is somewhat outside the scope of this book. The bottom line is that marketers need to consider all platforms when building new mobile-optimized content. Android is growing at a faster clip than the iPhone around the world. Therefore, you don't want to develop sites only for the iPhone. If you did that, you would risk missing out on or alienating a very large potential customer base.

The Explosion of Global Mobile Web Traffic

Just in the past two years, the amount of traffic Internet sites has received from mobile devices has exploded. According to StatCounter (see Figure 20.4), 1% of site traffic came from mobile devices as of December 2009. As of December 2012, that number had climbed to 13%. This is a staggering increase, and the trend line is only going to go higher as mobile device and smartphone adoption continues to rise.

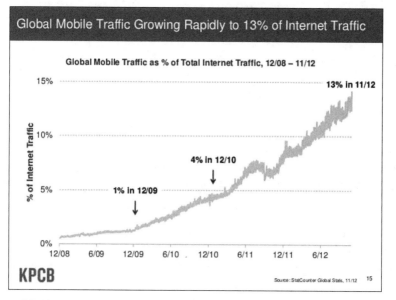

Figure 20.4   *Global mobile traffic as a percentage of Internet traffic. (Source: StatCounter Global Stats November 2012/Internet Trends by Mary Meeker, December 3, 2012.)*

What is even more amazing is that in some markets, the amount of traffic coming from mobile devices has surpassed the amount coming from desktops. In India, for example, over the past four years, the percentage of desktop Internet traffic has declined rapidly, whereas the percentage of mobile Internet traffic has grown exponentially. See Figure 20.5 for more details on this trend.

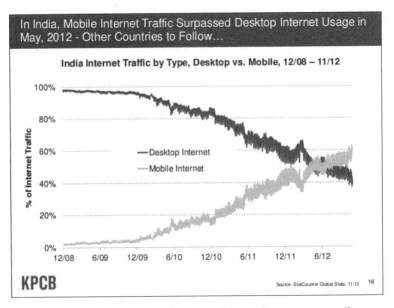

Figure 20.5 *Mobile and desktop Internet traffic in India: 2008–2012. (Source: StatCounter Global Stats November 2012/Internet Trends by Mary Meeker, December 3, 2012.)*

Again, what marketers can do to take advantage of this trend is a little outside the scope of this book. However, the biggest takeaway should be ensuring that the content you are posting on the Web is mobile optimized. You probably know how frustrating it is to go to a website on your mobile device and not be able to read any of the content. In many cases, a simple fix makes it possible for the content to be read on the go, but at other times, the fix requires a more complex build. Talk to your information technology (IT) and interactive marketing departments to ensure that your content is mobile optimized to take advantage of the trend of growing mobile Internet traffic.

The Introduction of Mobile Advertising

The explosion of smartphone and other mobile use has resulted in the explosion of the development of applications and mobile advertising. Some marketers have jumped on the trend early, developing applications and serving up advertising to potential consumers on the go. The growth in mobile app development and mobile advertising is a trend worth watching. Figure 20.6 shows more information on mobile app and mobile advertising revenue for the time period 2008–2012.

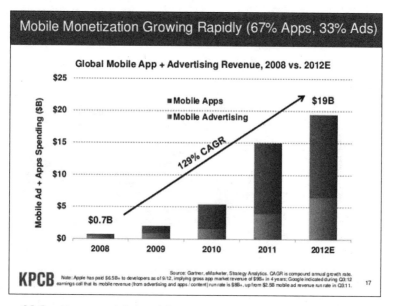

Figure 20.6   *Compare global mobile app and advertising revenue in 2008 with 2012. (Source: Gartner, eMarketer, Strategy Analytics/Internet Trends by Mary Meeker, December 3, 2012.)*

The upside to advertising through mobile devices is very large. As more people turn to their phones or tablets (or some other mobile device) to consume media, the percentage of advertising spending that companies need to allocate to mobile devices will increase. Figure 20.7 outlines the potential opportunity to increase mobile advertising spending.

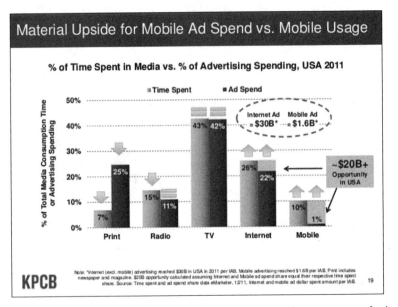

Figure 20.7 *The percentage of time spent in media versus the percentage of advertising spending in the United States in 2011. (Source: IAB and eMarketer/Internet Trends by Mary Meeker, December 3, 2012.)*

Notice that only 1% of the advertising spending is currently being allocated to mobile advertising, even though 10% of a person's time spent consuming media is happening on a mobile device. The report indicates that this is a $20 billion opportunity for the market. Most mobile advertising has not been very successful to date because either the call to action isn't strong or the content on the other end of the advertisement is not compelling. However, if brands develop a strong call to action and have mobile-optimized and original content on the other end, there might be a dramatic shift toward more mobile advertising spending.

With the explosion in the use of mobile devices comes the creation of new technologies and techniques to reach the customers on their favorite devices. In the next section, we build on the trends we just identified and talk about what is next for mobile marketing in general.

Identifying What Is Next for Mobile Marketing

In an area that is growing as fast as mobile marketing, it can often be difficult to pinpoint where the industry will grow next. There are certainly industry experts, such as Mary Meeker, that we can turn to for some insight, but even the trends the experts identify are best guesses. There could be an even bigger economic slowdown that causes the purchase and adoption of smartphones to wane. Desktops and laptops could see a resurgence in popularity with the adoption of new technology. We do not necessarily think these things will happen; we have stated them as example of the types of market forces that cause predictions to look a little foolish.

This section covers some future trends that are being predicted by experts in this area. A common thread throughout the next few pages is that these future trends are based on the current trends covered in the "Understanding the Current Mobile Market Landscape" section. It is our opinion that the trends Meeker has identified in her report have staying power, regardless of the market forces at play.

Increased Use of Apple Passbook

Aaron Strout, group director and head of Location-Based Marketing for WCG and co-author of *Location-Based Marketing for Dummies* (2011, Wiley), is one of the foremost thought leaders on the subjects of mobile marketing, digital strategy, and social media. In addition to writing for WCG's Common Sense blog (http://blog.wcgworld.com) and the Citizen Marketer 2.1 blog (http://blog.stroutmeister.com), Strout is a frequent columnist for Marketing Land (http://marketingland.com), a news and information site on Internet marketing, marketing issues, and the online marketing industry.

In one of Strout's recent columns for Marketing Land, he outlined several mobile marketing trends for 2013. It is important to note that while these were meant to be trends for a 12-month period, it is our belief that what he has identified are trends that will likely span 24 to 36 months.

One of the first trends that Strout identified is related to Apple Passbook, which is an application that enables users to store airline boarding passes, movie tickets, retail coupons, loyalty cards, and more in one place. By utilizing existing applications on your iPhone, you can see when coupons expire, where your concert or sporting event seats are located, and what the current status of your flight is. You can also get into a movie and check your balance on a gift card. The possibilities for mobile commerce with the invention of Apple Passbook are limitless.

Strout is bullish on Passbook for four reasons:

- **Apple device penetration**—As shown in Figure 20.2, the number of iPhone units shipped over the past several years is astonishingly high. The number of new devices purchased is not slowing down, either, especially with the release of new iPhone versions. Given the number of people who own iPhones, Passbook will likely become a mobile marketing staple for many brands.

- **Permanence of Passbook on devices**—Because Apple has made it impossible to delete the application and it is very difficult to delete items from your Passbook, users will have their coupons and cards saved in their digital wallet almost indefinitely.

- **Time and location awareness**—As with Foursquare and other location-based services, the customer only needs to activate an item once in Passbook to allow for ongoing messaging.

- **Customization of items within Passbook**—Customization can include text messaging, barcodes, QR codes, and other scannable formats, allowing Passbook to connect with most point of sale (POS) systems of major retailers.

Improvements in Facebook's Mobile Functionality

Facebook is the 800-pound—well, more like the 1.2-billion-pound—gorilla in the room. According to recent data from comScore, there are 170 million Facebook users in the United States alone, and each has an average of 130 friends and spends nearly 400 minutes a month on the site. Even with the size of its user base and nearly 60% of its users accessing the site via mobile device, Facebook has struggled to unlock the true potential that mobile marketing could bring.

In 2010, Facebook launched a location-based service called Places that was pulled only a year later. The reality, though, is that users can still identify where they are at any given time when posting to the site. Facebook has also experimented with Facebook Deals, which is a Groupon-like feature that offers deals for local venues; the service has never really taken off.

According to Strout, Facebook's launch of Nearby might finally crack the code on mobile marketing by leveraging the nearly always-on state of Facebook's app/mobile website combined with the power of 1.2 billion global users who spend a heck of a lot of time feeding structured and unstructured data into the mix. Nearby essentially enables Facebook (minus the games) to out-Foursquare Foursquare. Strout also predicts that Facebook will do more to tap into major acquisitions such as the mobile photo-sharing site Instagram. One of the favorite pastimes of the Millennial generation is to share photos via mobile devices. With the Instagram integration, Facebook is well positioned to take advantage of that market.

What does this mean for marketers? Most of you who are reading this book likely have a Facebook presence already, but ensuring that the content or any paid media can be easily read on Facebook is important. The functionality is somewhat beyond a marketer's control, but partnering with Facebook to develop interesting and appealing content that's accessible on mobile devices will become imperative.

Expansion of Location-Based Technologies

Strout identifies two important trends: location-based applications becoming more passive and always on and the development of hyperlocal location technology. Strout suggests that passive check-in is becoming more prominent because it is time-consuming for a user to pull out his or her phone, look up the location, add a picture and/or add a picture or color commentary, and then check in. The goal of passive check-in was to encourage businesses to provide relevant offers to encourage customers to check in regularly. According to Strout, that unfortunately has not happened as frequently as it should.

In his Marketing Land column, Strout argues that the focus will now shift to more location-aware applications that collect data or alert a customer to something he has indicated is of interest. This can be as simple as reminding someone that he is in the bread aisle at the grocery store and that he needs to pick up bagels. Or it could tie into a loyalty program; for example, every time you visit the local hardware store, you are automatically checked in and get points/cash/coupons for your visit and/or purchase.

A series of applications that complement location-based applications appeared in early 2012. Applications such as Sonar, Banjo, and Highlight alert a user when other people in her network are nearby. These applications created a lot of controversy when they were launched because there were several concerns about breach of privacy. However, the end user of these services is always in control of what the other users see. Strout believes that these applications are useful but will likely be acquired by a larger network such as Twitter or Facebook, which will make the offerings smarter.

Strout believes the use of these applications will also become hyperlocal and important to big retailers with the adoption of geo-fencing and low-energy Bluetooth technology. He points to amusement parks, such as SeaWorld, that are already using hyperlocal mapping in their apps to help customers navigate the properties. Google is also providing hyperlocal or indoor maps in places like Las Vegas so visitors can find their way around some of the hotels/casinos, which can be a mile or two from one end to another.

When hyperlocal mapping is combined with geo-fencing technology, retailers will have the ability to know where their customers are in stores and help them find their favorite products more easily. Retailers will also be able to present real-time offers based on previous purchase behavior, demographics, and participation in loyalty programs.

What these trends really boil down to is an expansion and explosion in the growth of mobile commerce. Although Apple Passbook is helpful in facilitating the transaction of goods and services via a mobile device, we are likely to see mobile commerce become bigger and more sophisticated over the next 24 to 36 months. The concept of a digital wallet, like Passbook, is only the beginning. Having the ability to target a consumer in or around a store with a highly targeted deal delivered to the customer's mobile device is likely to become the norm over the next several years.

Increased Strength of Mobile Measurement

Another important trend is mobile measurement. As Strout notes in his column, mobile measurement and available data are currently weak. It is important to pay attention to mobile data trends, but this is not something that is typically considered or included when developing an integrated measurement scorecard.

As mobile marketing continues to grow in importance, it is our view that mobile analytics will grow in importance to senior leaders. Understanding mobile behavior is critical to creating deeper relationship with customers. According to recent data from IBM, more marketers will be considering mobile tactics in 2013 and beyond. In order for mobile budgets to grow and for marketers to adopt the technology more widely, the available data and analytics techniques must improve. We think that analytics providers will improve mobile analytics capabilities in the very near future. Marketers will request improvements, and as with the other tools we have talked about throughout the book, the tools will advance as market trends become clearer.

The Current State of Measuring Mobile Marketing Activities

Mobile analytics has been the purview of the web analytics providers, and it is likely to remain so for the foreseeable future. As mentioned earlier, there is a large, and growing, percentage of web traffic comes from mobile devices. This trend has required web analytics solutions, such as Google Analytics, Webtrends, IBM Coremetrics, and Omniture to include mobile data within their standard dashboard suites.

The current mobile analytics offerings can be categorized into three different buckets:

- **Type of mobile device**—This functionality enables you to understand which devices users are using to find a website.
- **Audience/visitor metrics**—Most web analytics tools offer high-level metrics on your audience that can be segmented by mobile or desktop device.

- **Mobile app performance**—This functionality can allow you to understand how your application is performing at a high level.

Mobile Device Reporting

Mobile device reporting in web analytics tools enables you to see visitor statistics by mobile device, brand, service provider, operating system, and often also by other dimensions, such as screen resolution. This type of report also often provides a map of the location from which the visits originate. As discussed previously, hyperlocal services are going to grow in importance. If you know where the majority of your site traffic is coming from with regard to mobile devices, you can offer content specific to that market. Targeted content often leads to greater results for the brand, which is what we are all searching for, right?

Understanding the trends of mobile site traffic can give you an indication of whether your site needs to be redesigned to accommodate both mobile and personal computing traffic or whether the site justifies a separate mobile site. We argued earlier that most brands should have some mobile optimized content, but knowing how much traffic comes from mobile devices can help you make that decision.

Viewing data about where mobile visits are coming from can help you understand the current origins of mobile traffic, as well as make predictions about where traffic will increase. For example, if you are seeing a high number of views from the United States but you also notice a rise in views from India, you might want to consider serving up some sort of specific mobile content for India to see if the number of visits will continue to rise.

Most web analytics solutions also offer you the ability to create customer segments for different devices or operating systems, so you can compare, for example, visits and revenue from Samsung Galaxy devices and iPads, or Android devices and iPhone devices. If your business revolves around products like mobile applications, you can see which operating systems are most prevalent in your traffic and design to that market.

Audience/Visitor Metrics

Audience/visitor metrics are the metrics that we are most familiar with when interfacing with web analytics tools. Users of the analytics tools can often see a line graph showing visits over the past month, new versus returning visitors, and several other metrics. In most cases, you can segment higher-level metrics by desktop and mobile devices. For example, some of these metrics include the following:

- **Visits**—Total number of visits to your site
- **Unique visitors**—Total number of unique visitors to your site
- **Pageviews**—Total number of pages viewed on your site
- **Pages per visit**—Average number of pages viewed per visit
- **Average visit duration**—Average visit length of all visitors
- **Bounce rate**—Percentage of single-page visits
- **New visitors**—Percentage of total visitors who visited your site for the first time

Users of the analytics tools can also often look at demographic characteristics, the type of mobile operating system used, the mobile service provider used, and the typical mobile screen resolution in conjunction with the metrics just listed. Although these metrics do not tell you a lot on their own, they can at least be instructive of how big your audience is or could be.

Mobile App Performance

Most web analytics solutions offer you the ability to capture mobile app–specific usage data that integrates with your existing account. Google Analytics is currently one of the best solutions for measuring app performance in this way. Within the Google Analytics suite, you can analyze and evaluate an app's performance based on the following metrics:

- Number of installations or downloads
- Devices and networks used to access the app
- Geographic location and languages spoken by the visitors
- In-app purchase totals
- Customized tracking of the number of installations
- The number of screens seen per visit and the order in which visitors move through the screens

The best part about the Google Analytics mobile app performance capabilities is the ability to set up goals and ecommerce to track certain objectives such as completed sign-ups and product sales from within the app.

If you don't want to use Google Analytics, there is a very good chance that your web analytics provider gives you the ability to track app performance within its platform. Check with your customer relationship agent to find out whether it's possible to add the capability.

You can see that the metrics listed earlier are very web analytics heavy. Although the information these metrics can obtain is helpful, mobile analytics can and should go further. In the final section of this chapter, we discuss how mobile measurement can evolve from here.

The Future State of Measuring Mobile Marketing Activities

As mentioned earlier, mobile measurement to date has been focused mostly on web analytics metrics. Those are important metrics to track, but understanding behaviors is where the current approach really falls down. Yes, you know how many people visit our site from a mobile device. Yes, you know the type of operating system they are using. Yes, you can learn how many pages, and what pages, they are visiting from a mobile device. You can even understand whether they are making purchases from their mobile devices while visiting the site. Unfortunately, those latter two metrics are not things marketers are tracking often enough.

Because of the growth trends of mobile marketing overall and because the decision has changed from "should we do mobile marketing?" to "how should we do mobile marketing?" we think more sophisticated return-on-investment models need to be developed in order to truly gauge the performance of mobile marketing plans. Such models could track conversions from the device or even include mobile traffic data within marketing mix models.

We also think that the big data trend will impact mobile marketing tremendously. Marketers will begin to look for data beyond what we described earlier to provide information on things like coupon clicks, organic versus retargeted engagement, and location of engagement.

There is also an opportunity to do A/B split testing for mobile campaigns that can become a regular part of app development and management. There is not a service that currently offers this capability, but with mobile marketing expanding, new analytics tools will help capture this data.

You can probably gather by now that we are predicting that more action-oriented metrics will make their way into mobile marketing measurement programs in the foreseeable future. Will we see a standard approach to mobile measurement emerge? Perhaps, but a common approach to digital and social measurement has not been agreed to yet. In any case, finding ways to track conversions from mobile devices will be key. Tracking visits and high-level metrics will be important, but only when tracking the conversions associated with those visits.

21

Social CRM

You don't need us to tell you that social media has exploded over the past five years. Facebook has more than 1 billion users. Twitter has more than 100 million active users. LinkedIn has recently crossed the 200 million registered users mark. Participating in social media has become a staple of how consumers behave on the Internet. Consider for a moment that, according to comScore, social networking sites reach 82% of the world's online population, which represents 1.2 billion users around the world. That is a staggering number of people who could be, or currently are, customers of your brand. Until recently, businesses used traditional customer relationship management (CRM) systems to handle interactions with customers. Simply put, CRM is a model for managing a company's interactions with current and future customers. It involves using technology to organize, automate, and synchronize sales, marketing, customer service, and technical support. The goal of any CRM program is to find, attract, convert and retain customers. Unfortunately, many CRM systems were ill equipped to handle the speed and volume of data created by interactions taking place online. Furthermore, they were not meant to capture the kind of information given to marketers via interactions with online customers. New processes and systems needed to be built to handle the data, the interactions, and the multitude of individuals interacting with customers every day. Here enters the concept of social CRM. According to Jacob Morgan, principal at Chess Media Group, social CRM is a customer engagement strategy that supports defined goals and objectives toward optimizing the customer experience. Social CRM does not replace CRM, says Morgan, but is an important extension that adds value for the benefit of the users and the customer. Social CRM is not an exception to the rule we have been talking about in this book: Integration is key, with both communications teams and data. The only way you can maximize your benefit from an increased number of customer interactions is if you don't treat social CRM as a standalone process. There is a lot of confusion about what social CRM really is. That has been caused by the introduction of unfamiliar jargon and abbreviations that many marketers are unfamiliar with. This chapter includes definitions of provided by some of the leading thinkers in the space. For now, consider some of these statistics about how companies are interacting with customers through social networks:

- Gartner predicts that by the end of 2013, more than 60% of Fortune 500 companies will "actively engage" customers with Facebook marketing, up from 20% in the fourth quarter of 2011.

- Only 25% of business-run social media accounts are defined by meaningful customer engagement and consistent content distribution (Altimeter Group).

- In the past year, 17% of customers have used social media to get a customer service response (American Express 2012 Customer Barometer).

- Customers who engage with companies via social media spend 20% to 40% more money with those companies than other customers (Bain & Company).

- More than 20% of consumers use social media to seek information or to find deals or recommendations (J.D. Power and Associates).

- One survey found that 60% of customers feel companies have generally improved their response times over social media channels (American Express 2012 Customer Barometer). In addition to offering some of the definitions of social CRM available today, this chapter also discusses how to make social CRM operational today, describes the tools available on the market, and previews what is coming in the future of social CRM.

Defining Social CRM

One of the biggest challenges to the adoption of social CRM is the myriad definitions created by people who work in the social media or CRM industries. We
believe that social CRM is simply an extension of CRM into a new channel. Yes,
there is data available to us through social media channels that was never available
when legacy CRM systems were built. However, that does not mean that traditional CRM activities should take place independently of social CRM.

If you have not picked it up already, we are big believers in bringing together communicators and data sources. Bringing together all the available data that you have
on your customers only leads to more focused, successful communications programs. It is the same thing with CRM. If your organization is currently engaging
customers online, why would you not capture that data in some sort of CRM database? You could be capturing names, demographic characteristics, email addresses,
tone and tenor of the conversation, the product or brand name mentioned, and
dates and times of interactions. These are all valuable things that your sales force
would like to see as they work with customers offline.

The following list shows how several industry experts define social CRM. The
people whose definitions we've included have a background in either social media
or legacy CRM systems:

- Social CRM enhances the relationship aspect of CRM and builds
  on improving the relationship with more meaningful interactions.
  (Definition provided by Altimeter.)

- Social CRM is the process by which organizations make clients an integral asset in the management of productive relationships. (Definition
  provided by Mark Bonnell, CEO, Modyo.)

- Social CRM is a business philosophy that expands the borders of
  traditional customer relationship management beyond information,
  process, and technology to people, conversations, and relationships.
  (Definition provided by Jas Dhillon, Chief Social Technology Officer,
  Ipsos.)

- Social CRM captures both the tools *and* the processes around the tools
  to (1) leverage crowd-sourcing customer ideas, (2) apply the wisdom of
  crowds to those ideas, (3) create a public customer ecosystem, (4) take
  the customer experience and communication to the time, place, and
  method the customer prefers, and (5) increase customer intimacy and
  empowerment. (Definition provided by Michael Fauscette, Group Vice
  President, Software Business Solutions, IDC)

- Social CRM is a strategy for harnessing communities to support customers and prospects, as well as sales, marketing, and customer service organizations, along a purposeful and mutually beneficial business process. (Definition provided by Gartner.)

- Social CRM is a philosophy and a business strategy, supported by a technology platform, business rules, workflow, processes, and social characteristics, designed to engage the customer in a collaborative conversation in order to provide mutually beneficial value in a trusted and transparent business environment. It's the company's programmatic response to the customer's control of the conversation. (Definition provided by Paul Greenberg, Owner, The 56 Group, LLC and Management Consulting Consultant.)

- Social CRM is the business strategy of engaging customers through social media, with goal of building trust and brand loyalty. (Definition provided by Harish Kotadia, PhD, Practice Leader, Data Analytics and Big Data.)

- Social CRM is customer relationship management fostered by communication with customers through social networking sites, such as Twitter and Facebook. (Definition provided by Jacob Morgan, Principal, Chess Media Group.)

It is easy to be confused by the definitions here. None of these definitions are technically incorrect, but they offer too many different ideas about what social CRM is. In large companies, the enemy of adoption is often complexity. Something that easily integrates with what a team is already doing has a greater chance of being adopted. The common thread among the definitions listed here is that any social CRM initiative is a combination of your interactions with customers and their nature and influence online.

Although defining the concept of social CRM can be challenging, defining it is far less complicated than deploying it. The next section describes how you could deploy a social CRM initiative within a company.

Rolling Out a Social CRM Initiative

One of the things both Chapter 4, "Tools: Social Media Listening," and Chapter 22, "The Future of Digital Data: Business Intelligence," cover is having data at your fingertips while you are working. Chapter 22 briefly touches on the concept of listening command centers. Although listening command centers show internal and external stakeholders that you are serious about how your customers are talking online, command centers hold limited value as day-to-day research operations.

You can accomplish just as much, if not more, with a scalable dashboard that sits on the desktop of every team member.

A dashboard combines social channel (Facebook, Twitter, YouTube, and so on) data with social conversations not currently being had by you and available customer data that is often not made publicly available. What if this dashboard also included all relevant and verified customer data? The dashboard could include recent purchase history, demographics, previous interactions, call support data, recent tweets, and Facebook updates. This combination of data would enable social media practitioners and customer support personnel to tailor a customer's online experience like never before.

Developing a dashboard requires several steps. In addition to gathering the appropriate tools (many of which are discussed in Chapters 4 through 9), you must develop a process that guides decision making on whether an action is required.

Jacob Morgan, principal at Chess Media Group, has developed a helpful five-step process that revolves around action, reaction, and management. (Morgan's acronym for this process is ARM.) The concept is that organizations create a structure by which every customer interaction can be successfully managed in near real time. Let us go through each of the step in more detail.

The first step in Morgan's ARM process is identifying what is being said online about your customer or the competition's customer. These conversations can come from your existing customers, prospects, influencers, third-party groups, advocates, and even partners. By using a social media listening solution (see Chapter 4), your organization can easily set up a dashboard to listen for key terminology that your customers might use. Many social media listening solutions offer the ability to create multiple dashboards. In this context, our recommendation is that you create a separate dashboard that utilizes mentions of your brand along with variations of the word *buy* or *recommend*. Although it is likely that you will pull in mentions that aren't of a CRM nature, this should give you a cleaner set of data than only looking at all mentions of the brand.

The second step is identifying where the conversations are taking place. As with the first step, a social media listening solution can help you identify whether the conversations are taking place on Twitter, Facebook, blogs, traditional news sites, LinkedIn, YouTube, or some other platform. The missing link here is often the exclusion of more traditional methods of contact, such as online customer support, contact forms, telephone exchanges, and mailed-in contact cards. Understanding what's being said and where it is being said can help you more effectively tailor the outreach to your customers.

Tip

> After the social CRM initiative is created and you begin reaching out to
> your customers, it is important that you do so where they "live." If you
> have noticed that a customer is corresponding or mentioning your brand
> on Twitter, your outreach to that customer should take place on the same
> channel. This goes for all other social networks as well.

The third component of ARM involves analyzing the sentiment, or intent, of your customer. Several chapters in this book mention sentiment and the complexities of measuring the sentiment of an online conversation. Some listening tools include natural language processing (NLP) engines in order to more effectively judge the tone of someone's comments. However, those NLP engines are at best 80% accurate. Although that is better than any other automated scoring system, being only 80% sure of how a customer feels about the brand before interacting can be a dicey proposition. It is a little easier when the customer interaction takes place via telephone because the tone can be discerned. This element of the ARM process is likely never to be automated. There will always need to be an analyst who can hand code the sentiment of online conversations before it is entered into any dashboard or database.

✉ *Note*

> What do we mean by the term "hand code?" An analyst within your organi-
> zation would read a post and then assign either a number (on a scale of 1
> to 5, for example) or a qualitative value (positive, negative, neutral) to it.

The fourth step is to gather all the available data that your organization already has stored on the customer and then compare it to what you have gathered through social media channels. Ideally, your organization has been using some version of a traditional CRM platform—such as Oracle, Salesforce.com, or Adobe—and the information can be easily exported from it. This information should contain the core customer data such as transaction history, support history, and demographics. Comparing the social data you have gathered in the first three steps of the ARM process with your traditional CRM data can help you understand the following things:

- When did the customer last buy the product, and is he or she talking about that product online?
- Has the person called customer support recently? Did the issue get resolved quickly and easily?

- Is the person who is talking online a lead or prospect? Is he a current customer?

- Where does the customer "live" online?

- Where does the customer live geographically? Does the customer's location match up to the location of conversations that are being had online?

- How does the demographic data of your customer offline compare to her offline data?

- What social properties does your customer currently participate in? Where is she the most active? Does she talk about brands on all the social channels she participates in?

- What is the size of the customer's social graph? How many followers does he have on Twitter? Does he have a large number of blog subscribers?

These are just some of the things you could learn by putting the two data sources next to each other. You might find as you undertake this exercise for your business that you glean things that aren't on this list. That is perfectly fine as long as you utilize that insight for something in the organization.

The fifth step of ARM is to establish the rules of engagement. Every company is different, and every company has a unique approach to gathering data and using it to interact with customers. These business rules are constantly in flux and change, depending on new products that are announced, new locations of customer conversations, or new topics of customer conversations. What is important here, as Morgan notes, is that every potential interaction is documented. An example of something that should be documented is the fact that a member of the community downloads or unsubscribes from a piece of content. In this case, a notification should go to the sales team for prompt follow-up.

For visual learners, Morgan has created a helpful visual that brings these five steps together. See Figure 21.1 for more detail on how the ARM process flows.

Action/Reaction/Management (ARM) Process

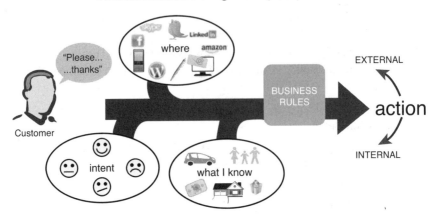

Figure 21.1   *The action, reaction, and management (ARM) process. (Source: Jacob Morgan, Chess Media Group.)*

Morgan's model is not the only one that exists for dissecting the concept of social CRM. However, we think it is the best one at breaking the process down in manageable, easy-to-understand steps. The other models, like that of Capgemini, utilize a similar approach of understanding social and offline interactions and then combining that knowledge with traditional CRM data. Figure 21.2 provides more detail on Capgemini's model.

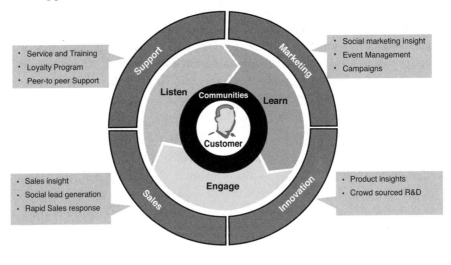

Social CRM, Onion model

Figure 21.2   *The onion model of social CRM. (Source: Capgemini.)*

Regardless of the model you prefer, combining traditional CRM data with social conversation and interaction data can be very powerful. One of the tricks to successful implementation is having many of the tools outlined in Chapters 4 through 9 as well as a social CRM—specific database to capture all the relevant information. The good news is that there are a number of high-quality solutions on the market.

Identifying a Social CRM Solution

As with social media listening tools, and frankly many of the other toolsets listed throughout the book, an abundance of social CRM tools are available on the market today. Some are more for small to medium-size businesses, whereas others cater to the enterprise market. The good news for marketers is that the tools integrate well with existing toolsets, regardless of industry or company size. Most of them integrate with traditional CRM databases and social media listening platforms. Integration is key because if you are planning to successfully implement the ARM process outlined in the preceding section, you need to be able to bring multiple data sets together. A lack of integration could make that transport much more complicated than it needs to be.

The following pages outline some of the best social CRM tools available on the market today. As mentioned throughout the book, the digital space is evolving rapidly. There could very well be tools that hit the market soon that take the place of these tools. However, if we were starting the search from scratch at this moment, this is where we would begin.

Batchbook from BatchBlue

BatchBlue's Batchbook is appropriate for small to medium-size businesses that are trying to develop relationships with their customers. The Batchbook solution enables you to easily create a customer relationship history, track conversations that mention the brand, and understand where conversations are taking place—in person or electronically via email, Twitter, Facebook, blogs, or LinkedIn. The best part of the solution is that it makes it easy for you to retweet, reply to, or save a tweet as a communication. You can also post to Facebook walls and friend pages. Batchbook includes the ability to pull in RSS feeds from blogs and social sites if you have identified a series of sites that you know your core customers frequent. Batchbook also enables you to record information about customers and create to-do items that are tied to specific people.

In addition, the Batchbook solution allows for easy importation and exportation of data. As we mentioned when discussing the ARM process, being able to easily import data into a social CRM solution is key for easy adoption and use by the organization. After all the data has been imported and organized in Batchbook, you can easily segment your contacts by task, location, last time contacted, and so on.

The Jive Social Business Platform

Jive brings together several different tools into one social business platform that allows for greater collaboration within the organization. Within one suite of services, Jive allows you to create communities that connect employees with customers and partners via social media; create new opportunities for internal collaboration; have greater access to customer data for sales, marketing, and customer support; and engage with customers via social media channels. The platform's many applications enable you to engage customers on Facebook, Twitter, and other social networks. One of the best components of the Jive platform is its ability to deliver performance metrics, which is something we have not talked about much in this chapter. Creating organizational efficiencies and being able to track that benefit to the organization is key.

The Lithium Social Customer Suite

Social Customer Suite from Lithium Technologies was designed to help companies improve customer engagement. It is recommended for enterprise companies. The suite has three components:

- **Community Platform**—This platform utilizes social conversations in order to help the organization spread a particular key message. These communities could be in the form of forums, idea communities, Q&A sites, ratings and reviews, photos and videos, contests, blogs, and groups. This is the legacy part of the business for Lithium, so expect this to be the best part of the Social Customer Suite.

- **Social Web**—Lithium Social Web equips customer service teams to respond to millions of messages across social channels, including Twitter, Facebook, blogs, and other types of online communities. Users of Lithium's Social Web read, task, and respond to social media posts; respond to posts in the community; embed links within the customer community; and monitor and measure the performance of agents in one platform.

- **Analytics**—The Analytics suite is organized into community, social web, and listening information. It gives high-level metrics on how your community is performing, identifies influencers, gives high-level background on the topics of conversation online, and provides metrics on response times to social media interactions. There are also advanced visualizations for the purposes of reporting to senior management.

The Meltwater Buzz Engage Module

The Buzz Engage module is a plug-in, of sorts, to the existing Meltwater monitoring solution. Having ease of integration with a social media listening provider is key. The Engage module is composed of a number of components:

- **Social inbox**—The social inbox centralizes your social media management across Twitter and Facebook into one location. You can set up alerts, immediately respond to customers, and task engagement to other members of the team.

- **Social profiles**—The social profiles provide you with a brand sentiment score, engagement and communications history, external social profiles, a network map of who the person is connected to, and the ability to custom tag and segment interactions.

- **Contact database**—The contact database is exactly what it sounds like: a listing of all your social interactions. You can sort the database by rank, reach, and social channel, and you can view heat maps of contacts by region.

- **Social action**—Based on the conversations you have identified mentioning the brand, you can directly engage with a customer on Facebook or Twitter.

- **Social calendar**—The social calendar enables you to view all the messages that have been sent and those that are scheduled for the future. You can use the social calendar, you can also post to Twitter and Facebook very easily.

- **Focused view**—Using heat map technology, you can see where interactions are taking place in a certain region by topic.

- **Multi-account**—You can manage multiple Twitter accounts and Facebook pages from the Engage module.

- **Engagement metrics**—With this component, you can understand what content is working, determine who is engaging with the brand most often, discover who is retweeting content the most, and track your brand's impressions.

This platform is one of the few that crosses the line between enterprise solution and small business solution. Meltwater has listening solutions that work for all sizes of businesses, and the Engage module is easy to use with those services.

Nimble

Nimble helps organizations build better relationships with their customers by integrating and unifying all points of contact and social communication. Nimble imports, merges, and unifies contacts, calendars, and communications from Google, IMAP, Skype, and social networks such as Facebook, LinkedIn, and Twitter. It enables you to read and respond to communications in just one place. Nimble also automatically searches social media sites, identifying relevant connections and ranking them in relevance. After key information is identified, you can share that data with anyone who needs it. In addition, Nimble's application programming interface (API) enables you to create your own social CRM widgets.

SugarCRM

SugarCRM is an open-source solution with social CRM built in, so organizations can integrate their social media feeds with their email marketing for online collaboration, document sharing, and sales intelligence from the get-go. With SugarCRM, you can read tweets of people you follow in the Activity Streams dashlet. You can read and respond to Facebook friends' news feeds and get up-to-date information on customers and prospects via the InsideView module. And if you want or need to create additional functionality or social CRM applications, you can do so using Sugar Studio, Sugar Cloud Connectors, and Module Builder.

We have talked about a lot of tools so far, but you might be wondering why we have not talked about Salesforce.com or Oracle in this chapter. Recall from Chapter 4 and Chapter 8, "Tools: Engagement Analysis," that we talk about the integrations the two companies were undertaking (the combination of Radian6 and Buddy Media in the case of Salesforce.com and the combination of Oracle's CRM solution with Vitrue). Chapter 22 also discusses Salesforce.com's new MarketingCloud product. Suffice it to say that both Salesforce.com and Oracle will be important players in the social CRM space in the near future.

Analyzing the Future of Social CRM

Social CRM will begin to disappear as a standalone term as more traditional CRM tools develop capabilities in this area. The reality is that CRM is CRM, whether you are gathering data on your customers when they're offline, online, or on a mobile device. The term social was added to provide clarification of the differences between the two activities (traditional and on social media). However, in the long-term, social CRM will need to be integrated with other, more traditional activities.

Where else will social CRM go? Michael Brito, senior vice president of Social Business Planning at Edelman Digital, has argued that it is time to move beyond social CRM and toward social business. We could not agree more. As Brito points out, social CRM is only one component of the customer and technology ecosystem. It is only one piece of the puzzle that organizations need to put together in order to change the way they communicate and engage with key stakeholders. Most importantly, it's only one attribute or proficiency that a company needs to develop in order to become a truly social business. It is time to move on and focus on the big picture.

22

The Future of Digital Data: Business Intelligence

In this book, we have armed you with everything you need to know about digital analytics to make your communications programs better and your business smarter. We have explained the basic digital analytics concepts, provided guidance on selecting tools (everything from social media listening tools to engagement tools), offered some digital analytics use cases, described how to formulate a research plan and measurement scorecard, and given you some additional things to think about, such as mobile analytics. Every chapter will help you and your organization harness the tremendous power of data and understand your customer in a way that has previously not been possible.

After reading the first 21 chapters, you might be thinking that implementing everything we have outlined is going to be difficult for your business. But do not worry. You may have started this book as an organization that utilizes only a social media listening provider. Eventually you may use (in some way) all the tools outlined in

Chapters 4 through 9, to create a process to conduct additional digital research, develop a best practice measurement scorecard and, most importantly, begin to utilize data to improve communications programs. This process does not take place overnight. The organizations that many people view as best-practice organizations in the industry (for example, Dell, Intel, Pepsi, Cisco, and American Express) did not develop strong analytics capability overnight.

You might be surprised to know that even though this industry is now several years old, only a small percentage of organizations are actually using social media to monitor activity. Even fewer companies are using digital data to measure corporate performance. According to a study conducted by Stanford University's Rock Center for Corporate Governance (http://www.gsb.stanford.edu/cldr/research/surveys/social.html), 35% of companies are using social media research to further understand their customers, and only 14% utilize social media research to measure corporate performance. What is even more staggering is that only 24% of senior managers and 8% of directors request reports on their company's social media engagement efforts and stakeholders' social media sentiment. If you read the first part of this book and thought you were behind, you should think again.

If you are not currently doing any social media monitoring or measurement, then that would be the best place for you to start. However, if you are looking for a formula for how to get started, you should do the following before developing your digital analytics program:

- **Develop company goals**—If you would like to develop a digital analytics capability, what are you trying to achieve by doing so? Is it to simply understand your customers better? Is it to understand how your digital marketing programs performed? You could have many goals, but before you go down the road of picking tools, knowing what you would like the end result to be is imperative.

- **Identify internal resources**—In almost every one of the chapters so far, we have talked about the importance of human and financial resources. You also need to think about your digital analytics program holistically. The resources need to be in place before you start picking tools, determining use cases, and putting the data to use.

- **Build reporting requirements**—If you have the go-ahead to create a digital analytics program, you should also start thinking about reporting requirements. Your bosses will want to know what they are getting for their investment in this program.

- **Develop a program schedule**—In all likelihood you will not be able to launch your program with every tool available from day one. You will need to create a Gantt chart or a program schedule that outlines how this new function will be built. This chart can include everything from when new tools will be researched to how head count for this new group will be acquired.

- **Achieve participation from other parts of the organization**—We have been involved in many digital analytics launches with clients of all sizes. One thing that consistently happens is that companies attempt to start small, but they don't stay small very long. When people in other parts of your organization realize the power of digital data, they will want to participate. Before launching your program, give thought to how other parts of the organization can participate. It could be something as simple as a financial contribution or something more rigorous, such as a set of digital media readiness standards.

At this point in the chapter, you might be wondering what getting started in digital analytics has to do with the future of the industry. The truth of the matter is that many companies that have implemented social media listening programs today are going through the motions. At one point in time, an organization may have realized that listening to customers is important, so the organization purchased a tool and started listening. Organizations often did this without thinking through the five things in the preceding list or any of the other best practices we have outlined throughout this book. We hope that in the future, companies will think about the listed items and everything else we have outlined in order to truly develop a best-practice digital analytics capability. Now, it's time to dig into how each of these disciplines will evolve over time.

Watching How the Digital Analytics Disciplines Evolve

In the next several pages, we talk about what the future holds for each of the toolsets outlined in Chapters 4 through 9. We also discuss what the future holds for the digital analytics industry more broadly. If you are just getting started building your digital analytics capability, be sure you have read the preceding chapters before reading this one. Getting your organization to this point requires the completion of a lot of the steps outlined in the rest of the book.

Predicting the Future of Social Media Listening

Very few specialties under the digital media umbrella have gone through as much transformation in the past five years as social media listening tools. When companies such as Radian6 and Sysomos launched their platforms, they provided incomplete data and had several user interface challenges. Now both of these tools are seen as the best in the industry and are used by many Fortune 1000 organizations.

They have since also been acquired by large organizations—Salesforce.com and Marketwire, respectively.

We think that the era of consolidation within social media listening tools will continue. Recall that in Chapter 4, "Tools: Social Media Listening," when we discussed the available options, we mentioned that there are literally hundreds of different tools available to companies today. It is impossible for companies to evaluate that many tools, and even if you were to try to do it, you would notice that there is not much differentiation between the various competitors. Some people have argued that consolidation in this space is a bad move because the tools have not fully evolved, but in our view, consolidation will not be the enemy of innovation.

Why do we feel that innovation will still occur with these listening providers? The primary reason is that listening data as a standalone input will slowly begin to lose its value. That isn't to say it has no value, but when it is presented by itself, it tells only a small part of the story. However, when it is presented alongside search behaviors, content engagement data, or even offline primary research, it can be much more powerful.

Social listening data can be even more powerful when it is presented alongside data from traditional customer relationship management (CRM) tools (along with the data inputs listed earlier in this chapter), which is why we believe Salesforce.com's MarketingCloud holds such tremendous potential. MarketingCloud will offer marketers the opportunity to analyze web data (through Webtrends) alongside social media monitoring data (through Radian6) and social media channel engagement data (provided by Buddy Media). MarketingCloud has many other applications beyond that, but this is the one most applicable to this book. How that application is rolled out in the near future will be critical to understanding the direction the other listening providers, like Sysomos, will move.

How else will listening providers change? We think that the dashboards listening providers offer to clients will become less important over time. As users become more familiar with the data that is provided and how to manipulate it, the static dashboards provided will significantly lose value. Having a reliable API where clients can easily access the data that is provided to them will become critical. An API that is not reliable will likely mean an exodus from that particular tool.

Finally, one of the growing trends we have seen over the past few years is the development of global command centers. A command center is a room, typically located at a company's headquarters, that is staffed by analysts or marketers for the purposes of listening to conversations online. Dell and Gatorade had two of the original command centers, and several other brands have since launched similar centers.

What is the value of having a command center? Because listening tools can be available literally on any desktop within your organization, you might be wondering why you should bother creating a specific physical space. During a panel discussion during South by Southwest Interactive 2012, one of the world's largest interactive and technology shows, Mason Nelder, director of Social Media and Digital Strategy at Verizon, was asked this very question. His response was that a command center is an internal rallying point. It is a symbol to the organization that listening to the customer is important and that social and digital media are important to the organization's communications efforts. In that context, you can see how the command center space might be valuable.

Do you need a command center? The answer, as usual, is that it depends. If you are looking for something around which your organization can rally, then it might make sense to create a command center. If you are looking to build a strong listening capability in order to more fully understand your customer's behaviors, then building the space might be a secondary concern. This isn't to say that you cannot have both goals and build the space; rather, it is typically one or the other in companies. Most companies have not evolved the command center concept beyond a singular use case.

The social media listening market has changed substantially since 2007, and we have no indication that the next five years will be any less tumultuous. However, as soon as more of the listening providers move in the direction that Radian6 has already moved, the greater the likelihood that we will hear less about social media listening and more about customer intelligence programs that have multiple data inputs.

Diving into Search Analytics

The difference between search analytics and social analytics is that the former is very well established. For search analytics, there are established tools such as Google AdWords that help a communicator understand what words are being used most often and in what volume. An established set of metrics are accepted by the industry, such as click through rate (CTR), total clicks, cost per click (CPC), and cost per acquisition (CPA).

The way those metrics have been calculated hasn't changed in years. It could be argued that it might be time to change the search analytics model or at least examine whether the established metrics are still appropriate, but that would require a significant amount of "reprogramming" within companies. Companies have used the same method of calculating the effectiveness of their search programs for years, and we don't see that changing anytime soon.

With that in mind, what do we see changing? In Chapters 5, "Tools: Search Analytics," and 17, "Search Analysis," we talk about the link between search and social media. Think about your own online behavior for a moment. There is a very good chance that you will read about a brand or product on a social media network and turn to a search engine to learn more about the product. Similarly, knowing what words people are searching for most often in conjunction with your brand or product name can be instructive as you develop your social media content.

Most marketers instinctively understand the link between search and social media, but rarely are they looking at the data side-by-side. We think that needs to change if for no other reason than it will make your social media content more visible to the audience that isn't talking or engaging. As much as Facebook and Twitter have grown, there are still industries or topics where people search more often than they engage or "speak." If you work in or represent a client in one of those industries, then knowing the words people use most often and how people react to certain paid media programs can be critical in content development. Even if the search marketing team is separate from the team that manages the social media presence, you should be making every attempt to compare data. Doing so will make both teams better.

Looking into the Audience Analysis Crystal Ball

The area of audience analysis is likely to see significant innovation over the next several years. Listening tools have attempted to provide data on demographics, geographies, and audience characteristics, but they still rely heavily on self-reporting from channels such as Facebook and Twitter. That isn't to say that the data Sysomos, for example, provides on audience characteristics is completely invalid. That data can definitely be valuable for marketers to analyze. However, because so few individuals report those characteristics openly and honestly, it is very difficult to truly understand the characteristics of those who are talking.

Because the automated solutions are currently inadequate, other techniques must be implemented. In Chapter 6, "Tools: Audience Analysis," we talk about conversation typing, which is essentially hand-coding mentions for certain audience characteristics. Currently, this is the most reliable method, provided that there is a set of standards each analyst can follow when reading and coding. Unfortunately, this method can be incredibly time-consuming. If you work for or represent a brand that gathers thousands of conversations per day, then hand-coding might not be a practical option.

Tip

One potential workaround for the issue with the volume of content that would be hand-coded is taking a statistically significant random sample. Instead of reading thousands of posts, an analyst is responsible for reading only hundreds. Traditional market researchers use this method, so it should be widely accepted by your organization.

The key for audience analysis to expand beyond hand-coding will be increasing the intelligence of the tools that currently gather this data. The tool might never be perfect in identifying audience characteristics, but some further level of automation will be required. Marketers do not just want to know what content is being engaged with or what themes are being mentioned in conversation most often. They want to know who is doing the engaging or talking. Right now, analysts can give only an incomplete picture. Soon though, marketers will begin demanding a greater level of specificity about the audience.

Forecasting the Content Analysis of the Future

In Chapter 7, "Tools: Content Analysis," we talk at length about tools such as Chartbeat and Woopra, which help brands better understand how content is performing. This is not a book about content marketing, so we don't dive deeply into what types of content perform best. For the purposes of this book, it is important to understand that content is the lifeblood of any marketing program, digital or otherwise. If your content is not appropriately tailored for the audience you are trying to reach, the program will fail. It really is that simple.

The good news is that tools like Chartbeat and Woopra can help you tailor your content to your audience. We know we sound like a broken record, but data sources need to converge more often to tell the complete story. For example, if you are responsible for developing content for your organization and are not looking at social media listening data, you are not doing your job well. Social media conversations are a great tip-off for the types of content that resonate the best. One of the individuals likely to be involved in all phases of content development is a community manager. For content analysis to evolve, we think the role of a community manager must evolve as well.

In March 2012, Chuck wrote a blog post for Spredfast in which he argued that it is time to ditch the community manager and hire the community analyst. He was not advocating that all community managers should be fired. Rather, he was arguing that community managers needed to evolve to be better with data and more flexible with content development.

Take a second to understand the differences between these two roles. Ask people who only loosely pay attention to the social media industry what their definition of *community management* is, and you're likely to receive several different versions. The most likely of them would include something about answering a customer's complaint on Twitter. We are not community managers but have worked with many of them over the years and know that community managers do much more than that. At a high level, a community manager is your company's first line of defense. It is often because of a community manager that a potential consumer knows about your company in the first place. More specifically, a community manager is intimately involved with the development of content.

Ask that same group of people for their definition of *analytics*. Or, better yet, ask them to describe an *analyst*. You'll probably get the same variation in responses, but you would likely be able to sum it up in two words: "data geek." In the past, that might have been seen as a pejorative label, but the explosion of social media has made those data geeks high-priced commodities. Social media has created so much data that brands and agencies alike are in a race to find people who can crunch numbers and create actionable insights. We describe that phenomenon in the last section of this chapter.

The community manager and analyst roles probably both make sense to you. Chances are good that you have one, if not both, on your team already. The bigger question, and really the crux of this section, is, "Are you bringing your community manager(s) and analyst(s) together?" More importantly, are you looking to fill both roles with one person?

A community manager sees posts as they come in, routes them or responds appropriately, and then catalogs them for eventual use in reporting. That's the ideal scenario, right? Where does your analytics team come in? Are those team members involved in reporting? Do they conduct the listening and feed conversations to your community manager? Whatever the setup, are your analytics and community management teams talking to each other? In our experience, there is a better than 50/50 chance that they are not. Why? Each role has something of value to offer the other. Why not take advantage of that? At a minimum, you should be looking for ways to foster more collaborative work environments with these two people (or teams, if appropriate). The best-case scenario has you sitting and working in close proximity to expedite workflow and make your content smarter.

We asked earlier where we think social media needs to move. Even though we have made the first solution sound like an easy fix, the reality is that working in teams is hard. Teams often have different goals, even though each team's goals should align with what the company is trying to achieve. The right approach is finding a person who is comfortable with the numbers and able to be your company's first line of defense in online communities. We realize that this is a rare breed of person, but think about the efficiencies and value this person would lend to a brand or an agency. A person like this would be able to gather data, crunch data, develop insights, and create content at a pace more in line with the pace of social media. There's a good chance you have hybrid people on your staff already; it's a matter of deploying them in the right way.

The blending of these two roles makes sense. Doing so would invariably make content analysis, development, and deployment more efficient. The tricky part is finding people who meet the needs of both roles, but we believe that marketers are becoming more conscious of the data available to them. Combine that with an already high level of comfort with content development and content across the Web should improve.

What else are we expecting as content analysis evolves? It isn't necessarily an innovation as there are some in the industry who have taken this approach, but we expect content indexes to become more prominent. It sounds like a very complex topic, but in practice it is very easy to execute if you have knowledge of Microsoft Excel.

The idea behind a content index is that you are presented with a series of metrics to evaluate your content (for example, likes, comments, shares, and clicks on Facebook) that are on different scales and carry different levels of importance for your business. A content index would take every piece of content you have created on that channel, gather the relevant metrics, and apply a weighted score to each metric. This approach allows you to more accurately assess content performance based on your organization's priorities instead of just counting a particular activity (likes, comments, shares, and so on).

Content analytics will continue to evolve because of its importance to digital marketing programs. New tools, new approaches, and new content types will push this particular practice forward. It's the newest of the types of analyses we have discussed throughout the book, so there is likely to be a period of rapid innovation over the coming years.

Extrapolating the Path of Engagement Analytics

Where engagement analytics tools go from here likely mirrors the path that social media listening tools are currently on, with the likely exception of the small to medium-sized businesses discussed in Chapter 8, "Tools: Engagement Analysis." As mentioned in the preceding section, the opportunity to combine engagement analytics with social media listening data will improve content and the performance of your digital marketing program. This value proposition is why Salesforce.com purchased Buddy Media to complement Radian6. Being able to read posts, develop content, respond to customers, and gauge the effectiveness of that response in one tool is very powerful.

Consolidation in this industry has already started (see Chapter 8 for more explanation), and we expect it to continue. With Buddy Media and Vitrue being acquired, very few enterprise solutions remain. In Chapter 8 we talk about the race that Sprinklr and Spredfast are currently waging to develop a strong user interface, build a robust analytics dashboard, and provide excellent customer service. As time passes, we will likely see these companies continue to battle it out for enterprise clients.

Unfortunately (or fortunately, depending on your perspective), we think that the future of Sprinklr and Spredfast has less to do with feature enhancements and happy customers and more to do with their ability to partner with a third-party listening provider. A smart solution would be for Marketwire (the parent company of Sysomos) or another one of the premium listening providers covered in Chapter 4 to work on partnering with either Sprinklr or Spredfast. That partnership would allow for either tool to be more competitive with MarketingCloud or the comparable offering to Oracle's Social Relationship Management solutions.

Knowing the Influencer Analysis Landscape

Before we get into any additional discussion in this section, let us dispel one notion you might be considering: Klout will not be going anywhere. We are sorry to break the news, but Klout's ubiquity would seemingly leave it in a place where it cannot be unseated. Now, other tools might evolve to the point where scores are reliable and context is an important part of the algorithm, but Klout's programs, especially Klout Perks, have delivered value for brands. Unless another tool is developed that offers a similar program and a reliable tool, we see Klout being a part of the landscape for the foreseeable future.

That said, we do expect other tools to be developed that offer a more reliable influence score for marketers. One such tool, Appinions, has begun gaining favor with marketers as it presents lists of influencers based on opinions and not exclusively on volume of activity. It certainly takes into account how active someone has been, but including brand or topic perceptions is a critical and valuable addition to influence tools. In addition, tools like Appinions are beginning to take context and credibility into account in their algorithms. Again, those sorts of additions can only make the scores these tools provide more valuable.

We do not provide extensive commentary on the concept of social scoring except to say that scoring is at least valuable in ranking the importance of a potential influencer. Whether that score is useful is in the eye of the user, but ranking individuals does help with prioritizing outreach targets.

Finally, we expect more organizations to begin creating their own influencer algorithms. As mentioned in Chapter 9, "Understanding Digital Influence," all the data that tools like Klout, PeerIndex, and Appinions gather is publicly available. Not only is it publicly available, most of it is available through application programming interfaces (APIs), which allows for easy data transfer. To create your own influencer approach, you need knowledge of those APIs and Microsoft Excel. There is a very good chance that someone on your information technology (IT) team can help you with the APIs, and we hope that you are at least vaguely familiar with Microsoft Excel so that you could manipulate the data. Why use someone else's data and approach when you can create your own?

This leads us into the last section of this chapter, in which we discuss the future of digital analytics more broadly. Before we leave the individual digital analytics disciplines, it is worth repeating that the tools and approaches have evolved at an insane pace. Regardless of whether we are talking about social media listening or influencer analysis, we expect that pace to continue.

Understanding Where Digital Analytics Goes from Here

The tools and individual disciplines that we have discussed are only one part of the equation. The other part—and it is a big part—is the enterprise itself evolving. Recall that at the beginning of this chapter, we cited a statistic from Stanford University which indicates that few companies are leveraging the true power of digital data. This is troubling for many reasons, but primarily because marketers should be looking for as much intelligence on their customers as they can glean. Not only that, but listening to social media conversations and gathering digital data is just smart reputation management.

Part of the reason that digital analytics in one form or another hasn't achieved widespread adoption is the lack of available talent. There are not many people with the appropriate skills to effectively implement a best practice digital analytics capability within a company. That is slowly changing as the value of analytics becomes more visible, but for the time being, companies are faced with a clear talent gap.

The following sections discuss the challenges and the solutions to building robust digital analytics capabilities. We firmly believe that digital analytics will become a growing part of the enterprise's marketing function, but there are some steps that need to be taken first.

Bridging the Analytics Talent Gap

Over the past few years, communicators have had a ringside seat to the biggest shift in their profession since, well, the creation of broadcast television. Consider for a moment that Facebook has now crossed 1 billion users, Pinterest reached

10 million unique visitors faster than any standalone site ever, and Twitter has more than 100 million active users. Communicators are now faced with a burgeoning community of creators, not consumers. Sure, the largest online population is still composed of those who consume content, but the numbers of people who contribute and share is growing substantially. This has several implications for communicators, not the least of which is factoring in new channels.

The other implication—and this is something that is more difficult to control—is the number of people looking to break into the business for companies or agencies. Unfortunately, the digital media space is moving at a pace that far outstrips the availability of quality talent. We don't mean to be unfair about this, but the number of people who have executed digital media campaigns for the Fortune 500 is small. It isn't a matter of setting up a Facebook page or managing a Twitter account. The best professionals are part marketer, part behavioral psychologist, part businessperson, and part number cruncher. Ah, the numbers. You knew we were getting there eventually, right?

If the talent gap in digital media is huge, the analytics talent gap is equally big. Whenever someone tweets, likes, comments, or clicks, she has created a data point that requires analysis. However, analyzing those top-level metrics is only one part of the equation. Can you take those metrics and turn them into a communications or business insight? Many people know how to collect data and put it into a presentation. Fewer people know how to collect the data and put it into a presentation that highlights insights that improve the business or a communications program.

The addition of digital marketing analytics professionals to corporate teams is not going to be a trend that slows down. We have seen a significant uptick in the number of openings at agencies and companies for positions of director or vice president in digital analytics. These organizations hope that by hiring such a person, a digital analytics capability will follow. Will it work? Only time will tell, but hiring a leader of digital analytics is a prudent first step in making it happen. Unfortunately, as two people who have been looking to fill these roles at several agencies, we can tell you that they do not grow on trees. Most of the people who have been successful in the analytics world come from diverse backgrounds.

If you are currently looking for such a person, what can you do to land the correct talent? Aside from scouring colleges and universities for more junior talent (not a bad idea, by the way), there are a few other steps you can take:

- **Understand what goes into a proper analytics job description—** Knowledge of social media listening tools is important, but it is not nearly the only thing you should be looking at to evaluate candidates. A senior analytics person should be able to help your organization source talent, have familiarity with a broad range of analytics and marketing concepts, and have the ability to present to upper management when necessary. Keep in mind that this is someone who will be responsible not only for understanding your customer but also building the capability. Strong business acumen is just as critical as the math and tool skills.

- **Have an open mind**—There are not a lot of people who have extensive experience in digital analytics. Sometimes you have to step outside your hiring comfort zone to hire the right person. You might want to consider someone from the social sciences who has strong research skills. It is our experience that strong research skills translate to these roles better than weak research but strong digital media skills.

- **Remember that some skills do not show up on a resume or LinkedIn profile**—You need to find someone who is naturally inquisitive, but when was the last time you saw "naturally inquisitive" on a resume? I know we haven't very often. That's probably something that you'll have to snuff out in an interview. This speaks a little bit to the point we just made, but the skills of an analyst don't easily translate to the traditional resume or LinkedIn profile.

- **Look for those people evangelizing on behalf of the space**—There are not many digital analytics bloggers who are active writers. If you do encounter someone who is writing often, it would behoove you to check him out. He might be someone who does a lot of writing and not a lot of doing, but it is worth investigating to see if he can back up his knowledge in a real-world environment.

Let's assume for a moment that you have the right person inside the organization already or are at least close to bringing someone in. Where should this person sit within your organization? This is a very important decision because that person's career trajectory will be greatly affected by where she sits within the organization. Many digital analytics professionals sit with the marketing team, and that does make some sense. However, we believe that digital analytics professionals should sit within the broader market research function because digital data is valuable, but it's infinitely more so when paired with other data sources. The market research team has access to a lot of proprietary business performance data that can be valuable as you are assessing overall digital marketing programs. It is the source of offline market research, which is very helpful in understanding consumer behavior. Finally, an important factor is the existing headcount within that team. As we just mentioned, it is often easier to teach digital media skills than it is to teach strong research skills. Having a group that consists of strong researchers will make the development of a digital analytics capability easier.

The integration of market research and digital analytics teams leads us to our final point, which is the internal gathering and application of this data.

Housing Your Customer Data

If you think about all the tools we have talked about here and in Chapters 4 through 9, you see that there is one common denominator: You do not own any of the data. What does this mean exactly? It means that every time you embark on a new digital research assignment, you must go to one of the tools, develop something akin to a profile, export the data, and then analyze the data. That is certainly fine if you are familiar with the tools and research processes. What happens, though, if you aren't as familiar but need information on how your customers behave online?

Herein lies what we think is the biggest revolution coming to digital analytics. Over the coming months, and most likely years, companies will be building internal repositories for this data. We have mentioned this throughout, but these tools have very easy-to-use APIs, which allow users to easily extract data. There are also data sources that your organization likely has (sales data being the biggest one) that aren't publicly available to many stakeholders or even your agencies. Wouldn't it be nice if you could build a tool that is easily accessible for all and includes all the available data inputs? It certainly is possible, and we think it should be done more often. If you are going to build such a repository, these are some things you should take into consideration:

- **Build a cross-functional team**—This sort of effort isn't going to be completed by one person from the social media or marketing team. The likelihood that someone on the marketing team has the technical skills required isn't very high. In order to build this capability, you need a cross-functional team that includes marketing, market research, IT, social or digital media, and analytics.

- **Detail all the data inputs**—Housing this much data could quickly go from manageable to completely unwieldy. Before moving toward the actual build and implementation, ensure that you have catalogued all the data you would like to capture and which tool it is going to be captured by.

- **Gather technical specifications**—Your IT team will come in handy in developing the technical specs in order to build this tool. However, do not let the IT folks create the tool in isolation. If you do, there is a very good chance that it will be written in a language that will not be easy for everyone else to decipher.

- **Ensure that you have the ability to query the database**—Whichever data inputs you select, there is probably going to be too much data available for the brand marketer. That is okay, as long as the user has the ability to select the data inputs or variables that matter to her.

- **Make it easy to extract the data**—It is one thing to have the data all housed in a dashboard, but it is another to make it easy to extract. Make sure you build in an export function in order to get the data out of the tool for further manipulation.

This sort of approach is not for companies that are just getting started with digital analytics. It is for those that are utilizing the tools we have discussed here, analyzing and implementing findings, and looking for a greater level of sophistication with their digital analytics approach. If you are just getting going, follow the steps we have outlined throughout this book. Before you know it, you'll be building an internal analytics repository for your organization.

The field of digital analytics has grown significantly in the past five years, and it will continue to grow for the foreseeable future. Companies are beginning to realize the true power of digital data and its impact on marketing programs. That impact is not going to lessen, and the companies that are leveraging this data effectively will be the ones that win. Wouldn't you like to be on the winning side?

Index

F

G

H

I

FREE
Online Edition

Assessing Intelligence

Applying a Bio-Cultural Model

Eleanor Armour-Thomas
Sharon-ann Gopaul-McNicol

REMP
Racial & Ethnic
Minority Psychology

SAGE Publications
International Educational and Professional Publisher
Thousand Oaks   London   New Delhi

For information:

SAGE Publications, Inc.
2455 Teller Road
Thousand Oaks, California 91320
E-mail: order@sagepub.com

SAGE Publications Ltd.
6 Bonhill Street
London EC2A 4PU
United Kingdom

SAGE Publications India Pvt. Ltd.
M-32 Market
Greater Kailash I
New Delhi 110 048 India

Printed in the United States of America

Library of Congress Cataloging-in-Publication Data

Armour-Thomas, Eleanor.
    Assessing intelligence: applying a bio-cultural model / by Eleanor
Armour-Thomas, Sharon-ann Gopaul-McNicol.
        p. cm. — (Ethnic minority psychology; vol. 1)
    Includes bibliographical references and index.
    ISBN 0-7619-0520-0 (alk. paper). — ISBN 0-7619-0521-9 (pbk.:
alk. paper)
    1. Intelligence tests. 2. Nature and nurture. 3. Cognition and
culture. I. Gopaul-McNicol, Sharon-ann. II. Title. III. Series.
BF431.A578 1998
153.9'3—dc21   97-45335

This book is printed on acid-free paper.

98 99 00 01 02 03 10 9 8 7 6 5 4 3 2 1

Acquiring Editor:	Jim Nageotte
Editorial Assistant:	Fiona Lyon
Production Editor:	Sherrise M. Purdum
Production Assistant:	Lynn Miyata
Typesetter/Designer:	Janelle LeMaster
Indexer:	Juinee Uneide
Print Buyer:	Anna Chin

To our families—*Bernard, Renaté, Bianca, Ulric, Monique Mandisa, and Monica*—with gratitude and love

And in loving memory of our parents
Cleaver and Celita Armour and *St. Elmo Gopaul*

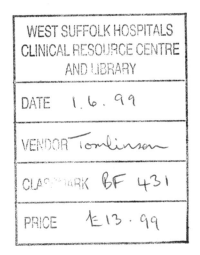

Contents

Series Editor's
Introduction

During the past two decades, Racial and Ethnic Minority Psychology has become an increasingly active and visible specialty area in psychology. Within the American Psychological Association, The Society for the Psychological Study of Racial and Ethnic Minority Issues was formed as Division 45 in 1986. This Division is now actively pursuing the publication of their own journal devoted to ethnic minority issues in psychology.

In APA we have also seen the publication of five bibliographies devoted to racial and ethnic minority groups. The first one was focused on Black males (Evans & Watfield, 1988) and the companion volume was focused on Black females (Iijima-Hall, Evans, & Selice, 1989). In 1990, the APA bibliography on Hispanics in the United States was published (Olmedo & Walker, 1990) followed by one on Asians in the United States (Leong & Witfield, 1992). The fifth bibliography was focused on North American Indians and Alaskan Natives and published in 1995 (Trimble & Bagwell, 1995).

As another indication of the increasing importance of racial and ethnic minority psychology, a brief review of the studies published on racial and ethnic differences in journals cataloged by Psychlit revealed a significant pattern. Between 1974 and 1990 (16 years), Psychlit cataloged 2,445 articles related to racial and ethnic differences. Between 1991 and 1997 (6 years), the number of articles related to racial and ethnic differences was 2,584. Put another way, between 1974-1990, an average of 153 articles were published each year on racial and ethnic differences. For 1990-1997, that number had jumped to an average of 430 articles published each year on racial and ethnic differences.

This pattern as well as many others have shown that racial and ethnic minority psychology is becoming an important and central theme in psychology in the United States. In recognition of this development, a new book series on **Racial and Ethnic Minority Psychology** (REMP) was launched at Sage Publications in 1995.

The REMP series of books is designed to advance our theories, research, and practice related to racial and ethnic minority psychology. It will focus on, but not be limited to, the major racial and ethnic minority groups in the United States (i.e., African Americans, Hispanic Americans, Asian Americans, and American Indians). For example, books concerning Asians and Asian Americans will also be considered. Books on racial and ethnic minorities in other countries will also be considered. The books in the series will contain original materials that address the full spectrum of methodological, substantive, and theoretical areas related to racial and ethnic minority psychology.

Within the field of racial and ethnic minority psychology, one of the earliest and recurring themes is concerned with the assessment of intelligence. This has been and remains a controversial topic in psychology as evidenced by the reactions to the work of Arthur Jensen and more recently to the publication of *The Bell Curve* by Herrnstein and Murray. The question of the so-called "significant racial differences in intelligence scores" remains a vexing one for psychology. From those who maintain that the differences in scores are real to those who argue that intelligence tests are biased against racial and ethnic minority groups, one thing is quite clear and stimulates little debate: Intelligence testing with racial and ethnic minority children and adolescents is not likely to disappear as a practice in the United States. It is therefore quite fitting that the first volume in the Sage series on **Racial and Ethnic Minority Psychology** is devoted to a well-reasoned and constructive approach to the use of intellectual assessment tools with racial and ethnic minority children and adolescents.

In this volume, Eleanor Armour-Thomas and Sharon-ann Gopaul-McNicol wonderfully integrate their many years of clinical experience in administering and interpreting intelligence test results on ethnic minority children to parents and teachers with the latest scientific knowledge. Based on the integration, they present a scientifically-based and culturally sensitive approach to using intelligence tests with racial and ethnic minority children and adolescents. Using a four-tier system, this integrated approach will be a significant contribution to the field and to the countless psychologists and educators who face the daily challenge of translating psychometrically-sound intelligence tests to the culturally complex and contextualized lives of their students, clients, families, and schools.

—Frederick T. L. Leong
Series Editor

Preface

In assessment circles, there seems to exist an implicit assumption that because teaching and learning concern the transfer and assimilation of knowledge and skill by persons uniquely equipped to do so, the assessment process should sample the pool of knowledge, skill, and competence. This logic seems to be based on the further assumption that if one can produce evidence of having mastered the assimilated knowledge and skill on demand, one not only knows but also can use these abilities whenever they are required. This basic conceptual model for assessment seems to ignore the fact that the traditional assessment process is also heavily dependent on the ability of the person being tested to recall and symbolically represent specific knowledge and to select iconic representations of skills. Some of us who have compared intellectual work in school and out of school have concluded that although these assumptions may be correct and may operate for some learners, there are vast differences between the ways in which mental work is experienced in school and in real-life settings. In real life, one actually engages in performances that contribute to the solution of real problems rather than producing, on demand and in artificial situations, symbolic samples of one's repertoire of developed abilities. In real life, one works with others to solve problems and often complements one's own knowledge and skill with those of others. Even more likely is the collective production of new knowledge and technique in response to experience with real problems that have special meaning to the persons encountering them. When we put these differences together with the relatively low correlations between scores on standardized tests and performance in real life, we recognize that there is some dissonance between what we typically do in the assessment of intellect and the ways in which humans exercise intellective functions in real life.

It is not only the arbitrary assumptions and processes that are associated with standardized tests that some consider to be problematic. In the latter part of this century, we have seen a plethora of activity directed at new approaches to educational assessment. Some of this ferment has been influenced by several years of agitation and complaint concerning the appropriateness of traditional standardized tests for the diverse populations served by modern schools. The most radical of these activities was the call, in the mid-1960s, for a moratorium on the use of standardized tests. Some courts placed restrictions on the use of such tests as the sole source of data in making certain decisions. At one point, some well-intentioned professionals called for the development of population-specific norms for groups known to show different patterns of scores on tests of educational achievement and intelligence. In recent years, we have seen calls for changes in the nature of what is measured, changes in the canons from which content is drawn, diversity in the performance modalities tapped by tests, the introduction of respondent choice, a shift to greater use of performance measures, and a variety of accommodations of test procedures to the special characteristics and needs of persons being tested. Considerable effort has recently been given to the design and implementation of performance assessment and portfolios. These adaptations and changes have been directed at the development of more "authentic" and valid measures of developed abilities and at making our tests more appropriate for diverse populations. Critics of standardized tests have argued that these proposed changes would improve the tests in addition to making them more "fair."

Perhaps it is the changing nature of the populations served by mass education and the changing criteria for what it means to be an educated person that have forced greater attention to this paradox. When the population was more homogeneous and society could absorb its school failures in a nonconceptually demanding workforce, the fact that schooling did not work for some of our members seemed less important. As the proportion of folks for whom school did not work increased, and as we became aware that even persons for whom schools once were adequate are not being enabled to function at intellective levels appropriate to changing societal demands, the potential crisis became more obvious. Teachers and schools became the targets of closer examination. Concern for how both of them can be held more accountable began to gain the focus of public attention. Because what teachers and schools produce is thought to be the achievements of their students, and because these achievements were increasingly viewed as inadequate, attention also came to be focused on educational tests and the processes by which we make judgments about the outcomes of schooling. It is this closer scrutiny that seems to have revealed to serious observers the contradiction between what it is we do in teaching and assessment, on the one hand, and optimally what should be happening in teaching, learning, and assessment on the other hand.

Despite this considerable amount of discussion and activity, it is interesting to note that the psychometric industry has not rushed to embrace these ideas. Rather, considerable effort has been directed at defending the validity of the extant psychometric technology and at seeking out and eliminating sources of bias in existing approaches to testing. The implicit assumption seems to be that the core practices are appropriate and do produce valid data, whereas many of the suggested changes present new problems, the most serious being the challenges of such innovations to the validity and reliability of extant assessment processes. It is a middle ground that is taken by the authors of this book.

It is in the context of this ferment for change and this assertion of stability and validity by the industry that Armour-Thomas and Gopaul-McNicol have produced this book. Rather than rejecting existing psychometric technology, these authors advocate its expansion to include a broader range of intellect-related behaviors and the contexts in which they are expressed. Asking the rhetorical question, "Are you a psychologist or a psychometrician?" they assert "that the psychologist is a clinician and a diagnostician, which means that he or she must go beyond IQ tests to assess intelligence, whereas the psychometrician relies purely on standardized tests of intelligence to determine a child's intellectual functioning" (p. 88). What is to form the basis for that clinical and diagnostic work and how the assessment is to be conducted constitute the focus of this book.

The central messages of this work involve (a) the origins and nature of intelligence, (b) a culture-embedded approach to assessment practices, and (c) the implications of a bicultural assessment system for policy determination and professional development. These three messages are delivered against a background of concern for the problems posed for assessment by the juxtaposition of increased concern with diversity in the population and broader respect for the pursuit of social justice in our society. The authors' treatment of issues related to practice, policy, and professional development isv grounded in the extensive discussion of the nature of intelligence with which they open this work.

Approximately a quarter of a century ago, Anne Anastasi suggested that we might better think of intelligence as the manifestation of developed mental abilities. She was trying to avoid the problems associated with those conceptions of intellect that privileged genetically determined and fixed states. Without addressing the nature-nurture controversy, Anastasi asserted that intellect is best thought of as a product—a result. No matter what the source, what is being measured is what has been developed. From those developed abilities, we infer the quality or level of intelligence.

In this book, we find a similar view of intelligence. The authors assert some biological substrate, but they think that the quality of cognitive function reflects the organism's interactions with its physical and cultural ecology. Consequently, to understand the character and quality of intellective development, its assessment must include these broader dimensions of cultural and ecological diversity, in which and as a result of which developed abilities are shaped. The authors argue that three interrelated and dynamic dimensions of intelligence can be identified. They are (a) biological cognitive processes, (b) culturally coded experiences, and (c) cultural contexts. They assert that these interacting multidimensional aspects of intellect must also be respected in the assessment process. To capture the complexities of this theoretical model, a four-tier biocultural assessment system is proposed that includes (a) psychometric achievement, (b) psychometric potential, (c) ecological conditions, and (d) other intelligences. In Part II, the authors describe the system and its use in the context of a critique of standardized tests. Part III is devoted to discussions of implications for professional development and public policy. We are indebted to the authors for a thoughtful analysis of a complex set of issues and for a rational approach to psychometric practice that is informed by their biocultural model for understanding human intellective competence.

—Edmund W. Gordon
John M. Musser Professor
of Psychology, Emeritus
Yale University

Acknowledgments

To our immediate family—Bernard, Renaté, Bianca, Monica Gopaul, Ulric, and Monique Mandisa—we extend our most profound gratitude. Your love, patience, and unflagging support throughout this challenging time will be remembered in our hearts forever.

To our parents, who instilled in us a sense of confidence and pride about "being the best you can be," we extend much gratitude, respect, and tenderness.

To our siblings, Cleavy, Edward, Margaret, Gail, Wendy, Kurt, and Nigel, our nieces and nephews, Ricardo, Brian, Jerry, Paula, Gena, Catrice, Wesley, Reid, Michael, Kja, Michelle, Skyler, and Kris, and our cousins, Doreen, and Maria, we thank you for your ongoing support and patience.

To our professional colleagues and special friends who have helped to nurture a respect for cross-cultural inquiry, we thank you immensely. In particular, we extend our appreciation to the following individuals: Norris Haynes, Miriam Azaunce, Coleen Clay, Brenda Allen, Ernest Washington, Randolf Tobias, David Rollock, Jesse Vasquez, Earl George, Janet Brice-Baker, Ann Francis-Okongwu, Nancy Boyd-Franklin, A. J. Franklin, Frederick Harper, Wade Boykin, Veronica Thomas, James Williams, Mary Conoley, Constance Ellison, Nicola Beckles, William Proefriedt, Aldrena Mabry, Lauraine Casella, Arthur Dozier, George Irish, Delroy Louden, Michael Barnes, Dawn Arno, Alice Artzt, Emery Francois, Jefferson Fish, Alina Camacho-Gingerich, Willard Gingerich, Tony Bonaparte, Frank Leveness, Tony Gabb, Erika Wick, James Curley, Joya Gomez, Charmaine Edwards, Headley Wilson, Susan Lokai, Seretse McHardy, Koreen Seabrun, Sandra Hosein, Jennifer D'Ade, and Joanne Julien.

To our research assistants—Grace Reid, Orlean Brown, Steve Choi, Renaté and Bianca Thomas, Samuel Korobkin, Andrew Livanis, Sibel Diaz, Robert Schmidt, Jessica Nava—and other students in training who provided much support, we extend our gratitude.

To the leading thinkers in the field who most influenced our work—Edmund W. Gordon, Lev Vygotsky, Janet Helms, Robert Sternberg, Ulric Neisser, Stephen Ceci, Barbara Rogoff, Howard Gardner, Jean Lave, Michael Cole, Stanley Sue, Jim Cummins, Robert Williams, A. Wade Boykin, Asa Hilliard, III, Esteban Olmedo, and Richard Figueroa—we extend our deepest respect and gratitude.

To the communities and students of Queens College, Howard University, and St. John's University, we thank you for your support in the nurturing of our thinking.

To our deceased loved ones, Cleaver and Celita Armour, St. Elmo Gopaul, Christopher Edwards, and Josephine Fritzgerald, may God bless you all.

Introduction

This book is divided into three parts. Part I examines the issues pertaining to intellectual assessment in a multicultural society (Chapter 1). The conceptions of the nature of intelligence are discussed in Chapter 2. Part I also delves into biological influences on cognition as well as cultural influences on cognition (Chapter 3). Chapter 4 proposes a new perspective of intelligence—a biocultural model developed by the authors.

Part II explores a new model for assessing all children—the four-tier biocultural assessment system (Chapters 5 and 6). Chapter 7 provides a critical review of four commonly used intelligence tests—the Wechsler scales, the Stanford Binet, the Kaufman, and the Woodcock. Chapter 8 presents sample reports, culminating in the most culturally sensitive psychological report based on the four-tier biocultural assessment system. Finally, an evaluation of the assessment system is performed in Chapter 9.

Part III offers training suggestions for teachers, parents, counselors, and psychologists for enhancing the intellectual potential of all children (Chapter 10). Finally, implications for future research and clinical work, as well as a vision for policymakers as to how to ensure culturally sensitive assessment and tutelage, are suggested in Chapter 11.

PART I

Intelligence: Major Issues and Challenges

1

Intellectual Assessment in a Multicultural Society

Unlike other reform movements in U.S. education, educational goals in the 1990s are centered around the three E's: economics, excellence, and equity. The national prosperity of the nation is perceived as dependent on the capacity of schools to produce workers with deep conceptual understanding in various domains of knowledge and demonstrations of advanced skills of reasoning, problem solving, and higher-order thinking. Although concern for equality of educational opportunity is not a new concept in U.S. education, it is new to envision academic excellence for all children, irrespective of race, class, ethnicity, gender, language, or any other dimension of human diversity by which individuals and groups are categorized in the society. This vision of education for the nation's children seems incompatible with the continuing use of intelligence test data to make selection and placement decisions of children for certain types of educational program. Implicit in the use of standardized intelligence test data for these purposes is a notion that differences in test scores reflect fundamental differences in intellectual capacities and that the goal of assessment is to objectively sort children according to these underlying differences. Once accurately sorted, educational programs can be more readily matched to these underlying differences. The scientific legitimacy of this notion, however, is in serious question when judgments about intellectual capacity and educational placements parallel race, class, and language differences. For example, it is a well-documented finding that the average performance of children from African descent differ by as much as one standard deviation on any standardized test of intelligence. It is also common knowledge that racial and ethnic minorities judged as "low ability" are placed in low-tracked and remedial classes or in special education programs (Persell, 1977; Rosenbaum, 1980; Slavin, 1987). What exactly do differences in IQ scores mean and what are the origins of such variation have been controversial questions since Jensen's (1969) declaration that the differences are real and substantial—a sentiment echoed in Herrnstein and Murray's book, *The Bell Curve* (1994).

In this chapter, we examine the principles of equal educational opportunity and multiculturalism and show how the purposes and practice of intelligence testing are at odds with those principles. The chapter begins with a discussion of key concepts in educational opportunity that serves as an entry point to a critical examination of the selection and placement purposes of standardized tests of intelligence. Next, a discussion of key issues in multiculturalism follows that also serves as an entry point for a critical examination of the assumptions of standardized tests of intelligence as these relate to children from certain racial and ethnic groups in U.S. society. The chapter ends with a brief exploration of new directions for intellectual assessment for this population of children.

Equal Educational Opportunity

The concept of equal educational opportunity reflects a core principle of democracy that ensures that all children, regardless of race, ethnicity, culture, language, gender, and other socially constructed characteristics of persons, should be entitled to equal access to the best and most appropriate education available. Gordon and colleagues (Gordon & Bonilla-Bowman, 1994; Gordon & Shipman, 1979) distinguish this notion of distributive equality from the concept of distributional appropriateness and sufficiency as essential criteria for educational equity. Building on Rawls's (1973) principles of justice, Gordon and Bonilla-Bowman (1994) argue that

> Educational treatments like medical treatments must be appropriate to the condition and characteristics of the person being treated and sufficient to their support and correction. To give all patients sulfa drugs when some need penicillin does not meet the condition of appropriateness. To give all one dose when some need three doses does not meet the condition of sufficiency. (p. 30)

Thus, Gordon introduces social justice attributes of need and circumstance criteria into the characterization of educational equity such that the emphasis is not on providing all children with the same educational treatments but rather on the appropriateness and sufficiency of treatment to the functional needs and characteristics of the persons being educated.

In a somewhat different vein, Howe (1992) calls attention to three key issues that any defensible interpretation of the principle of equality of educational opportunity must accommodate: (a) freedom and opportunities worth wanting—that is, the ability to deliberate effectively, and the opportunity to exercise it. This latter condition requires the availability of necessary information for deliberation and that social conditions do not serve as constraints or barriers for persons acting on the results of deliberations that are disproportionate to the burden of other deliberators; (b) equal educational opportunity as enabling—that is, taking advantage of early educational opportunities enables the acquisition of other ones later that, in turn, serve as the gateway for other societal goods such as adequate income, desirable employment, and political power; and (c) equal opportunity and children—that is, until they attain a certain age, children are not likely to pursue freedom and opportunities genuinely worth wanting or enabling. Schools, parents, or both, however, should ensure that one day children should be able to enjoy these benefits.

Both Gordon's and Howe's conceptions of equal educational opportunity make no conditional constraints on access to the nation's resources for all its children, regardless of the amount or quality of their intellectual endowments and the source of its distribution. Historically, variation in performance on standardized tests of intelligence has been used as a basis to select and place children in programs that are worth wanting or enabling for some children. For other children, however, such programs are neither worth wanting or enabling.

Consider the following findings of a *U.S. News & World Report* ("Separate and Unequal," 1993, p. 54) analysis of data from the Department of Education in 39 states:

Retarded: Black, 26%; white, 11%; Hispanic, 18%

Learning disabled: Black, 43%; white, 51%; Hispanic, 55%

Emotionally disturbed: Black, 8%; white, 8%; Hispanic, 4%

Speech impaired: Black, 23%; white, 30%; Hispanic, 23%

Compared to their percentage in the overall student population, black and Hispanic students are overrepresented in some special education programs. Closer examination of these statistics shows that in comparison to whites, a higher proportion of blacks are labeled mentally retarded and emotionally disturbed. They are less likely than whites, however, to be labeled with less stigmatizing labels of speech impaired or learning disabled.

A deficit explanation of biological inferiority is likely to be the heredity view for the overrepresentation of racial and ethnic minorities in special education programs. An alternative explanation and one that we support, however, has to do with a complex mix of factors involving (a) teaching and learning experiences reflective of the dominant group values in U.S. society, (b) the learning experiences of children reflective of the sociocultural milieu in which they are socialized, (c) a categorical approach to intellectual assessment that locates the problem of academic and intellectual dysfunction within the students themselves, and (d) the use of IQ tests that reflect a value system and experiences similar to those of the dominant group in the society and the schools that serve their children. We contend that many racial and ethnic minority children, particularly those from a low-income background, experience academic difficulty in adjusting to the norms and expectations of the dominant group values in U.S. society as reflected in the curriculum, instruction, and assessment practices in the classroom. Without appropriate guidance and support or an incentive system that works for them, these children experience academic difficulties so acute that inevitably they are referred for a psychological evaluation that includes an achievement test and a conventional IQ measure. Because IQ and academic achievement tests are correlated, it is not surprising that low to very low scores are obtained on both measures, thereby making plausible, although erroneous, the location for the source of the academic difficulties within the children themselves. The dominant categorical model so pervasive in intellectual assessment and special education will most likely identify a category among its complex array of labels (mentally retarded, mildly retarded, slow learner, specific learning disability, emotionally disturbed, language impaired, etc.) to match the "observed" dysfunction. This explanation is consistent with those of Cummins (1984, 1991), Mercer (1979), and Samuda (1975).

Other critics question whether standardized test data should even be used to inform educational decision making and instruction. For example, Glaser (1977) claimed that such tests give go/no-go selective decisions but do not provide information that is sufficiently diagnostic for the conduct of instruction. Gordon (1977) made a similar point when he argued that at best, test data analysis provides gross characterization of success and failure of students in relation to some reference group, but such analysis provides little information about the process by which individuals engage the task and is insensitive to an individual's differential response tendencies. As Gordon asserted, however, the description of these characteristics of behavioral individuality is of crucial importance in the design and management of teaching and learning transactions.

The Association of Black Psychologists (Williams, 1970) summed up the disillusionment of critics of the use of mental test data for children of African heritage when it charged that tests label black children as uneducable, place black children in special classes, potentiate inferior education, assign black children to lower-education tracks than whites, deny black children higher-educational opportunities, and destroy positive intellectual growth and development of black children (p. 5).

Almost 30 years later, the skepticism about the validity of intelligence tests for making educational decisions for racial and ethnic minorities still remains in many quarters (Armour-Thomas, 1992; Cummins, 1984; Figueroa, 1990; Gopaul-McNicol, 1992a; Hilliard, 1991; Lipsky & Gartner, 1996).

The specter of biological determinism and inequitable educational opportunity pose a serious moral dilemma for a society committed, at least in principle, to the ideals of equal educational opportunity for all its children irrespective of the cultural and linguistic background from which they come. We turn next to a discussion of the principle of multiculturalism and consider what it means for the intellectual assessment of children whose cultures are different from the culture of the dominant group in our society.

Multiculturalism

Multiculturalism is the term used to describe the existence of groups within a society that share ways of life or cultures that are rooted in distinct histories. Defining attributes of these ways of life include norms, values, and beliefs that govern the daily interactions of its members, that give meanings to these interactions, and that help shape the development and maintenance of a common identity. This perspective of cultures is consistent with those of the noted anthropologist Geertz (1973), who conceived of these sets of shared meanings as webs of significance that provide organization and maintain the cohesiveness of daily life of members of a cultural group.

Multiculturalism described in this way suggests to us that different cultures would have different perspectives that embody different value systems about how its members should behave among themselves as well as toward others outside their group. There is more, however, than simple recognition that different value systems exist in a multicultural society such as the United States. There are expectations for how different cultural groups should engage each other in conversations about their respective diversities. There must be not only acknowledgment of members of a cultural group's moral right to define their "webs of significance" on their terms but also a responsibility that other cultural groups will respect their right to do so. These norms of engagement are not easy to implement, as Moon (1993) pointed out:

> Moral pluralism does not simply involve the existence of . . . incompatible values—values that may come into conflict with each other depending upon circumstances. Rather, it arises when different people resolve these conflicts in systematically different ways, or when they come to hold ends or principles that are inherently incompatible. (p. 23)

Of course, there are a number of ways that democratic societies such as the United States seek to accommodate multiculturalism (e.g., perspectives of tolerance, common values, and search for universals). When we get beneath the surface rhetoric of these seemingly enlightened positions, however, the terms of accommodation or standards of acceptability are neither apolitical or morally neutral. Indeed, in a provocative essay on how dominance is concealed through diversity, Boyd (1996) pointed out the inadequacies of current perspectives on cultural pluralism in dealing with the dilemma of diversity: accommodating cultural relativism within a broader evaluative commitment to some generalizable morally binding constraints on all individuals and groups. Too often, according to Boyd, failure to deal with the dilemma leaves the prescriptive preferences of the dominant view in control.

Ostensibly, the idea of dominance in any form is incompatible with the principle of equity, a central tenet of U.S. democracy. It seems almost heretical to consider the notion of asymmetrical power relations among groups in a society for whom the metaphor *e pluribus unum* holds such significance in its developmental history. The seemingly intractable nature of the problem of access to education, however, essentially and sufficiently responsive to the needs of some learners, has led many to question whether the principle of equal educational opportunity operates in the same way for all children. The disproportionate and persistent nature of the problem of underachievement of some racial, linguistic, and ethnic groups and the centrality of the use of IQ tests in both explaining the reason for the underachievement and making subsequent educational placements have fueled the suspicion that something else is in the equity pot! Over the years, scholars from diverse disciplines have given name to the "something else" and have speculated with respect to how it functions. For example, DeVos (1984) used the term *caste thinking* to characterize the belief that there is some biological, religious, or social inferiority—unalterable—that distinguish members of a minority group from those of the dominant group in the society. He thinks that dominant-group members usually rationalize their exploitation of others with this form of thinking. Using this concept, Ogbu (1987) coined the term *castelike minorities* to refer to those groups that have been incorporated into the United States through conquest (e.g., Native Americans and Mexicans) or through slavery (individuals of African ancestry). Ogbu, like DeVos, believes that these historically subordinated groups have been the object of systematic discrimination in all realms of experience, including the provision of inequitable educational experiences. Other scholars use the terms *hegemony* (Apple, 1979; Boykin, 1983), *communicentric bias* (Gordon, Miller, & Rollock, 1990), and *eurocentrism* (Asante, 1988) to describe essentially the same phenomenon and to call attention to the inability of some members in the society who are too vulnerable or powerless to escape its pernicious effects.

Considerations of these issues of multiculturalism led us to suspect that a hidden dominance lurks within the structure and practice of standardized tests of intelligence. More specifically, we think that children from certain racial and ethnic minority groups (e.g., Native Americans, African Americans, Mexican Americans, and Caribbean Americans) are not allowed the right to develop and express their intelligence on their terms. Rather, their intellect is constantly being subjected to comparisons with other cultural groups (children from European descent) using criteria that "prove" their intellectual incompetence over and over again. In the next section, we elaborate on this claim of eurocentric bias through a critical analysis of the underlying assumptions of standardized tests of intelligence. In the process of this analysis, we examine how these assumptions are problematic when applied to children whose culture is substantively different from that of the dominant group in U.S. society.

Assumptions of Standardized Tests of Intelligence

Generally, proponents of standardized measures of intelligence justify the comparison made about intellectual performance between different cultural groups on the grounds that such measures meet at least four implicit criteria: (a) The tasks as constructed are culturally fair—that is, items do not favor any particular cultural group; (b) the tasks assess the cognitive abilities underlying intellectual behavior; (c) the tasks could sufficiently elicit the deployment of particular mental operations; and (d) accurate interpretations could be made from comparing the average IQ scores of different cultural groups. When these criteria are applied in the assessment of intellectual functioning of children from certain racial and ethnic groups, numerous difficulties arise that raise serious questions about the validity of comparative judgments about their performance. In the following sections, some problems of standardized tests for these populations are discussed.

Item Selection Bias

Any intelligence test construction procedure involves the standardization of the test on a representative sample. This means, in the case of U.S. society, the majority of subjects will come from the dominant group—Anglo- or European Americans. A minority of groups will make up the rest of the sample—groups of non-European origin including Native Americans, African Americans, Mexican Americans, Caribbean Americans, Asian Americans, and Pacific Islander Americans. During the early stage of item development, the majority of items selected for tryout will obviously reflect the prior learning experiences of the Anglo- or European American group. Because academic achievement correlates with any standardized test of intelligence, this means that the learning experiences are similar to those acquired through schooling.

It cannot be assumed that the learning experiences of the majority group are similar to those of the minority groups (e.g., Boykin, 1986; Ogbu, 1986). Nor can it be assumed that the learning experiences derived from schooling for majority children are similar to those of minority groups, particularly those from low-income backgrounds (e.g., Oakes, 1990). Even if items reflective of the prior learning experiences of minority groups were included in the early phase of item development, they would more than likely be screened out during item analysis. A common psychometric practice in test construction is to retain only those items that correlate with the total test and that are of moderate difficulty. Items that are appropriate for minority groups more often than not will be difficult for the majority group and will not correlate well with the total test (e.g., Williams's [1975] Black Intelligence Test of Cultural Homogeneity). Thus, the process of item selection for an intelligence test does involve some bias against minority groups (see Cummins, 1984, for a comprehensive discussion of the issues pertaining to item selection bias).

Lack of Specificity About Cognitive Processes

Although psychometric studies of cognitive abilities have identified a number of cognitive processes that underlie performance on intellectual tasks (e.g., Carroll, 1993; Horn, 1991a), there is no consensus about how many and which processes combine to produce behavior indicative of intelligence. Horn (1991b), in describing the difficulty of identifying these processes with precision, remarked that "Specifying different features of cognition is like slicing smoke— dividing a continuous, homogeneous, irregular mass of gray into . . . what?" (p. 198).

Lack of specificity of cognitive processes when describing intellectual behavior in assessment situations is likely to favor some cultural groups but hinder others. Almost three decades ago, Messick and Anderson (1970) called attention to the fact that these same tests may measure different processes in minority children from low-income backgrounds than in white middle-class children. A similar concern was articulated by Farnham-Diggory (1970), who suggested that the multiplicity of cognitive processes in Thurstone's Primary Abilities

Test made it difficult to determine which of these processes pose difficulties for children of African heritage. In our own work, it was not always clear that, when children from culturally and linguistically diverse backgrounds answered items incorrectly, these errors were due to inaccurate or inefficient deployment of cognitive processes.

Content Bias

When comparisons are made between cultural groups on standardized measures of intelligence, inaccurate assumptions about aspects of the task requiring the deployment of mental processes may be made. In other words, differences in cognitive processes may be a function of variability in dimensions of tasks within a particular cultural context. Many cross-cultural studies have reported that the familiarity or unfamiliarity of content may constrain or promote the efficient or accurate elicitation of cognitive processes in tasks involving memory, reasoning, perception, and problem solving (e.g., Cole, Sharp, & Lave, 1976; Greenfield, 1974; Laboratory of Comparative Human Cognition [LCHC], 1982; Lave, 1977; Rogoff, 1981; Saxe, 1988). In these studies, researchers focused on the domain-specific thinking of people as they solve problems routinely encountered in their culture. For example, in an early cross-cultural study, Gay and Cole (1967) assessed classification competencies between schooled and unschooled Liberians and U.S.-schooled children by using tasks involving culturally appropriate content: bowls of rice and geometric blocks. African subjects performed as competently when the tasks involved rice as the stimulus as their U.S. counterparts who used geometric shapes. In contrast, decrements in performance were observed for both groups when the contents of the stimulus materials were reversed. In other words, African children classified geometric shapes as poorly as the U.S. children sorted rice. Recently, several researchers have used concepts such as everyday cognition (e.g., Guberman & Greenfield, 1991; Rogoff & Chavajay, 1995) and practical intelligence (Neisser, 1979; Sternberg, 1985; Sternberg & Wagner, 1986) to better understand the thinking competencies of individuals and groups that underlie their performance on culturally familiar tasks in their own communities.

The LCHC (1982) used the concept of "functional stimulus equivalence" to account for these content-specific findings. This means that to make valid comparisons of intellectual performance between cultural groups, it is critical that the stimulus attributes of the task be equivalent for both groups in their ability to elicit the cognitive processes under investigation. From our experiences with standardized tests of intelligence with children from culturally diverse backgrounds, it does not appear that test designers have sufficiently addressed the issue of functional equivalence in item construction or selection.

Unfamiliar Sociolinguistics

One of the hallmarks of intelligence testing is the adherence to standardized procedures during its administration. One aspect of these procedures has to do with examiner-examinee interactions. When to probe for more information, how to respond to the examinee's queries, and how much feedback to give are all governed by a strict protocol using a standard format. Such constraints of the testing environment, however, may preclude an accurate estimation of intellectual competence of some children from culturally diverse backgrounds. An example of this problem concerns the dynamics of sociolinguistics among ethnic minority children from low-income backgrounds. Sociolinguistic variables are courtesies that govern verbal interactions that can have a positive or negative impact on student motivation to engage in a task. Miller-Jones (1989) provided some excellent examples of the verbal interactions between an examiner and an African American child that demonstrate how such interactions of the testing context may result in erroneous judgments of intellectual functioning of that child. The question and response exchange clearly indicated that the child did not understand or was not familiar with the social dynamics within the testing context. In short, in a standardized testing context, the norms of discourse are predetermined, and performance differences could result to the extent that children's sociolinguistic patterns of communication are different from the examiner's script.

Test Interpretation Bias

Comparisons of intelligence test scores on the basis of ethnic classification are likely to lead to bias in interpretation because there is considerable heterogeneity within such groups in terms of family structure, geographical region, social class, language, and education (e.g., Harrison, Wilson, Pine, Chan, & Buriel, 1990; McLoyd, 1990). For example, Phinney (1996) identified at least the following three aspects of ethnicity for ethnic groups of color in the United States (e.g., Native Americans, African Americans, Latinos, Asians, and Pacific Islanders) that may have psychological relevance for influencing behavior:

- Cultural values, attitudes, and behaviors that differentiate ethnic or racial groups
- Identity—the perceptions of what it means to the individual to belong to an ethnic or racial group
- Experiences associated with minority status in the United States (e.g., discrimination, prejudice, and a sense of powerlessness)

These features of psychological characteristics are similar to those identified by Sue (1991), who, like Phinney (1996), viewed them as overlapping and confounded constructs.

Thus, an ethnic label alone is not enough to interpret differences in performance between ethnic groups. To understand intellectual behavior would require an unpacking of the multiple psychological processes associated with the label as a number of researchers have recommended (e.g., Betancourt & Lopez, 1993; Phinney, 1996; Poortinga, van de Vijver, Joe, & van de Koppel, 1989; Whiting, 1976).

One of the methodological difficulties associated with the unpackaging of psychological processes, however, is that researchers and pollsters may not have fully understood or appreciated their importance in influencing behavior. As Betancourt and Lopez (1993) noted, research instruments and surveys often require subjects to indicate race by selecting among confounded status variables (e.g., white, black, Latino, Native American, and Asian). Zuckerman (1990) cautioned that the loose way in which race, culture, and ethnicity are treated may contribute to interpretations of findings of observed differences between groups that reinforce racist conceptions of human behavior.

Even in cases in which researchers try to minimize the confounding of status characteristics, it is not clear that they succeed. For example, by statistically controlling for the effects of socioeconomic status among Latinos or Asians children in a study of, for example, intelligent behavior, a researcher can unwittingly mask the effects of language and culture. To the extent that these two latter characteristics are differentially experienced by members who are located in different class positions, one can misattribute to socioeconomic status the influence of language or culture or both.

Comparisons of average IQ test scores of black and white children are equally problematic when using the race label to make group classifications. As Helms (1992, p. 1085) noted, tremendous variation may exist within black and white populations because of

a. Voluntary and involuntary interracial procreation
b. The tendency of researchers to assign subjects to one group or another on the basis of physical appearance
c. The decision of some visible racial or ethnic groups that appear white to disappear into white society (a process called passing in black culture)
d. The possibility that immigrants who would be considered black if they were born of similar parentage in this country classify themselves as white or other than black

Variations in perceptions of race also exist in other countries. In a recent review of conceptions of race as a socially constructed phenomenon, Eberhardt and Randall (1997) described the fluid continuum by which race is defined in Brazil, Latin America, and Caribbean countries. Factors such as economic and geographic mobility are allowed along the continuum as are a wide range of colors. In Caribbean and Latin American countries, it is not uncommon for individuals to change color or to have different perceptions of physical attributes such as hair texture and skin pigmentation as a function of economic mobility. According to these researchers, in these countries, money "whitens."

Thus, an interpretation of differences of IQ scores between subjects of European and African decent on the basis of racial categorization is indefensible and downright racist.

New Directions for Intellectual Assessment

The discussion of equity and multiculturalism principles in relation to standardized tests of intelligence raises many troubling questions about their selection and placement purposes and its use with children from certain racial and ethnic groups in U.S. society. It is our view that in a multicultural society, nondiscriminatory assessment would require an informed understanding and appreciation of the cultural influences on children's intellectual behavior. Furthermore, it would also require an understanding of the mechanism by which such factors function to promote or constrain the deployment of cognitive processes. As we argue in Chapter 5, no one measure can fulfill these multiple expectations of intellectual assessment. Rather, multiple forms of assessment need to be developed that

- Sample a broad range of cognitive processes
- Sample content that is functionally equivalent for the groups targeted for assessment
- Are sufficiently diagnostic so as to uncover strengths and weaknesses of manifest cognitions as well as emerging cognitive potentials
- Allow sufficient time to demonstrate accurate use of cognitive processes
- Are sensitive to the sociolinguistic patterns that children bring to the assessment environment
- Provide a scaffold for easier elicitation of the cognitive processes in a given domain of knowledge
- Allow opportunity to learn the process and knowledge demand of the task
- Assess the manifestation of these processes in more real-world environments
- More precisely inform prescriptive pedagogical or rehabilitative interventions

A fuller development of these issues is found in Chapter 6, in which we lay out in detail the four-tier approach to assessing intelligence.

Conclusion

A democratic society committed to equity and multiculturalism requires that fair and nondiscriminatory measures be used to assess children's intellectual competencies regardless of their background characteristics. When judgments about intelligence parallel race, language, and ethnicity and when such judgments are used to make educational placements of dubious quality, the principle of equity is doubly compromised for children. We hope, however, that increased awareness and genuine respect for cultural pluralism will lead to the development and use of measures that have greater psychodiagnostic and prescriptive utility than those that currently exist. A just and humane society demands no less for its children.

2

Conceptions of Human Intelligence and Implications for Its Assessment

What is human intelligence?" is one of the most intriguing questions in the study of psychology. As early as 2000 years ago in ancient China and Greece, philosophers pondered this question as have the psychologists in the 20th century, but a definitive response remains elusive. When, in 1921, the "Journal of Educational Psychology" published a number of papers on intelligence written by distinguished psychologists, there was remarkably little agreement among the 14 definitions ("Intelligence and Its Measurement," 1921). Recently (Sternberg & Detterman, 1986), a symposium was held to reexamine the concept but, yet again, the experts still do not agree. The theoretical ambiguity about the construct makes it difficult to gather valid and reliable evidence about intellectual behavior or to make accurate interpretations and inferences from differences in IQ scores. The absence of consensus does not mean inconsequential knowledge about the nature of the construct or its measurement because numerous handbooks and journal articles have been published on both topics during the past 90 years. Despite the continuing proliferation of perspectives of intelligence and its assessment, the field of intelligence and intelligence testing remains contentious.

To the extent that we see value in assessing intellectual competencies of individuals and groups, then continuing the search for greater understanding of the construct is a worthwhile endeavor. In this society, intelligence test scores have been used not only to make selection and placement decisions but also to predict how individuals will perform in the future or on other tests. The more theoretically grounded the construct, the greater our faith in the results from its assessment. Thus, for very practical reasons, the theoretical basis of intelligence needs to be determined. The chapter begins with a more elaborate discussion of a rationale for a conceptually driven assessment of intelligence. Next, criteria for a theory of intelligence that would inform a particular perspective of assessment are set forth. Philosophical, subjective, and objective conceptions of intelligence are advanced and evaluated against these criteria. The chapter ends with an identification of a number of theoretical propositions that form the conceptual basis for an assessment system of intelligence.

Rationale for a Conceptually Driven Assessment of Intelligence

Assessment is a process of gathering evidence of an individual's performance on a given task and of making interpretations and inferences about behavior on the basis of such evidence for a variety of purposes. Intelligence or IQ tests (e.g., the Wechsler scales) represent one form of assessment and are designed to enable systematic observation of individual and group differences in intellectual performance in a controlled setting. Biological or environmental influences are often used to account for differential performances, and purposes served by test data include decision making about selection, placement, and prediction about certain types of school achievement and job performance. For example, test scores are used, in part, to determine eligibility for gifted, mentally retarded, and special education programs and to predict who will do very well or poorly academically as measured by academic achievement tests. For the past three decades, proponents and critics have argued about the appropriateness of IQ tests for these purposes and the scientific legitimacy of biological or environmental interpretations for observed difference in performance. Given the fact that data from IQ tests are used, in part, to make decisions with respect to allocation of the nation's resources and opportunities, it is understandable why the IQ controversy has generated such strong emotional debate. Because of the high "stakes" consequences of intelligence and the irresolution of the nature-nurture question, we think that any measure purporting to measure such an enigmatic construct should be grounded in theory. Furthermore, we contend that any effort to assess intelligence should first inform diagnostic and prescriptive decision making. Only when decision makers have a broad and deep understanding of the sources of observed differences in intellectual performance and the prescriptive utility of such information should considerations about selection and prediction be explored.

What, then, are some reasonable criteria for any perspective of intelligence? This is a difficult question because the construct itself is a cultural invention created for the purpose of appraising who has how much of it according to the value system of any given society at any point in time! It is quite possible that a researcher or test designer may have a particular view of intelligence and can systematically observe behavior in task performance purporting to embody the construct. What counts for evidence, however, and how much is enough are questions for which there can be endless debate. We share Gardner's (1983) view that two prerequisites of a theory of intelligence should be that (a) it captures a sufficiently broad range of abilities that are genuinely useful and important at least in certain cultural contexts and (b) it should be verifiable.

Criteria for Conceptions of Intelligence

Our review of the literature about intelligence testing and our own experiences in this area during the past 10 years suggest that when these prerequisite conditions are met, there are at the very minimum the following four criteria that any conception of intelligence should meet:

1. Operational definition of the nature of the mental activity in tasks defined as "intellectual": To make an accurate determination of individual and group strengths and weaknesses, precise definition of the nature of the mental operations or cognitions underlying performance indicative of intelligence needs to be made.

2. Identification of a symbol system on which cognition(s) operates: Information is represented through language, numbers, pictures, gestures, or other types of symbol systems. The meanings and knowledge an individual acquires depend, in part, on the efficiency of operation of cognitions on any given symbol system. Explanations of differences in observed performance on intellectual tasks must take into account the symbol system on which cognition must operate.

3. Specification of the experiences within the context relevant for intellectual functioning: The kinds of experiences to which individuals are exposed may constrain or enable the efficiency and accuracy of the deployment of cognition. Because all experiences unfold within a particular setting or context, explanations of differences in observed performance on intellectual tasks must consider both the experiential and contextual realms within which cognitions are embedded.

4. Specification of the degree of susceptibility of cognition to biological and environmental influences: If prognosis for the future functioning of the individual is favorable, then the responsiveness of the cognitions to training or environmental manipulation needs to be ascertained. If, however, prognosis for future intellectual behavior is unfavorable, then the resistance of the cognitions to external stimulation would also need to be determined.

These are the criteria that we use to examine the philosophical, subjective, and objective conceptions of intelligence.

Philosophical Conceptions

Although the term *intelligence* had not been widely used until the seminal work of Binet and Simon in 1905, philosophical conceptions of the mind, intellect, the soul, and rationality can be traced back to ancient Greece. Robinson (1994) reviewed the evolution of philosophical views of intelligence from ancient through medieval and modern periods and found some consistency in the thinking of many philosophers regarding the nature of intelligence. For example, from examination of Plato's dialogues, Robinson (1994) found that Plato conceived of the intellect as an innate and god-given construct and equated it with wisdom-knowledge of universally true and unchanging principles. Moreover, it is to be distinguished from mere craft or skill that is acquired through sense-based experiences. For Plato, acquisition of wisdom used interchangeably with pure rationality could only be attained through a lifetime of the right kind of philosophical reflection and contemplation. Aristotle, Plato's star pupil, shared a similar view of intelligence as the rational awareness of universal principles to be distinguished from factual knowledge acquired through experience.

In medieval times, as Robinson (1994) pointed out, conceptions of intelligence were consistent with those of the ancient Greek philosophers. For example, Thomas Acquinas (1225-1274), in an effort to distinguish rote memory and sensory-based knowledge from cognitive abstractions, proposed a two-process perspective of intelligence: a passive intellect acted on by sensory information and an active intellect that engages the passive intellect in ways that enable the discernment of universal principles.

In the 16th century, Juan Huarte de San Juan, a Spanish physician and scholar, considered intelligence as a three-faceted construct: As reported by Linden and Linden (1968), Huarte described intelligence as (a) docility in learning from a master, (b) understanding and independence of judgment, and (c) inspiration without extravagance. It is claimed (Franzbach, 1965) that this characterization of intelligence influenced the thinking of German philosophers during the 18th and 19th centuries.

During the 17th and 18th centuries, according to Robinson (1994), three distinct conceptions of intelligence were advanced. The first one was rationalistic and was closely associated with the ideas of René Descartes and Gottfried Wilhelm von Leibnitz. Both, in the tradition of the Greek philosophers, held the view that intelligence was the capacity to comprehend abstract principles, and they argued for the prior existence of the intellect within the individual to make intelligible the multitude of experiences perceived through sensory stimulation. The second perspective—the empiricist—was associated with the writings of John Locke and David Hume who, using the principle of association, proposed that all knowledge can be reducible to objects as experienced through the senses. The third perspective was a biological one put forth by a number of philosophers who based their views on the assumption of a relationship of the organization of an animal's body and its adaptive abilities. According to this view, intelligence is defined as the problem-solving abilities made possible by the degree of efficiency of this organization.

It was not until the 19th century, however, with the publication in 1859 of Darwin's *Origin of the Species*, that investigations concerning the nature of intelligence became more pragmatic and less philosophical. Two provocative notions emerged from Darwin's work that were later explored by his half-cousin, Francis Galton. First is the proposition that the development of intelligence over the life span may, in some respects, resemble the development of intelligence from lower to higher species. Second is the assumption that development is continuous and therefore human beings could be subjected to the same type of scientific investigations as those conducted with animals.

Ten years later, Galton, in *Hereditary Genius* (1869), suggested that intellectual genius tends to run in families and is therefore inherited. In one of the chapters, "Classification of Men According to Their Natural Gifts," he alluded to the presence of specific and general abilities as the basis for individual differences in intelligence. In 1883, he published *Inquiries Into the Human Faculty and Its Development Among Human Beings* in which he explored the difficulties in measuring mental aptitudes and proposed a series of psychophysiological measures to discriminate the mentally strong from the mentally weak. From 1884 to 1889, he sought empirical validation of these claims using a variety of simple physical and sensory tasks at his anthrometric laboratory.

Commentary

None of the philosophical conceptions of intelligence met the prerequisites or criteria very well. All described intelligence as a mental activity, although the nature of the cognition differed. The ancient Greeks, the early Christians, and the rationalists considered that the capacity to frame and understand universal or abstract principles was an essential quality of the nature of mental life. The empiricists, however, proposed a theory of the mind as a collection of elementary sensation, combining to form simple to complex ideas through the principle of association. Although the issue of experience was discussed, its role in intellectual functioning differed. The Greeks, the early Christians, and the rationalists argued that although experience may enable rote memory and sense-based knowledge, these cannot account for the capacity to acquire knowledge of universal principles—the essence of intelligence. In contrast, the empiricists believed that all knowledge is reducible to stimuli acquired through the senses. None gave explicit attention to the role of a symbol system. With regard to the criterion pertaining to biological or environmental influences, the Greek scholars believed that intelligence was an innate and god-given construct. Some modern-day scholars, although not attributing divine blessing to those who possess it, believed that the genesis of intelligence was located in the organization of the body and nervous system. Although these conceptions may have met the prerequisite criterion of being useful or important in some cultural contexts, they did not meet the other prerequisite of a broad range of human abilities. Perhaps the greatest threat to these conceptions of intelligence, however, is the absence of verifiable evidence about its nature.

Subjective Conceptions of Intelligence

Subjective views of intelligence are based on people's commonsense theorizing or beliefs about the nature of intelligence. Unlike the methodologies used to study objective conceptions of intelligence, research uses self-report measures with a Likert-type format to elicit peoples' stated positions regarding intellectual functioning. Speculating that the construct was no more than society's cultural invention of it as a prototype of what its members value as a culture, Neisser (1979) used this approach to examine laypersons' conceptions of intelligence. These findings confirmed his earlier distinction between academic (used in classroom tasks) and practical (used in tasks people face in their everyday lives).

Many cross-cultural studies have found variations within and among cultural groups in their conceptions of intelligence. For example, Wober (1972) found that Ugandan teachers and groups influenced by Western ideas characterized intelligence in terms of speed, whereas the Ugandan villagers associated intelligence with words such as careful, active, and slow. In a later study of views of intelligence from different tribes in Uganda, Wober (1974) found that in Batoro tribes, people associate intelligence with terms such as obedient, yielding, and soft, whereas members of the Baganda tribe associated intelligence with words such as persistent and hard.

Super (as cited in Sternberger, 1985c) found that the concept of intelligence had different meaning when applied to children and adults among Kokwet people in western Kenya. For example, the connotation of cleverness, inventiveness, and unselfishness was associated with the word *utat* when applied to adults. The connotation of fluency and quickness in verbal comprehension on complex tasks and interpersonal skills was associated with the term *ngom* when applied to children.

Sternberg, Conway, Ketron, and Bernstein (1981) asked samples of experts in the field of intelligence and samples of laypersons in a train station, library, and supermarket to define and rate characteristics of intelligent people. Both groups had similar conceptions of intelligence that distinguished between competent performance on practical and academic tasks. Finally, Okagaki and Sternberg (1993) compared views of immigrant parents from Cambodia, Mexico, the Philippines, and native-born Anglo-Americans and Mexican Americans regarding their conceptions of intelligence of a typical first-grade child. They found that, with the exception of Anglo-Americans, all other groups identified intelligent characteristics, such as social skills, practical school skills, and motivation, as equally or more important than cognitive characteristics.

Commentary

Subjective conceptions of intelligence met the prerequisites and some criteria but not others. On the positive side, these conceptions define a very broad array of cognitions, spanning those used in school-like tasks and in a real-world environment. All these views considered experiences and context as important dimensions of intelligence. Lack of precision in terms of the actual behaviors indicative of these cognitions, however, renders judgments of them tentative at best. Consensus among the views of laypersons and experts in the area of intelligence research gives some validity to these conceptions. None of the conceptions addressed the criterion regarding the susceptibility of cognition to biological influences.

Objective Conceptions of Intelligence

Objective conceptions of intelligence are derived from findings from observation of individual differences in performance on intellectual tasks. Methodological developments have influenced these perspectives in the 20th century, including factor analytic and information-processing models and standard psychometric and information-processing tests of mental abilities. In addition, clinical studies in neuropsychology and field research in anthropology and psycholinguistics using observational methods and conversational analysis are shedding new light to an old question. In the following sections, we examine some of the more common conceptions of intelligences that have used these procedures to study individual differences in behavior indicative of intelligence.

Psychometric Theories of Intelligence

Psychometric theories of intelligence seek an understanding of intelligence in terms of the way it is measured through the use of a statistical-mathematical technique called factor analysis. It involves the examination of a matrix of intercorrelations or covariances for a set of cognitive tasks (most often standardized scores on psychometric tests of mental ability) to uncover common patterns of individual differences in performance on these tasks. The observed patterns or factors sometimes referred to as latent traits are presumed to be manifestations of individual differences in cognitive abilities or potentials as hypothesized by the theorist. The cognitive tasks used to identify individual differences in cognitive abilities are similar in many respects to the ones initially developed by Binet and Simon in 1905. Successive factorization of correlation matrices yields different numbers of factors at varying levels of generality, and such information is used to infer the structure or organization of the human intellect. Consider some examples of conceptions of intelligence with varying factors and structures that have been widely cited in psychology texts.

Spearman

Charles Spearman (1927) was among the first to propose a two-factor theory of intelligence—a general factor and specific factors. The general factor, which he termed g, is an index of general mental ability that accounts for the patterns of intercorrelations observed among performance on various cognitive tasks or intelligence tests. Specific factors that underlie only a single task or test are indicative of specific abilities. He believed that the general factor of intelligence reflected individual differences in three mental processes: "apprehension of experience"—perceiving and understanding the task of interest; "eduction of relations"—inferring some logical abstraction such as a similarity or comparison from two or more stimuli; and "eduction of correlates"—finding a second idea logically related to a previously stated one. (See *The Nature of "Intelligence"* and the *Principles of Cognition* for a detailed discussion of these attributes of intelligence.)

He also speculated that individual differences in these mental abilities, particularly the ability to educe relations and correlates, may be explained in terms of mental energy or power that might have a physiological base.

Thurstone

Thurstone (1938) proposed a seven-factor theory of intelligence. It is different from the one common factor in Spearman's model in that he contends that seven common factors describe all the intercorrelations observed on performance on cognitive tasks or tests. Thus, for Thurstone, seven primary abilities are represented by these factors. The nature and content of these abilities are described as follows:

Verbal comprehension: the ability to demonstrate knowledge of vocabulary and comprehension skills

Verbal fluency: the ability to generate rapid production of words quickly and in a limited time

Number facility: the ability to do computational arithmetic and reason quantitatively

Spatial visualization: the ability to mentally manipulate geometric designs making same-different comparisons

Memory: the ability to remember associations with words and pictures

Reasoning: the ability to deduce and induce logical abstractions from concepts or symbols

Perceptual speed: the ability to recognize quickly symbols embedded among an array of other symbols

Wechsler

Wechsler (1944), like Spearman, conceived of intelligence as a global or aggregate capacity to think rationally, act purposefully, and cope effectively with the environment. The Wechsler scales (for adults, children, and preschoolers) are based on this conception of intelligence. Despite the general nature of the construct, Wechsler believed that intelligence can be expressed in various ways. It is for this reason that he constructed his scales into two domains, verbal and performance, with many subtests within each domain. The verbal subtests assess verbal comprehension, verbal concept formation, and verbal reasoning, and the performance subtests assess perceptual organizational abilities, visual and motor abilities, and abstract nonverbal reasoning. Thus, the scales yield two scores— verbal and performance IQ—in addition to a full scale IQ. He did not equate these IQ scores with intelligence because he maintained that other nonintellective factors (persistence, drive, and motivation) were involved in intelligent behavior. No specific quantitative index of these nonintellective factors accompanied the IQ scores, however. As a clinician, he advocated weighing both the intellective and nonintellective factors in the assessment of intelligence.

Guilford

Guilford (1967) conceived of intelligence as comprising three components: the mental operation, the content of the material, and the

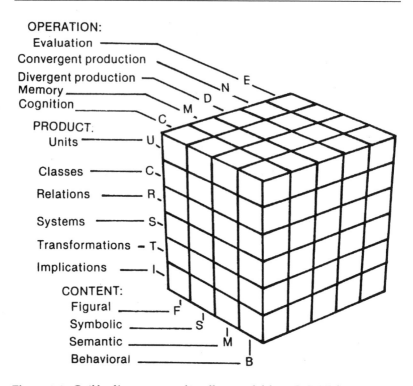

Figure 2.1. Guilford's structure of intellect model from B. B. Wolman (1985), *Handbook of Intelligence: Theories, Measurements, and Applications.* Reprinted by permission of John Wiley & Sons.

product. There are five kinds of operations: evaluation, convergent production, divergent production, memory, and cognition. There are four types of content: figural, symbolic, semantic, and behavioral. There are six kinds of products: units, classes, relations, systems, transformations, and implications. These components are independently defined so that, in combination, the four contents, five operations, and six products can produce 120 three-way combinations of mental abilities. The cubic structure of the intellect is shown in Figure 2.1.

Abilities manifested by the performance on certain cognitive tasks depended on the manner in which they were presumed to sample facets of operations, content, and product. Guilford (1967) claimed that it was possible to arrange these primary factors into a distinctive model popularly known as the Structure of the Intellect model. Similar to Thurnstone but unlike Spearman, he did not share a unitary conception of intelligence.

Horn

Horn (1991a) proposed that human intelligence comprises at least nine broad Gf-Gc (general/fluid-general/crystallized) abilities. For the past 25 years, studies indicating covariability among abilities have led to the conception of the theory as a system of factors among factors. Initially, however, the theory was based on the seminal work of Cattell (1941, 1943), who argued that general intellectual ability was of two types: fluid ability and crystallized ability. Fluid ability was conceived as being able to flow into many diverse types of mental activities. In contrast, crystallized ability was presumed to underlie the end product of an individual's exposure to education, training, or other types of experiences. Fluid ability was presumed to consist of basic reasoning and related higher-order mental processes particularly evident in novel situations. Crystallized ability, however, was presumed to reflect the ability of an individual, partly on the basis of fluid ability, to learn and benefit from exposure to experiences within one's culture. Over the years, the theory has undergone change as new evidence from numerous studies (Cattell & Horn, 1978; Gustafsson, 1984; Horn, 1965; Woodcock, 1990) revealed seven other factors in addition to the ones indicative of fluid and crystallized ability. Nonetheless, the term Gf-Gc has been retained and is associated with the work of both Horn and Cattell. As depicted in Figure 2.2, the structure of the intellect is hierarchical. Consider the nature and content of the following nine broad dimensions of the Horn-Cattell Gf-Gc theory:

> *Fluid intelligence:* the ability to understand relations among stimuli and to make inferences and to understand implications between and among stimuli particularly with complex novel tasks
>
> *Crystallized intelligence:* the ability to acquire the breadth and depth of knowledge from the dominant culture

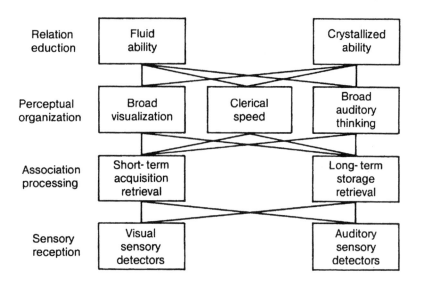

Figure 2.2. Horn's Hierarchical Model of Intelligence (Simplified Version) from B. B. Wolman (1985), *Handbook of Intelligence: Theories, Measurements, and Applications.* Reprinted by permission of John Wiley & Sons.

Quantitative ability: the ability to use quantitative information and to manipulate number symbols

Long-term storage and retrieval: the ability to store information in long-term memory over a long period of time (minutes, hours, weeks, and years) and to fluently retrieve it later through association

Short-term memory: the ability to maintain awareness of information and to recall it within a few seconds

Processing speed: the ability to quickly scan and respond to simple but timed tasks

Correct decision speed: the ability to quickly decide and respond accurately to tasks of moderate difficulty

Auditory processing: the ability to perceive sound patterns, to maintain awareness of order and rhythm among sounds under distortion or distraction, and to understand relationships between and among different groups of sounds

Visual processing: the ability to perceive and manipulate symbols of varying shape and to identify varying spatial configuration of them

Carroll

In a recent review and synthesis of factor analytic studies, Carroll (1993) proposed a three-stratum theory that involves the classification of abilities according to the generality of factors across domains of cognitive performances or tasks as well as the level and speed by which these tasks or performances are to be differentiated. The abilities located at each of the strata may be categorized as narrow (Stratum 1), broad (Stratum 2), and general (Stratum 3). Narrow, first-stratum abilities are indicative of a large number of specialized abilities presumed to reflect the effects of experience and learning. Broad, second-stratum abilities are indicative of moderate specialization of abilities and are particularly useful for understanding the breadth and scope of human cognition (fluid intelligence, crystallized intelligence, general memory and learning, broad visual perception, broad auditory perception, broad retrieval ability, broad cognitive speediness, and processing speed). According to Carroll (1993), these abilities represent "basic constitutional and long-standing characteristics of individuals that can govern or influence a great variety of behaviors in a given domain" (p. 634). As shown in Figure 2.3, general, third-stratum ability is indicative of general intelligence that reflects the domination of the second-order factors by a third factor.

Intelligence as a Multidimensional Construct

Conceptions of intelligence as a multidimensional construct have emerged in recent years. Theorists who subscribe to this view consider the internal and external world of the individual. Although cognitive processes represent an important characteristic of intelligence, the kinds of experiences in which these cognitive processes are developed and displayed and in what kinds of context are also important components of intelligence. Three theorists who share this view of intelligence are presented.

Stratus III

3G*
General Intelligence

Stratus II

2F*
Fluid Intelligence

2C*
Crystallized Intelligence

2Y
General Memory and Learning

2V
Broad Visual Perception

Stratus I

Level factors:
General Sequential Reasoning (RG)
Induction (I)
Quantitative Reasoning (RQ)
Piagetian Reasoning (RP)

Speed factors:
Speed of Reasoning (RE?)

Level factors:
Language Development (LD)
Verbal (Printed) Language
    Comprehension (V)
Lexical Knowledge (VL)
Reading Comprehension (RC)
Reading Decoding (RD)
Cloze Ability (CZ)
Spelling Ability (SB)
Phonetic Coding (PC)
Grammatical Sensitivity (MY)
Foreign Language Aptitude (LA)
Communication Ability (CM)
Listening Ability (LS)
Foreign Language Proficiency (KL)

Speed and level factors:
Reading Speed (RS)
Oral Production and Fluency (OP)
Writing Ability (WA)

Level factor:
Memory Span (MS)

Rate factors:
Associative Memory (MA)
Free Recall Memory (M6)
Meaningful Memory (MM)
Visual Memory (MV)
Learning Ability (LI)

Level factor:
Visualization (VV)

Speed factors:
Spatial Relations (SR)
Closure Speed (CS)
Flexibility of Closure (CF)
Serial Perceptual Integration (PI)
Spatial Scanning (SS)
Perceptual Speed (P)

Miscellaneous:
Imagery (IM)
Length Estimation (LE)
Perception of Illusions (IL)
Perceptual Alternations (PN)

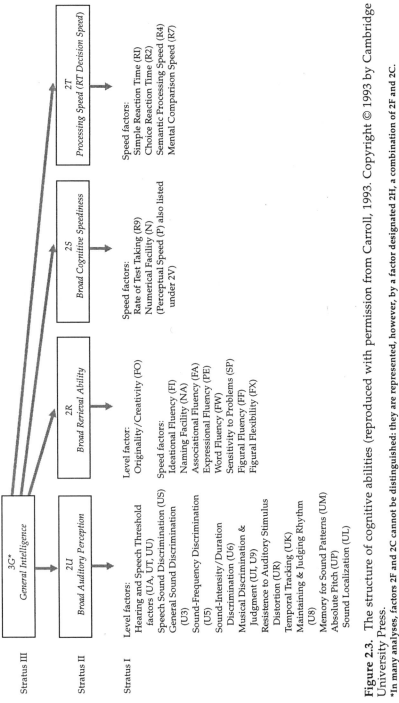

Figure 2.3. The structure of cognitive abilities (reproduced with permission from Carroll, 1993. Copyright © 1993 by Cambridge University Press.

*In many analyses, factors 2F and 2C cannot be distinguished: they are represented, however, by a factor designated 2H, a combination of 2F and 2C.

35

Sternberg's Triarchic Theory

Robert Sternberg (1985c) conceives of intelligence as a triarchic construct involving three interrelated subtheories; first, a componential theory that focuses on the cognitive processes that the individual uses in the performance of intellectual tasks. Sternberg distinguished three classes of processes: (a) metacomponents—general, executivelike processes used to plan, monitor, and evaluate one's performance on a task; (b) performance components—specific processes used in the actual performance of the task; and (c) knowledge-acquisition processes—specific processes used in the learning of new words. Together these processes form the bases for the other contextual and experiential subtheories. Second, according to Sternberg, the contextual subtheory describes the purposeful use of cognitive processes in adaptation to, selection, and shaping of a real-world context important to one's life. Third, the experiential subtheory posits that the individual may use these cognitive processes in situations that require the ability to deal with novel kinds of tasks and the ability to automatize the processing of information. For Sternberg, the basic unit of analysis for explaining individual differences in intellectual functioning is the cognitive process or component. A task or situation, however, is said to measure intelligence to the extent to which processes are deployed in contextually meaningful situations that are relatively novel or to which individuals respond with automaticity. Components of intelligence and the triarchic theory are illustrated in Figures 2.4 and 2.5, respectively.

Ceci's Bioecological Treatise on
Intellectual Development

Stephen Ceci's perspective on intelligence is both developmental and contextual. For Ceci (1990), a child is born with a number of biologically constrained cognitive muscles (the biological architecture to remember, to develop expectancies, classify, etc.) that are moderated by certain factors within the ecology in which the child grows and functions. These experiences within the environment to which the child is exposed set in motion biologically constrained potentials along multiple pathways, each of which has relevance for

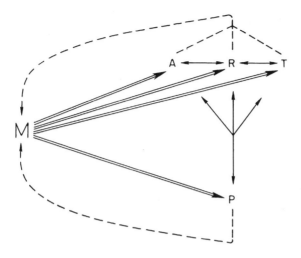

Figure 2.4. Components of intelligence. Interrelations among components serving different functions. *M*, a set of metacomponents; *A, R,* and *T,* a set of knowledge acquisition components as they function in the acquisition (*A*), retrieval (*R*), and transfer (*T*) of information; *P,* a set of performance components. Direct activation of one kind of component by another is represented by solid double arrows. Indirect activation of one kind of component by another is represented by single solid arrows. Direct feedback from one kind of component to another is represented by single broken arrows. Indirect feedback from one kind of component to another proceeds from and to the same components as does indirect activation and so is shown by the single solid arrows (reproduced with permission from Sternberg, 1980, p. 578. Copyright © 1980 by Cambridge University Press).

the crystallization of intellectual competencies that form the basis of adult intelligence. Thus, for Ceci, there are four facets to the development of intelligence: (a) multiple intellectual potentials; (b) context—an ecology that can either support or constrain the development and expression of the intellectual potentials; (c) domain-specific knowledge—the amount and quality of knowledge that can positively or negatively influence the efficiency and accuracy of the use of these intellectual processes; and (d) appropriate elicitors must be present within the ecology to motivate the development and expression of these intellectual potentials.

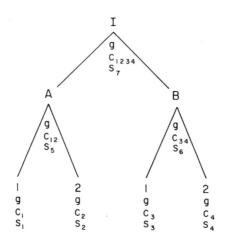

Figure 2.5. The triarchic theory: subtheories. Interrelations among components of different levels of generality. Each node of the hierarchy contains a task, which is designated by a roman or arabic numeral or by a letter. Each task comprises a set of components at the general (g), class (c), and specific (s) levels. Abbreviations used: g, a set of general components; c_i and c_j each refer to a set of class components; c_{ij} refers to a concatenaged set of class components that includes the class components from both c_i and c_j; s_i refers to a set of specific components (reproduced with permission from Sternberg, 1980, p. 579. Copyright © 1980 by Cambridge University Press).

Gardner's Theory of Multiple Intelligences

Howard Gardner is among a growing number of psychologists to argue that the human mind is quite modular in design and that separate and independent cognitive processes seem to underlie the performance on intellectual tasks. On the basis of his own studies of the development and breakdown of cognitive- and symbols-using capacities as well as those from the neuropsychological literature, Gardner and colleagues (Gardner, Howard, & Perkins, 1974; Gardner & Wolf, 1983) hold the view that an individual's precocity with one form of symbol use may not necessarily carry over to other forms. That is, individuals use different cognitive processes when engaged in tasks involving numerical, pictorial, linguistic, gestural, and other kinds of symbolic systems. He elaborated on this cognition and symbol system relationship in his 1983 *Frames of Mind*. Here, he coined the concept of multiple intelligences and proposed that individuals are capable of intellectual functioning in at least seven relatively autonomous areas and that they may have strengths or weaknesses in one or several areas. These multiple intelligences are logical-mathematical, linguistic, musical, spatial, bodily kinesthetic, interpersonal, and intrapersonal. Gardner believed that environmentally enriched contexts are likely to enable the nurturance of multiple emerging capacities.

Perspectives of Intelligence as Situated Cognition

The conception of intelligence as situated in its historical, social, cultural, and physical environment is shared by researchers from diverse disciplines, including anthropology, sociology, psychology, and psycholinguistics. A core feature of the situationist view is the reciprocal nature of the relationship between the person and the environment such that one cannot study cognition disembedded from the context in which it develops and finds expression. Using methodologies from traditions such as critical theory, ethnography, and conversational analysis, researchers examine human behavior in natural settings: the individual's interactions with others, the specifics of the person's situation, as well as the larger cultural and historical forces that embody these microlevel activities.

Vygotsky

Lev Vygotsky studied human cognitive functioning from a developmental perspective that holds that sociocultural processes are key influences on development. He makes a conceptual distinction between two classes of cognitive processes: lower (natural) and higher (cultural). He considered elementary perception, memory, and attention as rudimentary processes that create a biological predisposition for the child's development. According to Vygotsky, these lower cognitive processes become transformed into higher cognitive processes, such as reasoning, planning, and logical memory, through mediated activity and psychological tools. Three assumptions guided his work: (a) The individual cognitive processes have their origin in social interaction; (b) the zone of proximal development (the difference in performance with and without adult guidance or in collaboration with more capable peers) is one of the primary mechanisms that accounts for the development of individual cognitive functioning; and (c) the development of individual cognitive processes is mediated by tools, language, signs, or other symbolic systems. Thus, for Vygotsky, intellectual ability is not a natural entity but a sociocultural phenomenon that emerges through social mediation.

Boykin

A. Wade Boykin is among a growing number of researchers in racial and ethnic minority psychology to make the case for the relationship between cultural contexts and cognitive performance. For Boykin and colleagues, cognitive performance is inextricably wedded to the individual's views and values about what tasks should and would want to be performed. His research program is conceptually anchored within a framework of cultural integrity as it pertains to African American culture and children's cognitive performance. For Boykin, African American culture is characterized by three nonoverlapping realms of experience: mainstream, minority, and Afrocultural. Mainstream experience describes the beliefs, values, and behavioral styles common to most members of the U.S. society. Minority experience denotes certain defense mechanisms or coping strategies developed by members of ethnic and linguistic minority groups within a dominant society. Afrocultural experience refers to the beliefs, values, and behavioral styles of African descendants throughout the diaspora and traditional West African worldviews. The conflicts created by these three divergent psychological realities at once create what Boykin (1986) calls a "triple quandary" for most African Americans: "They are incompletely socialized to the Euro-American cultural system; they are victimized by racial and economic oppression; they participate in a culture that is sharply at odds with mainstream ideology" (p. 66).

For more than 15 years, Boykin and colleagues (Allen & Boykin, 1991; Boykin, 1977, 1979, 1982a; Boykin & Allen, 1988; Boykin, De-Britto, & Davis, 1984; Boykin & Toms, 1985) have engaged in research that examined the degree of success and failure of African American children on cognitive tasks in contexts reflective of these multiple experiences.

Lave

Since the early 1970s, the research investigations of Lave and colleagues have provided consistent evidence for the conception of cognition as a situated sociocultural process. Examples of this position include her observations of cognitive asymmetry in the performance of Liberian tailors on school-based and non-school-based mathematics (1977) and the context specificity of cognition in everyday mathematics tasks among grocery shoppers (1988). Moreover, observations of the opportunities afforded by certain cultures to involve children in the mature practices of their communities have added ecological validity to the notion of intelligence as a situated cognitive process. Collectively, from these works she has developed a theoretical account for the interdependence of learning and cognition as individuals become members of their communities of practice.

Commentary

For ease of discussion of the objective conceptions of intelligence in relation to the criteria, we outline each of the criteria and consider the extent to which they were met by the various perspectives. The goal here is not to do an exhaustive analysis of each perspective but rather to determine which among them offers the best guidance for diagnostic and prescriptive assessment.

Operational Definition of Cognition(s)
Underlying Performance of Intellectual Tasks

Psychometric conceptions of intelligence have a vast amount of evidence in support of the mental operations involved in tasks purporting to measure intelligence. These perspectives all seem to share the view that the mental activity underlying the performance on certain types of tasks involves the capacity to perceive, to remember, to reason, and to acquire knowledge efficiently. What seems to be the point of contention, however, is to determine the relative importance of these underlying cognitions in defining the essence of intelligence and to agree on a structure of the mind that best represents this essence. Conceptually, to the extent that these cognitions have differential meaning in different cultural contexts and the extent to which differential standards are expected of individuals or groups who execute them, there will continue to be differences in its conceptions. A similar claim can be made methodologically as well. Differences are also likely to occur to the extent that there is no consensus regarding a prior criteria for use of factor analytic techniques in the analysis and interpretation of observed differences on intellectual tasks. These caveats make more understandable the seemingly endless variations in the types of cognitions underlying intelligent behavior (e.g., Carroll's, Spearman's, and Wechsler's hierarchical structure of general intelligence; Thurstone's unordered arrangements; Horn's and Cattell's second-order system; and Guilford's cubic organization of multiple intelligences).

Despite the agreement among psychometric theorists regarding the mental operations underlying the performance on intellectual tasks, there is no agreed on understanding of the number and organization of these cognitions. Individual tasks of perception, memory, reasoning, comprehension, and knowledge are more likely to be less complex than tasks requiring different combinations of cognition. Even within particular cognitions there is variation in terms of how they cluster in a given universe of tasks. For example, Guilford's structure of the intellect and Thurnstone's primary abilities represent different combinations of the same cognitions. Also, Carroll's three-stratum model and Horn-Cattell Gf-Gc models identify similar cognitions, but Carroll's conceives of intelligence as involving narrow, broad, and general cognitions, whereas Horn and Cattell consider intelligence to consist of nine broad intellectual capabilities. These diverse ways by which different cognitions are clustered suggest that the search for the exact or precise nature of intelligence may be a fruitless one.

There is also empirical evidence and consensus for the nature of the cognitions underlying performance on intellectual tasks for both the multidimensional and the situated cognition views of intelligence. Like the psychometric perspectives, however, there is still no consensus about their exact nature.

Susceptibility of Cognitions to Biological
or Environmental Influences

To our knowledge, there is no conception of intelligence that does not give some consideration to both the biological and the environmental influences on human cognition(s). What distinguishes one theorist from another is the relative weight given to biology or environment. The role of these two influences is important because either one has implications for change in subsequent intellectual functioning. To the extent that the operation of a cognition(s) is constrained by biological forces, its stable or fixed quality would render it relatively impervious to significant modification through intervention. If, however, the cognition(s) is responsive to environmental manipulation, then its labile or dynamic nature would permit modification through intervention. Many studies of the genesis of intelligence in the psychometric literature suggest that the heritability of intelligence ranges from .50 (Scarr & Carter-Salzman, 1982) to .58 (Plomin, 1985) and .70 (Bouchard, Lykken, McGue, Segal, & Tellegen, 1990). Other studies have provided moderate to strong correlational evidence of the relationship between speed or efficiency of neurophysiological processes and intellectual behavior as measured by IQ tests (e.g., Jensen, 1987, 1991; Vernon, 1990).

Other theorists (e.g., Gardner, 1983; Sternberg, 1988), however, while acknowledging the relevance of biology in intellectual functioning, seem more inclined to seek empirical evidence of the malleability of the construct and its responsiveness to training or schooling. Gardner and colleagues' work in Arts PROPEL (Gardner et al., 1989) and Project Spectrum (Krechevsky & Gardner, 1990) as well as Sternberg's (1988) program to train intellectual skills in Venezuelan schools are examples of the positive outcomes of intervention to modify cognition.

Vygotsky does not dismiss the role of heredity in behavior but seem more interested in discussing the modification of cognition through instruction. Followers in the Vygotskian tradition, other researchers (e.g., Feuerstein, Rand, & Hoffman, 1979; Lidz, 1991) have provided encouraging evidence of change in cognitive functioning through mediated interactions.

Identification of a Symbol System
on Which Cognitions Operate

All conceptions of intelligence describe intellectual behavior within some symbolic domain. For example, psychometric multidimensional and situated cognition theorists examine the operation of cognition in different types of tasks requiring linguistic, spatial, numerical representation. Gardner (1983), however, considers other symbolic domains (e.g., music and dance) wherein intelligence might find expression. Also, for situation theorist Vygotsky, symbolic tools, such as signs and linguistic and mathematical systems, play a crucial mediating role in the development and expression of cognition. Although most theorists would acknowledge variation in performance as a function of the modality in which intellectual content of tasks are embedded, it is not clear how much researchers attribute differences in intellectual performance to the way individuals represent information. Ceci (1990) and Gardner (1983) consider intellectual functioning inseparable from the symbol system in which it is embedded and consequently argue for conceptually different manifestations of cognitions. Psychometric theorists (e.g., Carroll, 1993; Spearman, 1927), however, argue that the intercorrelations of intellectual tasks involving different symbol systems demonstrate the existence of a general ability.

Specification of the Context and Experiences
Relevant for Intellectual Functioning

All conceptions of intelligence recognize that experiences within certain types of settings influence intellectual functioning. For example, a common and consistent finding of studies in the psychometric tradition is that there is a positive correlation between IQ scores and academic achievement (.50) and certain types of job performance (.30). One explanation for these findings is that certain types of experiences in school and in the workplace require intellectual competence as defined by IQ tests. Other researchers who argue that there is more to intelligence than what is measured on an IQ test provide evidence of experiences in nonschool settings that also require intellectual competence. For example, Sternberg, Wagner, Williams, and Horvath (1995) found that tasks that are embedded in and require everyday experiences are important for demonstrating what they call practical intelligence. Similarly, other researchers (e.g., Boykin, 1982; Ceci & Liker, 1986b; Gardner, 1983; Lave, 1988) found evidence of intellectual functioning on tasks outside the school context.

Implications of Conceptions of Intelligence for Intellectual Assessment

Some of the conceptions of intelligence reviewed in this chapter met the criteria, and others did not. Some had empirical and consensual support, and others did not. At some level, it is not surprising that all conceptions did not meet these requirements. It may be recalled that these criteria emerged as a "wish list" of attributes that we believe should guide the development or an assessment procedure that serves both diagnostic and prescriptive purposes. Second, it is an unreasonable expectation that any one theory would meet all the requirements for an assessment procedure, particularly one with such high-stakes consequences in our society. These caveats notwithstanding, the review did provide some conceptual justification for attributes associated with intelligence that do have implications for intellectual assessment. What, then, are the theoretical perspectives that met our criteria for assessment? Table 2.1 presents a list of those theoretical propositions that, when taken together, provide a more comprehensive conception of human intelligence than any single perspective.

We applied these propositions in the development of a four-tier system to assessing intelligence (see Chapter 6 for an elaboration).

Conclusion

Today, we are no more definitive in our understanding of the concept of intelligence as when the ancient Greek philosophers sought to make distinctions between its principled and sensory-based characteristics. During the past nine decades, however, the objective and subjective conceptions have broadened our knowledge of the complexity and multifacetedness of the phenomenon. In addition, methodological advances in factor analytic and information-processing

TABLE 2.1 Major Theoretical Propositions of Each Conception of Intelligence

Theorist	Propositions on Intelligence
Psychometric theorists (e.g., Carroll, Horn, Wechsler, and Guilford)	Cognitive abilities underlie performance on intellectual tasks
Situated cognition theorists (e.g., Boykin, Lave, and Vygotsky)	Cognitive processes have their origin in social interaction
	Emergent cognitive processes could be identified through cooperative interaction between child and adult
	Cognitive processes are developed and manifested in culturally familiar tasks and contexts
Triarchic theorist (Sternberg)	The basic unit of intelligence is the cognitive process or processes
	Novel and familiar experiences influence how cognitive processes are deployed
	Different contexts elicit different manifestations of cognitive processes
	Cognitive processes can be modified through intervention
Bioecological theorist (Ceci)	Intelligence consists of multiple cognitive processes
	The structure of knowledge influences the development and manifestation of cognitive processes
	The ecology impedes or fosters the development of biologically constrained cognitive potentials
	The ecology contains elicitors for the manifestation and development of cognitive potentials
Multiple Intelligence theorist (Gardner)	Intelligence as emerging cognitive capacities develop in multiple contexts and through multiple symbol systems

procedures and clinical and observational techniques have been useful in providing some insights with respect to the observed individual differences in performance on intellectual tasks. In the course of the review, it became apparent that experiences and the context in which these experiences are embedded play a role in intelligent behavior as do cognitive capacities that are more intrinsic to the individual. These notions about intelligence have very clear implications for diagnostic and prescriptive assessment: (a) to design measures that would identify individual strengths and weaknesses in cognitive processing as well as the contextual and experiential factors that enabled or constrained its expression and (b) to ensure that these assessment probes yield information at a sufficient level of detail to inform pedagogical planning and intervention. These issues are explored more fully in Chapter 6.

3

Culture and Cognition

Human cognition describes the mental activities that manipulate, translate, and transform information represented in any modality. Thus, for example, it can change verbal information into spatial representation or pictorial information into numerical representation. Variation in number, form, level, and organization of human cognition will depend on the density or complexity of information to be operated on. As indicated in Chapter 2, the more commonly cited cognitions involved in intellectual activities are those related to short- and long-term memory, reasoning, vocabulary, comprehension, visual processing, auditory processing, and speed of processing. We also learned that some contemporary theorists argue that these cognitions do not function in isolation but depend, in part, on certain kinds of experiences in contexts for their development and expression. In this chapter, we explore these issues further through an examination of the relationship of culture and cognition. First, various conceptions of culture are identified, and then an overview of the relevant research in this area is presented. From this review, we distill those psychologically relevant attributes of culture that systematically influence how and when cognitions are deployed in a given task or situation.

Conceptions of Culture

According to the historian Stocking (1968), the modern concept of culture emerged at the end of the 19th and the beginning of the 20th century. The research of early anthropologists through their field studies of various cultural groups throughout the world sought to understand the factors responsible for variation in thinking among various groups. This early position was in direct contrast to the views of Tylor (1874) and social scientists of the midcentury who, guided by Darwinian notions, had constructed an evolutionary model of culture. By tracing the development of culture, some societies were presumed to evolve through stages from less to more developed culminating naturally in modern culture with its technological, intellectual, and artistic traditions. This ethnocentric view was refuted, however, by other cultural anthropologists who, through systematic and prolonged observation and field notes, sought to understand variation in thinking among various cultural groups. An early popular hypothesis from this early work as represented in the work of Rivers (1926) was that different patterns of thinking were related to different environmental demands across cultures.

Geertz (1973) put forth the following definition of culture that is widely cited in cross-cultural psychology: Culture is an "historically transmitted pattern of meanings embodied in symbolic form by means of which men communicate, perpetuate, and develop their knowledge about and attitudes toward life" (p. 89). Although there was no explicit reference to thinking in this definition, Geertz's notion of the inseparability of culture and cognition of more than 20 years is widely shared by many cultural psychologists today: "The human brain is thoroughly dependent upon cultural resources for its very operation; and those resources are, consequently, not adjuncts to but constituents of mental activity" (p. 730). Gordon (1991) has extended Geertz's notion of culture to include "structured relationships, which are reflected in institutions, social status, and ways of doing things, and objects that are manufactured or created such as tools, clothing, architecture, and interpretative and representational art" (p. 101).

In an effort to portray culture as an inclusive and overarching construct in the lives of any social group, Gordon (1991) conceives it as a multidimensional construct consisting of at least five dimensions: (a) the judgmental or normative, (b) the cognitive, (c) the affective, (d) the skill, and (e) the technological. Elaborations of these dimensions may be found in Gordon and Armour-Thomas (1991).

Transdisciplinary Research on Context and Cognition

During the past three decades, numerous studies have been conducted both within and across diverse cultural groups to examine differences in performance on cognitive tasks. These studies have been guided by different perspectives about context, learning, and cognition from disciplines including anthropology, sociolinguistics, education, psychology, and sociology. A common research inquiry across disciplines was the search for an explanation for the finding of context-specific cognition within and between individuals in diverse settings and cultures. In the following sections, we present, in capsule form, a select review of the theoretical and empirical research in this area.

Anthropological and Cultural and Psychological Research

Interpreting the variable findings in the early cross-cultural Piagetian studies, Cole, Gay, Glick, and Sharp (1971) made the following observation: "Cultural differences in cognition reside more in the situations to which particular cognitive processes are applied than in the existence of a process in one cultural group, and its absence in another" (p. 233).

Today, a vast knowledge base has accumulated that is essentially consistent with Cole et al.'s (1971) insightful observation. Many of these investigations were cross-cultural in nature in Western and non-Western cultural groups on cognitive tasks of memory (Kearins, 1981; Lancy & Strathern, 1981), reasoning (Gladwin, 1971), mental arithmetic (Lave, 1977; Murtaugh, 1985), and literacy (Cole & Scribner, 1977; Rogoff & Waddell, 1982). The English publication of *Mind in Society* (Vygotsky, 1978), which laid out the propositions of the sociohistorical theory of Vygotsky and colleagues, provided a theoretical frame for understanding the observed variation in performance on cognitive tasks. A basic tent of Vygotsky's sociocultural theory is that nascent cognitive potential emerges, develops, and is displayed in a sociocultural milieu. Since then, numerous empirical studies in this tradition have sought an understanding of people's "everyday cognition" by studying their thinking in real-world tasks in multiple real-world environments.

In synthesizing this body of work, Rogoff and Chavajay (1995) identified the following key assumptions common to disciplines that use a sociocultural approach to study differences in cognitive performance:

1. The use of the concept of activity as the unit of analysis to examine human cognition in tasks of a sociocultural nature
2. The dual analysis of development and cognitive process
3. Analysis of performance that integrates cognitive processes at the individual, interpersonal, and community level
4. The study of differences and similarities in performance
5. The research methods as tools in the service of research
6. The historical and cultural embeddedness of the research question itself

Cognitive, Experimental,
and Psychological Research

Within the past 15 years, empirical research findings in cognitive and experimental psychology have been consistent with those of anthropology and cultural psychology. Using a different theoretical lens, studies were based on the assumption that intelligence is more than what an IQ test measures. More specifically, researchers searched for proof of the elusive theory that is presumed to explain individual differences in performance on standardized measures of intelligence. For example, Sternberg (1988) has argued that an important aspect of intelligence is whether mental activity is directed toward "purposive adaptation to, and selection of, real-world environments relevant to one's life" (p. 45). Labeling such intelligence in context as "practical intelligence," Sternberg and colleagues (Sternberg & Wagner, 1986; Sternberg, Wagner, & Okagaki, 1993; Sternberg, Wagner, Williams, & Horvath, 1995) have conducted a series of studies across settings and cultures. These findings provide compelling evidence that performances on measures of practical intelligence, although related to measures of performance on real-world tasks, are relatively unrelated to standardized tests of intelligence. Sternberg and colleagues attribute success on practical intelligence tasks to procedural knowledge that is tacit but that is acquired with little direct help from others but is important to the attainment of goals that people value.

Similar to the practical intelligence research as well as that from anthropology and cultural psychology, studies from experimental psychology have also found evidence of lack of cross-task correlations, even though the mental activity was isomorphic across situations or contexts (Neisser, 1979). Perhaps the most compelling evidence for the context specificity of cognitive skills is provided by the prolific work of Ceci and colleagues (Ceci, Baker, & Bronfenbrenner, 1987; Ceci & Bronfenbrenner, 1985; Ceci & Cornelius, 1989; Ceci & Liker, 1986b, 1988; Chi & Ceci, 1987).

Ceci (1990) proposed a bioecological treatise on intellectual development in accounting for the consistency of these findings. According to Ceci, the individual is born with a number of biologically constrained cognitive potentials (e.g., the capacity to classify, remember, and habituate) that are moderated by aspects of the environment, such as domain-specific knowledge and appropriate elicitors from the context for the manifestation of cognitive potentials. From this perspective, conditions within a particular context can either impede or enable the development and eventual manifestation of certain cognitive potentials. Collectively, these psychologically laden environmental variables led to his conception of intelligence as an ecologically based construct.

*Research on Context-Specific
Attributes and Cognition*

A notion common in the previously cited research is that there are psychologically meaningful attributes within a particular context that influence the acquisition of specific types of knowledge and cognitive skills. It would appear that attributes of the task itself as well as conditions of its engagement enable or impede the individual's demonstration of knowledge and cognitive skills. Finally, knowledge and skill seem inseparable from the values and beliefs that are often implicitly reflected in the social interactions and tasks that a given culture deem appropriate or meaningful for its people. Given that we use these empirical findings as a basis for the biocultural thesis that we develop in Chapter 4, we comment again on specific studies that have examined the psychological significance of these context-specific variables on children's intellectual development.

Context. Numerous studies have examined the socialization of knowledge acquisition and cognition in various contexts, such as the home, the school, and the community. For example, some investigations focus on the various forms of language usage between significant others and children in the home in culturally and cognitively meaningful activities (Heath, 1983; Ochs & Schiefflin, 1984). Other studies examine child-rearing values and beliefs and their influence on the mother-child interactions on cognitive tasks (Guttierrez & Sameroff, 1990; Hale-Benson, 1986; Laosa, 1980; Serpell, Baker, Sonnenschein, & Hill, 1993; Steinberg, Dornbusch, & Brown, 1992). The longitudinal research of Bradley and Caldwell (1984) provides a comprehensive description of the kinds of stimuli and social interactions and structure operating within the home that are likely to influence cognitive growth and development: maternal involvement and responsivity with the child, maternal acceptance and encouragement of social competence, organization of the environment and provision of appropriate tools and material for play, and variety of stimulation in the home.

Several researchers have examined a number of factors related to schooling and intellectual development. Some studies focused on the amount of schooling, whereas others examined the quality of schooling. Specific studies are too numerous to mention here. Critical analyses of those findings, however, have been done by Ceci (1990), Nerlove and Snipper (1981), and Rogoff (1981). For example, in a recent synthesis of research on the cultural basis of cognitive development, Rogoff and Chavajay (1995) discussed the influence of schooling in fostering the following types of cognitive skills:

1. The deliberate remembering of disconnected bits of information
2. The organization of information to be remembered using taxonomic rules
3. The shifting to alternative dimensions of classification and verbalization of strategies used for their organization
4. The analysis of two-dimensional patterns through the use of media representing depth in two-dimensional drawings

Studies that have examined the role of community influence on children's intellectual development consider the parameters of children's social and intellectual work space and the opportunities to participate in apprenticeship situations (Munroe & Munroe, 1971; Munroe, Munroe, & Whiting, 1985; Parke & Bhavnagri, 1989; Whiting, 1980). Lave and Wenger (1991) argue for the legitimacy of "peripheral participation" when opportunities are structured and made available for children to observe the practices of more capable community members. It appears that these less direct social interactions but adult-directed activities foster knowledge and cognitive skills specific to the culturally sanctioned practices of the community.

Stimulus Attributes of the Task. All cognitive skills are assessed through some mode of representation (e.g., visual, spatial, and auditory). Many studies have examined how familiarity with these cultural tools and materials influence the efficacy with which cognitive skills are expressed. For example, Lantz (1979) found that Indian children showed better classification skills when the stimulus attributes of the task consisted of grains and seeds than when the same task used an array of colors. Similarly, Serpell (1979) compared the effects of media on performance on a pattern production task among children from Zambia and England. Zambian children performed better when reproducing the patterns in a familiar medium (modeling with strips of wire) than when they were asked to reproduce the patterns with a paper and pencil measure. In contrast, the English children performed better with the paper and pencil measure than with the wire medium. When a medium familiar to both groups (clay) was used, however, both groups performed equally well on the pattern reproduction task. Uttal and Wellman (1989) reported how the preschoolers' exposure to acquisition of spatial knowledge through maps may have accounted for their relative competence in subsequent map reading skills.

Communicative Conventions and Courtesies. A prerequisite for engaging in cognitively complex tasks may be related to the skill in the conventions within a community for acquiring and communicating knowledge and skills. An important question is whether children have the skill with certain communicative conventions for demonstrating the cognitive skills they already possess. Conversely, unfamiliarity with particular patterns of discourse may account for less than optimal performance on cognitive tasks. A number of researchers have found that variations in the mode of discourse accounted for differential performance on cognitive tasks (Gauvain & Rogoff, 1989; Kearins, 1981; Lancy & Strathern, 1981, 1989; Miller-Jones, 1989; Siegel, 1991).

Values and Beliefs of a Culture. Although, to our knowledge, there are no studies of human intelligence that have explicitly examined the values and beliefs of a culture as independent variables on cognition, these constructs are embedded in the very tasks and social interactions in which children engage and, consequently, serve an important socializing function in shaping intellectual development. During the past 20 years, Goodnow has commented on these constructs quite extensively. In accounting for the nonindependence of cognition from its contents and context in early cross-cultural studies, Goodnow (1976) argued that such findings reflect the goals and the values of a culture. According to her, cognitive problems or tasks neither exist in a vacuum nor are they ever connected to some abstract set of principles or framework. Rather, they are bounded by a culture's definition of the problem to be solved and its definition of "proper" methods of solution. Goodnow (1990) contends that cultural values contain tacit understandings of what constitutes an appropriate goal and proposes that individuals learn "cognitive values." In other words, culture defines not only what its members should think or learn but also what they should ignore or treat as irrelevant, aspects that she terms "acceptable ignorance or incompetence."

Conclusion

The research reviewed provides good empirical support for the influence of culture on human cognition. It would appear that within any given culture there are certain ecologies or contexts wherein an individual engages in experiences that influence the way cognitions are elicited and deployed for a given task. How much does the inevitable constraint that biology imposes on cognition affect the efficiency and accuracy of the operations of cognitions in such situations? Does the biological constraint channel cognitions along certain predetermined developmental tracks irrespective of the quality or quantity of cultural influences? How susceptible are these cognitions to modification given that the range for the development of cognitive potentials is limited by biological constraints? These are but a few of the questions that ultimately must be answered about human cognition but for which the literature reviewed was largely silent. In Chapter 4, we examine the influences of both biology and culture on the development of cognitions underlying human behavior in tasks defined as "intellectual."

4

Toward a Biocultural Perspective of Intellectual Development

The construct of intelligence has remained one of the most enduring and controversial topics in the history of psychology. Today, we still have not put to rest the genesis question of intelligence that was put forth more than a 100 years ago when Galton (1883), Darwin's cousin, published his heredity thesis about the construct. Jensen's (1969) *The Differences Are Real* and Herrnstein and Murray's (1994) *The Bell Curve* make similar claims that the evidence is substantial for the observed differences in behavior as measured by standardized tests of intelligence. In a different but related vein, other researchers point to the impressive evidence of neural efficiency in accounting for individual difference in intelligence, thus further bolstering the biological argument. There are other alternative explanations, however. Proponents of the cultural view also

provide compelling evidence that suggests that observed behavior
is not independent of the cultural forces that shape, support, and
guide its development and organization. Indeed, the situatedness of
human cognition perspective is in direct contradiction to the notion
that intelligence is essentially a construct located within the individual. Despite the strong claims on each side of this "either-or" and
"how much" debate, it is more likely that an interactionist perspective may shed light on the apparent causal ambiguity surrounding
the observed differences in behavior on intellectual tasks.

In this chapter, we examine in detail the major components of an
interactionist perspective of intelligence. We begin with a definition
of intelligence that is congruent with a biocultural concept. Next, we
put forth the underlying assumptions about intelligence and specify
what we consider are the key variables for understanding its development and expression. During the course of the discussion, we
show how the interdependence of biological potentials with cultural
experiences nested within particular cultural niches render attribu-
tions for individual differences in intelligence, in either biological or
cultural terms, untenable. More specifically, we examine the mechanisms by which cultural experiences within particular cultural niches
over time transform biological potentials into developed cognitions.
It is these developed cognitions, honed and socialized by cultural
experiences, that we believe account for the differences in behavior
that are observed and sometimes measured with standardized tests
of intelligence.

Definition of Intelligence

Intelligence is a culturally derived abstraction that members of any
given society coin to make sense of observed differences in performance of individuals within and between social groups. This notion
is similar to the one put forth by Neisser (1976) when he described it
as a cultural contrivance created by a people to define what they
value as a culture. In the previous chapters, we have come to the
realization that the search for an objective definition with universal
consensus is a futile endeavor. Horn (1991b) stated it best when he
said,

Efforts to define intellectual capabilities "once and for all" are doomed to failure because not only is the universe of these capabilities so vast that its boundaries are beyond comprehension, but also because it is constantly evolving into a new vastness. (p. 198)

Therefore, we too, like Neisser, have engaged in cultural inventing to define intelligence as the deployment of culturally dependent cognitions in adaptation to meaningful encounters in our environment in a purposive manner. Its expression as behavior reflects the gradual transformation of biologically programmed cognitive potentials into developed cognitions through a process of cultural socialization.

The Biocultural Perspective

The converging evidence from various disciplines that human cognition is context specific in addition to evidence of the strong influence of culture on cognitive development provide the empirical basis for the thesis that intelligence is a culturally dependent construct. More specifically, the evidence suggests that the mind functions and develops within cultural niches and as such the comingling of biological and cultural processes is inevitable. Although the range of cognitive potentials may be constrained by biological programming, which potentials become developed and expressed are under the control of cultural experiences. In this sense, the mental life of individuals is inseparable from the culture that gives it direction, regulation, and meaning; hence, intellectual behavior is more appropriately described as a biocultural phenomenon. From this perspective, individual differences in intelligence are best understood within a developmental framework wherein cultural forces shape the development of biologically programmed cognitive potentials along different pathways toward different end states.

Assumptions

There are four assumptions underlying the biocultural perspective: (a) The interactions between biologically derived cognitive potentials and forces operating within the child's culture are reciprocal, (b) the interdependence of knowledge and cognitive processing in the development of cognition, (c) instruction is a precursor to the development of cognition, and (d) motivation as energy activated from both within and outside the person. A brief explanation of each assumption follows.

Reciprocity

The biocultural perspective asserts that the characteristics of the individual and characteristics of specific characteristics within the child's culture are reciprocally interactive. Biologically derived potentials and other psychologically relevant characteristics are developed and shaped by culture, which itself undergoes change by developing cognitions. All human beings are born with capabilities that enable them to think in complex ways, such as the capacity to encode, scan, transform, reason, store, and retrieve information from memory. Selected attributes within the culture, however, determine when, how, and under what conditions these potentials develop and are manifested in behavior. Similarly, the nature and quality of social interactions and other kinds of cultural stimulation determine how well we organize our thinking and adapt to the ecologies in which we live and grow. The influence is therefore reciprocal or synergistic in that the interplay within and between biological and cultural characteristics results in changes that become the basis for greater and progressively more complex changes in both domains. For a more comprehensive discussion of the interactionist perspective on human development, see Bronfenbrenner (1989, 1993), Ceci (1990), Gordon (in press); Gordon and Terrell (1981), and Lewin (1935).

This process of change, with its reciprocal and synergistic effects, continues over the course of human development. At any point along the developmental continuum, the nature and quality of emerging cognitions are indivisible products of the dynamic weaving of biology and culture. Whether these emerging cognitions will reach their fullest possible expression, remain undeveloped, or show stunted or uneven development depends on two factors: (a) the opportunities and constraints within the culture that may foster or impede their growth and development and (b) the receptiveness or vulnerability of the organism at critical points in time toward these liberating and inhibiting forces operating with the culture. Thus, the number, type, and level of cognitions developed through this process of cultural socialization will consequently vary depending on the confluence of motivational, emotional, social, and cognitive forces operating within both the child's immediate ecologies and the larger culture.

Interdependence of Knowledge and Cognitive Processing

The biocultural perspective assumes that both knowledge and processing play important roles in cognitive development. Consequently, differences in observed behavior as measured by standardized tests of intelligence may be accounted for by differences in efficiency of cognitive processing as well as by differences in the nature and structure of one's knowledge. Empirical studies to date have not established the primacy of one over the other. Some scholars claim that the degree of elaborateness and differentiation of knowledge structures enable individuals to represent the knowledge in memory that makes possible the recognition of new relations and, consequently, the use of existing cognitive operations (Case, 1985; Ceci, 1990; Chi, 1978; Keil, 1984). Other scholars contend that it is the existence of the cognitive operation (Hunt, 1978; Jensen, 1980; Sternberg, 1977a, 1986) or the mental structures (Piaget, 1952) in the first place that enable the acquisition of knowledge. To our knowledge, the "chicken and the egg" question of which one is primary in its influence on cognitive development has not been settled. Nonetheless, it would appear that both the degree of elaboration and the differentiation of knowledge as well as the efficiency of cognitive processing play mutually supportive and complementary roles in the development of cognition.

Instruction and Cognition

Instruction as a form of transactional activity is another tenet of the biocultural perspective. It assumes that the development of cognition is facilitated when it becomes the object of instruction. It may be direct, as in significant other-child dyadic relationships, or it may involve less direct social processes, as in apprenticeships situations in which semistructured opportunities are created for observational learning by the child of expert practices in a given domain of interest. It is based on a Vygotskian notion that instruction is effective when it is directed at those cognitive functions not yet completely formed that lie in the zone of proximal development. The role of the instructor is to facilitate the emergence or development of these nascent cognitions.

Internal and External Motivation

The biocultural perspective holds that there are two aspects of motivation in the development and expression of cognition. The first describes the capacity of the individual to arouse attention and interest in environmental stimuli, to sustain the intensity of effort, and to direct one's energies toward the completion of a task without external feedback or reward. The second describes the mechanism within specific environmental stimuli that activates or triggers initial interest and attention in a task, which also serve to sustain intensity of effort in tasks and to direct one's energies toward fulfillment of goals. Banks and colleagues' (1979) conception of the embeddedness of relevance and interest in tasks, Gordon's (1991) prompting force within environmental stimuli, and Ceci's (1990) context elicitors all convey the notion that motivational forces also lie within the culture.

These are our working assumptions as we seek to develop a biocultural theory of intelligence. It is developmental and reflects a strong interactionist position of the dual role of biology and culture in accounting for its development and expression. We express the reciprocal interaction with the following equation:

$$D_t \rightleftharpoons B_t = f_{(t-p)}ST(PE)_{(t-p)}$$

where B represents intelligence as cognitive behavior and t is the particular point at which it is observed; the symbol f stands for function and is used as an indicator for developmental processes through which conditions and attributes of the person and the environment are reciprocally interactive in ways that produce continuous change in cognition overtime; $t - p$ is the prior period when the reciprocal interactions between person and environment conditions and attributes were occurring to produce the cognitive behavior observed at the particular point in time of observation; ST is the sustaining and threatening forces or conditions; PE is the person and environmental factors; D is cognition as a developmental outcome observed at a particular point in time; and the symbol $\rightleftharpoons$ is used to indicate that B_t and D_t can be used interchangeably.

Of course, representation of the interactionist perspective in equation form is not a new idea. More than 30 years ago, in his seminal study of the psychology of human behavior, Lewin (1935) advanced the notion that behavior is a joint function of person and environment: $B = f(PE)$. Since then, other scholars have transformed this classic formula with substitutions. For example, Gordon's (1977) conception of sustaining and threatening forces as well as existential and objective realities of the person in the person-environment interactions led to a reformulation: $B = f[o(SPE)o(TPE)e(SPE)e(TPE)]$. Bronfenbrenner (1993), couching person-environment interactions in developmental terms, argued that development is a joint function of person and environment $(D_t = f_{(t-p)} (PE)_{(t-p)}$. We have blended various aspects of the work of these scholars in the way we have represented the developmental nature of the reciprocity of person-environment interactions and its expression as behavior at a particular point in time. In the sections that follow, we examine the various components of our emerging biocultural theory of intelligence in greater detail.

Characteristics of the Developing Child

Cognitive functioning, although important, is indicative of but one aspect of a child's life. Other psychological processes—social, emotional, and motivational—play an important role as well. In our biocultural perspective, we begin with the position that differences in intelligence are more meaningfully understood within a developmental frame and as such consider other characteristics of the child as well. The section that follows begins with an examination of the concept of biologically derived cognitive potentials and culturally dependent cognitions. In addition, other psychologically relevant characteristics are considered that may have implications for the development of the human cognition that some of us regard as "intelligence."

Biologically Programmed Cognitive Potentials

Despite the seemingly irresolution of the genesis question of intelligence, it is difficult to dismiss the possibility that some basic cognitive functions as well as the dynamic organization and structure of the brain create a biological predisposition for human development. These biologically derived cognitive potentials include mental operations for attending, encoding, and scanning environmental stimuli as well as operations for transforming, storing, and retrieving environmental input. A speed factor appears to be pervasive within and across these cognitive operations. (See Ceci, 1990, for discussions of these natural cognitive functions.) We share Weinberg's (1989) view that our genes set limits in terms of the range of possible reactions for these labile cognitive potentials. The nature and quality of environmental encounters in a given culture, however, determine whether or not the full range of gene reactivity is developed and ultimately expressed.

Culturally Dependent Cognitions

We take the Vygoskian position that higher classes of cognitive function (e.g., reasoning, logical memory, planning, fluency in language, speed of decision making and retrieval of information from memory, etc.) are higher human functions conceptually distinct from the lower classes alluded to earlier. According to Vygotsky (1978), lower (natural) classes of cognitive functions are reorganized and transformed according to the means and social goals established by a culture. The transformation is made through social mediation, symbolic tools, and materials, all of which have psychological salience for the developing child. (For a more comprehensive discussion of these issues, see Newman & Holzman, 1993; Wertsch, 1985.)

We label these higher cognitive functions culturally dependent cognitions because it appears that it is through a developmental process of cultural socialization that account for their restructuring and transformation from lower cognitive functions (biologically constrained potentials). At any point in the developmental history of a child, through task analysis it should be possible to determine the nature and quality of these developed, culturally dependent cognitions. To the extent to which we need to use them to discriminate among individuals or groups, then a variety of quantitative and qualitative procedures may be used. As we argue later, differences in the expression of these cognitions may be more of a function of the nature and quality of learning experiences within certain cultural niches to which the child has been exposed rather than to defective genes or faulty neural processing. We make no claims for the number and level of thinking involved in these cognitions as other researchers using factor analytic and information processing models have done. This is not an attempt to dodge questions of generality versus specificity and one versus many regarding the nature of intelligence. Indeed, to date the status of our technology and statistical techniques are unable to address the causality of intelligence issue without polemical debate. As such, these questions have deliberately not been the focus of our attention.

Other Psychologically Relevant Characteristics

Demographics

Demographic characteristics of the person may or may not have implications for the developing child. In multicultural societies such as the United States, demographic characteristics, such as age, race, class, gender, and ethnicity, are not merely static variables used to conveniently distinguish different categories of people. Rather, for many individuals, they are psychologically charged constructs with implications for how individuals react to situations, events, or people in the environment as well as how others perceive and react to them. Phinney (1996) provided a discussion of the psychological importance of ethnicity in U.S. culture, but we think other demographic characteristics may have similar significance for some individuals as well. When these characteristics are considered in relation to cognitive development and more specifically intellectual functioning, they take on special meaning and relevance for individuals, particularly those who identify with a cultural group within a dominant social order. The ideological orientation, opportunity structures, and patterns of social, political, and economic interchange that are embedded within the dominant culture determine to a significant extent the course and conditions of cognitive development. There is reason to expect that the process of cognitive development may operate differently for ethnic and racial minorities as well as for males and females. To the extent that this is the case, any consideration of intellectual functioning must include its interactive influences with those aspects of demographics that have psychological relevance and meaning for some individuals and groups. (The interested reader is referred to Boykin, 1983, for a discussion of the psychological functioning of some racial and ethnic minority groups within the U.S. society.)

Response Tendencies

Our review of the literature suggests that there are a variety of cognitive, emotional, and cultural patterns of an individual's response to specific environmental stimuli—situations, persons, or events. To describe these idiosyncratic responses to situations, a variety of terms have been used: affective response tendency or temperamental style (Gordon, 1988; Thomas & Chess, 1977), cognitive style (Messick, 1976; Shade, 1982; Shipman & Shipman, 1985), learning style (Dunn & Dunn, 1978), cultural and behavioral style (Boykin, 1979; Hale, 1982; Hilliard, 1976), developmentally instigative characteristics (Bronfenbrenner, 1993), and cognitive response tendencies (Gordon, 1988, 1991). In reviewing this work, we were unable to find unequivocal findings for the relationship between these stylistic modes and behavior. Some of them appear to be dynamic dispositional traits that show a high degree of stability that may be minimally responsive to environmental stimulation. Others, however, seem quite labile and consequently are responsive to situational demands. Some of these latter "response tendencies," as Gordon (1988, 1991) labels them, are motivational and cognitive in nature in that the child shows initial interest and attention to certain types of tasks and remains engaged over a prolonged period of time until task completion. When these personologic qualities are considered in relation to cognitive development, and more specifically cognitive functioning, they are likely to interact with biologically derived potentials as well as with other psychologically relevant demographic characteristics of the child in nontrivial ways.

In summary, a developmental perspective allows a conception of the child as a functional whole wherein cognitive functioning does not operate in isolation of other psychological characteristics of the child. So as not to run the risk of overgeneralization or distortion regarding observed differences in behavior measured by intelligence tests, we consider other aspects of the child in our biocultural perspective of intelligence. Our reading of the literature suggests that these characteristics of the child are quite dynamically interactive and are likely to influence the course and outcome of subsequent cognitive development. Such characteristics, however, do not exist in isolation of the cultural environment in which development unfolds. Rather, they interact with certain characteristics of the cultural environment in ways that substantially affect the development of biologically derived cognitive potentials. The product of these interactions that we observe as behavior is consequently biocultural in nature. To better understand the psychological effects of culture, we turn now to a discussion of its defining attributes and the mechanisms by which it enables the transformation of biologically derived cognitive potentials into what we call *culturally dependent cognitions.*

Culture

The picture that emerges from both the theoretical and empirical research on culture, cognition, and behavior is one that suggests that culture permeates the daily life of a people and as such plays a pivotal role in human development. In terms of its location in cognitive development, and more specifically intelligent behavior, it seems to us that it has the potency to shape, direct, and transform biologically constrained potentials into developed cognitions. Over time, these developed cognitions, honed by the process of cultural socialization, are reflected in those special capabilities that members of a culture use to meet the demands of their social, economic, and technological environment.

Our position has been inspired by Vygotsky's (1978) sociocultural theory and thus many of our ideas are consistent with those of other researchers who argue that thinking does not exist outside of the activities in which people engage and the cultural practices that support and maintain desired patterns of cognitive development (Boykin & Allen, 1991; Ceci, 1990; Cole, 1988; Rogoff, 1990; Wertsch, 1985). From this work, both empirical and theoretical, we were able to discern at least three broad defining attributes of culture with psychological significance for the cognitive development of the child:

(a) belief system, (b) symbol system, and (c) language system. Although there is conceptual overlap among these systems, each one provides essential information regarding the relationship between cognition and behavior. A brief description of each attribute follows.

Belief System

Beliefs are interrelated concepts that govern the day to day lives of a social group. These include norms that describe the social standards and expectations for behaviors that, according to Berry (1976), people regard as right, proper, and natural. Beliefs are often implicitly understood and reflect a tacit consensus of assumptions about individuals and groups and their place within the society. Beliefs reflect a "mind-set" that remains deeply entrenched in the psyche of a people despite the passage of time. The term is sometimes used interchangeably with the notion of "worldview" or an "ethos" that according to Mbiti (1970) includes concepts such as understanding, attitude of mind, and perceptions that influence the way people think, act, and speak in various situations of life. Goals define the targets and expectations and give focus for people's energies and thought. Collectively, we refer to these interrelated concepts as a value system because it is likely that these concepts have their greatest impact as a cluster rather than a single entity. With respect to cognition and behavior, these intangible yet powerful attributes of a culture not only establish the opportunities and constraints for the types of cognitions about which judgments are made but also provide structure, direction, and regulation for its development. The daily activities in which individuals engage and the practices that support and maintain these values function as essential resources fueling their motivations and their thinking along particular pathways toward particular ends.

We find support for these ideas in Vygotsky's (1978) *Mind in Society*. In that work, he argued that at any given point in its history, a culture both defines and sets limits on options for individual development and it is to the flow of history that we look for evidence of psychological development across all domains—cognitive, emotional, and social. This means that the characteristics of the person as described earlier may be encouraged or discouraged depending on the social, economic forces operating within a culture at any given point in time and the structured relationships embedded within its institutions. More specifically, the nature and quality of cognitions are often indirectly shaped by the belief system that is implicitly reflected in these institutions. Brofenbrenner (1979, 1993) makes a similar point about the overarching influences of the macrosystem in his discussion of the role of ecology in cognitive development. Culture at this macrolevel, although critical, does not tell the full story of its impact on the developing child. For its influence at a more direct level—in face-to-face adult-child or capable peer collaborations—we turn to a discussion of culture's other defining attributes.

Symbol System

The symbol system describes the technologies (e.g., linguistic, pictorial, numerical, and gestural) that enable the development and ultimately the expression of cognition within any given culture. It is through the use of a symbol system that the child acquires knowledge, the differentiation and elaboration of which enable him or her to make connections to events, objects, and persons within his or her environment. Some cultures use more than one symbol system, so it is not uncommon that task demand reflect different permutations in content representation. For example, a task may require the processing of knowledge acquired through a dual modality of content: verbal-auditory, visual-spatialization, auditory-spatialization, pictorial-auditory, and kinesthetic-auditory. Of course, even more complex permutations of these dual modalities may be represented in some tasks. We speculate that the level of cognitive complexity of some tasks is to some extent a function of the sophistication in which the task content is represented. In principle, therefore, we make the case that the efficacy in which children are able to do Spearman-like tasks of "eduction of relations" and the "eduction of correlates" depends to a large extent on children's familiarity with the symbol system in which such reasoning tasks are represented. In cultural terms, we contend that the level of generality at which cognitions are expressed in behavior is dependent on the opportunities a given culture affords its members to access and use its symbol system(s) in meaningful tasks.

Again, we look to Vygotsky's (1978) conception of the symbolic feature of tool-mediated activity to better understand the mechanisms by which lower cognitive functions are transformed into higher cognitive functions. According to Vygotsky, the type of material tools places corresponding demands on one's human mental faculties. They are not merely a collection of individual implements. They take on psychological significance when used to represent phenomena in collective human interactions. In Vygotsky's seminal work (1978), he identified some ancient tools that served psychological functions such as "tying knots" and "counting fingers." Tying knots was used as a mnemonic tool to facilitate retrieval of information from memory. Using fingers to count functioned as a support in higher cognitive processing that involved basic arithmetic operations. He also mentioned other more advanced symbolic mediators that included artificial and natural languages.

Language System

A language system describes a number of different ways a culture systematically communicates ideas, feelings, and thoughts through the use of words, sounds, gestures, or signals with commonly understood meanings. It shares with the symbol system the modality for communicating environmental stimuli. Unlike the symbol system, however, the emphasis here is on the sociolinguistic conventions of a cultural group for organizing social interaction between an adult-child or peer collaborations or both. These culturally valued media act as a vehicle for dynamic and mutual engagement of cognitive tasks and through which the child's knowledge and thinking undergo organization, restructuring, and transformation. Over time, through these reciprocal processes between adult-child or capable peer collaboration, the child develops a system of knowledge structures and cognitive skills that are congruent with the symbol and belief systems of his or her cultural group. These culturally coded knowledge structures are then used as interpretative frameworks for using cognitions in the acquisition of new knowledge. Although the precise relationship between cognition and knowledge remains unclear, we concur with the positions of Keil (1981, 1984), Chi (1978), and Ceci (1990) that the degree of elaboration and differentiation in the representation is perhaps the mechanism that makes possible the recognition of new relations and consequently the use of existing cognitive processes. Also, it is from this perspective that we speculate that the efficiency or automaticity with which some children respond to intellectual tasks both in and outside of school may be a reflection of their well-elaborated and differentiated knowledge structures and developed cognition honed through this reciprocal process of the language system. Conversely, it is quite likely that the difficulties that children from linguistically diverse backgrounds experience on standardized tests of intelligence may have more to do with incompatibility between the sociolinguistics patterns of the child and the tester than with innate capacity to think abstractly or to retrieve information quickly. When we consider that the belief and symbol systems of these children may be different from those of the culture that supports the construction and administration of standardized tests of intelligence, their plight is multiplied exponentially.

Once more, we turn to Vygotsky and colleagues for the claims we make about the psychological salience of a language system. Earlier, we alluded to the symbolic aspects of tool-mediated activity. The other dimension of Vygotsky's mediated activity thesis involved another individual or capable peer. According to Vygotsky (1978, p. 57), "Every function in the child's cultural development appears twice: first on the social level, and later on the individual level; first between people (*interpsychological*)[italics added] and then inside the child (*intrapsychological*) [italics added]." He claimed that social mediation involves four concepts that account for its role in shaping cognitive development. First, knowledge in one's culture is socially transmitted by adults and capable peers to children. Second, joint participation in the range of activities determined by the culture allows for certain cognitive skills to be practiced and demonstrated by adults so that the children's current cognitive functioning may be modified or strengthened. In this way, the adult helps to shape the child's existing skills to better suit the demands of the culture. Third, new cognitions are cultivated when the adult or capable peer shares in the responsibility for the task with the child. Assuming the role of an expert tutor, the adult models, corrects, clarifies, and explains concepts to the child so that the child attempts and completes the task according to the criteria established by the culture. Finally, the independent use of new cognitive abilities is encouraged when the adult or more capable peer works with the child on cognitively challenging tasks that the child could not have successfully completed without guidance and support. Working with the child in their *zone of proximal development*, the adult models the task's appropriate behaviors, directs the child's attention to alternative procedures or approaches to the task, and encourages the child to try out his or her embryonic skills on some portion of the task. As the child's ability develops, the adult gradually reduces instructional support and allows the child to assume greater independence in task solution. It is this type of social scaffolding that Vygotsky suggested as the mechanism for change in cognitive development.

In summary, we think that each cultural system has psychological significance for the developing child. We speculate, however, that in any given culture, these systems interlock and the collective impact on the child is greater than is any one operating in isolation. How, then, do these influences coalesce in ways that affect the cognitive functioning of the child? We use two metaphors, "learning experience" and "cultural niche," as a way to operationally seek an understanding of the psychological dynamics operating within and across the three cultural systems.

Learning Experience

For us, the concept of learning experience comprises a cluster of social, emotional, motivational, and cognitive ingredients for enabling the transformation of biologically constrained cognitive potentials into culturally dependent cognitions. It embodies the defining attributes of culture in ways that the boundaries for the three symbol systems are virtually seamless. More specifically, every experience of the developing child has at least three features: persons (significant other(s) and the child), the tasks (symbolic mode of representation and level of complexity and motivational properties), and processes (social interaction). In practice, either tasks or processes may be subjected to manipulation as a way to better understand its unique effects on development or behavior of the person(s) under investigation. These localized treatments and influences, however, should not obscure the reciprocal interrelationships among these three variables and their impact on the developing child. In the following sections, we consider the findings from research that we think represent attempts to study selective aspects of experience.

Person-Process

Social interactions describe the dynamic processes of mutual engagement that occur between adults, capable peers, or any significant others and the child. They instantiate the language system of a culture by which the significant other, through mediation, structures the tasks in ways that encourage the child to focus on his or her thinking as he or she tackles the task.

The literature does provide some evidence for the importance of adult-child and peer collaboration in tasks requiring the demonstration of developed cognitions. For instance, Artzt and Armour-Thomas (1992) found that variation in mathematical problem solving was associated with the differences in the nature and quality of verbal interaction among seventh-grade students working in small groups. In that study, the ratio of metacognitive to cognitive behaviors was higher for groups that showed higher levels of peer collaborations. Other investigators have documented the gradual evolution of cognition when adults organize the learning environments of children using the principle of social scaffolding. For instance, in the studies conducted by Palinscar and Brown (1984) and Wertsch (1979), the adult was able, through different levels of interaction over time, to socialize the development of self-regulatory skills in children. Finally, Mackie (1980, 1983) studied the effects of social interaction on performance on spatial reasoning tasks among children from European descent and children from Maori and Pacific Island descent in New Zealand. The findings revealed that the children from Maori and Pacific Island descent were more passive in their interactions, especially when paired with more capable peers as partners, and their performance was lower than that of their counterparts from European descent. Mackie hypothesized that differences in the values regarding social interaction in the two cultural groups may have contributed to the differences in effort and performance.

Person-Tasks

Symbolic Representation of Information. Modes of representation are instantiations of a symbol system of a cultural group and include manipulatives, computers, maps, charts, various types of musical instruments, written script, and forms of counting. Acquisition and mastery of knowledge as well as the efficiency and accuracy of cognitions depend in part on the mode of representation of the task demands.

A growing body of cross-cultural research has reported differential effects of various symbol systems on children's cognitive performance. The underlying assumption of these studies suggests that the nature and quality of an individual's experience with the mode in which the task is represented will positively influence his or her performance in that task. For example, Stigler (1984) examined the use of the abacus as a tool for mathematical operations and mental calculations of Japanese students and found that intermediate and expert abacus users used a "mental abacus" when they performed mental calculations. It appears that a mental representation of problems on an abacus enhances remembering specific skills. In another investigation, Lave (1977) compared the arithmetic skills of Liberian tailors with school and tailoring experience using a format used in school with one used in tailoring. Findings indicated that experiences with schooling and with tailoring were related to solving arithmetic problems with the respective formats.

Motivational Stimuli. An important characteristic of a task that is likely to influence performance is the extent to which it has properties that are likely to attract and sustain attention and emotional investment until its completion. Again, we look to the culture and ask the following questions:

- What kinds of activities arouse individuals' attention and interest?

- What kinds of activities encourage them to sustain that effort with a level of intensity until task completion?

- What kinds of cultural practices support, maintain, and validate a high level of energy expenditure?

To the extent that the individual sees relevance and value for himself or herself or that the goal is worth pursuing, then positive outcomes can be expected.

To our knowledge, systematic study of this issue of the linkage between cultural motivation and developed cognition has remained relatively unexplored. There is some indirect evidence, however, that holds promise in this area. For example, Boykin (1982a) and Tuck (1985) reported that African American children's task performance was markedly better when the task context afforded a higher rather than a lower level of variability, the former being more congruent with the amount of variability present in the home life of these children. In a similar vein, Boykin and Allen (1988) and Boykin (1991) found that low-income African American children's task performance could be enhanced when the learning context afforded a greater rather than a lesser opportunity for movement expressiveness. Collectively, these studies suggest that the relatively high levels of sensate stimulation afforded in many African American home environments play a nontrivial role in observed task engagement and persistent behaviors. Similarly, motivational dynamics may have accounted for the efficacy in mathematical problem solving in Carraher, Carraher, and Schliemann's (1985) and Saxe's (1991) work with Brazilian street children. For example, the candy selling observed by Saxe was tied to the primary goal of the children—making money—and it is this motive that may have accounted for the speed and accuracy of their mathematical calculations.

Level of Cognitive Complexity. Level of complexity refers to the cognitive difficulty of the task—both its form of representation and its type and level of cognitive processing. Our reading of the empirical research suggests that researchers have different conceptions of this aspect of task demand that are correspondingly reflected in the analysis and interpretation of their findings. Some studies examined the level and type of cognitive processing in tasks involving reasoning (Pelligrino & Glaser, 1979; Sternberg; 1977), comprehension (Sternberg & Powell, 1983), and metacognition (Brown, 1978; Sternberg, 1986). Findings were usually interpreted in terms of differences in the efficiency of processing or use of cognitive strategies. Other studies examined the nature and quality of knowledge demands of the task (Ceci, 1990; Chi, 1978; Keil, 1984). Findings were often interpreted in terms of differences in knowledge representation. It may well be that both perspectives and interpretations are correct.

Knowledge and process appear to play different but complementary roles in cognitive development and, as such, behavior at any point in the child's development is likely to reflect the effects of a reciprocal interaction of knowledge representation and cognitive processing.

Contexts as Cultural Niches

We use the term *niche* in an effort to locate those particular ecologies within a culture that provide psychologically meaningful experiences for the developing child that are likely to nurture his or her development. It is a concept borrowed from biology—the "ecological niche"—used to describe the relationships between an organism and the environments in which it lives and grows. The term has also been used in developmental psychology. For example, Gauvain (1995) and Super and Harkness (1986) used it as a way of examining the simultaneous psychological and cultural influences on human development. Similarly, Bronfenbrenner (1979, 1993) used it to consider the multiple contexts wherein interactions of a changing organism in a changing environment unfold over the course of cognitive development. In an analogous manner, we think that experiences, as they relate to the development of biologically derived potentials, are embedded in settings in which person-process-task interactions occur. These settings must involve face-to-face relationships between the significant others and the child in which opportunities are provided on a consistent basis for mediating the child's engagement with the task demands. Feuerstein and colleagues (Feuerstein, 1990; Feuerstein, Rand, & Hoffman, 1979; Feuerstein, Rand, Hoffman, & Miller, 1980), building on Vygotsky's work, contend that it is at this face-to-face level where mediated learning takes place and constitutes what they call the proximal determinant on cognitive development. Other factors in the culture may influence cognitive development, but the effects of these distal determinants occur mainly through their influence on mediated learning experiences between the significant other and the child. Bronfenbrenner (1979, 1993) makes a similar argument in his discussion of the role of context in cognitive development.

The cultural niches wherein critical developmental processes between significant other and child occur include the home, the school, the peer group, and the community. Of course, other combinations of cultural niches can serve similar function. For example, for some adolescents, the peer group, the community, and the church may provide experiences that are likely to foster the development of biologically constrained potentials along certain trajectories. For other adolescents, the school, the home, the church, and the peer group through its learning experiences may foster the development of the same biologically constrained cognitive potentials but along different trajectories toward different ends. The point is that regardless of the type of cultural niche, each one is construed as a social-psychological nexus that, through the experiences made available for the child, offers structure, direction, and regulation for the development of biologically constrained potentials. Needless to say, not every culturally dependent cognition that emerges through this process of cultural socialization in every niche will be equally valued by the larger culture in which it is nested. Indeed, it is quite plausible that some cultural niches may have their own belief, language, and symbol systems that are different from those of other cultural niches as well as the larger culture. In multicultural societies such as the United States in which many cultural groups coexist, one can only wonder at the tremendous variations in culturally dependent cognitions that must have developed both within and across cultural groups. Figure 4.1 illustrates the types and level of relations within and across cultural niches as well as the social context of the larger culture within which these niches are embedded.

Conclusion

We have tried to make the case that observed behaviors at any point in a child's development are more precisely defined as culturally dependent cognitions. As members of the species *Homo sapiens*, we are born into this world with certain dynamic characteristics including cognitive potentials that create a biological predisposition for human development. How these characteristics develop, along what pathways, and toward what end states, however, are determined by the reciprocal interplay of these characteristics with equally dynamic experiences within particular zones of the culture wherein the child develops and functions. From this biocultural perspective, differ-

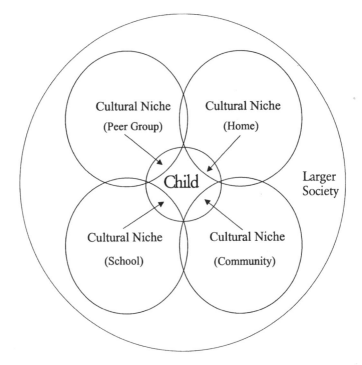

Figure 4.1. Biocultural System

ences in behavior that some of us label as intelligent reflect the extent to which the culture has differentially shaped the development of those biologically constrained cognitive potentials under investigation. These issues of person-process-context interactions, to our knowledge, have been unevenly explored in investigations of biology, culture, and intelligence. This is particularly troubling given the fact that in some cultures, such as the United States, judgments of intelligence have such far-reaching implications for how much and to whom the nation's resources are allocated. We hope that the biocultural perspective offers another lens through which to study the development of intelligence and to analyze, interpret, and draw implications of findings consistent with such a perspective. In Chapter 5, we describe the development of a four-tier assessment system of intelligence consistent with the notions of a biocultural perspective.

PART II

Intellectual Assessment and Culture: A New Paradigm

5

The Evolution of the Biocultural Assessment System

The Early Years

This assessment system has a long history that began in our private practice in 1986. It is based on the assessment of approximately 2,500 children who, over a 10-year period, were referred to Multicultural Educational and Psychological Services in Hempstead, New York. These children were referred from approximately 42 school districts and 150 schools in New York, Connecticut, New Jersey, California, and Washington. Approximately 7% of the children assessed were of African American heritage and 3% were Anglo-Americans. The remaining 90% were bicultural, originally from the United Kingdom, Puerto Rico, the Dominican Republic, Columbia, Peru, Ecuador, Mexico, Panama, Costa Rica, Haiti, Trinidad/Tobago, Barbados, Jamaica, Grenada, Guyana, Antigua/Barbuda, St. Kitts/Nevis, St. Vincent/Grenadines, St. Lucia, Montserrat, and Dominica.

As students in training in the early 1980s, there were some nagging concerns that the manner in which we were being trained to assess intelligence and interpret its findings was incongruent with our cross-cultural experiences given our understanding of intelligent behavior. The interpretation of differences on the IQ measure in terms of biological inferiority or cultural deprivation seemed equally untenable. When we examined the literature and the subjects for whom these judgments were made, they paralleled race, class, and linguistic differences. It was therefore rather disconcerting that the research on intelligence overwhelmingly revealed that minority (African American, Latino, and Native American) children on an average performed as much as one standard deviation (15 or 16-scale score IQ points) below that of their Anglo-American counterparts. In addition, the research also revealed that during a 3-year period children's IQ very rarely changed more than 3 IQ points as assessed by standardized tests of intelligence. We could not come to terms with our growing disenchantment with the assumptions that seemed to underlie the practice and interpretations of findings. We believe that all human beings have the capacity to remember, to reason, and to acquire and use knowledge. The speed and accuracy with which these capacities are deployed are dependent on the kinds of experiences from which individuals are socialized and the value system of the culture that supports the expression of these cognitions. This discomfort about this entire intellectual assessment enterprise led to a life-long commitment to investigate these issues more fully.

Upon graduation in the mid-1980s, we formed an agency—Multicultural Educational & Psychological Services—whose goals were

1. to provide psychological, educational, psychiatric, and speech for ethnic, linguistic, and other culturally diverse families.
2. to conduct research and provide workshops and consultation services to these families as well as to various agencies, school districts, and organizations throughout the tri-state areas.

Psychometric Assessment

When we first began assessing children at the multicultural agency, we adhered strictly to the standardized procedures as we were initially trained to do. Postassessment interviews of the 650 children assessed between 1986 and 1988, however, revealed that standardized measures of intelligence did not provide a complete understanding of the full range of a child's ability. Although cognitions related to memory, reasoning, and knowledge acquisition and application were present on the IQ tests, they still did not capture the breadth of the children's experiences and the multiple contexts in which these experiences were manifested differently. Anecdotes such as "I know this, but I can't describe it" and "Could I tell you what the word means in a different way" led to a theoretical review of the literature on the receptive and expressive vocabulary of the importance of contextually embedded words (Sattler, 1988; Sternberg, 1985). We also examined the literature on knowledge-acquisition processes from Sternberg's triarchic theory of intelligence and the general literature on the availability and accessibility of cognitive strategies from long-term memory. Furthermore, we became familiar with the works of Keil (1984) and Chi (1978) regarding knowledge and its structure in long-term memory. Hence, the idea of contextualizing vocabulary as a means of assessing a child's cognitive potentials was born.

Furthermore, many children, when faced with the arithmetic subtests that required them to solve problems mentally, claimed that "I can't do this in my head." When given the opportunity to use paper and pencil, upon completion of the testing, they were often correct. We found empirical support for this procedure from the research that examined the use of materials and tools to support mathematical understanding and accuracy (Stigler, 1984; Vygotsky, 1978). Hence, the idea of allowing the use of paper and pencil as a form of potential assessment was developed.

Another clinical observation that was evident during those early years was the fact that many children from culturally diverse backgrounds seemed totally lost when given blocks and puzzles to manipulate. On several occasions, some children asked, "What do I do with this?" even after the standardized explanation was provided by the examiner. When a more direct explanation of the task demands was provided and when the children were allowed to go beyond their ceiling points, significant gains were noted. It became clear that they were learning as they went along and that the task of building blocks and puzzles was novel and unfamiliar to these children. Therefore, the familiarity with blocks that was so endemic to the typical American 5-year-old child was foreign to many of these culturally diverse children. The theoretical insights of Vygotsky (1978) regarding the role of social mediation in ascertaining the zone of proximal development in children whose cognitions are not yet well formed were examined. Also, we examined the results of Feuerstein, Rand, Hoffman, and Miller's (1980) Instrumental Enrichment Program and Lidz's (1987) dynamic assessment strategies. Hence, the development of the test-teach retest assessment measure.

In general, an ongoing debate in intelligence testing is that of speed of mental functioning. Carroll (1993), De Avila (1976), Eysenck (1986, 1988), Horn (1991a), Jensen (1979), and Sternberg (1986) noted that assessing culturally different children via timed tests confuses the measurement of ability with measurement of aspiration because little regard is given to children who are not culturally trained to work under timed conditions. Gopaul-McNicol (1993) found that most Caribbean children have difficulty completing tasks under time pressures because this represents the antithesis of what their culture dictates. On the contrary, slow and careful execution of their work is highly valued so that even if the child is aware that he or she is being timed, he or she may ignore the request by the examiner for a quick response and instead execute the work methodically and cautiously. Several children stated in a jocular manner, "Is this a test? I want to get it right." They were more concerned about accuracy than completing the test in a speedy manner. As such, scores tend to be lower for such students on timed tests, which comprise most of the nonverbal subtests and some of the verbal ones. Although speed may be essential in such situations, most of everyday life's events do not require decision making in a few seconds typically allotted for problem solving on IQ tests. The important issue here should not be one of total time spent but rather time distribution across various kinds of processing and planning events. The practical point to be made from this is that students should not be penalized for not completing a task in the allotted time (speed test). Instead, they should be credited for successful completion of the task regardless of how much time it took (power test). As such, the idea of suspending time as a form of potential assessment was born.

The Later Years

Psychometric Potential Assessment

In 1988, we secured permission from parents to experiment on the various ways of best assessing a child's potential by "stepping away" from standardized procedures as mentioned previously. By 1990, after assessing approximately 625 more children, we felt we had mastered a standard procedure for potential assessment. Between 1990 and 1992, we utilized this standard procedure, which we called psychometric potential assessment; after assessing an additional 600 children, however, we found that many parents were disenchanted with our findings, often claiming that "my child knows more," "my child can do this," and "my child is not mentally retarded or deficient."

Ecological Assessment

Parents invited us to visit their homes and observe the children in their natural settings. A significant change in the development of our assessment procedure resulted after these home and community visits. It was clear to us that these children were by far more skilled in all the areas assessed, but for reasons unknown to us at the time, these children were unable to attain success on the IQ tests whether they were assessed to their potential or whether adherence to standardized testing was done. Children were seen building chairs and tables, fixing bicycles and cars, repairing fans, televisions, and other electrical appliances and yet they could not put blocks and puzzles together. The works of Helms's (1989, 1992) cultural and item equivalence and Sternberg's (1986) *Beyond IQ* were examined in 1992 and 1993 as we assessed approximately 350 more children. This led to the development of the third tier of our assessment system—the Ecological Taxonomy (Ceci, 1990).

Other Intelligences Inventory

Also in 1992 and 1993, we observed that many children who were found to be deficient on psychometric or potential psychometric tests were found to be talented in various athletic and musical arenas. One child who was clearly a Down syndrome boy played the violin and the piano with fluency and poise. One young man was such a genius in basketball that his parents encouraged him to pursue this talent. Today, he is a professional player and attributes his career choice to the support he received from his parents after they read the examiner's report. This observation and finding led to our examination of the literature that deals with content in which cognitions are embedded, including the work of Gardner's (1983) multiple intelligences. Out of this emerged the last tier of our assessment system—the Other Intelligences Inventory.

In 1993 and 1994, we assessed approximately 250 more children utilizing this four-tier assessment model, now coined the Biocultural Assessment System. In addition, assessment measures were developed to assist in this assessment process—the Family Assessment Support Questionnaire, the Stage of Acculturation Measure, and the Teacher Questionnaire. Together, these nonpsychometric measures beautifully complimented the psychometric IQ measure to give a more comprehensive picture of a child's cognitive functioning.

In 1994, we began to train graduate students in school psychology programs, and by 1995 several New York state school districts contracted us to conduct trainings with their professional staff psychologists using this comprehensive assessment system with the following goals:

1. Determine a more accurate profile of a youngster's potential for learning and for intervention
2. Help psychologists to understand that many variables contribute to and explain performance and that psychological assessment is both a formal and an informal process that occurs in several contexts—the school, the home, and the community

Length of Time for Training

From our experiences in the training of this model, we found that it takes a professional person who has been in the field for 2 or more years approximately 2 full days of training. A professional in the field with under 2 years requires approximately 4 days of training.

A student in training would need approximately one semester (two or three 1-hour classes per week) after he or she had been trained to use traditional psychometric IQ standardized tests for at least one semester. This is because to appreciate and value the benefits of this biocultural assessment system, some exposure to traditional measures of assessment may be useful.

Why the Need for Such a Large Sample and for Such a Long Time Period?

Because we were attempting to change the manner in which IQ testing is conducted, we tried to secure ecological validity by building on a large sample size because experts in the assessment of minority children (Cummins, 1991; Hamayan & Damico, 1991; Hilliard, 1996; Samuda, 1975) espouse the notion that a more comprehensive understanding of within-group differences of minority children is needed before intergroup comparisons can be made. These researchers emphasize that intergroup comparisons foster the view that minority children are abnormal, incompetent, and underdeveloped. They recommended that a thoughtful analysis of the role of situational, ecological, cultural, and systemic factors that shape the behavior of minority children need to be understood by studying these children in their own right. Of course, this position weakens the view that a control group of Anglo-American children is needed for adequate interpretation of the research findings of African American or other non-white children. Herein lies the rationale for studying such a large sample of children. The idea was to understand, in this case, a particular group of minority children before conducting a race-comparative study and then attempt to generalize the findings to other non-white children.

It must be emphasized that it was not as if we were unaware of another level of inquiry via traditional scientific methods with random sampling, control groups, and so on. We specifically wanted to look at culturally diverse children in greater detail than is normally done by researchers. We strongly believe it is faulty methodology to use Anglo-American children as the point of reference for all children in the United States.

Another issue was that it was necessary to examine reliability and validity factors not only in "stepping away" from standardized procedures but also in the development of the procedures for potential assessment. On the basis of the information using primarily the Wechsler scales, we have developed a standard procedure for potential assessment on several commonly used standardized IQ tests— the Wechsler scales, Woodcock, the Kaufman, and the Stanford Binet.

Future Research and Practice of the Biocultural Assessment System

Research is still being conducted with Anglo-American children and children residing in countries around the world to see if there is a significant difference in their performance when potential and ecological assessments are conducted. In addition, there is still concern about the item equivalency measure because validating cultural equivalence is extremely difficult. After an abundance of assessments, we conclude that it is not statistically possible to quantify cultural equivalence. Powerful information can be obtained clinically, however. Thus, psychologists who consider themselves clinicians and not psychometricians will still find this measure very beneficial.

Exploration of the other intelligences, in particular the interpersonal and intrapersonal areas, is still needed.

In general researchers should be mindful that when examining intelligent behavior, the task should have at least two attributes— cognition embedded within the items and the content base modality (verbal, spatial, auditory, motor, and kinesthetic) these cognitions are tapping.

Are Psychologists Prepared to Go Beyond the Role of a Psychometrician?

To gain a healthy appreciation for this biocultural assessment system, we often asked our workshop participants and graduate students in training to differentiate between a psychometrician and a psychologist. Generally, the responses reflect a clear understanding that the psychologist is a clinician and a diagnostician, which means that he or she must go beyond IQ tests to assess intelligence, whereas the psychometrician relies purely on standardized tests of intelligence to determine a child's intellectual functioning. Interestingly, despite this awareness, individuals who call themselves psychologists continue to rely solely on IQ tests because "it is a sin to step away from standard procedures." The challenge facing psychologists today is whether they are prepared to expand themselves beyond the IQ guild to embrace a more comprehensive approach to intellectual assessment— an approach that would afford them the opportunity to be more accurate in their assessment, diagnosis, placement, and ultimate treatment of children throughout the system.

According to our four-tier biocultural assessment system, psychometricians perform 25% of the work of psychologists (see Chapter 6). In other words, as far as we are concerned, where a psychometrician's work ends is the beginning point for a psychologist. We believe that those who continue to rely on standardized tests of intelligence to determine intellectual functioning really have a genetic predisposition to intelligence because the basis on which these tests is built is that intelligence is fixed and immutable. It is time for us to come straight out and let the public know where we stand. Are you a psychologist or a psychometrician? If one is a psychometrician, then like Herrnstein and Murray (1994) and Jensen (1979), such an individual believes that IQ is fixed, that it is explained more through its biological genetic structures, and that for the most part it determines success in the real world. If one is a psychologist, then he or she should understand the importance of recognizing the role of experience and context in a child's intellectual development. Such an individual endorses a more environmental, cultural explanation for a child's intelligence and believes that IQ is labile and can change with the appropriate intervention.

A Note to the Users of the Biocultural Assessment System

As you embark on this comprehensive approach to assessing children's intelligence, you will come to gain more confidence in your assessment skills. If you came out of a traditional mode of assessment, as most of us did, initially you may feel awkward adopting this new approach. As you gain more practice, however, you will experience great fulfillment in your ability to assess children more accurately and to avoid misdiagnosis, misinterpretation, and misplacement of children. It is a journey that when taken totally transforms you in such a way that you will never resume assessment in the manner you did previously.

You should be proud of yourself for your willingness to grow and question your previous educational experiences. This indeed requires great courage and much risk. Just when you think you understand it all, you are faced with the challenge of a child who comes from another culture that you may never have come into contact with in the United States. This demands that you grow more. Through that growth, however, you will be rewarded with the joy of knowing that you have a skill that can apply to any child from any part of the world. You will come to know that assessment is not something you do to get a result: it is an action that, in itself, gives you a glimpse of the future of that child and, therefore, fulfills its own purpose at each moment. You have the ability to make a tremendous difference in the life of a child. Remember that one child who is misassessed is one child too many. Therefore, please choose your assessment tools wisely.

6

The Biocultural Assessment System

Preassessment Activities to Conducting the Biocultural Assessment System

Before assessing any child and before administering any battery of tests, a differential diagnosis of other possible causes for the child's problems should be performed (Armour-Thomas & Gopaul-McNicol, 1997a). Only after ruling out the following possible causes of the child's learning or emotional difficulties should a psychometric or nonpsychometric assessment be done:

Health assessment: It is important to review the child's school records to determine that all is well physically. In addition, ask the parent about the child's medical history. This is important to ensure that the child is not suffering from dietary deficiencies or any other ailments that can impede his or her functioning on the testing situation. The health examination must be done by a licensed physician or evidence of such in the form of a health certificate. This is important to rule out basic impediments to learning. This includes sensorium functioning: vision and hearing. Dental check-up should also be done to rule out the possibility of dental pain being a depressing factor. Blood work should be done to ensure the child is not anemic or suffering from dietary deficiencies. The issues of pain and anxiety related to menstruation should be explored. Finally, issues related to enuresis should be examined.

Linguistic assessment: It is necessary to rule out linguistic issues that may be the contributing factor to cognitive delays—that is, does this child speak another language other than English and, therefore, does not fully comprehend what is being said to him or her?

Prior experiences: It is necessary to examine any educational or psychosocial previous experiences, such as the child's learning style, that may inhibit or facilitate the expression of intellectual behavior. Also, it is important to investigate whether the child was formally educated. Many children who come from politically unrested countries may never have been formally educated. As such, they may be educationally deprived even though they may show similar profiles to those of mentally deficient children.

Family issues: It is advised to explore what familial factors, such as a recent divorce, may be affecting the child's performance in the clinical or school setting.

After ruling out any other causes for a child's learning and emotional difficulties, the four-tier biocultural assessment system then follows in the sequence outlined in Table 6.1. Table 6.2 summarizes for the examiner a step by step view of the stages in conducting this comprehensive assessment.

Biocultural Approach to Intellectual Assessment

The biocultural approach to intellectual assessment emphasizes that behavior is "intelligent" to the extent that the nature and quality of experiences to which one is socialized require the exercise of these capacities in a given context. This assessment system comprises three interrelated and dynamic dimensions: (a) a set of biologically pro-

TABLE 6.1   The Biocultural Assessment System

Psychometric Assessment

Psychometric Potential Assessment
This tier consists of the following four components:
Suspending Time
Contextualizing Vocabulary
Paper and Pencil
Test-Teach-Retest

This section reveals the child's potential and estimated intellectual functioning. If the child showed an improvement in his or her performance, the examiner should state so.

Ecological Assessment
This ecological taxonomy of intellectual assessment consists of the following four components:
Family/Community Support Assessment
Observation to determine performance in the school, home, and community
  (item and cultural equivalence)
Stage of Acculturation
Teacher Questionnaire

These components are used to assess the child in the following three settings:
School (classroom, gym, and playground)
Home
Community (church, playground, other recreational sites, or all three)

In this section, a child is observed in his or her ecology—home, community, and school. Therefore, the examiner discusses all tasks that the child was able to perform in these settings but that he or she was unable to do in the IQ testing situation, even under potential IQ assessment.

Other Intelligences
This tier consists of the following four components:
Musical Intelligence
Bodily Kinesthetic Intelligence
Interpersonal Intelligence
Intrapersonal Intelligence

---

grammed cognitive processes or capacities similar to those tapped by traditional standardized tests of intelligence (e.g., capacities for reasoning, auditory processing, and retrieving information from long-term memory); (b) experiences that mediate the use of cognitive processes under consideration. These experiences vary in a number of ways, including organization, form, content, and degree of famil-

TABLE 6.2 Sequence for Administering the Biocultural Assessment System

The Biocultural Assessment must be done in the following order:
1. Do a Differential Diagnosis by first looking at the following:
   Review school and clinic records: Secure the child's medical history.
   Teacher interview: Ask about the child's medical history, linguistic, other intelligences, and teacher questionnaire.
   Parent interview: Interview the parents at school or in the clinic. Ask about the child's medical history, other intelligences, and conduct the family and community support assessment to ascertain linguistic, educational experiences, and family issues.
2. Assess the child's psychometric intelligence in school. You must have two scores: one for the standardized questions and one for the potential questions.
3. Assess the child ecologically by observing the child in the home and community.
4. Conduct a parent interview for further ecological assessment of the child in the home and community.
5. Conduct a teacher interview for further ecological assessment of the child. Observe the child in the classroom and playground.

iarity and complexity; and (c) cultural niches within which these experiences are embedded and that function to enable or constrain the deployment of cognitive processes. Ecological contexts include the home, the community, and various settings within the school (e.g., classroom, playground, and cafeteria). The assumption of the assessment system is that intellectual behavior will vary within and between cultural groups insofar as there are differences in the experiences that different ecological contexts enable or impede the application of biologically constrained cognitive processes. Therefore, the cognitive capacities required for intelligent behavior in one context may or may not be the same as those in another context (Armour-Thomas & Gopaul-McNicol, 1997b; Gopaul-McNicol, 1992a, 1992b; Gordon & Armour-Thomas, 1991; Neisser et al., 1996). Thus, to assess intellectual functioning fully, a comprehensive assessment system is required that appraises how well an individual or group applies different cognitive processes for any given experience across multiple contexts.

We propose a more flexible and ecologically sensitive assessment system that allows for greater heterogeneity in the expression of intelligence. Our four-tier biocultural approach outlined in this book incorporates both quantitative and qualitative information with respect to cognitive functioning through various modes of assessment that include (a) psychometric, (b) psychometric potential, (c) ecological taxonomy, and (d) other intelligences (see Table 6.1).

Biocultural Assessment System

Psychometric Assessment

The important point to remember is that there is no single psychometric measure that taps the three interrelated and dynamic dimensions of intelligence—biological cognitive processes, culturally coded experiences, and cultural contexts. Therefore, any psychometric measure or an amalgamation of tests (interbattery testing, the process approach to assessment, or cross-battery testing) that emphasize a score-oriented approach should be used in conjunction with nonpychometric ecological measures because they help to further gain an understanding of the child's potential intellectual functioning and his or her ability to function in other settings besides the school.

It is critical to emphasize that this assessment system gives pure psychometric assessment (biological explanation) only 25% of the entire weight for determining an individual's intellectual functioning (Figure 6.1). Psychometric potential, ecological assessment, and other intelligences are each weighted 25% as well. Thus, the biocultural assessment system relies more heavily (75%) on one's experiences nested within one's contexts in determining one's intelligence.

Given the breakdown in Figure 6.1, one will expect that only 25% of the diagnostic power comes from standardized tests of intelligence. Chapter 8 demonstrates this via a case study. Prescription and intervention strategies are directly formulated from the information gained through potential and ecological assessment (see Chapter 9 for more detail on diagnostic and prescriptive utility).

Psychometric Potential Assessment

The advantage of assessing a child's potential during the testing process itself is that one is able to witness the improvement in a

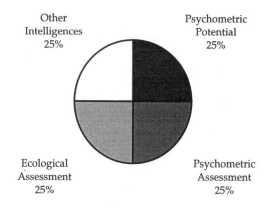

Figure 6.1. Four-Tier Biocultural Assessment System

child's performance immediately as opposed to waiting 3 years to see the gains when nonpotential psychometric assessment is used (Vygotsky, 1978). The psychometric potential assessment procedure consists of five measures that should be used in conjunction with the psychometric measure. They are used to provide supplementary information on cognitive functioning that goes beyond what is provided by the traditional standardized measure of intelligence. A description of each procedure is provided in the following sections.

Suspending Time

The assumption that to be smart is to be quick permeates the entire American society. Thus, many contemporary theorists (Carroll, 1993; Eysenck, 1982; Horn, 1991; Jensen, 1979; Woodcock, 1990) based their theories on individual differences in the speed of information processing and viewed speed as a major correlate of general intelligence. This assumption also underlies the majority of creative tests for gifted children. Several researchers differed with these researchers' positions and argued that there is still much doubt and uncertainty with respect to reaction time and psychometric intelligence (Carlson, 1985; Jones, 1985; Nettelbeck, 1985). Das (1985) noted that many American blacks have surpassed whites in the judicious use of their speed ability, especially in athletics and dancing, but on speeded tests they do not do as well as whites. The explanation must be in their familiarity or lack thereof of certain stimuli. Sternberg (1984) argues that although speed may be critical for some mental operations, "the issue ought not to be speed per se, but rather speed selection: Knowing when to perform at what rate and being able to function rapidly or slowly depending on the tasks or situational demands" (p. 7). Sternberg (1984) also argues that although speed of mental functioning has been associated with intelligence testing, it is well-known that snap judgments are not an important attribute of intelligence. Thurstone (1924) emphasized that a critical factor of intelligence is the ability to substitute rapid impulsive responses for rational, reflective ones. Noble (1969) found that children can be taught to increase their reaction time. Jensen and Whang (1994) agreed with Noble because they found that "the more the retrieval process has become automatic through practice, the faster it occurs" (p. 1). Therefore, the greater the speed, the greater the amount of practice. Baron (1981, 1982) also noted that with respect to problem solving, a reflective cognitive style is generally associated with intelligence. De Avila and Havassy (1974) noted that assessing culturally different children via timed tests confuses the measurement of ability with measurement of aspiration because little regard is given to children who are not culturally trained to work under timed conditions. Gopaul-McNicol (1993) found that most Caribbean children have difficulty completing tasks under time pressures because this represents the antithesis of what their culture dictates. On the contrary, slow and careful execution of their work is highly valued so that even if the child is aware that he or she is being timed, he or she may ignore the request by the examiner for a quick response and will rather execute the work methodically and cautiously. As such, scores tend to be lower for such students on timed tests, which comprise most of the nonverbal subtests. Of course, there are some professions, such as air traffic controller, in which one must consequentially make quick decisions as a part of one's daily life. Although speed may be essential in such situations, most of everyday life's events do not require decision making in a few seconds typically allotted for problem solving on IQ tests. The important issue here should not be one of total time spent but time distribution across various kinds of processing and planning events. The practical point to be made from this is that students should not be penalized for not completing a task in the allotted time.

Instead, they should be credited for successful completion of the task. Again, two scaled scores can be tabulated to compare how they function under timed conditions and how they function when tested to the limits. Thus, this measure involves the suspension of time and the tabulating of two scores—one timed and one in which time is suspended.

Contextualization Versus Decontextualization

Although McGrew (1995) found that vocabulary is only moderately influenced by American culture, Hilliard's (1979) question, "What precisely is meant by vocabulary?" is a valid one which advocates for IQ tests have not yet answered. Words may have different meanings in different cultures. For instance, although the word *tostone* means a quarter or a half dollar to a Chicano, it means a squashed part of a banana that has been fried to a Puerto Rican. Given such a situation, it is recommended that the child be permitted to say the words in a sentence to be sure that the child's understanding of the word meaning is the same as that on the American IQ test. Armour-Thomas and Allen (1993) found that 32 ninth-grade students' vocabulary were elevated when unknown words were presented in a context-embedded situation. These findings were consistent with those of other studies that found individual differences in the acquisition of word meanings in contextually embedded situations (Sternberg, Powell, & Kaye, 1982; Van Daalen-Kapteijns & Elshout-Mohr, 1981). The important issue here is that most of vocabulary is contextually determined—that is, it is learned in everyday contexts rather than through direct instruction. Children accomplish this decontextualization by embedding unknown words in simple contexts (Sattler, 1988; Sternberg, 1985a).

In the authors' private practice, we found that children who did not know the word meanings in isolation were able to figure out the words when placed in a surrounding context. Of course, on traditional IQ tests children are asked word meanings in isolation. Although this may be acceptable for children who have had adequate educational opportunities in adequate social environments, for children who have had little formal schooling, word definition without the surrounding context may lead to invalid findings of their intelligence, in particular knowledge acquisition. Gardner (1983) recommended against using formal instruments administered in a decontextualized setting but instead recommended that assessment should be part of the natural learning environment and should not be set apart from the rest of the classroom activity. With the biocultural assessment system, the examiner can contextualize all words by asking the child to say them in a sentence. For example, the examiner can say to the child, "Please say the word clock in a sentence." Potential credit is given only if the child says it in a sentence (not the examiner).

Paper and Pencil on the Arithmetic Subtests

During the past two decades, researchers have studied problem solving in mathematics from a cognitive information-processing perspective and found that a primary source of difficulty in problem solving lies in students' inability to monitor and regulate the cognitive processes that one engages in during problem solving (Artzt & Armour-Thomas, 1992). On most IQ tests, arithmetic taps skill, memory and attention, and speed. In the standard procedure, it is difficult to tell which is operating. Potential testing allows the examiner to rule out which factor is operating. For potential testing on the arithmetic subtest of the Wechsler scales, the examiner can say to the child who fails, "Please use this paper and pencil and try to solve the problem." This response will fall under a potential score.

Test-Teach-Retest Assessment Measure

Although Esquivel (1985) emphasized that "performance scales of standardized intelligence tests appear to have the greatest predictive validity for Limited English Proficient students, and may provide a more accurate estimate of their actual abilities" (p. 119), the nonverbal subtests, contrary to the claims that have been espoused, are not culture fair and are definitely not culture free. In fact, it is "the information (direct experience) components of these tests that carry their culture bound characteristics" (Cohen, 1969, p. 840). Nonverbal tests rely on one's ability to reason logically. In some respects, they embody more analytic mode of abstraction than the quantitative information components. This is because at times the task requires the individual to extrapolate and relate to relevant parts of the test items. Thus, the manner of cognitive organization is relevant for successful performance on nonverbal tests. The Block Design and Object Assembly subtests are highly influenced by the American culture, and individuals exposed to such items will find the experience less novel and thus their performance will be more automized. Hence, the tests will not be measuring the same skills across cultures and populations. Most children who are from rural areas in Third World countries have had little if any prior exposure to puzzles and blocks. Sternberg (1984) emphasized that "as useful as the tests may be for within group comparisons, between group comparisons may be deceptive and unfair for nonverbal subtests" (p. 10). A fair comparison between groups would require equitable degrees of familiarity or novelty in test items as well as comparable strategies. Sternberg (1984, 1985b, 1986) found that it was the ability to deal with novelty that was critical to measuring subjects' reasoning skills. Gopaul-McNicol (1993) found that in working with Caribbean children, other more complicated activities that also measure nonverbal abstract reasoning and visual integration—as do the Block Design and Object Assembly subtests, respectively—and are more relevant to the children's cultural experiences should be considered. The average child who comes from such countries is very handy and is able to help in constructing buildings, making furniture, creating a steel pan, maneuvering a motor boat, or cutting grass with a cutlass even though he or she has no formal education in these areas. These tasks are as or more complicated than putting blocks or puzzles together. Therefore, it would not be logical to label these children as delayed intellectually when they have honed other more complicated nonverbal skills. Evidently, their American counterparts are not labeled as deficient because they are unable to perform some of the previously mentioned activities that these children can so easily do. These skills, however, are not measured on the typical Anglo intelligence tests. Gardner (1983, 1993) noted that the performance gap between students from Western cultures versus those from non-Western cultures narrowed or even disappeared when familiar materials were used, when revised instructions were given, or when the same cognitive capacities were tapped in a form that made more sense within the non-Western context. Thus, nonverbal tests have not been freed from their culture-bound components. Clearly, the substantive information experiences are still culture bound. When testing the limits of culturally different children on the nonverbal subtests, it is quite common for students to answer the more difficult items correctly after they have passed their ceiling points or after time limits have been expended. It seems as if the children learn as they go along, and that lack of familiarity may have been why they did not do as well on the earlier items. Unfortunately, by the time they understand how to manipulate the blocks and put the puzzles together, it is time to stop those particular subtests because the children have already reached their ceiling point. Of course, in keeping with standardization procedures, one should not receive credit for items passed after the ceiling point has been attained.

Feuerstein (1979, 1980) produced evidence of the plasticity of the human organism that has made cognitive performance modifiable through mediated learning experiences. Through his Learning Potential Assessment Device (LPAD), Feuerstein found that a substantial reservoir of the abilities of Jewish children remained untapped when traditional assessment instruments were utilized to determine the intelligence of these children. This LPAD instrument, as the name implies, involved a radical shift from a static to a dynamic approach in which the test situation was transformed into a learning experience for the child. The focus was on learning rather than on its product and on the qualitative rather than on the quantitative dimensions of the individual's thought (Feuerstein, 1980, 1990). Many researchers (Beker & Feuerstein, 1990; Budoff, 1987a; Feuerstein et al., 1986b; Glutting & McDermott, 1990; Lidz, 1987, 1991; Missiuna & Samuels, 1988; Vygotsky, 1978) suggest that the best way to predict learning efficiency is to assess it in an actual learning and teaching situation. Thus, dynamic assessment links testing and intervention with the goal of enhancing a child's performance through a particular intervention. The objective of this approach is to identify obstacles that may be hindering the expression of a child's intellectual functioning and then to specify the conditions under which the child's intelligence may be enhanced. In summary, the child's modifiability is an important outcome of this dynamic approach to assessment.

Unlike in standardized testing conditions in which the examiner is neutral, the test-teach-retest approach proposed in the biocultural assessment system allows the examiner to be interactive, and his or her interactions are an integral part of the assessment process. The ultimate goal is to link the assessment findings directly to the development of individualized educational intervention programs.

The Test-Teach-Retest Assessment Measure is to be administered only if the examiner realizes that the child was not exposed to these types of items prior to the testing—that is, if the child never played with blocks, puzzles, and so on. Then, the examiner is to teach the child and then retest him or her. For instance, on the Block Design, Picture Arrangement, or Object Assembly subtests of the Wechsler scales, if a child fails the items on both trials, for potential psychometric assessment the examiner can teach and give the test again. Credit is given only under potential if the child gets it correct after the teaching period. The important point to remember is that the exact procedures are followed as in the standardized testing, except time is suspended, teaching is done, and potential scores are given after the child passes the teaching items.

In addition, please try to answer the following questions:

1. How much did the child benefit from the training intervention?
2. How much training is needed to raise the child's performance to a basic minimum level?
3. How well did the child retain the skills learned in the training period?
4. How much more training is needed to ensure that the child retains what he or she learned?
5. How well does the child generalize to other settings (home) what he or she has learned?
6. How easily is the child able to learn other difficult problems different from what he or she learned in training?

Ecological Taxonomy of Intellectual Assessment

Westernized thinking is indeed ethnocentric in its assumptions that Western education nurtures disembedded, context-free thinking. Although this may have been an attractive position years ago, there is now evidence that these cognitive processes are developed by various aspects of one's environmental experiences. Therefore, when a child is asked, "How are an apple and a banana alike" and he or she does not know the response but does know how a mango and a coconut are alike, then the crucial role of context in an individual's perception of the problem is ignored (Lave, Murtaugh, & de la Roche, 1984). Likewise, when an American Indian child has learned to develop speed by games such as a bow and arrow, the fact the he or she does not perform as well on the current speeded IQ tests in no way suggests that this child is limited in speed. Cultural taxonomies are risen out of one's cultural contexts. Therefore, one's cultural experiences and context are integral to the development of one's cognition. Culture dictates the amount of time a child will spend on a particular task. Therefore, the people of some former Soviet countries, Somalia, and Western Africa, who have to barter for food on a daily basis, tend to have a greater conceptual comprehension of volume because an error in bartering for a volume of rice could lead to suffering. Likewise, in many Third World countries, because there are no street signs a strong conceptualization of spatial orientation results. Accordingly, one can infer that the development of a specific set of skills can only occur within a specific cultural context in response to specific knowledge and experience. Thus, the implicit assumption that attributes are constant across place irrespective of the context in which one finds himself or herself is erroneous. The fact that an individual can perform one task very well may have little relevance for performing equally well another task that obviously entails the same cognitive ability albeit in different contextual settings. This is because it requires different types of values of attainment to respond to challenges in different environments. Several researchers (Lave, 1977; Murtaugh, 1985; Rogoff, 1978) found that competency in using arithmetic operations in carrying out everyday duties is not always predictive on standardized arithmetic tests, although they tap the same arithmetic operations. For example, Carraher, Carraher, and Schliemann (1985) found that "street children" in Brazil intuitively developed models of probability to serve as street brokers for lottery tickets. These same children, however, have difficulty applying these models to solve similar types of probability problems in the educational setting.

An examination of the literature on the consistency between IQ scores and real-life attainments calls into question the isomorphism between these two situations. For instance, the types of skills required for success on the Picture Arrangement and Similarities subtests of the Wechsler scales are similar to the deductive reasoning necessary for grocery shopping. Grocery shoppers tend to match prices, comparing how similar or dissimilar items are, as well as plan whether the volume of their purchase can fit in their refrigerator. As such, the goal is to allow for a few days of supply rather than a week. The previous examples confirm that there are many instances in which deficits in cognitive functioning disappear when the problem is couched in familiar terms or using familiar stimuli (Super, 1980). Therefore, cognition is indeed context sensitive and there exist multiple cognitive potentials instead of one cognitive potential or one central processor.

Because we have veered too far in the direction of formal testing, and in the light of these desiderata for new approaches to assessment, several researchers propose a more naturalistic, context-sensitive, and valid ecological mode of assessment (Ceci, 1990; Gardner, 1993; Vygotsky, 1978). This is not merely a call to regress to a subjective form of evaluation. There is no reason to feel less confident about such a thorough approach because reliability can be achieved in these ecological approaches as well. In fact, these nonpsychometric measures that are based on multiple assessment instruments in multiple contexts have more ecological validity than psychometric measures that were based on a child's functioning in a controlled testing situation. Another retort to this alleged objectivity of standardized formal tests is the fact that all tests are skewed toward a certain type of cognitive style. Thus, standardized tests are quite hostile and unfriendly to individuals who do not possess a blend of certain logical and linguistic intelligences and who are uncomfortable in decontextualized settings under impersonal and timed conditions. Correlatively, such tests are biased in favor of individuals who possess these strengths based on their prior cultural experiences.

Therefore, this "assessment view" seeks to connect school activities with after-school activities with emphasis on the individual's strengths (Figure 6.2). In other words, this approach calls for a broader menu of assessment options and an abandonment of the sophomoric mentality that relies on some type of rigid superficial conformity. A broader trained cadre of workers would make greater use of the many subsets of human talents by embracing this assessment approach. The reader should note that the authors are not

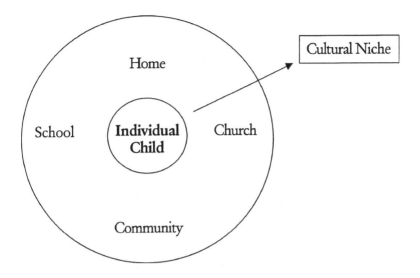

Figure 6.2. Biocultural Assessment System

asserting that psychometric tests are not relevant in the intellectual assessment enterprise. What is being asserted here is that assessment of intellectual functioning should be mindful of the multifaceted influences of culture on behavior.

Ecological Taxonomy of Intellectual Assessment

This ecological measure attempts to measure skills and behaviors that are relevant to the context in which a child lives (real-world types of intelligences, not just academic type of intelligence). Therefore, the child is assessed in several settings—the school, home, and the community. Observing children's interaction with their family and friends in their most natural settings brings to the assessment robust knowledge of the family dynamics and cultural experiences of the child. The examiner should look for

- The way they communicate
- The way they socialize
- The activities they engage in

- The friendships they have
- The roles they play
- The respect or lack thereof they are given by family and friends

In addition, the examiner should assess the child's intelligence by bringing some real-life experiences to the psychometric measure. For instance, if a child is unable to attain success on the mazes, take the child to a real-life maze situation and see if the child can maneuver his or her way out of the maze. Even intelligence experts such as Wechsler (1958) and Binet and Simon (1905) defined intelligence as one's ability to adapt to the real-world environment. Williams (1971) emphasized that the very fact that a child can learn certain familiar relationships in his or her own culture shows that he or she can master similar concepts in the school curriculum, as long as the curriculum is related to his or her background experiences.

Another example is the comprehension subtest; if the child does not know what he or she is supposed to do, then take him or her to a real situation and see if he or she is able to perform the task. For example, take the child to a store and see what he or she will do if he or she finds a wallet that you deliberately placed.

The second component within the ecological taxonomy is the Family/Community Support Assessment. This is a questionnaire designed to determine what support systems the child has at home or in the community, what has been the child's previous educational experiences, what language is spoken at home, and how the family can boost a child's intellectual functioning. Family assessment as part of intellectual assessment brings to the assessment robust knowledge of the family dynamics of the child. Therefore, parenting, child-rearing practices, disciplinary measures, punishments and re-inforcers, the language spoken at home, religious values, the child's relationship to the society at large, as well as society's impact on the child are indeed rich sources of knowledge for school psychologists.

There is an enormous amount of literature that shows the relation-ship between individual differences in intellectual functioning and individual differences in familial support (Nichols, 1981; Zajonc, 1976). The basic proposition is that there is a direct relationship between the intellectual environment of the family and the intellec-tual development of the child being socialized in that environment.

Parenting has been shown to exert a powerful influence on intellectual development, primarily through the inculcation of specific modes of learning strategies and motivational routes that influence problem-solving skills (Vaughn, Block, & Block, 1988). Therefore, child-rearing practices such as encouraging proper study habits are congruent with later intellectual development. There is substantial literature that documents social class differences in parenting that are linked to differences in intellectual functioning. Schaefer (1987) suggested that intellectual competence is mediated by an assortment of parental attitudes and values, such as the worth of schooling, and so on. Schaefer's environmental model posits that human intelligence is not fixed but can be changed by altering parental attitudes and values. Furthermore, various aspects of home environment and parental values are related to IQ and educational attainment (Siegel, 1984). Others have shown that the home environment is a better predictor of educational outcomes than cognitive variables, IQ, and socioeconomic status (SES), even when SES was controlled in a regression analysis. These studies clearly show that aspects of the home, such as its organization, are important independent determinants of intellectual development.

Family assessment has become a point of discussion in the school setting. This is because to really aid in promoting psychological well-being in children, individual assessment will have to be done in conjunction with family assessment, particularly with respect to at-risk families. Thus, the kind of support systems students have at home should be rated and ranked, as is done with other intellectual assessment measures. Thus, a student who is found to be of low average intelligence on an IQ test but has great family support has the potential to be an average to above average student. This is indeed a very critical issue for determining the potential, motivation, and achievement of a student. Likewise, very intelligent students who are not achieving commensurate to their ability may need to be given more familial support. Moreover, the relationship between parents' schooling and the intellectual functioning of their children suggests that public policymakers can exert a positive influence on the intellectual performance of children. By encouraging parents, especially those from culturally different backgrounds, to advance themselves educationally and to become more involved in their children's education an improvement in the intellectual performance of their children can result (Valencia, Henderson, & Rankin, 1981).

Interpersonal competence must also be examined with respect to the child's culture because ethnic groups vary in the value attached to certain kinds of interpersonal skills (Taylor, 1988). Certain behaviors that are reinforced in one group may not be in another. For instance, in the white American culture, children who are assertive are reinforced, whereas among African Americans and immigrant groups such behaviors are considered disrespectful and hence are not reinforced. Likewise, among many culturally different families, parents place different emphasis on independence at an early age. Adolescent autonomy is often not reinforced in such societies. Thus, the evaluator or clinician must be knowledgeable about the ethnic values toward this issue to more accurately determine whether the family respected its own cultural norms with respect to autonomy in children. Likewise, for children who are not assertive or are shy in the classroom, it would be wise to conduct a family assessment to determine if such behaviors are in fact reinforced at home. To encourage a child to completely abandon his or her familial cultural values is ill-advised given the disorientation this can cause to both the child and his or her family. It would be beneficial to assist the family in understanding what cultural adjustments the child is making to adjust to the school or community. This awareness should aid in the family's acceptance of some of the "strange" behaviors evidenced in their children.

Family/Community Support Assessment

Parent's name: _____ Date: _____

Child's name: _____

Regionality: USA—urban/inner city/suburban/rural

If country of origin is not in the USA: _____

Where is the native country? _____

How long is the child in the USA? _____

Are the parents/significant other residing in the USA? _____

Who else resides in the home? _____

What has been your child's previous educational experiences? _____

_____

_____

- ■ Was your child ever retained? _____

- ■ How often per week is your child absent? _____

- ■ What has been your child academic performance in

  Math—poor/fair/good/very good

  Reading—poor/fair/good/very good

- ■ Did your child participate in any supplemental instructional programs? If yes, what programs were they? _____

In the event there is one parent in the home, but there is a significant other residing at home, fill in the other relative instead of mother/father. If there is only one adult in the home, then leave the other parent section questions blank. _____

How many years has the mother been residing in the United States?

_____

How many years has the father been residing in the United States?

_____

What is the mother's place of birth? _____

What is the father's place of birth? _____

_____

Home Linguistic Assessment

1. Does mother speak English? Rank how well.

   Not fluently   Somewhat fluently   Very fluently

2. Does mother speak another language? What language?

   Not fluently   Somewhat fluently   Very fluently

3. Does mother read English? Rank how well.

   Not fluently   Somewhat fluently   Very fluently

4. Does mother read another language? What language?

   Not fluently   Somewhat fluently   Very fluently

5. Does mother write English? Rank how well.

   Not fluently   Somewhat fluently   Very fluently

6. Does mother write another language? What language?

   Not fluently   Somewhat fluently   Very fluently

7. Does father speak English? Rank how well.

   Not fluently   Somewhat fluently   Very fluently

8. Does father speak another language? What language?

   Not fluently   Somewhat fluently   Very fluently

9. Does father read English? Rank how well.

   Not fluently   Somewhat fluently   Very fluently

10. Does father read another language? What language?

    Not fluently   Somewhat fluently   Very fluently

11. Does father write English? Rank how well.

    Not fluently   Somewhat fluently   Very fluently

12. Does father write another language? What language?

    Not fluently   Somewhat fluently   Very fluently

In what language did the mother receive most of her education?

In what language did the father receive most of his education?

_____

What language does your child most often speak to his or her mother?

_____

What language does your child most often speak to his or her father?

_____

What language does your child most often speak to his or her siblings?

_____

What language does your child most often speak to his or her friends?

_____

In what language are radio or television shows most often received at home?

_____

How many hours per week does your child read? _____

In what language does your child most often read? _____

How many hours per week does your child see you reading? _____

In what language does your child most often see you reading? _____

   Linguistic proficiency: _____

   Linguistic dominance: _____

Family Educational Background

13. Mother level of education attained in native country or in the USA

    Did not finish HS   Finish HS   Finish college

14. Father level of education attained in native country or in the USA

    Did not finish HS   Finish HS   Finish college

15. Is anyone at home able to assist this child in his or her homework?

    Never   Sometimes   Always

16. Is the child able to study at home?

    Never   Sometimes   Always

    Why not? _____

17. Is anyone or organization in the community able to assist the child in his or her homework?

    Never   Sometimes   Always

Social/Community

18. Are you involved in any church/community organization?

    Never   Sometimes   Always

19. Is your child involved in any church/community organization?

    Never   Sometimes   Always

20. Are you involved in any interest group or club?

    Never   Sometimes   Always

21. Is your child involved in any interest group or club?

    Never   Sometimes   Always

22. Does your child go to any nonschool events with friends without adult supervision?

    Never   Sometimes   Always

23. Does your child go to any nonschool events with friends with adult supervision?

    Never   Sometimes   Always

24. Is your child involved in any sports in the community?

    Never   Sometimes   Always

25. Is your child involved in any form of employment?

    Never   Sometimes   Always

Examine the circled responses and comment on the level of support based on these answers, the clinical interview, behavioral/cultural observation, etc.

    More "never" responses—low

    More "sometimes" Responses—moderately low/adequate

    More "always" Responses—adequate/moderately high

Furthermore, to help the examiner to conduct the item equivalency assessment, it is necessary to ascertain from the parent or significant other how the child learned the common IQ constructs in his or her culture. Therefore, the following should be stated or asked of the parent:

Please assist me in understanding how your child learns or what type of experiences he or she had in his or her native country or culture by answering the following questions:

How are the constructs listed below taught or nurtured in your culture—that is, what games do children play, what songs do they sing, or what social experiences do they have to help develop these skills?

(These may have to be simplified to fit the parents' educational level)

Verbal abstract reasoning—similarities: How do children learn the differences and similarities in objects or items?

Social awareness—comprehension: How are children taught to be aware of social cultural issues (directly or indirectly)?

Word meaning—vocabulary: How do children learn new words? How is vocabulary developed?

Arithmetic: Check with the parents to find out what level of arithmetic skills the child attained commensurate to his or her age. (The examiner can allow the child to do paper and pencil tasks to assess his or her potential.)

General information: How is general information learned—read papers, teach civics?

Auditory short-term memory—digit span: How is memory developed—songs, rhymes, and history?

Visual discrimination—picture completion: How are children taught to pay attention to detail?

Visual integration—object assembly: How are children taught to build things up—puzzles, etc.?

Nonverbal comprehension/planning—picture arrangement: How are children taught to plan, organize, think sequentially, follow directions, etc.?

Nonverbal abstract reasoning—block design: How are children taught to break something down and build it back up?

Visual short-term memory—coding: How are children taught to memorize things they see in a short time?

Item Equivalencies Assessment Measure

The third component within the ecological taxonomy is the cultural and item equivalence. In some ways, standardized tests of intelligence are consistent with a biocultural approach. They all purport to measure many cognitive abilities indicative of intelligence and that many scholars agree are, in part, biologically determined. Test items do reflect learning experiences that are similar to the learning experiences common in some homes and in some school contexts. The caveat, of course, is that the experiences sampled on the tests are not common across populations. As such, it is indeed inappropriate to suggest that there is a resolution with respect to interracial or cultural equivalence on intelligence tests, and it is equally misleading to conclude that one is brighter by virtue of his or her score on these IQ tests. Therefore, existing tests should incorporate multiple methods that examine both biological and ecological factors.

Cummins (1984) points out that when referring to concept formation, evaluators must keep in mind that it is difficult for examinees to know similarities or differences in objects if they have had little or no experiences with the objects themselves. An alternative would be to determine if these children can perform comparable skills typical of their native lands and describe in a more qualitative type of manner their strengths and weaknesses with respect to the skills they can perform in their native countries, showing the similarities between these skills and those found on the traditional-type tests. For instance, Question 4 on the Similarities subtest of the Wechsler Intelligence Scale for Children—III reads, "In what way are a piano and a guitar alike?" Many children from Third World countries may not have ever seen or heard a piano. Perhaps the cuatro, another string instrument, could be substituted. The same solution may be applied to Question 6—"In what way are an apple and a banana alike?" Apples are not grown in tropical climates. Perhaps mango could be substituted. The important thing here is that the child knows the concept of fruits of different kinds. This idea of matching items to a child's culture has been emphasized by Sternberg (1986) and Helms's (1992) cultural equivalence perspective.

Many test developers have attempted to reduce or ignore cultural influences on cognitive ability tests by constructing "culture fair tests." McGrew (1994) spoke of the comprehensive nature of the Woodcock newly revised test of cognitive ability. These tests, however, are simply attempts to control the influence of different cultures instead of measuring them (Helms, 1992). Even the black IQ test that was developed by Williams (1975) was biased in favor of a specific social class and regional group rather than blacks as a cultural group. The insistence that white American culture is superior and universal and should be adopted by every racial group results in the devaluation of the unique and special cultural values of different groups. Few investigators have studied what blacks and other minorities have contributed to this society apart from being used as points of comparisons on IQ scores. Lonner (1981) discussed the following four types of equivalence:

1. Functional equivalence: the extent to which the test scores mean the same thing among different cultural groups and measure psychological characteristics that occur equally frequently within these groups

2. Conceptual equivalence: whether groups are equally familiar or unfamiliar with the content of the test items and therefore attribute the same meaning to them

3. Linguistic equivalence: whether the test developer has equalized the language used in the test so that it signifies the same thing to different cultural groups

4. Psychometric equivalence: the extent to which tests tap the same things at similar levels across different cultural groups

Butcher (1982) listed potential nonequivalent sources in cross-cultural research and emphasized that failure to consider these issues can result in committing the cultural equivalence fallacy. Helms (1992) pointed out the culture bias with respect to psychometric equivalence. Helms (1989) defined Eurocentrism as "a perceptual set in which European and/or European American values, customs, traditions and characteristics are used as exclusive standards against which people and events in the world are evaluated and perceived" (p. 643). Thus, permeating every question of these IQ tests is whether the answers are right or wrong, with the correctness being determined by the normative white response. Thus, the more intelligent individual is the one who can apply Eurocentric rules most effectively and expediently. Therefore, those who see alternative answers because they do not have access to the Eurocentric worldview are penalized and are deemed less intelligent. Matthews (1989) reported the incident when two white prelaw students convinced the Law School Admissions Services that a Law School Admissions Test question had two correct answers. Although these two men were socialized in a white culture, they saw an alternative and more creative response than did the test's constructors. Another example could be found in Gopaul-McNicol (1993). The author noted that many "lesser developed" cultures value functional responses rather than taxonomic responses because it is in keeping with the normal everyday life for many groups. Therefore, when a child gives a one-point response to "How are a car and a boat alike?" by saying that "you drive them," it is in keeping with the functional use of these items rather than the taxonomic response of them being vehicles or means of transportation. As Piaget (1952) pointed out, however, the taxonomic responses are considered more abstract and therefore show a more advanced form of cognitive ability.

Until test developers investigate the item equivalence on these tests, the lack of cultural equivalence on the IQ tests cannot be ruled out as an explanation for the between-group racial difference of IQ scores. Until test developers assess whether black or African culturally laden cognitive strategies turn out to be more effective strategies for equal or better outcomes for predicting performance, it should not be assumed that blacks are less intelligent. A recommendation would be to allow expert representatives of various ethnic, cultural, gender, linguistic, and social class groups to assist in the construction of the test items. The caveat, of course, is whether these consultants have the ability to step away from the Eurocentricism so endemic in their professional environment. Please note that we are not asserting that psychometric tests are not relevant in the intellectual assessment enterprise. What is being asserted here is that other cultural groups centered cognitive abilities require test developers to integrate ecological contextual factors into their thinking process. In other words, these other group information processing strategies might be some sort of implicit unmeasured aspect of ability tests in addition to their predictive criteria. In many cultures throughout the

world, teachers and parents do not always reward the obvious answer but rather reward the more creative, expansive responses. Thus,
when an individual who is socialized to develop and nurture innovative, expansive, interactive, and spontaneous thinking is placed in
a testing situation, it is difficult for him or her to reconcile the
contrasting Eurocentric world perspectives that underlie test construction. In many British colonized societies, for instance, a student's achievement is not assessed by multiple-choice exam questions but by the ability to respond to essays, resulting in a more
creative, integrative learning and response style. For these students,
multiple choice is viewed as simplistic and not a mature way of
assessing one's comprehensive knowledge (Gopaul-McNicol, 1993).
Students who have to adjust to a more detailed way of studying to
respond to the right and wrong multiple-choice format usually find
this frustrating.

In general, different responses are elicited on the IQ tests depending on the environment in which the child was reared and depending
on the culturally loaded biased items. An example of a biased item
is from the comprehension subtests of the WISC-III: "What is the
thing to do if a boy/girl much smaller than yourself starts to fight
with you?" In discussing this question, Helms (1992) stated that
researchers (Gordon & Rudert, 1979) contend that black children are
taught that the appropriate response is to "hit him/her back." After
testing black children, we often try to ascertain their cultural experiences by interviewing their parents. In response to why their child
may have responded in an "aggressive manner" to that question on
the comprehension subtest, black parents often say, "My child cannot
come home and tell me a white kid beat him or her up." It seems that
when the black child in the testing situation hears "boy/girl," the
child thinks white boy or white girl, so they know they are expected
to defend themselves as they are taught by their families. It is not so
unusual for black parents to teach their children to self-defend given
the racism in this society. The fact that the question recognizes the
need to say "boy" if it is a male child being tested as opposed to "girl"
if it is a female child being assessed tells us that the response would
have been different had the examiner asked a girl what she is supposed to do if a boy hits her. Mothers often tell their daughters to

never allow a boy or man to strike them. Thus, a girl would have probably given a more aggressive response if the question states that it is a boy doing the hitting as opposed to a girl. It is expected that black children's responses might be different if they think that it is a black instead of a white child doing the hitting. This item equivalency assessment measure attempts to equate a child's cultural experience in every item of every IQ test by matching the questions on the IQ test to the child's culture. As such, the child's broad-base information repertoire is recognized. A caveat is that it is not statistically possible to quantify cultural equivalence. Powerful information can be obtained clinically, however. Thus, psychologists who consider themselves more than just a psychometrician will still find this measure very helpful because they can clinically create a cluster of items that form the construct of intelligence for a particular cultural group. This cultural equivalence approach certainly also falls under the rubric of potential assessment.

Item Equivalencies Assessment Measure

Because the Wechsler scales are the most widely used of all intelligence tests, a cursory review of the Wechsler items will be examined to demonstrate the ecological nonpsychometric measures.

If the examinee did not obtain full score points on any subtest, the item equivalency measure should be administered.

Creating a cluster of items that form the construct of intelligence that are equivalent items for the culturally or linguistically different child is one way of tapping a child's intellectual potential. Tabulating two scores—one following standardization procedures and one measuring the child's potential —should result in a more accurate assessment of the child's intelligence.

Nonverbal equivalencies: The parent interview should assist you in matching the child's cultural experiences to the test constructs. Thus, assess if the child has the concept and how it is manifested in his or her culture.

In addition to suspending time for all the timed subtests, the following items can be matched to the child's culture.

Tests Administered	Subtest	Item Equivalency
WISC-III	Gen inf.	Match to culture
Verbal subtests	Similarities	Match to culture
	Vocabulary	Match to culture or contextualize all or both
	Arithmetic	Match to culture (paper and pencil)
	Comprehension	Match to culture; place the question in different context
Nonverbal subtests	Block Design	Match to culture or test or teach; retest or see what other skills measure this concept
	Object Assembly	Match to culture; what skills measure this or teach
	Picture Completion	Match to culture; what skills measure this; if the child points, score as correct; you are not assessing vocabulary
	Picture Arrangement	Match to culture; what skills measure this or teach
	Coding	Match to culture; what skills measure this (e.g., memory and card game); people have different symbols systems in their culture

Review each item of each of the verbal subtests and match them to the child's culture. For example, on the Wechsler verbal subtests:

General Information

Question 9: "What are the four seasons of the year?" A child who recently arrived from a tropical climate, where there are only two seasons—rain and sun—may be at a disadvantage. If the child knows the two seasons in his or her native country but is unfamiliar with the four seasons in the United States, two general information subtest scores should be tabulated: one following standardization procedure and one showing the child's potential.

Similarities Subtest

Cummins (1984) points out that when referring to concept formation evaluators must keep in mind that it is difficult for examinees to know similarities or differences in objects if they have had little or no experiences with the objects themselves.

Question 4: "In what way are a piano and a guitar alike?" Many children from Third World countries may not have ever seen or heard a piano. Perhaps the cuatro, another string instrument, could be substituted.

Question 6: "In what way are an apple and a banana alike?" Apples are not grown in tropical climates. Perhaps mango could be substituted. The important thing here is that the child knows the concept of fruits of different kinds.

Question 9: "In what way are a telephone and a radio alike?" Children who are not exposed to telephones may never have thought about this, and in many Third World countries, only the affluent have telephones. Therefore, some children may not have conceptualized in an abstract sense a telephone as it relates to a radio.

Comprehension Subtest

Question 8: "What is the thing to do when a boy or a girl much smaller than yourself starts to fight with you?" Most children from different cultures may answer tell his or her mother or tell the teacher. From a ecological standpoint, this is quite expected and acceptable. This response, however, results in only one point. For such children to get two points it may be necessary to ask, "Would you fight?" Usually, the child will say, "No, it is not good to fight." The important thing to keep in mind is that in such cultures not fighting and telling an adult are the most important things taught to children. In this culture, a child is not necessarily expected to tell an adult.

Question 13: "Why is it good to hold elections by secret ballot?" Children originally from nondemocratic societies, such as Haiti, Cuba, and so on, may have difficulty with this question because the idea of a secret ballot is foreign to them. The very concept is difficult for such children to understand because in their societies voting is not a private matter and in some cases there is no such thing as an election.

Question 15: "In what ways are paperback books better than hardcover books?" In some cultures, such as the United Kingdom and the English Caribbean, the term softcover rather than paperback is used, so it is best to use an equivalent term with such children.

Change the contexts of the question. For example, for Question 4, "What are you supposed to do if you find one's wallet or purse in a store?" the examiner can change the context—for example, change "in a store" to "in a police station" or "in the classroom."

It is important to remember that this subtest is not attempting to assess what a child would do but rather what he or she is expected to do in a social situation. In other words, in what contexts would the child choose to do what he or she knows he or she is supposed to do.

Digit Span

Examine how else auditory short-term memory is assessed in the child's culture (parent interview). In addition, remember people have different symbol systems in their culture. Therefore, using the more familiar letters than numbers may facilitate recall.

Two additional questionnaires make up the fourth component of the ecological taxonomy. These two questionnaires were designed to further assist the examiner in understanding the child. The stage of acculturation of a child provides information about the child's emotional functioning that may be impeding intellectual functioning and classroom or home adjustment. The teacher questionnaire allows us to view the child through the eyes of the teacher and gives us important information about the child's abilities and overall functioning in the classroom. All this information is critical in grasping the total picture of the child vis-à-vis his or her entire community.

Stage of Acculturation

Assess what cultural adjustment difficulties the individual may be experiencing. This is done because in working with children, in particular culturally different children, to some extent most people undergo some change (minimal as it may be) at unpredictable periods of time:

1. Physical changes: The individual must cope with living in a new place in which pollution and other environmental hazards can be a new experience.

2. Cultural changes: Linguistic and social institutions are different and thus the individual has to adjust to these differences. The individual has to function within new social networks both within his or her own group and outside his or her group.

3. Psychological changes: The individual may experience an alteration in his or her mental status due to culture shock as he or she adapts to the new milieu. This is a period of psychological transition from back-home values to host-home values. Individuals begin to understand the host culture and feel more in touch with themselves.

4. Acculturated: The individual has adjusted to the new culture but values his or her cultural morays as well. Thus, he or she is bicultural.

Teacher Questionnaire

- What has been the child's previous educational experiences?
- Was the child ever retained?
- How often per week is the child absent?
- What has been the child's academic performance in
    Math: poor/fair/good/very good
    Reading: poor/fair/good/very good
- Did the child participate in any supplemental instructional programs? If yes, what programs were they?
- What is the child's motivational or attention levels in class?
- How persistent is this child?
- How does the child relate to his or her peers?
- How does the child behave in class? In other words, is the child reflective or impulsive?
- Is the child responsible? How so?
- Is the child disciplined? How so?
- Does the child prefer to study alone or in a group?
- Does the child prefer dim or bright lights?

Also ask the music/dance/sports/drama teacher the questions from the Other Intelligences questionnaire.

Other Intelligences Inventory

The Other Intelligences Inventory is the fourth tier of the bicultural assessment system. This tier supports Gardner's (1983, 1993) position that most children can excel in one or more intelligences.

Gardner's theories of seven multiple intelligences shares the view that the human mind is a computational device that has separate and qualitatively different analytic ways of processing various kinds of information. He provides evidence for what he terms "factors of mind." He maintains that there are many types of intelligences rather than one, as IQ tests claim. He takes the position that all children can excel in one or more intelligences. Gardner regards his theory as an egalitarian theory, and what is most important to him is not whether one child outperforms another on some skills but that all children's skills are identified. Therefore, one child may have a propensity for interpersonal skills, whereas another may have a propensity for numerical reasoning. These propensities are not borne because a parent exposed their child to situations and activities involving these intelligences but rather because children have "jagged cognitive profiles," somewhat akin to the learning disabled child who does well in one area and poorly in another. Of all the theoretical positions, Gardner's is the one most outside the family of traditional intelligence researchers. He developed his thinking partly because he objected to what he viewed as the domination of thinking about intelligence by a few theorists. Many have criticized Gardner's thinking, claiming that he does not examine the possibility that various cognitive abilities exist within each type of intelligence. His theory has been criticized by psychologists on the basis that it cannot be subjected to adequate testing. In certain educational quarters, however, massive gains in children's motivational level and sense of self have been used to validate Gardner's theory.

James Comer, a professor at Yale University and the director of the leading school reform program in the country, the School Development Program, proposes a theory of development that includes multiple pathways (Haynes, 1995). Although Comer did not address IQ as a construct, Comer suggests that the effects of schooling are very significant and the environment is primarily responsible for successful development along six developmental pathways: physical, moral, linguistic, social and emotional, psychological, and cognitive and academic. Comer also emphasized that there is a physiological component by way of energy and drive that influences one's development along each pathway. Comer was most emphatic in stating that supportive environments, in which adults manifest much caring and nurturing, are most influential in children reaching their potential.

The Other Intelligences Inventory (Gopaul-McNicol & Armour-Thomas, 1997b) attempts to capture four of Gardner's intelligences. Therefore, asking the child, the parents, and the teacher questions to ascertain the child's musical intelligence, bodily kinesthetic intelligence, and inter- and intrapersonal intelligence—areas that are not represented on any of the commonly used standardized IQ tests (see Chapter 8)—is critical in understanding the breadth and depth of a child's comprehensive intellectual abilities.

Interviewing several different persons (child, teacher, and parent) is necessary to add reliability to the child's description of his or her other intelligences.

Other Intelligences Inventory

Does your child have a strength in any nonacademic type area? _____

_____

How do you define this as a strength? Give examples of such.

_____

_____

_____

Musical Intelligence

Interview With the Child

Do you (make music) play a musical instrument? Yes/No

If yes, what instrument? _____

How long have you been playing this instrument _____

Do you sing? Yes/No

If yes, what kinds of songs? _____

How long have you been singing? _____

What level of proficiency have you attained?

Beginner   Intermediate   Advanced

Please check off if you can do the following:

Listen to a piece of music then create a song

Could I obtain a copy of your certificate/diploma/teacher feedback in music/singing?

Do you have samples/audiotapes of musical/singing performances? Y/N

Do you have samples/audiotapes of compositions? Y/N

Do you have samples of written/performed/composed songs? Y/N

Do you have lyrics of raps, songs, or rhymes that you wrote? Y/N

Did you compile discographies? Y/N

Interview With the Parent and Music Teacher

Does your child (make music) play a musical instrument? Yes/No

If yes, what instrument? _____

How long has your child been playing this instrument? _____

Does your child sing? Yes/No

If yes, what kinds of songs? _____

How long has your child been singing? _____

What level of proficiency has your child attained?

Beginner   Intermediate   Advanced

Could you furnish me with a copy of your child/your student certificate/diploma/teacher feedback in music? _____

Do you have samples/audiotapes of musical performances of your child? Y/N

Do you have samples/audiotapes of compositions of your child? Y/N

Do you have samples of written/performed/composed songs of your child? Y/N

Do you have lyrics of raps, songs, or rhymes that your child wrote? Y/N

Did you compile discographies of your child? Y/N

Bodily Kinesthetic Intelligence

Interview With the Child

Do you play any sports? Yes/No

If yes, what sport(s)? _____

How long have you been playing this game? _____

What level of proficiency have you attained? _____

     Beginner   Intermediate   Advanced

Do you dance/act/paint/draw? Yes/No

If yes, what type of dance? _____

How long have you been dancing/acting/painting/drawing? _____

What level of proficiency have you attained?

     Beginner   Intermediate   Advanced

Could I obtain a copy of your certificate/diploma/teacher feedback
in sports/dance/drama? _____

Do you have videotapes of projects/demonstrations? Y/N

Do you have samples of projects actually made? Y/N

Do you have photos of hands-on projects? Y/N

Interview With the Parent and Sports/Dance/Drama/Art Teacher

Does your child play any sports? Yes/No

If yes, what sport(s)? _____

How long has your child been playing this sport? _____

What level of proficiency has your child attained?

     Beginner   Intermediate   Advanced

Does your child dance/act/paint/draw? Yes/No

If yes, what type of dance? _____

How long has your child been dancing/acting/painting/drawing?

What level of proficiency has your child attained?

    Beginner   Intermediate   Advanced

Could you furnish me with a copy of your child/your student certificate/diploma/teacher feedback in sports/dance/drama/art?

Do you have videotapes of projects/demonstrations of your child? Y/N

Do you have samples of projects actually made by your child? Y/N

Do you have photos of hands-on projects of your child? Y/N

Personal Intelligences

Intrapersonal

A self-concept scale should assist in assessing self-esteem (intrapersonal) issues. In addition, ask the following:

- Do you have self-assessment activities/checklist?
- What outside hobbies or activities are you involved?
- What are your strengths and weaknesses?

Break down into intellectual, social, and affective.

Interpersonal

Social skills scales such as the Social Skills Rating Scale should assist in assessing interpersonal intelligence. In addition, examine the following:

- Peer group reports
- Videos, photos, or write-ups of cooperative learning projects
- Certificates or other documentation of community service projects
- Written teacher reports
- Written parent reports

Break down further into intellectual, social, and affective.

Furthermore, the following questions can be asked:

Child Interview

Are you involved in any church/community organization?

Never   Sometimes   Always

Are you involved in any interest group or club?

Never   Sometimes   Always

Do you go to any nonschool events with friends without adult supervision?

Never   Sometimes   Always

Do you go to any nonschool events with friends with adult supervision?

Never   Sometimes   Always

Are you involved in any form of employment?

Never   Sometimes   Always

Do you accompany your parent or any relatives to the store or any agency and serve as a translator for him or her?

Never   Sometimes   Always

Are you responsible for caring or for supervising your younger siblings while your parents/relatives are not at home?

Never   Sometimes   Always

Could you cook/iron/go grocery shopping? Please circle the ones you do well.

Please list any other domestic/community chores for which you are responsible.

Parental Interview

Is your child involved in any church/community organization?

Never   Sometimes   Always

Is your child involved in any interest group or club?

Never   Sometimes   Always

Does your child go to any nonschool events with friends without adult supervision?

Never   Sometimes   Always

Does your child go to any nonschool events with friends with adult supervision?

Never   Sometimes   Always

Is your child involved in any form of employment?

Never   Sometimes   Always

Does your child accompany you or any relatives to the store or any agency and serve as a translator for you?

Never   Sometimes   Always

Is your child responsible for caring or for supervising his/her younger siblings while you are not at home?

Never   Sometimes   Always

Could your child cook/iron/go grocery shopping? Please circle the ones your child does well.

Please list any other domestic/community chores for which your child is responsible.

Implications for Psychologists

Routinely, school psychologists make diagnostic decisions without considering the possible effects of culture as mediating and intervening variables. In other words, intelligence is a multifaceted set of abilities that can be enhanced depending on the social and cultural contexts in which it has been nurtured, crystallized, and ultimately assessed. Therefore, there is a need to expand the notions of intelligence that have been developed within the psychometric and information-processing traditions. It is amazing that we live in a society so advanced in technology, but we use numbers and scores as primary bases for triage. The fact is that even among a group of children who are otherwise similar, there can be important ecological variations that contribute to their ecological development. This does not mean that information-processing theories and psychometric measures are not relevant in the field of intelligence. These theories, however, need to be expanded to include a more cultural and anthropological approach. The important point to note is that IQ is quite a labile concept and is quite responsive to a shift in context. Thus, contextual influences on more complex-type tasks inevitably cast doubt on current conceptualization of intelligence. It is wise to consider the research of others outside of the psychological IQ guild, such as anthropologists and sociologists, who bring the richness of the contextual influences into the testing situation.

The American Psychological Association (1993) has offered culturally relevant suggestions for practice for providers who work with culturally diverse families. The suggestions therein should be strongly considered. School psychologists should also familiarize themselves with the psychometric and nonpsychometric measures assessment tools that address the multifaceted nature of intelligence. The biocultural model of assessment is recommended as a comprehensive assessment system for the understanding of a qualitative, quantitative, cognitive, social, emotional, cultural, and behavioral comprehensive assessment. Although the recommended methods of administering and scoring these traditional tests may seem quite unconventional and not in keeping with standardization procedures, they are a guide for psychologists in tapping the potential of culturally different children. Reporting two IQ scores—one following standard procedures and one taking into consideration issues raised in potential assessment—may be the best way to understand these children's strengths and weaknesses. If school psychologists intend to serve children well, they should give greater attention to qualitative rather than quantitative reports that highlight all a child's past and present cultural experiences.

In summary, this "assessment view" seeks to connect school activities with after-school activities, with emphasis on the individual's strengths. In other words, this approach calls for a broader menu of assessment options and an abandonment of the sophomoric mentality that relies on some type of rigid superficial conformity. A broader trained cadre of workers would make greater use of the many subsets of human talents by embracing this assessment approach. The question that one should always keep in mind is whether the tasks on the decontextualized intelligence tests bear any resemblance to the values held by the surrounding community. Many traditional test developers still define intelligence as a unitary attribute with a cognitive overtone situated only in the individual's head. More contemporary researchers recognize that intelligence is really a flexible, mobile, culturally dependent construct. Testing in most North American contexts, however, is formalized and examines only the individual, not the individual vis-à-vis his or her community. These tests require people to examine decontextualized tasks rather than examining how people function when they can draw on their experiences and knowledge as they typically have to do in the real world. The extensive attention given to the cognitive information-processing components in testing situations is based on an assumption that the same processes are required to function in real-life contextual situations. Knowing about abstract analogies, or word meanings in isolation, does not mean that one's human intellectual performance is adequately represented. The ideal contemporary approach is one in which standardized tests are only one component of a broad-based intellectual evaluation and in which interviews with parents and observation of children in their natural setting—community, home, school, and so on—is equally valued.

All the information presented in this chapter should be incorporated in the report in a qualitative and descriptive manner (see Chapter 8 for a sample biocultural report). Table 6.3 provides a cursory view of the various biocultural measures that should be given to all involved in the assessment of a child.

TABLE 6.3   Checklist of Tests to Be Given to the Child, Parent, and Teacher

---

Child
  Child consent form
  Medical examination (observation of the child's school records—nutritional and
    physical)
  A psychometric measure or cross-battery testing
  Nonpsychometric measures
    Item Equivalency Assessment Measure
    Other Intelligences Assessment
    Test-Teach-Retest Assessment Measure
    Ecological Taxonomy of Intellectual Assessment
    Stage of Acculturation

Parent
  Parent consent form
  Family/Community Support Assessment of linguistic proficiency, dominance,
    and fluency
  Medical examination (ask the parent for the child's nutritional and physical status)
  Other Intelligences Assessment
  Some questions to help assess the item equivalencies (see Family/Community
    Support Assessment)

Teacher and school
  Medical examination (ask the school to observe the child's medical records)
  Teacher questionnaire
  Other Intelligences Assessment

7

A Critical Review of Standardized Tests and Approaches of Intelligence Using the Biocultural Assessment System

In 1987, a nationwide survey of school psychologists was conducted by Obringer (1988) in which respondents were asked to rank in order of their usage the following instruments: the Wechsler scales, the Kaufman Assessment Battery for Children (K-ABC), and the old and new Stanford-Binets. The results were as follows: The Wechsler earned a mean rank of 2.69, K-ABC of 2.55, followed by the old Stanford-Binet of 1.98 and the new Stanford-Binet Fourth Edition of 1.26. To date, no series of intelligence tests has yet to equal the success both in practice and in research of the Wechsler scales. Despite the volumes of criticisms, the Wechsler scales continue to "enjoy unprecedented popularity and have a rich clinical and research tradition" (Kamphaus, 1993, p. 125). As such, this test will be used as the main point of reference for teaching potential assessment. In Chapter 2, we gave an overview of the conceptions of human intelligence and a cursory glance at the history of intelligence tests. A more extensive and detailed representation of the history of IQ testing can be found in French and Hale (1990) and Sattler (1988).

This chapter contains a brief description of the major scales of intelligence, their assumptions about what constitute intelligent behavior, and their limitations. An exploration of how to use the bicultural model with two of the four commonly used IQ tests will be presented in this chapter as well.

In 1905, when Binet and Simon developed the Binet-Simon Scale it became known as the first practical intelligence test (Sattler, 1988) that initially served to diagnose levels of mental retardation and was considered the prototype of subsequent measures for assessing mental ability. The age scale format was revised in 1908 and 1911, and in 1916 it was renamed by Terman, a professor at Stanford University, the Stanford-Binet. This version was revised in 1937, 1960, 1972, and 1986, when it first became a point-scale format—the Stanford-Binet Intelligence Scale: Fourth Edition (Thorndike, Hagen, & Sattler, 1986).

The development of the Wechsler scales began in 1939 when David Wechsler, a clinical psychologist at Bellevue Hospital, introduced the Wechsler-Bellevue Intelligence Scale Form I, which was the forerunner to the Wechsler Intelligence Scale for Children (WISC) (1949) and its revision—The Wechsler Intelligence Scale for Children-Revised (1974). The most daring changes of the WISC were made in the 1991 Wechsler Intelligence Scale for Children-III (WISC-III) (Kamphaus, 1992). The Wechsler scales and its derivatives—the Wechsler Primary Preschool Scale of Intelligence-Revised and the Wechsler Adult Intelligence Scale-Revised continue to enjoy much popularity and are still the most widely used tests of intelligence possibly because of their ease in administration and scoring (Detterman, 1985). Opinions on the Wechsler scales range from glowing reports to outright condemnation (Witt & Gresham, 1985).

The K-ABC (Kaufman & Kaufman, 1983) has become quite popular within the past 10 years both in the school and in clinical settings.

TABLE 7.1   Assumptions Made in IQ Tests

			Test		
Assumption	Wechsler	Stanford	WJTCA-R	K-ABC	Biocultural
Speed is critical	X	X	X	X	✓
Linguistic equivalence	X	X	X	✓	✓
Do problems mentally	X	X	X	X	✓
Conceptual equivalence	X	X	X	✓	✓
Nonverbal culture fair	X	X	X	X	✓
Functional equivalence	X	X	X	X	✓
Psychometric equivalence	X	X	X	X	✓
No other intelligences are needed	X	X	X	X	✓
Do not need practical or tacit knowledge	X	X	X	X	✓
IQ is fixed	X	X	X	X	✓

X, This assumption is made by this test, thus limiting the accurate assessment of the child's intelligence.
✓, This assumption is not made by this test or model.

What has made the K-ABC most appealing is its attempt to enhance fair assessment of minorities, limited English-proficient children, individuals with speech and language difficulties, bilingual children, and youngsters with learning disabilities. A strength of the K-ABC is the fact that there are "teaching items" to ensure that children understand the demands of the tasks. Although we view the K-ABC as a promising innovative test with good technical quality, like its predecessors there are still limitations with respect to its assumptions (Table 7.1).

The Woodcock-Johnson Tests of Cognitive Ability-Revised (WJTCA-R) (1989) was first introduced in 1977 as the Woodcock-Johnson Tests of Cognitive Ability—a combined psychoeducational battery. Its revised form has been touted by its followers (McGrew, 1994) as the "first intelligence battery to incorporate a number of innovations in intelligence testing" (p. xiv). As such, the limitations of this intelligence test will be presented along with a demonstration of how to conduct potential assessment vis-à-vis the biocultural model. Of course, the main problem with the WJTCA-R is that it is organized around the Gf-Gc (general/fluid-general/crystallized) theory, a theory whose comprehensive empirical-based research emphasizes that the nature of intelligence is inferred by observable differences in intellectual functioning as measured by standardized tests of intelligence. Many experts in the IQ testing industry (Ceci, 1990; Gordon, 1988; Hilliard, 1996; Sternberg, 1986) have repeatedly echoed Anastasi's (1988) position that there is "no culture fair test" and that the heavy reliance on standardized assessment measures to determine intelligence runs counter to the guidelines recommended by many experts for nondiscriminatory assessment for culturally, ethnically, and linguistically diverse students.

In general, all the IQ tests make many assumptions about intelligence that have served as the major criticisms of standardized tests of intelligence. These assumptions will be discussed in the next section.

Assumptions and Criticisms of Intelligence Tests

Table 7.1 lists several assumptions that most IQ tests make about the intelligence of human beings throughout the world. An examination of these assumptions would shed some light on the limitations and criticisms of IQ tests as a whole. All these assumptions are discussed in Chapter 6, in which the biocultural model was presented.

The first and most obvious assumption is that speed of mental functioning is a critical component of intelligence. Hence the interjection of speeded items on most IQ tests.

A second assumption is that vocabulary is only moderately influenced by culture, resulting in the insertion of vocabulary words in a decontextualized manner on many commonly used IQ tests despite the fact that most vocabulary is contextually determined and some words have different meanings in a different context (linguistic equivalence) (Hilliard, 1979).

The third assumption is that children who cannot perform mathematical computations mentally are less skilled in math and less intelligent than their counterparts who are able to do so. This has led to the inclusion of mental computations without the aid of paper and pencil in many IQ tests. Such tests do not distinguish between whether the child has the skill, whether anxiety is impeding the child's functioning, or whether the child is unable to work in a speedy manner because many of these arithmetic tests are also timed.

The fourth assumption that characterizes most IQ tests is that all children enter the assessment process with the same level of novelty or experience irrespective of their cultural backgrounds (conceptual equivalence). Thus, most IQ tests fail to recognize that some children were never exposed to some items even though they may have been exposed to the concept itself in a different form. As such, with the exception of the K-ABC that allows for teaching to ensure understanding of the tasks, most IQ tests do not accommodate mediated learning experiences.

The fifth assumption is that nonverbal tests are more culture fair. This has resulted in the development of more nonverbal-type tasks on IQ tests within the past 5 years.

The sixth assumption is deeply embedded in Westernized ethnocentric thinking whereby it is believed that Western education nurtures disembedded, context-free thinking (functional equivalence). Therefore, most IQ tests assume that one's cultural experiences and context are integral to the development of one's cognition. As such, the tests leave no room for the probability that the child may have the same skill but may not be representing it in the way the IQ test dictates. Therefore, because the child may know how to build a fan but not know how to put a puzzle together (as required on an IQ test)—two different tasks that demand a similar type of skill—the individual is not credited for having the ability because this skill or knowledge is not captured in the exact manner on the IQ test.

The seventh assumption is that the IQ test can capture the broad-based nature of a person's intelligence and therefore there is no need for a broader menu of assessment options (psychometric equivalence). Hence the reason IQ tests are used in isolation of the child's various other ecologies, such as the family and the community.

The eighth assumption is that all cognitive abilities exist within the IQ tests themselves. Hence, most psychometricians believe that children who do not perform well on the IQ tests have no other intelligences, such as musical and bodily kinesthetic intelligences.

The ninth assumption is that emotional and practical intelligence (tacit knowledge) is not a criterion for cognitive intelligence. Of course, cognitive theory has yet to address why the "most intelligent" child in the class may not always be the most successful or why some people stay buoyant when faced with great challenges when the same situations tend to sink a person who is less resilient. Not one IQ test takes into consideration emotional factors even though "the majority of variance in real-world performance is not accounted for by intelligence tests scores" (Sternberg, Wagner, Williams, & Horvath, 1995, p. 913).

The tenth assumption is that because of the genetic nature of intelligence, that intelligence is fixed and cannot be changed. This position has prohibited psychologists from functioning as diagnosticians, and instead they function as psychometricians whereby they are expected to adhere strictly to standardized procedures.

The Demise of Standardized Tests as a Sole Means of Determining Intelligence

We have begun to witness the demise of the term IQ, which has been touted as outdated by some researchers (Kamphaus, 1993). With the exception of the Wechsler scales, which have maintained an IQ score, a standard score has been given in its place by several standardized tests, such as the Stanford-Binet (composite standard score), the K-ABC (mental processing composite score), and the Woodcock (standard score and grade and age equivalent). The days of the term IQ seem to be numbered, and this is probably symptomatic of the changing climate of intelligence testing as a sole means of assessing intelligence. Given the limitations of all these IQ tests and the ongoing debate with IQ tests as a whole, Kamphaus (1993) hypothesizes that the term intelligence test may become extinct. If standardized tests are to be preserved, especially in a multiethnic and multicultural society, potential and ecological assessment must be part of the overall assessment system that we term the four-tier biocultural assessment system.

The next section presents an overview of how potential assessment can be performed with two intelligence tests.

TABLE 7.2 Correcting the Biases on the Wechsler Scales Through the Biocultural Assessment System

Subtest	Assumption	Potential Assessment
General information	Functional Equivalence	Cultural/Item Equivalence
Similarities	Functional Equivalence	Cultural/Item Equivalence
Vocabulary	Linguistic Equivalence	Linguistic Equivalence Contextualize Words
Arithmetic	Do problems mentally Speed	Paper and Pencil Suspend Time
Comprehension	Functional Equivalence	Cultural/Item Equivalence
Block Design	Conceptual Equivalence Functional Equivalence Speed	Test-Teach-Retest Cultural/Item Equivalence Suspend Time
Object Assembly	Conceptual Equivalence Functional Equivalence Speed	Test-Teach-Retest Cultural/Item Equivalence Suspend Time
Picture Completion	Speed Functional Equivalence	Suspend Time Cultural/Item Equivalence
Picture Arrangement	Conceptual Equivalence Functional Equivalence Speed	Test-Teach-Retest Cultural/Item Equivalence Suspend Time
Coding	Speed	Cultural/Item Equivalence

Administration Procedures for Potential Assessment for Two Standardized Tests of Intelligence

Wechsler Intelligence Scale for Children-III

Please follow the standardized testing procedures unless stated below (see Table 7.2 for a cursory view).

Divide your protocol in half on each subtest. Write in black or blue for actual testing scores and red for the potential testing scores. Place actual testing scores to the left and potential testing scores to the right.

If the child has reached his or her ceiling point on standardized testing but not on potential, you are to continue doing potential testing until the child has reached the ceiling point. In potential assessment, time should be suspended on all timed tests.

Picture Completion:[1] Suspend time and let the child go beyond the "20." Note in the Response column "Time 25" and put in red in the potential column "1" if the child got the answer correct.

General Information: Match to culture. Give potential scores in red.

Coding: Match to culture. Give potential scores in red.

Similarities: Match to culture. Give potential scores in red.

Picture Arrangement (teach and suspend time):[1] Begin with the sample item as in the standardized manual. If the child passes the sample item, move along to Item 1 for children ages 6 to 8 and Item 3 for children ages 9 to 16. Items 1, 2, and 3 can be used as teaching items. Therefore, if a 9-year-old child fails Item 3, teach it, then go back and allow the child to do it again. Credit the child under potential and continue with Item 1 and 2 in normal sequence as in the standardized procedures. If the child passes Items 1 and 2, continue to Item 4, as you would have in the standardized procedure. Remember for Items 1 and 2 to give both trials. Teaching comes after the second trial. The important point to remember is that the exact procedures are followed as in the standardized testing, except time is suspended, teaching is done, and potential scores are given after the child passes the teaching items. Remember to circle the correct points (based on the timed completed) under potential scores as you would have in the standard procedure.

Arithmetic:[1] For potential testing, use paper and pencil and say to the child who fails: "Please use this paper and pencil and try to solve the problem." Circle in red the correct response because this falls under potential testing. Another version of potential is to allow the child to read all the questions as he or she would have done in Questions 17 to 19. Arithmetic taps skill, memory, attention, and speed. In the standard procedure, it is difficult to tell which is operating. In the first potential example, we can rule out speed as a factor, whereas in the second potential example, we can rule out speed, memory, and attention. Reading may be a confounding variable, however.

Block Design:[1] Begin with Design 1 for children ages 6 and 7 and Design 3 for children ages 8 to 16. If a child fails the beginning item on both trials, teach it and give the test again. Give credit under potential if the child gets it correct. Then follow standardized procedures by going to the next item in normal sequence. Therefore, for children ages 8 to 16, teach at Item 3 and give credit if the child gets it correct after the teaching. Then go back to Items 1 and 2, give credit if correct, then go to Item 4. Remember on Items 1, 2, and 3 to give both trials. Teaching comes after the second trial. The important point to remember is that the exact procedures are followed as in the standardized testing, except time is suspended, teaching is done, and potential scores are given after the child passes the teaching items. Remember, place in the incomplete design column in red the time it took, and circle the correct points (based on the timed completed) under potential scores as you would have in the standard procedure.

Vocabulary:[1] Contextualize all words by asking the child to say them in a sentence. Credit is only given if the child (not the examiner) says it in a sentence. Follow the standardized procedures for querying. Thus, if the child is on potential and he or she gives a query response, query it. If, after querying, the child gets it correct, give credit under potential. You can keep querying if the child is in a query category as in the standardized procedure, but the responses fall under potential scores.

Object Assembly:[1] Begin with the sample item for all as in the standardized procedures. Then proceed to Item 1. If the child fails Item 1, even if he or she got the sample item correct, teach Item 1 and give the credit under potential. Only the sample item and Item 1 can be used for teaching. Remember to suspend time and circle in red the potential score and give the correct points based on the timed completed.

Comprehension: Match to culture.

Digit Span: Match to culture.

Woodcock-Johnson Test of Cognitive Ability-Revised

Please follow the standardized testing procedures unless stated below (see Table 7.3 for a cursory view).

Divide your protocol in half on each subtest. Write in black or blue for actual testing scores and red for the potential testing scores. Place actual scores to the left and potential scores to the right.

If the child has reached his or her ceiling point on standardized testing but not on potential, continue doing potential testing until the child has reached the ceiling point.

In potential assessment, time should be suspended on all timed tests.

TABLE 7.3   Correcting the Biases on the Woodcock Through the
Biocultural Assessment System

Subtest	Assumption	Potential Assessment
Visual matching	Speed	Suspend Time
Visual closure	Speed Conceptual Equivalence Functional Equivalence	Suspend Time Test-Teach-Retest Cultural/Item Equivalence
Picture vocabulary	Speed Conceptual Equivalence Functional Equivalence	Suspend Time Test-Teach-Retest Cultural/Item Equivalence
Analysis-synthesis	Speed	Suspend Time
Visual-auditory learning	Speed	Suspend Time
Cross out	Speed	Suspend Time
Picture recognition	Speed Functional Equivalence	Suspend Time Cultural/Item Equivalence
Oral vocabulary	Linguistic Equivalence	Linguistic Equivalence Contextualize Words
Concept formation	Speed	Suspend Time
Listening comprehension	Functional Equivalence	Cultural/Item Equivalence
Verbal analogies	Functional Equivalence	Cultural/Item Equivalence

In general, there are many tests of memory on the WJTCA-R. Therefore, this can be used to supplement the memory tests on the Wechsler scales. Also, the symbols on the WJTCA-R are unfamiliar symbols for any child from any culture. Thus, to a large extent, they are more universal symbols.

Test 3—Visual Matching:[1] Suspend time.

Test 4—Incomplete Words: Allow for different pronunciation based on different accents. If you are unsure, allow someone from the child's culture to administer this subtest.

Test 5—Visual Closure:[1] Suspend time. Also, please note that some culturally different children may not have had exposure or experience with some of these pictures (Examples include Nos. 11, 17, 18, 22-26, 28, 29, 33, 44, and 46).

Test 6—*Picture Vocabulary:* Please note that some culturally different children may not have had exposure or experience with some of these pictures (Examples include Nos. 6, 8, 19, 30, 35, 40, and 47).

Test 7—*Analysis-Synthesis:*[1] Items 26 through 35—suspend time.

Test 8—*Visual-Auditory Learning:*[1] Suspend time.

Test 10—*Cross Out:*[1] Suspend time.

Test 11—*Sound Blending:* Allow for different pronunciation based on different accents. If you are unsure, allow someone from the child's culture to administer this subtest.

Test 12—*Picture Recognition:*[1] Suspend time.

Test 13—*Oral Vocabulary:* (Note that even in the standard procedure, the child is not penalized for speech pronunciation differences.) On this test, you can contextualize all words by asking the child to say them in a sentence. Credit is given only if the child (not the examiner) says the words in a sentence. Follow the standardized procedures for querying. Thus, if the child is on potential and he or she gives a query response, query it. If, after querying, the child gets it correct, give credit under potential. You can keep querying if the child is in a query category as in the standardized procedure, but the response falls under potential scores.

Test 14—*Concept Formation:*[1] For Items 22 through 34, suspend time.

Test 18—*Sound Patterns:* Allow for different pronunciation based on different accents. If you are unsure, allow someone from the child's culture to administer this subtest.

Test 20—*Listening Comprehension:* (Note that even in the standard procedure the child is not penalized for speech pronunciation differences.) Also, please note that some culturally different children may not have had exposure or experience with some of these items (e.g., No. 3; in many Third World countries, a shower is more commonly found than a bathtub).

Test 21—*Verbal Analogies:* (Note that even in the standard procedure, the child is not penalized for speech pronunciation differences.) Some questions assume that the child may have been exposed to these items (Examples include Nos. 2, 8, 18, 27, and 29).

Although the assumptions and limitations of the Stanford-Binet and the K-ABC were presented in Table 7.1, a detailed subtest analysis will not be discussed here. Examiners, however, could use the previous format in developing potential assessment for any tests because all standardized tests are limited with respect to ecological assessment. Gopaul-McNicol, Elizalde-Utnick, Nahari, and Louden (1998) gave a critical review of 16 commonly used intelligence tests with bilingual children. A perusal of this series will prove helpful in understanding the limitations of other tests not discussed in this chapter, such as the McCarthy scales, the Detroit Test of Learning Aptitude 3, the Differential Ability Scales, the Leiter, the System of Multicultural Pluralistic Assessment, and the Peabody Picture Vocabulary Test and its Spanish companion, the Test de Vocabulario Imagenes Peabody.

Inter-Battery, Cross-Battery, or Process-Oriented Approach

Thomas (1990) helped to bring to the forefront the blending of IQ tests at the American Psychological Association Convention in Boston in 1990. In her discussion on how best to assess the intelligence of Hispanic children, Thomas mapped out how another aspect of the child's cognitive functioning can be ascertained by using an amalgamation of IQ tests—the Wechsler, the Stanford-Binet, the Test of Non-Verbal Intelligence, and the Kaufman. Thomas, a licensed clinical, school, and bilingual (Spanish) psychologist, personally assessed approximately 600 children during a 10-year period utilizing this interbattery approach and concluded that "it is still just another IQ test." As such, "It must be used in conjunction with nonpsychometric measures to best capture the range of a child's intelligence in various contexts and with varied experiences."

Proponents of interbattery testing, termed by other psychometricians (McGrew & Flanagan, 1995) as cross-battery testing or the process-oriented approach (neuropsychology), do not recognize that adding more items and mixing various tests in no way strengthens the validity of these tests in assessing the intelligence of children. The grave question that comes to mind with this interbattery approach to assessing intelligence is the issue of norming. Questions such as the following need to be answered:

1. Which population sample was used from each of the various tests to form this new test?
2. Why were the items selected from the various tests chosen over other items?
3. At what point is it safe to say that the examiner has exhausted all possibilities of assessing the particular concept under study? In other words, should we use three, four, or five different tests?
4. What happens if the child still fails the interbattery? Does this prove without a doubt that the child is really limited in that area being assessed? In other words, is the examiner going to conclude that it now justifies the biological explanation although item equivalence via ecological assessment was not done?

Even with this interbattery approach, the following question still remains: How can one tell that these abilities are not tainted by cultural factors? In other words, how could one know that it is ability and not experience and context that are operating? Could one say emphatically that all cultures and all people demonstrate abstract reasoning in the way they do on standardized tests of intelligence. We view this cross-battery approach as no more than a last attempt by desperate psychometricians to hold on to the cornerstone of traditional IQ tests.

Note

1. These subtests are most applicable to potential assessment.

8

Report Writing Utilizing the Four-Tier Biocultural Assessment System

Traditionally, many school psychologists consider report writing a burdensome task and tend to assume this challenge only when forced to at the end of the semester when writing the report cannot be further postponed. Despite its unpopularity, however, documented written reports are critical to the role of psychologists. First, they provide accountability and proof of the examiner's findings that have long-term effects on a child's life. Surber (1995) noted that "Probably no other profession or specialty do legislative regulations have such an important effect on the information presented in a written report" (p. 161). The purpose of the psychological report has traditionally been to address the reason the student is having difficulty in learning, behaving, and so on and to determine what services or class placement the child may need. A tremendous void in most reports is the conversion of the assessment data into specially designed tailored interventions that really fit the child's needs and that can lead to improved student performance in the areas of concern. This chapter first demonstrates how the four-tier biocultural assessment system can assist school psychologists in writing more culturally sensitive reports instead of narrowly focused reports that are endemic to psychometricians or "tester-technicians" (Tallent, 1993) who restrict their reporting to test results only. When the psychologist's role is expanded to that of a diagnostician or a clinician, the approach to report writing is more prescriptive and relates more to educational implications for classroom practice (Gopaul-McNicol & Armour-Thomas, 1997a). Hence, the second purpose of this chapter is to assist school psychologists to develop interventions that can assist the teacher and the parent in reducing the discrepancy between the child's current functioning as assessed by classroom-type tasks and the child's potential functioning as assessed by this comprehensive biocultural assessment system. It is critical to note that in assessing students from linguistically and culturally diverse backgrounds, their personal competencies, such as their ability to negotiate an environment that is highly different from that of their culture of origin, along with their many other intelligences and personal strengths, are important in understanding the strengths of the child. Also with these children, it is necessary to conduct differential diagnoses for intellectual assessment. In other words, it is important to rule out whether the child's deficits are a result of mental retardation, educational deprivation, learning disability, a linguistic factor, or a mere misassessment of the child's strengths due to using only standardized measures of assessment.

Recommendations

After reporting all the findings, it is recommended that a Diagnostic Impression section and an Educational/Clinical Implications section—that is, what are the implications of the findings for the child's functioning in the classroom setting—be included. It is important to remember that the recommendations should be based more on the results of the intellectual potential findings, ecological findings, and other intelligences rather than only on the standardized psychometric intelligence tests scores. In addition, the recommendations must be based on the diagnostic impressions. Thus, after doing potential intellectual assessment, the examiner should recommend what he or she believes are the best ways the teacher, the parent, and the mental health worker can intervene in working with the child. In other words, if teaching helped, then recommend one on one teaching for a particular number of sessions. If extending time helped, then recommend that the child be given extra time and more opportunity for practice. If contextualizing words helped, recommend that initially as the child acclimates to the new environment that he or she be given an opportunity to receive his or her assignment in a surrounding context. If it was found that the child did better on paper and pencil tasks than on tasks requiring mental computations, then recommend that paper and pencil assessment be allowed. If the child has other intelligences, recommend programs in which these can be further enriched.

It is also important to utilize all the resources in the community—church, social and recreational community programs, after-school programs, legal aid, psychotherapeutic programs, and so on. The important role of the psychologist is to assist the school-based support team, the teacher, the family, and the child to develop a course of treatment that would maximize every opportunity for the child to move from his or her actual functioning to his or her potential functioning in a 3-year period. In other words, the child should show significant gains after the intervention period in all areas assessed.

To best address the purpose of this chapter, a review of a traditional psychological report and a biocultural report conducted on the same child will aid the examiner in detecting how the differences in assessment and report writing can lead to differences in recommendation and improved life chances for children with special needs. The following is information on the child discussed in this chapter:

Name: Miguel   Date of testing: 5/21/94
School: JHS   Date of birth: 8/19/81
Grade: 6th   Age: 12 years, 9 months
Language: Spanish

Reason for Referral and Background Information

Miguel was referred for an initial evaluation by his teacher due to academic difficulties. Miguel arrived from Colombia in August of 1993 at age 12. His parents had migrated to the United States when he was 7 years old. While in Colombia, Miguel was said to be a pleasant boy who related well to his aunts with whom he resided while his parents were in the United States.

The social history conducted in March 1994 by the school social worker revealed that since Miguel arrived in the United States, he has had serious difficulty adjusting to the classroom not because of linguistic factors "Because he is more proficient and more dominant in English since he attended English classes in his native country to prepare for his migrating to the USA." According to the social worker and the teacher, Miguel clearly has no skills, and the school psychologist's report revealed deficient intellectual functioning when tested with standardized tests of intelligence.

The social history revealed that Miguel lives with his mother, father, an older brother, maternal aunt, and grandmother. All family members present themselves as a cohesive unit with strong extended family ties and good family support systems. According to Miguel's mother, all developmental milestones were attained at age-expectant levels. There were reports of delays in reading even in Colombia, however, but his mother said, "He was certainly able to read what was necessary to get by. He is definitely not stupid as the school is making him out to be."

Test Administered and Test Results: Traditional School Report

Wechsler Intelligence Scale for Children-III

Psychometric Assessment	Range
Verbal Scale IQ	Deficient
Performance Scale IQ	Borderline
Full-Scale IQ	Deficient

Wechsler Intelligence Scale for Children-III (continued)

Current Scale Score	Range	Current Scale Score	Range
Information	Deficient	Picture Completion	Borderline
Similarities	Deficient	Coding	Borderline
Arithmetic	Deficient	Picture Arrangement	Borderline
Vocabulary	Deficient	Block Design	Borderline
Comprehension	Deficient	Object Assembly	Borderline
Digit Span	Low average	Mazes	Borderline

Given the previous findings, the standardized psychological report reflected that Miguel is functioning in the mentally deficient range of intelligence, and even when tested to potential (extending the time limits in some of the nonverbal areas), he was at best borderline. He was unable to do basic math commensurate to his age and grade peers. He was deficient in his vocabulary skills, and could not define words such as nonsense, ancient, and thief. When given the blocks and puzzles to manipulate, he became noticeably frustrated, stating "I do not know what to do," while pushing the blocks away. On the general information subtests, Miguel was unable to respond to basic questions such as "Name two kinds of coins." The report recommends that Miguel be placed in a self-contained class in which he can receive special educational services in all areas to address his obvious delays in academic-type tasks and his overall intellectual deficiencies.

Test Administered and Test Results:
Biocultural Assessment System

Wechsler Intelligence Scale for Children-III

Psychometric Potential Assessment	Range
Verbal Scale IQ	Borderline
Performance Scale IQ	Average
Full-Scale IQ	Low average

Potential Scale Score	Range	Potential Scale Score	Range
Information	Deficient	Picture Completion	Low average
Similarities	Deficient	Coding	Borderline
Arithmetic	Low average	Picture Arrangement	Low average
Vocabulary	Average	Block Design	Average
Comprehension	Borderline	Object Assembly	Average
Digit Span	Average	Mazes	—

Medical examination: No medical difficulties

Ecological Intellectual Assessment
Estimated overall functioning   Average

Other intelligences assessment
   Bodily kinesthetic (soccer)   Advanced
   Artistic (painting)   Advanced
   Musical intelligence (guitar)   Advanced
   Family Support Assessment   Adequate

Vineland Behavior Adaptive Scales—Parent edition	Range
Communication	Low
Social	Adequate
Daily Living scales	Adequate

Social History
Clinical Interview
Parent Interview
Teacher Questionnaire

Language Dominance   English

Language Proficiency

Vocabulary Subtest	Proficiency Rating
Spanish Expressive Vocabulary	Deficient
English Expressive Vocabulary	Borderline

Behavioral Observation

Miguel, a pleasant young man, presented himself in a cooperative, compliant manner. He had a good disposition and was motivated to do all the tasks assigned to him. Even on completion of the testing, Miguel asked the examiner if he could do more. He was not fatigued and believed these types of tests were reinforcing to him. In general, his response time was slow, and he approached the testing in a cautious, reflective manner. When he clearly did not know the answer, he still persisted but became noticeably frustrated and embarrassed. He would sigh, frown, and seemed upset that he did not know the answer to a question that he initially perceived as easy. All in all, it was a pleasure testing Miguel because he tried hard and was willing to please.

Language Assessment

Miguel's language proficiency was tested through the administration of the vocabulary subtest of the Wechsler Intelligence Scale for Children-III (WISC-III) in both Spanish and English. He is clearly more dominant and more proficient in English. He spoke mainly in English, but on several occasions he requested that the examiner speak in Spanish. When he engaged in social play on the playground, he spoke in both languages. In general, his English receptive and expressive skills are better developed than his Spanish skills. It is possible that the years of English instruction he received prior to coming to the United States and the fact that his parents speak only in English at home aided in his developing such proficiency and fluency in English. At this time, although Miguel can function well in a predominantly English-speaking class, the supportive environment of a bilingual paraprofessional may prove beneficial when he is faced with very difficult tasks.

Test Interpretation

Psychometric Assessment

On the WISC-III, Miguel obtained a full-scale IQ score that placed him in the deficient range of intelligence. His verbal and nonverbal scores fell in the deficient and borderline ranges, respectively.

Subtest analysis indicates considerable subtest variability within both the verbal and nonverbal spheres. In the verbal area (crystallized), Miguel was deficient in general information, suggesting that on this psychometric test, Miguel is not as alert to the social and cultural factors typical of American society as measured by the WISC-III. His deficiency in comprehension is also indicative of his limited understanding of the social mores in the United States as assessed on the WISC-III. Miguel was also deficient in verbal abstract reasoning, suggesting that, on this test, Miguel has difficulty placing objects and events together in a meaningful group. In arithmetic and vocabulary, Miguel was also deficient. This is indicative of inadequate arithmetic skills as assessed by the standardized procedures of the WISC-III as well as poor language development and limited word knowledge as defined by the WISC-III. In auditory short-term memory, Miguel was low average. Therefore, one can expect Miguel to be relatively good at rote memory and sequential processing.

In the nonverbal area (fluid intelligence), Miguel was borderline in identifying essential missing elements from a whole, suggesting delayed visual alertness, visual discrimination, and long-term visual memory on the Wechsler scales. In visual integration, Miguel was borderline, suggesting limited perceptual skills, poor long-term visual memory, and limited constructive ability commensurate to his peers nationwide on the Wechsler scales. Miguel, however, was persistent and tried to put the puzzles together. There was a sense that he was unfamiliar with these items. As such, when he was taught how to connect the pieces, he tended to be more relaxed, although he continued to perform poorly. In visual motor coordination and motor speed, Miguel was also borderline, suggesting slow response time, poor visual short-term memory, and limited visual acuity on the Wechsler scales. In nonverbal comprehension, Miguel was borderline, suggesting a delayed ability to anticipate the consequences of his actions, to plan, and to organize ahead of time. In nonverbal abstract reasoning, Miguel was also low average, suggesting below average ability to perceive, analyze, and synthesize blocks on the Wechsler scales.

Psychometric Potential Assessment

When Miguel was tested to the limits such as when time was suspended, and also when item equivalencies were done, his scores improved by 14 IQ points in the verbal area, 16 IQ points in the nonverbal area, and 16 IQ points in overall intelligence. Thus, when the test-teach-test technique was implemented and when time was suspended with the blocks and puzzles, Miguel went from borderline to average, displaying much confidence on these tests during potential assessment. Because Block Design is the best measure of nonverbal intelligence on the Wechsler scales, Miguel is of average potential in the nonverbal area.

Another important fact is that when Miguel was offered the opportunity to use paper and pencil, he was able to perform many of the mathematical tasks that presented difficulty under standardized procedures. For instance, he clearly knew multiplication, division, and even simple fractions. Thus, by allowing Miguel to use paper and pencil, instead of relying on mental computations only, the examiner was able to determine that Miguel did master some arithmetic skills but was unable to perform them without the aid of paper and pencil. Because in real-life situations one is usually allowed the opportunity to work with pencil and paper, one can expect that Miguel will be able to do basic calculations to function adequately well in his day to day duties. Moreover, although Miguel was unable to name two American coins on the psychometric test, he was able to correctly name and identify the *escudo* and the *peso*, two monetary units from South America. Furthermore, when the vocabulary words were contextually determined—that is, Miguel was asked to say the words in a surrounding context (Miguel said, "I migrated to the USA recently," even though he did not know the word "migrate" in isolation)—Miguel score rose from deficient to average. He knew almost every word commensurate to his age and grade peers when allowed to contextualize them. Because vocabulary is the best measure of general intelligence, Miguel is of average potential in the verbal area. Incidentally, if the substitute test was used to tabulate his verbal IQ score instead of general information (the most biased of the verbal subtests), Miguel's verbal score would have been low average, albeit his overall IQ score would have still been low average.

Ecological Assessment

At home, in school, on the playground, and in the community, Miguel is described as "bright and promising" by his family and friends. According to his mother, Miguel helps with the groceries and assists with basic household tasks commensurate to those of his peers. Moreover, in observing Miguel on the community playground, it was clearly evident that he was able to perform several of the tasks found on the IQ test. For instance, although he was unable to put the puzzles and blocks together on the Wechsler scales, he was adept at fixing a car. On one occasion, when his aunt's car was unable to start, he checked the carburetor and other car parts and deciphered the problem. His aunt mentioned that he is responsible for repairing any electrical appliances that malfunction in the home. Evidently, this activity involves the same visual motor coordination skills as putting puzzles together. The fact that Miguel was unable to reintegrate the pieces of puzzles on the IQ test, but could have assembled smaller, more complex parts of a car, suggests that cultural factors must be impeding his ability to perform such a similar task on the standardized IQ test. Clearly, he is at least average in visual motor integration skills, albeit this was not evident on the psychometric measure. Also significant was Miguel's ability to remember a 14-item grocery list, although he was unable to recall as many as seven numbers on the Digit Span subtest of the Wechsler scales. Equally impressive is his ability to do arithmetic computations mentally at the grocery store, although he demonstrated deficient mathematical skills on the psychometric IQ test. Thus, in Miguel's ecology—that is, in a real-life situation away from the testing environment—he showed good planning ability, good perceptual organization, good mathematical skills, and good short-term memory. Unfortunately, none of these skills were manifested on the standardized traditional IQ test, albeit gains were noted when he was tested for his cognitive potential via the same IQ measure. Evidently, from an ecological perspective, in real-life situations Miguel's cognitive ability is approximately average.

Other Intelligences Assessment

Miguel's family and his gym teacher described him as "multi-talented." He is said to be very athletic, particularly in his ability to play soccer. His gym teacher described him as well coordinated. He is artistic in that he paints and draws all sorts of abstract images as well as cartoon-like figures. His art teacher described his skills as advanced in artistic ability and said that Miguel was the best student in his class in all artistic-related fields, such as painting, designing, architecture, and so on. Thus, with respect to his bodily kinesthetic ability, Miguel was above average to superior commensurate to his peers. Another intelligence that Miguel possesses is his musical ability. He plays the clarinet and formulates melodic and harmonic images with fluency after only 1 year of playing the guitar. His mother stated that he also has an interest in other musical instruments such as the flute. An interview with his music teacher revealed that Miguel plays the piano "for fun" and composes songs and music so creatively that in the realm of musical intelligence he would be considered superior intellectually.

An interview with the after-school community director revealed that he is a "well-rounded, talented" young man who manifests accuracy, grace, speed, power, and great team spirit in all artistic and sports-like endeavors. He is said to have a well-developed sense of timing, coordination, and rhythm when it pertains to playing music. Also reported by the director is his ability to remain composed under great pressure. An observation of him playing soccer allowed the examiner the opportunity to note his bodily intelligence in its purest form with much flexibility and high technical proficiency. He is indeed of superior ability in the area of gross and fine motor motions. Also of note is the social feedback offered by the director: "Everyone likes Miguel, both young children and his peers. Everyone wants him to lead the team. He inspires his peers to do their best." Interpersonal skills are described as excellent because Miguel is a "warm, pleasant, and sociable young man."

Diagnostic Impression and Educational and Clinical Implications

Intellectually, Miguel is functioning in the mentally deficient range on the WISC-III psychometric test and low average range on psychometric potential assessment. Because Miguel attended school in his native country on a regular basis, he cannot be said to be educationally deprived. Also, a diagnosis of mental retardation cannot be given because adequate functioning was noted on two sections of the Vineland Adaptive Behavior Scales. To be diagnosed as mentally retarded, low functioning in all areas of social adaptation should be evident. It is only on communication skills that he was found to be low, which was commensurate to his score on the WISC-III psychometric test. Besides, after conducting a family assessment, it is clear that Miguel functions adequately in the his community and is respected by his peers. Thus, despite communication delays, there are no overall social adaptive deficiencies to characterize him as mentally deficient. At this juncture, Miguel's intellectual functioning best fits the category of Learning Disabled Not Otherwise Specified. This category is for learning disorders that do not meet the criteria for any specific learning disorder, and it may include problems in all three core areas of reading, mathematics, and written expression.

Given the obvious delays in several academic skill areas, and because of the psychometric IQ test scores, one (such as the school psychologist) may be solely inclined to provide Miguel with intensive instruction in all academic cognitive skill areas on a daily basis in a small classroom special educational setting. Clearly, he does require the supportive environment of supplemental instruction. Given his performance when assessed in other settings beyond the IQ testing environment, however, a less restrictive setting outside of the special education self-contained realm should be explored. For instance, Miguel should be encouraged to pursue music, in particular the guitar. Likewise, he should be encouraged to embellish his athletic skills given his intellectual prowess in this area. As such, the typical special education self-contained class, in which there is little emphasis on honing one's career and occupational skills, is not recommended.

Evidently, Miguel's obvious intelligence in music renders him a prime candidate for a scholarship at a music school. As such, opportunities for career-related academic skill development, which includes essential work-adjustment skills, and direct work experience through daily practice in a music school are needed for this young man to attain his potential and be self-supportive.

Clinically, Miguel was lacking in self-confidence and was noticeably frustrated when faced with demanding classroom-type tasks.

When observed in the home and in his music and sports classes, however, no frustration nor anger were noted. Likewise, the after-school instructor reported that Miguel had a good sense of himself—the opposite to what his general classroom teacher had stated. It was indeed important that assessment of this youngster in various settings was done to ensure a more accurate diagnosis of his overall functioning.

Summary and Recommendations

Miguel is a 12-year-old young man who showed delays on both the psychometric and the potential psychometric assessment measures in general information, comprehension, arithmetic, and verbal abstract reasoning. As a result, remediation should focus on exposure to a broad range of everyday facts and practical reasoning in social situations. Miguel should be encouraged to read American literature or the newspaper on a daily basis to gain more insight into world events and the mainstream cultural views to help improve his general information. Other forms of resources are museums, educational television shows, tapes, and film documentaries. Teaching same-different concepts should aid in improving verbal abstract reasoning. In addition, vocabulary skills can be enhanced by encouraging Miguel to learn new words by reading more. Teaching computational skills commensurate to his grade peers should aid in improving arithmetic skills.

Miguel can function in a monolingual class, although the supportive environment of a bilingual paraprofessional may prove beneficial when he is faced with difficult tasks. In addition, the recommendation for Miguel also included a referral to Operation Athlete, an organization in New York City that provides scholarships for gifted athletes. This organization has an after-school program whose goal is to recruit intelligent athletes who can go on and become professionals in their areas of expertise. Miguel was recently offered a scholarship for soccer, but he must finish high school while maintaining passing grades in all core courses.

Miguel was also referred to Sesame Flyer, a Caribbean organization that teaches immigrant families to play various musical instruments.

Moreover, counseling aimed at increasing frustration tolerance surrounding his academic delays was offered for 8 weeks.

A follow-up of Miguel's progress 1 year after the completion of the evaluation revealed a continued superiority in the nonacademic-type tasks such as sports and a slight increment in the academic areas. Miguel was taught to transfer his knowledge from his ecology to the classroom setting by various exercises offered by the examiner who continued treatment following the evaluation. Teacher and family consultation to assist those who work more closely with Miguel was offered on an ongoing basis. The most recent teacher report revealed "significant gains in reading, math, and spelling," and no frustration was evident when faced with difficult tasks. On the contrary, Miguel repeatedly stated, "This is my weak area, but I have many strengths." Miguel has learned to rely on his other intelligences—bodily kinesthetic and music—and hopes to pursue one of these vocational arenas.

Miguel should be monitored closely and tested next year to see what progress he is making and if a more or less restrictive setting would be beneficial.

Conclusion

The linking of assessment and diagnosis to intervention continues to be one of the most challenging demands faced by school psychologists. The important factor to note at this juncture is that assessment programs that fail to take into account the differences among individuals' cultural experiences are anachronistic. To take these variations into account, it would require those in the formal testing enterprise to suspend some of the major assumptions of standardized testing, such as uniformity of individuals' experiences and the penchant for one type of cost-efficient instrument. Surber (1995) emphasizes that incorporating a multimethod, multitrait approach to assessment and intervention can better ensure that the outcomes for students are nondiscriminatory. He suggests conducting more comprehensive assessment and writing more integrated reports. Indeed, such an approach allows the examiner to answer more readily the major question—What is interfering with the child's ability to learn? Such an approach expands the psychologist's role beyond that of a psychometrician who administers only standardized tests.

Psychologists in training should be taught about individual differences by being introduced formally to such distinctions. It is going to be quite difficult for students in training to arrive at such empirically valid taxonomies of differences in individuals on their own. Such exposure should occur during their professional training. Once exposed to different profiles in the course of their apprenticeships, it is easier for them to be more flexible in their assessment practices. Chapter 10 discusses issues in the training of psychologists.

Furthermore, it is equally important for students in training to be cognizant of their individual state regulations regarding bilingual and bicultural assessment. In several states, there are Chancellor's disclaimant statements for assessing bilingual children. The reader should see Table 6.2, which presents a summary of the stages in the biocultural assessment system in a biocultural report. More examples of how to word biocultural sections of a report can be found in Table 8.1. A sample disclaimant statement for bilingual children is also provided in Table 8.1.

In summary, the most critical dimension to assessment is getting at the strengths of a youngster and helping that child to feel a sense of empowerment and success despite any obvious academic deficiencies.

Although these recommended methods of administering and scoring traditional tests are not in keeping with standardization procedures, they certainly can assist psychologists in tapping the potential of all children. If psychologists intend to serve children well, they should focus on qualitative rather than quantitative reports that highlight all of a child's past and present cultural experiences.

TABLE 8.1   Examples of How to Write Sections of a
Biocultural Report

Psychometric Assessment

For those who opt to interpret this test via the Gf-Gc factors, write a paragraph on each of the nine abilities (McGrew, 1994). For example:

Processing speed (GS) (coding) was found to be borderline. This suggests that Miguel may experience difficulty performing automatic intellectual tasks quickly.

Visual processing (GV) (block design and object assembly) was average. This suggests that Miguel has the ability to analyze, synthesize, and think with visual patterns. His strength clearly is his ability to manipulate visual shapes, especially those that are figural and geometric in nature. Therefore, it is not surprising that Miguel demonstrates exceptional talent in painting.

Psychometric Potential Assessment

Example 1

The Block Design and Object Assembly subtests are highly influenced by the American culture. When Miguel was assessed by other more comparable measures, such as building a chair, he was found to be very superior given the quick and accurate manner in which he executed the task.

Example 2

Miguel's scores were elevated when he was asked questions more related to his cultural experiences. For instance, although he did not know who Anne Frank was on the IQ tests, he knew Rafael Pombo—the author of the Colombian national anthem. Clearly, Miguel has some general fund of information endemic to his culture of origin. One could expect that with time, he will equally master the general type of knowledge more specific to the American cultural experiences.

Example 3

Although Miguel did not know who discovered America or who was Christopher Columbus, he knew that Pedro De Valdivia founded Santiago. Thus, if given time to acclimate to this society, it is expected that Miguel will learn American history and concepts, resulting in a higher intellectual functioning.

Example 4

On the Block Design subtest, Miguel got the more difficult items correct after he passed his ceiling point or after time limits had been expended. In his native country, blocks and puzzles are not games commonly played by children. As such, he was never exposed to block building. It seemed as if he was learning as he went along, and that lack of familiarity and ultimately anxiety may have been why he did not do as well on the earlier items. As a result, two IQs were tabulated: one following standardization procedures and one tapping his

(continued)

TABLE 8.1   (continued)

potential as evidenced by summing all points attained even after he had reached his point of discontinuation.

Example 5

Miguel was asked, "In what way are an apple and a banana alike?" and he did not know the answer. Interestingly, however, when he was asked how a mango and a banana are alike, he gave a correct answer. The important thing here is that he knew the concept of fruits.

Example 6

Although Miguel did not know the word "migrate" in isolation, he knew it when used in a sentence. Thus, if contextualized, Miguel's word knowledge and ability to express verbal ideas at varying degrees of abstraction was much higher. In the same manner, although Miguel was unable to articulate how a wheel and a ball were alike, he was able to draw how they were both alike and then to state that they were both round. It seems as if he had to first conceptualize their similarity via visual stimuli and then form the concept of sameness before being able to express the common factor between these two objects. Therefore, it is not that Miguel has not conceptualized this relationship but rather that he has to go through a longer process to retrieve and articulate the similarity of such a concept.

Example 7

Miguel was able to respond to questions previously misunderstood or unanswered when Spanish dialectical terminologies were utilized. Thus, although he did not understand the question, "Why do you recycle paper?" he was able to respond appropriately to "Why do you separate paper in a separate garbage can?" Likewise, although Miguel did not understand the question, "Why do games have rules?" he clearly was able to produce a two-point response when asked, "Why are rules needed to play marbles?" Thus, merely rewording the directions helped with understanding and resulted in an increased performance of 10 points.

Example 8

In observing (Sternberg's) atomization information process approach (Triarchic Model), when given the opportunity to slowly process nonverbal reasoning tasks by trial and error, the ability to correctly complete the tasks became successively more automatic.

Example 9

When standardization procedures were not followed, Miguel's potential demonstrated an 8-point difference. For instance, instead of presenting the visual stimuli for 5 seconds as in the standard procedure, the gestalt was shown for 10 seconds (15 seconds for more complicated gestalts), and word or number sentences were slowly repeated. This process allowed for, and resulted in, the ability to process information, increase concentration, decrease anxiety, and

TABLE 8.1 (continued)

correctly respond. This suggests that when given more time to process and practice learned problem-solving skills, he can perform quite better.

Example 10

Although initially Miguel did not understand the Block Design subtest, when a test-teach-retest technique was used (i.e., when he was taught how to build blocks and puzzles other than those used on the Wechsler scales and was then tested again), he was able to correctly synthesize the more difficult items and to correctly strategize and respond to two of three previously incorrect questions. Thus, with respect to nonverbal abstract reasoning, he is more average than borderline, as was the result when standard procedures were followed. This also shows that Miguel is capable of learning various tasks once they are explained and he is given the opportunity to practice the tasks.

Example 11

When Miguel was tested to the limits—for instance, when he was not placed under time pressure—and when item equivalencies as well as the test-teach-test techniques were implemented, Miguel's score went from borderline to low average/average in the verbal area, borderline to average in the nonverbal area, and borderline to low average/average in overall intelligence. When Miguel was asked to perform comparable skills to the puzzles on the Wechsler scales, he went from borderline to average. Likewise, when the vocabulary words were contextually determined—that is, the words were structured in a surrounding context ("Miguel migrated to the USA recently") instead of asking for a definition of the word migrate in isolation—Miguel went from low average to average. Because vocabulary is the best measure of general intelligence, Miguel is of average potential in the verbal area. In the nonverbal area, Miguel went from deficient to low average on the Block Design subtest when he was taught (test-teach-retest) to manipulate the sample block. Thus, Miguel is of low average potential in the nonverbal area because Block Design is the best measure of nonverbal intelligence on the Wechsler scales. Overall, Miguel's potential intellectual functioning is borderline.

Ecological Assessment

Observation of the child in various settings, such as on the playground or in his or her community, offers interesting information.

Example 1

Although Miguel had difficulty putting the puzzles together on the WISC-III, at home Miguel had no difficulty dismantling a fan and putting it back together in a 1-hour period. Thus, when he was exposed to a more familiar stimulus, he was able to integrate parts into a meaningful whole, which is very characteristic of the Object Assembly subtest of the Wechsler scales.

(continued)

TABLE 8.1   (continued)

Example 2

The television and Nintendo were recently broken, and Miguel was able to disconnect the wires and repair these appliances. This task is equivalent to tasks on the IQ tests, such as building puzzles and attending to detail, that require the same analysis and synthesis and visual stimulation as repairing the television and the Nintendo.

Example 3

Miguel showed the examiner a table made from logs that he assisted his neighbor in building. This task is equivalent to that of building blocks on the IQ test.

Other Intelligences Assessment

Example 1: Musical intelligence

Despite Miguel's deficiencies in the verbal area, he is able to formulate melodic, rhythmic, and harmonic images into elaborate ideas although he never studied music. For instance, he plays the steel pan, the piano, and the cuatro without sheet music and with fluency. He also composes music so creatively that in the realm of musical intelligence he would be considered superior intellectually.

Example 2

According to Miguel's parents, he is very musical and plays the guitar for various Hispanic events. His father says that he has a desire to compose music and he does it so creatively that in the realm of musical intelligence he would be considered superior intellectually.

Example 3: Bodily kinesthetic intelligence

Miguel is able to dance energetically. His dances allow one an opportunity to observe his bodily intelligence in its purest form with flexibility and high technical proficiency. He is indeed of superior ability in this area.

Example 4

Miguel is athletic and is able to excel in grace, power, speed, accuracy, and teamwork. His ability to pitch the ball shows his analytic power and resourcefulness. Also noted was his ability to remain poised under great pressure. A well-developed sense of timing, coordination, and rhythm result in his being well executed and powerful in his gross and fine motor motions. His bodily intellectual strength is indeed superior.

Example 5

Miguel has an adequate amount of social competence to deal with issues in his community. For instance, he knows which areas in his neighborhood are drug infested and how to avoid going to those areas. He repeatedly said, "Here is where the drug people hang out, so don't go there." He also knew that it was

TABLE 8.1   (continued)

unsafe to flash money around and cautioned the examiner about opening her wallet even in the supermarket.

Example 6

Miguel displayed great leadership skills in the school yard. He initiated the organization of games with ease and confidence. He delegated responsibility so that the work was evenly divided among the team players and examined the regulations of the game. Miguel was particularly sensitive to his peers' feelings, ensuring that everyone was included.

Writing a Language Assessment section

Miguel's receptive skills are stronger than his expressive skills because he had more difficulty expressing verbal ideas than understanding what was said to him. Receptively and expressively, he is more dominant in Spanish because he only responded in Spanish, even when the examiner spoke to him in English. Of note is that Miguel is also more proficient in English because he was better able to perform mathematical computations in English and to read and write in English. He counted up to three in Spanish and knew some of the letters in Spanish. In English, however, he was able to construct sentences and to do applied mathematical problems. It is possible that because he receives instruction in the classroom only in English, his English skills far surpass his Spanish skills despite being more socially dominant in his native language. The fact that the Spanish translation improved his score in all verbal areas indicates that Miguel requires the supportive environment of bilingual instruction and should be evaluated bilingually when tested psychologically, educationally, and linguistically.

Given the fact that Miguel is bilingual and that a Latino or Hispanic population was not used as part of the standardization sample, in keeping with the Chancellor's regulations, the scores should be interpreted with caution and should be used only as a guide for school personnel. The results should be interpreted from both a biological and a contextual approach.

A Disclaimant Statement for
Bilingual and Bicultural Children

At the end of the behavioral observation section, it is suggested by state officials that the following disclaimant statement for bilingual and bicultural children be included:

Because this test was not standardized on an Asian/Latino/Caribbean etc. population, the following scores should be interpreted with caution in keeping with the Chancellor's regulations in assessing bilingual and bicultural children. Thus, these scores should only be used solely as a guideline in assisting school personnel in designing the best program for this child.

Test Results: Scores

Many school districts do not permit scores to be placed in the body of the report. Miguel's scores are listed here for the reader to review the changes in scores from psychometric to potential assessment.

Wechsler Intelligence Scale for Children-III

Psychometric Assessment	Scale Score	Range
Verbal Scale IQ	62	Deficient
Performance Scale IQ	74	Borderline
Full-Scale IQ	65	Deficient

Psychometric Assessment	Scale Score	Psychometric Assessment	Scale Score
Information	3	Picture Completion	6
Similarities	2	Coding	6
Arithmetic	4	Picture Arrangement	6
Vocabulary	4	Block Design	5
Comprehension	3	Object Assembly	6
Digit Span	8	Mazes	6

Psychometric Potential Assessment		Range
Verbal Scale IQ	76	Borderline
Performance Scale IQ	90	Average
Full-Scale IQ	81	Low Average

Potential	Scale Score	Potential	Scale Score
Information	3	Picture Completion	8
Similarities	4	Coding	6
Arithmetic	7	Picture Arrangement	8
Vocabulary	10	Block Design	9
Comprehension	5	Object Assembly	11
Digit Span	9	Mazes	8

9

Evaluation of the Biocultural Assessment System

In Chapter 4, we proposed a biocultural perspective of intelligence in which we have argued that behaviors observed as "intelligent" should be more appropriately termed culturally dependent cognitions because, to a large extent, we think they reflect the outcomes of person-environmental interactions developed over time in particular cultural niches. For the past 10 years, we have sought confirmation of this basic thesis through our work at the Multicultural Educational and Psychological Services Agency. Toward this end, we developed the Four-Tier Assessment System of Intelligence to seek answers to the following four questions about children's intellectual functioning:

1. What is the nature of the actual cognitive strengths and weaknesses as measured by a traditional psychometric measure of intelligence?

2. What is the nature of the potential cognitive strengths and weaknesses not observed on the IQ measure?

3. In what context and for what types of experiences other than the formal testing environment are cognitive strengths displayed?

4. Do children demonstrate other intelligences beyond those that seem to be measured on the IQ test?

In this chapter, we describe the results of our work to date. We begin with the examination of data using a widely used measure of intelligence: The Wechsler scales. This is followed by a presentation of findings using procedures for cognitive potential elicitation during the actual administration of the psychometric IQ measure. Next, we present data of cognitive competencies obtained from our observations of children in contexts beyond the testing environment. In addition, we provide data on other intellectual competencies from reports of parents, teachers, and the children themselves. Finally, we end with other self-reported data from workshops and seminars conducted with practitioners and psychologists in training.

Psychometric Data

Studies From the Research Literature on Intelligence

Psychometric data were derived from three sources: factor analytic and other studies as well as our own assessment of children in two broad age groupings (6-11 and 12-16). Our review of the literature indicated that the Wechsler scales are among the more commonly used measures of intelligence in the field. Review of the factor analytic studies indicated that there was substantial evidence for a number of verbal and nonverbal cognitive abilities underlying the tasks on this measure (e.g., Reynolds, 1990; Sattler, 1988). From our biocultural perspective, we define these competencies as culturally dependent cognitions because all the subtests, to some degree, measure previously acquired knowledge and cognitive skills developed from particular experiences in particular cultural niches. There is also some support for this judgment in the intelligence test literature, although the theoretical lens through which the judgment is made is different from ours. Consider, for example, the following view of Kaufman (1979), another well-known intelligence test developer:

> The WISC-R [Wechsler Intelligence Scale for Children-Revised] subtests measure what the individual has learned. . . . From this vantage point, the intelligence test is really a kind of achievement test . . . a measure of past accomplishments that is predictive of success in traditional school subjects. When intelligence tests are regarded as measures of prior learning, the issue of heredity versus environment becomes irrelevant. Since learning occurs within a culture, intelligence tests obviously must be considered to be culture-loaded—a concept that is different from culture biased. (pp. 12-13)

More direct evidence for our conception of intelligence as culturally dependent cognitions comes from the work of Ribeiro (1980), who analyzed the data from the WISC-R administered to 350 low-income Portuguese-speaking children in Massachusetts. Ribeiro, himself a Portuguese immigrant who came to the United States as an adult, attributed the low scores obtained by these children to cultural differences in the experiences of the children. Similar findings of culture saturation have been reported by others who seek to assess children's intelligence using the Wechsler scales (e.g., Mercer, 1979).

The WISC-III or the EIWN-R (Spanish WISC-R), depending on the children's level of proficiency in English or Spanish, were administered to 244 children, 140 of whom were ages 6 to 11 and 104 ages 12 to 16. These measures were also administered to another sample of 51 children with ages also ranging between 6 and 16. Proficiency was determined by the Family Support Assessment questionnaire and the New York State School/Home Language Survey. Due to academic, behavioral, or adjustment difficulties, these children were referred for psychological evaluation by their parents or by the teachers of various New York state school districts to determine the best program placement. Table 9.1 presents a breakdown of the background characteristics of these children.

Table 9.1 Background Characteristics of Children

Sample (Grade)	Gender		Ethnicity*			School Type			
	Boys	Girls	SP-C	Eng-C	AF-A	Kindergarten	Elementary	Middle	High
6-11	90	51	135	6	0	6	135		
12-16	71	33	95	4	5	0	27	48	13

	Language						Program Type				
	Dominant Language			Proficient Language							
	Spanish	English	West Indian Creole	Spanish	English	Bilingual	Instructional Services-1	Supplemental Instructional Services-1	Other	Special Education	Regular Education
6-11	34	82	1	26	102	13	29	8	24	15	80
12-16	32	64	3	23	78	3	28	9	25	21	42

	Age										
	6	7	8	9	10	11	12	13	14	15	16
6-11	15	20	22	22	28	33					
12-16							21	29	32	21	1

NOTE: *SP-C = Spanish Caribbean; Eng-C = English Caribbean; AF-A = African American

Psychometric Potential Data

As described in Chapter 6, the basis for the psychometric potential procedures was initially derived from our clinical observations during standardized administration of the Wechsler scales as well as our postadministration interviews with children and their families. To obtain more direct evidence for our hypothesis that there was more to the children's cognitive functioning than was possible to measure from the standardized administration of the Wechsler scales, we used a number of complementary procedures (contextualization, paper and pencil, teach-test-retest, and suspending time) during the actual administration of the IQ test. We assessed two groups of children (ages 6-11 and 12-16) at two different points in time (1991 and 1992) and found far more substantial diagnostic information from the psychometric potential procedures than from the use of the IQ measure alone. A description of the samples and a comparison of the data for the psychometric and psychometric potential are found in Tables 9.2 and 9.3, respectively.

The data showed wide variation in performance between the standard and potential scores (full-scale, verbal, and performance tests). Statistical tests revealed significant differences for each age cohort (ages 6-11 and 12-16) between standard and potential scores. These findings lend support to the validity of the potential procedures to elicit information about cognitive functioning beyond what was obtained under standardized administration.

Ecological Data

Using the data obtained from the psychometric and psychometric potential procedures for the second sample of 51 children (Table 9.4), we sought firsthand evidence of the child's cognitive functioning in settings other than the testing context. We observed the child in the home, the playground, and, in some cases, the community (e.g., grocery store and the video game parlors) and used the ecological taxonomy to record the evidence. From these ecologies, we gathered a great deal of qualitative information about the children's cognitive competencies as they interacted with peers and adults in these non-contrived contexts.

TABLE 9.2   Standard and Potential Profiles of Children Aged 6 to 11

Range of Intellectual Functioning	Full Scale		Verbal		Performance	
	Standard	Potential	Standard	Potential	Standard	Potential
Mentally retarded	6	4	14	6	2	2
Deficient	9	6	21	9	7	4
Borderline	6	15	34	30	12	9
Low average	39	48	33	39	40	28
Average	45	60	37	56	62	78
Above average	4	5	1	0	11	11
Superior	1	2	0	0	3	5
Very superior	0	0	0	0	3	3

(Score)

TABLE 9.3   Standard and Potential Profiles of Children Aged 12 to 16

Range of Intellectual Functioning	Full Scale		Verbal		Performance	
	Standard	Potential	Standard	Potential	Standard	Potential
Mentally retarded	5	0	7	0	5	0
Deficient	5	3	21	1	5	1
Borderline	34	3	32	19	16	5
Low average	31	28	29	29	25	8
Average	22	50	11	48	39	49
Above average	7	11	4	7	8	17
Superior	0	9	0	0	4	11
Very superior	0	0	0	0	2	13

(Score)

Analysis of the data revealed that more than 80% of the children showed evidence of cognitions related to memory, reasoning, and knowledge. They did grocery shopping, performed complex housekeeping tasks, repaired electrical appliances and automotive vehicles, and engaged in conversations with their siblings, peers, and adults that revealed a rich source of information and vocabulary. In short, on tasks of everyday cognitions, these children excelled—a finding for which there is substantial supportive evidence in the literature of both experimental and cultural psychology and anthropology (Cole, Gay, Glick, & Sharp, 1971; Lave, 1977; Rogoff and Waddell, 1982; Saxe, 1988; Serpell, 1979).

Other Intelligences Data

As described in Chapter 6, from our early informal conversations with parents and observations of children we speculated that children were far more cognitively proficient than what the IQ measure revealed. We surmised that if children did indeed possess other intellectual competencies, then elicitation of them may provide two useful functions: (a) boost the children's self-image as cognitively competent beings and (b) knowledge of their own competencies may serve as a motivational carrot to encourage them to engage in tasks in which their IQ-like competencies appeared to be less than optimally developed.

The Other Intelligences Inventory was administered to the parents, teachers, and the children themselves, who comprised the second sample (Table 9.5). The analysis of data revealed consistency of the reports from all three groups. Again, more than 80% of the children were reported to possess intermediate and advanced intellectual competencies in music, dramatization, dance, and other bodily-kinesthetic domains. Table 9.4 and 9.5 present a description of the background characteristics of the sample and a breakdown of the other intelligences findings.

Other Support for the Bioecological Assessment System

Psychologists in Training

Students in graduate programs in clinical and school psychology have used the bioecological assessment system as part of their pre-

Table 9.4 Background Characteristics of Children

	Cultural Background					Language				
Anglo	African American	Spanish	French	English	Other	Spanish/ French	English	Other	Spanish/ French	English	Other
23	3	14	0	3	7	11	24	0	4	47	0

Table 9.5 Performance on Other Intelligences Scale

Bodily Kinesthetic (n = 37)			Musical (n = 10)			Spatial (n = 4)		
Beginner	Intermediate	Advanced	Beginner	Intermediate	Advanced	Beginner	Intermediate	Advanced
4	18	15	2	3	5	2	2	0

paratory fieldwork experience in intellectual assessment. During initial training, some students had reservations about the use of the psychometric potential measure, admitting that they felt that they had "sinned" when they stepped away from standard procedures for the IQ administrations. Once they were fully trained with the entire system and saw the diagnostic and prescriptive power of the approach, however, they were more comfortable with the concept of "stepping away" from formal assessment of intelligence.

End of semester evaluations revealed that students felt more confident in their ability to conduct more culturally sensitive assessments and to appreciate the diagnostic and prescriptive utility of such an approach.

Psychologist-Practitioners

During the 1995 and 1996 academic year, we conducted a series of workshops on the Biocultural Assessment System for the New York City Board of Education for practitioner-psychologists at their regional offices in the five boroughs. An evaluation questionnaire was administered to each group following completion of the workshop. From a sample of 175 participants, more that 80% indicated the following:

- Their knowledge was broadened regarding the cognitive capabilities of students, particularly those with linguistically and ethnically diverse backgrounds.

- The assessment system had merit for writing the psychological report in a manner that included more diagnostic information about the child's cognitive functioning.

- They had a greater appreciation for qualitative information to complement the psychometric description of the child's cognitive functioning.

Many of them, however, expressed reservations that the assessment may have limited usefulness unless changes were made in policy guidelines for administration of standardized tests of intelligence.

Conclusion

The evidence to date is promising with respect to the development of the four-tier approach to assessing intelligence. The psychometric potential procedures have yielded consistent evidence of the Vygotskian zone of proximal development—that is, the difference in performance when the psychometric and psychometric potential procedures are used. The qualitative information acquired through the ecological taxonomy provided further confirmation for our notion that cognitions are shaped by experiences in particular cultural niches. It is not that some children do and others do not possess the cognitions tapped on traditional tests of intelligence, as IQ scores on the IQ measure suggest. Rather, to make this determination far greater diagnostic probing in multiple ecologies in which the child functions is required than is currently allowed in any standardized intelligence testing context. We were also encouraged by the findings from the Other Intelligence Inventory that suggest that, at least for some children, the experiences and the ecologies that sustain them seemed to have nurtured some cognitions and not others. As we indicate in Chapter 11, we are continuing to refine our procedures in an effort to generate stronger validity and standardizability for the assessment system. Currently, we are exploring the generalizability of our procedures with other commonly used psychometric measures of intelligence. We hope that in time we will have the kinds of empirical data that are both necessary and essential for the emerging biocultural perspective of intelligence that we espouse.

PART III

Training and Policy Implications of the Biocultural Assessment System

10

Training of
Mental Health Workers,
Educators, and Parents to
Enhance the Intellectual
Functioning of Children

Can Intelligence Be Taught?

Many avid supporters of IQ tests contend that IQ cannot be boosted (Herrnstein & Murray, 1994; Jensen, 1969). Over the years, however, a number of programs have mushroomed that are designed to increase intellectual skills. These programs are based on the assumption that intelligence is dynamic and mutable and as such can be enhanced through intervention strategies. The more notable programs in which significant gains were seen include Abel (1973),

Adams (1989), Armour-Thomas (1992), Budoff (1987b), Feuerstein's Instrumental Enrichment (1980), Herrnstein, Nickerson, de Sanchez, and Swets (1986), Kornhaber, Krechevsky, and Gardner (1990), Moyer (1986), Scarr and Ricciuti (1991), Sternberg (1985a, 1985b, 1986), Sternberg and Davidson (1989), Thompson and Hixson (1984), Whimbey (1975), and Whimbey and Lochhead (1982). A rather interesting conflict was noted in the works of Richard Herrnstein, coauthor of *The Bell Curve*, which generated much discussion and controversy. In 1986, Herrnstein et al. found that, after working with 400 Venezuelan seventh graders, "Cognitive skills can be enhanced by direct instruction" and that all of the researchers "came away with the strengthened belief in the possibility of teaching intellectual competence more directly than conventional school subjects do" (p. 1289). In his book on the Bell Curve (Herrnstein & Murray, 1994), however, no mention was made to his earlier findings with this cross-cultural population. In any event, we undoubtedly believe that a child's intelligence can be boosted through teaching and coaching, which can be accomplished through several significant groups of people—mental health workers, parents, and teachers.

Training for Psychologists

Assessment

In addition to the issues raised in Chapters 6, 7, and 8, psychologists in graduate training must receive two semesters of training in assessment; the first must provide exposure to psychometric tests such as the Wechsler scales and any other tests that the institution deems necessary. Thus, a prerequisite for training in the biocultural assessment model is a course on psychometric intellectual assessment. It is in the second semester of training in the assessment of intelligence that the biocultural assessment system should be introduced. It is important to remember that only after one has been taught the psychometric properties can one fully appreciate their limitations and when to "step away" from standardized procedures in assessment.

On the basis of experiences of the authors, training in the biocultural assessment system can take place in one semester. The following is an example of what was found to be most effective:

Lecture 1: This lecture provides a review of psychometric testing and an overview of the biocultural assessment system.

Lectures 2, 3, 4, and 5: These lectures provide an exploration of the second tier—psychometric potential assessment. Each component within this tier should be examined in one lecture. Time should be allotted for role play and case samples.

Lectures 6, 7, 8, and 9: These lectures provide an exploration of the third tier—ecological assessment. Each component within this tier should be examined in one lecture. Time should be allotted for role play and case samples.

Lectures 10 and 11: These lectures provide an exploration of the fourth tier—other intelligences. A lecture should be allotted for musical intelligence and for bodily kinesthetic intelligence.

Lectures 12, 13, and 14: These lectures discuss report writing, implications for classroom intervention, and so on. Case reports should be discussed as they apply to this model.

In addition, the curriculum should take on a more interdisciplinary approach, utilizing the contributions from related fields such as social work, psychiatry, and anthropology. Intradiscipline by way of exposure to cross-cultural issues in clinical, counseling, social, developmental, and educational psychology can be quite beneficial in cross-cultural training. Moreover, areas such as psycholinguistics, bilingual and multicultural education, cross-cultural theory, and cross-cultural assessment are all necessary requisites in developing this interdisciplinary competence. Ethical and legal issues in multicultural assessment, consultation, supervision, research, and so on should be infused in each course. Ridley (1985) suggested that every effort should be made to ferret out the principles that are universal in nature so that a basis for determining where cultural variability begins and cultural generalization ends would be established. Exposure to various cultural groups should afford students the opportunity to be part of a viable programmatic experience.

Further Training for Psychologists and Other Mental Health Workers

Treatment Intervention: Cognitive and Behavioral Therapy

Whimbey (1975) proposed a cognitive therapy approach to training intelligence whereby children could be trained in concept formation, classification, categorization, generalization, a graded series of block designs, analytic reasoning, sequential analysis, and sequential deduction. Tasks such as "if-then" reasoning in everyday situations could be explored. Teaching children to be reflective before responding, to use a sort of Socratic dialogue to encourage reflective thinking, and to foresee consequences is critical to the training of intelligence. Cause and effect reasoning stimulated through questions, such as "Why do we need to stay indoors if it is raining?" helped build sequential thinking skills.

Gains in the IQ score of children from the Milwaukee Project in Wisconsin were reported when their intelligences were trained via a three-part process—language development and expression, reading, and mathematics and problem solving. In general, these training techniques increased the children's IQ score between 9 and 15 points. Through lengthy Socratic discussions in an 8-week training program, Gopaul-McNicol and Armour-Thomas (1997b) offer suggestions to mental health workers to further advance the cognitive skills of children through exposing children to intelligence tests items. Whimbey (1975) referred to this as "teaching test-taking ability" and "teaching intelligence since the capacity to analyze problems in this way is exactly what intelligence is" (p. 61).

Training for Parents

Via the Portage Project, Shearer and Loftin (1984) propose a guide for teacher and community leaders on how to assist parents to teach their children to enhance their potential at home. Structured and informal activities for the parent and the child that are generalized to the community at large are offered. Sternberg (1986) offered several strategies for enhancing the memory of children, including categorical clusters whereby an individual is taught to group things by categories instead of trying to memorize in an unordered fashion. Interactive imagery is another technique to aid in memorizing objects or events. If the items cannot fit into a convenient category, Sternberg recommends generating the unrelated words in interactive images such as by the method of loci. Of course, remembering objects by forming acronyms by noting the first letter of each word and making an acronym can increase memory.

Whitehurst et al. (1991) found that severe language problems in children can be ameliorated with a home-based intervention that uses parents as therapists. Parents were given seven standard assignments on a biweekly basis that lasted about 30 minutes each. Role play and other behavioral interventions aided the children in increasing their expressive vocabulary, and this was generalized to other situations and maintained over time.

Rueda and Martinez (1992) proposed a "fiesta educativa" program whereby parents play an active role through community programs to address the needs of their learning disabled youngsters. Essentially, many Latino families worked in tandem to oversee the assessment process, the remedial services, and the overall mental health services. Educating the parents on their children's educational rights was a critical component of this program. Strom, Johnson, Strom, and Strom (1992a, 1992b) found that schools can better serve communities when opportunities for growth are provided to both parents and children. The main point is that Latino parents can help enhance their children's intellectual skills by encouraging their children to ask more questions and to experiment with problem solving in a more independent fashion. Allowing their children the freedom to engage in fantasy and play was also an important characteristic for enhancing intelligence. In general, it was found that children's divergent and convergent thinking, memory, and creative problem solving were increased by teaching these skills through a 4-week (each session lasting 2 hours) parent curriculum, which was as follows:

1. The first session focused on the folly of defining giftedness via a single criterion. Then a more comprehensive perspective (Gardner's multiple intelligences) was presented. Before the end of this session, par-

ents were taught how to identify their children's other intelligences, skills, and gifts.

2. The second session dealt with the kinds of activities that teachers can use in the classroom to enhance critical thinking. An individualized instructional plan for each child was shared with parents. Adequate time was allotted for questions and answers.

3. Session three allowed parents to identify their own strengths and to evaluate their ability to be tolerant of persistent and inopportune questions raised by their children and their ability to be supportive of their children engaging in conversation with adults.

4. Session four gave specific handouts to parents on how to continue enhancing their children's intellectual potential. Guidelines for follow-up sessions were given so parents could continue to be supportive to each other after the group had terminated through a type of steering committee.

We endorse programs such as that outlined previously. We propose, however, a longer training period for parents—an additional 4 more weeks during which parents are taught to enhance their children's intellectual skills by exposing them to tasks commensurate to the type of tasks found on IQ tests and then generalizing these skills to the classroom. Cultural transmission from the home to the school is essential for optimal functioning. Therefore, if the results reveal that a child has a particular concept in one way, but the school ecology needs it to be reflected in another, then it is incumbent on the parent and the school official to train that child to master the skill in the way the school desires. For instance, when a child can put a fan together and is unable to put pieces of a puzzle in a unified whole—tasks that are conceptually quite similar—then such a child can be directly taught through mediated learning experiences (Feuerstein, 1980; Lidz, 1991) how to transfer this knowledge from one context to another. Thus, children can be exposed to puzzles, blocks, and sequential types of tasks such as storytelling via pictures and games that have different and similar features to help nurture abstract thinking. Parents should be encouraged to teach their children to remember in a rote manner their timetables (as is done in the British educational system) so as to develop the ability to do computations mentally. Gopaul-McNicol and Armour-Thomas (1996) offer a step by step practical guide to parents, teachers, and community members on how best to nurture and enhance the intellectual abilities of children. Moreover, the *Guidelines for Providers to the Culturally Diverse* (American Psychological Association, 1993) offers culturally relevant suggestions for practice. More community visits during which contact is established with families, community leaders, and church representatives are critical in understanding the learning styles of children and in using these systems as support to aid in the best assessment practices of children. In general, the research supports that children can be trained to think creatively and enhance their intellectual potential if the appropriate intervention is put in place.

Training for Teachers

Teachers' implicit theories of children's intelligence help to shape the manner in which they respond to them in the classroom (Murrone & Gynther, 1991). We found that teachers were more demanding of children with above-average IQ scores as measured by standardized tests of intelligence. As such, teacher attitudes and perceptions of intelligence tests scores need to be changed through a reeducation process. Maker (1992, p. 32) emphasized that "Not only do standardized tests not predict success in nonacademic settings, but they also are poor predictors of success in school." Maker (1992) also found that the intelligences of children can be enhanced by teaching them Tangram activities (logical mathematical reasoning) in an enrichment program.

Riley, Morocco, Gordon, and Howard (1993) examined what it takes for complex ideas to become rooted in the daily instruction of teachers. Therefore, the authors explored how teachers could design their curriculum to include the needs and strengths of all students. They recommended analog experiences (writing and reading in different genre, conferencing, and role playing) to activate the children's higher cognitive abilities. They also recommended posing questions to children in a directive manner. Thus, children were always expected to develop their responses in a more elaborative type of response.

Armstrong (1994) expanded Gardner's (1993) multiple intelligences in the classroom and in so doing aided teachers in enhancing the varied skills of all children. The concern of proponents of the multiple intelligences theory is that "traditionally, schools have focused on students' analytic, mathematic, and linguistic intelligence which comprise a general intelligence as measured by the IQ test" (Murray, 1996, p. 46). Contrary to this psychometric school of thought, the other intelligences of children are being nurtured as a form of recognizing, respecting, nurturing, and enhancing the holistic intellectual potential of all children.

Authentic Teaching, Learning, and Assessment for All Students (ATLAS) is a comprehensive reform program that combines the work of four organizations: the Coalition of Essential Schools, the School Development Program, the Educational Development Center, and the Development Group of Project Zero. ATLAS emphasizes all the initiatives of these organizations—personalized learning environment, home-school collaboration, an active hands-on type of learning, and ongoing assessment through a curriculum-based approach that responds to the students' strengths.

Lee Katz (1991) spoke of the home-school connection. She spoke of scripts that we all acquire through our experiences and through various contexts. Many children are socialized in the home to a particular script and, when they enter the school setting, the script is different. Therefore, a child who was taught to be emotionally expressive in his or her adult-child interactions at home and then comes to the school, in which the interaction is emotionally cool, must be taught a new script. This is commonly the case with many African American children (Allen & Boykin, 1992), who were found to have more emotionally expressive experiences in their homes. The school psychologists, the teachers, and the special education prevention specialists can assist such children in understanding when one script is preferred over the other. In other words, the idea should not be to inform the child that his or her script is inferior but rather that in the school setting, he or she must recognize when to use which script. The child has to be taught the various scripts that he or she can use. This is analogous to a bilingual child who learns that in the classroom he or she speaks English but can engage his or her peers socially in his or her native language. If we are going to improve learning for all children, the teachers, parents, and significant others must work in a collaborative manner to bring the scripts from the home, the community, and the school closer together.

Adams (1989) offers a thinking skills curricula that first include ecologically valid materials, such as real-world experiences, followed by more abstract materials typically found on psychometric tests. *The Odyssey: A Curriculum for Thinking* (Adams, 1989) focused on the foundations of reasoning, understanding language, verbal reasoning, problem solving, decision making, and inventive thinking in a seven-part creative thinking program.

Armour-Thomas and Allen (1993) developed a cognitive training-intervention program based on Sternberg's triarchic theory of intelligence. The purpose of the program was to help teachers understand the nature of cognitions, in this instance, (a) Sternberg's (1986) meta-components, performance components and knowledge-acquisition components; (b) the function of these cognitive processes in student's learning; and (c) the importance of explicitness in the use of thinking processes in three major areas of teachers' work—instructional objectives, teacher-student interactions during instruction, and assessment.

Evaluation of the program revealed certain characteristics of teachers classified as high users of process: (a) There was a consistency in their high use of process in all three stages of teaching—the objectives for their students were process focused; (b) the interactions with students during instruction were also process-focused. The kinds of questions they asked and the quality of the feedback given to students demonstrated that not only did they model the process but also they encouraged student awareness and use of these processes; and (c) the emphasis on process was also apparent in the way they designed their assessment procedures—variation in the format, variation in the level of complexity of the tasks, and content equivalent to what students had learned in class.

A multidisciplinary approach to enhancing the performance of children has been touted as the new model of the millennium. Haynes and Comer (1993) recommend a theme concept approach to address the needs of children. At the Yale University Child Study Center, this team of professionals works closely with the home in a collaborative manner. This School Development Program is at the foundation of a holistic development perspective developed by James Comer, now known as the Comer Process for Reforming Education (Comer, Haynes, Joyner, & Ben-Avie, 1996). This model looks to the mental health team, the central organizing body in the school, to involve parents and teachers alike in a decision-making capacity to address the sociocultural needs of the child. This approach is one of collaboration rather than autocracy. Parents are selected by their fellow parents to represent their views on school planning. This indeed bridges the gap between the home and the school. We endorse all the previous initiatives and in particular we emphasize the importance of including people from the community in effecting these changes. We are increasingly mindful that the classroom is quite different from the context of the research lab, which is decontextualized and free from the ongoing activity of the typical classroom. Also, although teachers are trying to include a more dynamic approach to tutelage, they are also dealing with the increase in student diversity that is making teaching the most challenging vocation of our time. Enabling a high level of proficiency in cognitive competence in students will require much more than training in the use of process-based pedagogical strategies in planning, instruction, and assessment—the major areas of the teacher's work. In addition, teacher training programs need to provide experiences for teachers to

appreciate the cognitive strengths that children bring to the classroom;

think of cognitive weaknesses as experience specific and not as general person-specific deficits;

explore ways by which children's everyday cognitions could be applied to school tasks;

engage teachers in self-reflective practices in which they confront their beliefs about children whose cultural socialization may be different from theirs.

These experiences are likely to be rewarding to the extent that training programs

forge more meaningful collaborations with the home and community so as to more fully appreciate the other cultural niches in children's lives;

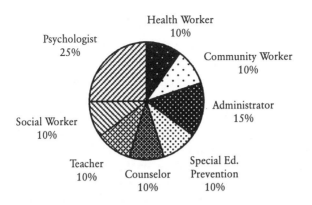

Figure 10.1. A Multisystem Interdisciplinary Model

ensure that teachers are supported with extra resources in the classroom so that they may more effectively apply information gathered from the biocultural assessment system.

As such, we recognize the need to share the responsibility in the schools. We envision the psychologist as playing a prominent role in linking all the disciplines in a multidisciplinary team approach as outlined in the following section.

Psychologists' New Role as Consultant to Parents, Teachers, and the Special Education Prevention Specialists

Currently, in the school and clinical systems there are many disciplines that function as multidisciplinary teams in that each discipline works almost as a separate unit and comes together primarily at Committee on Special Education meetings mainly to decide on placement for the child. We hope that the various disciplines can begin to see the need to be more interdisciplinary than multidisciplinary (Figure 10.1).

Our vision is that administrators such as psychologists can serve as leaders in the school and community systems to bring these various disciplines together and we hope that this will enhance the quality of education and, in particular, bring about a reduction in special education placement.

Thus, with more interdisciplinary training, psychologists can team up with health workers so that school officials will understand how health issues impede or enhance the child's functioning. Likewise, psychologists can work with all school administrators to see how their assessment findings can be used in a prescriptive manner to assist the teachers in the classroom. At this juncture, special education teachers will intervene as special education prevention specialists. Therefore, with the help of these three subdisciplines, children will learn to use all their strengths to work on their weaknesses. This should result in a reduction of special education placement.

Moreover, psychologists can work with the social workers and community resource people to develop a pool of resources outside of the school settings to best empower the child and his or her family.

If the family is involved in any sort of treatment by psychotherapists, psychologists, psychiatrists, and so on, the psychologists can serve as a liaison and can aid school personnel in understanding how the treatment program is enhancing or impeding the child's progress.

Finally, psychologists can work with guidance counselors and serve in consulting capacity—a sort of mediator between the school and vocational orgánizations outside of the school setting. This is to ensure that there is a connection between completion of high school and job or advanced educational opportunities.

For school psychology to survive with dignity, a multimodal, multisystems approach is needed to address the needs of people from varying ethnic and cultural backgrounds.

If such an interdisciplinary program is initiated, we envision this type of program becoming the model training program for the 21st century.

Example of an Interdisciplinary Training Program at the University Level

Johnson (1982, 1987, 1990) developed a two-part course that included theory, current research, and a laboratory experiential-type section.

Practica in all areas of their training should be available to ensure that all students receive hands-on training in assessing children, especially culturally and linguistically diverse children. To accomplish an innovative interdisciplinary training program, the following step-by-step guidelines are suggested:

1. A written academic policy emphasizing a clear statement of purpose and commitment to an interdisciplinary cultural diversity type of training as well as the consequences to the program if these policies are violated should be provided. Included in this statement must be definite quantifiable, tangible program objectives that must be achieved during a particular time frame.

2. Cultural and ethnic content should be infused in each course and not taught as a single course. Thus, when teaching psychological assessment, students should first be exposed to adherence of standardized procedures, and then they should be taught how to assess the cognitive potential of children via techniques such as Item Equivalency Assessment, Other Intelligences Assessment, Test-Teach-Retest Assessment, Ecological Assessment, and Suspending Time.

3. There should be a more aggressive recruitment of faculty members and students of various cultural backgrounds. Working with an ethnically diverse student and faculty body adds enrichment to the program because one can view issues from various perspectives.

4. Faculty members should be encouraged to update their interdisciplinary and cross-cultural expertise by attending continuing education courses, seminars, and so on. The university should give a reduction in faculty members' teaching load for 1 year to allow for this type of training.

5. A consultant or a full-time faculty member with interdisciplinary expertise should be available to consult with all faculty members to assist them in redesigning their curriculum to reflect a culturally diverse interdisciplinary content.

6. Funds should be set aside for a few research students to be assigned strictly to this interdisciplinary and cross-cultural thrust—building a resource file, assisting in student and faculty recruitment, linking with community people to recruit more ethnic minority practicum supervisors, coordinating experts of different cultural backgrounds to speak at colloquia, and so on.

7. For the first 2 years, an ongoing review of the program to ensure that the goals are being met should be done on a monthly basis at regular staff meetings. After 2 years of smooth functioning, it should be done on a quarterly basis, and after 5 years, an annual basis should suffice. Every faculty member should be required to sit in on these meetings.

8. Without all of the above in place and without financial support to fund all these innovative efforts, failure is most likely to occur. Because the ultimate goal of innovation should be institutionalization, hard-line financial endowments are needed (Ridley, 1985).

A biocultural interdisciplinary curriculum should therefore be multifaceted, consisting of a combination of assessment, review of the ethnic literature, personal involvement, and the development of a small classroom group project (Parker, Valley, & Geary, 1986). This approach utilizes the cognitive, affective, and behavioral domains. The students should first be assessed on their knowledge, attitudes, and perceptions of interdisciplinary and cross-cultural experiences as well as their comfort level in interacting with others from different ethnic and racial groups. This assessment process serves as a guide to the professor for future training.

Part 2 of the course involves the readings and discussions about the variability within majority and minority groups so that no one ethnic group will be stereotyped. Part 3 is very action oriented in that it involves behavioral activities geared to helping students increase biocultural assessment skills and cultural knowledge, sensitivity, and effectiveness. Students initially observe from a distance videotapes and so on and gradually move to participate directly. In the final stage, the students are expected to work on a small group activity in class. Such a project allows the students to become aware of their own stereotypical values and assumptions about intelligence and about other cultural and ethnic groups.

A true commitment to interdisciplinary and multicultural training requires at a minimum the implementation of all the previously discussed guidelines. If this program has only the bare skeleton of a commitment, then it creates no more than false generosity (Freire, 1970), dishonesty, and continued disrespect. The goal should be to produce competent psychologists capable of working with children from any linguistic, cultural, and ethnic background.

11

Implications for Future Research and Policy

It may be recalled that the biocultural assessment system was developed in response to our concern that standardized tests of intelligence provided an incomplete appraisal of children's cognitive functioning. Guided by the assumptions of our emerging biocultural theory, a number of cognitive enhancement procedures were used in conjunction with the traditional IQ measure—the Wechsler Intelligence Scale for Children-III (WISC-III)—to identify cognitive strengths and weaknesses of children. We are encouraged with the results, which demonstrate that improvements on intellectual tasks are to be expected when children are

allowed opportunity to contextualize words in sentences;

given time, paper, and pencil to solve verbal problems involving memory and quantitative reasoning;

given time and opportunity to understand and solve spatial problems involving memory, understanding, and reasoning.

In addition, we have observed that many children who perform poorly on standardized IQ tasks are able to demonstrate comparable skills in their everyday lives. Finally, we found that many children, including those with below-average performance on the IQ measure, possess other intellectual competencies at varying degrees of proficiency. Consideration of these results from a biocultural perspective would suggest that a standardized measure of intelligence is insufficiently sensitive to discriminate which cognitions are well formed from those that are still in an embryonic stage of development. Furthermore, such a measure tells us nothing about the prior experiences of children or the ecologies in which they grow and function and how these culturally specific experiences may have influenced the performance observed at the time of assessment. In contrast, the results from the other procedures, psychometric potential and other intelligences, were far more diagnostically useful in probing for both emerging cognitions and those that are already well formed but may be in need of further development. The observation that children who seem "unintelligent" in the testing environment but are cognitively adept in their homes and communities provided additional confirmation of our conception of intelligent behavior as culturally dependent cognitions.

These findings present some interesting challenges for researchers (Table 11.1) regarding the types of questions they may wish to consider regarding intelligence and its assessment as well as the kinds of research design and methodology that such questions would necessitate. We think, however, that the findings pose a more pressing challenge to those who set guidelines and standards for intelligence testing, particularly as these relate to nondiscriminatory practices for children from linguistically and ethnically diverse backgrounds (Table 11.2). This chapter gives an overview of some of these challenges.

Research Implications

IQ Studies

Through administration of the IQ measure, we were able to discern some diagnostic information regarding strengths and weak-

TABLE 11.1 Ideas for Future Research

Develop new theories to examine the relationship between cognitive processes and ecology.

Examine the validity of the current assessment measures that assess linguistically and culturally different children.

Explore the use of the biocultural approach to cognitive assessment with all children.

Train mental health workers to more accurately assess all children.

Design studies in ways that allow the interpretation of the differences found to be in line with the measures used. For example, the Other Intelligences Inventory was developed to address the concept of multiple intelligences.

More longitudinal studies are needed to address the cultural deprivation and biological inferiority positions that exist in traditional research.

Develop research that examines diagnosis as informing prescription not describing deficits—a more enhancement model.

TABLE 11.2 Main Policy Issues for the New Millennium

We need a clear policy regarding the principles and standards of intelligence testing beyond the standardized testing instruments. The challenge is to remove the paradigm from reliance on prediction to understanding prescription.

We need clarity of policy on the federal level. Currently, it is left up to the individual districts and states. Therefore, the American Psychological Association and National Association of School Psychologists should support such a policy because many decisions are made on children's lives that center around the IQ tests.

We need policies that provide clear standards for desirable competencies among practitioners, both psychologists-in-training and practicing psychologists and clinicians.

We need a clear policy regarding the more dynamic role that psychologists should play in guiding the teacher, parent, and other school staff in best serving all students.

We need to have a policy regarding the role of the special education prevention specialists, who can serve as mediators between the classroom and special education.

nesses in cognitive functioning as indicated in Chapter 9. It is quite likely, however, that far more educationally meaningful information may be derived from an IQ test than we were able to extract. Gordon (1977, 1995) offers the following step-by-step procedure for the analysis of test scores that may yield other diagnostically useful information:

1. Identify, through logical analysis, the dimensional or functional demands of selected standardized tests.

2. Determine the rationale utilized in the development of each of several tests to identify the conceptual categories for which items were written and in which item response consistencies might cluster empirically.

3. Determine the learning task demands represented by the items of selected tests and classify those demands into functional categories.

4. Appraise the extent to which selected tests provide adequate coverage of the typical learning task demands found in educational settings.

5. Utilize the categories produced by any or all of the previous strategies in the metric and nonmetric factorial analysis of test data to uncover empirical dimensions of test responses.

The intent of the first four tasks is to unbundle the cognitive competencies embedded in test items. The fifth step involves the actual analysis of performance data to reveal their factorial demand structure and to ascertain the extent to which they yield empirical evidence for those item clusters or require a reconceptualization of response processes. Assuming that there is congruence between the fifth task and the other four tasks, the resulting data may reveal diagnostic patterns that then become the basis for prescriptive instruction.

Other Intelligence Studies

We were able to identify consistently other intellectual competencies that children possessed in varying degrees of proficiency. If, as a society, we value these intelligences as adult end states, then it is important for research to seek a more informed understanding of the content and context of their development. For example, if musicians, mathematician, dancers, computer scientists, and aerospace engineers are valued by a society, then opportunities should be made available for the development of intellectual competencies related to the knowledge and skills related to these professions. The work of Gardner and Hatch (1989) in the Arts PROPEL and Project Spectrum demonstrates the kinds of experiences in multiple domains of knowledge that are likely to nurture the growth and development of spatial, linguistic, musical, and other intellectual competencies. Apprenticeships or mentoring relationships are other types of learning experiences in particular domains of knowledge (e.g. architecture, visual arts, and music) whereby emerging intelligences can be nurtured and developed. Schools, community organizations, and other institutions of a society, such as art, music, math, and science museums or galleries, provide a rich variation of tools, materials, and culturally meaningful information from which children can acquire and apply different forms of knowledge. Longitudinal studies could be designed that begin with the collection of baseline data on children's emerging intellectual competencies in cultural niches wherein certain types of experiences are valued and are made available by the community. Subsequently, at different periods in time, these person-environmental interactions could be assessed to better understand the nature and quality of change and continuity of the nascent intellectual competencies observed earlier.

Cognitive Enhancement Studies

We used a variety of strategies to elicit cognitive potential masked by the standardized IQ measure. To the extent that these competencies represent meaningful adult end states in a society—and they do in the U.S. culture—then every effort should be made to foster these malleable cognitions in the teaching and learning experiences both within and outside the classroom. We concur with the theoretical and empirical work of a number of researchers (e.g., Feuerstein, 1990; Feuerstein, Rand, & Hoffman, 1979; Gardner, 1983; Lave & Wenger, 1991; Sternberg, 1986; Vygotsky, 1978; Whimbey & Lockhead, 1982) regarding the trainability of intellectual skills. We think, however, that the design of cognitive enhancement studies should ensure that essential and sufficient opportunities are provided for transfer of cognitive competencies to other tasks and settings. The following suggestions are made for critical person-task-context conditions if intervention effects are to be expected:

1. There must be opportunity to acquire and use knowledge and cognitive skills in the preferred symbol system of the cultural group.
2. There must be opportunity for the social mediation (direct and indirect) of acquisition of knowledge and cognitive skills within the selected symbolic system of the cultural group.
3. There must be opportunity for independent practice of knowledge and cognitive skills within the symbol system in which the initial knowledge and cognitive skills were acquired.
4. There must be opportunity for social mediation (direct and indirect) in the application of previously acquired knowledge and skills in relatively new and more complex tasks represented through a familiar symbol system.
5. There must be opportunity for independent use of previously acquired knowledge and cognitive skills in relatively new and cognitively more complex tasks represented in a familiar symbol system.
6. There must be opportunity for social mediation (direct and indirect) in the application of previously acquired knowledge and skills in relatively new and progressively more complex cognitive tasks represented in an unfamiliar symbol system.
7. There must be opportunity for independent practice of previously acquired knowledge and cognitive skills in relatively new and progressively more complex cognitive tasks represented in an unfamiliar symbolic system.

These recommendations assume that generalizability of learning from one context to another is contingent on careful manipulation of the person-task-context variables and is consistent, for the most part, with the strategies identified in the cognitive science literature (e.g., Anderson, Reder, & Simon, 1996).

Perhaps, as important, intervention studies should be longitudinal in design to allow sufficient time for reinforcement and generalizability of effects to other contexts. It may well be that Head Start and other intervention studies for improving intelligence showed little enduring results due to the brevity of the treatment. During the course of development of some children, threatening person-environment interactions may far outweigh the sustaining person-environment ones. To offset the negative impact of the former, longer and more enriching interventions are likely to produce more lasting cognitive change. As Horowitz and O'Brien (1989) noted,

Development is not a disease to be treated. It is a process that needs constant nurturance. There is no reason to expect that an intensive program of early stimulation is an inoculation against all further developmental problems. No one would predict that a child given an adequate amount of vitamin C at 2 years of age will not have vitamin C deficiency at 10 years of age. Currently, according to the most viable models of development that apply to both at-risk and normal children, developmentally, functional stimulation is desirable at every period of development and not only in early years. (p. 444)

Ecology Studies

The prescriptive utility of our findings, particularly as they relate to schooling, was identified in Chapter 9. These interventions, if explored, are unlikely to lead to enduring results unless sustaining conditions and forces are operating within ecologies beyond the school in which children grow and function. More than 30 years ago, Coleman et al. (1966) called attention to relative influence of schooling on the cognitive outcomes of children by stating the following:

The school brings little influence to bear on a child's achievement that is independent of his background and general social context; and that this very lack of an independent effect means that the inequalities imposed on children by their home, neighborhood, and peer environment are carried along to become the inequalities which control life at the end of school. For equality of educational opportunity through the school to be effective, one must imply a strong effect of schools that is independent of the child's immediate social environment, and that strong independent effect is not present in American schools. (p. 325)

We know from previous research that socialization practices of the peer group (e.g., Steinberg, Dornbusch, & Brown, 1992) and the home (e.g., Allen & Boykin, 1991) both directly and indirectly influence children's behavior in school. This would suggest that researchers seeking to understand the impact of in-school cognitive intervention programs should simultaneously examine the nature and quality of experiences in the primary ecologies in which children function (e.g., the home and the peer group). In other words, the researcher needs to determine whether sustaining or threatening person-environments interactions or both operating outside the school are likely to reinforce or weaken the effects of the in-school intervention program. It is hoped that the use of such a methodology would minimize a common knee-jerk interpretation in terms of biologically constrained cognitive abilities for the nonsignificant or short-lived effects of many cognitive enhancement programs.

Personal Characteristics Studies

Although our sample came from diverse linguistic, ethnic, and racial backgrounds in the United States, further research is needed on the generalizability of the biocultural approach to intelligence testing to societies beyond the culture of the United States. Also, in generating the data we did not control for individual or groups with contrasting characteristics (e.g., race, gender, ethnicity, or socioeconomic status) because that was not the focus of our work as was explained in Chapter 10. We know from previous research, however, that demographic characteristics (Boykin & Toms, 1985; Gaines & Reed, 1995; Gordon, Marin, & Marin, 1991; Ogbu, 1986; Phinney, 1996; Sue, 1991) and response tendencies (Boykin, 1979; Gordon, 1988; Hale-Benson, 1986; Hilliard, 1992; Shade, 1982) play a crucial role in cognitive behavior. Indeed, we suspect that these person characteristics render some individuals resilient or vulnerable toward environmental encounters and stimuli and as such should be carefully considered in any interpretation of differences in observed cognitive performance. Thus, researchers investigating differences in intelligent behavior should describe samples at a sufficient level of detail so as to better understand the relative contributions of person characteristics in the observed differences in performance.

Instrument Refinement and Development

Through the application of our psychometric potential techniques, ecological taxonomy, and other intelligence measures, we are confident in our findings that there is more to intelligence than the traditional IQ test measures. As we gain a more informed understanding and appreciation of cognitions developed through person-environment interactions in multiple cultural niches in which children develop and function, however, we need to ensure that our measures are ecologically valid as well. Currently, we are refining some of the measures in the Other Intelligence Inventory and expanding the ecological taxonomy to include observational procedures of other intelligences.

Policy Implications

Over the years, professional organizations, such as the American Psychological Association and the National Council of Measurement in Education, have reflected concerns regarding discriminatory practices in intelligence testing through their bylaws, ethical principles, and standards. These noble sentiments, however, seemed to have had minimal impact on the construction of standardized tests or their practice. As indicated in Chapter 6, interpretation and use of test results have been particularly inimical to ethnic and linguistic children, particularly those from low-income backgrounds. It is as if test developers and practitioners have been oblivious to the theoretical and empirical research regarding the situatedness of cognition during the past two decades or to the influence of linguistic and cultural diversity in intelligent behavior. Even more disheartening, however, they seem unaware of the devastating consequences of their judgments that place large numbers of children on educational paths that are neither enabling nor worth wanting. Indeed, the literature is replete with inequitable schooling of children placed in low-track classes or in unwarranted special educational programs (e.g., Kozol, 1991; Lipsky & Gartner, 1996; Oakes, 1990; Skrtic, 1991). Perhaps, a list of principles and standards, no matter how well intentioned, is insufficient insurance against discriminatory practice in standardized intellectual testing. What is needed, in our judgment, is greater democratic reciprocity in discussions among practitioners, test developers, and client representatives in the development of principles and standards setting with respect to intellectual assessment practices. Equally important is the need for enforceable principles that are truly reflective of our commitment to equity and cultural pluralism. Though not exhaustive, in the following sections we submit recommendations for consideration.

Principles Development and Standards Setting

Professional organizations in psychology and education, through their principles and standards, have provided ethical guidelines for practitioners. It is not always clear, however, that the terms of conversation as well as the content of deliberations genuinely reflect the views of parents and community stakeholders who have had firsthand evidence of the deleterious effects of standardized testing of intelligence. Also not clear is whether the principles and standards emerged from the kinds of discourse that Moon (1993), Boyd (1996), and Rawls (1993) identify as critical for the commitment to the principle of cultural pluralism. In other words, have participants engaged in discussions of reasonable pluralism about incompatible conceptions of the human good or ideals of excellence or the dilemma of cultural relativism and universal ethical principles?

These and other questions are the kinds of uncomfortable moral challenges that, in our judgment, should form the agenda for policy-makers if the hidden ugliness of multiculturalism is to be truly unmasked. We submit for consideration the following questions:

Is there representation of diverse epistomologies at the discussion table?

Do the terms of conversation allow for genuine and open discussions of culturalism, pluralism, and universal ethical principles?

Are the principles and standards essentially and sufficiently accommodating of multiple cultural perspectives?

Are the principles and standards supportive of multiple expressions of intelligent behavior?

Are the principles and standards supportive of the assessment of cognitive potential?

Are the principles and standards supportive of evidence of intelligence beyond the standardized testing context?

Is there a mechanism for principles and standards revision or modification?

Do the principles and standards provide clear implications for desirable competencies among practitioners, both psychologists-in-training and practicing psychologists and clinicians?

Do these competencies include skill in intellectual assessment within and outside the standardized testing context?

Do these competencies include skill in assessment of cognitive potential?

Do these competencies include skill in report writing that includes both quantitative and qualitative evidence of intellectual functioning?

Are there mechanisms for the incorporation of these competencies in accreditation criteria?

Principles Enforcement Strategies

Most psychologist-in-training programs have vision and goal statements that describe a commitment to the principles of cultural diversity. In addition, such programs can identify courses with cultural diversity topics and reading lists dealing with the topic. To ensure that the principles and standards as enunciated by the professional organizations are operationalized in practice, however, satisfactory answers should be sought for the following questions by accreditation teams when they visit training programs:

1. Do the end-of-training competencies include concrete evidence of understandings of diverse epistomologies or worldviews?

    appreciation and genuine respect for cultural pluralism?

    culturally sensitive strategies used in assessment?

    skill in gathering data on intellectual functioning within and beyond the testing context?

    skill in analyzing quantitative and qualitative data from assessment?

    skill in writing psychological reports with diagnostic and prescriptive utility?

2. Do courses on intelligence and its assessment explicitly indicate theoretical assumptions about intelligence?

    limitations of standardized tests of intelligence in terms of culturally compatible fallacies?

3. Do supervisors have demonstrable competencies commensurate with those of the end-of-training competencies of the psychologist-in-training?

Conclusion

The biocultural assessment system has greater diagnostic and prescriptive utility than any single standardized measure of intelligence. The data are highly relevant and useful for instructional purposes both within and outside the classroom. It has yielded information from which testable research hypotheses could be made regarding the cultural dependency of human cognition in terms of both its development and its teachability. The early promise of these findings, however, is likely to be ignored or dismissed as have those of other researchers before us unless all those connected to the intelligence testing movement do more than pay lip service to the country's commitment to equality and cultural pluralism. As the new millennium approaches, the question is clear: Are we, the community of custodians of the nation's children, ready and able to provide equitable educational opportunities through culturally responsive assessments or will we, like other generations of custodians before us, shirk our responsibility to do right by those entrusted in our care for service? It may be helpful to remember that the calling of stewardship requires neither scientific evidence nor protective policies as a prerequisite to action but only the moral impulse to do right, especially by those most vulnerable and placed at risk in our society. We are optimistic that the nobler and gentler side of this generation's community of custodians will emerge and that greater efforts will be made to provide education that is both enabling and worth wanting for more of the nation's children.

References

Abel, T. M. (1973). *Psychological testing in cultural contexts*. New Haven, CT: College & University Press.

Adams, M. J. (1989). Thinking skills curricula: Their promise and progress. *Educational Psychologist, 24*(1), 25-75.

Allen, B., & Boykin, A. W. (1991). The influence of contextual factors on black and white children's performance. Effects of movement opportunity and music. *International Journal of Psychology, 26*, 373-387.

Allen, B. A., & Boykin, A. W. (1992). Children and the educational process: Alienating cultural discontinuity through prescriptive pedagogy. *School Psychology Review, 21*(4), 586-596.

American Psychological Association. (1993). Guidelines for providers of psychological services to the ethnic, linguistic and culturally diverse populations. *American Psychologists, 48*, 45-48.

Anastasi, A. (1988). *Psychological testing* (6th ed.). New York: Macmillan.

Anderson, J. R., Reder, L. M., & Simon, H. A. (1996). Situated learning and education. *Educational Researcher, 25*(4), 5-11.

Apple, M. (1979). *Ideology and curriculum*. London: Routledge & Kegan Paul.

Armour-Thomas, E. (1992a). Assessment in the service of thinking and learning for low achieving students. *High School Journal, 75*(2), 99-118.

Armour-Thomas, E. (1992b). Intellectual assessment of children from culturally diverse backgrounds. *School Psychology Review, 21*(4), 552-565.

Armour-Thomas, E., & Allen, B. (1993). The feasibility of an information-processing methodology for the assessment of vocabulary competence. *Journal of Instructional Psychology, 20*(4), 306-313.

Armour-Thomas, E., & Gopaul-McNicol, S. (1997a). The bioecological approach to cognitive assessment. *Cultural Diversity and Mental Health, 3*(2), 131-144.

Armour-Thomas, E., & Gopaul-McNicol, S. (1997b). In search of correlates of learning underlying "learning disability" using a bioecological assessment system. *Journal of Social Distress and the Homeless, 6*(2), 143-159.

Armstrong, T. (1994). *Multiple intelligences in the classroom.* Alexandria, VA: Association for Supervision and Curriculum Development.

Artzt, A. F., & Armour-Thomas, E. (1992). Development of a cognitive-metacognitive framework for protocol analysis of mathematical problem solving in small groups. *Cognition and Instruction, 9,* 137-175.

Asante, M. K. (1988). *Afrocentricity.* Trenton, NJ: Africa World Press.

Banks, W. C., McQuater, V., & Hubbard, J. L. (1979). Toward a reconceptualization of the social-cognitive bases of achievement orientation in blacks. In A. W. Boykin, A. J. Franklin, & J. F. Yates (Eds.), *Research directions of black psychologists* (pp. 294-311). New York: Russell Sage.

Baron, J. (1981). Reflective thinking as a goal of education. *Intelligence, 5,* 291-309.

Baron, J. (1982). Personality and intelligence. In R. J. Sternberg (Ed.), *Handbook of human intelligence.* New York: Cambridge University Press.

Beker, J., & Feuerstein, R. (1990). Conceptual foundations of the modifying environment in group care and treatment settings for children and youth. *Journal of Child and Youth Care, 4*(5), 23-33.

Berry, J. (1976). *Human ecology and cognitive style.* New York: John Wiley.

Betancourt, H., & Lopez, S. R. (1993). The study of culture, ethnicity, and race in American psychology. *American Psychologist, 48*(6), 629-637.

Binet, A., & Simon, T. (1905). Méthodes nouvelles pour le diagnostic du niveau intellectuel des anormaux. [New methods for diagnosing the intellectual level of abnormals]. *Année Psychologique, 11,* 191-336.

Bouchard, T. J., Jr., Lykken, D. T., McGue, M. L., Segal, N. L., & Tellegen, A. (1990). Sources of human psychological differences: The Minnesota study of twins reared apart. *Science, 250,* 223-228.

Boyd, D. (1996). Dominance concealed through diversity: Implications of inadequate perspectives on cultural pluralism. *Harvard Educational Review, 66*(3), 609-630.

Boykin, A. W. (1977). On the role of context in the standardized test performance of minority group children. *Cornell Journal of Social Relations, 12,* 109-124.

Boykin, A. W. (1979). Black psychology and the research process: Keeping the baby but throwing out the bathwater. In A. W. Boykin, A. J. Franklin,

& J. P. Yates (Eds.), *Research directions of black psychologists*. New York: Russell Sage.

Boykin, A. W. (1982). Task variability and the performance of black and white schoolchildren. *Journal of Black Studies, 12,* 469-485.

Boykin, A. W. (1983). The academic performance of Afro-American children. In J. T. Spence (Ed.), *Achievement and achievement motives* (pp. 322-371). San Francisco: Freeman.

Boykin, A. W. (1986). The triple quandary and the schooling of Afro-American children. In U. Neisser (Ed.), *The school achievement of minority children* (pp. 57-92). Hillsdale, NJ: Lawrence Erlbaum.

Boykin, A. W., & Allen, B. A. (1988). Rhythmic movement facilitation of learning in working-class Afro-American children. *Journal of Genetic Psychology, 149,* 335-348.

Boykin, A. W., DeBritto, A., & Davis, L. (1984). *The influence of social process factors and contextual variability on school children's task performance.* Unpublished manuscript, Howard University, Washington, DC.

Boykin, A. W., & Toms, F. (1985). Black child socialization: A conceptual framework. In H. McAdoo & J. McAdoo (Eds.), *Black children: Social, educational, and parental environments* (pp. 32-51). Beverly Hills, CA: Sage.

Bradley, R. H., and Caldwell, B. M. (1984). The relation of infants' home environments to achievement test performance in first grade: A follow-up study. *Child Development, 52,* 708-710.

Bronfenbrenner, U. (1979). *Toward the ecology of human development.* Cambridge, MA: Harvard University Press.

Bronfenbrenner, U. (1993). The ecology of cognitive development: Research models and fugitive findings. In R. H. Wozniak & K. W. Fischer (Eds.), *Development in context: Acting and thinking in specific environments* (The Jean Piaget Symposium Series, pp. 3-44). Hillsdale, NJ: Lawrence Erlbaum.

Bronfenbrenner, U. (1989). Ecological systems theory. In R. Vasta (Ed.), *Annals of Child Development Research, 6,* 185-246.

Brown, A. L. (1978). Knowing when, where, and how to remember: A problem of metacognition. In R. Glaser (Ed.), *Advances in instructional psychology* (Vol. 1, pp. 77-165). Hillsdale, NJ: Lawrence Erlbaum.

Budoff, M. (1987a). The validity of learning potential assessment. In C. S. Lidz (Ed.), *Dynamic assessment: An international approach to evaluating learning potential.* New York: Guilford.

Budoff, M. (1987b). Measures for assessing learning potential. In C. S. Lidz (Ed.), *Dynamic assessment: An interactional approach to evaluating learning potential.* New York: Guilford.

Butcher, J. N. (1982). Cross-cultural research methods in clinical psychology. In P. C. Kendall & J. N. Butcher (Eds.), *Handbook of research methods in clinical psychology* (pp. 273-308). New York: John Wiley.

Carlson, J. S. (1985). The issue of g: Some relevant questions. *The Behavioral and Brain Science, 8*(2), 224-225.

Carraher, T. N., Carraher, D., & Schliemann, A. D. (1985). Mathematics in the streets and in schools. *British Journal of Development Psychology, 3*, 21-29.

Carroll, J. B. (1993). *Human cognitive abilities: A survey of factor-analytic studies.* New York: Cambridge University Press.

Case, R. (1985). *Intellectual development: Birth to adulthood.* Orlando, FL: Academic Press.

Cattell, R. B. (1941). Some theoretical issues in adult intelligence testing. *Psychological Bulletin, 38,* 592.

Cattell, R. B. (1943). The measurement of adult intelligence. *Psychological Bulletin, 40,* 153-193.

Cattell, R. B., & Horn, J. L. (1978). A check on the theory of fluid and crystallized intelligence with description of new subtest designs. *Journal of Educational Measurement, 15,* 139-164.

Ceci, S. J. (1990). *On intelligence . . . more or less: A bioecological treatise on intellectual development.* Englewood Cliffs, NJ: Prentice Hall.

Ceci, S. J., Baker, J., & Bronfenbrenner, U. (1987). *The acquisition of simple and complex algorithms as a function of context.* Unpublished manuscript, Cornell University, Ithaca, NY.

Ceci, S. J., & Bronfenbrenner, U. (1985). Don't forget to take the cupcakes out of the oven: Strategic time-monitoring, prospective memory, and context. *Child Development, 56,* 175-190.

Ceci, S. J., & Cornelius, S. (1989, April 29). *Psychological perspectives on intellectual development.* Paper presented at the biennial meeting of the Society for Research in Child Development, Kansas City, MO.

Ceci, S. J., & Liker, J. (1986a). A day at the races: A study of IQ, expertise, and cognitive complexity. *Journal of Experimental Psychology: General, 115,* 225-266.

Ceci, S. J., & Liker, J. (1986b). Academic and non-academic intelligence: An experimental separation. In R. J. Sternberg & R. K. Wagner (Eds.), *Practical intelligence: Origins of competence in the everyday world.* New York: Cambridge University Press.

Ceci, S. J., & Liker, J. (1988). Stalking the IQ-expertise relationship: When the critics go fishing. *Journal of Experimental Psychology: Human Learning and Memory, 6,* 785-797.

Chi, M. T. H. (1978). Knowledge structures and memory development. In R. S. Siegler (Ed.), *Children's thinking: What develops?* Hillsdale, NJ: Lawrence Erlbaum.

Chi, M. T. H., & Ceci, S. J. (1987). Content knowledge: Its restructuring with memory development. *Advances in Child Development and Behavior, 20,* 91-146.

Cohen, R. (1969). Conceptual styles, culture conflict, and non-verbal tests of intelligence. *American Anthropologist, 71*(5), 828-857.

Cole, M. (1988). Cross-cultural research in the sociohistorical tradition. *Human Development, 31,* 137-152.

Cole, M., Gay, J., Glick, J. A., & Sharp, D. W. (1971). *The cultural context of learning and thinking*. New York: Basic Books.

Cole, M., & Scribner, S. (1977). Cross-cultural studies of memory and cognition. In R. V. Kail & J. W. Hagen (Eds.), *Perspectives on the development of memory and cognition*. Hillsdale, NJ: Lawrence Erlbaum.

Cole, M., Sharp, D. W., & Lave, C. (1976). The cognitive consequences of education. *Urban Review, 9*, 218-233.

Coleman, J. S., Campbell, E. Q., Hobson, C. J., McPartland, J., Mood, J., Winfield, F. D., & Work, R. L. (1966). *Equality of educational opportunity* (No. OE 38001). Washington, DC: U.S. Office of Education.

Comer, J., Haynes, N., Joyner, E., & Ben-Avie, B. (1996). *Rallying the whole village: The Comer process for reforming education*. New York: Columbia University Press, Teachers College.

Cummins, J. (1984). *Bilingualism and special education: Issues in assessment and pedagogy*. San Diego: College Hill.

Cummins, J. (1991). *Bilingualism and special education: Issues in assessment and pedagogy*. San Diego: College Hill Press.

Das, J. P. (1985). Interpretations for a class on minority assessment. *The Behavioral and Brain Science, 8*(2), 228-229.

De Avila, E. (1974, November/December). The testing of minority children— A neo Piagetian approach. *Today's Education*, pp. 72-75.

Detterman, D. K. (1985). Review of Wechsler Intelligence Scale of Children— Revised. In J. V. Mitchell (Ed.), *The ninth mental measurement yearbook* (Vol. 2, pp. 1715-1716). Lincoln, NE: Buros Institute of Mental Measurements.

DeVos, G. A. (1984, April). *Ethnic persistence and role degradation: An illustration from Japan*. Paper presented for the American-Soviet Symposium on Contemporary Ethnic Processes in the U.S.A. and the U.S.S.R., New Orleans, LA.

Dunn, R., & Dunn, K. (1978). *Teaching students through their own behavioral teaching style*. Reston, VA: Prentice Hall.

Eberhardt, J. L., & Randall, J. L. (1997). The essential notion of race. *American Psychological Society, 8*(3), 198-203.

Esquivel, G. (1985). Best practices in the assessment of limited English proficient and bilingual children. In A. Thomas & J. Grimes (Eds.), *Best practices in school psychology I* (pp. 113-123). Washington, DC: National Association of School Psychologist.

Eysenck, H. J. (1982). Introduction. In H. J. Eysenck (Ed.), *A model for intelligence*. Berlin: Springer-Verlag.

Eysenck, H. J. (1986). Inspection time and intelligence: A historical introduction. *Personality and Individual Differences, 7*, 603-607.

Eysenck, H. J. (1988). The biological basis of intelligence. In S. H. Irvine & J. W. Berry (Eds.), *Human abilities in cultural context* (pp. 87-104). New York: Cambridge University Press.

Farnham-Diggory, S. (1970). Cognitive synthesis in Negro and white children. *Monograph of the Society for Research in Child Development, 35*(2), Serial No. 135.

Feuerstein, R. (1979). *The dynamic assessment of retarded performers.* Baltimore, MD: University Park Press.

Feuerstein, R. (1980). *Instrumental enrichment: An intervention program for cognitive modifiability.* Baltimore, MD: University Park Press.

Feuerstein, R. (1990). The theory of structural cognitive modifiability. In B. Z. Presseisen (Ed.), *Learning and thinking styles: Classroom interaction* (pp. 68-134). Washington, DC: National Education Association.

Feuerstein, R., Hoffman, M., Rand, Y., Jensen, M., Morgans, R. J., Tzuriel, D., & Hoffman, D. (1986b). Learning to learn: Mediated learning experiences and instrumental enrichment. *Special Services in the Schools, 3*(1-2), 49-82.

Feuerstein, R., Rand, Y., & Hoffman, M. B. (1979). *The dynamic assessment of retarded performers: The learning potential assessment device, theory, instruments, and techniques.* Glenview, IL: Scott, Foresman.

Feuerstein, R., Rand, Y., Hoffman, M. B., & Miller, R. (1980). *Instrumental enrichment: An intervention program for cognitive modifiability.* Baltimore, MD: University Park Press.

Feuerstein, R., Rand, Y., Jensen, M., Kaniel, S., Tzuriel, D., Ben Shachar, N., & Mintzker, Y. (1986a). Learning potential assessment. *Special Services in the Schools, 3*(1-2), 85-106.

Figueroa, R. A. (1990). Best practices in the assessment of bilingual children. In A. Thomas & J. Grimes (Eds.), *Best practices in school psychology II* (pp. 93-106). Washington, DC: National Association of School Psychologists.

Franzbach, M. (1965). *Lessings Huarte-Uebersetzung (1752): Die Rezeption und Wirkungsgeschichte des "Examen de Ingenios para las Ciencia" (1575) in Deutschland* [Lessing's translation (1752) of Huarte: History of the reception and impact of "Examen de Ingenios para las Ciencias" (1575) in Germany]. Hamburgz: Cram, de Gruyter.

Freire, P. (1970). *Pedagogy of the oppressed.* New York: Seabury.

French, J., & Hale, R. (1990). A history of the development of psychological and educational testing. In C. R. Reynolds & R. W. Kamphaus (Eds.), *Handbook of psychological and educational assessment of children's intelligence and achievement* (pp. 3-28). New York: Guilford.

Gaines, S., Jr., & Reed, E. (1995). Prejudice from Allport to DuBois. *American Psychologist, 50*(3), 103.

Galton, F. (1869). *Hereditary genius: An enquiry into its laws and consequences.* London: Collins.

Galton, F. (1883). *Inquiry into human faculty and its development.* London: Macmillan.

Gardner, H. (1983). *Frames of mind: The theory of multiple intelligences.* New York: Basic Books.

Gardner, H. (1989). Zero-based arts education: An introduction to Arts PROPEL. *Studies in Art Education, 30,* 71-83.

Gardner, H. (1993). *Multiple intelligences.* New York: Basic Books.

Gardner, H., & Hatch, T. (1989). Multiple intelligences go to school: Educational implications of the theory of multiple intelligences. *Educational Researcher, 18*(8), 4-10.

Gardner, H., Howard, V., & Perkins, D. (1974). Symbol systems: A philosophical, psychological and educational investigation. In D. Olson (Ed.), *Media and symbols* (pp. 37-55). Chicago: University of Chicago Press.

Gardner, H., & Wolf, D. (1983). Waves and streams of symbolization. In D. R. Rogers & J. A. Sloboda (Eds.), *The acquisition of symbolic skills* (pp. 19-42). London: Plenum.

Gauvain, M. (1995). Thinking in niches: Sociocultural influences on cognitive development. *Human Development, 38,* 25-45.

Gauvain, M., & Rogoff, B. (1989). Ways of speaking about space: The development of children's skill at communicating spatial knowledge. *Cognitive Development, 4,* 295-307.

Gay, J., & Cole, M. (1967). *The new mathematics and an old culture.* New York: Holt, Rinehart & Winston.

Geertz, C. (1973). *Interpretation of cultures.* New York: Basic Books.

Gladwin, H. (1971). *East is a big bird.* Cambridge, MA: Harvard University Press.

Glaser, R. (1977). *Adaptive education: Individual diversity and learning.* New York: Holt, Rinehart & Winston.

Glutting, J., & McDermott, P. (1990). Principles and problems in learning potential. In C. R. Reynolds & R. W. Kamphaus (Eds.), *Handbook of psychological and educational assessment of children's intelligence and achievement* (pp. 296-347). New York: Guilford.

Goodnow, J. J. (1976). The nature of intelligent behavior: Questions raised by cross-cultural studies. In L. B. Resnick (Ed.), *The nature of intelligence.* Hillsdale, NJ: Lawrence Erlbaum.

Goodnow, J. J. (1990). The socialization of cognition: What's involved? In J. W. Stigler, R. A. Shweder, & G. Herdt (Eds.), *Cultural psychology* (pp. 259-286). Cambridge, UK: Cambridge University Press.

Gopaul-McNicol, S. (1992a). Understanding and meeting the psychological and educational needs of African American and Spanish speaking students. *School Psychology Review, 21*(4), 529-531.

Gopaul-McNicol, S. (1992b). Implications for school psychologists: Synthesis of the miniseries. *School Psychology Review, 21*(4), 597-600.

Gopaul-McNicol, S. (1993). *Working with West Indian families.* New York: Guilford.]

Gopaul-McNicol, S., & Armour-Thomas, E. (1996, February). *A practical guide for enhancing the intellectual potential of children: A biocultural perspective.* Presented at the annual professional development workshops for school psychologists: New York City Board of Education: Brooklyn.

Gopaul-McNicol, S., & Armour-Thomas, E. (1997a). A bioecological case study: A Caribbean child. *Cultural Diversity and Mental Health, 3*(2), 145-151.

Gopaul-McNicol, S., & Armour-Thomas, E. (1997b). The role of bioecological assessment system in writing a culturally sensitive report: The importance of assessing other intelligences. *Journal of Social Distress and the Homeless, 6*(2), 129-141.

Gopaul-McNicol, S., Elizalde-Utnick, G., Nahari, S., & Louden, D. (1998). *A test review guide for bilingual children: Cognitive assessment.* New York: National Nursing League.

Gordon, E. W. (1977). Diverse human populations and problems in educational program evaluation via achievement testing. In M. J. Wargo & D. R. Green (Eds.), *Achievement testing of disadvantaged and minority students for educational program evaluation* (pp. 29-40). New York: CTB/McGraw-Hill.

Gordon, E. W. (1988). *Human diversity and pedagogy.* New Haven, CT: Yale University, Institute for Social and Policy Studies.

Gordon, E. W. (1991). Human diversity and pluralism. *Educational Psychologist, 26,* 99-108.

Gordon, E. W. (1995). Toward an equitable system of educational assessment. *Journal of Negro Education, 64*(3), 360-372.

Gordon, E. W., & Armour-Thomas, E. (1991). Culture and cognitive development. In L. Okagaki & R. J. Sternberg (Eds.), *Directors and development: Influences on the development of children's thinking.* Hillsdale, NJ: Lawrence Erlbaum.

Gordon, E. W., & Bonilla-Bowman, C. (1994). Equity and social justice in educational achievement. In R. Berne & L. O. Picus (Eds.), *Outcome equity in education.* Thousand Oaks, CA: Corwin Press.

Gordon, E. W., Miller, F., & Rollock, D. (1990). Coping with communicentric bias in knowledge production in the social sciences. *Educational Researcher, 19*(3), 14-19.

Gordon, E. W., & Shipman, S. (1979). Human diversity, pedagogy and educational equity. *American Psychologist, 34*(1), 1030-1036.

Gordon, E. W., & Terrell, M. (1981). The changed social context of testing. *American Psychologist, 36,* 1167-1171.

Gordon, R. A., & Rudert, E. E. (1979). Bad news concerning IQ tests. *Sociology of Education, 52,* 174-190.

Greenfield, P. M. (1974). Comparing dimensional categorization in natural and artificial contexts: A developmental study among the Zenacantecos of Mexico. *Journal of Social Psychology, 93,* 157-171.

Guberman, R., & Greenfield, P. M. (1991). Learning and transfer in everyday cognition. *Cognitive Development, 6,* 233-260.

Guilford, J. P. (1967). *The nature of human intelligence.* New York: McGraw-Hill.

Gustafsson, J.-E. (1984). A unifying model for the structure of intellectual abilities. *Intelligence, 8,* 179-203.

Guttierrez, J., & Sameroff, A. (1990). Determinants of complexity in Mexican-American and Anglo-American mothers' conceptions of child development. *Child Development, 61*, 384-394.

Hale, J. (1982). *Black children: Their roots, culture, and learning styles.* Provo, UT: Brigham Young University Press.

Hale-Benson, J. E. (1986). *Black children: Their roots, culture and learning styles* (Rev. ed.). Baltimore, MD: Johns Hopkins University Press.

Hamayan, E. V., & Damico, J. S. (Eds.). (1991). *Limiting bias in the assessment of bilingual students.* Austin, TX: Pro-Ed.

Harrison, A., Wilson, M., Pine, C., Chan, S., & Buriel, R. (1990). Family ecologies of ethnic minority children. *Child Development, 61*, 347-362.

Haynes, N. (1995). How skewed is the bell curve? *Journal of Black Psychology, 21*(3), 275-299.

Haynes, N., & Comer, J. (1993). The Yale School Development Program: Process, outcomes and policy implications. *Urban Education, 28*(2), 166-169.

Heath, S. B. (1983). *Ways with words: Language, life and work in communities and classrooms.* Cambridge, UK: Cambridge University Press.

Helms, J. E. (1989). Eurocentrism strikes in strange places and in unusual ways. *The Counseling Psychologist, 17*, 643-647.

Helms, J. E. (1992). Why is there no study of cultural equivalence in standardized cognitive ability testing? *American Psychologist, 47*(9), 1083-1101.

Herrnstein, R., & Murray, C. (1994). *The bell curve.* New York: Free Press.

Herrnstein, R., Nickerson, R., de Sanchez, M., & Swets, J. (1986). Teaching thinking skills. *American Psychologist, 41*(11), 1279-1289.

Hilliard, A. (1991). Do we have the will to educate all children? *Educational Leadership, 49*(1), 31-36.

Hilliard, A. (1996). Either a paradigm shift or no mental measurement: The nonscience and the nonsense of the bell curve. *Cultural Diversity and Mental Health, 2*(1), 1-20.

Hilliard, A. G., III. (1976). *Alternatives to IQ testing: An approach to the identification of "gifted" minority children.* Final report to the California State Department of Education, Special Education Support Unit. (ERIC Clearinghouse on Early Childhood Education No. ED 146 009)

Hilliard, A. G. (1979). Standardization and cultural bias as impediments to the scientific study and validation of "intelligence." *Journal of Research and Development in Education, 12*(2), 47-58.

Horn, J. L. (1965). *Fluid and crystallized intelligence: A factor analytic study of the structure among primary mental abilities.* Unpublished doctoral dissertation, University of Illinois. (University Microfilms No. 65-7113)

Horn, J. L. (1991a). Measurement of intellectual capabilities: A review of theory. In K. S. McGrew, J. K. Werder, & R. W. Woodcock (Eds.), *WJ-R technical manual.* Chicago: Riverside.

Horn, J. L. (1991b). Measurement of intellectual capabilities: A review of theory. In K. S. McGrew, J. K. Werder, & R. W. Woodcock (Eds.), *A reference on theory and current research to supplement the Woodcock-Johnson-Revised Examiner's Manuals* (pp. 197-245). Allen, TX: DLM.

Horowitz, F. D., & O' Brien, M. (1989). A reflective essay on the state of our knowledge and the challenges before us. *American Psychologist, 44,* 441-445.

Howe, K. R. (1992). Liberal democracy, equal educational opportunity and the challenge of multiculturalism. *American Educational Research Journal, 29*(3), 455-470.

Hunt, E. B. (1978). Mechanics of verbal ability. *Psychological Review, 85,* 109-130.

Intelligence and its measurement: A symposium. (1921). *Journal of Educational Psychology, 12,* 123-147, 195-216, 271-275.

Jensen, A. R. (1969). How much can we boost IQ and scholastic achievement? *Harvard Educational Review, 39*(1), 1-123.

Jensen, A. R. (1979). Outmoded theory or unconquered frontier? *Creative Science and Technology, 2,* 16-29.

Jensen, A. R. (1980). *Bias in mental testing.* New York: Free Press.

Jensen, A. R. (1987). Unconfounding genetic and nonshared environmental effects. *Behavioral and Brain Sciences, 10,* 26-27.

Jensen, A. R. (1991). General mental ability: From psychometrics to biology. *Diagnostique, 16,* 134-144.

Jensen, A. R., & Whang, P. A. (1994). Speed of accessing arithmetic facts in long term memory: A comparison of Chinese-American and Anglo-American Children. *Contemporary Educational Psychology, 19,* 1-12.

Johnson, S. D. (1982). *The Minnesota, multiethnic counselor education curriculum: The design and evaluation of an intervention for cross-cultural counselor education.* Unpublished doctoral dissertation, University of Minnesota, Minneapolis.

Johnson, S. D. (1987). Knowing that versus knowing how: Toward achieving expertise through multicultural training for counseling. *The Counseling Psychologist, 15,* 320-331.

Johnson, S. D. (1990). Towards clarifying culture, race and ethnicity in the context of multicultural counseling. *Journal of Multicultural Counseling and Development, 18*(4), 16-31.

Jones, L. V. (1985). Interpreting Spearman's general factor. *Behavioral and Brain Science, 8*(2), 233.

Kamphaus, R. (1993). *Clinical assessment of children's intelligence.* Boston: Allyn & Bacon.

Kaufman, A. S., & Kaufman, N. L. (1983). *K-ABC: Kaufman Assessment Battery for Children.* Circle Pines, MN: American Guidance Service.

Kearins, J. (1981). Visual spatial memory in Australian Aboriginal children of desert regions. *Cognitive Psychology, 13,* 434-460.

Keil, F. C. (1981). Constraints on knowledge and cognitive development. *Psychological Review, 88,* 197-227.

Keil, F. C. (1984). Mechanisms of cognitive development and the structure of knowledge. In R. J. Sternberg (Ed.), *Mechanisms of cognitive development*. San Francisco: Freeman.

Kiselica, M. S. (1991, September/October). Reflections on a multicultural internship experience. *Journal of Counseling and Development, 70,* 126-130.

Kornhaber, M., Krechevsky, M., & Gardner, H. (1990). Engaging intelligence. *Educational Psychologist, 25*(3/4), 177-199.

Krechevsky, M., & Gardner, H. (1990). The emergence and nurturance of multiple intelligences: The Project Spectrum Approach. In M. J. A. Howe (Ed.), *Encouraging the development of exceptional skills and talents* (pp. 222-245). Leicester, UK: British Psychological Society.

Laboratory of Comparative Human Cognition. (1982). Culture and intelligence. In R. J. Sternberg (Ed.), *Handbook of human intelligence* (pp. 642-719). New York: Cambridge University Press.

Lancy, D. F., & Strathern, A. J. (1981). Making two's: Pairing as an alternative to the taxonomic mode of representation. *American Anthropologist, 83,* 773-795.

Lantz, D. A. (1979). A cross-cultural comparison of communication abilities: Some effects of age, schooling and culture. *International Journal of Psychology, 14,* 171-183.

Laosa, L. M. (1980). Maternal teaching strategies in Chicano and Anglo-American families: The influence of culture and education on maternal behavior. *Child Development, 51,* 759-765.

Laosa, L. M. (1981). Maternal behavior: Sociocultural diversity in modes of family interaction. In R. W. Henderson (Ed.), *Parent-child interaction: Theory, research, and prospects* (pp. 12-167). New York: Academic Press.

Lave, J. (1977). Tailor-made experiments and evaluating the intellectual consequences of apprenticeship training. *Quarterly Newsletter of the Institute for Comparative Human Development, 1,* 1-3.

Lave, J. (1988). *Cognition in practice: Mind, mathematics and culture in everyday life.* Cambridge, UK: Cambridge University Press.

Lave, J., Murtaugh, M., & de la Roche, D. (1984). The dialectic of arithmetic in grocery shopping. In B. Rogoff & J. Lave (Eds.), *Everyday cognition: Its development in social context.* Cambridge, MA: Harvard University Press.

Lave, J., & Wenger, E. (1991). *Situated learning: Legitimate peripheral participation.* Cambridge, UK: Cambridge University Press.

Lee Katz, L. (1991). Cultural scripts: The home-school connection. *Early Child Development and Care, 73,* 95-102.

Lewin, K. (1935). *A dynamic theory of personality.* New York: McGraw-Hill.

Lidz, C. S. (Ed.). (1987). *Dynamic assessment.* New York: Guilford.

Lidz, C. S. (1991). *Practitioner's guide to dynamic assessment.* New York: Guilford.

Linden, K. W., & Linden, J. D. (1968). *Modern mental measurement: A historical perspective.* Boston: Houghton Mifflin.

Lipsky, D. R., & Gartner, A. (1996). Inclusion, school restructuring, and the remaking of American society. *Harvard Educational Review, 66*(4), 762- 796.

Lonner, W. J. (1981). Psychological tests and intercultural counseling. In P. B. Pedersen, J. G. Draguns, W. J. Lonner, & J. E. Trimbie (Eds.), *Counseling across cultures* (pp. 275-303). Honolulu: East West Center/University of Hawaii.

Mackie, D. (1980). A cross-cultural study of intra- and interindividual conflicts of concentrations. *European Journal of Social Psychology, 10,* 313-318.

Mackie, D. (1983). The effect of social interaction on conservation of spatial relations. *Journal of Cross-Cultural Psychology, 14,* 131-151.

Maker, C. J. (1992, Fall). Intelligence and creativity in multiple intelligences: Identification and development. *Educating Able Learners,* pp. 12-19.

Matthews, J. (1989, March 25). Aspiring lawyers already finding a way to mak a point. *The Washington Post,* p. A3.

Mbiti, J. (1970). *African religions and philosophy.* Garden City, NJ: Anchor.

McGrew, K., & Flanagan, D. (1995). *An intelligence test desk reference: The cross-battery approach to test interpretation.* Paper presented at the National Association of School Psychologist Convention, Atlanta.

McGrew, K. S. (1994). *Clinical interpretation of the Woodcock Johnson Tests of Cognitive Ability—Revised.* Boston: Allyn & Bacon.

McGrew, K. S. (1995). Analysis of the major intelligence batteries according to a proposed comprehensive Gf-Gc framework of human cognitive and knowledge abilities. In D. P. Flanagan, J. L. Genshaft, & P. L. Harrison (Eds.), *Beyond traditional intellectual assessment: Contemporary and merging theories, tests and issues.* New York: Guilford.

McLoyd, V. (1990). Minority children: Introduction to the special issue. *Child Development, 61,* 263-266.

Mercer, J. R. (1979). In defense of racially and culturally nondiscriminatory assessment. *School Psychology Digest, 8*(1), 89-115.

Messick, S. (1976). Personality consistencies in cognition and creativity. In S. Messick (Ed.), *Individuality in learning* (pp. 4-22). San Francisco: Jossey-Bass.

Messick, S., & Anderson, S. (1970). Educational testing individual development and social responsibility. *The Counseling Psychologist, 2*(2), 93-97.

Miller-Jones, D. (1989). Culture and testing. *American Psychologist, 44,* 360-366.

Missiuna, C., & Samuels, M. (1988). Dynamic assessment: Review and critique. *Special Services in the Schools, 5*(1-2), 1-22.

Moon, J. D. (1993). *Constricting community: Moral pluralism and tragic conflicts.* Princeton, NJ: Princeton University Press.

Moyer, J. (1986, May/June). Child development as a base for decision making. *Childhood Education,* pp. 325-329.

Munroe, R. H., Munroe, R. L., & Whiting, B. B. (Eds.). (1981). *Handbook of cross-cultural human development.* New York: Garland.

Munroe, R. L., & Munroe, R. H. (1971). Effect of environmental experience on spatial ability in an East African society. *Journal of Social Psychology, 125,* 23-33.

Murray, B. (1996). Developing phoneme awareness through books. *Reading and Writing: An Interdisciplinary Journal, 8*(4), 307-322.

Murray, H. A. (1938). *Explorations in personality.* New York: Oxford University Press.

Murrone, J., & Gynther, M. (1991). Teachers' implicit "theories" of children's intelligence. *Psychological Reports, 69,* 1195-1201.

Murtaugh, M. (1985, Fall). The practice of arithmetic by American grocery shoppers. *Anthropology and Education Quarterly, 23.*

Niesser, U. (1976). Genera, academic, and artificial intelligence. In L. Resnick (Ed.), *Human intelligence: Perspectives on its theory and measurement* (pp. 179-189). Norwood, NJ: Ablex.

Neisser, U. (1979). The concept of intelligence. *Intelligence, 3,* 217-227.

Neisser, U., Boodoo, G., Bouchard, T., Boykin, W., Brody, N., Ceci, S., Halpern, D. F., Loehlin, J. C., Perloff, R., Sternberg, R., & Urbina, S. (1996). Intelligences: Knowns and unknowns. *American Psychologist, 51*(2), 77-101.

Nerlove, S. B., & Snipper, A. S. (1981). Cognitive consequences of cultural opportunity. In R. H. Munroe, R. L. Munroe, & B. B. Whiting (Eds.), *Handbook of cross-cultural human development.* New York: Garland.

Nettelbeck, T. (1985). What reaction times time. *Behavioral and Brain Science, 8*(2), 235-236.

Newman, F., & Holzman, L. (1993). *Lev Vygotsky: Revolutionary scientist.* London: Routledge.

Nichols, R. (1981). Origins, nature and determinants of intellectual development. In M. Begab, H. C. Haywood, & H. Garber (Eds.), *Psychosocial determinants of retarded performance, Vol. 1.* Baltimore, MD: University Park Press.

Noble, C. E. (1969). Race, reality and experimental psychology. *Perspectives in Biology and Medicine, 13,* 10-30.

Nobles, W. (1980). African philosophy: Foundations for black psychology. In R. Jones (Ed.), *Black psychology* (pp. 23-35). New York: Harper & Row.

Oakes, J. (1990). *Multiplying inequalities: The effects of race, social class, and tracking on opportunities to learn mathematics and science.* Santa Monica: Rand Corporation.

Obringer, S. J. (1988, November). *A survey of perceptions by school psychologists of the Stanford-Binet IV.* Paper presented at the meeting of the Mid-South Educational Research Association, Louisville, KY.

Ochs, E., & Schiefflin, B. (1984). Language acquisition and socialization: Three developmental stories and their implications. In R. Shweder & R. LeVine (Eds.), *Culture and its acquisition.* Chicago: University of Chicago Press.

Ogbu, J. U. (1986). The consequences of the American caste system. In *The school achievement of minority children: New perspectives*. London: Lawrence Erlbaum.

Ogbu, J. U. (1987). Variability in minority responses to schooling: Nonimmigrants vs. immigrants. In G. Spindler (Ed.), *Interpretive ethnography of education at home and abroad* (pp. 255-278). Hillsdale, NJ: Lawrence Erlbaum.

Okagaki, L., & Sternberg, R. J. (1993). Parental beliefs and children's school performance. *Child Development, 64*, 36-56.

Palinscar, A. S., & Brown, A. L. (1984). Reciprocal teaching of comprehension-fostering and comprehension-monitoring activities. *Cognition and Instruction, 1*, 117-175.

Parke, R. D., & Bhavnagri, N. P. (1989). Parents as managers of children's peer relationships. In D. Belle (Ed.), *Children's social networks and social supports*. New York: John Wiley.

Parker, W. M., Valley, M. M., & Geary, C. A. (1986). Acquiring cultural knowledge for counselors in training: A multifaceted approach. *Counselor Education and Supervision, 26*, 61-71.

Pellegrino, J. W., & Glaser, R. (1979). Cognitive correlates and components in the analysis of individual differences. In R. J. Sternberg & D. K. Detterman (Eds.), *Human intelligence: Perspectives on its theory and its measurement*. Norwood, NJ: Ablex.

Persell, C. H. (1977). *Education and inequality: The roots and results of stratification in America's schools*. New York: Free Press.

Phinney, J. S. (1996, September). When we talk about American ethnic groups, what do we mean? *American Psychologist, 51*(9), 918-927.

Piaget, J. (1952). *The origins of intelligence in children*. New York: International University Press.

Plomin, R. (1985). Behavioral genetics. In D. Detterman (Ed.), *Current topics in human intelligence* (Vol. 1). Norwood, NJ: Ablex.

Poortinga, Y., van de Vijver, F., Joe, R., & van de Koppel, J. (1989). Peeling the onion called culture: A synopsis. In C. Kagitcibasi (Ed.), *Growth and progress in cross-cultural psychology* (pp. 22-34). Berwyn, PA: Swets North American.

Rawls, J. (1973). *A theory of justice*. London: Oxford University Press.

Rawls, J. (1993). *Political liberalism*. New York: Columbia.

Ribeiro, J. L. (1980). Testing Portuguese immigrant children: Cultural patterns and group differences in responses to the WISC-R. In D. P. Macedo (Ed.), *Issues in Portuguese bilingual education* (pp. 90-101). Cambridge, MA: National Assessment and Dissemination Center for Bilingual Education.

Ridley, C. R. (1985). Imperatives for ethnic and cultural relevance in psychology training programs. *Professional Psychology: Research and Practice, 16*(5), 611-622.

Riley, M. K., Morocco, C. C., Gordon, S. M., & Howard, C. (1993). Walking the talk: Putting constructivist thinking into practice of constructivist principles. *Educational Horizons, 71*(4), 187-196.

Rivers, W. H. R. (1926). *Psychology and ethnology*. New York: Harcourt Brace.

Robinson, D. (1994). Philosophical views of intelligence. In *Encyclopedia of human intelligence*. New York: Macmillan.

Rogoff, B. (1978). Spot observations: An introduction and examination. *Quarterly Newsletter of the Institute for Comparative Human Development, 2,* 21-26.

Rogoff, B. (1981a). Schooling's influence on memory test performance. *Child Development, 52,* 260-267.

Rogoff, B. (1981b). Schooling and the development of cognitive skills. In H. Triandis & A. Heron (Eds.), *Handbook of cross-cultural psychology, Vol. 4* (pp. 233-294). Rockleigh, NJ: Allyn & Bacon.

Rogoff, B. (1990). *Apprenticeship in thinking*. New York: Oxford University Press.

Rogoff, B., & Chavajay, P. (1995). What's become of research on the cultural basis of cognitive development? *American Psychologist, 50*(10), 859-877.

Rogoff, B., & Waddell, K. J. (1982). Memory for information organized in a scene by children from two cultures. *Child Development, 53,* 1224-1228.

Rosenbaum, J. E. (1980). Social implications of educational grouping. *Review of Research in Education, 8,* 361-401.

Rueda, R., & Matinez, I. (1992). Fiesta educativa: One community's approach to parent training in developmental disabilities for Latino families. *Journal of the Association of Severe Handicaps, 17*(2), 95-103.

Samuda, R. (1975). From ethnocentrism to a multicultural perspective in educational testing. *Journal of Afro-American Issues, 3*(1), 4-17.

Sattler, J. M. (1988). *Assessment of children* (3rd ed.). San Diego: Author.

Saxe, G. (1988). The mathematics of street vendors. *Child Development, 59,* 1415-1425.

Saxe, G. (1991). *Culture and cognitive development: Studies in mathematical understanding*. Hillsdale, NJ: Lawrence Erlbaum.

Scarr, S., & Carter-Salzman, L. (1982). Genetics and intelligence. In R. J. Sternberg (Ed.), *Handbook of human intelligence* (pp. 792-896). Cambridge, UK: Cambridge University Press.

Scarr, S., & Ricciuti, A. (1991). What effects do parents have on their children? In L. Okagaki & R. J. Sternberg (Eds.), *Directors of development: Influences on the development of children's thinking*. Hillsdale, NJ: Lawrence Erlbaum.

Schaefer, E. S. (1987). Parental modernity and child academic competence: Towards a theory of individual and societal development. *Early Development and Care, 27,* 373-389.

Separate and unequal. (1993, December 13). *U.S. News & World Report,* pp. 46-60.

Serpell, R. (1979). How specific are perceptual skills? A cross-cultural study of pattern reproduction. *British Journal of Psychology, 70,* 365-380.

Serpell, R., Baker, L., Sonnenschein, S., & Hill, S. (1993, May). *Contexts for the early appropriation of literacy: Caregiver meanings of recurrent activities.* Paper presented at the annual meeting of the American Psychological Society, Chicago.

Shade, B. J. (1982). Afro-American cognitive style: A variable in school success? *Review of Educational Research, 52*(2), 219-244.

Shearer, D., & Loftin, C. (1984). The Portage Project. In R. Dangel & R. Polster (Eds.), *Parent foundations of* (p. 93). New York: Guilford Press.

Shipman, S., & Shipman, S. (1985). Cognitive styles: Some conceptual, methodological and applied issues. In E. W. Gordon (Ed.), *Review of research in education* (Vol. 12, pp. 229-291). Washington, DC: American Educational Research Association.

Siegel, L. S. (1984). Home environmental influence on cognitive development in pre-term and full-term children during the first five years. In A. W. Gottfried (Ed.), *Home environment and early cognitive development* (pp. 19- 34). Orlando, FL: Academic Press.

Siegel, M. (1991). *Knowing children: Experiments in conversation and cognition.* London: Lawrence Erlbaum.

Skrtic, T. M. (1991). The special education paradox: Equity as the way to excellence. *Harvard Educational Review, 61*(2), 148-206.

Slavin, R. E. (1987). *A review of research on elementary ability grouping.* Baltimore, MD: Johns Hopkins University Press.

Spearman, C. (1923). *The nature of "intelligence" and the principles of cognition.* London: Macmillan.

Spearman, C. (1927). *The abilities of man: Their nature and measurement.* New York: Macmillan. (Reprinted 1981, New York: AMS)

Steinberg, L., Dornbusch, S. M., & Brown, B. B. (1992). Ethnic differences in adolescent achievement: An ecological perspective. *American Psychologist, 47*(6), 723-729.

Sternberg, R. J. (1977a). *Intelligence, information processing, and analogical reasoning: The componential analysis of human abilities.* Hillsdale, NJ: Lawrence Erlbaum.

Sternberg, R. J. (1977b). Component processes in analogical reasoning. *Psychological Review, 84,* 353-378.

Sternberg, R. J. (1980). Sketch of a componential subtheory of human intelligence. *Behavioral and Brain Sciences, 3,* 573-584.

Sternberg, R. J. (1984, January). What should intelligence tests test? Implications of a triarchic theory of intelligence for intelligence testing. *Educational Researcher,* pp. 5-15.

Sternberg, R. J. (1985a). Teaching critical thinking, Part 1: Are we making critical mistakes? *Phi Delta Kappan, 67*(3), 104-108.

Sternberg, R. J. (1985b). Teaching critical thinking, Part 2: Possible solutions. *Phi Delta Kappan, 67*(4), 277-280.

Sternberg, R. J. (1985c). *Beyond IQ: A triarchic theory of human intelligence.* New York: Cambridge University Press.

Sternberg, R. J. (1986). *Intelligences applied.* New York: Harcourt Brace Jovanovich.

Sternberg, R. J. (Ed.). (1988). *The nature of creativity: Contemporary psychological perspectives*. New York: Cambridge University Press.

Sternberg, R. J., Conway, B. E., Ketron, J. L., & Bernstein, M. (1981). People's conception of intelligence. *Journal of Personality and Social Psychology, 41,* 37-55.

Sternberg, R. J., & Davidson, J. (1989). A four-prong model for intellectual development. *Journal of Research and Development in Education, 22*(3), 22-28.

Sternberg, R. J., & Detterman, D. K. (Eds.). (1986). *What is intelligence? Contemporary viewpoints on its nature and definition*. Norwood, NJ: Ablex.

Sternberg, R. J., & Powell, J. S. (1983). Comprehending verbal comprehension. *American Psychologist, 38,* 878-893.

Sternberg, R. J., Powell, J. S., & Kaye, D. B. (1982). The nature of verbal comprehending. *Poetics, 11,* 155-187.

Sternberg, R. J., & Wagner, R. K. (1986). *Practical intelligence: Nature and origin of competence in the everyday world*. New York: Cambridge University Press.

Sternberg, R. J., Wagner, R. K., & Okagaki, L. (1993). Practical intelligence: The nature and role of tacit knowledge in work and at school. In H. Reese & J. Puckett (Eds.), *Advances in lifespan development* (pp. 205-227). Hillsdale, NJ: Lawrence Earlbaum.

Sternberg, R. J., Wagner, R. K., Williams, W. M., & Horvath, J. A. (1995). Testing common sense. *American Psychologist, 50*(11), 912-926.

Stigler, J. W. (1984). "Mental abacus": The effect of abacus training on Chinese children's mental calculation. *Cognitive Psychology, 16,* 145-176.

Stocking, G. (1968). *Race, culture and evolution*. New York: Free Press.

Strom, R., Johnson, A., Strom, S., & Strom, P. (1992a). Designing curriculum for parents of gifted children. *Journal for the Education of the Gifted, 15*(2), 182-200.

Strom, R., Johnson, A., Strom, S., & Strom, P. (1992b). Educating gifted Hispanic children and their parents. *Hispanic Journal of Behavioral Sciences, 14*(3), 383-393.

Sue, S. (1991). Ethnicity and culture in psychological research and practice. In J. Goodchilds (Ed.), *Psychological perspectives on human diversity in America* (pp. 51-85). Washington, DC: American Psychological Association.

Super, C. M. (1980). Cognitive development: Looking across at growing up. *New Directions for Child Development: Anthropological Perspectives on Child Development, 8,* 59-69.

Super, C. M., & Harkness, S. (1986). The development niche: A conceptualization at the interface of child and culture. *International Journal of Behavioral Development, 9,* 545-569.

Surber, J. (1995). Best practices in a problem-solving approach to psychological report writing. In Thomas, A., & Grimes, J. (Eds.). (1977). *Best practices in school psychology III*. Washington, DC: The National Association of School Psychologists.

Tallent, N. (1993). *Psychological report writing* (4th ed.). Englewood Cliffs, NJ: Prentice Hall.

Taylor, C. W. (1988). Various approaches to the definitions of creativity. In R. J. Sternberg (Ed.), *The nature of creativity: Contemporary psychological perspectives* (pp. 37-49). New York: Cambridge University Press.

Thomas, A., & Chess, S. (1977). *Temperament and development.* New York: Brunner/Mazel.

Thomas, T. (1990, August). *Is it learning disability, mental retardation, or educational deprivation: An exploration with Hispanic children?* Paper presented at the American Psychological Association Annual Convention, Boston.

Thompson, R. W., & Hixson, P. (1984). Teaching parents to encourage independent problem solving in preschool-age children. *Language, Speech and Hearing Services in the Schools, 15,* 175-181.

Thorndike, R. L., Hagen, E. P., & Sattler, J. M. (1986). *Stanford-Binet Intelligence Scale: Fourth edition.* Chicago: Riverside.

Thurstone, L. L. (1924). *The nature of intelligence.* New York: Harcourt Brace.

Thurstone, L. L. (1938). Primary mental abilities. *Psychometrika Monographs, 1.*

Tuck, K. (1985). *Verve inducement effects: The relationship of task performance to stimulus variability and preference in working class black and white schoolchildren.* Unpublished Doctoral Dissertation, Howard University, Washington, DC.

Tylor, E. B. (1874). *Primitive culture.* London: John Murray.

Uttal, D. H., & Wellman, H. M. (1989). Young children's representation of spatial information acquired from maps. *Developmental Psychology, 25,* 128-138.

Valencia, R., Henderson, R., & Rankin, R. (1981). Relationship of family constellation and schooling to intellectual performance of Mexican American children. *Journal of Educational Psychology, 73*(4), 524-532.

Van Daalen-Kapteijns, M. M., & Elshout-Mohr, M. (1981). The acquisition of word meaning as a cognitive learning process. *Journal of Verbal Learning and Verbal Behavior, 20,* 386-399.

Vaughn, B. E., Block, J. E., & Block, J. (1988). Parental agreement on child-rearing during early childhood and the psychological characteristics of adolescents. *Child Development, 59,* 1020-1033.

Vernon, P. A. (1990). The use of biological measures to estimate behavioral intelligence. *Educational Psychologist, 25*(3-4), 293-304.

Vygotsky, L. S. (1978). *Mind in society: The development of higher psychological processes.* Cambridge, MA: Harvard University Press.

Wechsler, D. (1944). *The measurement of adult intelligence* (3rd ed.). Baltimore, MD: Williams & Wilkins.

Wechsler, D. (1958). *The measurement and appraisal of adult intelligence* (4th ed.). Baltimore, MD: Williams & Wilkins.

Wechsler, D. (1974). *Manual for the Wechsler Intelligence Scale for Children—Revised (WISC-R).* New York: Psychological Corporation.

Weinberg, R. A. (1989). Intelligence and IQ: Landmark issues and great debates. *American Psychologist, 44*(2), 98-104.

Wertsch, J. V. (1979). From social interaction to higher psychological processes: A clarification and application of Vygotsky's theory. *Human Development, 22,* 1-22.

Wertsch, J. V. (1985). *Culture, communication, and cognition: Vygotskian perspectives.* Cambridge, UK: Cambridge University Press.

Whimbey, A. (1975). *Intelligence can be taught.* New York: Dutton.

Whimbey, A., & Lochhead, J. (1982). *Problem solving and comprehension: How to sharpen your thinking skills and increase your IQ.* Philadelphia: Franklin Institute.

Whitehurst, G., Fischel, J., Lonigan, C., Valdez-Menchaca, M., Arnold, D., & Smith, M. (1991). Treatment of early expressive language delay: If, when and how. *Topics in Language Disorders, 11*(4), 55-68.

Whiting, B. (1976). The problem of the packaged variable. In K. Riegel & J. Meacham (Eds.), *The developing individual in a changing world* (pp. 303-309). Chicago, Aldine.

Whiting, B. (1980). Culture and social behavior: A model for the development of social behavior. *Ethos, 8,* 95-116.

Williams, R. (1970). Danger: Testing and dehumanizing black children. *Clinical Child Psychology Newsletter, 9*(1), 5-6.

Williams, R. (1971, Spring). Abuses and misuses in testing black children. *Washington University Magazine, 41*(3), 34-37.

Williams, R. (1975). The BITCH-100: A culture-specific test. *Journal of Afro-American Issues, 3,* 103-106.

Witt, J. C., & Gresham, F. M. (1985). Review of Wechsler Intelligence Scale of Children-Revised. In J. V. Mitchell (Ed.), *The ninth mental measurement yearbook* (Vol. 2, pp. 1715-1716). Lincoln, NE: Buros Institute of Mental Measurements.

Wober, M. (1972). Culture and the concept of intelligence: A case in Uganda. *Journal of Cross-Cultural Psychology, 3,* 327-328.

Wober, M. (1974). Toward an understanding of the Kiganda concept of intelligence. In J. W. Berry & P. R. Dasen (Eds.), *Culture and cognition: Readings in cross-cultural psychology.* London: Methuen.

Woodcock, R. W. (1990). Theoretical foundations of the WJ-R measures of cognitive ability. *Journal of Psychoeducational Assessment, 8,* 231-258.

Woodcock, R. W., & Johnson, M. B. (1977). *Woodcock-Johnson Psycho-Educational Battery.* Chicago: Riverside.

Woodcock, R. W., & Johnson, M. B. (1989). *Woodcock-Johnson Psycho-Educational Battery-Revised.* Chicago: Riverside.

Zajonc, R. (1976). Family configuration and intelligence. *Science, 192,* 227-236.

Zuckerman, M. (1990). Some dubious premises in research and theory on racial differences: Scientific, social, and ethical issues. *American Psychologist, 45,* 1297-1303.

Name Index

224

Subject Index

About the Authors

Eleanor Armour-Thomas, originally from Trinidad and Tobago, West Indies, is Associate Professor in the School of Education at Queens College, City University of New York. She graduated from the University of the West Indies. From 1978 to 1984, she attended Columbia University, where she received a master's degree in applied human development and guidance, a master's degree in education, and a master's degree in behavioral analysis. In 1984, she received her doctorate in education psychology (schooling). Following completion of her graduate work, she continued her postdoctoral studies at Yale University. Her publications are in the areas of intellectual assessment of children from culturally diverse backgrounds and assessment of teaching in mathematics. In addition, as a consultant, she does evaluative research for educators and policymakers in several states.

238

Sharon-ann Gopaul-McNicol, originally from Trinidad and Tobago, West Indies, is Associate Professor in the School of Education at Howard University. She is an international expert in multicultural assessment. During the past 10 years, she assessed children both nationally and internationally. She is the author of three cross-cultural books and several journal articles, and she has given presentations throughout the world on electronic media. She has a bachelor's degree in psychology from New York University (1981), a master's degree in child and adolescent psychology from Columbia University (1982), a master's degree in general psychology from Hofstra University (1984), and a master's degree in school psychology from Hofstra University (1985). In 1986, she completed her doctorate in clinical psychology at Hofstra University.